TRADE FINANCE DURING THE GREAT TRADE COLLAPSE

TRADE FINANCE DURING THE GREAT TRADE COLLAPSE

Jean-Pierre Chauffour and Mariem Malouche
Editors

THE WORLD BANK
Washington, D.C.

ISBN: 978-0-8213-8748-1
eISBN: 978-0-8213-8749-8
DOI: 10.1596/978-0-8213-8748-1

Library of Congress Cataloging-in-Publication Data

Chauffour, Jean-Pierre.
  Trade finance during the great trade collapse / Jean-Pierre Chauffour and Mariem Malouche.
     p. cm.
  Includes bibliographical references and index.
  ISBN 978-0-8213-8748-1 — ISBN 978-0-8213-8749-8 (electronic)
  1. Export credit.   2. Exports—Finance.   3. Financial crises.   4. International trade.   I. Malouche, Mariem, 1973-   II. Title.
  HG3753.C435 2011
  332.7'42—dc22

                                                                                      2011012219

CONTENTS

Boxes

Figures

Tables

FOREWORD

The bursting of the subprime mortgage market in the United States in 2008 and the ensuing global financial crisis were associated with a rapid decline in global trade. The extent of the trade collapse was unprecedented: trade flows fell at a faster rate than had been observed even in the early years of the Great Depression.

G-20 leaders held their first crisis-related summit in November 2008. The goal was to understand the root causes of the global crisis and to reach consensus on actions to address its immediate effects. In the case of trade, a key question concerned the extent to which a drying up of trade finance caused the observed decline in trade flows.

There are different types of trade finance. Banks offer a number of trade finance instruments that vary in terms of risk. A large share of global trade finance is also provided on an interfirm basis—that is, involving contracts between buyers and suppliers. It rapidly became obvious that the data on global trade finance flows (by type of products, providers, or markets) were incomplete. This dearth of data complicated the estimation of a possible trade finance "market gap" and of whether trade finance was indeed a major factor driving the fall in global trade. An implication for policy was whether governmental intervention in favor of a specific segment of the financial system—the trade finance market—was necessary and, if so, what form such support should take.

The G-20 quickly reached broad agreement that the international community needed more information and knowledge about trade finance markets and also needed to consider expanding trade finance liquidity. International agencies, the financial industry, and analysts cooperated to act on three fronts: (a) collecting data to better inform decision makers on the prevalence of trade finance market constraints; (b) helping design a quick and effective institutional and governmental response to restore confidence and liquidity in the trade credit market; and (c) better understanding the effects of the changes in the international regulatory framework for the banking sector on the supply of trade finance.

In response to the crisis, the International Finance Corporation—the private sector arm of the World Bank—doubled the capacity of its Global Trade Finance Program in late 2008 and, in collaboration with other development finance institutions, set up a Global Trade Liquidity Program in July 2009 to channel additional liquidity to finance trade transactions. In addition, the World Bank undertook a series of bank- and firm-level surveys in developing countries to gauge the impact of the crisis, complementing other institutional surveys conducted in advanced and emerging economies.

This book brings together a range of projects and studies undertaken by development institutions, export credit agencies, private bankers, and academics to shed light on the role of trade finance in the 2008–09 great trade collapse. It provides policy makers, analysts, and other interested parties with analyses and assessments of the role of governments and institutions in restoring trade finance markets. A deeper understanding of the complexity of trade finance remains critical as the world economy recovers and the supply of trade finance improves. The international community continues to know too little about the fragility of low-income economies in response to trade finance developments and shocks, as well as about the ability and conditions of access to trade finance by small and medium enterprises and small banks in developing countries. Similarly, there is uncertainty regarding the impact on trade finance of recent changes in the Basel III regulatory framework.

We hope that the contributions to this volume are just the start of a broader effort to undertake more research and analysis on an important, and neglected, segment of the financial market. Such analysis is conditional on the availability of timely and comprehensive data on the cost and volume of trade finance as well as the probability of default trade finance products. As discussed in a number of chapters in this book, generating such data requires a collective effort, which we hope will be put in place and sustained in the coming years.

Bernard Hoekman
Director, International Trade Department
Poverty Reduction and Economic
  Management
World Bank

Georgina Baker
Director, Short Term Finance
International Finance Corporation
World Bank Group

ACKNOWLEDGMENTS

The editors are grateful to all the contributors in this book who have willingly embarked on this endeavor and offered their time, energy, and ideas to help advance our collective knowledge on the role of trade finance during the 2008–09 global economic crisis. We have been particularly blessed to count on most actors that played a significant role during the financial crisis, be it international or regional institutions, government bodies, private sector players, or academia. This rich and unique combination of views and analyses on the relationship between trade and trade finance in times of crisis constitutes the real value added of this book. It would not have been possible without the willingness of all the contributors to share their considerable expertise and their devotion to the purpose of this book.

The production of such a book would not be possible without the involvement, commitment, and dedication of many other individuals. Bernard Hoekman, director of the World Bank International Trade Department, provided the overall intellectual guidance for this project under the direction of Otaviano Canuto, Vice President of the Poverty Reduction and Economic Management (PREM) Network. Mona Haddad, manager of the PREM Trade Unit provided unfailingly generous support, suggestions, and help, whenever needed. The book also immensely benefited from the inputs and comments from peer reviewers: Hamid Alavi, senior private sector specialist, and Valeria Salomao Garcia, senior financial sector specialist, at the World Bank; and Michael Hadjimichael, deputy director at the Institute of International Finance (IIF).

But a book cannot exist without an effective production team. This book benefited from the impeccable professionalism of the World Bank's Office of the Publisher. Stephen McGroarty, Theresa Cooke, and Andres Meneses managed the publication process so efficiently and diligently that we hardly noticed it. Mary A. Anderson carefully edited all of the contributions to deliver a harmonized manuscript. We would also like to thank the dedicated and professional support provided by the administrative team in the International Trade Department, including Cynthia Abidin-Saurman, Rebecca Martin, Anita Nyajur, Marinella Yadao, and Amelia Yuson. Special thanks also to Charumathi Rama Rao, who provided support on the financial management aspects of the project, and to Stacey Chow for her infectious energy throughout the publication and dissemination phases.

Last but not least, we would like to thank the governments of Finland, Norway, Sweden, and the United Kingdom for their financial support under the Multi-donor Trust Fund for Trade and Development (MDTF-TD). The MDTF-TD supports the World Bank's international trade strategy, which focuses on helping developing countries benefit from their integration into the global economies and making the world trading system more supportive of development.

The editors

ABOUT THE EDITORS AND CONTRIBUTORS

Jean-Pierre Chauffour is a lead economist in the International Trade Department of the World Bank, in the Poverty Reduction and Economic Management Network, where he works on regionalism, competitiveness, and trade policy issues. Prior to joining the Bank in 2007, he spent 15 years at the International Monetary Fund, where he held various positions, including mission chief in the African department and representative to the World Trade Organization and United Nations in Geneva. Mr. Chauffour has extensive economic policy experience and has worked in many areas of the developing world, most extensively in Africa, the Middle East, and Eastern Europe. He holds master's degrees in Economics and in Money, Banking, and Finance from the Panthéon-Sorbonne University in Paris. He is the author of *The Power of Freedom: Uniting Human Rights and Development* (Cato Institute, 2009).

Mariem Malouche is an economist in the International Trade Department of the World Bank, in the Poverty Reduction and Economic Management Network. She joined the Bank in the Middle East and North Africa Region in 2004. Before joining, Ms. Malouche obtained her Ph.D. in International Economics from University Paris-Dauphine. Her areas of interest are trade policy, nontariff measures, regional integration, and export diversification.

Contributors

Hyung Ahn, International Finance Corporation, World Bank Group

Donna K. Alexander, Bankers' Association for Finance and Trade–International Financial Services Association

Irena Asmundson, International Monetary Fund

Marc Auboin, World Trade Organization

Steven Beck, Asian Development Bank

Ghazi Ben Ahmed, African Development Bank

Nicolas Berman, Graduate Institute of International and Development Studies

Cosimo Beverelli, World Trade Organization

Daniela Carrera, Inter-American Development Bank

Thomas Dorsey, International Monetary Fund

Tore Ellingsen, Stockholm School of Economics, Stockholm University

Daniela Fabbri, University of Amsterdam

Thomas Farole, World Bank

Bonnie Galat, International Finance Corporation, World Bank Group

Adnan Ghani, Royal Bank of Scotland

Jean-Jacques Hallaert, OECD and Groupe d'Économie Mondiale (GEM), Institut d'Études Politiques de Paris

John Humphrey, Institute of Development Studies

Tan Kah Chye, Standard Chartered Bank

Armine Khachatryan, International Monetary Fund

Leora Klapper, World Bank

Madina Kukenova, World Trade Organization

Jean-François Lambert, HSBC

Andrei A. Levchenko, University of Michigan and National Bureau of Economic Research

Logan T. Lewis, University of Michigan and National Bureau of Economic Research

Inessa Love, World Bank

Philippe Martin, Institut d'Études Politiques de Paris

Anna Maria C. Menichini, University of Salerno and Centre for Studies in Economics and Finance

Jesse Mora, U.S. International Trade Commission

Fabrice Morel, Berne Union

Ioana Niculcea, International Monetary Fund

William Powers, U.S. International Trade Commission

Rudolf Putz, European Bank for Reconstruction and Development

Douglas Randall, World Bank

Nadia Rocha, World Trade Organization

Christian Saborowski, World Bank

Mika Saito, International Monetary Fund

Thierry J. Senechal, International Chamber of Commerce

Ahmet I. Soylemezoglu, World Bank

Linda L. Tesar, University of Michigan

Koen J. M. van der Veer, De Nederlandsche Bank

Jonas Vlachos, Stockholm University

ABBREVIATIONS

$	All references to "dollars" or dollar amounts ($) are U.S. dollars (US$) unless indicated otherwise.
AfDB	African Development Bank
ADB	Asian Development Bank
AGOA	African Growth and Opportunity Act
ALADI	Latin American Integration Association
ATL	Agro Traders Ltd.
AVC	asset value correlation
BAFT-IFSA	Bankers' Association for Finance and Trade–International Financial Services Association (merged association)
BANCOLDEX	Banco de Comercio Exterior de Colombia
BCBS	Basel Committee on Banking Supervision
BIS	Bank for International Settlements
BPLR	Benchmark Prime Lending Rate
BU	Berne Union
CCF	credit conversion factor
CEPII	Centre d'Etudes Prospectives et d' Informations Internationales (Centre for Research on the International Economy)
CIS	Commonwealth of Independent States
DFI	development finance institution
EBRD	European Bank for Reconstruction and Development
ECA	export credit agency
ECGD	Export Credits Guarantee Department
EFD	external financial dependence
EFIL	Export Finance Insurance Corporation (Australia)
EMIB	emerging-market issuing bank
ES	Enterprise Survey (World Bank)
EU	European Union

FCS	Financial Crisis Survey (World Bank)
FI	financial intermediary
FY	fiscal year
G-20	Group of 20 (countries') Finance Ministers and Central Bank Governors
GDP	gross domestic product
GTFP	Global Trade Finance Program (IFC)
GTLP	Global Trade Liquidity Program (IFC)
ICC	International Chamber of Commerce
IDA	International Development Association
IDB	Inter-American Development Bank
IDS	Institute of Development Studies
IFC	International Finance Corporation (World Bank Group)
IFI	international financial institution
IMF	International Monetary Fund
IMF-BAFT	International Monetary Fund–Bankers' Association for Finance and Trade
ISIC	International Standard Industrial Classification
IT	information technology
KYC	know-your-customer
LIBOR	London interbank offered rate
LC	letter of credit
LOC	line of credit
MFA	Multifibre Arrangement
MLT	medium/long-term (export credit insurance)
NAICS	North American Industry Classification System
NFIB	National Federation of Independent Business
OECD	Organisation for Economic Co-operation and Development
RBI	Reserve Bank of India
RBS	Royal Bank of Scotland
SBSA	Standard Bank of South Africa
SCF	supply chain finance
SMEs	small and medium enterprises
ST	short-term (export credit insurance)
SWIFT	Society for Worldwide Interbank Financial Telecommunication
TCD	trade credit dependence
TFI	Trade Finance Initiative (AfDB)
TFP	Trade Facilitation Program (EBRD)
TFP	Trade Finance Program (ADB)

TFFP	Trade Finance Facilitation Program (IDB)
TFRP	Trade Finance Reactivation Program (IDB)
TWCC	trade-weighted credit contraction
UB	utilization bank
WTO	World Trade Organization

OVERVIEW

Introduction

On September 15, 2008, Lehman Brothers, the fourth-largest U.S. investment bank, filed for bankruptcy, marking the largest bankruptcy in U.S. history and the burst of the U.S. subprime mortgage crisis. Concerns about the soundness of U.S. credit and financial markets led to tightened global credit markets around the world. Spreads skyrocketed. International trade plummeted by double digits, as figure O.1 illustrates. Banks reportedly could not meet customer demand to finance international trade operations, leaving a trade finance "gap" estimated at around $25 billion. The liquidity problem spread from the United States and the European Union (EU) to developing countries' markets. As the secondary market dried up in late 2008, the trade finance gap reportedly increased to up to $300 billion.

In the midst of the crisis, these alarming developments were at the epicenter of world leaders' attention. When the G-20 leaders held their first crisis-related summit in Washington, D.C., in November 2008, their primary objective was to reach a common understanding of the root causes of the global crisis and agree on actions to address its immediate effects, including providing liquidity to help unfreeze credit markets.

The purpose of this book is to provide policy makers, analysts, and other interested parties with a comprehensive assessment of the role of trade finance in the 2008–09 "great trade collapse" (Baldwin 2009) and the subsequent role of governments and institutions to help restore trade finance markets.

The 1997–98 Asian crisis had already illustrated the critical role that trade finance plays during a financial crisis—especially its effects on trade—but that crisis remained regionally confined, and international institutions and regulators largely blamed the opaque financial sector in the affected economies for the crisis. In contrast, the 2008–09 crisis originated in the United States, one of the most

Figure O.1. Trade Fluctuations by Region, 2007–10
export volume, three-month moving average (seasonally adjusted)

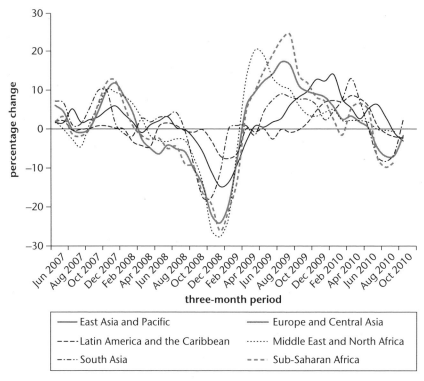

Sources: Authors' calculations and data from Datastream.

transparent and sophisticated financial markets, and quickly spilled over to the EU and the rest of the world.

Policy makers, central bankers, and finance ministers from around the world found themselves in largely uncharted territories. They had to contemplate policy actions to channel liquidity into the real economy in support of trade transactions. However, because of the dearth of data on trade finance, they had no gauge to estimate the magnitude of the market gap or even to know whether trade finance was indeed a main factor behind the drop in trade. It was also not clear whether governments' intervention in favor of a specific segment of the financial system—the trade finance market—was justified and warranted.

Trade finance covers a wide spectrum of payment arrangements between importers and exporters—from open accounts to cash-in-advance, interfirm trade credit, and bank-intermediated trade finance. Moreover, assessment of trade finance conditions is notoriously difficult in the absence of organized markets for bank-intermediated trade finance and given the proprietary nature of bank information about customer relationships. With these considerations in mind, estimation of the effect of a potential trade finance shortfall on the decline in trade volumes during the crisis was even more convoluted. Against this background, the World Bank commissioned firm and bank surveys in developing countries to assess the impact of the financial crisis on trade and trade finance developments. The International Monetary Fund (IMF), in association with the Bankers' Association for Finance and Trade (BAFT)—now merged with International Financial Services Association (BAFT-IFSA)—and others, conducted additional surveys of commercial banks in developed and emerging countries to collect information on commercial bank trade finance conditions.

Governments and international institutions were encouraged to intervene on the basis of information that some 80–90 percent of world trade relies on some form of trade finance and that trade credit markets were tight.[1] To help overturn the trade collapse and a possible further deepening of the global economic recession, the G-20 called on international institutions at its Washington, D.C., summit to provide trade financing to assist developing countries affected by the crisis. At a second summit in London in April 2009, the G-20 adopted a broad package to provide at least $250 billion in support of trade finance over two years.

This book assembles 23 contributions to tell the story of trade finance during the 2008–09 global economic crisis and to answer four main questions:

1. What do we know about the specifics and determinants of trade finance during financial crises, especially the role of interfirm trade credit versus bank-intermediated trade finance?
2. Was the availability and cost of trade finance a major constraint on trade during the crisis?
3. What are the underpinnings and limits of national and international public interventions in support of trade finance markets in times of crisis?
4. How effective was the institutional support for trade finance put in place during the crisis, and to what extent (if any) did the new banking regulations under Basel II and Basel III exacerbate the trade finance shortfall during the crisis and in the postcrisis environment?

What Is Trade Finance, and Why Does It Matter?

The global financial crisis demonstrated that trade finance is a broad concept that encompasses various products, mechanisms, and players. When trade collapsed in the fall of 2008, trade finance rapidly became the focus of attention. Foremost, the crisis illuminated the dearth of data and information on trade finance.

Trade finance differs from other forms of credit (for example, investment finance and working capital) in ways that have important economic consequences during periods of financial crisis. Perhaps its most distinguishing characteristic is that it is offered and obtained not only through third-party financial institutions, but also through interfirm transactions. Table O.1 lists the major trade finance products.

The vast majority of trade finance involves credit extended bilaterally between firms in a supply chain or between different units of individual firms.[2] According to messaging data from the Society for Worldwide Interbank Financial Telecommunication (SWIFT), a large share of trade finance occurs through interfirm, open-account exchange. Banks also play a central role in facilitating trade, both through the provision of finance and bonding facilities and through the establishment and management of payment mechanisms such as telegraphic transfers and documentary letters of credit (LCs). Among the intermediated trade finance products, the most commonly used for financing transactions are LCs, whereby the importer and exporter entrust the exchange process to their respective banks to mitigate counterparty risk. The IMF/BAFT-IFSA bank surveys during the crisis helped gather information on the market shares of financing products and suggested that about one-third of trade finance is bank intermediated, as figure O.2 shows.

Relative to a standard credit line or working-capital loan, trade finance— whether offered through banks or within the supply chain—is relatively illiquid, which means that it cannot easily be diverted for another purpose. It is also highly collateralized; credit and insurance are provided directly against the sale of specific products or services whose value can, by and large, be calculated and secured.[3] This suggests that the risk of strategic default on trade finance should be relatively low, as should be the scale of loss in the event of default.

Figure O.2. Trade Finance Arrangements, by Market Share

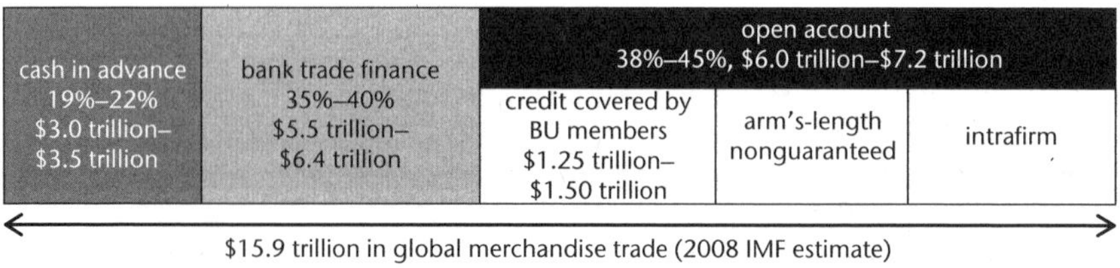

cash in advance	bank trade finance	open account 38%–45%, $6.0 trillion–$7.2 trillion		
19%–22% $3.0 trillion– $3.5 trillion	35%–40% $5.5 trillion– $6.4 trillion	credit covered by BU members $1.25 trillion– $1.50 trillion	arm's-length nonguaranteed	intrafirm

←———————————————————————————————→
$15.9 trillion in global merchandise trade (2008 IMF estimate)

Sources: IMF staff estimates from IMF/BAFT-IFSA surveys of commercial banks (IMF-BAFT 2009; IMF and BAFT-IFSA 2010) and Berne Union database.
Note: BU = Berne Union. IMF = International Monetary Fund. BAFT-IFSA = Bankers' Association for Finance and Trade–International Financial Services Association.

Table O.1. Overview of Trade Finance Products

Category	Product	Description
Interfirm or supply-chain financing	Open account	• Contract settled between importer and exporter without third-party security or risk management arrangements, either directly or (most commonly) through transfers between their banks; extension of credit by one party (normally the exporter) by way of accepting payment after a certain delay (usually 30–90 days)
"Traditional" bank financing	Investment capital	• Medium-term finance for investment in the means of production (for example, machinery)
	Working capital	• Short-term finance to cover ongoing costs (addressing mismatch in timing between cash receipts and costs incurred), including payment of suppliers, production, and transport; also used to cover risks of (or real) delays in payments, effects of currency fluctuations, and so on
	Preexport finance	• Similar to working capital, but bank takes a security interest in the goods being shipped and a right to receive payment for those goods directly from the importer; typically used for commodity production
Payment mechanisms and liquidity	Letter of credit (LC)	• Provided by importer's bank to exporter's bank; when exporter fulfills LC conditions, the relevant documents of proof submitted to exporter's bank, which submits them to importer's bank, which remits funds to exporter's bank, which then pays exporter (importer subsequently remits funds to importer's bank) • Designed to mitigate the counterparty risk inherent in open-account transactions • Could be issued under various modalities (for example, confirmed, standby, deferred, revocable, transferable, usance, or back-to-back)
	Supplier credit	• Extended or deferred payment terms offered by the supplier to the buyer but typically linked with bank financing to enable exporter to receive cash on delivery (for example, factoring)
	Buyer credit	• Term financing provided to finance cash payments due to supplier
	Countertrade	• Addresses liquidity (particularly access to foreign exchange, thus especially relevant in emerging economies) by promoting two-way trade of equivalent-value merchandise (for example, barter, buy-back, or counterpurchase)
	Factoring and forfaiting	• Factoring as a financial service that purchases an exporter's invoices or accounts receivable at a discount and assumes the risk of nonpayment; addresses both liquidity and risk mitigation • Forfaiting similar to factoring but typically involves medium-term accounts receivables for exporters of capital goods or commodities with long credit periods

(continued next page)

Table O.1. *(continued)*

Category	Product	Description
Risk management	Advance payment guarantees	• Security provided to importer when exporter requires mobilization payment; usually a matching amount callable on demand
	Performance bonds	• Security provided to importer (normally in case of capital goods export); callable if exporter fails to perform (compensates for costs of finance, rebidding, and so on)
	Refund guarantees	• Security provided to importer when importer is required to make stage payments during manufacturing by exporter (normally in case of large capital-goods export); callable if goods are not delivered
	Hedging	• Security (for example, through a financial instrument issued by a bank) to offset market (rather than counterparty) risks, including fluctuations in exchange rates, interest rates, and commodity prices
Export credit insurance and guarantees	Export credit insurance	• Exporters insured against a range of risks, including nonpayment, exchange rate fluctuations, and political risk; can be used to securitize other forms of trade and nontrade finance from banks
	Export credit guarantees	• Instruments to protect banks providing trade finance; facilitates the degree to which banks can offer trade finance products (for example, to SMEs without sufficient export track records)

Source: Chauffour and Farole 2009.
Note: SMEs = small and medium enterprises.

The remainder of this overview offers a brief review of the content of this book and its 23 chapters and concludes with a number of key takeaways.

Section 1: Interfirm Trade Credit and Trade Finance during Crises

With the collapse of major financial institutions, the global financial crisis first took the form of a major global liquidity crisis, including a trade finance crisis. Many banks reported major difficulties in supplying trade finance.

The conditions of access to interfirm trade credit also worsened in the aftermath of the crisis. Interfirm trade credit refers to finance provided to importers from exporters to buy the goods from overseas and to exporters to help them produce the goods to export as well as to allow them to finance their extensions of credit to importers. Interfirm trade credit is a particularly important source of short-term financing for firms around the world (Petersen and Rajan 1997), and it tends to be relatively more prevalent for firms in developing countries (Demirgüç-Kunt and Maksimovic 2001; Beck, Demirgüç-Kunt, and Maksimovic 2008). Although bank-intermediated trade finance and interfirm trade credit should be perfect substitutes in a world free of information asymmetries and the like, the two sources offer firms alternatives to deal with the frictions and market imperfections of the real world.

Chapter 1: Trade Credit versus Bank Credit

Inessa Love reviews the main rationale for the provision of trade credit by suppliers and highlights four main considerations that may lead firms to prefer interfirm trade credit when possible:

1. Trade credit suppliers have a cost advantage over banks in acquisition of information about the financial health of the buyers.
2. In the event of nonpayment, trade credit providers are better able than specialized financial institutions to liquidate the goods they repossess.
3. Trade credit serves as a guarantee for product quality.
4. Potential moral hazard problems on the borrower's side are reduced when trade credit is extended to suppliers because in-kind credit is difficult to divert to other uses.

Better understanding the determinants of interfirm trade credit is particularly important during financial crises, when the cost of trade finance increases and banks become more risk averse. Interfirm trade credit could play an important role and substitute for lack of liquidity in the financial system. Its use tends to increase in times of crisis (Calomiris, Himmelberg, and Wachtel 1995; Love, Preve, and Sarria-Allende 2007). Yet Inessa Love also points to evidence from the Asian financial crisis that interfirm trade credit and bank trade finance are imperfect substitutes and could complement each other (Love, Preve, and Sarria-Allende 2007). The findings suggest that trade credit cannot fully compensate for long-term contraction in bank finance that stems from a financial crisis. A contraction in trade credit may even exacerbate a contraction in bank finance, which in turn may lead to a collapse in trade credit.

Chapter 2: Firms' Trade-Financing Decisions

Assuming that firms' suppliers are better able than banks or other financial institutions to extract value from the liquidation of assets in default and have an information advantage over other creditors, Daniela Fabbri and Anna Maria C. Menichini then investigate the determinants of trade credit and its interactions with borrowing constraints.

They find that rationed and unrationed firms alike use trade credit to exploit the supplier's liquidation advantage. Moreover, they find that the use of trade credit goes together with the transfer of physical inputs within the supply chain and that the bias toward more physical inputs increases as financial constraints tighten and creditor protection weakens.

Chapter 3: Interfirm Trade Finance: Pain or Blessing?

Anna Maria C. Menichini identifies a number of theoretical economic rationales that could underpin policy actions in favor of trade credit financing in times of crisis, with a focus on constraints faced by developing countries. She looks at whether interfirm credit has features that can shield it from a general credit squeeze or whether, instead, it constitutes an additional element of tension.

She finds two main and opposing effects: Interfirm finance may be a way to overcome informational problems associated with standard lender-borrower relations due to information asymmetries and principal-agent problems. However, interfirm finance may also contribute to propagation of shocks among firms along the supply chain, especially for firms operating in developing countries with little access to alternative finance.

Menichini proposes a few policy schemes to help reduce contagion by focusing on the breaking points in the supply chain—mainly firms more exposed to the risk of insolvency and more likely to start the chain of defaults.

Chapter 4: Financial Crisis and Supply-Chain Financing

The analysis of the link between interfirm trade credit and bank trade finance during the 2008–09 global crisis has been blurred by the fact that the financial crisis swiftly spilled over to the real economy and constrained firms' cash reserves and revenues, putting additional pressure on their capacity to extend trade credit. As such, both interfirm trade credit and bank trade finance dropped in the midst of the crisis.

To document the financial behavior of firms under competitive pressure, Leora Klapper and Douglas Randall use data from the World Bank's Financial Crisis Surveys of 1,686 firms in Bulgaria, Hungary, Latvia, Lithuania, Romania, and Turkey in 2007 and 2009. They find that in countries hit hardest by the crisis, firms under competitive pressure were relatively more likely to extend trade credit, suggesting an additional financial burden for some firms.

Section 2: The Role of Trade Finance in the 2008–09 Trade Collapse

The 2008 financial crisis and the ensuing trade collapse immediately prompted policy makers and analysts to link the two events: Trade dropped in part because of a lack of supply of trade finance. Given the lack of data and the relative secure nature of trade finance, however, some analysts raised doubts about the prominent role of trade finance. A review of financial crises over the past three decades found that trade elasticity to gross domestic product has increased significantly over time, which in turn may explain why trade dipped so much (Freund 2009).

Survey data also suggest that the trade finance market tightened during the crisis but may not have played the alleged dominant role in the drop in trade. Lack of data spurred the IMF and BAFT-IFSA and the International Chamber of Commerce (ICC) to launch a series of commercial- and investment-bank surveys to gauge the impact of the financial crisis on trade finance availability and constraints.

The ICC surveys indicate that it became more difficult to raise money to finance trade in the aftermath of the Lehman Brothers collapse and that both the availability and the price of trade finance severed in late 2008. The surveys indicate that the supply of trade finance remained constrained both in value and in volume in 2008–09. They also find considerable evidence that the weaker emerging economies were hit first (for example, Bangladesh, Pakistan, and Vietnam), but fast-growing developing economies also suffered from the contraction in trade finance (ICC 2009, 2010).

Chapter 5: Evidence from Commercial Bank Surveys

Analyzing the IMF/BAFT-IFSA surveys of commercial banks, Irena Asmundson, Thomas Dorsey, Armine Khachatryan, Ioana Niculcea, and Mika Saito find evidence that credit limits on trade finance tightened during the crisis. However, they also find that increases in the price of trade finance products did not stand out from those for other commercial bank products.

Their results suggest that factors other than trade finance—chiefly the collapse of global demand and the decline in commodity prices—played a more important role in the 2008–09 trade collapse. Nevertheless, increased pricing and tightened credit conditions undoubtedly discouraged some trade transactions that might have taken place otherwise. These results have been corroborated by the World Bank's surveys of firms, which chapter 10 covers in greater detail.

Chapter 6: Global Perspectives on Trade Finance Decline

Jesse Mora and William Powers examine broad measures of financing—including domestic lending in major developed economies and cross-border lending among more than 40 countries—and review eight survey-based results.

Their findings suggest that a decline in global trade finance had a moderate role, at most, in reducing global trade. Furthermore, in most cases, trade finance declined much less sharply than exports and broader measures of financing. Empirical firm-based data analyses confirm the importance of the demand side effect. They also observed a compositional shift in trade financing as heightened uncertainty and increased counterparty risk led exporters to move away from risky open accounts and toward lower-risk letters of credit and export credit insurance.

Chapter 7: A Skeptic's View of the Trade Finance Role

Using highly disaggregated international trade data for the United States, Andrei A. Levchenko, Logan T. Lewis, and Linda L. Tesar examine whether financial variables can explain the cross-sectoral variation in how much U.S. imports or exports fell during the crisis. Overall, they find little evidence that financial factors played a role in the collapse of U.S. trade at the aggregate level, in sharp contrast to other measures that were found to matter significantly in earlier studies, such as vertical production linkages and the role of durables. Their results might point out that when aggregating across partner countries up to the sector level, the effect disappears.

Moreover, the authors recognize that although the United States is widely seen as the epicenter of the financial crisis, its financial system is nonetheless one of the deepest and most resilient in the world. Thus, even if their analysis finds no effect of financial factors for U.S. trade, these factors may be much more important in other countries with weaker financial systems.

Chapter 8: Trade Finance in Africa

Although trade finance constraints may not have constrained advanced economies' exporters and importers, developing-country policy makers were concerned about the impact of exports from low-income countries—particularly from African countries. John Humphrey, through firm interviews, looks at the impact of the financial crisis on African exporters.

He reports that most interviewed firms in Africa did not experience direct difficulties with trade finance. Yet, indirectly, the financial crisis—through its effects on global demand and price volatility—led to deterioration of firms' creditworthiness and a decline in their access to trade finance. Moreover, the survey underscores the differentiated impact the crisis may have had by firm type: Scarce bank finance reportedly was channeled mainly to firms with established exporting records and regular customer relations, leaving small and medium enterprises (SMEs) and new entrants that lacked relationships with banks and customers in a dire situation.

Chapter 9: Financial Crises and African Trade

Nicolas Berman and Philippe Martin also focus their analysis on the impact of the crisis on Sub-Saharan Africa. The authors find that African exporters are more vulnerable to a financial crisis in importing countries given the concentration of African exports in primary goods as well as the high dependence of African exports on trade finance.

Nonetheless, they also find that the direct effects of the crisis may have been weaker because of the relative insulation and underdevelopment of the financial system in most Sub-Saharan African countries, and that the indirect effect through trade may be stronger. During a financial crisis—when uncertainty and risk are high, and trust and liquidity are low—banks and firms in importing countries tend to first cut exposure and credit to countries that they perceive as financially riskier.

Chapter 10: The World Bank's Firm and Bank Surveys in Developing Countries

Mariem Malouche reaches similar conclusions in her report on a larger-scale firm survey commissioned by the World Bank in 14 developing countries. As of

April 2009, the low-income African countries where the survey was conducted (Ghana, Kenya, and Sierra Leone) seem to have been relatively insulated from the financial crisis. Yet the crisis did add strains on their underdeveloped domestic financial systems and adversely affected SMEs and new export firms that are seeking to diversify away from commodity exports. The firm surveys also indicated that the crisis generally affected SMEs more than large firms across regions and income levels because of a weaker capital base and bargaining power in relation to global buyers as well as banks.

SMEs also have been subject to relatively higher increases in the cost of trade finance instruments. Many SMEs operating in global supply chains or in the sectors most affected by the global recession (such as the auto industry) have been constrained through both the banking system and the drop in export revenues and buyers' liquidity. Moreover, SMEs have been more likely constrained to purchase guarantees and insurance to access trade finance. However, echoing previous survey results, most SMEs declared that, overall, their exports were severely or moderately constrained by the financial crisis, mainly because of lack of orders and directly related lack of finance on buyers' part (trade credit). Lack of finance from banks seems to have played a lesser constraining role.

Chapter 11: Private Trade Credit Insurers: The Invisible Banks

Koen J. M. van der Veer examines the role of trade finance guarantees and insurance during the crisis and estimates to what extent the reduction in the availability of trade credit insurance has affected trade.

Using a unique bilateral data set that covers the value of insured exports, premium income, and paid claims of one of the world's leading private credit insurers during 1992–2006, he finds that, on average, every euro of insured exports generates 2.3 euros of total exports. Van der Veer further estimates that, during the 2008–09 crisis, up to 9 percent of the drop in world exports and up to 20 percent of the drop in European exports could be explained by a combination of decreases in private trade-credit insurance limits and increases in insurance premiums.

Chapter 12: Trade Finance in Postcrisis Recovery of Trade Relations

Looking forward, Cosimo Beverelli, Madina Kukenova, and Nadia Rocha discuss the speed of trade recovery after a banking crisis. Using an annual data set of product-level exports to the United States from 157 countries from 1996 through 2009, they estimate the duration of each export relationship and find that, on average, 23 percent of trade relationships were interrupted by a banking crisis between 1996 and 2008.

The authors also find that trade is likely to recover faster with "experience," defined as the number of years an export relationship had been active before a banking crisis hit. Moreover, trade finance, measured by firms' financial dependence, does not appear to affect the recovery of trade relations after a banking crisis. These findings corroborate earlier results that small and relatively inexperienced firms are likely to be the most vulnerable to banking crises, and they also indicate that these firms will have more difficulty surviving crises and recovering.

Section 3: Government Trade Finance Intervention during Crises

Notwithstanding uncertainty about the size of the trade finance gap and its potential role in the drop in trade, governments around the world were compelled in the fall of 2008 to intervene to mitigate the impact of the crisis on their domestic economies. The exceptional character of the crisis called for immediate actions:

- U.S. and European governments with fiscal capacity instituted bailout programs for their financial sectors.
- Governments in developing countries and emerging economies instituted expansionary fiscal and monetary policies.
- International institutions rapidly scaled up their trade finance programs and lending to budget-constrained countries.

As is often the case when governments intervene to correct supposed market distortions, some policy analysts wondered how to make such interventions the most effective and the least distortionary.

Chapter 13: The Theoretical Case for Trade Finance Intervention

On a theoretical level, Tore Ellingsen and Jonas Vlachos argue in favor of trade finance intervention during a liquidity crisis because it mitigates the problems that arise—particularly for international finance—when firms hoard cash. Because international loan enforcement is weaker than domestic enforcement, sellers are less willing to keep international loans on their books, and it is the seller's insistence on immediate payment that creates the demand for liquidity in the first place.

The authors also contend that multilateral organizations should support trade finance specifically, rather than providing funding more broadly, because domestic policy initiatives are likely to place a relatively low weight on foreigners' gains.

Because the support of trade finance typically involves supplying funds to the buyer's bank, while primarily benefiting the seller, it is easy to see how these transactions will suffer under purely domestic policies.

Chapter 14: Risks in Boosting the Availability of Trade Finance

In contrast, Jean-Jacques Hallaert argues against boosting the availability of trade finance. First, like other analysts, he argues that trade finance is unlikely to have contributed significantly to the plunge in international trade in the 2008–09 crisis. The cost of trade finance was a greater problem than its availability. Rather than trying to increase the supply of trade finance per se, policy makers should help credit flows in general to return to normal.

Second, Hallaert contends that boosting the supply of trade finance is risky and probably not the best use of scarce public resources. Moreover, encouraging export credit agencies (ECAs) to take more risks could result in fiscal contingent liabilities.

Chapter 15: Trade Finance during Crises—Market Adjustment or Market Failure?

For Jean-Pierre Chauffour and Thomas Farole, a critical question is therefore whether the supply of trade finance declined because of market or government failures, and, hence, whether there is a rationale for public intervention to address such failures. Two broad cases that would create a real trade finance gap would be (a) insufficient supply ("missing markets") or (b) supply at prices temporarily too high to meet demand ("overshooting markets")—both of which may have had temporary relevance in fall 2008.

Drawing upon the lessons from past crises, Chauffour and Farole devise a set of 10 principles for effective public actions in support of trade finance:

1. Targeting interventions to address specific failures
2. Ensuring a holistic response that addresses the wider liquidity issues of banks
3. Channeling the response through existing mechanisms and institutions
4. Ensuring collective action in the response across countries and regions
5. Addressing both risk and liquidity issues
6. Recognizing the importance of banks in developed countries to free up trade finance for emerging-market exporters
7. Promoting greater use of interfirm credit and products such as factoring
8. Maintaining a level playing field in terms of risk weight

9. Improving transparency in the trade finance market
10. Avoiding moral hazard and crowding out commercial banks by setting clear time limits and exit strategies for intervention programs and by sharing rather than fully underwriting risk.

Chapter 16: Export Credit Agencies in Developing Countries

Jean-Pierre Chauffour, Christian Saborowski, and Ahmet I. Soylemezoglu assess the case for policy makers to support setting up ECAs in response to financial crises—focusing in particular on low-income economies, which often suffer from sovereign debt problems, weak institutional capacity, poor governance practices, and difficulties in applying the rule of law.

Although expansion of ECA operations can mitigate credit risk and keep trade finance markets from drying up, they argue that a developing country should establish an ECA only after careful evaluation of its potential impact on both the financial and the real sectors of the economy. The authors advise extreme caution in setting up ECAs in low-income contexts and highlight the factors that policy makers should consider.

Section 4: Institutional and Regulatory Support for Trade Finance

In response to the financial crisis, many governments put in place programs that either injected liquidity in banks or provided fiscal and monetary stimulus to the economy, sometimes directly in support of affected exporting firms. Central banks with large foreign exchange reserves could supply foreign currency to local banks and importers, generally through repurchase agreements. And government intervention was not reserved to developed countries. The central banks of Argentina, Brazil, India, Indonesia, the Republic of Korea, and South Africa, to name a few, also massively supported their local banks.

The measures helped mitigate the global decline in output and trade flows and directly and indirectly supported the provision of trade finance—stimulating more confidence in the outlook of individual countries, reducing risk premiums, and providing more direct financing to financial institutions. However, many developing countries were not in a position to extend credit or expand existing trade finance facilities and therefore needed support.

While economists and other experts argued about the suitability of intervening or not intervening, policy makers and development institutions were facing a historic trade collapse and felt the pressure to act swiftly. A look back at their actions indicates that the 10 principles described above were largely followed. The response of international financial institutions was immediate and of a magnitude unseen in recent history. In particular, multinational and regional development banks mostly scaled up existing instruments and acted in cooperation with other trade finance institutions. Capacities in certain activities were enhanced significantly as early as fall 2008. As soon as the world economy and trade flows showed signs of picking up, governments began to withdraw the support measures put in place at the peak of the crisis.

The expansion of trade finance programs notwithstanding, another important concern has been the possible adverse effect of the new banking regulations under Basel II and Basel III on the provision of trade finance. In the immediate aftermath of the crisis, the World Trade Organization (WTO), the ICC, BAFT-IFSA, a number of private banks, and others sought to draw attention to (a) the preferential regulatory treatment of trade finance under the Basel I framework, in recognition of its safe, mostly short-term, and self-liquidating character, and (b) their concerns that the implementation of some Basel II provisions had proved difficult for trade. At the 2009 G-20 summit in London, flexibility in the application of these provisions was explicitly requested. Moreover, the WTO and the banking sector argue that Basel II and proposed Basel III rules, as they apply to trade finance, may significantly affect banks' ability to provide trade finance at affordable prices to businesses, to increase trade pricing, and to reduce trade finance capacity and world trade, especially in the direction of poor countries.

Chapter 17: World Trade Organization Response

Marc Auboin rationalizes the government actions in support of trade finance because of the potential damage to the real economy from shrinking trade finance. International supply-chain arrangements globalized not only production, but also trade finance. Sophisticated supply-chain financing operations—including those for SMEs—rely on a high level of trust and confidence in global suppliers that they will deliver their share of the value added and have the necessary financial means to produce and export it in a timely manner. Any disruption in the financial sector's ability to provide working capital or preshipment export finance, to issue or endorse letters of credit, or to deliver export credit insurance could create a gap in complex, outward-processing assembly operations and lead by itself to a contraction in trade and output.

As such, Auboin underlines the institutional and economic case for the WTO to be concerned and involved in trade finance. He also stresses the importance of cooperation, arguing that one clear lesson from the Asian financial crisis is that— in periods prone to lack of trust and transparency as well as to herd behavior—all actors, including private banks, ECAs, and regional development banks, should pool their resources to the extent practicable. Cooperation among players is particularly important in the absence of a comprehensive and continuous data set on trade finance flows.

Chapter 18: World Bank Group's Response

As Bonnie Galat and Hyung Ahn recount, the World Bank Group, through the International Finance Corporation (IFC), was quick to act—strengthening its trade facilitation programs between November 2008 and April 2009. The IFC Global Trade Finance Program (GTFP) doubled its revolving ceiling to $3 billion in late 2008 in support of emerging markets' trade finance.

Leveraging the experience gained from the GTFP, the IFC launched the Global Trade Liquidity Program (GTLP) in July 2009 to rapidly mobilize and channel funding to support underserved developing-country markets by providing trade credit lines and refinancing portfolios of trade assets held by selected banks. Additionally, the new program was premised on leveraging the IFC funding by creating a historic collaboration with other international financial institutions, which also contributed their financial resources to the GTLP. Both programs have successfully facilitated trade during the crisis period. As the world economy recovers from the crisis, the IFC will bring the GTLP to an end, starting in 2012.

Chapter 19: Regional Development Banks' Response

Rudolf Putz, Ghazi Ben Ahmed, Steven Beck, and Daniela Carrera describe the impact of the financial crisis on regional trade and trade finance as well as the way four regional development banks quickly responded by scaling up their trade finance facilities.

The European Bank for Reconstruction and Development increased the overall program limit of its Trade Facilitation Program from €800 million to €1.5 billion. The Asian Development Bank ramped up the activities of its Trade Finance Program to support $2 billion in trade in 2009, an increase of more than 300 percent over 2008. Further enhancements of these programs were agreed on at the G-20 summits, in particular the already-noted IFC's establishment of a liquidity pool allowing cofinancing operations with banks in developing countries. From this perspective, the African Development Bank established a $1 billion Trade Finance Initiative in January 2009 as part of its broader package of crisis response initiatives.

For its part, the Inter-American Development Bank (IDB) had already put in place its Trade Finance Reactivation Program (TFRP) when the crisis hit. The TFRP supported the IDB's fast response in Latin America and the Caribbean, strengthening supply-side capacity and trade-related infrastructure. In addition, the Trade Finance Facilitation Program (TFFP), implemented in 2005, proved an effective fast-delivery vehicle for not only mitigating the effects of the liquidity crisis, but also expanding trade finance for financial intermediaries and their clients.

Chapter 20: Berne Union Response

The Berne Union (BU)—the leading global association for export credit and investment insurance—counts the major private credit insurers as well as most ECAs worldwide among its members. As Fabrice Morel explains, ECAs stepped in during the 2008–09 financial crisis to provide programs for short-term lending of working capital and credit guarantees aimed at SMEs.

For certain countries, the BU commitment was substantial (for example, in Germany and Japan). In some countries, large lines of credit were granted to secure supplies with key trading partners (for example, in the U.S. relationships with China and Korea), while in some other countries, cooperation centered on support for regional trade (in particular, supply-chain operations).

Chapter 21: International Chamber of Commerce Response

Over the past three years, the ICC developed intelligence gathering initiatives in trade finance to promote a banking model that would continue to finance a sustained expansion of international trade, even in difficult times. Thierry J. Senechal illustrates how the ICC addressed the lack of reliable information in trade finance.

He reviews measures undertaken by ICC in the midst of the financial crisis, then discusses the market intelligence projects developed by the ICC Banking Commission—in particular, the Global Surveys on Trade and Finance designed to gain an accurate snapshot of the prevailing market trends and to gauge future expectations for global trade and traditional trade finance. Senechal also discusses key findings of the ICC research contained in the Trade Finance Register, including the initial finding from a first set of data that trade finance is a relatively low-risk asset class (ICC 2011), and concludes by discussing future patterns of international cooperation and the need to establish a new set of regulations to supervise banks.

Chapter 22: Private Bankers' Response

Donna K. Alexander of BAFT-IFSA and representatives of three global banks—Tan Kah Chye (Standard Chartered Bank), Adnan Ghani (Royal Bank of Scotland), and Jean-François Lambert (HSBC)—describe their experience from the ground at the climax of the crisis and the bankers' efforts to maintain their trade finance credit lines throughout the crisis.

Although the trade finance market has largely recovered from its trough in late 2008, the authors are also adamant that implementation of the Basel III recommendations by the Basel Committee on Banking Supervision (BCBS) could result in decreased trade flows for trade-focused banks at a time when those flows are essential to supporting global economic recovery. They argue that the new prudential liquidity and capital requirements may result in an increase in the cost of lending across the board but would disproportionately affect trade finance. In their view, trade finance exposures are small in size, self-liquidating, and transactional in nature. They also tend to be short term (often 180 days or less) and more geographically diversified. Finally, they note that trade exposures historically have had low default rates and, even in default scenarios, have had better and quicker recoveries than other asset classes because clients tend to repay working capital first to keep their cash-flow engines running.

In the view of bank regulators and others, the changes in the Basel rules aim to achieve a sounder banking sector and to establish more risk-sensitive means for calculating risk weights for various obligors. In response to these concerns, the BCBS conducted a comprehensive quantitative impact study to assess the impact of capital adequacy standards announced in July 2009 and the Basel III capital and liquidity proposals published in December 2009. As a result, the BCBS maintained the proposed capital and liquidity standards, which it claims will help strengthen the regulatory environment by gradually raising the level of high-quality capital in the banking system, increasing liquidity buffers, and reducing unstable funding structures. Although under Basel III the risk-based capital required to be held against all credit exposures will be higher—because of both the higher capital ratios and the increased emphasis on equity capital—the increase in capital for trade finance exposures is not any greater than for other exposures. In December 2010, the BCBS issued the Basel III rules text previously endorsed by the G-20 at its November 2010 summit in Seoul.

Chapter 23: Trade Finance Issues under the Current Basel Regulatory Framework

Marc Auboin expresses hope that the regulatory debate will remain open and will lead to a better understanding of both bankers' and regulators' views, ultimately resulting in a set of regulations perceived as right and fair. Data collection and further analysis of the impact of the new rules are necessary.

The ICC has contributed to this debate by focusing its efforts on addressing the lack of reliable information in trade finance and mobilizing resources to engage in a constructive dialogue with regulators to bridge the information gap. This kind of coordination would assist in developing user-friendly intelligence for both the public and the private sectors.

The WTO and the World Bank have recommended that the G-20 examine the potential impact of the Basel II and III provisions on the availability of trade finance—with a particular focus on developing-countries' trade—and take stock of such examination at the 2011 G-20 summit in Cannes, France.

Main Takeaways from the Crisis

1. *Lack of trade finance data is impeding the formulation of policies.* The absence of data capturing all kinds of trade finance (bank-intermediated and interfirm) has proven a major constraint to measuring the extent of the trade finance shortfall and its effect on trade flows during the financial crisis. The ICC's buildup of the Trade Finance Register is a significant step forward because it will create a living database of the trade finance market and may help demonstrate the resilience of the trade finance business.

2. *Trade finance matters for trade.* Results from bank and firm surveys undertaken during the crisis to overcome the lack of trade finance data, as well as postcrisis empirical analyses, all indicate tighter trade finance conditions during the crisis and significant adverse effects on trade flows.

3. *Not all forms of trade finance are equal.* Although the crisis constrained both bank-intermediated trade finance and interfirm trade credit, empirical findings suggest that interfirm trade credit may be more resilient than bank-intermediated trade finance in times of crisis. Trade credit offers features that make it safer, given the better information that buyers and suppliers have on creditworthiness of clients and the liquidating feature of trade credit. Although trade credit (in particular, among supply chains) could be a factor of contagion leading to sharp drops in trade during crises, it also contributes to a quicker rebound when economies recover—a pattern observed in Southeast Asia during the crisis.

4. *Trade finance was not the main driver behind the 2008 trade collapse.* The shortfall in trade finance seems to have been a moderate factor in the sharp 2008–09 drop in trade flows. Trade finance and trade volumes dropped mostly as a result of the spillover of the financial crisis to the real economy, including through lower activity and destocking. The demand effect was further amplified for firms operating in global supply chains or in sectors that were most affected by the slow global economy, such as the auto industry.

5. *SMEs have been particularly vulnerable to the tightening of trade finance conditions.* The lack of access to affordable trade finance has been particularly

detrimental for certain firms (for example, SMEs and new exporters), especially in developing countries with underdeveloped financial systems and weak contractual enforcement systems. SMEs have been more affected than large firms because of a weaker capital base and bargaining power in relation to global buyers and banks. Also, SMEs have been more subject to high increases in the cost of trade finance instruments, with banks being more risk averse and preferring to work with sounder large, multinational firms.

6. *New Basel regulations may have unnecessarily constrained trade finance supply during the crisis and in the postcrisis environment.* Bankers and some international institutions consider Basel II regulations to have further constrained the supply of trade finance during the crisis, especially for banks based in low-income countries (as well as second- and third-tier banks in middle-income countries). They have called on regulators to carefully study the potential unforeseen impact of proposed Basel III changes on trade finance. In particular, banks argue that the increase in the new liquidity and capital prudential requirements and the nonrecognition of trade assets as highly liquid and safe would lead to a significant increase in the cost of banks providing trade finance, which in turn will lead to a lower supply, higher prices, or both. Conversely, regulators have maintained the view that, under Basel II and III, the increase in capital for trade finance exposures is not any greater than for other exposures. The new leverage ratio and the new liquidity rules will not have any systematic impact on trade finance, though they may affect a few large, complex, or wholesale-funded banks, albeit for reasons unrelated to their trade finance activities. Even in those cases, the impact on trade finance is not expected to be greater than on any other class of asset. Given the diverging views, the BCBS has established a working group to study impacts of regulation on trade finance, and—at the request of the World Bank and the WTO—the G-20 will take stock of the situation at its 2011 meeting.

7. *The international community responded swiftly to the trade finance crisis.* The G-20 orchestrated quick and collective actions from governments and the international financial community. This led to a set of cofinancing arrangements among development banks, export credit agencies, foreign commercial banks, private insurance underwriters, and investment funds. While part of the G-20 support was directed mostly at a handful of large banks and international banking groups, the support of the IFC and regional development banks—in terms of both insurance and liquidity—has targeted mainly smaller banks and banks in developing countries.

8. *A timely exit from trade finance support programs is key.* As the global economy recovers and demand rises, some governments appropriately cut back their trade finance programs to avoid displacing legitimate private sector activity.

Similarly, the IFC will wind up the GTLP, set up in response to the crisis, beginning in 2012. Setting clear time limits and exit strategies for intervention programs and sharing, rather than fully underwriting, risk are important considerations to limit moral hazard and the crowding out of commercial banks in times of financial crises.

9. *Maintaining specific programs in support of vulnerable segments of the trade finance market is also key.* Continued uncertainty in some markets (for example, low-income countries with underdeveloped financial systems and weak contractual enforcement) or among some firms (for example, SMEs and new exporters) calls for vigilance on the suitability and timing of the retrenchment of international organizations' trade finance programs. Although lack of liquidity does not seem to be the most prominent constraint anymore, the director-general of the WTO and the president of the World Bank, with the support of the heads of regional development banks, have flagged the risk that a substantial number of countries could be increasingly left out of trade finance markets and thereby unable to benefit fully from the recovery of global trade. At the Seoul G-20 meeting of November 2010, the international community expressed particular concern about low-income countries that may still be facing severe difficulties in accessing trade finance at affordable cost, particularly in import finance.

10. Finally, *an important knowledge gap remains* on the effect of trade finance on trade and the role of trade finance during crises, as well as on the appropriate banking regulations and supervisory standards for banks' trade finance portfolio exposure. This calls for a continuing analysis of the issues by academics, practitioners, and other interested stakeholders.

Notes

1. Although this range of 80–90 percent was widely reported, the source and evidence for the claim remain unclear.

2. Estimates from FImetrix (IMF-BAFT 2009) suggest that 10–20 percent of trade finance is composed of cash-in-advance payments (these mainly involve small and medium enterprise [SME] buyers, inordinately in developing countries); 45–80 percent is on open account (of which 30–40 percent is intrafirm); and 10–35 percent is bank-intermediated.

3. This is, of course, not true in all cases. Specific problems occur with products that are perishable (whose value erodes quickly or immediately) or extremely differentiated (where there is little or no market value outside the intended buyer) as well as with services (which generally cannot be collateralized).

References

Baldwin, Richard, ed. 2009. *The Great Trade Collapse: Causes, Consequences and Prospects.* VoxEU.org publication. London: Centre for Trade and Economic Integration. http://www.voxeu.org/reports/great_trade_collapse.pdf.

Beck, Thorsten, Asli Demirgüç-Kunt, and Vojislav Maksimovic. 2008. "Financing Patterns around the World: Are Small Firms Different?" *Journal of Financial Economics* 89 (3): 467–87.

Calomiris, Charles W., Charles P. Himmelberg, and Paul Wachtel. 1995. "Commercial Paper, Corporate Finance and the Business Cycle: A Microeconomic Perspective." Working Paper 4848, National Bureau for Economic Research, Cambridge, MA.

Chauffour, Jean-Pierre, and Thomas Farole. 2009. "Trade Finance in Crisis: Market Adjustment or Market Failure?" Policy Research Working Paper 5003, World Bank, Washington, DC.

Demirgüç-Kunt, Asli, and Vojislav Maksimovic. 2001. "Firms as Financial Intermediaries: Evidence from Trade Credit Data." Policy Research Working Paper 2696, World Bank, Washington, DC.

Freund, Caroline. 2009. "The Trade Response to Global Downturns: Historical Evidence." Policy Research Working Paper 5015, World Bank, Washington, DC.

ICC (International Chamber of Commerce). 2009. "Rethinking Trade Finance 2009: An ICC Global Survey." ICC, Paris.

———. 2010. "Rethinking Trade Finance 2010: An ICC Global Survey." ICC, Paris.

———. 2011. "Rethinking Trade and Finance 2011: ICC Global Survey on Trade and Finance." ICC, Paris.

IMF-BAFT (International Monetary Fund-Bankers' Association for Finance and Trade). 2009. "Trade Finance Survey: A Survey among Banks Assessing the Current Trade Finance Environment." Report by FImetrix for IMF and BAFT, Washington, DC.

IMF and BAFT-IFSA (International Monetary Fund and Bankers' Association for Finance and Trade-International Financial Services Association). 2010. "Trade Finance Services: Current Environment & Recommendations: Wave 3." Report by FImetrix for IMF and BAFT-IFSA, Washington, DC.

Love, Inessa, Lorenzo Preve, and Virginia Sarria-Allende. 2007. "Trade Credit and Bank Credit: Evidence from the Recent Financial Crises." *Journal of Financial Economics* 83 (2): 453–69.

Petersen, Mitchell, and Raghuram Rajan. 1997. "Trade Credit: Theories and Evidence." *The Review of Financial Studies* 10 (3): 661–91.

SPECIFICITY OF TRADE CREDIT AND TRADE FINANCE DURING CRISES

TRADE CREDIT VERSUS BANK CREDIT DURING FINANCIAL CRISES

Inessa Love

The 2008–09 global financial crisis is one of historic dimensions. Few would dispute its rank as one of the broadest, deepest, and most complex crises since the Great Depression. Its origins were in the U.S. subprime housing finance market, which showed signs of trouble in the first half of 2007. After Wall Street investment firm Lehman Brothers collapsed in September 2008, the crisis spread rapidly across institutions, markets, and borders. Both developed and developing countries faced massive failures of financial institutions and a staggering collapse in asset values.

This financial crisis was characterized by a severe credit crunch as the banks became reluctant to lend to even the highest-quality firms. Financing constraints tightened for many firms, leading them to cut investments in capital as well as research and development (R&D) and to bypass attractive investment projects (Campello, Graham, and Harvey 2009). Trade credit is an alternative source of finance provided by suppliers of raw materials and other inputs. It potentially serves as an important source of finance to financially constrained firms because suppliers might be better able than financial institutions to overcome informational asymmetries and enforcement problems. This advantage may enable suppliers to lend more liberally than banks, especially during downturns.

This chapter explores the role of trade credit and its relationship to bank credit during financial crises, including the following discussions:

- Theories of trade credit
- The relationship between trade credit and bank credit, with a focus on financial crises
- Empirical evidence from two related papers—(1) a study of the effect of the 1997 Asian financial crisis on large, publicly listed firms using data from the Worldscope database (Love, Preve, and Sarria-Allende 2007); and (2) a study of the same crisis using data on small and medium enterprises (SMEs) from World Bank enterprise surveys (Love and Zaidi 2010)—with a comparison of results from the two studies and explanations for the differences
- Findings based on the comparative analysis of the two studies.

Theories of Trade Credit

Numerous theories seek to explain the provision of trade credit by suppliers. These theories often pertain to particular aspects of market structure and product characteristics and suggest that certain industries or firms may have a greater ability to use trade credit than others. Most theories of trade credit provision fall into one of the following categories, each of which is briefly reviewed below:

- Comparative advantage in information acquisition
- Comparative advantage in liquidation
- Warranty for product quality
- Price discrimination by suppliers
- Sunk costs and customized products
- Moral hazard.

Comparative Advantage in Information Acquisition

One common explanation for existence of trade credit is based on the premise that *suppliers have a cost advantage over banks in acquisition of information* about the financial health of the buyers. For example, Mian and Smith (1992) argue that monitoring of credit quality can occur as a by-product of selling if a manufacturer's sales representatives regularly visit the borrower. Similarly, suppliers often offer a two-part trade credit, which includes a substantial discount for relatively early repayment such as a 2 percent discount for payments made within 10 days. The failure of a buyer to take this discount could serve as a strong early signal of financial distress.

Biais and Gollier (1997) assume that suppliers receive different signals than banks do about the customer's probability of default and, furthermore, that the bank will extend more credit if it observes that the supplier has offered trade credit. Similarly, Smith (1987) argues that the choice of trade credit terms can be used as a screening device to elicit information about buyers' creditworthiness.

Comparative Advantage in Liquidation

Another hypothesis about the availability of trade credit concerns *suppliers' relative advantage in liquidating repossessed goods.* Trade credit providers can liquidate the goods they repossess in the event of nonpayment much easier than specialized financial institutions can. Therefore, several authors have suggested that credit provision becomes more likely when resale of the product is easier because the credit extension allows the seller to seize and resell its product if default occurs (Mian and Smith 1992; Frank and Maksimovic 1998).

Warranty for Product Quality

Some argue that *trade credit serves as a guarantee for product quality,* under the theory that the supplier willingly extends credit to allow the customer sufficient time to test the product (Long, Malitz, and Ravid 1993). Similarly, the choice of trade credit terms offered by the supplier can signal product quality (Lee and Stowe 1993; Emery and Nayar 1998).

Price Discrimination by Suppliers

Another theory involves *price discrimination as a motive for trade credit provision by suppliers.* Low competition among suppliers in an input market may create incentives to discriminate between cash and credit customers (Brennan, Maksimovic, and Zechner 1988). This price discrimination would happen if, first, the demand elasticity (or the reservation price) of credit customers is lower than that of cash customers, and second, if there is adverse selection in the credit market.

In addition, trade credit could be used as a strategic instrument in the oligopolistic supplier market. Recent empirical evidence confirms that firms with less market power do indeed extend more credit (Fabbri and Klapper 2009) and that a customer that generates a large share of its supplier's profits tends to be offered more credit (Giannetti, Burkart, and Ellingsen 2008).

Sunk Costs and Customized Products

Repeated interactions between suppliers and customers can also result in *sunk costs, which can drive trade credit provision.* Cuñat (2007) offers a model in which supplier-customer relationships that involve tailor-made products, learning by doing, or other sources of sunk costs, generate a surplus that increases with the length of the relationship. This surplus increases the amount of credit that suppliers are willing to provide because it ties firms to particular suppliers, thereby increasing the scope for punishment of nonpayment.

One theory includes product quality guarantees, market power, and sunk costs to generate a model of trade credit terms that are uniform within industries and differ across industries (Smith 1987). Ng, Smith, and Smith (1999) present empirical support for this model by documenting wide variation in credit terms *across* industries but little variation *within* industries.

Moral Hazard

Burkart and Ellingsen (2004) argue that *moral hazard is the key reason for existence of trade credit.* Firms with access to funding to buy illiquid assets are less tempted to engage in activities that are undesirable from the investors' point of view. Because in-kind credit is too difficult to divert to other uses, potential moral hazard problems on the borrower's side are reduced when trade credit is extended.

Relationship between Bank Credit and Trade Credit

So far, this chapter has discussed the reasons for the existence of trade credit. Because trade credit is, in some ways, similar to short-term bank credit (especially working capital finance offered by the banks), it is important to examine the relationship between trade credit and bank credit. This relationship has important implications for trade finance policy.

There is no clear-cut evidence concerning whether trade credit and bank credit are complements or substitutes. Some researchers posit that trade credit is complementary to bank credit. For example, Biais and Gollier (1997) hypothesize that the extension of trade credit reveals favorable information to other lenders, thereby increasing their willingness to lend. Giannetti, Burkart, and Ellingsen (2008) find empirical support for this argument, specifically that firms that use trade credit tend to borrow from a larger number of banks, use more distant banks, and have shorter relationships with their banks. Additionally, these firms receive better deals from banks—in particular, lower fees for their credit lines. This analysis suggests that trade credit and bank credit are complements rather than substitutes.

Other literature has argued that trade credit could compensate for unavailable bank credit, serving as a substitute. For example, Fisman and Love (2003) find that firms in industries with greater reliance on trade credit exhibit faster growth in countries with low levels of financial development. They argue that trade credit provides an alternative source of funds, which allows higher growth rates in industries that can be characterized as intense trade credit users.

In addition, trade creditors may have more incentives than banks to support firms that experience temporary liquidity shocks. For example, because trade credit is predominantly based on long-term relationships and likely to involve sunk costs, suppliers have an interest in keeping their customers in business (Cuñat 2007). To maintain a product-market relationship, trade creditors that are more dependent on their customers' business grant more credit to financially distressed customers than banks do (Wilner 2000). During monetary contractions, small firms are more likely to rely on supplier credit (Nilsen 2002). In addition, credit-constrained firms extend less trade credit to their customers and take more trade credit from their suppliers (Petersen and Rajan 1997).

Whether they are complements or substitutes, trade credit and bank credit have an important relationship during financial crises, which are characterized by the sharp contraction of bank lending. During financial crises, the banks become more reluctant to lend, thus exacerbating the financing constraints. In turn, firms cut investments in capital and R&D and are more likely to bypass attractive investment projects (Campello, Graham, and Harvey 2009). A priori, it is not clear whether trade finance can serve as a substitute for bank finance during the crisis, or whether, because of their complementarity, the collapse in one may exacerbate the collapse in the other.

In a systemic financial crisis, liquidity shocks experienced by some firms might be transmitted to other firms through supply credit chains. The existing theoretical models (for example, Cuñat 2007 and Wilner 2000) deal only with a single customer's distress event rather than systemic shock that might affect all suppliers and customers alike. During such periods, the supply chains might instead propagate and amplify the liquidity shocks (Raddatz 2010).

The intuition behind the propagation mechanism is straightforward: a firm that faces a default by its customers may run into liquidity problems that force it to default on its own suppliers. Therefore, in a network of firms that borrow from each other, a temporary shock to the liquidity of some firms may cause a chain reaction in which other firms also suffer financial difficulties, resulting in a large and persistent decline in aggregate activity. Liquidity shocks are passed down the supply chain from defaulting customers to a firm's suppliers, while firms with access to outside liquidity absorb these shocks with their "deep pockets" (Boissay and Gropp 2007).

During a financial crisis, such "liquidity shock chains" can operate in reverse. Firms that face tightening financing constraints as a result of bank credit contraction may withdraw credit from their customers. Thus, they pass the liquidity shock up the supply chain; that is, their customers might cut the credit to their customers, and so on. The firms that are privileged enough to have access to outside finance—that is, the "deep pockets" (Boissay and Gropp 2007)—might be the ones most severely affected by the crisis. After all, if a firm does not have bank finance to start with, the banking crisis will have little direct effect on its financial condition. The suppliers to financially constrained firms may also reduce the trade credit they extend, either because they are financially constrained (if the liquidity shocks are highly correlated) or because they choose to withdraw credit from their less-creditworthy customers. Thus, the supply chains might propagate the liquidity shocks and exacerbate the impact of the financial crisis.

Impact of Financial Crisis on Trade Credit: Empirical Evidence

Two recent studies examined trade credit behavior during the 1997 Asian financial crisis. This section summarizes the empirical results from each paper, and the next section discusses the papers' commonalities and differences.

Trade Credit in Large, Publicly Traded Firms

Love, Preve, and Sarria-Allende (2007) studied two of the four major financial crises during the 1990s: the Mexican devaluation of late 1994 and the Southeast Asia currency crisis of mid-1997, which affected Indonesia, Malaysia, the Philippines, the Republic of Korea, and Thailand. The authors used data from the Worldscope database, which contains observations on publicly traded firms representing about 95 percent of the world's market value.[1] Because this database focuses largely on those firms in which there is significant international investor interest, the sample represents the largest firms in each country.

The nature of this dataset, which comes from audited financial statements, dictated the trade credit measures used in the analysis. The two main variables of interest are accounts payable and accounts receivable, which show the amount of trade credit that firms obtain from suppliers and provide to customers, respectively. These trade credit variables are scaled using sales (for receivables) and cost of goods sold (for payables). These ratios capture the importance of trade credit in the financing of economic activity. Using ratios scaled by flow variables controls for declines in economic activity (such as sales) that are commonly associated with crises.

The study presents two types of results: the aggregate behavior of trade credit (the average for all firms) and an analysis of the heterogeneous responses of firms of varying financial health preceding the crisis.

Aggregate behavior of trade credit

Love, Preve, and Sarria-Allende (2007) found two main aggregate results: (a) a short-lived *increase* in the amount of trade credit provided and received immediately after a crisis and (b) a pronounced *decline* in the amount of credit provided (as opposed to credit received) in the aftermath of the crisis, an amount that continued to contract for several years.

The first result has a straightforward plausible explanation: after a crisis hits, buyers stop paying suppliers, and credit accumulates until either the suppliers take the write-downs or the buyers resume repayment. In other words, in the chaos of a crisis, everybody stops paying back their trade credit debt, at least temporarily. Indeed, Cuñat (2007) argues that the ability to delay repayment on trade credit in the case of temporary illiquidity is among the likely reasons for the high costs of trade credit.

However, the second result—the prolonged decline in trade credit provided—is harder to disentangle because there are two alternative explanations: on the one hand, a decline in the provision of trade credit could be the result of a supply effect; that is, firms that lack access to bank financing reduce the supply of credit they are willing to extend to their customers. On the other hand, this same pattern could be consistent with a demand-side story—that customers of these firms become less willing to accept more credit.

Analysis of heterogeneous firm responses

To disentangle the reason for decline in trade credit after the crisis, Love, Preve, and Sarria-Allende (2007) analyze the heterogeneous responses of firms, allowing a unique identification strategy that relies on precrisis indicators of a firm's vulnerability to financial crises. Firms in more vulnerable financial positions are more likely to be negatively affected by crisis-related events and are thus more likely to reduce their supply of credit to customers while increasing their own use of credit from suppliers. The authors used a firm's reliance on short-term debt as the main indicator of financial vulnerability to a crisis. Firms with a high proportion of short-term debt are more likely to be disadvantaged by a crisis because they would need to roll over their debt at a time when it is either impossible or extremely costly to do so (because interest rates increase sharply during the crisis).

The main findings of the heterogeneous analysis is that firms with high short-term debt reduce their provision of trade credit relatively more in response to an aggregate contraction in bank credit, which is consistent with a reduction in the supply of trade credit caused by the crisis. The authors also find similar results using alternative indicators of a firm's financial health, such as foreign currency-denominated debt, cash stocks, and cash flows.

These results are consistent with the redistribution view advanced by Meltzer (1960), Petersen and Rajan (1997), and Nilsen (2002), among others. This view posits that firms with better access to capital will redistribute the credit they receive to less-advantaged firms through trade credit. However, for redistribution to take place, some firms first need to raise external finance to pass on to less-privileged firms. For example, during monetary contractions in the United States, large firms have increased the issuance of commercial paper (Calomiris, Himmelberg, and Wachtel 1995) and accelerated bank credit growth, while small firms have reduced these instruments (Gertler and Gilchrist 1994). Such access to alternative sources of finance in the United States likely explains the aggregate increase in trade credit during monetary contractions (Nilsen 2002). However, during a financial crisis, alternative sources of financing become scarce as stock markets crash and foreign lenders and investors pull out their money. That is, as all the potential sources of funds dry up, there may be nothing left to redistribute through trade credit.

Love, Preve, and Sarria-Allende (2007) argue that their findings expand the traditional "redistribution view" because redistribution shuts down when all sources of finance dry up, such as during a financial crisis. The credit crunch that affects financial lenders also affects nonfinancial lenders of trade credit. Consistent with this argument, the authors also find that countries that experience a sharper decline in bank credit also experience a sharper decline in trade credit.

Trade Credit in SMEs

Love and Zaidi (2010) extend the work of Love, Preve, and Sarria-Allende (2007) along two dimensions. First, they study trade credit behavior of SMEs, which commonly have less access than large public firms to bank finance. Small firms also differ in their trade credit behavior (Nilsen 2002; Boissay and Gropp 2007). Second, the authors use detailed data on trade credit terms—the length of payables and receivables and early payment discounts—while Love, Preve, and Sarria-Allende (2007) use only data on the amount of credit from firms' balance sheets.

Love and Zaidi (2010) use a unique dataset based on a World Bank survey after the 1997 financial crisis in four East Asian countries: Indonesia, Korea, the Philippines, and Thailand. About 3,000 firms were surveyed about the impact of crisis, access to sources of finance before and after the crisis, and their prospects for recovery.

As in the earlier study, Love and Zaidi obtained two types of results: aggregate average trade-credit behavior after the crisis and the heterogeneous results for firms with various financial positions.

Aggregate behavior of trade credit

The aggregate results show that, on average, the use of trade credit declines after the crisis—shown in the decline in the percentage of inputs the sample firms buy on credit from their suppliers (accounts payable) and the percentage of sales they extend on credit to their customers (accounts receivable). In addition, the length of payables declines in three out of four countries, but there is mixed evidence on the length of receivables.

Notably, the cost of credit increases because firms offer higher discounts on cash repayments after the crisis. Thus, trade credit use becomes more expensive and more restrictive during the crisis than it was before the crisis.

Analysis of heterogeneous firm responses

In studying the heterogeneous responses of financially constrained firms, the authors use two key indicators. The first is an objective measure that separates firms that applied for a bank loan but were declined the loan before or after the crisis. Firms that submitted a loan application have revealed their demand for more bank finance, and the rejection indicates financing constraints. The second measure is a subjective perception measure based on survey responses that access to domestic bank finance became more restrictive during the crisis.

Love and Zaidi (2010) find two main results from the heterogeneous responses. First, financially constrained firms extend less credit to their customers (in terms of both percentage of output sold on credit and length of time they allow their customers for payment), and they charge more for the trade credit they do offer. Second, financially constrained firms buy a smaller percentage of inputs on credit, have a shorter length of time to repay the credit to their suppliers, and have to pay a higher cost for trade credit.

The first finding has an easy interpretation: firms that face financial constraints have to cut the credit they provide to their customers. Thus, they pass on their liquidity shock upstream to their customers, who in turn may cut trade credit to their own customers. In this way, the liquidity shock travels along the supply chain, consistent with the previous evidence in Boissay and Gropp (2007) and Raddatz (2010).

The second finding is more difficult to disentangle because the dataset does not contain any information on the financial position of the firm's suppliers. Two possible cases might affect the interpretation of this finding. First, the suppliers of the financially constrained firms might themselves be financially constrained. Note that, on average, all firms are expected to become more constrained during the crisis because of the systematic nature of financial crisis. However, some firms are likely to be more constrained than others, and the suppliers of more severely constrained firms might also be more severely constrained than an average firm. In other words, this case implies a high correlation between suppliers' and customers' financing constraints, which is consistent with Raddatz (2010). If this is the case, the second result has the same interpretation as the first: that suppliers simply pass their liquidity shock up the supply chain to their customers.

However, an alternative interpretation is possible if suppliers' financing constraints are not highly correlated with their customer's financing constraints. In other words, suppliers of firms identified as financially constrained might, on average, be no different (at least in the degree of financing constraint) from suppliers of firms identified as unconstrained. In this case, the second result suggests that suppliers of financially constrained firms are not willing to lend them a "helping hand," and they withdraw credit from less-creditworthy firms.

Although Love and Zaidi (2010) cannot disentangle which of the two possibilities is indeed the case, their results unambiguously show that negative shocks to the supply of bank credit cannot be mitigated by an increase of trade credit—and this finding has clear policy implications.

Comparison of the Two Studies

The aggregate results of both studies appear to tell the same story—of a prolonged decline in trade credit provision after financial crises. Thus, one of the main results is the same in both studies.

The ancillary aggregate result of Love, Preve, and Sarria-Allende (2007)—that of a temporary increase in trade credit during the initial stage of the crisis—is not borne out in the second study (Love and Zaidi 2010). The differences in the datasets can easily explain this difference. Love, Preve, and Sarria-Allende (2007) used a panel of annual observations that allowed the authors to track responses of firms over time—that is, in Year 0 (the year of the crisis) and several subsequent years. However, Love and Zaidi (2010) used data containing only two observations—one before crisis and another after the crisis. Thus, no time series patterns can be observed. It is plausible that SMEs also experienced a short-lived increase in trade credit before the prolonged decline; this finding would still be consistent with the observed patterns.

The two studies show both differences and similarities among the heterogeneous results. Both find that firms in more difficult financial positions cut trade credit to their customers. This is an important finding, which is robust to different samples (large firms versus SMEs) and different definitions of financial position (short-term debt in one case and subjective or objective measures of financial constraints in another case). Thus, on the receivable side, both papers' findings are similar.

The differences, however, exist on the payable side—that is, the credit that sample firms obtained from their suppliers. Love and Zaidi (2010) find that financially constrained firms received less trade credit from their suppliers during the crisis, either because suppliers themselves were constrained or because they were unwilling to offer assistance to their distressed customers. However,

Love, Preve, and Sarria-Allende (2007) find that more-constrained firms (firms with higher proportions of short-term debt) increased their reliance on trade credit during the crisis.

This difference may arise because of the differences in the sample composition. In Love, Preve, and Sarria-Allende (2007), the sample consisted of large, publicly traded firms, while the Love and Zaidi (2010) sample consisted mainly of private SMEs. Large, publicly traded firms have more market power, which increases their suppliers' willingness to extend them extra trade credit (Brennan, Maksimovic, and Zechner 1988; Giannetti, Burkart, and Ellingsen 2008). Consistent with this hypothesis, Love and Zaidi (2010) look separately at the largest firms in their sample (dominated by SMEs) and find that larger firms increased their reliance on trade credit during the crisis (in terms of increasing the percentage of inputs bought on credit).

Despite the differences in the datasets, sample firms, and study design, the two studies appear to have more similarities than differences. The aggregate results of both papers suggest a prolonged decline in trade credit after the crisis. The heterogeneous results suggest that this decline is due to the supply effect because firms that are more constrained in their access to bank finance cut their trade credit provision more than firms that are less constrained. Both studies are consistent with the view that liquidity shocks propagate along the supply chain (Raddatz 2010).

Conclusions

The studies discussed above show that trade credit cannot fully compensate for the long-term contraction in bank credit that stems from a financial crisis. These findings also suggest a complementarity of bank credit and trade credit, which can operate in both directions. In other words, a contraction in trade credit may exacerbate a contraction in bank credit, or a contraction in bank credit may lead to a collapse in trade credit.

These findings have a clear implication for trade finance policy during financial crises. Specifically, they suggest that there is sufficient rationale for supporting trade finance during a crisis. Such support may come in the form of liquidity injection, risk mitigation, addressing specific market failures, providing information, and mitigating externalities that exist in supply credit chains.

Note

1. The Worldscope database, a Thomson Reuters product, is accessible online at http://thomson reuters.com/products_services/financial/financial_products/a-z/worldscope_fundamentals/.

References

Biais, Bruno, and Christian Gollier. 1997. "Trade Credit and Credit Rationing." *The Review of Financial Studies* 10 (4): 903–37.

Boissay, Frédéric, and Reint Gropp. 2007. "Trade Credit Defaults and Liquidity Provision by Firms." Working Paper 753, European Central Bank, Frankfurt. http://www.ecb.int/pub/pdf/scpwps/ecbwp753.pdf.

Brennan, Michael, Vojislav Maksimovic, and Josef Zechner. 1988. "Vendor Financing." *The Journal of Finance* 43 (5): 1127–41.

Burkart, Mike, and Tore Ellingsen. 2004. "In-Kind Finance: A Theory of Trade Credit." *American Economic Review* 94 (3): 569–90.

Calomiris, C., C. Himmelberg, and P. Wachtel. 1995. "Commercial Paper, Corporate Finance and the Business Cycle: A Microeconomic Perspective." *Carnegie-Rochester Conference Series on Public Policy* 42 (1): 203–50.

Campello, Murillo, John R. Graham, and Campbell R. Harvey. 2009. "The Real Effects of Financial Constraints: Evidence from a Financial Crisis." Paper presented at the American Finance Association Annual Meeting, Atlanta, March 11. http://ssrn.com/abstract=1357805.

Cuñat, Vicente. 2007. "Suppliers as Debt Collectors and Insurance Providers." *The Review of Financial Studies* 20 (2): 491–527.

Emery, Gary, and Nandkumar Nayar. 1998. "Product Quality and Payment Policy." *Review of Quantitative Finance and Accounting* 10 (1998): 269–84.

Fabbri, D., and L. Klapper. 2009. "Trade Credit and the Supply Chain." Unpublished manuscript, University of Amsterdam. http://www1.fee.uva.nl/pp/bin/859fulltext.pdf.

Fisman, R., and I. Love. 2003. "Trade Credit, Financial Intermediary Development, and Industry Growth." *The Journal of Finance* 58 (1): 353–74.

Frank, Murray, and Vojislav Maksimovic. 1998. "Trade Credit, Collateral, and Adverse Selection." Unpublished manuscript, University of Maryland, College Park.

Giannetti, Mariassunta, Mike Burkart, and Tore Ellingsen. 2008. "What You Sell Is What You Lend? Explaining Trade Credit Contracts." *The Review of Financial Studies* (online). http://rfs.oxfordjournals.org/content/early/2007/12/31/rfs.hhn096.full.pdf.

Gertler, M., and S. Gilchrist. 1994. "Monetary Policy, Business Cycles, and the Behavior of Small Manufacturing Firms." *The Quarterly Journal of Economics* 109 (2): 309–40.

Lee, Yul W., and John D. Stowe. 1993. "Product Risk, Asymmetric Information, and Trade Credit." *Journal of Financial and Quantitative Analysis* 28 (2): 285–300.

Long, Michael, Ileen Malitz, and Abraham Ravid. 1993. "Trade Credit, Quality Guarantees, and Product Marketability." *Financial Management* 22 (4): 117–27.

Love, Inessa, Lorenzo Preve, and Virginia Sarria-Allende. 2007. "Trade Credit and Bank Credit: Evidence from the Recent Financial Crises." *Journal of Financial Economics* 83 (2): 453–69.

Love, Inessa, and Rida Zaidi. 2010. "Trade Credit, Bank Credit and Financial Crisis." *International Review of Finance* 10 (1): 125–47. http://onlinelibrary.wiley.com/doi/10.1111/j.1468-2443.2009.01100.x/full.

Meltzer, A. H. 1960. "Mercantile Credit, Monetary Policy, and Size of Firms." *The Review of Economics and Statistics* 42 (4): 429–37.

Mian, Shehzad L., and Clifford Smith. 1992. "Accounts Receivable Management Policy: Theory and Evidence." *The Journal of Finance* 47 (1): 169–200.

Ng, Chee K., Janet Kiholm Smith, and Richard Smith. 1999. "Evidence on the Determinants of Credit Terms Used in Interfirm Trade." *The Journal of Finance* 54 (3): 1109–29.

Nilsen, J. H., 2002. "Trade Credit and the Bank Lending Channel." *Journal of Money, Credit, and Banking* 34 (1): 226–53.

Petersen, M., and R. Rajan. 1997. "Trade Credit: Theories and Evidence." *The Review of Financial Studies* 10 (3): 661–91.

Raddatz, Claudio. 2010. "Credit Chains and Sectoral Comovement: Does the Use of Trade Credit Amplify Sectoral Shocks?" *The Review of Economics and Statistics* 92 (4): 985–1003.

Smith, Janet. 1987. "Trade Credit and Information Asymmetry." *The Journal of Finance* 42 (4): 863–872.

Wilner, B. 2000. "The Exploitation of Relationships in Financial Distress: The Case of Trade Credit." *The Journal of Finance* 55 (1): 153–78.

FIRMS' TRADE-FINANCING DECISIONS DURING CRISES

Daniela Fabbri and Anna Maria C. Menichini

Firms procure funds not only from specialized financial intermediaries, but also from suppliers, generally by delaying payments. The empirical evidence on trade credit raises questions that are hard to reconcile with existing theories:

- What justifies the widespread use of trade credit by financially unconstrained firms that have access to seemingly cheaper alternative sources?
- Why is the reliance on trade credit not always increasing in the degree of credit rationing?
- Does input lending affect the borrower's choice of inputs?
- Does the degree of creditor protection affect financing and input choices?

This chapter addresses these questions in a unified framework.

A consensus exists that trade credit is most common among firms that face borrowing constraints. This follows from the assumption that trade credit is more expensive than bank loans. According to this view, reliance on trade credit should increase in credit rationing, but the empirical evidence is not generally consistent with this common belief. Large U.S. firms (presumably less likely to be credit-constrained) rely more heavily than small firms on trade credit, with accounts payable averaging 11.6 percent and 4.4 percent of sales for large and small firms, respectively (Petersen and Rajan 1997). Similarly, in the Italian manufacturing sector, trade credit finances, on average, 38.1 percent of the input purchases of nonrationed firms and 37.5 percent of rationed ones (Marotta 2005).

A common feature in the use of trade credit, which is independent of the degree of credit rationing, is that the supplier's lending is tied closely to the value of the input. Given that not all inputs can be purchased on account, trade credit is likely to go together with some bias in the input combination. This relation seems to be confirmed by scattered evidence on financing and technological choices. Some papers find greater use of trade credit in countries with less creditor protection, such as developing countries (Rajan and Zingales 1995; La Porta et al. 1998; Demirgüç-Kunt and Maksimovic 2001; Fisman and Love 2003). Further evidence shows that firms in developing countries have a higher proportion of fixed assets and fewer intangibles than firms in developed countries (Demirgüç-Kunt and Maksimovic 1999). Although fragmented, these findings suggest a cross-country correlation between financing and input choices and identify the degree of creditor protection as a possible explanation.

To account for the foregoing stylized facts, we propose a model with collateralized bank and trade credit. Firms face uncertain demand and choose between two inputs with different degrees of observability and collateral value: tangibles and intangibles. Firms are opportunistic in that they can divert borrowed resources for private uses, but they get a lower return when diverting inputs instead of cash. Borrowers' opportunism might generate credit constraints.

Firms choose between two types of financier: banks and suppliers. Banks are specialized intermediaries and have a cost advantage in providing finance. Suppliers have both information and liquidation advantages in providing finance. The information advantage derives from suppliers' ability to observe costlessly that an input transaction has taken place. Coupled with the lower profitability of input diversion, this advantage mitigates borrowers' opportunism and relaxes firms' financial constraints. The liquidation advantage derives from the suppliers' ability to extract a greater liquidation value from the inputs collateralized in case of default. Uncertainty and multiple inputs in a model with moral hazard are the key notions used to address the open questions above.

An original feature of the model presented here is the explanation of why firms with unused lines of bank credit could demand trade credit: even they could benefit from the liquidation advantage of their suppliers. This advantage makes trade credit cheaper than bank loans, offsetting the banks' lower cost of funds.

The liquidation advantage is sufficient by itself to explain the demand for trade credit by financially unconstrained firms. The interaction between the liquidation and the information advantages helps show why reliance on trade credit does not always increase with the stringency of financing constraints. Financially constrained firms could take trade credit for both reasons. If it is for the incentive (to relax financial constraints), credit-rationed firms finance a larger share of their inputs by trade credit than do nonrationed firms, as theoretical literature holds. Conversely, when the liquidation motive dominates, the share of inputs purchased on account remains constant across firms with different degrees of credit rationing.

Regardless of the motives underlying the use of trade credit, suppliers always finance the inputs they sell but they never lend cash. The absence of cash lending by suppliers implies that trade credit can be used to finance only specific inputs, which in this setting are tangibles. It follows that whenever trade credit is used to relax financial constraints, a credit-rationed business can benefit from it only by distorting its input combination. This introduces a link between financing and input decisions, which the authors explore here to derive new predictions. More intensive use of trade credit goes together with a technology biased toward tangible assets, and the bias increases as the legal protection of creditors weakens. These predictions reconcile the scattered international evidence.

The chapter is related to the literature on trade credit that has sought to explain why agents should want to borrow from firms rather than from financial intermediaries. The traditional explanation is that trade credit facilitates the transaction (Ferris 1981; Brennan, Maksimovic, and Zechner 1988; Long, Malitz, and Ravid 1993; Summers and Wilson 2002) and relaxes borrowing constraints (Biais and Gollier 1997; Burkart and Ellingsen 2004), thus playing both nonfinancial and financial roles. What these theories fail to explain is why trade credit is also used by financially unconstrained firms and why resorting to trade credit does not necessarily increase with the severity of financial constraints, as the empirical literature shows.

This chapter proposes a new rationale for trade credit use in the liquidation advantage that suppliers have over other creditors, and it claims that when that advantage exceeds the bank's intermediation advantage, trade credit is used by rationed and unrationed firms alike.

Finally, the literature has disregarded the relationship between financing and input decisions and offered no explanation of why firms lend only inputs. The use of a multi-input technology allows us to fill these gaps.

The Model

A risk-neutral entrepreneur has an investment project that uses a tangible and an intangible input. The tangible input can be interpreted as raw material and physical capital, and intangibles as skilled labor. Inputs can be purchased q and then invested in the production process I. The amount of input purchased is observed only by the suppliers, while the amount invested is totally unobservable and is converted into a verifiable output whose value depends on the demand conditions. At times of high demand, with probability p, invested inputs produce output according to an increasing and concave production function $f(I_t, I_{nt})$. At times of low demand, there is no output, and the firm's worth is only the scrap value of unused inputs.

The entrepreneur is a price taker in both the input and output markets. The output price is normalized to 1, and so are the prices of tangible and intangible inputs.

To carry out the project, the entrepreneur uses observable internal wealth A as well as external funding from competitive banks L_B or suppliers L_S or both. Banks lend cash. The supplier of intangibles provides the input, which is fully paid for in cash. The supplier of tangibles sells the input but can also act as a financier, lending both inputs and cash.

Moral Hazard

Unobservability of investment to all parties, and of input purchases to parties other than the supplier, raise a problem of moral hazard. The entrepreneur might not invest the funds raised, either in cash or in-kind, in the venture but divert them to private uses. This problem limits the amount of credit the entrepreneur can obtain from financiers. However, the supplier can observe whether inputs have been purchased. This advantage, together with the lesser liquidity of inputs than cash, implies that moral hazard is less severe when funding comes from the supplier and not the bank.

In particular, one unit of cash gives the entrepreneur a return $\phi < 1$ if diverted, where ϕ can be interpreted as the degree of vulnerability of creditor rights; one unit of the tangible input q_t gives a return $\phi \beta_t$ if diverted, where $\beta_t < 1$ denotes the tangible input liquidity. When β_t is close to 1, the input can be resold at near the purchase price and converted into a monetary benefit. Last, diverting the intangible input gives a zero return.

Collateral Value

Tangible inputs have value when repossessed in default, while intangibles have zero collateral value. Hence, the total value of pledgeable collateral is I_t. However, different financiers have different liquidation abilities. We define $\beta_i I_t$ as the liquidation value extracted by a given financier in case of default, with $i = B$, and S referring to the bank or supplier. The supplier has a better knowledge of the resale market, so we assume $\beta_S > \beta_B = 0$, for simplicity. This makes it always efficient to pledge the collateral to the supplier in case of default.

Finally, the cost of raising one unit of funds on the market is assumed to be higher for the supplier than for the bank ($r_B < r_S$). This is consistent with the special role of banks.

Contracts

The entrepreneur-bank contract specifies the credit granted by the bank L_B and the entrepreneur's repayment obligation in case of high-demand R_B. The contract between the entrepreneur and the supplier of the tangible input specifies the credit granted by the supplier L_S, the input provision q_t, and the entrepreneur's repayment obligation R_S in case of high demand. Unlike the bank, the supplier can condition the contract also on the input purchase q_t. Last, given that the intangible input is fully paid for when purchased, the contract between entrepreneur and supplier specifies the amount of the input purchased, q_{nt}. All parties have limited liability protection.

The sequence of events is as follows:

1. Banks and suppliers make contract offers specifying the size of the loan, the repayment obligations, and the amount of inputs purchased, q_t, q_{nt}.
2. The entrepreneur chooses among contract offers.
3. The investment or diversion decisions are taken, I_t, I_{nt}; uncertainty resolves.
4. Repayments are made.

The Optimization Problem

Firms carry out production, which is financed with internal funds, with the cash provided by banks or with the cash or in-kind resources lent by suppliers of the tangible input. Because banks have a comparative advantage in raising funds ($r_B < r_S$), entrepreneurs would prefer bank financing to trade credit. However, trade credit has two advantages relative to bank's financing: First, the supplier is better at liquidating the inputs if repossessed from a defaulting firm. Second, lending inputs rather than cash reduces the scope for diversion due to their lower liquidity and thus mitigates the entrepreneur's moral hazard problem.

So trade credit arises from two motives: a liquidation motive (to exploit the supplier liquidation technology) and an incentive motive (to relax financial constraints created by moral hazard problems). In this section, we discuss the conditions under which each of the two motives becomes relevant and the way they interact.

Firms maximize profits, which can be split into two components: the returns from production (*EP*) and from diversion (*D*). The expected return from production is

$$EP = p\{f(I_t, I_{nt}) - R_B - R_S\}. \tag{2.1}$$

The return from diversion is

$$D = \phi\{\beta_t(q_t - I_t) + (A + L_B + L_S - q_t)\}$$

where the term in round brackets denotes the return from tangible input diversion, net of the amount invested in production, and that in square brackets denotes the return from residual cash diversion (the amount of cash not spent on the input purchase).

Because intangibles have zero liquidity, an opportunistic entrepreneur purchases only tangibles ($q_t \geq I_t \geq 0$) and never intangibles for diversion ($q_{nt} = I_{nt} = 0$). Moreover, because the diversion technology is inefficient ($\phi < 1$), partial diversion is never optimal. Thus, either all funds (and inputs) are used for investment ($D = 0$) or they are diverted, in which case none of the purchased inputs is invested: $I_t = 0$.

To prevent the entrepreneur from diverting all resources in equilibrium, the return from investment must exceed the maximum return from cash and input diversion, that is

$$EP \geq \phi(A + L_B), \tag{2.2}$$

$$EP \geq \phi[\beta_t q_t + A + L_B - (q_t - L_S)], \tag{2.3}$$

where (2.2) is the incentive constraint in relation to the bank, which prevents the entrepreneur from diverting internal funds as well as the credit raised from the bank, while (2.3) is the incentive constraint in relation to the supplier, preventing the entrepreneur from diverting inputs, plus any spare cash left after the input purchase. If the above constraints hold, there is no diversion in equilibrium, so that $D = 0$ and $q_t = I_t$.

Banks and suppliers participate in the venture if their expected returns cover at least the opportunity cost of funds:

$$pR_B = L_B r_B \tag{2.4}$$

$$pR_S + (1 - p)\beta_S C = L_S r_S. \tag{2.5}$$

To make the problem interesting, we assume that creditor protection is sufficiently poor (ϕ high) to constrain the investment of a zero-wealth entrepreneur.

The rest of this section derives two types of demand for trade credit: (a) a demand for liquidation, arising from the supplier's liquidation advantage and depending on the collateral value of the firm's assets, and (b) a demand for incentive, arising from the informational advantage and depending on the firm's borrowing constraints and input liquidity.

The Liquidation Motive

Assume that conditions (2.2) and (2.3) are slack; (2.4), (2.5), and (2.6) identify the liquidation motive LM for trade credit demand. Because $\beta_S > \beta_B$, pledging the collateral to the supplier relaxes its participation constraint more than the bank's. As a consequence, the total repayment due from the entrepreneur in the good state decreases, and total surplus increases. However, $r_B < r_S$ implies that the entrepreneur prefers bank credit to trade credit, that is, $L_S = 0$. Having the supplier acting as a liquidator without taking trade credit implies, using equation (2.5), that $R_S < 0$. Because the interest is in the supplier's role as financier, such contracts are not allowed for and repayment is required to be nonnegative (equation [2.6] holds):

$$R_S = \beta_S C. \tag{2.6}$$

Solving equation (2.5) for R_S, condition (2.6) implies a lower bound on trade credit demand equal to the collateral value of the inputs pledged to the supplier:

$$L_S = (\beta_S / r_S) I_t. \tag{2.7}$$

Condition (2.7) sets the trade credit demand for liquidation motives $L_{S,LM}$ equal to the discounted value of the collateral to the supplier.

The Incentive Motive

In addition to extracting more value from assets, trade credit can relax the entrepreneur's financial constraints. Because diverting inputs is less profitable than diverting cash, the supplier is less vulnerable than banks to borrowers' opportunism and could thus be willing to provide credit when the bank is not (condition [2.2] is binding). In this case, the demand for trade credit is above the level defined by condition (2.7), and trade credit is taken for incentive motives. However, suppliers are not willing to meet all possible requests because supplying too many inputs on credit could induce the entrepreneur to divert them all. The maximum trade credit extended for incentive motives IM is

$$L_{SIMmax} = (1 - \beta_t) I_t, \tag{2.8}$$

which obtains when both incentive constraints (conditions [2.2] and [2.3]) are binding. $(1 - \beta_t)$ measures the extent to which the supplier's informational advantage reduces moral hazard. If inputs are as liquid as cash ($\beta_t = 1$), this advantage is ineffective. The supplier cannot offer any trade credit when banks ration cash. Conversely, if inputs are illiquid, the informational advantage becomes important. The maximum line of trade credit is positive, and the less liquid the inputs, the greater the line of credit.

From the foregoing, it follows that two regimes could arise, depending on whether the demand for liquidation motives LM (2.7) exceeds the maximum credit line extended for incentive motives IM (2.8). This condition can be redefined exclusively in terms of the parameters of the model as follows:

$$\beta_S/r_S - (1 - \beta_S) \lessgtr 0. \tag{2.9}$$

When inputs are illiquid (β_t low) or have low salvage value (β_S low), the incentive motive outweighs the liquidation motive ($IM > LM$) and condition (2.9) is strictly negative. Vice versa, when inputs are liquid (β_t high) or have high collateral value (β_S high), the liquidation motive outweighs the incentive motive ($LM \geq IM$) and condition (2.9) is weakly positive.

Results

Our results are presented in three parts. The first subsection identifies two regimes and examines how trade credit varies with the entrepreneur's wealth between regimes. The second focuses on the trade credit demand of financially unconstrained firms. The third investigates the relation between financing, technology, and borrowing constraints.

Trade Credit and Two Alternative Regimes

As shown in the previous section, trade credit could be taken for liquidation or for incentive reasons. The way these two motives interact across different levels of wealth depends on inequality (2.9). When strictly negative, wealthy entrepreneurs take trade credit for liquidation motives, and the less-wealthy take trade credit for incentive motives. The share of inputs purchased on credit is nonincreasing in wealth and larger for entrepreneurs that are credit-rationed. We define this regime as the *dominant incentive motive*. When inequality (2.9) is positive or zero, all entrepreneurs, regardless of wealth, take trade credit for liquidation reasons, and the share of inputs purchased on credit is the same for rationed and nonrationed firms. We define this regime as the *dominant liquidation motive.*

Our theoretical results reconcile an apparent conflict between the theoretical literature and the empirical evidence. On the one hand, in arguing that trade credit mitigates credit rationing by banks, the theoretical literature has highlighted a positive relationship between trade credit and borrowing constraints (Biais and Gollier 1997; Burkart and Ellingsen 2004). On the other hand, some empirical literature finds that reliance on trade credit is practically unaffected by the degree of credit rationing (Petersen and Rajan 1997; Marotta 2005). This section accounts for both these cases.

Dominant incentive motive

The dominant incentive motive regime is illustrated in figure 2.1. The population of entrepreneurs is distributed into four wealth areas with different degrees of credit rationing. For each area, the figure shows the motive for trade credit demand (liquidation or incentive) and the share of inputs purchased on account.

Sufficiently rich entrepreneurs ($A \geq A_3$) finance the first-best investment by taking a constant amount of trade credit, equal to the discounted value of collateralized assets, and a variable amount of bank credit.[1] Each unit of trade credit below this amount costs less than bank credit because the supplier exploits the

Figure 2.1 Regime where the Incentive Motive Dominates

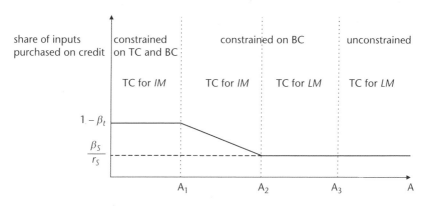

Source: Authors.
Note: The figure shows the degree of credit rationing and the motive for trade credit demand for different levels of wealth (A). Entrepreneurs can be constrained on trade credit (TC), or bank credit (BC), or be unconstrained. TC can be demanded for an incentive motive (*IM*) or a liquidation motive (*LM*). The solid line shows the share of inputs purchased on credit for different levels of wealth. $1 - \beta_t$ is the proportion of inputs that cannot be diverted, and β_S/r_S is the scrap value of collateral inputs.

greater liquidation revenues accruing in the bad state to decrease the repayment required in the good state.

The price of one unit of trade credit and bank credit is given by r_S and r_B/p, respectively. An extra unit of trade credit above the level set in equation (2.7) costs more than bank credit because there is no more collateral to pledge. This is the amount of trade credit for liquidation motives. As wealth comes down toward A_3, trade credit stays constant while bank credit increases to compensate for the lack of internal wealth, as follows:

- For $A < A_3$, the loan needed to finance the first-best investment implies a large repayment obligation that leaves the entrepreneur with a return lower than the return from diversion. Banks must therefore ration the entrepreneur to prevent opportunistic behavior, hence credit rationing. Suppliers are still willing to sell inputs on credit because they face a less severe incentive problem.
- For $A_2 \le A < A_3$, however, firms do not yet increase trade credit demand because the cost of an extra unit is still higher than the cost of bank credit. Thus, they are forced to reduce the investment below the first-best, and also trade credit and bank finance, but they keep the share of inputs purchased on account constant.
- For $A < A_2$, the shadow cost of bank credit exceeds the marginal cost of trade credit. Firms start demanding trade credit also for incentive motives, that is, to relax financial constraints. Thus, bank credit stays constant, but both trade credit and the share of tangible inputs purchased on account rise to their maximum. This is reached at $A = A_1$, when the incentive constraint in relation to the supplier also binds.
- For $A < A_1$, the entrepreneur is constrained on both credit lines and forced to reduce investment further. Both trade and bank credit decrease, but the share of inputs purchased on credit stays constant at its maximum $(1 - \beta_t)$.

In summary, across the wealth areas described in figure 2.1, the share of inputs purchased on account is nondecreasing in credit rationing.

Dominant liquidation motive

Figure 2.2 illustrates the dominant liquidation motive regime and has the same interpretation as figure 2.1.

In this regime, there are only two wealth areas:

- For $A \ge \hat{A}_1$, firms are wealthy enough to finance the first-best investment without exhausting their credit lines. They use a constant amount of trade

Figure 2.2 Regime where the Liquidation Motive Dominates

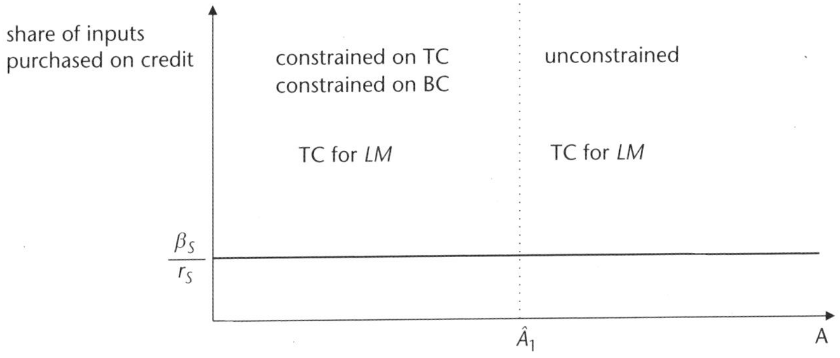

Source: Authors.
Note: The figure shows the degree of credit rationing and the motive for trade credit demand for different levels of wealth (A). Entrepreneurs can be constrained on trade credit (TC), or bank credit (BC), or be unconstrained. Trade credit is demanded for a liquidation motive (LM). The solid line shows the share of inputs purchased on credit for different levels of wealth. β_S/r_S is the scrap value of collateral inputs.

credit, equal to the scrap value of collateral assets and, as wealth decreases, an increasing amount of bank credit. The funding from banks ceases when $A = \hat{A}_1$. Because the amount of inputs financed on credit is large, the total funding obtained is so great that an extra amount of it induces the entrepreneur to divert all resources.

- Thus, for $A < \hat{A}_1$, being financially constrained on both credit lines, entrepreneurs are forced to reduce both sources of external financing as well as the investment level. In contrast with the previous regime (the dominant incentive motive), they keep financing a constant share of input by trade credit equal to β_S/r_S for any level of wealth. They have no incentive to alter it because this would increase the total cost of financing. Each unit of trade credit above the scrap value is more expensive than bank loans. Similarly, each unit below this amount can be replaced only by more costly bank credit.

Thus, in contrast with earlier financial theories, trade credit use is independent of financial constraints: both rationed and nonrationed firms purchase the same share of inputs on account, as the empirical evidence to date indicates. In this second regime, trade credit is never demanded to mitigate borrowing constraints but only for liquidation motives.

Trade Credit Demand of Financially Unconstrained Firms

The right sides of figures 2.1 and 2.2 describe the use of trade credit by unconstrained firms and deliver a common prediction: financially unconstrained firms take trade credit to exploit their suppliers' liquidation advantage. The amount of trade credit used equals the collateral value of tangible inputs pledged to the supplier.

This result also posits that the use of trade credit is bound to the value of the inputs as collateral, in line with Mian and Smith (1992) and Petersen and Rajan (1997), because the supplier's liquidation advantage makes trade credit cheaper than bank loans only up to this collateral value. Therefore, this liquidation story requires that the input has a positive collateral value; it is worth suffciently more to the supplier than to the bank in case of default, which implies the supplier's contractual seniority; and the bankruptcy law does not alter the contractually agreed-on claims held by creditors. It follows that whether the liquidation motive arises depends on traded goods characteristics—in that not all goods have a liquidation value in case of default—as well as the characteristics of the legal system.[2]

This result also implies that, even though the opportunity cost of funds is higher for input suppliers than for banks, trade credit can be cheaper than bank loans. This finding contrasts with the rather high interest rates implied by standard buyer-seller agreements generally cited in the related literature. In line with this prediction, several recent papers show that trade credit can be cheaper than bank loans (for example, Fabbri and Klapper 2009).

Input Tangibility, Financial Decisions, and Creditor Protection

Regardless of the motives underlying the use of trade credit, suppliers always finance the inputs they sell, but they never lend cash. It follows that when a constrained entrepreneur uses trade credit to relax a borrowing constraint, he also distorts the input mix toward tangibles. This implies a link between financing and input choices across different levels of wealth and borrowing constraints.

In particular, greater use of trade credit goes together with an input bias toward tangible assets, and the bias becomes stronger when creditor vulnerability increases. The intuition is that because bank credit is more sensitive than trade credit to moral hazard, weaker creditor protection raises the relative cost of bank financing. Rationed entrepreneurs consequently rely more on trade credit and tangible inputs.

Figures 2.3 and 2.4 display trade credit intensity and input tangibility, respectively, for different wealth levels.

Figure 2.3 Trade Credit Intensity, Wealth, and Creditor Protection

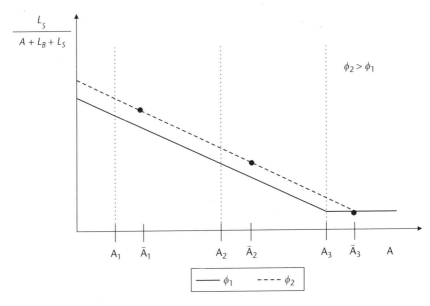

Source: Authors.
Note: The figure shows trade credit intensity $[L_S /(A + L_B + L_S)]$ for different levels of wealth (A) and for high and low degrees of creditor rights protection, ϕ_1 and ϕ_2, respectively.

Firms with $A \geq A_3$ are unconstrained on both credit lines, so both the price ratios between trade and bank credit and those between inputs are invariant in wealth. Both trade credit intensity and input tangibility hold constant for levels of wealth above A_3. For $A < A_3$, the moral hazard problem in relation to the bank becomes binding.

Reductions in wealth within the interval $A_2 \leq A < A_3$ increase the shadow cost of bank credit and thus decrease the price ratio between the two sources of funding. Firms give up more bank credit than trade credit, increasing trade credit intensity (in figure 2.3, the solid line in the interval $A_2 \leq A < A_3$). The higher price of bank credit also affects the input prices but by a different amount. It is translated fully into a higher price of intangibles because they are totally financed by bank credit and only partially into a higher price of tangibles, given that only a share $(1 - \beta_S/r_S)$ is financed by bank credit. The input price ratio thus falls for decreasing levels of wealth, inducing entrepreneurs to increase input tangibility (in figure 2.4, the solid line in the interval $A_2 \leq A < A_3$).

When wealth falls below A_2, the shadow cost of bank credit equals the cost of trade credit. For $A_1 \leq A < A_2$, firms are indifferent between financing sources.

Figure 2.4 Input Tangibility, Wealth, and Creditor Protection

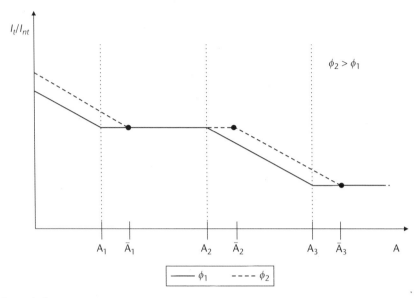

Source: Authors.
Note: The figure shows input tangibility, that is, the ratio between tangible and intangible assets (I_t/I_{nt}), for different levels of wealth (A) and for high and low degree of creditor rights protection, ϕ_1 and ϕ_2, respectively.

Although constrained by banks, they are still unconstrained by suppliers and can take trade credit at a constant price to compensate for their lesser wealth. Thus, trade credit intensity increases (in figure 2.3, the solid line in the interval $A_1 \leq A < A_2$). This extra credit is used to finance the purchase of tangibles, freeing resources to intangibles and leaving the input combination unchanged (in figure 2.4, the solid line in the interval $A_1 \leq A < A_2$).

Finally, when $A < A_1$, entrepreneurs are financially constrained on both credit lines. The prices of both sources rise, but more for bank credit, given its greater exposure to moral hazard. Because the tangible input is financed partly by trade credit, while the intangible is financed entirely by bank credit, the input price ratio decreases, increasing input tangibility (in figure 2.4, the solid line in the area $A < A_1$).

The dotted lines in figures 2.3 and 2.4 show how trade credit intensity and input tangibility, respectively, respond to an increase in creditor vulnerability. Any increase in ϕ moves all the thresholds of wealth rightward, given that all incentive constraints bind at higher wealth. Firms with $A \geq \bar{A}_3$ are unconstrained on both credit lines, and neither trade credit intensity nor asset tangibility varies. When wealth decreases ($\overline{A}_2 \leq A < \overline{A}_3$), the incentive constraint on the bank becomes stringent, and the shadow cost of bank credit rises. When $\overline{A}_1 \leq A < \overline{A}_2$, the two sources of finance cost the same, but firms are not constrained by suppliers and can use trade credit to keep investment and input combination constant (the dotted line does not shift upward in figure 2.4) and increase trade credit intensity (the dotted line shifts upward in figure 2.3). When $A < \overline{A}_1$, the change in ϕ makes the entrepreneur's moral hazard more severe in relation to both bank and supplier. Thus, both trade credit intensity and asset tangibility increase, as shown by the upward shift of the dotted lines in both figures.

The preceding analysis allows the authors to obtain the following predictions:

- *Prediction 1.* Credit-constrained firms have higher trade credit intensity and use technologies more intensive in tangible assets than unconstrained ones. Moreover, assuming that countries differ only in the degree of creditor protection, that leads to prediction 2.
- *Prediction 2.* In countries with weaker creditor protection, credit-constrained firms have higher trade credit intensity and a technological bias toward tangibles. Unconstrained firms have the same trade credit intensity and input tangibility across countries with different degrees of creditor protection.

If one takes into account that credit-constrained firms are more widespread in countries with weaker creditor protection, prediction 2 is consistent with two distinct sets of empirical evidence. First, there is a greater use of trade credit in countries with less creditor protection, including developing countries (for example, Rajan and Zingales 1995). Second, firms in developing countries have a higher proportion of fixed to total assets and fewer intangible assets than those in developed countries (for example, Demirgüç-Kunt and Maksimovic 1999). This chapter thus offers a theory that reconciles these distinct findings.

Conclusions

The chapter has investigated the determinants of trade credit and its interactions with borrowing constraints, input combination, and creditor protection. By interacting two motivations for trade credit use (liquidation and incentive motive), which the literature had so far dealt with separately, the paper has derived a set of new predictions, presented here as answers to the questions posed in the introduction.

1. *What justifies the widespread use of trade credit by financially unconstrained firms that have access to seemingly cheaper alternative sources?*

An important result presented in this chapter is that financially unconstrained firms (with unused bank credit lines) take trade credit to exploit the supplier's liquidation advantage.

2. *Why is the reliance on trade credit not always increasing in the degree of credit rationing?*
If inputs purchased on account are sufficiently liquid, the reliance on trade credit does not depend on credit rationing, but on the liquidation advantage.

3. *Does input lending have an impact on the borrower's choice of inputs?*
The second major contribution presented in this chapter is the analysis of the link between financing and input decisions. Specifically, more intensive use of trade credit goes together with a technology biased toward tangibles, and the bias increases as financial constraints tighten and creditor protection weakens. In short, greater reliance on trade credit is associated with more intensive use of tangible inputs.

4. *Does the degree of creditor protection affect financing and input choices?*
Better creditor protection decreases both the use of trade credit and the input tangibility.

Notes

1. The model implicitly assumes the entrepreneur's wealth is never so high as to finance entirely the first-best investment.
2. For a discussion of this issue, see Fabbri and Menichini 2010.

References

Biais, B., and C. Gollier. 1997. "Trade Credit and Credit Rationing." *The Review of Financial Studies* 10 (4): 903–37.
Brennan, M., V. Maksimovic, and J. Zechner. 1988. "Vendor Financing." *The Journal of Finance* 43 (5): 1127–41.
Burkart, M., and T. Ellingsen. 2004. "In-Kind Finance: A Theory of Trade Credit." *American Economic Review* 94 (3): 569–90.
Demirgüç-Kunt, A., and V. Maksimovic. 1999. "Institutions, Financial Markets, and Firm Debt Maturity." *Journal of Financial Economics* 54: 295–336.
———. 2001. "Firms as Financial Intermediaries: Evidence from Trade Credit Data." Policy Research Working Paper 2696, World Bank, Washington, DC.
Fabbri, D., and L. Klapper. 2009. "Trade Credit and the Supply Chain." Unpublished manuscript, University of Amsterdam. http://www1.fee.uva.nl/pp/bin/859fulltext.pdf.
Fabbri, D., and A. Menichini. 2010. "Trade Credit, Collateral Liquidation and Borrowing Constraints." *Journal of Financial Economics* 96 (3): 413–32.
Ferris, J. S. 1981. "A Transaction Theory of Trade Credit Use." *The Quarterly Journal of Economics* 96 (2): 247–70.

Fisman, R., and I. Love. 2003. "Trade Credit, Financial Intermediary Development, and Industry Growth." *The Journal of Finance* 58 (1): 353–74.

La Porta, R., F. Lopez-de-Silanes, A. Shleifer, and R. W. Vishny. 1998. "Law and Finance." *Journal of Political Economy* 106 (6): 1113–55.

Long, M. S., I. B. Malitz, and S. A. Ravid. 1993. "Trade Credit, Quality Guarantees, and Product Marketability." *Financial Management* 22 (4): 117–27.

Marotta, G. 2005. "Is Trade Credit More Expensive than Bank Credit Loans? Evidence from Italian Firm-Level Data." Unpublished manuscript, Department of Political Economy, University of Modena and Reggio Emilia, Italy.

Mian, S. L., and C. W. Smith. 1992. "Accounts Receivable Management Policy: Theory and Evidence." *The Journal of Finance* 47 (1): 169–200.

Petersen, M. A., and R. G. Rajan. 1997. "Trade Credit: Theories and Evidence." *The Review of Financial Studies* 10 (3): 661–91.

Rajan, R. G., and L. Zingales. 1995. "What Do We Know about Capital Structure? Some Evidence from International Data." *The Journal of Finance* 50 (5): 1421–60.

Summers, B., and N. Wilson. 2002. "Trade Credit Terms Offered by Small Firms: Survey Evidence and Empirical Analysis." *Journal of Business and Finance Accounting* 29 (3–4): 317–35.

INTERFIRM TRADE FINANCE: PAIN OR BLESSING DURING FINANCIAL CRISES?

Anna Maria C. Menichini

The severe recession that hit the global economy in 2008–09, causing low or even negative growth rates, caused widespread contractions in international trade in both developed and developing countries. The World Trade Organization reported that global trade volume contracted by 12.2 percent in 2009 because of the collapse in global demand brought on by the biggest economic downturn in decades (WTO 2010).

The contraction in international trade has been accompanied by a sharp decline in the availability of trade finance and an increase in its cost. The decline is only partly explained by the contraction in demand; a joint qualitative survey by the International Monetary Fund and the Banker's Association for Trade and Finance—now merged with International Financial Services Association (BAFT-IFSA)—found that trade finance has been constrained and its cost has increased, particularly in some developing countries, suggesting that part of the reduction in trade transactions reflects a disruption of financial intermediation (IMF-BAFT 2009). Although recent survey updates report signs of timid improvement in credit availability, the recovery prospects of trade finance markets remain weak (IMF-BAFT 2009; Malouche 2009).

The situation has raised concern, especially for firms operating in developing countries that trade in low-margin products in long manufacturing supply chains and rely heavily on trade finance to support both their exports and imports. With restricted access to financing and increased cost, these firms may have difficulties maintaining their production and trade cycle. Fear that these difficulties could further slow world trade has triggered government initiatives to support trade finance (Chauffour and Farole 2009).

This chapter focuses on interfirm trade finance—the finance that exporters provide to importers to buy goods from overseas and that exporters also receive to help them produce the goods to export and finance their extensions of credit to importers.[1]

Three stylized facts are striking and suggest that a closer look should be devoted to this specific form of financing:

- Interfirm trade finance is one of the most important sources of short-term financing for firms around the world (Petersen and Rajan 1997).[2]
- It tends to be relatively more prevalent for firms in developing countries (Demirgüç-Kunt and Maksimovic 2001; Beck, Demirgüç-Kunt, and Maksimovic 2008).
- Its use tends to increase in times of crisis (Calomiris, Himmelberg, and Wachtel 1995; Love, Preve, and Sarria-Allende 2007).

Given these facts, this chapter aims to convey an understanding of whether interfirm finance presents features that can shield it from a general credit squeeze or, rather, constitutes an extra element of tension (especially from the viewpoint of developing and low-income countries) that justifies specific, differential treatment by policy makers.

According to these features, the chapter identifies measures to increase access to this form of finance—measures that go in the direction, on one side, of creating the conditions to fully exploit its potential advantages, and, on the other, of identifying market participants that are more likely to be exposed to market failures. These measures include

- creating or improving information sharing mechanisms;
- promoting institutional reforms to increase the efficiency of the legal and judicial system; and
- creating the conditions for exploiting the benefits of structured financing schemes, especially in developing countries.

The rest of the chapter explores the main features that distinguish interfirm international trade finance from alternative sources of financing; evaluates the potential effects of a financial crisis on reliance on this form of financing among firms in developing countries; and discusses measures to increase access to this financing in times of crisis.

Features of Interfirm Trade Finance

Firms simultaneously take credit from their suppliers and provide credit to their customers. Thus, their balance sheets present both financial assets (receivables from the customer) and liabilities (payables to the supplier). Although it may seem puzzling that, in the presence of specialized financial intermediaries, firms both receive and extend trade credit, the dual practice can be rationalized in various ways.

Offering trade credit may be profitable because accounts receivable can be collateralized and used to obtain additional financing against them (Burkart and Ellingsen 2004). Alternatively, demanding trade credit may allow firms to hedge their receivables risk (Fabbri and Klapper 2009). Or it may result from firms having trouble collecting from their own customers and being forced to delay paying their suppliers (Boissay and Gropp 2007).

Alternative rationales stress the advantages that interfirm credit presents over other forms of credit. The problem of borrower opportunism that plagues any lender-borrower relationship is less severe with interfirm trade finance than with other sources of financing for various reasons. First, the supplier might have private information regarding the customer's creditworthiness that other financial intermediaries do not have (Biais and Gollier 1997)—because, for example, their repeated business relations facilitate the establishment of a relational contract, which is especially valuable when contract incompleteness renders contract enforcement difficult and costly. In such cases, agreements must be enforced informally or be self-enforcing; through repeated relations, parties abide by the agreements because they know that compliance will be rewarded with future business gains. Reputation, therefore, becomes sufficiently valuable that neither party wishes to renege on the deal.

Another factor behind the ameliorated incentive problem of interfirm financing has to do with the nature of the supplier-customer lending relationship, which, unlike other credit relationships, involves an exchange of goods rather than cash. Because goods are not as liquid as cash, defaulting on the supplier may provide limited benefits to the customer (Burkart and Ellingsen 2004). Moreover, because some tradable goods are less liquid than others, the benefits of defaulting may be further reduced. Thus, the less-severe incentive problem implied by goods lending is strictly related to the characteristics of traded goods.

Besides providing low benefits, defaulting on the supplier may also be costly. When the client cannot easily and rapidly secure the same goods elsewhere or when the goods supplied are tailored to the needs of a single customer, the supplier has considerable market power; it can threaten to stop deliveries if clients fail to pay and, thus, can enforce debt repayment better than financial intermediaries can (Cuñat 2007). As a result of the reduced buyer opportunism in all the above cases suppliers are willing to lend more liberally.

Another possible determinant of trade credit use lies in the supplier's better ability to liquidate the goods supplied in case of the customer's default (Frank and Maksimovic 2004; Fabbri and Menichini 2010). The viability of this solution depends again on traded-goods characteristics (in that not all goods have a liquidation value in case of default) as well as on the characteristics of the legal system. Although these advantages may be significantly diluted when firms trade internationally, some of them may still be relevant. In particular, it is still true that when traded goods are highly specific, there is little scope for the customer to behave opportunistically, even in an international context, or that strong supplier-customer relationships can develop among firms that trade internationally because of either long-term business interaction or difficulties in replacing the supplier. The next section elaborates further on some of the aspects that seem most relevant, both theoretically and empirically, in a crisis scenario.

The Role of Traded-Goods Characteristics

Some of the theories briefly surveyed imply that the willingness to extend trade credit may be related to the characteristics of the goods traded. Three factors related to those characteristics could facilitate interfirm credit relationships: (a) the possibility of diverting the goods traded; (b) the ease of switching to alternative suppliers; and (c) the traded goods' collateral value. To highlight the relevance of these factors, the goods are classified into three broad categories:

- *Standardized goods* can be used by many different customers and thus have a high resale value. Consequently, it is easy for the buyer to divert them. Moreover, because of their widespread use, any agent can easily sell them, which implies that their suppliers are easily replaceable. Last, they may have high liquidation value in case of the buyer's default if they have not been transformed into finished goods.
- *Differentiated goods* are more specific and often tailored to the needs of particular customers, making it more difficult for customers to switch to alternative suppliers. Because of their specificity, differentiated goods are particularly valuable in the hands of the original customer—and, because there are fewer alternative users, they are worth more in the hands of the original supplier and more difficult to divert.
- *Services* have no collateral value and are almost impossible to divert. Moreover, when the service provided is highly specific, it may be hard to find alternative suppliers.

The above analysis suggests that, because buyer opportunism is less severe for firms in sectors offering differentiated goods and services, these firms should extend more trade credit to their customers than firms selling standardized goods (moral hazard hypothesis). Similarly, because differentiated goods are worth more in the hands of the original supplier if the buyer defaults, firms selling (respectively buying) differentiated goods should offer (respectively receive) more trade credit (liquidation hypothesis).

Using a sample of small U.S. firms, Giannetti, Burkart, and Ellingsen (2008) show that service firms as well as firms producing differentiated products grant more trade credit, while firms offering standardized goods offer less trade credit. This evidence seems to support the moral hazard hypothesis but does not clearly disentangle whether the driver of the results is the different diversion value of the goods or the different cost in switching to alternative suppliers. McMillan and Woodruff (1999) provide a direct investigation into the relevance of this last motivation. Using survey data collected on a sample of Vietnamese firms, they show that customers lacking alternative suppliers receive more trade credit.[3]

Regarding the collateral hypothesis, Giannetti, Burkart, and Ellingsen (2008) provide some limited supporting evidence because firms offering differentiated goods offer more trade credit, and firms buying a larger proportion of differentiated goods receive more trade credit. Petersen and Rajan (1997) also provide evidence in support of this hypothesis, using as a proxy for the liquidation advantage the fraction of the firm's inventory not consisting of finished goods.

The Role of Credit Chains

One distinguishing feature of trade credit is that it appears on both sides of the firms' balance sheets. In addition, because firms' customers tend to belong to specific sectors, trade credit is not well diversified at the firm level. Debtors' lending and lack of diversification may constitute an element of great risk in times of crisis, particularly in light of the increasing organization of production in global supply chains—that is, in a network of different types of companies that participate in the production of goods and services and ultimately deliver them to the final consumer.

Aside from the aspects concerning technology improvements and efficiency increasing methods of production, a key element in determining the competitiveness of each company along the chain, and ultimately of the whole chain of production, is related to financing. To guarantee themselves production orders, suppliers have to offer their customers attractive payment options. However, to finance their credit extensions, they themselves need financing, which may be extended by upstream suppliers or by financial intermediaries. When firms are perceived as potentially risky, or the financial sector is poorly developed—often the case for firms in developing countries—access to credit for weak firms in the chain may be difficult and costly.

All of this implies that, besides the supplying relationship, there may be strong financial links among the various parties that interact along a supply chain. It is no surprise, therefore, that interfirm trade finance becomes a particular issue of concern in times of crisis, especially for developing countries, for a number of reasons:

- Large international companies in developed countries have increasingly outsourced their production to low-cost sourcing markets. Disruptions in production may then arise if these suppliers have insufficient credit to finance the shipment of their production to the next stage of the chain or even to carry out production.
- Exports from emerging markets may highly depend on imports from developed-country firms along the chain. A collapse in import financing may further depress emerging countries' exports, thus causing further disruptions in production.
- Shocks to the liquidity of some firms, caused by the default of customers in a depressed sector, may in turn cause default or postponement of debt repayments on their suppliers and propagate through the supply chain. With a large proportion of their debts financed with trade credit (Demirgüç-Kunt and Maksimovic 2001; Beck, Demirgüç-Kunt, and Maksimovic 2008), firms in emerging countries might face stronger risks of propagation of shocks. The scale of the damage depends on the length of the supply chain between constrained agents. In a recession, such chains are longer because more firms suffer negative shocks to their flow of funds. However, the presence of firms with sufficient access to outside finance to absorb defaults without transmitting them along the supply chain (deep-pockets firms) can weaken the credit-chain propagation mechanism (Kiyotaki and Moore 1997).

The latter theory has received some empirical support. Raddatz (2010) provides evidence of the presence and relevance of credit chains for the transmission and amplification of shocks. Boissay and Gropp (2007) find evidence in favor of the existence of trade credit default chains. In particular, firms that face default are themselves more likely to default. Liquidity shocks are transmitted along the trade credit chain until they reach deep-pockets firms, which ultimately absorb the shock. This theory suggests that external effects may be associated with supply-chain productions that might amplify the downsides of a credit crunch.

However, if it is true that interfirm trade finance may be a mechanism of propagation of shocks, it is also true that the repeated business interactions among these firms may provide relevant benefits, especially during a financial crisis. The typical fear that lack of trust in times of extreme uncertainty may squeeze intermediated trade finance, exacerbating the effects of the crisis, may be less of a problem for firms operating along supply chains. These firms are often involved in long-term relationships and, thus, are less likely to experience an uncertainty-driven contraction in financing.[4]

This might also explain why trade credit is often countercyclical.[5] In times of recession, banks are more concerned about credit risk and less willing to extend credit. Firms that rely more on relational contracts can increase their reliance on trade credit; the relationship of trust with the supplier makes up for the higher credit risk. Conversely, firms that rely on intermediated finance (formal contracts) are likely to be squeezed by the credit contraction because the higher credit risk and the lack of a credit history will discourage suppliers from extending them credit.

The Role of Institutions

One factor of crucial importance in determining the availability of international trade finance is the legal system in which trading countries operate. Inefficiency of the judicial system or of the legal system in general—in the form of inadequate contract law or bankruptcy law—increases enforcement costs and thus commercial risk. This inefficiency affects the cost and the availability of financing, thus hampering international trade.

How does the legal system affect interfirm credit? A number of papers find evidence that trade credit is relatively more prevalent in countries with worse legal institutions and lower investor protection (Demirgüç-Kunt and Maksimovic 2001; Beck, Demirgüç-Kunt, and Maksimovic 2008). This seems puzzling because one may expect that better legal institutions facilitate all types of borrowing, including trade credit. This finding can nevertheless be explained by noting that, unlike financial intermediaries, trade creditors may be able to more effectively enforce contracts without resorting to the legal system by stopping future supplies. This intuition seems to be confirmed by a study, based on 1997 survey data from small and medium-size manufacturers in transition countries, concluding that ongoing relationships are more likely to be preserved when goods are complex, assets are specific, and it is difficult for customers to resort to alternative suppliers (Johnson, McMillan, and Woodruff 2002).

According to other studies, the varying efficiency of countries' legal systems might be related to their varying legal origins (La Porta et al. 1998). More precisely, countries belonging to the common law tradition are found to have more efficient judicial systems, and thus lower enforcement costs, than those belonging to the civil law tradition. This variation results in an ample variety of codes and procedures across countries (as shown by, among others, Djankov et al. 2002, 2008) that may introduce extra elements of uncertainty in the buyer-seller relationship and that parties certainly take into account when choosing trading partners and deciding whether to extend them credit.

Given the documented greater prevalence of trade credit in countries with worse legal institutions and lower investor protection, how does uncertainty in enforcement affect the provision of credit to suppliers? Johnson, McMillan, and Woodruff (2003) find that although interfirm credit does occur even under a poor enforcement of contracts, thanks to relational contracts, efficient courts are nevertheless important at the start of a trading relationship, encouraging firms to take on new partners and thus promote future long-lasting relationships. Thus, workable courts have positive external effects because, by facilitating new trading relationships, they improve on relational contracting and boost overall productivity. This role is even more important in times of crisis because increased uncertainty may increase the perception of the risk underlying a trading relationship and induce suppliers to refrain from extending credit. The institutional framework, therefore, plays a direct role in favoring interfirm trade finance.

However, legal institutions also may affect interfirm trade finance through alternative channels. For example, a low-quality legal system may jeopardize both the effective use of structured financing schemes—whereby the lender extends a loan to the borrower by securitizing its assets—and the possibility of exploiting the supplier's better ability to liquidate the goods supplied and not yet transformed in case of default.

Policy Implications

The analysis so far has highlighted some factors that may affect the provision of interfirm finance, stressing those raising greater concern in times of crisis. This section focuses on policy instruments that could address those concerns.

Improved Information Sharing

Some literature—both theoretical (Biais and Gollier 1997) and empirical (McMillan and Woodruff 1999; Johnson, McMillan, and Woodruff 2002)—has rationalized the use of trade credit based on the informational advantage the supplier has over other creditors regarding the buyer's creditworthiness. This advantage may descend from existing business relationships or from prior investigations of the customer's reliability—for example, through information sharing mechanisms.

Acquiring information about the customer's repayment history across a range of suppliers can be valuable in making credit extension decisions. Kallberg and Udell (2003) provide evidence of this, showing that trade credit history in Dun & Bradstreet reports improves default predictions relative to financial statements alone. In a crisis scenario in which banks are more concerned about credit risk and less willing to extend credit, these factors may be crucial in limiting the potential damages of a trade finance shortage and preventing such a shortage from adding to the downturn in demand.

In particular, relevant benefits may be gained from improving cross-country information sharing mechanisms—for example, by extending public credit registries and voluntary exchange mechanisms to developing countries (where these systems are often still being designed) and by promoting the sharing of this information across trading countries.

Exploitation of Traded-Goods Characteristics

The previous discussion confirmed that interfirm trade financing presents some advantages over other lending relationships, related to the characteristics of traded goods. In particular, the moral hazard hypothesis, which predicts that firms selling (or buying) standardized goods should offer (or receive) less trade credit, has found some empirical support (Giannetti, Burkart, and Ellingsen, 2008).

One may then expect the problems brought about by the financial crisis to be particularly exacerbated for firms more exposed to moral hazard, which may find it harder to raise credit, especially during a financial crisis. By implication, different firms operating along a supply chain may "suffer" the effects of a credit crunch differently. Commodities, for instance, are sold to manufacturers that process them into intermediate inputs or directly into finished goods. Having a high resale value, these goods can be classified as standardized. In times of crisis, suppliers of commodities may be reluctant to extend credit against them to downstream firms. Intermediate inputs, instead, tend to be much more customized to their intended buyers than commodities or even final goods and hence have a low resale value that mitigates moral hazard problems. A similar argument can be made for suppliers of offshore services. The consequences of a credit crunch may thus be different for firms along the chain, and this analysis may provide some useful indications regarding the candidate "weak links." Possible ways of dealing with them are discussed in the next section.

Regarding the liquidation advantage, although the literature has provided some evidence in support of it (Petersen and Rajan 1997; Giannetti, Burkart, and Ellingsen, 2008), it is generally true that trade credit is a junior claim and that, in an international trade scenario, the chances for the supplier to repossess the goods supplied are extremely low, especially when the trading countries operate in different legal environments. Absent the ability to repossess goods, suppliers may not be willing to supply goods on credit and thus may require cash payments, with a subsequent efficiency loss.

One way to preserve the liquidation advantage would be for the supplier to secure the goods. By doing so, in the event of default, the supplier might reclaim any goods not yet transformed into output. Of course, not all types of goods can be secured because some of them can be easily hidden or diverted and therefore subtracted from the bankrupt party's estate. Other goods, such as equipment or heavy machineries, may be less easily diverted and, thus, may become the object of a secured claim. The willingness to extend credit may therefore be boosted by encouraging the creation of liens on the goods supplied to avoid actions from other creditors in case of default. The viability of this option depends, of course, on the specific provisions of the trading countries' bankruptcy codes and on their efficiency in enforcing creditor's rights (again, depending on institutional factors).[6]

Rejoining the "Broken Chains"

A downside of interfirm finance is that it may be a mechanism that propagates and amplifies shocks. However, the evidence in support of the existence of trade credit default chains that stop when they reach large, liquid firms with access to financial markets (Boissay and Gropp 2007) suggests that there is some room for intervention.

In these circumstances, it is important to identify breaks in the chain (firms more exposed to the risk of insolvency and more likely to start the chain of defaults discussed previously, such as sellers of commodities or of final goods) and devise interventions to prevent disruptions in the chain. However, depending on the type of intervention, many new issues arise. First, it may be difficult to discriminate between a firm that is facing a temporary liquidity shock and one that is insolvent (for which a targeted intervention only postpones the decision to shut down). Moreover, moral hazard problems may arise in adopting schemes of financial support for vulnerable firms because these might divert the financing obtained to alternative uses.

One way to overcome these problems might be to design schemes aimed at extending the maturity period of trade credit while not challenging the financial health and ongoing viability of other firms along the supply chain—that is, ensuring that suppliers can collect payments as soon as possible. For example, receivables-backed finance programs are normally used to finance exports, allowing firms to get the receivables off their books and promote a greater extension of trade credit.[7]

A similar scheme, used largely to finance imports, is payables-backed supplier finance, also known as reverse factoring, by which the buyer delegates to a bank or to other financial intermediaries the handling of its payables. It allows buyers to extend payment terms and allows suppliers to receive early payment or payment at maturity, according to their actual working capital needs. It can be particularly important to finance the working capital of risky exporting firms in emerging countries with little access to credit and to reduce the processing costs of the buyer, which can make fewer payments to a single creditor (the factor) rather than various payments to multiple suppliers. The extension of the maturity period of trade credit that this arrangement permits would, at least temporarily, relax buyers' financial constraints and may make it possible to screen for viable firms facing occasional liquidity shocks as opposed to the distressed ones. More important, the possibility for the supplier to receive early payment, rather than payment at maturity, would inject fresh liquidity into the chain and possibly absorb negative shocks.

Some of these schemes are already effectively in use in many supply-chain finance programs (GBI 2007),[8] but in times of uncertainty and lack of confidence and with their own access to finance drying up, many financiers may be more reluctant to provide them. In these circumstances, the response of public-backed institutions may prove important to mitigate risk and encourage the implementation of such measures.[9]

Institutional Reforms to Increase Access to Trade Finance

The above discussions have highlighted the importance of institutional factors to interfirm finance. By increasing uncertainty for traders, heterogeneous or inefficient institutional structures give rise to legal or administrative barriers that can strongly hamper cross-border transactions. In particular, poor or uncertain creditor protection may limit the willingness to extend credit, worsen the conditions under which credit is granted, and jeopardize future potentially profitable trading relationships. These consequences are especially likely in newly established relationships—in which it is not possible to base the credit extension decision on previous credit histories or trust—and may prove especially harmful for developing countries needing export financing or seeking to finance their imports.

A harmonization of the rules and more efficient judicial systems are therefore imperative to keep international trade finance going, and possibly growing, and to level the playing field for firms in developing countries seeking to export to developed countries.[10] This issue is clearly important because an efficient judicial system maximizes the total value available to be divided between debtor and creditors and reduces the ex ante cost of credit. However, institutional reforms are also important to address the possible implications of the crisis for corporate failure rates. Based on the discussion in the previous section, especially for firms along supply chains, distress may have self-reinforcing effects and cause systemic defaults. A question therefore arises about whether existing bankruptcy regimes can adequately deal with situations of this type or whether reforms are needed to alleviate the effects of the crisis.

The issue is taken up by Djankov (2009), who discusses a menu of possible reforms designed to deal with situations of distress following a crisis: the "super-priority" of fresh capital, prepackaged bankruptcy, and "super-bankruptcy." The super-priority of fresh capital is particularly interesting in the light of the discussion on interfirm finance as a mechanism of propagation of shocks. As argued previously, in times of crisis it is important that financing be available along the chain to absorb negative shocks and prevent inefficient liquidation. One possible solution is to reform bankruptcy codes in the direction of allowing new capital to take priority over all old creditors, including secured ones. This reform gives an extra incentive to lend to distressed businesses, thereby allowing an injection of fresh capital in the chain.

Conclusions

The chapter has focused on interfirm international trade finance, identifying theoretical economic rationales that could underpin policy actions in favor of this form of financing in times of crisis, with a focus on constraints faced by developing countries. To this aim, it has identified some distinguishing features shown to influence firms' reliance on, and provision of, trade credit to understand under which circumstances these features constitute either an issue of concern in times of crisis or a "shield" for financially squeezed firms.

Two main and opposing aspects have emerged from the analysis. On one side, interfirm finance may be a way to overcome informational problems associated with standard lender-borrower relations because of the lower incentive problem its use involves. On the other side, due to firms' interconnection along supply chains, interfirm finance may be a mechanism that propagates shocks, especially for firms operating in developing countries.

Although the advantages of interfirm trade finance could remain largely unexploited because of developing countries' poor legal institutions, the disadvantages could be exacerbated because of their greater exposure to a default chain. Based on these arguments, the chapter has identified choices for policy makers to boost firms' access to interfirm trade finance in times of crisis.

Notes

1. The study does not address issues related to trade finance intermediated by banks per se, although the bank-intermediated segment does represent a conspicuous share of trade finance.

2. According to Global Business Intelligence, a consulting firm specializing in supply-chain matters, accounts payable and receivable represent 78 percent of international trade (GBI 2007).

3. A distinctive feature of the Vietnamese economy is the absence of legal enforcement of contracts. The authors interpret the existence of interfirm credit in this environment as evidence of relational mechanisms in place.

4. Anecdotal evidence shows that the increase in the perception of risk induced by the crisis has promoted supply-chain solutions and that supply-chain finance is being increasingly used to mitigate risk and increase firms' capital needs.

5. Calomiris, Himmelberg, and Wachtel (1995) and Love, Preve, and Sarria-Allende (2007), for example, show that in the United States and emerging markets, respectively, the extension of trade credit increases during financial crises.

6. Several business laws do allow trade creditors to include specific liquidation rights in the sale contract, but the degree of legal protection guaranteed to secured creditors differs across countries. In some bankruptcy codes, secured creditors can enforce their contractual rights and recover the collateral outside the ongoing insolvency proceedings. In others, they are included in the bankruptcy process, generally for a specified period of time, during which the administrator can either sell the firm as a going concern or sell assets piecemeal. In this second case, secured creditors are first in the order of priority.

7. Being off the balance sheet, this instrument would not reduce the exporter's existing credit limits. Moreover, it would overcome the problems created by banks' reluctance to lend against receivables, especially in emerging markets, when a large percentage of these receivables are international.

8. The reverse factoring, for instance, is used in various countries by large international retailers with supermarket chains to support their suppliers' cash flows while optimizing their own working capital management. Finance is structured so that trade payables on the retailers' balance sheets are classified as trade credit rather than bank debt, thereby avoiding a reduction in their credit limits. Similarly, being structured as receivables purchased from the supplier, which is without recourse, this finance is off the balance sheet for the supplier as well. Therefore, it has positive effects for both the retailers and their suppliers.

9. Along these lines, the supply-chain finance group at the International Finance Corporation (of the World Bank Group) has recently attempted to boost short-term trade finance by creating a temporary secondary market for receivables. Export credit agencies are also implementing programs for short-term lending of working capital and credit guarantees aimed at small and medium enterprises.

10. Letters of credit were originally introduced to deal with this problem and ensure enforceable contracts.

References

Biais, Bruno, and Christian Gollier. 1997. "Trade Credit and Credit Rationing." *The Review of Financial Studies* 10 (4): 903–37.

Beck, Thorsten, Asli Demirgüç-Kunt, and Vojislav Maksimovic. 2008. "Financing Patterns around the World: Are Small Firms Different?" *Journal of Financial Economics* 89 (3): 467–87.

Boissay, Frederic, and Reint Gropp. 2007. "Trade Credit Defaults and the Liquidity Provision by Firms." Working Paper 753, European Central Bank, Frankfurt am Main.

Burkart, Mike, and Tore Ellingsen. 2004. "In-Kind Finance: A Theory of Trade Credit." *American Economic Review* 94 (3): 569–90.

Calomiris, Charles W., Charles P. Himmelberg, and Paul Wachtel. 1995. "Commercial Paper, Corporate Finance, and the Business Cycle: A Microeconomic Perspective." Working Paper 4848, National Bureau of Economic Research, Cambridge, MA.

Chauffour, Jean-Pierre, and Thomas Farole. 2009. "Trade Finance in Crisis: Market Adjustment or Market Failure?" Policy Research Working Paper 5003, World Bank, Washington, DC.

Cuñat, Vicente. 2007. "Trade Credit: Suppliers as Debt Collectors and Insurance Providers." *The Review of Financial Studies* 20 (2): 491–527.

Demirguc-Kunt, Asli, and Vojislav Maksimovic. 2001. "Firms as Financial Intermediaries: Evidence from Trade Credit Data." Policy Research Working Paper 2696, World Bank, Washington, DC.

Djankov, Simeon. 2009. "Bankruptcy Regimes during Financial Distress." Unpublished manuscript, World Bank, Washington, DC.

Djankov, Simeon, Oliver Hart, Caralee McLiesh, and Andrei Shleifer. 2008. "Debt Enforcement around the World." *Journal of Political Economy* 116 (6): 1105–49.

Djankov, Simeon, Rafael La Porta, Florencio Lopez-de-Silanes, and Andrei Shleifer. 2002. "Courts: The Lex Mundi Project." Working Paper 8890, National Bureau of Economic Research, Cambridge, MA.

Fabbri, Daniela, and Leora Klapper. 2009. "Trade Credit and the Supply Chain." Unpublished manuscript, University of Amsterdam. http://www1.fee.uva.nl/pp/bin/859fulltext.pdf.

Fabbri, Daniela, and Anna Maria C. Menichini. 2010. "Trade Credit, Collateral Liquidation and Borrowing Constraints." *Journal of Financial Economics* 96 (3): 413–32.

Frank, Murray Z., and Vojislav Maksimovic. 2004. "Trade Credit, Collateral, and Adverse Selection." Unpublished working paper, University of Maryland, College Park.

GBI (Global Business Intelligence). 2007. "Global Supply Chain Finance, First Edition." Unpublished manuscript, GBI, Vancouver.

Giannetti, Mariassunta, Mike Burkart, and Tore Ellingsen. 2008. "What You Sell Is What You Lend? Explaining Trade Credit Contracts." *The Review of Financial Studies* (online). http://rfs.oxfordjournals.org/content/early/2007/12/31/rfs.hhn096.full.pdf.

IMF-BAFT (International Monetary Fund-Bankers' Association for Finance and Trade). 2009. "Trade Finance Survey: A Survey among Banks Assessing the Current Trade Finance Environment." Report by FImetrix for IMF and BAFT, Washington, DC.

Johnson, Simon, John McMillan, and Christopher M. Woodruff. 2002. "Courts and Relational Contracts." *Journal of Law, Economics, and Organization* 18 (1): 221–77.

Kallberg, Jarl G., and Gregory F. Udell. 2003. "The Value of Private Sector Business Credit Information Sharing: The U.S. Case." *Journal of Banking and Finance* 27 (3): 449–69.

Kiyotaki, Nobuhiro, and John Moore. 1997. "Credit Chains." *Journal of Political Economy* 105 (2): 211–48.

La Porta, Rafael, Florencio Lopez-de-Silanes, Andrei Shleifer, and Robert W. Vishny. 1998. "Law and Finance." *Journal of Political Economy* 106 (6): 1113–55.

Love, Inessa, Lorenzo A. Preve, and Virginia Sarria-Allende. 2007. "Trade Credit and Bank Credit: Evidence from the Recent Financial Crises." *Journal of Financial Economics* 83 (2): 453–69.

Malouche, Mariem. 2009. "Trade and Trade Finance Developments in 14 Developing Countries Post-September 2008." Policy Research Working Paper 5138, World Bank, Washington, DC.

McMillan, John, and Christopher M. Woodruff. 1999. "Interfirm Relationships and Informal Credit in Vietnam." *Quarterly Journal of Economics* 114 (4): 1285–320.

Petersen, M. A., and R. G. Rajan. 1997. "Trade Credit: Theories and Evidence." *The Review of Financial Studies* 10 (3): 661–91.

Raddatz, Claudio. 2010. "Credit Chains and Sectoral Comovement: Does the Use of Trade Credit Amplify Sectoral Shocks?" *The Review of Economics and Statistics* 92 (4): 985–1003.

WTO (World Trade Organization). 2010. "Trade to expand by 9.5% in 2010 after a dismal 2009, WTO reports." Press Release 598, March 26.

FINANCIAL CRISIS AND SUPPLY-CHAIN FINANCING

Leora Klapper and Douglas Randall

Supply-chain financing is an important source of funds for both small and large firms around the world. The 2008–09 financial crisis, however, brought significant firm- and market-level disruptions that were likely to affect interfirm financing decisions.

This chapter explores the use of trade credit during the financial crisis of 2008–09 and therefore contributes to the related literature exploring why buyers depend more on trade credit for short-term financing during periods of contraction in bank credit (Calomiris, Himmelberg, and Wachtel 1995; Nilsen 2002; Love, Preve, and Sarria-Allende 2007). One hypothesis is that customers in financial distress can more easily extract credit concessions from their suppliers, who are interested in maintaining a long-term relationship, than they could from lenders in a competitive credit market (Evans 1998; Wilner 2000). Alternatively, it has been observed that the higher interest rates charged by suppliers, compared with the banking sector, serve as a premium for an arrangement in which the supplier provides extra liquidity to the customer in the event of a shock (Cuñat 2007).

The authors used data from the World Bank's Financial Crisis Survey (FCS), which extended the Enterprise Survey (ES) database to create a panel of 1,686 firms in Bulgaria, Hungary, Latvia, Lithuania, Romania, and Turkey[1] in 2007 and 2009. The data provide novel evidence that the degree to which market competition and liquidity affected a firm's decision to extend trade credit in 2009 varied with the country-level severity of the crisis. The chapter focuses on two key measures of supply-chain financing: first, whether the firm extended trade credit to its customers; and second, a unique and timely variable of whether the firm increased, maintained, or decreased the volume of goods sold on trade credit during the crisis.

Rationales for Trade Finance

Previous literature on the extension of trade credit by suppliers to their customers confirms that it is an essential component of external firm financing. The diversity of firms and industries that use supplier credit suggests that no single reason drives its popularity. Rather, its use is motivated by several rationales (Petersen and Rajan 1997; Fabbri and Klapper 2008).

First, trade credit extensions may be linked to market power and used as a form of price discrimination, enabling customers to demand better terms from suppliers if they make up a large share of the supplier's business (Brennan, Maksimovic, and Zechner 1988). Indeed, Klapper, Laeven, and Rajan (2010) show that the largest and most creditworthy buyers receive contracts with the longest maturities from smaller, investment-grade suppliers. Similarly, suppliers in competitive markets are at the mercy of their customers' market power and may offer attractive trade credit terms to attract new customers and maintain the loyalty of existing ones (Fisman and Raturi 2004; Giannetti, Burkart, and Ellingsen 2008).

The extension of trade credit may also serve as a risk management mechanism to reduce informational asymmetries between buyers and sellers, allowing buyers to ensure the quality of the products and sellers to reduce payment risks through two-part payment terms (Ng, Smith, and Smith 1999).

In addition, trade credit extensions serve as a substitute for bank credit. Customers are likely to demand trade credit extensions if they face obstacles in obtaining affordable bank credit or believe that their suppliers have cheaper access to financing and a comparative advantage in passing it on (Ng, Smith, and Smith 1999). Empirical research has shown that firms with access to credit from banks or their own suppliers extend a greater amount of credit to their customers (Petersen and Rajan 1997; McMillan and Woodruff 1999; Fabbri and Klapper 2008). The substitution of trade credit for bank credit is particularly relevant in economies with poorly developed financial markets, although empirical evidence on the relationship between trade credit and growth is mixed (Demirgüç-Kunt and Maksimovic 1999; Fisman and Love 2003; Cull, Xu, and Zhu 2009).

Data and Summary Statistics

The FCS provides unique insight into the use of trade credit during the financial crisis in a representative cross-section of firms in six Eastern European countries.

The firms included in the FCS are a subsample of firms drawn from the set of firms previously interviewed in the ES. Because the last ES round refers to the fiscal year 2007, the ES data allow an examination of the precrisis behavior and structure of firms and also facilitate the isolation of cause and effect in the econometric analysis.

In 2009, FCS participants were asked, "In the last completed month, did this establishment sell goods or services on credit?" Forty-three percent of the firms reported extending trade credit to their customers, with an econometrically significant variation across countries. In Lithuania, 80 percent of firms reported extending trade credit, while the figure was only 16 percent among Hungarian firms, as figure 4.1 shows.

To examine how the extension of trade credit changed as a result of the 2008–09 financial crisis, the FCS asked the subsample of firms that had sold goods on credit in the previous month, "Comparing last month's sales on credit with the month before, did they increase, decrease, or remain the same?" Across countries, almost half the firms that extended trade credit maintained a steady extension of credit during the crisis, while an almost even percentage reported a decrease or increase in the volume of goods sold on credit (29 percent versus 23 percent, respectively).

Hungarian firms experienced a comparatively large contraction in trade credit offerings; only 3 percent reported an increase in the volume of goods offered on trade credit. The situation was notably different in Lithuania and Romania, where more than 40 percent of firms reported increases in the volume of goods sold on trade credit, as shown in figure 4.2.

Figure 4.1 Extension of Trade Credit, by Country
share of firms offering trade credit

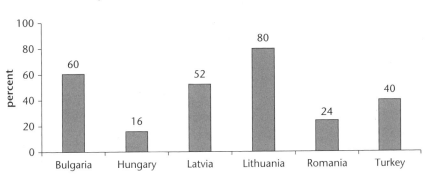

Source: World Bank 2009.

Figure 4.2 Changes in the Extension of Trade Credit, by Country
share of surveyed firms

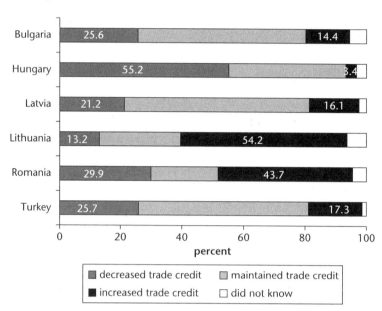

Source: World Bank 2009.

Sample Description

Of the firms in the sample, 33 percent are small (fewer than 20 employees), 35 percent are medium-size (20–99) employees, and 32 percent are large (100 or more employees). Firms in the manufacturing sector constitute 55 percent of the sample, while the retail and other services sectors represent 21 percent and 24 percent, respectively. Twenty-three percent of all firms are located in their countries' capital cities, 41 percent export either directly or indirectly, and 9 percent are foreign-owned.

Measures of Market Competition

Among the variables that might explain a firm's decision to offer trade credit to its customers is the use of trade credit as a competitive gesture—that is, to help firms distinguish themselves from their competitors (Fisman and Raturi 2004; Giannetti, Burkart, and Ellingsen 2008). In 2007, before the crisis, firms were asked to rate the importance of domestic competitors to the firm's production cost decisions. They were also asked to rate the importance of domestic competitors to their new

Table 4.1 Description of FCS Sample

	Bulgaria	Hungary	Latvia	Lithuania	Romania	Turkey
Observations (no.)	150	187	226	239	370	514
Composition by size (%)						
Small (< 20 employees)	47	34	36	39	31	28
Medium (20–99 employees)	35	30	31	34	35	38
Large (100+ employees)	18	36	33	27	34	34
Composition by sector (%)						
Manufacturing	36	40	35	38	38	95
Retail	28	25	32	29	31	1
Other services	36	35	33	33	31	4
Composition by characteristic (%)						
Capital city	29	35	50	22	16	10
Exporter	25	33	36	39	17	75
Foreign-owned	9	19	15	8	11	2

Source: World Bank 2007.
Note: FCS = Financial Crisis Survey.

product development decisions. Finally, the firms were asked both questions about foreign competitors. If the firm responded "very important" (highest on a scale of four) to any of the four questions, the firm was considered to be operating in a competitive market. Across the sample, approximately 41 percent of firms operated in competitive markets.

Similarly, innovative firms looking to expand into new markets may also regard trade credit as a useful device for luring new customers away from their existing suppliers. Innovative firms, defined as those who introduced a new product or service in the 2005–07 period, accounted for 52 percent of the sample.

Measures of Financial Access

Given that the extension of trade credit implies a delay in output payments with nontrivial consequences on a firm's liquidity, it follows that financial constraints affect a firm's decision to extend trade credit (Petersen and Rajan 1997; McMillan and Woodruff 1999; Fabbri and Klapper 2008). In 2007, 57 percent of the surveyed firms reported having a loan or line of credit from a financial institution, with significant variations across countries, as figure 4.3 illustrates.

Just as they offer trade credit to their customers, firms may also turn to their own suppliers for extensions of trade credit to provide liquidity, establishing a system of supply-chain financing. Approximately 71 percent of the firms reported using supplier credit in 2007—a figure that, again, varied among the countries in the sample, as figure 4.3 also shows. Although Hungary has the lowest rate of

Figure 4.3 Access to Bank and Supplier Financing, by Country
share of surveyed firms

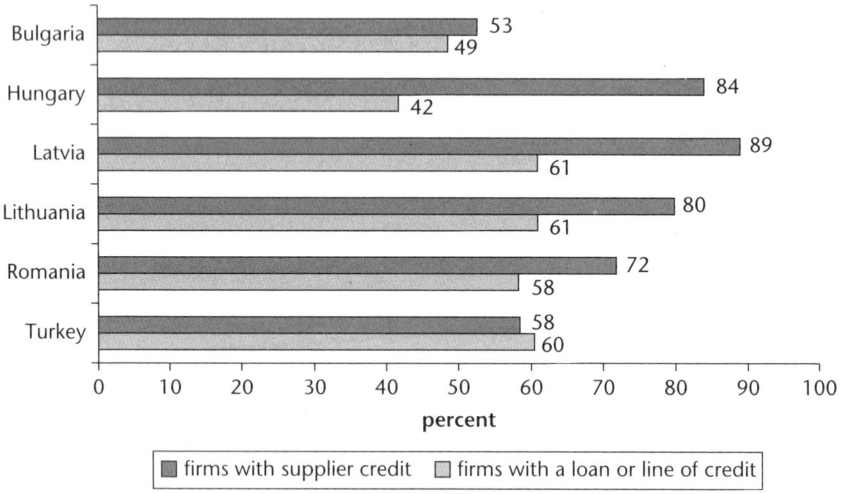

Source: World Bank 2007.

formal credit users, it has the second-highest rate of firms using supplier credit, which might support prior evidence that firms turn to supplier credit when formal credit (which is generally cheaper) is not available.

Measure of Crisis Severity

A measure from Didier and Calderon (2009) is used to gauge the country-level severity of the financial crisis. The Index of Economic Turbulence is based on a factor analysis summarizing six financial and real indicators of crisis severity, including growth in exports, growth in real gross domestic product, and variation in industrial production between the first quarters of fiscal 2008 and fiscal 2009. The more negative the value, the greater the crisis severity. Notably, except for Turkey, all of the surveyed countries were among the 10 hardest-hit economies, listed in table 4.2, among 65 countries for which the measure was calculated.

Empirical Results

The main results are shown in Table 4.3.[2] All independent variables are lagged, using data from the ES that corresponds to fiscal year 2007, which allows for the isolation of cause and effect.

Table 4.2 Countries Hardest Hit by the 2008–09 Crisis

Rank	Country	Index of Economic Turbulence
1	Ukraine	−2.39
2	Iceland	−2.36
3	**Latvia**	**−2.05**
4	**Lithuania**	**−2.03**
5	Estonia	−1.65
6	**Bulgaria**	**−0.82**
7	**Romania**	**−0.77**
8	Russian Federation	−0.70
9	Ireland	−0.69
10	**Hungary**	**−0.66**
26	**Turkey**	**−0.15**

Source: Didier and Calderon 2009.

The base regressors include age (log years since the firm's foundation); size (binary variables equal to 1 if the firm is small or medium, with large being the excluded category); ownership (binary variables equal to 1 if more than 50 percent of the firm is foreign or state owned); location (binary variable equal to 1 if the firm is located in the capital city); export orientation (binary variable equal to 1 if the firm exports directly or indirectly); and country and sector fixed effects.

Simple univariate tests suggest that several firm characteristics are associated with the extension of trade credit:

- *Size.* Among small firms, 41 percent extend trade credit, compared with 44 percent of large and medium-size firms.
- *Exporters.* In addition, 49 percent of exporters offer trade credit, compared with 40 percent of nonexporting firms.
- *Age.* Older firms were also more likely to extend trade credit.
- *Location.* Among firms in capital cities, 49 percent reported extending trade credit to their customers, contrasted with 41 percent in the subsample of firms that are not in capital cities.
- *Sector.* In the wholesale sector, 55 percent of firms offer trade credit, compared with 43 percent of firms in other sectors. In particular, firms in the information technology and garments sectors made comparatively little use of trade credit.

Regression analyses largely confirm these findings: older firms, firms that export directly or indirectly, wholesalers, and firms in capital cities were more

Table 4.3 Regression Results

		Extends trade credit						
	(1)	(2)	(3)	(4)	(5)	(6)	(7)	(8)
Competitive		0.26** [0.030]		0.27** [0.025]			-0.05 [0.804]	
Innovative			0.45*** [0.000]		0.44*** [0.000]			0.19 [0.300]
Loan or line of credit		0.41*** [0.001]	0.40*** [0.001]					
Use supplier credit				0.29** [0.035]	0.24* [0.090]			
Competitive × crisis severity							-0.27* [0.083]	
Innovative × crisis severity								-0.31** [0.046]
Crisis severity						-0.96*** [0.000]	-0.83*** [0.000]	-0.73*** [0.000]
Log age	0.19* [0.069]	0.20* [0.052]	0.23** [0.031]	0.20* [0.050]	0.23** [0.029]	0.21** [0.030]	0.21** [0.032]	0.23** [0.018]
Foreign–owned	-0.07 [0.734]	-0.01 [0.962]	-0.01 [0.964]	-0.07 [0.753]	-0.07 [0.753]	-0.37* [0.059]	-0.37* [0.060]	-0.39** [0.045]
State–owned	-0.91 [0.372]	-1.07 [0.292]	-0.99 [0.311]	-0.99 [0.301]	-0.9 [0.330]	-1.12 [0.147]	-1.17 [0.117]	-1.16 [0.113]

	(1)	(2)	(3)	(4)	(5)	(6)	(7)	(8)
Firm size: small	−0.28*	−0.23	−0.18	−0.29*	−0.24	−0.08	−0.08	−0.04
	[0.072]	[0.149]	[0.275]	[0.070]	[0.138]	[0.590]	[0.578]	[0.806]
Firm size: medium	−0.01	0.01	0.04	0	0.02	0.09	0.08	0.11
	[0.934]	[0.925]	[0.763]	[0.982]	[0.867]	[0.505]	[0.560]	[0.425]
Capital city	0.24	0.29**	0.31**	0.25*	0.28*	0.11	0.11	0.12
	[0.105]	[0.049]	[0.036]	[0.084]	[0.060]	[0.423]	[0.448]	[0.403]
Exporter	0.30**	0.24	0.17	0.27*	0.21	0.49***	0.48***	0.43***
	[0.035]	[0.106]	[0.242]	[0.057]	[0.150]	[0.000]	[0.000]	[0.001]
Constant	−0.80*	−1.19***	−1.34***	−1.15***	−1.25***	−1.85***	−1.81***	−1.95***
	[0.060]	[0.007]	[0.003]	[0.009]	[0.005]	[0.000]	[0.000]	[0.000]
Observations (number)	1,546	1,537	1,534	1,536	1,533	1,546	1,546	1,542
Adjusted R-squared	0.15	0.16	0.164	0.157	0.161	0.0858	0.089	0.0968
Country fixed effects	yes	yes	yes	yes	yes	no	no	no
Sector fixed effects	yes	yes	yes	yes	yes	yes	yes	yes

Source: World Bank 2009 and authors' analysis.

Note: Dataset comprises 1,546 firms. The dependent variable is a binary variable equal to 1 if the firm reported extending trade credit to its customers in 2009, 0 otherwise. All independent variables are lagged, using data from the Enterprise Surveys that correspond to fiscal 2007. All variables are defined in the text of the "Data and Summary Statistics" and "Empirical Results" sections. More negative values for the crisis severity variable indicate greater severity. P-values are displayed in brackets below the coefficients. Columns (1)–(5) include country and sector fixed effects. Columns (6)–(8) include sector fixed effects, but do not include country fixed effects because the crisis severity measure is on the country level. All findings are robust to replacing country fixed effects with gross domestic product per capita and controlling for a financial crisis turbulence measure and clustering the standard errors by country.

*p = 0.1.
**p = 0.05.
***p = 0.01.

likely to offer trade credit, even when accounting for basic firm-, sector-, and country-level differences in the multivariate analysis (table 4.3, column [1]).

A significant relationship between the competitive structure of the output market and the extension of trade credit was found in the sample during the crisis period, similar to the findings in other literature during noncrisis periods. Innovative firms and firms that reported operating in competitive markets in 2007 were significantly more likely to offer trade credit to their customers in 2009 than were firms that did not innovate or firms that did not face stiff competition from their competitors. In summary, 48 percent of competitive firms offered trade credit during the crisis, while only 40 percent of noncompetitive firms offered trade credit. The contrast is even starker for innovative firms: 51 percent of innovative firms extended trade credit, while only 34 percent of noninnovative firms extended trade credit.

The data confirm that a supplier's liquidity is an important determinant of the extension of trade credit. Firms in the sample that had loans or lines of credit from financial institutions in 2007 were significantly more likely to extend trade credit in 2009, as figure 4.4 illustrates. Among firms that had loans or lines of credit in 2007, 48 percent offered trade credit, compared with 37 percent of those that did not have loans or lines of credit.

There is also strong evidence that the use of supplier credit affects a firm's decision to offer trade credit to its own customers. On average, in the subsample of firms that reported receiving supplier credit in 2007, 45 percent extended trade credit to their customers in 2009, compared with 38 percent in the subsample of firms that had not reported receiving supplier credit.

Columns (2)–(5) in table 4.3 confirm the results of the univariate tests summarized above. Even when one accounts for differences in basic firm, sector, and country characteristics, competitive and innovative firms are significantly more likely to extend trade credit. Additionally, firms with access to bank and supplier financing are significantly more likely to offer trade credit to their customers.

An examination of recent changes in trade credit extensions among firms that reported extending trade credit shows that firms that operate in a competitive market were also more likely to report increasing the volume of goods sold on trade credit during the crisis. This is based on a multivariate Ologit regression with the controls from the previous model plus controls for recent sales trends (not shown). The dependent variable, changes in trade credit extensions, has a value of 0 for "decreasing trade credit," a value of 1 for "maintained trade credit," and a value of 2 for "increased trade credit." The relationship between competition and the increase of trade credit is significant at the 5 percent level.

Figure 4.4 Trade Credit and Liquidity
share of surveyed firms extending trade credit

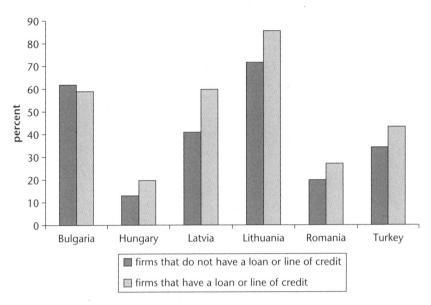

Source: World Bank 2007, 2009.

Interestingly, foreign-owned firms in competitive markets were especially likely to increase the amount of trade credit offered during the crisis, possibly because they have better access to financing that allows them to finance increased amounts of trade credit, which might offer a comparative advantage during periods of lower customer demand (Perotti and Vesnaver 2004). The relationship between increasing trade credit and the interaction term between competition and foreign ownership is significant at the 10 percent level.

Impact of the Financial Crisis on Trade Credit Decisions

According to this analysis, the degree to which a competitive market is associated with the extension of trade credit varies with the relative severity of the crisis in a given country. Using a country-level indicator of the severity of the financial crisis, there is strong evidence that a firm operating in a relatively more competitive environment is more likely to extend trade credit, and this is especially so in countries more severely affected by the crisis. The same applies for innovative firms: relative to noninnovating firms, an innovating firm is more likely to extend trade credit, and this is especially so in countries hit harder by the crisis (table 4.3, columns [6]–[8]).

At first blush, this result seems counterintuitive: if liquidity is an important determinant in whether a firm offers trade credit, why would a firm that has been hit hard by the crisis and is operating in a competitive environment with low profit margins want to suffer the additional financial constraints that come with extending trade credit? These results support the theory that due to the firm's lack of market power and because its customers have also likely been hit by the crisis, the firm has no choice but to extend trade credit as a matter of survival, consistent with the market-power theory outlined in the earlier section, "Rationales for Trade Finance." It is clear that the crisis exerted additional financial pressure on suppliers that had become credit-constrained themselves.

Hungary: A Special Case

In many respects, Hungary is an outlier when it comes to trade credit. It has, by far, the lowest percentage of firms that reported extending trade credit (16 percent, compared with an average of 51 percent among the other five countries) and the largest percentage of firms that reported decreasing the amount of goods they sell on trade credit (55 percent, compared with 23 percent among the other five countries).

This deviance from the other country-level results might be explained by a related finding that Hungary also has the lowest percentage of firms that reported having a loan or line of credit from a financial institution—which our model shows is the most significant predictor of financial intermediation among firms in our sample (table 4.3).

Conclusions

Supplier financing is a critical source of financing for firms in emerging markets, yet the determinants of the extension of trade credit are not well understood. First, the firm and market characteristics associated with the extension of supplier financing are identified. An analysis finds that the firms that operated in a competitive market or recently innovated are significantly more likely to offer trade credit to their customers, suggesting that supplier financing is often used as a competitive gesture. In addition, firms with greater liquidity to finance the extension of credit, measured as access to a line of credit or credit from their own suppliers, are more likely to extend credit.

Second, upon examination of the impact of the financial crisis on supply-chain financing decisions, the analysis finds that firms that operated in a competitive market are also more likely to increase the volume of goods sold during the crisis.

Third, a study of the heterogeneous effects of trade credit finds that, in countries hit harder by the crisis, firms in competitive markets are more likely to extend credit than firms in less-competitive markets.

Overall, these results suggest that firms in competitive markets faced an additional burden during the crisis, one that might have increased their financial vulnerability.

Notes

1. The sample of firms from Turkey covers only the manufacturing sector.
2. Complete results are available upon request.

References

Brennan, Michael, Vojislav Maksimovic, and Josef Zechner. 1988. "Vendor Financing." *The Journal of Finance* 43 (5): 1127–41.

Calomiris, Charles, Charles Himmelberg, and Paul Wachtel. 1995. "Commercial Paper, Corporate Finance and the Business Cycle: A Microeconomic Perspective." Working Paper 4848, National Bureau for Economic Research, Cambridge, MA.

Cull, Robert, Lixin Colin Xu, and Tian Zhu. 2009. "Formal Finance and Trade Credit During China's Transition." *Journal of Financial Intermediation* 18 (2): 173–92.

Cuñat, Vicente. 2007. "Trade Credit: Suppliers as Debt Collectors and Insurance Providers." *The Review of Financial Studies* 20 (2): 491–527.

Demirgüç-Kunt, A., and V. Maksimovic. 1999. "Institutions, Financial Markets, and Firm Debt Maturity." *Journal of Financial Economics* 54 (3): 295–336.

Didier, T., and C. Calderon. 2009. "Severity of the Crisis and its Transmission Channels." Latin America and the Caribbean Region Crisis Briefs Series, World Bank, Washington, DC.

Evans, Jocelyn D. 1998. "Are Lending Relationships Valuable to Equity Holders in Chapter 11 Bankruptcy?" Unpublished manuscript, Georgia State University, Atlanta.

Fabbri, Daniela, and Leora Klapper. 2008. "Market Power and the Matching of Trade Credit Terms." Policy Research Working Paper 4754, World Bank, Washington, DC.

Fisman, Raymond, and Inessa Love. 2003, "Trade Credit, Financial Intermediary Development, and Industry Growth." *The Journal of Finance* 58 (1): 353–74.

Fisman, R., and M. Raturi. 2004. "Does Competition Encourage Credit Provision? Evidence from African Trade Credit Relationships." *Review of Economics and Statistics* 86 (1): 345–52.

Giannetti, Mariassunta, Mike Burkart, and Tore Ellingsen. 2008. "What You Sell Is What You Lend? Explaining Trade Credit Contracts." *The Review of Financial Studies* (online). http://rfs.oxfordjournals.org/content/early/2007/12/31/rfs.hhn096.extract.

Klapper, Leora, Luc Laeven, and Raghuram G. Rajan. 2010. "Trade Credit Contracts." Policy Research Working Paper 5328, World Bank, Washington, DC.

Love, Inessa, Lorenzo A. Preve, and Virginia Sarria-Allende. 2007. "Trade Credit and Bank Credit: Evidence from Recent Financial Crises." *Journal of Financial Economics* 83 (2): 453–69.

McMillan, John, and Christopher Woodruff. 1999. "Interfirm Relationships and Informal Credit in Vietnam." *Quarterly Journal of Economics* 114 (4): 1285–320.

Ng, Chee K., Janet Kilholm Smith, and Richard L. Smith. 1999. "Evidence on the Determinants of Credit Terms Used in Interfirm Trade." *The Journal of Finance* 54 (3): 1109–29.

Nilsen J. H. 2002. "Trade Credit and the Bank Lending Channel." *Journal of Money, Credit, and Banking* 34 (1): 226–53.

Perotti, C. Enrico, and Luka Vesnaver. 2004. "Enterprise Finance and Investment in Listed Hungarian Firms." *Journal of Comparative Economics* 32 (1): 73–87.

Petersen, Mitchell A., and Raghuram G. Rajan. 1997. "Trade Credit: Theories and Evidence." *The Review of Financial Studies* 10 (3): 661–91.

Wilner, Benjamin S. 2000. "The Exploitation of Relationships in Financial Distress: The Case of Trade Credit." *The Journal of Finance* 55 (1): 153–78.

World Bank. 2007. Enterprise Survey (database). World Bank, Washington, DC. http://www.enterprise surveys.org.

———. 2009. Financial Crisis Survey (database). World Bank, Washington, DC. http://www.enterprise surveys.org/financialcrisis.

TRADE FINANCE DURING THE 2008–09 CRISIS: INNOCENT OR GUILTY?

TRADE FINANCE IN THE 2008–09 FINANCIAL CRISIS: EVIDENCE FROM IMF AND BAFT–IFSA SURVEYS OF BANKS

Irena Asmundson, Thomas Dorsey, Armine Khachatryan, Ioana Niculcea, and Mika Saito

The banking system provides short-term trade finance arrangements such as lending, insurance against nonpayment, or both in support of international trade. Trade finance covers a spectrum of payment arrangements between importers and exporters:

Open-account financing, the largest share of global merchandise trade, allows importers to repay exporters directly after receipt of goods, without either insurance or lending from third parties. In this context, exporters both supply working capital to importers and take on the risk of nonpayment.

Cash-in-advance arrangements, at the opposite end of the spectrum from open-account financing, allows importers pay for goods before they are shipped, placing both nonperformance risk and the burden on working capital on the importer.

Bank-intermediated trade finance allows importers or exporters to shift some of the nonpayment or nonperformance risk to banks or to obtain bank financing to allow the exporter to receive payment before the importer is required to make it.

This chapter is an excerpt from a previously published paper by I. Asmundson, T. Dorsey, A. Khachatryan, I. Niculcea, and M. Saito, "Trade and Trade Finance in the 2008–09 Financial Crisis" (Working Paper 11/16, International Monetary Fund, Washington, DC).

The views expressed herein are those of the authors and should not be attributed to the International Monetary Fund, its executive board, or its management.

Figure 5.1 Trade Finance Arrangements, by Market Share

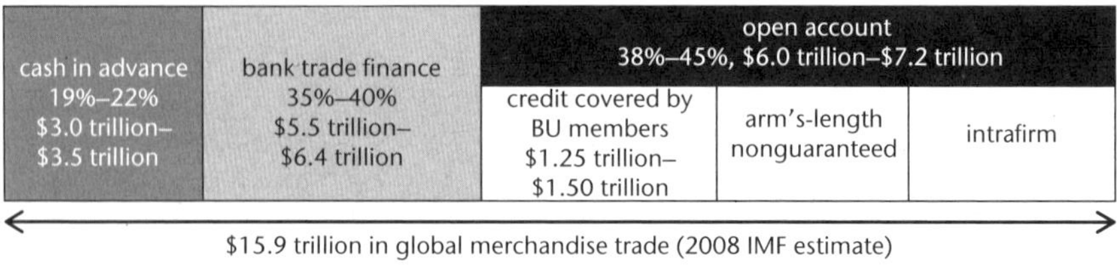

cash in advance	bank trade finance	open account 38%–45%, $6.0 trillion–$7.2 trillion		
19%–22% $3.0 trillion– $3.5 trillion	35%–40% $5.5 trillion– $6.4 trillion	credit covered by BU members $1.25 trillion– $1.50 trillion	arm's-length nonguaranteed	intrafirm

←———————————————————————————————————————→
$15.9 trillion in global merchandise trade (2008 IMF estimate)

Sources: IMF staff estimates from IMF/BAFT-IFSA surveys of commercial banks (IMF-BAFT 2009; IMF and BAFT-IFSA 2010) and Berne Union database.
Note: BU = Berne Union. IMF = International Monetary Fund. BAFT-IFSA = Bankers' Association for Finance and Trade–International Financial Services Association.

Public sector entities such as export credit agencies (ECAs) and multilateral development bank programs also play a role that overlaps with that of commercial banks.

Figure 5.1 summarizes the market shares of each of these arrangements within the worldwide trade finance market.

Assessment of trade finance conditions is complicated by the absence of organized markets for bank-intermediated trade finance and the proprietary nature of bank information about customer relationships. To fill this gap during the current crisis, the International Monetary Fund (IMF) staff and the Bankers' Association for Finance and Trade (BAFT)—now merged with International Financial Services Association (BAFT-IFSA)—conducted four surveys of banks about trade finance between December 2008 and March 2010 that covered developments from the fourth quarter of 2007 through the fourth quarter of 2009 and the banks' outlook for 2010.[1] In addition, the authors discussed trade finance with many representatives of commercial banks, ECAs, and other market participants in the context of outreach, conferences, and bilateral discussions.

Trade and Financial Market Developments in 2008–09

Global trade entered the financial crisis already unsettled by other developments. The sharp drop in trade in late 2008 came after a period of turmoil in global commodities trade. In 2007 and early 2008, prices of both food and fuel increased sharply, with wheat prices doubling and rice prices almost tripling. Following difficult harvests in Australia and India (among other places), several countries banned exports to maintain lower food prices for staples internally. Fuel prices in 2007 rose by around 50 percent, mostly from increased demand, which also affected fertilizer prices (some of which is produced from natural gas), in turn lowering potential agricultural output.

Against this backdrop, futures contracts reportedly were being broken because the high prices on the spot market more than compensated for having to pay penalties. This development led to fears that more widespread market break-downs would occur, and buyers became more worried about counterparty risk.

The disruption to trade finance in late 2008 and early 2009 did not occur in isolation; it occurred against a backdrop of sharply falling international trade and a broader disruption to global financial markets. The bankruptcy of Lehman Brothers in September 2008, coming on the heels of lesser financial market failures, exacerbated concerns over counterparty risk in the financial sector, caused short-term funding costs to spike, and the turmoil in financial markets spilled over into goods markets. Emerging markets, which had been assumed to have decoupled from developed country growth, were shown to remain dependent on exports. The magnitude and timing of developments in international trade and broader financial markets provides some context for assessing developments in trade finance and the influence of these markets on trade finance and vice versa.

International Trade

International trade had a sharp and globally synchronized fall in the second half of 2008 and early 2009. Exports of advanced, emerging, and developing economies were all growing robustly through mid-2008 before dropping sharply in the second half of 2008 and early 2009, as figure 5.2 illustrates.

The reversal was most pronounced for developing economies, where a commodity price boom and decline reinforced the roughly simultaneous effects of rising partner-country demand for commodities until mid-2008 and the subsequent sharp fall in demand. Although exports of advanced, emerging, and developing economies stabilized in early and mid-2009 and recovered sharply in late 2009–early 2010 in most major economies, trade was still much lower in early 2010 than at the mid-2008 peak.

Financial Markets

The financial crisis touched off by the September 2008 collapse of Lehman Brothers manifested in sharply tightened credit conditions in September and October of 2008. Borrowing costs for even the strongest banks rose immediately as London interbank offered rates (LIBOR) rose by roughly one full percentage point, as figure 5.3 illustrates. However, policy rates of major central banks responded quickly and brought LIBOR rates down to pre-Lehman levels within a few weeks and by more than three percentage points from pre-Lehman levels by the second quarter of 2009.

Figure 5.2 Merchandise Trade Index, 2007 to mid-2010

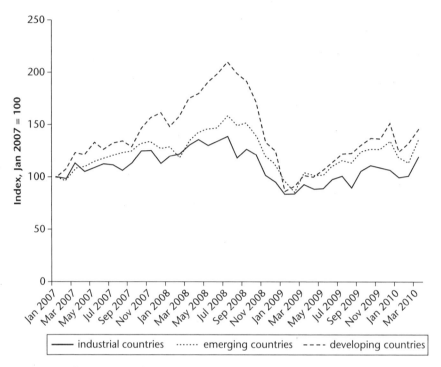

Sources: IMF staff estimates based on Haver Analytics data and WTO 2010.
Note: January 2008 = 100, in U.S. dollars. Trade data on industrial, emerging, and developing countries
are based on Haver Analytics reporting of 31, 32, and 20 countries, respectively.

The impact of the increased cost of funds was spread unevenly across the markets, banks, and nonbank financial institutions of advanced and emerging
economies. The interest-rate spreads above policy rates rose and fell rapidly in the
advanced economies, as shown in figure 5.4, coming close to precrisis levels by
January 2009 and dropping below precrisis levels by mid-2009.

As for the emerging markets, debt market spreads rose by much larger margins, fell much more gradually, and remained above pre-Lehman levels in the first
quarter of 2010, as figure 5.5 illustrates.

The disruption to lending correlated with the distance between the borrower
and the ultimate holder of the debt. Lending volumes quickly reflected the declining economic activity and the financial shock of the crisis. Loans to nonfinancial
firms dropped in the Euro Area and the United States by 1 percent and 14 percent,
respectively, between the fourth quarter of 2008 and the third quarter of 2009, as
shown in figure 5.6.

Figure 5.3 Global Funding Pressure, 2008 to mid-2010
average of Euro Area, U.K., and U.S. rates, by percent

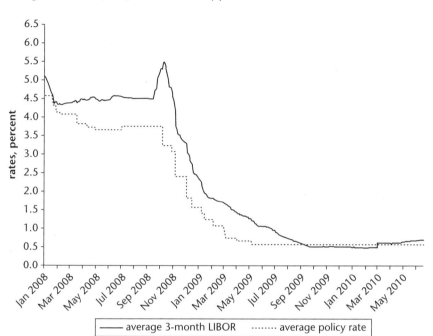

Source: Bloomberg database.
Note: LIBOR = London interbank offered rate.

However, over the same period, the decline in commercial paper volumes was much more pronounced, falling by 22 percent and 40 percent for U.S. financial and nonfinancial issuers, respectively, as figure 5.7 shows. The much sharper decline in traded commercial paper may have reflected the widely reported lack of trust in all securitized debt following the onset of the crisis, even though commercial paper is a direct obligation of the underlying borrower.

Evidence on Bank-Intermediated Trade Finance

The crisis affected both bank trade finance and other financial markets. However, bank-intermediated trade finance largely held up during the crisis. Banks were increasingly cautious with real-sector customers and counterparty banks, and pricing margins often increased. However, these factors were more than offset by an increase in risk aversion on the part of exporters seeking protection from risk. As a result, the share of world trade supported by bank-intermediated trade

Figure 5.4 Three-Month LIBOR Spreads in Advanced Markets

overnight index swap, in basis points

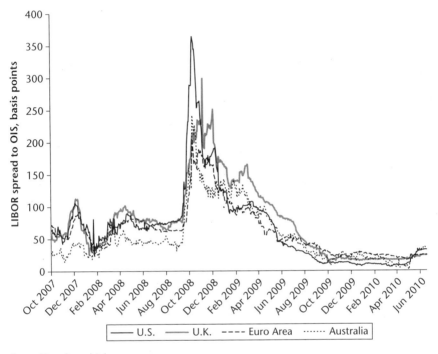

Source: Bloomberg database.

Note: LIBOR = London interbank offered rate. OIS = overnight indexed swap.

finance appears to have *increased* during the crisis. The causes of the increased price and decreased value of trade finance appear to be mostly spillovers from broader financial markets and the recession-induced decline in the value of international trade rather than specific problems in the trade finance markets themselves.

IMF staff, with BAFT-IFSA and the assistance of many other organizations, conducted four surveys of commercial banks to fill gaps in information about commercial-bank trade finance since December 2008, as box 5.1 further describes. The survey responses came from banks of widely varying sizes in countries representing all income groups and major geographic regions. Table 5.1 shows summary data on the characteristics of banks responding to the fourth survey. The average bank responding to the survey is active in trade finance in three major regions and has branches in two regions. Except in Sub-Saharan Africa, one-fifth or more of the banks were active in each region, with coverage of emerging Asia, industrial countries, and Latin America being particularly high.[2]

Figure 5.5 External Debt Market Spreads in Emerging Markets, 2008 to mid-2010
basis points over treasury rates

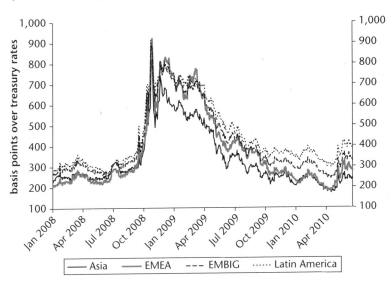

Source: Bloomberg database.
Note: EMEA = Europe, Middle East, and Africa. EMBIG = Emerging Markets Bond Index Global.

Figure 5.6 Loans to Nonfinancial Firms in the Euro Area and U.S., 2007 to mid-2010

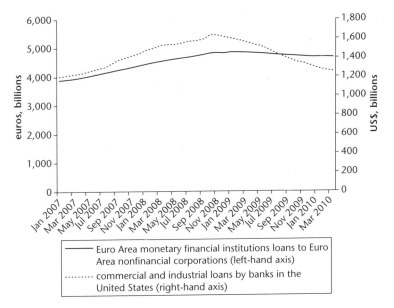

Source: DDP database (U.S. Federal Reserve) and Statistical Data Warehouse (European Central Bank).

Figure 5.7 U.S. Commercial Paper: Outstanding Accounts, 2008 to mid-2010

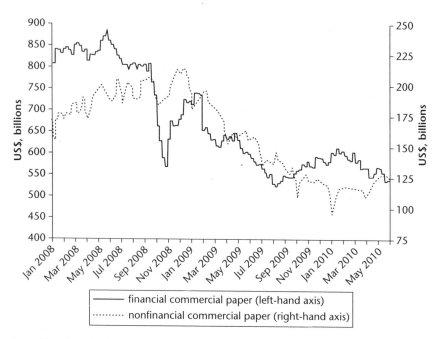

Source: Bloomberg database.

Value of Trade Finance

The value of trade covered by bank-intermediated trade finance held roughly stable and even rose during the first phase of the crisis (fourth quarter of 2008 versus fourth quarter of 2007), even as the value of trade fell sharply, as table 5.2 and figure 5.8 show. During the most intense period of the crisis (from October 2008 to January 2009), trade finance did decline in value by amounts on the order of 10 percent, but the value of merchandise trade fell much more sharply during the same period.

In almost all regions and periods through the second quarter of 2009, the value of trade finance activities declined less than merchandise trade, or trade finance value rose even while exports were falling. The smaller decline in trade finance presumably reflected a sharply heightened risk aversion of the part of real sector trade participants and their attempt to address this risk aversion by shifting some of the transaction risk to the banks. Trade also showed signs of recovery— and a more widespread recovery—by the fourth quarter of 2009 as the recovery in

Box 5.1 The IMF/BAFT-IFSA and Other Bank Surveys

Market conditions for trade finance are difficult to assess because of the absence of data. Bank trade finance is generally based on relationship banking with individual clients. Pricing and availability of bank-intermediated trade finance depends on a complex web of relationships between client, counterparty, and counterparty banks. As such, data are intermingled with proprietary information about bank-client relationships and are difficult to come by. Data on open-account and cash-in-advance transactions are similarly tied into individual customer relationships, but data are even harder to come by in the absence of the information clearinghouse role provided with transactions channeled through banks.

The IMF and BAFT-IFSA conducted four surveys of commercial banks since late 2008 to fill these informational gaps. All four surveys were designed mostly by IMF staff with the participation of BAFT-IFSA and member banks and direct input from the European Bank for Reconstruction and Development (EBRD) and HSBC. The surveys were distributed primarily by BAFT (BAFT-IFSA for the fourth survey) with the assistance of many cooperating public and private sector organizations. In particular, valuable assistance in further distribution was provided by FELABAN (Federación Latinoamericana de Bancos). Data were compiled and summarized by FImetrix for the second through fourth surveys. The third and fourth surveys also benefited from collaboration on survey design with the Banking Commission of the International Chamber of Commerce (ICC) and from the assistance of the Asian Development Bank (ADB) and EBRD in promoting responses in their regions of operations. The ICC has also conducted its own surveys and published the results (ICC 2009, 2010). Although the IMF/BAFT-IFSA and ICC surveys have different focuses and different sets of respondents, the results tended to be broadly similar where the survey questions overlapped.[3]

the value of merchandise trade outstripped the growth in the value of trade finance in most regions, as figure 5.9 illustrates.

The relatively resilient value of trade finance is also reflected in an increased share of global trade moving from open-account to bank-intermediated trade finance as the crisis progressed. Banks estimate that open-account transactions fell below the level of bank-supported trade finance in the second quarter of 2009, as figure 5.10 shows. These trends appear to reflect increased risk aversion on the part of both banks (increased margins) and nonfinancial corporations (decline in the open-account share). The slight decline in bank-intermediated trade finance in the most recent period presumably reflected a return toward the long-term trend of a shift to open-account transactions as the crisis abated.

Why the Value of Trade Finance Changed

Banks attributed both the declines and the increases in the value of trade finance mostly to demand factors. Of these factors, the change in the value of trade was by

Table 5.1 Summary of Bank Survey Respondent Characteristics
percentage of 100 respondents

	Industrial countries	Sub-Saharan Africa	Emerging Europe	Southeast Europe and Central Asia	Emerging Asia including China and India	Developing Asia	Middle East and the Maghreb	Latin America
Primary location of trade finance activities	69	9	31	28	75	24	26	42
Location of trade finance branch	50	6	21	22	29	17	15	41
Location of global headquarters	45	1	6	9	5	6	4	24
Most recent total assets			small banks (< $5 billion) 33		medium-size banks 33		large banks (> $100 billion) 34	

Source: IMF and BAFT-IFSA 2010.

Table 5.2 Changes in Merchandise Exports and Trade Finance, by Country Group
percentage of growth

	Q4 CY08 vs. Q4 CY07		Q1 CY09 vs. Q4 CY08[a]		Q2 CY09 vs. Q4 CY08[b]		Q4 CY09 vs. Q4 CY08	
	Goods exports	Trade finance	Goods exports	Trade finance	Goods exports	Trade finance	Goods exports	Trade finance
Industrial countries	-12.4	2.4	-31.0	-9.2	-13.5	-9.1	2.6	0.4
Sub-Saharan Africa	-11.2	1.4	-43.2	-8.1	-13.2	-3.0	4.9	6.5
Emerging Europe	-14.9	4.3	-33.0	-11.1	-11.8	-10.4	9.2	0.7
Southeast Europe and Central Asia	-8.1	-4.3	-54.5	-13.2	-30.6	-7.8	-3.4	0.2
Emerging Asia including China and India	-0.4	9.1	-29.0	-9.7	-18.0	0.0	3.8	6.1
Developing Asia	0.4	4.2	-8.8	-9.1	0.8	-3.8	10.1	1.8
Middle East and the Maghreb	1.0	2.2	-20.4	-5.3	1.4	-5.3	11.1	4.4
Latin America	-10.4	4.8	-37.4	-9.5	-10.4	-13.7	1.9	2.2
Overall	-10.3	3.4[c]	-32.2	-9.6[d]	-14.7	-7.5	2.9	2.2[c]

Sources: IMF-BAFT 2009; IMF and BAFT-IFSA 2010; Haver Analytics; International Financial Statistics (IMF); WTO 2010.

Note: CY = calendar year. The respondents' samples differ across surveys.

a. Based on March 2009 IMF-BAFT survey. Country categories in this survey are broadly consistent, though not identical, to the categories in the July 2009 and March 2010 surveys.

b. Based on July 2009 IMF-BAFT survey.

c. Weighted average of regional changes by activity level in respective region.

d. Overall figure computed using weights in July 2009 IMF-BAFT survey.

Figure 5.8 Overall Changes in Merchandise Exports and Trade Finance

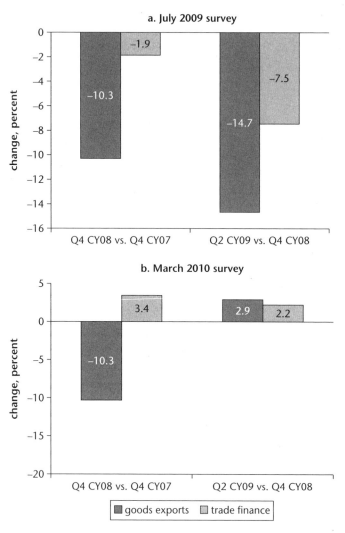

Sources: IMF-BAFT 2009; IMF and BAFT-IFSA 2010; Haver Analytics; International Financial Statistics (IMF); WTO 2010.
Note: CY = calendar year. The respondents' samples differ across surveys. The overall change in trade finance is computed as the weighted average of regional changes by activity level in respective region.

Figure 5.9 Changes in Merchandise Exports and Trade Finance, by Country Group

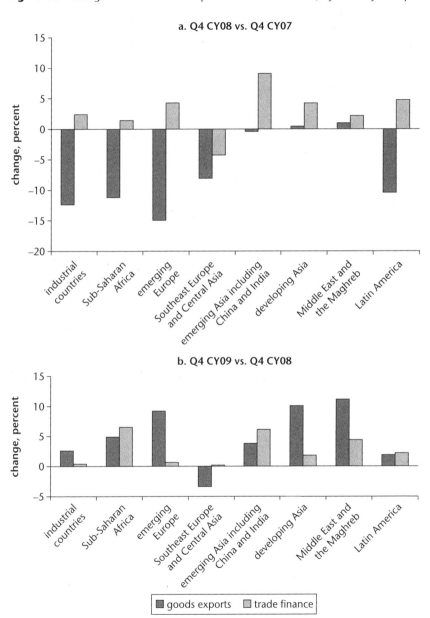

a. Q4 CY08 vs. Q4 CY07

b. Q4 CY09 vs. Q4 CY08

■ goods exports   □ trade finance

Sources: IMF and BAFT-IFSA 2010; Haver Analytics; International Financial Statistics (IMF); WTO 2010.
Note: CY = calendar year.

Figure 5.10 Estimated Composition of the Trade Finance Industry

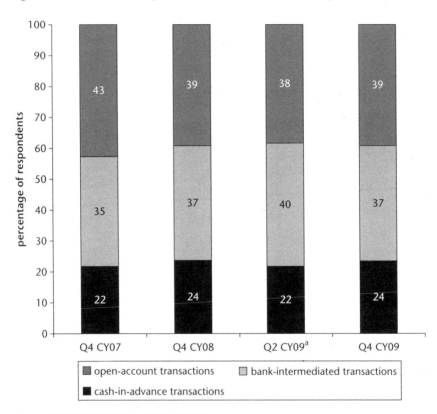

Sources: IMF-BAFT 2009; IMF and BAFT-IFSA 2010.
Note: CY = calendar year. The data show respondents' answers to this survey question: "What is your 'best' estimate for the composition of the trade finance industry as a whole?" The respondents' samples differ across surveys.
a. Figures for Q2 CY09 are from the July 2009 survey, which did not have the same set of respondents as the 2010 survey and therefore may not be fully comparable to the figures in other columns. However, the survey results for equivalent periods between the July 2009 and March 2010 surveys line up closely, suggesting a broad consistency in results across both surveys.

far the most important, with the rise or fall in commodity prices a distant second, as table 5.3 shows. Significant minorities of institutions cited supply-side factors (such as credit availability at either their own institution or counterparties) and shifts to or from open-account or cash-in-advance transactions. Looking across different size classes of banks, credit availability factors seemed to be relatively more important at large banks, presumably reflecting the greater need for deleveraging at some of the largest institutions.

Table 5.3 Reasons for Decline in Value of Trade Finance
percentage of respondents

	All banks	Small banks	Medium-size banks	Large banks
Fall in the demand for trade activities	85	81	90	80
Fall in the price of transactions (e.g., commodity prices)	38	25	24	56
Less credit availability at your own institution	30	19	24	40
Less credit availability at your counterparty banks	30	6	24	48
Shift toward open-account transactions	23	19	33	16
Shift toward cash-in-advance transactions	21	31	14	20
Decline in support from export credit agencies	8	0	5	16
Decline in credit from multilateral institutions	0	0	0	0
Other reasons	18	31	10	16

Source: IMF and BAFT-IFSA 2010.
Note: Small banks = < $5 billion in assets; medium-size banks = $5 billion–$100 billion in assets; large banks = > $100 billion in assets. Data reflect only the views of the 61 respondents that reported a decline in value of trade finance in at least one geographic region presented and that subsequently marked at least one option for the question.

Banks adopted stricter risk management practices in response to higher risks, as figure 5.11 and tables 5.4 and 5.5 illustrate. They differentiated more, depending on the individual client, the business segment (trading, retail, commodities, and so on), and home country. Banks have also limited their own risk through expanded insurance, shorter loan maturities, and stronger covenants and by requiring higher cash deposits or other collateral from clients. Large banks were more cautious than small and medium-size banks relative to countries seen as posing high financial risks, and they were also more likely to request confirmations or export credit insurance. On the other end of the size spectrum, small and medium-size banks were more likely than large banks to manage risk by requiring greater collateral or stronger covenants. The 2010 ICC survey also examined Society for Worldwide Interbank Financial Telecommunication (SWIFT) message data and found evidence of increased risk aversion by banks and customers, including refusals to honor letters of credit (LCs) because of discrepancies in documents (ICC 2010).[4]

Most banks of all sizes indicated in the March 2010 survey that they could satisfy customer demands for trade finance, although a substantial minority of large

Figure 5.11 Overall Change in Trade-Related Lending Guidelines, Q4 CY09 vs. Q4 CY08

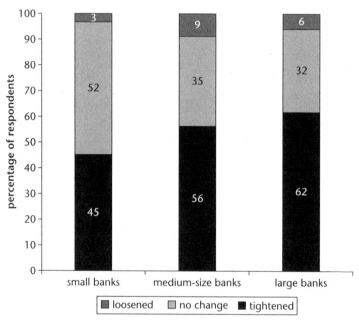

Source: IMF and BAFT-IFSA 2010.
Note: CY = calendar year. Small banks = < $5 billion in assets; medium-size banks = $5 billion–$100 billion in assets; large banks = > $100 billion in assets.

banks indicated that they could not, as figure 5.12 shows. This result was consistent with the greater emphasis on credit availability concerns at large banks and also with the perception that large banks had been more heavily affected by the need for deleveraging.

Bank Pricing and Credit Conditions for Trade Finance

The survey evidence on pricing is also consistent with a demand-driven story in which the decline in trade finance plays no more than a modest role in the decline in merchandise trade. The survey results indicate some increased pricing for trade finance, at least relative to banks' cost of funds. Other things being equal, the increased pricing should have reduced the use of bank-intermediated trade finance as a share of trade. The increased share of bank-intermediated trade finance in spite of increased pricing also suggests that demand factors such as exporter risk aversion dominated.

Table 5.4 Change in Trade-Related Lending Guidelines: Tightening
percentage of respondents

	All banks	Small banks	Medium-size banks	Large banks
Became more cautious with certain sectors	74	71	78	71
Became more cautious with certain countries	77	57	67	100
Requested more collateral (including equity contributions and cash deposits)	62	64	83	43
Requested shorter tenors	58	57	56	62
Requested stronger covenants	47	64	56	29
Faced more regulatory controls	43	57	33	43
Requested more DC or LC (including standby and confirmed LC)	42	21	44	52
Requested more export credit insurance	28	21	11	48
Other	2	0	0	5

Source: IMF and BAFT-IFSA 2010.
Note: DC = documentary credit. LC = letter of credit. Small banks = < $5 billion in assets; medium-size banks = $5 billion–$100 billion in assets; large banks = > $100 billion in assets. Data reflect only the views of the 53 respondents that reported a tightening in trade-related lending guidelines from Q4 CY08 to Q4 CY09 and that subsequently answered this question.

Table 5.5 Change in Trade-Related Lending Guidelines: Loosening
percentage of respondents

	All banks	Small banks	Medium-size banks	Large banks
Became less cautious with certain sectors	83	100	67	100
Became less cautious with certain countries	50	0	33	100
Requested less collateral (including equity contributions and cash deposits)	67	100	67	50
Requested longer tenors	50	100	33	50
Requested weaker covenants	50	100	67	0
Faced fewer regulatory controls	17	0	33	0
Requested fewer DC or LC (including standby and confirmed LC)	33	0	33	50
Requested less export credit insurance	33	0	0	100
Other	0	0	0	0

Source: IMF and BAFT-IFSA 2010.
Note: DC = documentary credit. LC = letter of credit. Small banks = < $5 billion in assets; medium-size banks = $5 billion–$100 billion in assets; large banks = > $100 billion in assets. Data reflect only the views of the six respondents that reported a loosening in trade-related lending guidelines from Q4 CY08 to Q4 CY09 and that subsequently answered this question.

Figure 5.12 Ability to Satisfy "All Customer Needs"

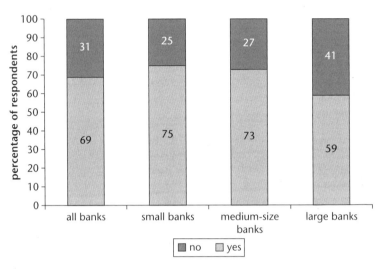

Sources: IMF and BAFT-IFSA 2010.
Note: Small banks = < $5 billion in assets; medium-size banks = $5 billion–$100 billion in assets;
large banks = > $100 billion in assets.

Average pricing margins for trade finance rose during the crisis, but fewer than half of the banks increased pricing in any single period. More banks increased pricing than decreased pricing relative to their costs of funds. However, most banks either held pricing steady or reduced pricing during the following periods:

- Fourth quarter of 2007 to fourth quarter of 2008 (table 5.6)
- Fourth quarter of 2008 to second quarter of 2009 (table 5.7)
- Fourth quarter of 2008 to fourth quarter of 2009 (table 5.8).

However, because the large banks account for a substantial majority of trade finance, average pricing margins for trade finance as a whole almost certainly increased. The largest banks were much more likely to increase pricing, and by larger average amounts, than the unweighted averages for all banks shown in the tables. These data suggest that pricing pressures eased in 2009 as the shares of banks reporting pricing increases, as opposed to decreases, fell sharply, as figure 5.13 illustrates.

The average increases in pricing were moderate for most of those banks reporting increases, particularly in 2009, as shown in figure 5.14.

There is some differentiation, according to bank size, in the factors that banks see as affecting the pricing of trade finance. Roughly similar shares of large,

Table 5.6 Pricing Changes by Bank Size, Q4 CY08 vs. Q4 CY07
percentage of respondents

	All banks	Small banks	Medium-size banks	Large banks
Letters of credit				
Increased	38	23	19	70
No change	52	63	71	24
Decreased	10	13	10	6
Mean change	31	17	26	50
Median change	0	0	0	50
Export credit insurance				
Increased	29	22	4	57
No change	62	61	88	39
Decreased	9	17	8	4
Mean change	14	23	0	21
Median change	0	0	0	0
Trade-related lending				
Increased	48	41	31	69
No change	40	44	48	28
Decreased	13	15	21	3
Mean change	48	64	29	53
Median change	0	0	0	20
Average across products				
Increased	38	29	18	65
No change	51	56	69	31
Decreased	10	15	13	4
Mean change	31	35	18	41
Median change	0	0	0	23

Source: IMF and BAFT-IFSA 2010.
Note: CY = calendar year. Small banks = < $5 billion in assets; medium-size banks = $5 billion–$100 billion in assets; large banks = > $100 billion in assets. Mean figures are percentage changes in the pricing margin above bank cost of funds. Mean and median figures do not include responses for which detailed pricing data were not provided.

medium-size, and small banks reported that they increased pricing margins because of the increased bank cost of funds; the share of banks citing this factor fell from about two-thirds in late 2008 to just under half in the first half of 2009. However, the increased risk of trade finance lending relative to other bank lines of business was a greater concern for small and medium-size banks in the latter period, as table 5.9 shows. Conversely, increased capital requirements were cited more often by large banks.

Large banks diverged widely from other banks in their views about the impact of Basel II capital requirements.[5] For example, large banks were more concerned

Table 5.7 Pricing Changes by Bank Size, Q2 CY09 vs. Q4 CY08
percentage of respondents

	All banks	Small banks	Medium-size banks	Large banks
Letters of credit				
Increased	46	38	48	54
No change	36	41	33	33
Decreased	18	21	19	13
Mean change	23	16	25	31
Median change	0	0	0	0
Export credit insurance				
Increased	41	32	48	45
No change	50	60	43	45
Decreased	9	8	9	10
Mean change	19	1	36	18
Median change	0	0	0	0
Trade-related lending				
Increased	45	33	44	61
No change	35	45	30	26
Decreased	20	21	26	13
Mean change	28	24	14	57
Median change	0	0	0	22
Average across products				
Increased	44	35	47	53
No change	40	49	35	35
Decreased	16	17	18	12
Mean change	23	14	25	35
Median change	0	0	0	7

Source: IMF-BAFT 2009.
Note: CY = calendar year. Small banks = < $5 billion in assets; medium-size banks = $5 billion–$100 billion in assets; large banks = > $100 billion in assets. Mean figures are percentage changes in the pricing margin above bank cost of funds. Mean and median figures do not include responses for which detailed pricing data were not provided.

about the impact of Basel II on their ability to provide trade finance, as table 5.10 shows. This finding is consistent with the more frequent citation of increased capital requirements as a factor behind increased pricing margins.

Consistent with the survey results on the factors driving increased pricing, no small banks and only a minority of medium-size banks cited Basel II as having a negative impact on their ability to provide trade finance. Interestingly, a minority of banks of varying size cited Basel II as having a positive impact on their ability to provide trade finance. As with the banks' divergent responses about pricing, this finding may reflect that differing initial capital and risk requirements have

Table 5.8 Pricing Changes by Bank Size, Q4 CY09 vs. Q4 CY08
percentage of respondents

	All banks	Small banks	Medium-size banks	Large banks
Letters of credit				
Increased	40	47	35	39
No change	36	33	55	21
Decreased	23	20	10	39
Mean change	6	9	–5	15
Median change	0	0	0	0
Export credit insurance				
Increased	32	39	24	32
No change	49	43	64	39
Decreased	20	17	12	29
Mean change	3	–13	5	11
Median change	0	0	0	0
Trade-related lending				
Increased	47	56	41	44
No change	23	15	38	16
Decreased	31	30	21	41
Mean change	11	25	–11	23
Median change	0	0	0	0
Average across products				
Increased	40	47	34	38
No change	36	31	52	25
Decreased	25	22	14	36
Mean change	6	7	–4	16
Median change	0	0	0	0

Source: IMF and BAFT-IFSA 2010.
Note: CY = calendar year. Small banks = < $5 billion in assets; medium-size banks = $5 billion–$100 billion in assets; large banks = > $100 billion in assets. Mean figures are percentage changes in the pricing margin above bank cost of funds. Mean and median figures do not include responses for which detailed pricing data were not provided.

increased the relative competitiveness of the more conservative banks once Basel II requirements are in effect.

In addition to capital requirements and banks' costs of funds, the probability of default decreased over the course of 2009, as shown in figure 5.15.

Most of the respondents indicated that there was no change in defaults. A net of only 13 percent (the difference between the percentage reporting an increase and the percentage reporting a decrease) reported an increase in default risk in 2009, against a net of 30 percent between the fourth quarter of 2007 and the fourth quarter of 2008.

Figure 5.13 Effect of "Recent Developments" on Pricing of Trade Instruments

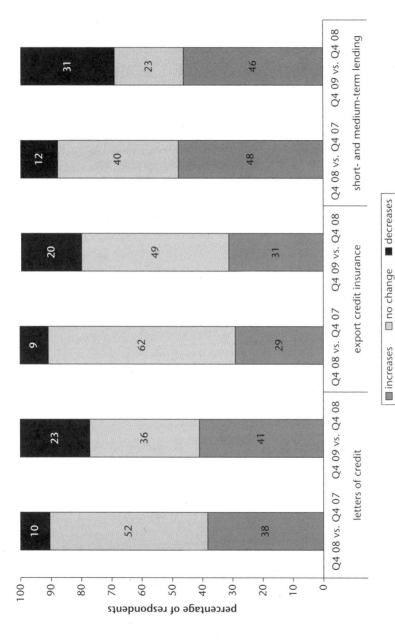

Sources: IMF and BAFT-IFSA 2010.

Figure 5.14 Change in Trade Instrument Pricing

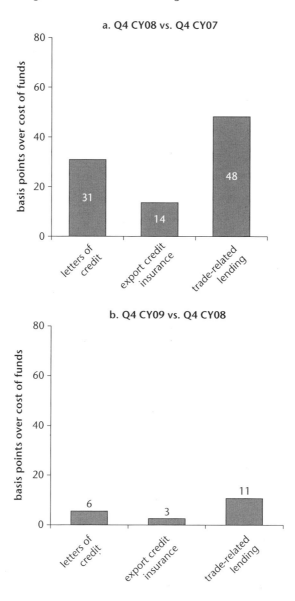

Sources: IMF and BAFT-IFSA 2010.
Note: CY = calendar year.

Table 5.9 Reasons for Trade Finance Price Increases
percentage of respondents

	Q4 CY08 vs. Q4 CY07				Q4 CY09 vs. Q4 CY08			
	All banks	Small banks	Medium-size banks	Large banks	All banks	Small banks	Medium-size banks	Large banks
Own institution's increased cost of funds	57	45	44	72	41	47	24	48
Increased risk of trade finance products relative to other working capital lending to the same nonfinancial corporate borrowers	36	30	28	45	42	42	47	39
Increased capital requirements	34	20	28	48	42	21	35	65
Other	18	25	17	14	25	37	18	22

Source: IMF and BAFT-IFSA 2010.
Note: CY = calendar year. Small banks = < $5 billion in assets; medium-size banks = $5 billion–$100 billion in assets; large banks = > $100 billion in assets. Data reflect only the views of respondents that reported an increase in pricing and that subsequently answered this question.

Table 5.10 Impact of Basel II on Trade Finance Availability
percentage of respondents

	Q4 CY08 vs. Q4 CY07				Q4 CY09 vs. Q4 CY08			
	All banks	Small banks	Medium-size banks	Large banks	All banks	Small banks	Medium-size banks	Large banks
Not applicable (including Basel II has not been implemented)	17	50	0	14	12	25	0	13
No impact	52	50	80	43	42	75	71	20
Positive impact	9	0	0	14	12	0	14	13
Negative impact	22	0	20	29	35	0	14	53
Other	0	0	0	0	0	0	0	0

Source: IMF and BAFT-IFSA 2010.
Note: CY = calendar year. Small banks = < $5 billion in assets; medium-size banks = $5 billion–$100 billion in assets; large banks = > $100 billion in assets. Includes only respondents reporting price increases due to increased capital requirements and that subsequently marked at least one option for the question.

However, perceptions of higher default risks continue to increase the price of credit. Among the July 2009 survey respondents that indicated they had increased prices, 47 percent identified default risk as a significant force in higher margins, and 52 percent cited the increased cost of funds as a leading reason for higher margins.

Figure 5.15 Change in Probability of Default, 2007–09

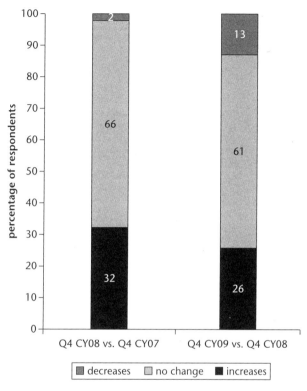

Sources: IMF and BAFT-IFSA 2010.
Note: CY = calendar year.

The increased pricing margins that came with the crisis may persist regardless of developments in defaults and Basel II (or Basel III) requirements. Although the surveys did not address this persistence, market participants widely believe that markets are unlikely to return to precrisis conditions because trade finance pricing margins were artificially low before the crisis (as was also the case with other types of short-term financing). This belief is consistent with the banks' view that trade finance was often a "loss leader" service provided to maintain client relationships and that banks were putting insufficient capital behind risk in general. In equilibrium, prices may have to remain higher than they were before the crisis, but it is unclear at what level they should settle.

Summary of Survey Results

Bank-intermediated trade finance largely held up during the 2008–09 financial crisis even as it came under several sources of strain. The value of trade finance fell

---

Box 5.2 Key Findings and Observations from the Fifth Trade Finance Survey

In fall 2010, IMF and BAFT-IFSA initiated the fifth survey administered by the market-research firm FImetrix. The fifth survey gathered responses from 118 banks in 34 advanced, emerging-market, and developing countries.

The survey results demonstrate that the trade finance industry has steadily recovered from the crisis. The value of trade finance activities has increased, especially in industrial countries, emerging Asia, and Latin America. Improvement in trade finance activities has also been observed across all trade finance instruments. The most frequently cited factors contributing to the increase seem to be recovery in global demand and easing of constraints on availability of financial resources. (The· latter appears to be a principal reason among banks with less than $100 billion in assets.)

The developments in pricing are broadly in line with the story of improvement in trade finance activities; more banks reported a pricing decrease than an increase, particularly for letters of credit (LCs). The decline in pricing for LCs is most evident among banks in Latin America and emerging Europe. The large banks ($100 billion or more in assets) are the primary drivers of the shift in pricing.

The decline in defaults and increase in the use of secondary markets for risk mitigation purposes is also consistent with the signs of recovery and returning market confidence.

Nevertheless, the banks continue to revisit trade-related exposure and lending guidelines. More than half of the survey participants reported changes in trade-related guidelines, with about 40 percent noting tightening in guidelines.

The outlook for trade finance activities continues to improve, especially in emerging Asia and Latin America. Two-thirds of the banks responding to this survey expect market conditions to improve in emerging Asia in the coming year, while half expect improvement in Latin America.

The fifth survey added a question to explore banks' perceptions and assessment of the impact of Basel III on trade finance activities. Banks seem to remain concerned about the potential impact of Basel III on trade finance activities—a concern that is particularly strong regarding LCs and among larger banks. However, due to the lack of quantitative analysis of the impact of Basel III on trade finance, the opinions varied: more than half of all respondents were either unsure or neutral regarding the impact that Basel III will have on trade finance activities.

Finally, the official sector response continues to be viewed positively. The larger the bank in terms of asset size, the more likely it is to view the response of the official sector positively.

---

at the peak of the crisis, but it fell by consistently smaller percentages across regions than did the export declines in the same regions. As a result, the share of bank-intermediated trade finance in world trade increased during the crisis. This larger share developed in spite of considerable headwinds.

Banks supplying trade finance shared the general increase in risk aversion observed in broader financial markets, and they restricted their supply of trade finance to certain countries or sectors and otherwise tightened credit conditions.

Banks also increased pricing margins, driven by both increased perceptions of default risk and higher capital requirements, the latter in part due to Basel II requirements.

However, the impact of increased default risk and higher capital requirements seems to have been more than offset by a parallel increase in risk aversion by real-sector customers because these customers had become increasingly willing to pay banks to absorb risk, even at an increased cost.

Moreover, the lower total cost of credit may also have supported the value of trade finance because the decline in banks' costs of funds (for example, LIBOR) more than offset the increased pricing margins for many banks.

Notes

1. Main findings of a fifth survey, conducted in late 2010, are summarized in box 5.2.

2. The classification of country groups in the survey is the same classification used in the winter 2009 IMF *World Economic Outlook* except to place China and India in emerging Asia rather than developing Asia.

3. The IMF and BAFT-IFSA surveys are designed mostly to support economic analysis of changes in bank trade finance. The ICC surveys, on the other hand, have focused more on banks' experience with the functioning of legal and procedural aspects of trade finance transactions.

4. SWIFT provides financial messaging services that distinguish, inter alia, between issuance, modification, and refusal of letters of credit. The ICC report analyzed the number of messages in different categories to draw conclusions about trends in bank and real-sector client risk aversion. As the ICC report notes, because SWIFT data provide a count of messages but no information on the size of transactions, they cannot be used to measure the value of different types of trade finance transactions.

5. The four surveys, conducted from 2008 to early 2010, covered issues related to the impact of Basel II on trade finance. With acceleration of the Basel III measures (tentatively set for implementation by the end of 2012), the latest survey covers questions related to the impact of Basel III on trade finance industry, as box 5.2 further describes. Some suggest that the application of credit conversion factor proposed under the Basel III may negatively affect the trade finance industry (Auboin 2010).

References

Auboin, Marc. 2010. "International Regulation and Treatment of Trade Finance: What Are the Issues?" Working Paper ERSD-2010-09, World Trade Organization, Geneva. http://www.wto.org/english/res_e/reser_e/ersd201009_e.pdf.

DDP (Data Download Program) (database). U.S. Federal Reserve, Washington, DC. http://www.federalreserve.gov/datadownload/default.htm.

ICC (International Chamber of Commerce). 2009. "Rethinking Trade Finance 2009: An ICC Global Survey." ICC, Paris.

———. 2010. "Rethinking Trade Finance 2010: An ICC Global Survey." ICC, Paris.

IMF-BAFT (International Monetary Fund-Bankers' Association for Finance and Trade). 2009. "Trade Finance Survey: A Survey among Banks Assessing the Current Trade Finance Environment." Report by FImetrix for IMF and BAFT, Washington, DC.

IMF and BAFT-IFSA (International Monetary Fund and Bankers' Association for Finance and Trade-International Financial Services Association). 2010. "Trade Finance Services: Current

Environment & Recommendations: Wave 3." Report by FImetrix for IMF and BAFT-IFSA, Washington, DC.

International Financial Statistics (database). International Monetary Fund, Washington, DC. http://www.imfstatistics.org/imf.

Statistical Data Warehouse (database). European Central Bank, Frankfurt am Main, Germany. http://sdw.ecb.europa.eu.

WTO (World Trade Organization). 2010. *International Trade Statistics 2010.* Geneva: WTO. http://www.wto.org/english/res_e/statis_e/its2010_e/its10_toc_e.htm.

GLOBAL PERSPECTIVES IN THE DECLINE OF TRADE FINANCE

Jesse Mora and William Powers

The collapse of Lehman Brothers in September 2008 is widely viewed as the spark that triggered the global economic crisis—what has become known as the "Great Recession." Global credit markets froze, which may have affected the specialized financial instruments—letters of credit and the like—that help grease the gears of international trade. Some analysts view the credit market freeze as contributing to the 31 percent drop in global trade between the second quarter of 2008 and the same quarter in 2009 (Auboin 2009).

Evidence presented in this chapter suggests that declines in global trade finance had, at most, a moderate role in reducing global trade. The chapter also examines broad measures of financing, including domestic lending in major developed economies and cross-border lending among more than 40 countries. Supplementing the data are the results of eight recent surveys to provide a more thorough examination and greater confidence in the role of trade finance during the crisis. This investigation highlights several aspects of trade finance during the crisis:

- Trade finance is dependent on both domestic and cross-border funding. While both fell substantially in 2008, neither the timing nor the magnitude of

The authors thank Hugh Arce, Richard Baldwin, and Michael Ferrantino for their helpful comments and support. This piece represents solely the views of the authors and does not represent the views of the U.S. International Trade Commission or any of its commissioners.

domestic declines matched the drop in trade finance. Cross-border funding declines presented more troubling trends, however, with supply falling earlier and exceeding the drop in demand for funds.

- Trade finance began to recover in the second quarter of 2009 for most developed and developing countries. Latin America and Africa showed the least progress but have recently stabilized. Among all regions, Asia has had the strongest recovery.
- Reduced trade finance played a moderate role in the trade decline at the peak of the crisis. Banks and suppliers judged reduced trade finance as the second greatest contributor to the decline in global exports, behind falling global demand.
- The crisis has led to a compositional shift in trade finance. Because of heightened uncertainty and increased counterparty risk, exporters shifted away from risky open-account transactions and toward lower-risk letters of credit and export credit insurance.
- Financing has been a larger problem for exports than for domestic sales.

Effect of Crisis on Corporate Finance

The crisis negatively affected every type of financing that companies use to fund their domestic production and international trade. Companies get financing in many ways, such as by issuing bonds or equity, obtaining bank loans, or self-financing through retained earnings. The crisis negatively affected all of these channels: Interest rates on bonds and loans rose, while equity prices and profits fell—and, hence, retained earnings (Guichard, Haugh, and Turner 2009). Indexes of financial conditions based on all types of financing began falling in 2007 (or earlier) in Japan, the European Union, the United Kingdom, and the United States. U.S. financial conditions did not return to normal until the end of 2009 or the beginning of 2010 (Hatzius et al. 2010).

Although strains had appeared in domestic banking markets before the trade collapse, there is no evidence that large declines in domestic lending preceded the decline in trade. (Box 6.1 describes the mechanics of how trade is exposed to financing shocks.) Strains in domestic financial markets became apparent in developed countries long before the global downturn. One early indicator of banking sector constraints was credit standards for commercial loans. In most developed countries, these standards became progressively tighter after the third quarter of 2007, as figure 6.1 illustrates.

Despite the tighter standards, commercial lending actually expanded until the end of 2008, although the declines that began in 2009 generally continued into 2010, as figure 6.2 shows.

Box 6.1 Common Types of Trade Finance and the Risk for Exporters

Worldwide, firms exported about $16 trillion of goods in 2008. Firms finance most exports through open accounts—that is, the importer pays for goods after they are delivered—just as is the usual practice for sales among firms in the same nation. This is the riskiest form of financing for an exporter, as figure B6.1 illustrates. Estimates vary, but sources report that open accounts are used for between 47 percent (Scotiabank 2007) and 80 percent (ICC 2009b, 2010) of world trade. Cash-in-advance arrangements, the least risky form of financing for exporters, account for a small share of total financing.

Banks finance the remaining portion of global trade. Most bank financing involves a letter of credit, a transaction in which a bank assumes the nonpayment risk by committing to pay the exporter after goods have been shipped or delivered. This method provides greater security to the exporter and is particularly popular with small firms and in developing countries. Regardless of the type of financing, exporters can also buy export insurance to reduce risk; about 11 percent of world trade was insured in 2009.

The role of bank financing is increased if one includes working capital loans, which are short-term loans to buy the inputs necessary to produce goods. Working capital loans are more important for financing export shipments than for domestic shipments because of the increased time between production and payment for exports (Amiti and Weinstein 2009).

Figure B6.1 Payment Risk

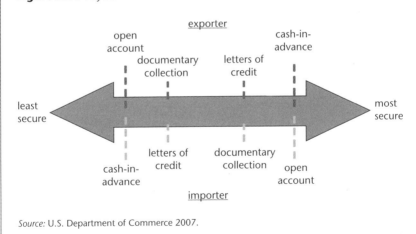

Source: U.S. Department of Commerce 2007.

The declines averaged about 2.3 percent per quarter—far below the decline in global merchandise exports, as figure 6.3 shows.

As this chapter will also show, the domestic financing drop was similar in magnitude to declines in other short-term, cross-border financing. In developing

Figure 6.1 Tightening Domestic Loan Standards

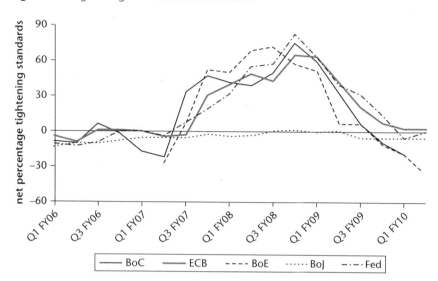

Sources: Bank of Canada 2010; Bank of England 2010; Bank of Japan 2010; ECB 2010; U.S. Federal Reserve 2010.

Note: Data show credit standards reported by central banks for large firms, except for Canada, which reports an overall measure. The Bank of England does not report a single measure of credit tightening, but separate measures for fees, spreads, loan covenants, and collateral requirements all behaved similarly; fees to large firms are included here. BoC = Bank of Canada, BoE = Bank of England, BoJ = Bank of Japan, ECB = European Central Bank, Fed = U.S. Federal Reserve.

countries, lending continued to grow in 2008 and 2009, even in Asia, which had the largest decline in exports.[1] Throughout the world, the lending declines that became evident later in the crisis were generally accompanied by a similarly large drop in demand for funds. For example, U.S. demand for commercial and industrial loans plunged at the beginning of 2009 (ECB 2009; U.S. Federal Reserve 2010). In emerging markets, particularly Asia, where trade decline was the largest, loan growth continued to grow throughout 2009. Thus reduced domestic financing seems an unlikely cause for the trade finance decline in most markets.

It is, of course, possible that trade financing from domestic banks fell even as overall lending rose. For example, several bank surveys report that the Basel II capital adequacy requirements overstate the risks of trade financing and divert funding away from exports. And Basel II has become quite widespread; 105 countries have implemented its standards, or plan to implement them, including many emerging economies in Africa, Asia, the Caribbean, and Latin America (BIS 2008). Countering this possible trade finance-specific decline, though, were numerous nonbank sources of domestic support targeted specifically to trade financing. Many central banks and government stimulus programs targeted domestic

Figure 6.2 Domestic Commercial Lending

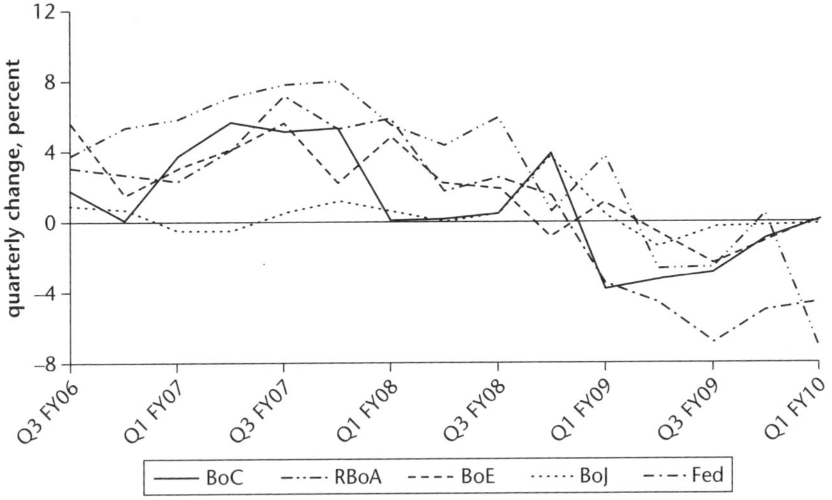

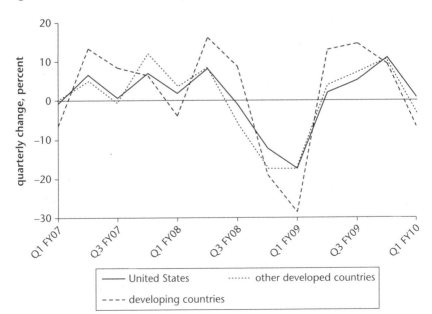

Sources: Bank of Canada 2010; Reserve Bank of Australia 2010; Bank of England 2010; Bank of Japan 2010; U.S. Federal Reserve 2010.
Note: Bank of Japan data reflect total loans, not only commercial loans. BoC = Bank of Canada, BoE = Bank of England, BoJ = Bank of Japan, Fed = U.S. Federal Reserve, RBoA = Reserve Bank of Australia.

Figure 6.3 Global Merchandise Exports

Source: IMF 2010.

financing for exports (for example, Brazil, the Republic of Korea, and Singapore), in particular after the G-20 declaration in April 2009 (Mora and Powers 2009).

Cross-Border Banking Decline Preceded Other Flows

Although both domestic and international banks provide financing for trade, an examination of cross-border lending in the crisis is more instructive for several reasons:

- Cross-border data are more complete and detailed because of centralized reporting by the Bank for International Settlements (BIS), so the data present a more complete picture of changes.
- Cross-border data show more troubling trends; particularly, cross-border declines are earlier and larger than changes in domestic bank flows or local currency lending of bank subsidiaries (McCauley, McGuire, and von Peter 2010, among other sources).
- Firms relying on cross-border financing seemed more likely to experience shortfalls. Unlike the decline in domestic lending, in which demand plummeted with supply, supply factors largely drove the fall in cross-border bank lending during the crisis, at least to emerging markets (Takáts 2010).

The decline in the value of global cross-border banking preceded the failure of Lehman Brothers in September 2008 and thus preceded the merchandise trade decline, as shown in figure 6.4. The decline in global outflows, and the subsequent decline in domestic lending in most countries, directly reduced the availability of all types of financing. Perhaps because the United States was among the first to enter the downturn, U.S.-based financial outflows recovered earlier than those of other countries and have since grown a bit faster than in other regions. The strength of U.S. outflows indicates a return to interbank dollar-denominated lending and highlights the need for dollar funding even as real gross domestic product (GDP) around the world contracted (McGuire and von Peter 2009).

Because much of trade is dependent on short-term lending (either directly through bank-intermediated export financing, such as letters of credit, or indirectly through working-capital financing), the decline in short-term banking activity, illustrated in figure 6.5, is also an important indicator. Although short-term flows are generally quite volatile, the contraction of short-term funding has been shallower and more protracted than the decline in merchandise trade. The figure also shows that inflows into the United States, unlike outflows, continued to decline through the end of 2009.

Figure 6.4 Global Cross-Border Banking Activity
amounts outstanding, in all currencies, relative to all sectors

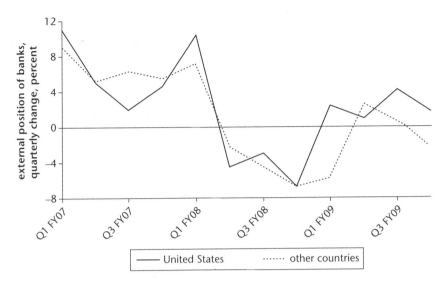

Source: BIS 2010.

Figure 6.5 Short-Term Financing Received

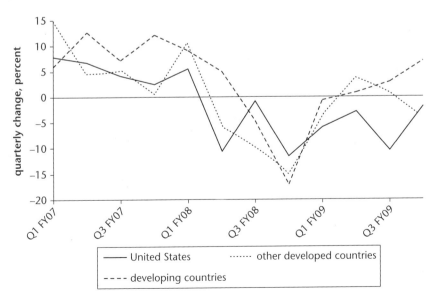

Source: BIS 2010.

Trade Finance More Resilient than Exports

In many ways, the changes in trade finance during the crisis reflected conditions in overall credit and banking markets during the period. The cost of trade finance, for example, briefly reached several hundred basis points in some markets, reflecting abnormally high financing costs throughout the financial system in the fourth quarter of 2008. Availability declined and credit standards tightened for all types of financing to firms worldwide during the period.

Trade finance does have some characteristics that differ from other types of financing. Trade finance is generally priced as a share of the value of goods shipped, so it is more directly tied to the level of exports than are other financial markets, and trade finance generally reflects the seasonality exhibited by a country's exports. Furthermore, as discussed in the survey section below, global demand for more secure types of trade finance increased during the crisis, in contrast to falling demand for other corporate financing (ECB 2009). Strong demand resulted in lower declines in trade finance than in global exports. Because all exports must be financed, at least by the exporter itself, a smaller decrease in bank financing than exports must be matched by a move away from exporter-financed open accounts.

These differences also affected the timing of the decline in trade financing. Although overall financial flows declined before the trade collapse, trade-specific financing moved together with trade. Short-term export credit insurance exposure is a measure of the amount of trade financing provided by private and public insurers.[2] Such insurance fell by 22 percent between the second quarter of 2008 and the same quarter of 2009. Trade financing debt incurred by countries is an imperfect proxy for the amount of financing that countries receive.[3] Such debt fell by 13 percent. Figures 6.6 and 6.7 show the quarterly changes for these measures of trade finance.

Data from the Society for Worldwide Interbank Financial Telecommunication (SWIFT) provide a count of trade messages sent through the SWIFT network (ICC 2010; SWIFT 2009, 2010). These transactions accounted for about $1.5 trillion in letters of credit, or about 12 percent of global trade value.[4] During the crisis, global traffic fell by more than 20 percent in 2008 and rose by about 10 percent in 2009.[5] As trade finance improved in 2009, letters of credit increased while less-secure methods such as documentary collections remained flat. This finding agrees with the survey results discussed below (such as ICC 2010), which report that exporters continue to move toward more secure forms of trade financing.

Comparing different regions, most of the improvement during 2009 occurred in the Asia and Pacific region, with other regions showing no change or only a slight rise in volume. In the first half of 2010 (January to May), volumes in all regions improved, though the Asia and Pacific region again showed the greatest growth (22 percent).[6]

Figure 6.6 Export Credit Insurance Exposure

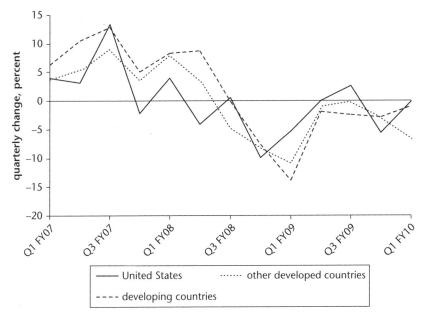

Source: JEDH 2010.

Both the value and volume data show that changes in trade finance have been more moderate than changes in trade, during both the downturn and the recovery, especially as follows:

- By nearly all measures, trade finance declined less than trade from mid-2008 to mid-2009. Figure 6.8 shows that this was true for individual regions as well, except in Latin America.
- As trade recovered in 2009 and early 2010, however, export credit insurance and trade finance debt remained largely flat, with only letters of credit showing any substantial increase during 2009. The Asia and Pacific region exhibited the largest growth in both transactions and value; Latin America has grown in value, making up for its losses in the downturn, while both volume and trade decreased in developed European countries.

Survey Results

Because much of trade finance is not distinguishable in official statistics—for example, our data account for only about 23 percent of total global trade—data

Figure 6.7 Trade Financing Debt, by Country

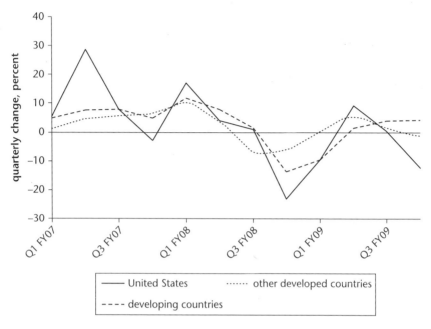

Source: JEDH 2010.

Figure 6.8 Relative Declines in Exports, Export Insurance Exposure, and Trade Finance Debt, by Region, Q2 FY08 to Q2 FY09

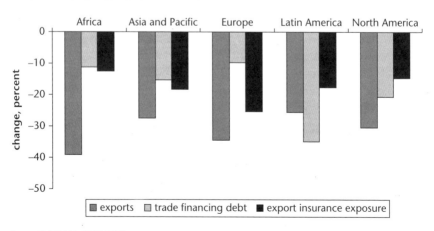

Source: IMF 2010; JEDH 2010.

comparisons are intrinsically imperfect and incomplete.[7] To address the informational gap, the World Bank, International Monetary Fund, World Trade Organization, and International Chamber of Commerce have conducted surveys of global participants in the trade credit world.

Overall, the surveys confirm the trends discussed above about the timing and geographic differences in trade finance. They also provide otherwise unavailable information about the effects of financing on exports; distinguish the effects of reduced bank finance supply from increased exporter demand; and highlight the importance of multilateral support during the crisis.

Trade Finance the No. 2 Reason for Trade Decline at Crisis Peak

Surveys show that declines in trade finance contributed directly to the decline in global trade in the second half of 2008 and early 2009. At the peak of the crisis, banks and suppliers report, reduced trade finance was the second-greatest cause of the global trade slowdown, behind falling international demand.

Estimates of the relative contribution of trade finance fell in later surveys as other factors rose in prominence. In July 2009, only 40 percent of banks reported that lower credit availability contributed to declining trade, and this share decreased to less than one-third by April 2010. By the beginning of 2010, the banks reported that price declines were a larger drag on export values than trade finance limits.

Financing has been less of a concern for domestic shipments, at least in the United States. The National Federation of Independent Business (NFIB) monthly surveys of small businesses, whose sales are largely domestic, show that less than 5 percent of U.S. small businesses report that financing is their single most important problem (NFIB 2010). This share did not exceed 6 percent at any time during the crisis.[8] The share of NFIB members citing poor sales as the top problem doubled during the crisis and has held at about 30 percent since late 2008. A substantially higher share of exporters cited financing as a top problem in the survey results we examine below.

Collectively, these results support the argument that financing is more important for exports than for domestic shipments (Amiti and Weinstein 2009), though all surveys agree that poor demand was more important than reduced financing in limiting sales.

Surveys Help Distinguish Changes in Supply and Demand

Surveys provide the best evidence distinguishing changes in trade finance supply from changes in demand.[9] After September 2008, the risks of exporting and financing rose substantially because of downgraded credit ratings of firms, banks, and countries. Macroeconomic difficulties also mattered—declining GDPs, fluctuating exchange rates, and falling prices. The rising uncertainty increased demand for more secure types of financing, such as insurance and letters of credit, to reduce the risk of nonpayment. Demand for export credit insurance rose, with the share of insured shipments rising to 11 percent of global exports in 2009 from 9 percent in 2008 (ICC 2010).[10] Exporters also demanded more trade financing from banks, and half of banks reported increased demand for products such as letters of credit.

As exporters tried to obtain less-risky financing, however, banks began to restrict financing to some customers to limit their own lending risk. Most surveyed banks (between 47 percent and 71 percent, depending on the survey) reduced the supply of trade financing in the last quarter of 2008. For example, the value of letters of credit fell by 11 percent in that quarter. Supply bottomed out in the first half of 2009. The value of all trade finance then rose gradually in the second half of 2009, making up for losses earlier in the year but still well below pre-crisis levels.

Prices of letters of credit rose early in the crisis, reflecting both increased risk and the banks' substantially higher cost of raising funds. As the crisis continued, increased demand and reduced supply drove trade finance prices even higher. In 2009, surveys report, prices for exporters continued to rise, even as banks were able to obtain funding more cheaply. The latest surveys report that demand remained high and was expected to increase further in 2010, while prices were not expected to fall in the short term.

Conclusions

This survey has included the most comprehensive measures of trade financing available, accounting for over one-fifth of global trade, and has supplemented the data with a number of trade finance surveys. This combination provides the best look to date at the changes in trade finance during the 2008–09 financial crisis.

The evidence does not support the view that declines in trade finance were exceptional during the crisis. Overall, the declines have not been large relative to changes in trade or other financial benchmarks. For example, measures of trade finance fell by about 20 percent from peak to trough, while global exports fell by over 30 percent. Relative to other types of financing, the decline in trade finance is about the same as the decline in overall cross-border, short-term lending.

Nor did trade finance have an outsize impact on trade during the crisis. Surveys show that trade finance played a moderate role at the peak of the crisis and that this role declined over time. Although prices remain high, companies no longer report that financing costs are a major impediment to trade. Financing remains a larger problem for exporters than for domestic shippers, however, for two reasons: trade financing contracted substantially more than domestic financing, and exports require more financial support than domestic shipments.

Data and surveys agree that trade finance did rebound considerably in 2009, but 2010 data have been mostly flat and conflict with the rosier gains and predictions that surveys reported. The value of all trade finance rose in the second half of 2009, making up for losses earlier in the year, but it remains well below precrisis levels. Those regions that were lagging in earlier surveys (Latin America and Africa) have seen trade finance stabilize or have begun to make up ground. The latest surveys report that exporter demand remained high and was expected to increase further in 2010. The data also show, however, that only the safest forms of trade finance rose in 2010, with total value flat or even declining.

Overall, given the easing of access to credit, the trade finance situation is expected to improve. Still, as with improvement in macroeconomic conditions, the turnaround in bank attitudes and financing of all types will likely be gradual—and, to a large degree, further gains in trade finance will be tied to increases in global exports.

Notes

1. For loan growth in emerging Asia, see Monetary Authority of Singapore (2009).

2. France, Germany, Italy, and the United States are the top providers of this insurance, accounting for about 25 percent of the global total. Globally, firms and agencies had close to $900 billion of such exposure before the crisis. About 90 percent of the credit guarantees are provided by private companies (Berne Union 2009).

3. The figure includes only short-term nongovernmental trade financing debt, which had a global value of $572 billion before the crisis. Debt depends on trade financing received as well as repaid, so debt may underrepresent the decline in trade financing in countries that experienced fiscal difficulties during the downturn.

4. Value data were provided for the four quarters from the fourth quarter of 2008 to the third of 2009.

5. That is, the number of transactions was about 10 percent higher in December 2009 than in December 2008, although the yearly total in 2009 was lower than the total in 2008.

6. The value of trade financing also rose in most regions during 2009, with the exception of Europe and the Middle East. Because only four quarters of value data have been reported, we cannot calculate the change for the same quarter in two consecutive years.

7. It would be possible to increase this share slightly with the currently available data. Including medium-term trade financing data from the Berne Union and documentary collection data from SWIFT would increase the covered share of global trade by about 6 percentage points. BIS also reports guarantees extended by financial institutions, including letters of credit and credit insurance in addition to contingent liabilities of credit derivatives (for example, credit default swaps). This series would be a promising source of information on trade financing if a means were devised to remove the portion related to credit default swaps, which dominate the series for some developed countries such as the United States (BIS 2009).

8. Financing has not been a top concern of small U.S. businesses in any recession since the 1980s.

9. The surveys include ICC 2009a, 2009b, 2010; IMF-BAFT 2009a, 2009b; IMF and BAFT-IFSA 2010; and Malouche 2009.

10. The share reported in ICC (2010) includes medium-term financing. The share of exports covered by short-term financing, which this report focuses on, also rose, but by less than 1 percent.

References

Amiti, Mary, and David E. Weinstein. 2009. "Exports and Financial Shocks." CEPR Discussion Paper 7590, Centre for Economic Policy Research, London.

Auboin, Marc. 2009. "The Challenges of Trade Financing." Commentary, VoxEU.org, Centre for Economic Policy Research, London. http://www.voxeu.org/index.php?q=node/2905.

BIS (Bank for International Settlements). 2008. "2008 FSI Survey on the Implementation of the New Capital Adequacy Framework in non-Basel Committee Member Countries." Financial Stability Institute, Basel, Switzerland. http://www.bis.org/fsi/fsiop2008.pdf.

———. 2009. "Credit Risk Transfer Statistics." Committee on the Global Financial System Paper 35, Basel, Switzerland.

———. 2010. *BIS Quarterly Review.* June 2010 statistical annex, BIS, Basel, Switzerland. http://www.bis.org/statistics/bankstats.htm.

Bank of Canada. 2010. "Senior Loan Officer Survey on Business-Lending Practices in Canada." Bank of Canada, Ottawa. http://www.bankofcanada.ca/en/slos/index.html.

Bank of England. 2010. "Credit Conditions Survey: Survey Results." Bank of England, London. http://www.bankofengland.co.uk/publications/other/monetary/creditconditions.htm.

Bank of Japan. 2010. "Senior Loan Officer Opinion Survey on Bank Lending Practices at Large Japanese Firms." Bank of Japan, Tokyo. http://www.boj.or.jp/en/statistics/dl/loan/loos/index.htm.

Berne Union. 2009. *Yearbook.* London: Exporta Publishing & Events Ltd.

ECB (European Central Bank). 2009. *Monthly Bulletin.* November issue, Executive Board of the ECB, Frankfurt.

———. 2010. "The Euro Area Bank Lending Survey: January 2010." ECB, Frankfurt. http://www.ecb.int/stats/pdf/blssurvey_201001.pdf?09898ebfbb522a57fa3477bc3e5022e0.

Guichard, Stephanie, David Haugh, and David Turner. 2009. "Quantifying the Effect of Financial Conditions in the Euro Area, Japan, United Kingdom, and United States." Economics Department Working Paper 677, Organisation for Economic Co-operation and Development, Paris.

Hatzius, Jan, Peter Hooper, Frederic Mishkin, Kermit Schoenholtz, and Mark Watson. 2010. "Financial Conditions Indexes: A Fresh Look after the Financial Crisis." Paper presented at the U.S. Monetary Policy Forum, New York, February 25.

ICC (International Chamber of Commerce). 2009a. "ICC Trade Finance Survey: An Interim Report – Summer 2009." Banking Commission Report, ICC, Paris.

———. 2009b. "Rethinking Trade Finance 2009: An ICC Global Survey." Banking Commission Market Intelligence Report, ICC, Paris.

———. 2010. "Rethinking Trade Finance 2010." Banking Commission Market Intelligence Report, ICC, Paris.

IMF (International Monetary Fund). 2010. International Financial Statistics Online (database). IMF, Washington, DC. http://www.imfstatistics.org/imf.

IMF-BAFT (International Monetary Fund–Bankers' Association for Finance and Trade). 2009a. "Global Finance Markets: The Road to Recovery." Report by FImetrix for IMF and BAFT, Washington, DC.

———. 2009b. "IMF-BAFT Trade Finance Survey: A Survey among Banks Assessing the Current Trade Finance Environment." Report by FImetrix for IMF and BAFT, Washington, DC.

IMF and BAFT-IFSA (International Monetary Fund and Bankers' Association for Finance and Trade-International Financial Services Association). 2010. "Trade Finance Services: Current Environment & Recommendations: Wave 3." Report of Survey by FImetrix for IMF-BAFT, Washington, DC.

JEDH (Joint External Debt Hub). 2010. Joint BIS-IMF-OECD-WB Statistics (database). JEDH, http://www.jedh.org.

Malouche, Mariem. 2009. "Trade and Trade Finance Developments in 14 Developing Countries Post-September 2008." Policy Research Working Paper 5138, World Bank, Washington, DC.

McCauley, Robert, Patrick McGuire, and Goetz von Peter. 2010. "The Architecture of Global Banking: From International to Multinational?" *BIS Quarterly Review* (March): 25–37.

McGuire, Patrick, and Goetz von Peter. 2009. "The U.S. Dollar Shortage in Global Banking." *BIS Quarterly Review* (March): 47–63.

Monetary Authority of Singapore. 2009. *Financial Stability Review*. Macroeconomic Surveillance Department report, Monetary Authority of Singapore. http://www.mas.gov.sg/publications/MAS_FSR.html.

Mora, Jesse, and William Powers. 2009. "Did Trade Credit Problems Deepen the Great Trade Collapse?" In *The Great Trade Collapse: Causes, Consequences and Prospects*, ed. Richard Baldwin, 115–26. VoxEU.org E-book, Centre for Economic Policy Research, London. http://www.voxeu.org/index.php?q=node/4297.

NFIB (National Federation of Independent Business). 2010. "Small Business Economic Trends." Survey report, NFIB, Nashville, TN. http://www.nfib.com/research-foundation/surveys/small-business-economic-trends.

Reserve Bank of Australia. 2010. "Banks—Assets: Commercial Loans and Advances." Statistical tables, Reserve Bank of Australia, Sydney. http://www.rba.gov.au/statistics/tables/index.html.

Scotiabank. 2007. "2007 AFP Trade Finance Survey: Report of Survey Results." Report for the Association for Financial Professionals, Bethesda, MD.

SWIFT (Society for Worldwide Interbank Financial Communication). 2009. "Collective Trade Snapshot Report." Trade Services Advisory Group, SWIFT, La Hulpe, Belgium.

———. 2010. "Data Analysis: SWIFT Traffic and Economic Recovery." *Dialogue* Q3 2010: 47–50.

Takáts, Elöd. 2010. "Was It Credit Supply? Cross-Border Bank Lending to Emerging Market Economies during the Financial Crisis." *BIS Quarterly Review* (June): 49–56.

U.S. Department of Commerce. 2007. "Trade Finance Guide: A Quick Reference for U.S. Exporters." International Trade Administration guide, U.S. Department of Commerce, Washington, DC. http://trade.gov/media/publications/pdf/trade_finance_guide2007.pdf.

U.S. Federal Reserve. 2010. "Senior Loan Officer Opinion Survey on Bank Lending Practices." Survey report, Federal Reserve Board, Washington, DC. http://www.federalreserve.gov/boarddocs/SnLoanSurvey/201002/.

THE ROLE OF TRADE FINANCE IN THE U.S. TRADE COLLAPSE: A SKEPTIC'S VIEW

Andrei A. Levchenko, Logan T. Lewis,
and Linda L. Tesar

The contraction in trade during the 2008–09 recession was global in scale and remarkably deep. From the second quarter of 2008 to the second quarter of 2009, U.S. real goods imports fell by 21.4 percent and exports by 18.9 percent. The drop in trade flows in the United States is even more dramatic considering that both import and export prices simultaneously fell relative to domestic prices, which normally would have resulted in an expansion of trade flows.

Several recent papers have suggested that credit constraints contributed significantly to the global decline in trade (for example, Auboin 2009; IMF 2009; Chor and Manova 2010). To be sure, financial intermediaries were at the epicenter of the global crisis, and it is clear that credit conditions facing firms and households tightened in fall 2008. These constraints could be particularly important for firms engaged in international trade because they must extend credit to their foreign counterparties before the shipment of goods. If these lines of credit are suspended, importing firms will cancel their orders for foreign goods, and foreign firms will reduce production.

As reasonable as this hypothesis sounds, it is a difficult empirical challenge to isolate the impact of tightening credit constraints on the collapse in trade flows, for the following reasons:

- It is hard to tell whether the credit extended to firms dropped because of a supply-side constraint (banks won't extend credit) or because of a drop in demand (demand falls, so firms import fewer goods and require less credit).

- Although a firm's dependence on credit is observable, it is difficult, if not impossible, to obtain precise data on the cost of credit associated with the international shipment of goods.
- Given the importance of multinational firms in international trade, it is an open question whether multinationals require credit to acquire goods from their own affiliates or long-term trade partners. Moreover, to the extent they do require credit, how will such financial flows appear in the firms' balance sheets?

This chapter explores the role of financial factors in the collapse of U.S. imports and exports. Using data disaggregated at the six-digit North American Industry Classification System (NAICS) level (about 450 distinct sectors), the chapter examines the extent to which financial variables can explain the cross-sectoral variation in how much imports or exports fell during this episode. To do this, the authors employ a wide variety of possible indicators, such as standard measures of trade credit and external finance dependence, proxies for shipping lags at the sector level, and shares of intrafirm trade in each sector. In each case, the hypothesis is that if financial factors did play a role in the fall of U.S. trade, one should expect international trade flows to fall more in sectors with certain characteristics, a strategy reminiscent of Rajan and Zingales (1998).

Based on the analysis here, overall, there is at best weak evidence for the role of financial factors in the U.S. trade collapse. Imports or exports *did not* fall systematically more in (a) sectors that extend or receive more trade credit; (b) sectors that have a higher dependence on external finance or lower asset tangibility; (c) sectors in which U.S. trade is dominated by countries experiencing greater financial distress; or (d) sectors with lower intrafirm trade. All of these are reasonable sectoral characteristics to examine for evidence of financial factors in trade, as detailed in each case below.

For imports into the United States, some evidence does exist that shipping lags mattered. Sectors in which a high share of imports is shipped by ocean or land experienced larger reductions in trade, relative to sectors in which international shipments are primarily by air. In addition, sectors with longer ocean-shipping delays also experienced significantly larger falls in imports. This is indirect evidence for the role of trade finance during the recent trade collapse. Trade finance instruments, such as letters of credit, are typically used to cover goods that are in transit. Thus, trade finance is likely to matter more for sectors in which goods are in transit longer—either because they are mostly shipped by land or sea or because they tend to be shipped over greater distances. In turn, the finding that these sectors experienced larger reductions in U.S. imports can be seen as supportive of the role of financial factors in the trade collapse. All in all, however, the bottom line of this exercise is that, in the sample of highly dis-aggregated U.S. imports and exports, evidence of financial factors has proven hard to find.

U.S. Trade Flows and Measures of Trade Finance

This analysis uses quarterly nominal data for U.S. imports from, and exports to, the rest of the world at the NAICS six-digit level of disaggregation from the U.S. International Trade Commission. This is the most finely disaggregated monthly NAICS trade data available, yielding about 450 distinct sectors. The empirical methodology follows Levchenko, Lewis, and Tesar (2010), which can also serve as the source for detailed data documentation. In each sector, the year-on-year percentage drop in quarterly trade flows is computed, from the second quarter of 2008 to the second quarter of 2009. This period corresponds quite closely to the peak-to-trough period of the aggregate U.S. imports and exports.

The working hypothesis is that if financial factors did matter in the fall in U.S. trade during this period, the financial contraction should have affected certain sectors more than others. Thus, the empirical analysis is based on the following specification:

$$\gamma_i^{trade} = \alpha + \beta CHAR_i + \delta \mathbf{X}_i + \varepsilon_i, \qquad (7.1)$$

where i indexes sectors,

γ_i^{trade} = the percentage change in the trade flow (alternatively exports or imports),

$CHAR_i$ is a sectoral characteristic meant to proxy for the role of financial factors.

All of the specifications include a vector of controls $\mathbf{X}_i$. The baseline controls are (a) the share of the sector in overall U.S. imports and exports, a proxy for size; (b) elasticity of substitution among the varieties in the sector, sourced from Broda and Weinstein (2006); and (c) labor intensity of the sector, computed on the basis of the U.S. input-output matrix.

Levchenko, Lewis, and Tesar (2010) used a similar framework to test the rela-tive importance of vertical production linkages, trade credit, compositional effects, and the distinction between durables and nondurables. Two sectoral char-acteristics were robustly correlated with declines in trade: the extent of down-stream linkages and whether the sector was durable. Based on these findings, all specifications include Levchenko, Lewis, and Tesar's (2010) preferred measure of downstream linkages (average use of a sector as an intermediate in other sectors) and a dummy for durability as controls in all specifications.

This chapter focuses on the hypothesis that financial variables played a role in—and tests whether a variety of proxies for financing costs can account for— the cross-sectoral variation in trade flows. The sectoral characteristics considered are trade credit, external finance dependence, tangible asset levels, partner country credit conditions, shipping lags, and intrafirm trade.

Trade Credit

The analysis evaluates the hypothesis that, because of the credit crunch, firms were no longer willing to extend trade credit to their suppliers. Under this view, international trade would fall, for instance, because U.S. buyers could no longer extend trade credit to foreign firms from which they normally purchase goods. To test this hypothesis, two measures of trade credit intensity are built. The first is accounts payable as a share of cost of goods sold, which records the amount of credit extended to the firm by suppliers, relative to the cost of production. The second is accounts receivable as a share of sales, which measures how much credit the firm extends to its customers.

Accounts payable relative to the cost of goods sold and accounts receivable relative to sales are the two most standard indices in the trade credit literature (for example, Love, Preve, and Sarria-Allende 2007) and are constructed using firm-level data from Compustat.[1] If importing and exporting firms are dependent on trade credit, these two measures of credit dependence should appear with a negative coefficient (sectors with more trade credit dependence should experience a larger reduction in trade flows).

External Finance Dependence

The second set of measures is inspired by the large literature on the role of financial constraints in sectoral production and trade. Following the seminal contribution of Rajan and Zingales (1998), external finance dependence is computed as the share of investment not financed out of current cash flow.

This measure is based on the assumption that in certain industries, investments by firms cannot be financed with internal cash flows, and these are the industries that are especially dependent on external finance. If financially dependent industries were in systematically greater distress during this crisis, the coefficient on this variable should be negative (greater dependence leads to larger falls in trade).

Tangible Assets

A related measure is the level of tangible assets (plant, property, and equipment) as a share of total assets by sector. Firms with greater tangible assets should have better collateral and therefore an easier time obtaining credit.

This variable should have a positive coefficient in the regressions (more pledgeable assets means it is easier to raise external finance, and thus a credit crunch will have less of an impact on production or cross-border trade). As with measures of trade credit, external finance dependence indicators were built using standard definitions and data from Compustat.

Partner Country Credit Conditions

The next hypothesis tested is that trade should fall disproportionately more to and from countries that experienced greater financial distress. This approach is inspired by the work of Chor and Manova (2010), who find a link between credit conditions in the trading partner and the volume of bilateral trade. To capture this effect, a trade-weighted credit contraction (*TWCC*) measure for imports and exports is created, as in Levchenko, Lewis, and Tesar (2010):

$$TWCC_i^{trade} = \sum_{c=1}^{N} \Delta IBRATE_c \times a_{ic}^{trade}, \qquad (7.2)$$

where c indexes countries,

   trade refers to either imports or exports,

   $\Delta IBRATE_c$ = change in interbank lending rate over the crisis period in country c,

   a_{ic} = precrisis share of total U.S. trade in sector i captured by country c.

For imports, a_{ic} is thus the share of total U.S. imports coming from country c in sector i. For exports, a_{ic} is the share of total U.S. exports in sector i going to country c.

In the case of imports, the value of *TWCC* will be high if, in sector i, a greater share of U.S. precrisis imports comes from countries that experienced a more severe credit crunch. Therefore, if the credit crunch hypothesis is correct, the coefficient on this variable will be negative (tighter partner-country credit conditions lead to a greater contraction in trade flows).[2]

Shipping Lags and Trade Finance

Auboin (2009) and Amiti and Weinstein (2009) emphasize the role of trade finance instruments in international trade. These instruments, such as letters of credit, are used by firms to cover costs and guarantee payment while goods are in transit. The authors are not aware of any sector-level measures of trade finance used by U.S. firms engaged in international trade. However, if the needs for trade finance are positively related to the time it takes goods to reach their destination, one might expect trade finance costs to increase with distance and delivery lags. For ocean transit, shipping times can be as long as several weeks (Hummels and Schaur 2010), during which the exporting firm would typically be waiting for payment.

If these considerations matter, one should expect trade to fall more in sectors with longer shipping lags. To test for this possibility, bilateral trade data, disaggregated by mode of shipping, are used to compute several indicators of delays.[3] The first is simply the average distance traveled by a dollar's worth of imports or exports in each sector. The second is the share of imports and exports that traveled by air, ship, and over land. The hypothesis is that in sectors dominated by air shipping, trade finance would matter much less because air shipping time is almost never greater than one or two days (Hummels 2007). However, in sectors dominated by other forms of shipping, delays are substantially longer, and thus, a disruption in trade finance is potentially more damaging.

Finally, data on average ocean shipping times from each country to the United States are used to calculate a proxy for the average shipping time in each sector:

$$TIME_i = \left(\sum_{c=1}^{N} a_{ic,ocean}^{trade} \times ShipDays_c \right) \times a_{i,ocean}^{trade} + 2 \times \left(a_{i,air}^{trade} + a_{i,other}^{trade} \right), \qquad (7.3)$$

where c indexes countries,

   $trade$ can refer to either imports or exports,

   $a_{ic,ocean}^{trade}$ = share of country c's ocean trade in total U.S. ocean trade in sector i,

   $a_{i,ocean}^{trade}$ = share of U.S. trade in sector i that is shipped by ocean,

   $ShipDays_c$ = the ocean shipping time from country c to the United States.

Shipping time measures for shipments by air and other means are not available. In calculating the measure, one assumes that shipment by air or other means (usually truck or pipeline) takes two days.

Thus, $TIME_i$ is the average shipping time, in days, for a dollar's worth of imports or exports in sector i. If firms must raise finance to cover the period that goods are in transit, one would expect a negative coefficient on the variables reflecting shipping delays (larger delays mean a greater role for trade finance, implying a larger fall in trade).[4]

Intrafirm Trade

Finally, it is hypothesized that trade finance used for insuring exporters against nonpayment for the shipment will matter less if trade is intrafirm. Thus, a contraction in trade finance will have less of an impact, if any, on the more than one-third of U.S. trade that is intrafirm. To check for this possibility, the fall in trade in a sector is regressed on the share of intrafirm trade in total trade in the sector. This variable is computed by combining multinational affiliate sales data from the U.S. Bureau of Economic Analysis with standard international trade data and averaging over the 2002–06 period. Sectors with a greater share of intrafirm trade should experience smaller reductions in trade—a positive coefficient.

Table 7.1 reports summary statistics (mean, standard deviation, minimum and maximum across the sectors) for the variables used in the analysis.

The top panel shows statistics for the two dependent variables: the percentage change in imports and exports from the second quarter of 2008 to the

Table 7.1 Summary Statistics, Q2 2008–Q2 2009

	Mean	Standard deviation	Minimum	Maximum
Dependent variables				
Change in imports (%)	−25.3	22.7	−100.0	86.1
Change in exports (%)	−20.9	21.4	−96.9	74.4
Credit indicators				
Accounts payable/cost of goods sold	0.469	0.141	0.194	1.733
Accounts receivable/sales	0.532	0.131	0.156	0.817
External finance dependence	0.703	0.476	−2.977	1.852
Asset tangibility	0.735	0.669	0.096	6.619
TWCC (imports)	−2.691	0.493	−5.594	−1.178
TWCC (exports)	−2.721	0.392	−4.190	−0.411
Shipping delays indicators				
Average distance shipped (imports)	6650	2533	549	15201
Average distance shipped (exports)	5233	1869	781	11192
Share shipped by truck and pipeline (imports)	0.330	0.254	0.000	1.000
Share shipped by truck and pipeline (exports)	0.442	0.224	0.000	0.942
Share shipped by vessel (imports)	0.527	0.267	0.000	1.000
Share shipped by vessel (exports)	0.364	0.235	0.000	0.997
Average time to ship, in days (imports)	22	4	4	36
Average time to ship, in days (exports)	19	4	6	33
Control variables				
Share in total imports	0.002	0.007	0.000	0.088
Share in total exports	0.002	0.005	0.000	0.045
Elasticity of substitution	6.817	10.705	1.200	103
Labor intensity	0.633	0.229	0.049	0.998
Average downstream use	0.001	0.002	0.000	0.013
Durable dummy	0.587	0.493	0.000	1.000

Source: Authors' calculations.
Note: TWCC = trade-weighted credit contraction. This table presents the summary statistics for the variables used in estimation. Variable definitions and sources are described in detail in the text. See also Levchenko, Lewis, and Tesar (2010).

second quarter of 2009. The mean sectoral decline is 25.3 percent for imports and 20.9 percent for exports. There is considerable heterogeneity across sectors; some sectors even saw an expansion of trade, while others experienced a large contraction. Thus, a great deal of cross-sectoral variation could potentially be exploited.

Estimation Results

Regarding the results of the regression analysis, table 7.2 presents the results when the dependent variable is U.S. imports by sector, and table 7.3 presents the results when the dependent variable is U.S. exports.

Throughout, the tables report the standardized beta coefficients, obtained by first renormalizing each variable to have a mean of 0 and a standard deviation of 1. Thus, all the regression coefficients correspond to the number of standard deviations' change in the left-hand side variable that would be due to a 1 standard deviation change in the right-hand side variable. This also implies that the magnitudes of the coefficients are comparable across variables that may have very different scales when not normalized.

The controls for sector size in trade and labor intensity come in as strongly significant across the board. In addition, the main two variables found to be significant in Levchenko, Lewis, and Tesar (2010)—durability and vertical production linkages—remain strongly significant, with all p-values less than 1 percent in the case of U.S. imports.

The coefficients on the financial variables are less consistent. Columns (1) and (2) of each table report the results for the trade credit variables (accounts payable and accounts receivable). For imports, the coefficients are not significant, and the point estimates are close to zero. For exports, accounts payable is not significant with a near-zero point estimate, while the accounts receivable variable is significant at the 10 percent level, but with the "wrong" sign: exports in sectors that extend trade credit more intensively fell by *less*.

Columns (3) and (4) of tables 7.2 and 7.3 report the results for the measures of external finance dependence and asset tangibility. Although for both directions of trade flows, the Rajan and Zingales (1998) measure of external dependence is insignificant with a near-zero beta coefficient, asset tangibility is significant, but once again with the "wrong" sign: sectors with a greater share of tangible assets should have a relatively easier time getting credit during a crunch; those sectors also had *larger* falls in both imports and exports.

Column (5) reports the results for the trade-weighted credit contraction in the partner countries. Once again, while the coefficient is nearly zero for U.S. imports, for exports it is significant at 10 percent with the "wrong" sign: exports from the

Table 7.2 U.S. Imports and Financial Variables, Q2 2008–Q2 2009

	(1)	(2)	(3)	(4)	(5)	(6)	(7)	(8)	(9)
Dependent variable change in imports (%)									
Accounts payable/cost of goods sold	0.076 (0.085)								
Accounts receivable/sales		0.056 (0.071)							
External finance dependence			0.035 (0.041)						
Asset tangibility				-0.185*** (0.071)					
TWCC					-0.008 (0.069)				
Average distance shipped						0.087 (0.063)			
Share shipped by truck and pipeline							-0.133** (0.067)		
Share shipped by vessel							-0.148** (0.063)		
Average time to ship								-0.123** (0.058)	
Share of intrafirm imports[a]									0.022 (0.049)
Durable dummy	-0.206*** (0.059)	-0.215*** (0.054)	-0.194*** (0.048)	-0.258*** (0.046)	-0.185*** (0.050)	-0.193*** (0.047)	-0.212*** (0.047)	-0.220*** (0.046)	-0.191*** (0.049)

(continued next page)

Table 7.2 *continued*

	(1)	(2)	(3)	(4)	(5)	(6)	(7)	(8)	(9)
Average downstream use[b]	-0.200***	-0.195***	-0.203***	-0.154***	-0.192***	-0.178***	-0.172***	-0.197***	-0.205***
	(0.042)	(0.044)	(0.043)	(0.047)	(0.040)	(0.045)	(0.043)	(0.041)	(0.046)
Share in total[c]	-0.092*	-0.073*	-0.069*	-0.027	-0.064*	-0.071**	-0.074**	-0.074**	-0.061
	(0.047)	(0.038)	(0.039)	(0.042)	(0.037)	(0.035)	(0.031)	(0.034)	(0.037)
Elasticity of substitution[d]	-0.076	-0.073	-0.08	-0.064	-0.078	-0.075	-0.07	-0.068	-0.078
	(0.061)	(0.061)	(0.062)	(0.058)	(0.061)	(0.059)	(0.061)	(0.062)	(0.060)
Labor intensity[e]	-0.113**	-0.129**	-0.126**	-0.135**	-0.122**	-0.121**	-0.114**	-0.124**	-0.110**
	(0.054)	(0.054)	(0.055)	(0.054)	(0.051)	(0.058)	(0.055)	(0.052)	(0.053)
Observations	415	415	423	432	435	436	436	434	437
R-squared	0.124	0.122	0.124	0.138	0.116	0.114	0.119	0.133	0.112

Source: Authors' calculations.

Note: Standardized beta coefficients reported throughout. Robust standard errors are in parentheses. The dependent variable is the percentage reduction in U.S. imports in a six-digit NAICS category from Q2 2008 to Q2 2009 (year-to-year). The financial variables are described in detail in the text.

a. "Share of intrafirm imports" is total U.S. imports, computed from U.S. Bureau of Economic Analysis multinationals data and averaged over the period 2002–06.

b. "Average downstream use" is the average use output in a sector as an intermediate input in other sectors.

c. "Share in total" is the share of a sector in total U.S. imports.

d. "Elasticity of substitution" between varieties in a sector is sourced from Broda and Weinstein (2006).

e. "Labor intensity" is the compensation of employees as a share of value added, from the U.S. 2002 Benchmark Input-Output Table (BEA 2002).

* significant at 10 percent.

** significant at 5 percent.

*** significant at 1 percent.

Table 7.3 U.S. Exports and Financial Variables, Q2 2008–Q2 2009

	(1)	(2)	(3)	(4)	(5)	(6)	(7)	(8)	(9)
Dependent variable change in imports (%)									
Accounts payable/cost of goods sold	0.012 (0.068)								
Accounts receivable/sales		0.105* (0.063)							
External finance dependence			0.01 (0.050)						
Asset tangibility				−0.156** (0.062)					
TWCC					0.120* (0.065)				
Average distance shipped						0.093 (0.064)			
Share shipped by truck and pipeline							−0.093 (0.062)		
Share shipped by vessel							−0.083 (0.070)		
Average time to ship								−0.042 (0.056)	
Share of intrafirm imports[a]									0.016 (0.050)
Durable dummy	−0.094 (0.058)	−0.137** (0.055)	−0.100** (0.050)	−0.152*** (0.054)	−0.082 (0.051)	−0.111** (0.050)	−0.125** (0.052)	−0.104** (0.050)	−0.106** (0.050)

(continued next page)

Table 7.3 *continued*

	(1)	(2)	(3)	(4)	(5)	(6)	(7)	(8)	(9)
Average downstream use[b]	-0.098**	-0.090**	-0.100**	-0.054	-0.091**	-0.073*	-0.07	-0.095**	-0.098**
	(0.042)	(0.043)	(0.043)	(0.048)	(0.041)	(0.044)	(0.044)	(0.041)	(0.041)
Share in total[c]	-0.191***	-0.194***	-0.189***	-0.199***	-0.196***	-0.210***	-0.208***	-0.190***	-0.188***
	(0.067)	(0.064)	(0.067)	(0.062)	(0.064)	(0.068)	(0.061)	(0.065)	(0.064)
Elasticity of substitution[d]	-0.049	-0.042	-0.049	-0.036	-0.05	-0.062	-0.049	-0.045	-0.05
	(0.087)	(0.085)	(0.087)	(0.082)	(0.079)	(0.079)	(0.081)	(0.083)	(0.083)
Labor intensity[e]	-0.135**	-0.134***	-0.129**	-0.156***	-0.133***	-0.145***	-0.156***	-0.143***	-0.145***
	(0.054)	(0.050)	(0.050)	(0.052)	(0.050)	(0.050)	(0.050)	(0.050)	(0.050)
Observations	415	415	423	432	437	436	436	436	437
R-squared	0.097	0.106	0.098	0.116	0.117	0.113	0.112	0.105	0.104

Source: Authors' calculations.

Notes: Standardized beta coefficients reported throughout. Robust standard errors are in parentheses. The dependent variable is the percentage reduction in U.S. exports in a six-digit NAICS category from Q2 2008 to Q2 2009 (year-to-year). The financial variables are described in detail in the text.

a. "Share of intrafirm imports" is total U.S. imports, computed from the U.S. Bureau of Economic Analysis multinationals data and averaged over the period 2002–06.

b. "Average downstream use" is the average use output in a sector as an intermediate input in other sectors.

c. "Share in total" is the share of a sector in total U.S. imports.

d. "Elasticity of substitution" between varieties in a sector is sourced from Broda and Weinstein (2006).

e. "Labor intensity" is the compensation of employees as a share of value added, from the U.S. 2002 Benchmark Input-Output Table (BEA 2002).

* significant at 10 percent.

** significant at 5 percent.

*** significant at 1 percent.

United States fell by *less* in sectors dominated by trading partners with greater credit contractions.

Columns (6), (7), and (8) report the results of using shipping lags measures (average distance shipped, share shipped by truck and pipeline, share shipped by vessel, and average time to ship). For U.S. exports, these do not seem to matter. For imports, there is some evidence for the role of shipping lags. Although the simple average distance shipped is not significant (column [6]), the mode of transportation is. Sectors with higher shares of imports shipped by ocean and other means (usually truck and pipeline) experienced larger falls than sectors with higher shares of air shipping (column [7]). Furthermore, sectors with longer shipping times (column [8]) had larger falls in imports. The magnitudes of the beta coefficients are also economically significant: a 1.0 standard deviation change in share shipped by ocean is associated with a 0.148 standard deviations' greater fall in imports. Similarly, a 1.0 standard deviation change in shipping time leads imports to fall by 0.123 standard deviations.

One difficulty in interpreting the shipment coefficients is that the mode of shipping could be an endogenous variable. For instance, firms choose the shipping mode optimally in response to demand volatility (Hummels and Schaur 2010). A second problem is that the mode of shipping is likely to be correlated with the type of goods (for example, automobiles account for a substantial fraction of the decline in trade and are never shipped by air). Although other industry characteristics that are explicitly controlled for may sweep out some of this variation, others could be missing from the analysis.

Finally, column (9) reports the results of regressing imports and exports on the share of intrafirm trade in the sector; although the coefficient has the "right" sign, it is very close to zero and insignificant.

Conclusions

It is widely recognized that the current global downturn was triggered by a large-scale financial crisis. At the same time, the world experienced a collapse in international trade of a magnitude unseen since World War II. If one puts the two events together, it is a reasonable hypothesis that financial factors contributed to the collapse in trade. However, hard evidence for this has proven elusive. This chapter tests a battery of hypotheses concerning how financial factors could have affected U.S. imports and exports at the sector level. Overall, the results show little evidence that financial factors contributed to the trade collapse. This finding is in sharp contrast to the other measures that were found, in earlier studies, to matter a great deal: vertical production linkages and the role of durables.

The remainder of this section highlights some boundaries of this empirical analysis. First, though there is hardly any effect of financial variables on overall U.S. import and export volumes in each sector, financial variables could have been partly responsible for collapses in bilateral trade from individual countries in particular sectors. This possibility is consistent with the results of Chor and Manova (2010), who found that countries experiencing greater credit contractions reduced their exports to the United States disproportionately in financially dependent sectors. These results point out that when one aggregates across partner countries up to sector level, the impact of financial factors on trade volumes disappears.

In light of historical experience, this finding is not surprising. Relative to the level of economic activity, the fall in U.S. trade during the 2001 recession was almost as large as in 2008–09 (Levchenko, Lewis, and Tesar 2010). However, the 2001 recession was not accompanied by a contraction in credit, suggesting that other mechanisms are probably responsible for falls in cross-border trade during economic downturns.

Second, although the United States is widely seen as the epicenter of the financial crisis, its financial system is nonetheless one of the deepest and most resilient in the world. Thus, even if financial factors had no effect on U.S. trade, these factors could have been much more important in other countries with weaker financial systems. Indeed, in a wide sample of countries, past banking crises did affect international trade flows (Iacovone and Zavacka 2009).

Third, even if financial characteristics were found to have a significant impact on international trade volumes, such a result would not necessarily be evidence of financial factors in international trade specifically because production may have fallen by just as much in each sector. Thus, a conclusive test of the role of financial variables in the trade collapse would have to find that financial factors were responsible for changes in trade *over and above the change in output*. This critique applies also to the other existing studies of finance and trade, though it is less of a problem for the negative results here because a robust effect is not found even on unadjusted trade volumes.

Notes

1. Data were obtained on all firms in Compustat from 2000 to 2008. These ratios were computed for each firm in each quarter, and the median value was taken for each firm (across all the quarters for which data are available). The median value across firms is then taken in each industry. Medians are taken to reduce the impact of outliers, which tend to be large in firm-level data. Taking means instead leaves the results unchanged. Because coverage is uneven across sectors, trade credit intensity is calculated over at least 10 firms. This implies that sometimes the level of variation is at the five-, four-, and even three-digit level, although the trade data are at the six-digit NAICS level of disaggregation. See Levchenko, Lewis, and Tesar (2010) for more details.

2. The authors are grateful to Davin Chor and Kalina Manova for sharing the interbank rate data used in Chor and Manova 2010.

3. The authors use 2007 data collected by the U.S. Census Bureau and made available by Peter Schott on his website: http://www.som.yale.edu/faculty/pks4/sub_international.htm.

4. The authors are grateful to David Hummels and Georg Schaur for computing these measures using their ocean shipping time data.

References

Amiti, Mary, and David E. Weinstein. 2009. "Exports and Financial Shocks." Discussion Paper 7590, Centre for Economic Policy Research, London.

Auboin, Marc. 2009. "Restoring Trade Finance: What the G20 Can Do." In *The Collapse of Global Trade, Murky Protectionism, and the Crisis: Recommendations for the G20*, ed. Richard Baldwin and Simon Evenett, 75–80. VoxEU.org, E-book. London: Centre for Economic Policy Research.

BEA (U.S. Bureau of Economic Analysis). 2002. U.S. 2002 Benchmark Input-Output Database. BEA, Washington, DC. http://www.bea.gov/industry/io_benchmark.htm.

Broda, Christian, and David Weinstein. 2006. "Globalization and the Gains from Variety." *The Quarterly Journal of Economics* 121 (2): 541–85.

Chor, Davin, and Kalina Manova. 2010. "Off the Cliff and Back? Credit Conditions and International Trade during the Global Financial Crisis." Working Paper 16174, National Bureau of Economic Research, Cambridge, MA.

Hummels, David L. 2007. "Transportation Costs and International Trade in the Second Era of Globalization." *The Journal of Economic Perspectives* 21 (3): 131–54.

Hummels, David L., and Georg Schaur. 2010. "Hedging Price Volatility Using Fast Transport." *Journal of International Economics* 82 (1): 15–25.

Iacovone, Leonardo, and Veronika Zavacka. 2009. "Banking Crises and Exports: Lessons from the Past." Policy Research Working Paper 5016, World Bank, Washington, DC.

IMF (International Monetary Fund). 2009. "Survey of Private Sector Trade Credit Developments." Memorandum, IMF, Washington, DC.

Levchenko, Andrei A., Logan T. Lewis, and Linda L. Tesar. 2010. "The Collapse of International Trade during the 2008–2009 Crisis: In Search of the Smoking Gun." *IMF Economic Review* 58 (2): 214–53.

Love, Inessa, Lorenzo A. Preve, and Virginia Sarria-Allende. 2007. "Trade Credit and Bank Credit: Evidence from Recent Financial Crises." *Journal of Financial Economics* 83(2): 453–69.

Rajan, Raghuram G., and Luigi Zingales. 1998. "Financial Dependence and Growth." *The American Economic Review* 88 (3): 559–86.

TRADE FINANCE IN AFRICA: A SURVEY OF FIRMS

John Humphrey

Over the past two decades, development policy has encouraged producers in developing countries to export labor-intensive manufactures and nontraditional agricultural exports as an effective means of reducing poverty. How did these industries fare in the wake of the 2008–09 global crisis? Given the unprecedented financial nature of this crisis and its impact through the banking system, were exporters from low-income countries hit by cuts in the finance needed for trade?

Concern has been expressed about this issue by trade specialists and policy makers from a wide range of international organizations. The final communiqué of the April 2009 G-20 London Summit identified withdrawal of trade credit as a factor exacerbating trade declines, and the G-20 leaders committed $250 billion to support trade finance. Many commentators welcomed this announcement, but notes of skepticism have also been registered. For example, economist Richard Baldwin, policy director of the Centre for Economic Policy Research, has suggested that expanding trade finance is an easy option that encounters little political opposition (Baldwin 2009). In fact, whether trade finance has a discernible effect on levels of trade—and to what extent—is far from clear, as is whether

This paper was written with financial support from the U.K. Department for International Development. Paul Kamau at the Institute for Development Studies, University of Nairobi, and Steve Homer at Biospartners (www.biospartners.co.uk) interviewed the companies. The author is also grateful to Ian Sayers at the International Trade Centre in Geneva for providing information about trade credit issues for developing-country exporters.

exporters from the poorest countries are affected to the same extent as those in more-developed countries.

This chapter provides some evidence about whether export-oriented garment production and high-value export horticulture in Sub-Saharan Africa have experienced problems in obtaining trade finance. The findings are based on telephone interviews with companies in these two sectors of the African export market.

Trade Finance and How Firms Use it for Trade

Trade finance can take many forms. For simplification, this chapter focuses on three types, as shown in table 8.1: letters of credit (LCs), domestic bank lending, and trade credit.

LCs are specifically designed to facilitate trade by providing both finance and assurances about payment to the exporting company. LCs require confidence and liquidity to be maintained at various points along the chain of payment—from the importer to the issuing bank, to the advising or confirming bank, and ultimately to the exporter.

The other two forms of trade finance are extensions of credit facilities that operate in domestic economies. Companies may use domestic bank lending to finance both capital investment and working capital. Such lending can be used to facilitate trade. Similarly, firms extend credit to each other when payment takes place before or after receipt of goods. Such credit is widely used in domestic transactions. Firms that have well-developed trading relationships may adopt the same practice. To the extent that sophisticated global value chains linking firms in different countries often involve repeat transactions and long-term relationships, conducting trade on these terms is not uncommon.

Policy Makers' Concerns

The possible impact of the global financial crisis on trade finance and the capacity of developing-country exporters to finance their trade became a salient issue in the final few months of 2008. The International Chamber of Commerce argued that uncertainties in global markets were leading firms to be more risk-averse, shifting from open-account trading to LCs, while financial markets themselves were providing less trade finance (ICC 2008). These concerns were taken up by World Trade Organization (WTO) Director-General Pascal Lamy, who announced the formation of a WTO task force to monitor the issue. The Institute of International Finance suggested that private financial flows to emerging markets were falling dramatically (IIF 2009). Anecdotal evidence also emerged about trade credit drying up, international banks becoming less willing to lend, and the

Table 8.1 Potential Impacts of Financial Crises on Trade Finance, by Type

Trade finance type	Potential impacts of crisis
Letters of credit (LCs) Importers use LCs issued by their banks (the issuing banks) as a means of assuring exporters that they will be paid. Payment is made to the exporter upon production of required documentation (for example, invoices or bills of lading) to its (confirming) bank.	• The importer's creditworthiness is undermined, and the issuing bank will not assume the risk. • The issuing bank lacks sufficient funds to extend credit to the importer. • The confirming bank lacks confidence in the issuing bank. • Trade finance institutions reduce their overall exposure or exposure to particular countries during a financial crisis.
Domestic bank lending Domestic banks provide credit to exporters to cover preshipment or postshipment costs. Such funding is similar to provision of working capital in general.	• Financial outflows reduce liquidity in the domestic banking system. • International banks operating in the domestic market reduce credit to cut the exposure of parent banks. • Shortages of foreign currency prevent banks from lending the foreign exchange needed for import of inputs or export freight charges.
Trade credit Companies extend credit to each other when buyers delay or advance payments to suppliers. This is called trade credit, even within the domestic market. In open-account trade, importers pay invoices once goods are received. Equally, importers can extend credit to exporters if they pay for goods in advance.	• General shortages of credit in domestic markets prevent importers and exporters from extending credit to each other. • As credit becomes scarce, not only do banks reduce lending to their customers, but more-creditworthy firms also reduce lending to less-creditworthy ones as their own access to finance is reduced (Love, Preve, and Sarria-Allende 2007). • Firms reduce credit extended to suppliers or buyers because of the increased risk of nonrepayment by these firms.

Source: Compiled by the author.

cost of trade finance rising. Central banks and international financial institutions extended new lines of finance for trade.

However, problems were perhaps more anticipated than actual. Lamy noted, for example, that "he was not aware of any shipments being stopped as a result of the crisis. 'No member has come to me saying we got stranded in this harbour because of the credit crunch'" (Lynn 2008). Similarly, *Asia Today* quoted Angus Armour, managing director of Australia's Export Finance Insurance Corporation (EFIC), as saying "there are anecdotes of people having difficulties in obtaining trade finance, but EFIC 'is struggling' to find data to confirm these reports" (*Asia Today International* 2008).

Evidence from Past Crises

What do we learn from past crises about how shortages of trade finance developed during financial crises and how they affected trade and businesses? During a succession of crises affecting emerging economies in the 1990s, shortages of trade finance appeared to be a substantial and direct consequence of broader economic problems. In fact, commentators seem to agree that the collapse in short-term trade finance was more substantial than might have been expected—or possibly greater than during financial crises in the 1980s. "During the financial crises in the late 1990s and the early years of the new century, trade financing to the crisis countries fell dramatically. . . . Bank-financed trade credits declined by as much as 30 to 50 percent in Brazil and Argentina [in 2002], by about 50 percent in [the Republic of] Korea in 1997–98, and from $6 billion to $1 billion in Indonesia during the Asian crisis" (Wang and Tadesse 2005).

In some cases, such as in Indonesia, trade finance fell so much and so sharply during the 1997 Asian financial crisis that "'cross-border' international trade finance for imports became a particular problem at the peak of the crisis in Indonesia. . . . Indonesia's growth of exports was seriously affected by the difficulty of financing imported raw materials, spare parts, and capital equipment used in its export sectors" (Auboin and Meier-Ewert 2003).

When financial crises centered on particular countries or regions, foreign lenders responded by reducing lending across the board, including trade finance, to reduce their country risk exposure.

There is also evidence from emerging markets that intercompany lending (trade credit) fell during these crises, as analyzed by Love, Preve, and Sarria-Allende (2007). They argue that companies that are good credit risks obtain credit from the financial system and pass some of this credit on to other companies through expanding trade credit. If credit in the economy as a whole dries up, then—after a short period in which involuntary trade credit mounts up as debtors have difficulty repaying—trade credit falls.

In spite of these findings, some unknowns remain:

- *How relevant are these findings on emerging markets to the situation in Africa now?* It is frequently suggested that poorer countries in Africa still have small, relatively insulated banking sectors. Will the impact of the crisis on trade credit be correspondingly smaller?
- *Will the effects of the current crisis be similar to those of past banking crises?* In the 1990s, banking crises were focused on particular countries or regions, and the impact on these regions was immediate and large. It is not clear whether the 2008–09 crisis would play out in the same way.

• *Which firms are more vulnerable to the credit crunch?* Even when trade financing availability is drastically reduced, it is not eliminated altogether. As Auboin and Meier-Ewert (2003) note, "Small local suppliers, who sell specialised products to international importers on a one-off basis, are much less likely to be able to obtain company financing, since they do not have an established relationship with their buyers." Conversely, companies that do have established relationships may continue to trade on preexisting terms.

The link between trade finance and the capacity to export remains unclear. In previous financial crises, substantial declines in short-term capital availability in crisis countries were very weakly associated with declines in exports (Ronci 2005). There was a positive correlation, but "the elasticity of export volume with respect to trade financing is estimated at between 0.02 and 0.04" (Ronci 2005).

Trade Finance in the Crisis: Garment and Horticulture Firms

To find out more about the impact of the financial crisis on exporting firms in Africa, the Institute of Development Studies at the University of Sussex arranged a small telephone survey in the first two months of 2009. The focus was on two sectors: garments and horticulture. These two sectors have been at the forefront of Africa's drive to increase exports of high-value agricultural products and manufactures.

In the case of garments, the African Growth and Opportunity Act (AGOA, introduced by the United States in 2000) led to a substantial expansion of garment production in eastern and southern Africa. Factories produced garments for the U.S. market, predominantly using inputs imported from Asia and taking advantage of duty-free access and the absence of Multifibre Arrangement (MFA) quotas. Although the phase-out of the MFA had a substantial impact on this sector (Kaplinsky and Morris 2006), export activities still continued in 2008.

In the case of horticulture, export promotion activities have been extensive, with particular recent interest in ensuring that African producers and exporters meet increasingly stringent public and private standards in export markets (Humphrey 2008).

Researchers in the United Kingdom and Kenya telephoned 30 firms in Sub-Saharan Africa and asked them how they financed their exports and imports and whether the availability of trade finance—from domestic banks, through LCs, and from customers—had changed. Nineteen firms were interviewed in the garment industry in five countries in Sub-Saharan Africa. Nine firms were interviewed in the horticulture sector, spread across six countries. Contact was made with an additional three horticulture firms in Ghana and Uganda through another source. The uniformity of responses from these firms led to a broadening of the research focus. Two horticulture firms, in Guatemala and Thailand, were interviewed to see whether their experiences were similar. This process was followed by contact with some U.K. importers and the International Trade Centre in Geneva. In addition, informants from two banks in Kenya provided a lender's perspective on trends in trade finance and the impact of the financial crisis.

The overall findings are clear: in both the garment and horticulture sectors, most of the African exporters interviewed had not (as of February–March 2009) experienced significant cutbacks in trade finance availability. The capacity of these firms to continue exporting was not being affected by credit cutbacks from either their customers, the international banking system (LCs), or domestic banks. The crisis had already had some negative impacts in both sectors, but these were not related to trade finance. The finding that trade credit issues were not undermining the capacity to trade, which applies to well-established exporting firms in Africa, cannot be extended to other regions or to all types of firms, as will be discussed further below. The reasons for this finding differ in the two sectors.

Impact on the Garments Sector

The garment exporters included subsidiaries of companies from Asia and the United States, domestic firms, and some firms with investors from the Middle East. The clear majority of these firms processed imported inputs for export to the United States under the AGOA regime. Finance was required both for imports of raw materials and intermediates and also for coverage of the time lag between exports of garments to customers and receipt of payment. For these firms, trade credit was, to some considerable extent, the responsibility of the parent companies, particularly for imported inputs.

Some of the firms interviewed indicated that finance for either imports or exports had been affected in 2008, but none suggested this had affected their capacity to export. These subsidiaries did rely to some extent on domestic bank credit for working capital. Even here, the availability of bank finance from within the host country had remained unchanged. Credit had generally been difficult to obtain and expensive, but that had always been the case. The domestic banking system was not used for trade finance.

For locally owned firms, too, trade finance did not appear to be a problem. Firms in Ethiopia, Kenya, and Tanzania either borrowed from banks to finance their imports and exports or relied on their own financial resources to bridge the gap between production and the receipt of payment from customers. These firms were still able to obtain credit from their locally based banks. As long as these companies could show themselves to be good risks and to provide collateral where necessary, trade finance was still available. In Ethiopia, firms had difficulties in obtaining foreign exchange, but this was the consequence of government exchange-rate policy rather than trade finance issues.

There were two exceptions to this picture. First, a company linked to a Middle East investor reported that the company's head office in the Middle East had experienced a credit squeeze in the international financial market. This resulted in a fall in the supply of finance from the parent company. Second, a garment company in South Africa reported credit shortages as a result of the financial crisis. Garment firms are not considered good risks by the South African banking system, according to one of the respondents, and so they were affected by this problem.

Interviews with two banks in Kenya provided a complementary perspective on trade credit for garment firms. Both banks, one domestic and the other a subsidiary of an international bank, had garment companies on their loan books. Both confirmed that the financial crisis had not restricted their lending to companies. The domestic bank continued—in fact, increased—lending to companies. The financial crisis had had a marked impact on overseas remittances used to buy property in Kenya, but this had not undermined the bank's capacity to lend. The international bank provided loans to garment firms in the export processing zone, and it was continuing as before. The bank financed imports through LCs and provided credit to facilitate exports.

The main factors governing lending to these firms were the financial stability and creditworthiness of the borrower. In the case of garments, export receipts often went directly to the parent company, and this made the bank especially wary of bad debts.

Impact on the Horticulture Sector

In the case of horticulture, interviews were arranged with six African exporters to European markets. To analyze firms with potentially different access to trade (interfirm) credit, the sample included exporters supplying large retailers (supermarkets) as well as exporters supplying European wholesale markets, where business was more likely to be conducted through arm's-length trading relationships. The interviewees cited the following reasons for the absence of trade finance problems:

- *Local banks consider the horticulture sector in Sub-Saharan Africa to be a good risk.* Therefore, lending has continued. There was some risk that exports of high-value food would be more affected by the recession than exports of basic commodities, but one key informant from the Kenyan export horticulture sector reported in early 2009 that export volumes for fresh vegetables had not fallen.

- *Firms are operating in well-established value chains.* Even firms supplying wholesale markets in Europe had well-established relationships with their importers and established lines of trade finance. These transactions often involved open-account trading. Unless the financial position of the creditor company in the relationship deteriorates, trade can be sustained. Where local banks did provide finance, they were continuing to lend, and the established patterns of trade finance had continued.

These findings are confirmed by broader findings relating to trade in horticulture and agriculture. A variety of exporters of agricultural products are sustaining trade. For example, one major European importer of coffee and cocoa from West Africa reported that there were no problems with trade finance. Most transactions are conducted between well-known parties who do not use LCs. Trust between the parties means that they rely on open-account trading (payment following delivery) or documentary collections. These require less external financing commitment, and although they place risk on the exporter, risk exposure is mitigated by well-established trade ties.

Affected Regions and Firms

That these particular types of exporters were not affected by availability of trade finance does not mean that substantial impacts cannot be found in other types of firms and in other countries. In at least one West African country, for example, there is a credit shortage in the domestic market; as a result, prefinancing of trade in cocoa is curtailed. This has an impact on local intermediaries that buy produce in rural areas and transport it to the docks.

The big local buyers working with transnational companies are not affected because their customers provide finance, but smaller buyers are finding it difficult to borrow the cash they need to buy supplies at the farm gate or from cooperatives. This disparity will have distribution and poverty consequences. Smaller producers and niche producers may find themselves marginalized because credit is available only for large buyers buying in large quantities. Given the uneven impact of the financial crisis, there is a clear need to target any public provision of trade finance and domestic credit.

On the regional level, there were also substantial problems with trade finance in Central America, the Caribbean, and parts of South America. This issue was emphasized by one large U.K. fruit importer that had well-established, long-term relationships with fruit growers across this region. For some producers in Central America, the U.K. importer prefinanced production, paying up to half the purchase price in advance of shipping or at the point of shipment. In late 2008, its growers in Costa Rica faced a crisis when the domestic banking system withdrew credit, and the U.K. importer had to choose between extending further credit to its suppliers or risking the loss of the advances it had already made. Being cash-rich, the importer was able to provide further advances, but producers in a similar situation but without an established link with a cash-rich buyer would have been in much more serious difficulties.

The position of this particular exporter was not an isolated case. The banking industry in Central America and the Caribbean reportedly has had significant problems that appeared to create many problems for small and medium-size producers, shippers, and exporters of agricultural products. These problems not only reveal the potential impact of the global financial crisis on working capital but also suggest that the African banking system had, up to mid-2009, escaped some of the impact of the crisis being felt in other parts of the developing world.

There are two ways of interpreting these results. One is to suggest that Africa is generally more isolated from the global financial crisis; banks are still lending to companies, and they still have money available, particularly for good credit risks. The other interpretation is that the financial crisis is merely delayed in Africa; the impacts of the global financial crisis merely take time to work through. At this point, it is not possible to say which view is correct. However, the next section makes the case that African firms are feeling the effects of the crisis in different ways that might eventually affect trade finance.

Further Impacts: Exchange Volatility and Falling Demand

Having established that most of the Africa-based firms in the garment and horticulture sectors have not experienced difficulties with trade finance, it is important to recognize that the financial crisis is nonetheless having clear and substantial impacts. These impacts are not uniform, but various respondents have reported two in particular: exchange rate volatility and falling demand.

Exchange Rate Volatility

In the garment industry, contracts are priced in dollars, and companies have been largely insulated from exchange-rate fluctuations. For the horticulture sector, in contrast, exchange-rate fluctuations are a major issue.

In Kenya, the substantial devaluation of the U.K. pound against the dollar, amounting to a little more than 25 percent in the second half of 2008, created two problems. Exporters to the United Kingdom, the biggest market, mostly had contracts priced in pounds, but many inputs were priced in dollars. For companies that export Cost, Insurance, and Freight (CIF), air freight (a substantial part of the landed price in the United Kingdom) is also priced in dollars. Furthermore, the appreciation of the Kenya shilling against the U.K. pound by 12 percent between March 2008 and February 2009 (average rates for both months) meant that domestic costs increased relative to export revenues.

Falling Demand

Garment producers were facing reduced orders. Lead times for African garment producers are long; in early 2009, they were completing orders negotiated in mid-2008. However, the companies reported that buyers were holding back new orders and pushing for much lower prices. Almost all the garment companies reported falls in demand and poor prospects for new orders. Fresh vegetable producers had not yet registered declines in demand for what is a premium product (fresh produce from Africa), but flower exporters did experience sharp falls in demand and pressure on prices, according to one well-placed local informant in Kenya.

Both of these effects could undermine company finances, leading to deterioration in their creditworthiness and a decline in their access to trade finance. More difficult trading conditions and increased uncertainty about sales and profit could undermine access to trade finance.

Public Policy Responses and Implications

The financial crisis has affected these companies in various ways. Therefore, public policies to address the immediate impacts of the crisis require targeting of measures to sustain trade finance to the firms that most need it.

Overall, the mechanisms to sustain trade finance are well-established. In past financial crises, national governments, international financial institutions, regional development banks, and parts of national banking systems stepped in to increase the supply of trade finance. There is ample evidence that the same bodies acted to improve the supply of trade finance in the current crisis, prompting trade finance-related announcements from the International Finance Corporation of the World Bank Group, various national governments, and regional development banks.

Trade finance support must be targeted to be effective. The impacts of the crisis on firms vary by region and by sector and also according to the nature of intercompany trading relations. Broadly targeted support to increase lending capacity in the banking system—in both importing and exporting countries—will not necessarily reach the firms that are in greatest need. Scarce bank finance is likely to go to firms with established exporting records and regular customers. Difficulties in obtaining trade finance are more likely to affect small firms and new entrants that do not have established relationships with banks and customers. These firms will continue to be categorized as higher-risk. In particular, it was seen in West Africa that smaller exporters, producer groups, and cooperatives might be particularly vulnerable. The financial crisis might have more impact on new entrants to global markets that have been encouraged by recent development policy to venture into export markets. Therefore, programs should identify and target these companies.

In the longer term, there are further implications for development policy. Firms that have done well from linking into dynamic global value chains, such as producers of fresh vegetables for U.K. supermarkets, are particularly vulnerable to adverse global conditions. Export-oriented production has linked these firms to powerful customers. In the crisis, the powerful customers have the capacity to transfer the risks and consequences of turbulence and unpredictable markets to their suppliers. To the extent that exporters have investment in market- or customer-specific assets (such as sophisticated processing and packaging plants for supplying the U.K. market), customers can transfer the costs and risks of the crisis down the chain. U.K. supermarkets tried to maintain the pound sterling price of imports irrespective of exchange-rate fluctuations. They also vary purchase quantities according to short-term fluctuations in demand. As a result, most of the risks and uncertainties fall on the supply chain. Large and powerful customers can provide strong and stable demand in times of expansion, but they are more difficult to deal with in difficult times.

References

Asia Today International. 2008. "Export Credit Agencies to Step Up Loan Books." *Asia Today International* 26 (6): 18.

Auboin, Marc, and Moritz Meier-Ewert. 2003. "Improving the Availability of Trade Finance during Financial Crises." Discussion Paper 2, World Trade Organization, Geneva.

Baldwin, Richard. 2009. "Trade and the London Summit Outcome." Commentary, VoxEU.org, Centre for Trade and Economic Integration, London. http://www.voxeu.org/index.php?q=node/3417.

Humphrey, John. 2008. "Private Standards, Small Farmers and Donor Policy: EUREPGAP in Kenya." Working Paper 308, Institute of Development Studies, Brighton, U.K.

ICC (International Chamber of Commerce). 2008. "Trade Finance in the Current Financial Crisis: Preliminary Assessment of Key Issues." Banking Commission report, ICC, Paris.

IIF (Institute of International Finance). 2009. "Capital Flows to Emerging Market Economies." Report, IIF, Washington, DC.

Kaplinsky, Raphael, and Mike Morris. 2006. "Dangling by a Thread: How Sharp Are the Chinese Scissors?" Research Report, Institute of Development Studies, Brighton, U.K.

Love, Inessa, Lorenzo Preve, and Virginia Sarria-Allende. 2007. "Trade Credit and Bank Credit: Evidence from Recent Financial Crises." *Journal of Financial Economics* 83 (2): 453–69.

Lynn, Jonathan. 2008. "WTO Creates Financial Crisis Taskforce." *Insurance Journal*, October 16. http://www.insurancejournal.com/news/international/2008/10/16/94686.htm.

Ronci, Marcio. 2005. "Trade Credit and Financial Flows: Panel Data Evidence from 10 Crises." In *Access to Trade Finance in Times of Crisis*, ed. Jian-Ye Wang and Marcio Ronci, 24–38. Washington, DC: International Monetary Fund.

Wang, Jian-Ye, and Helaway Tadesse. 2005. "Overview." In *Access to Trade Finance in Times of Crisis*, ed. Jian-Ye Wang and Marcio Ronci, 1–15. Washington, DC: International Monetary Fund.

FINANCIAL CRISES AND AFRICAN TRADE

Nicolas Berman and Philippe Martin

Early in the 2008–09 global financial crisis, a common view was that Africa's low level of financial integration may be a blessing in disguise, insulating the region from the direct impact of the crisis. Indeed, the direct wealth effect may have been less important in Africa than in other regions such as East Asia, Latin America, and Central and Eastern Europe, where countries have more-open financial flows than African countries. African banks may indeed have bought fewer "toxic" assets than did banks in other parts of the world, but this reduced exposure was not enough to mitigate the negative effects of the crisis in this region. African countries, although not involved in the origin of the crisis, have been hard-hit by its expansion. The potential explanations are many:

- Fluctuations in commodity prices may have particularly affected African countries; global slowdown of demand had no reason to spare African products.
- Because the crisis deeply affected migrants in developed countries, workers' remittances may have plummeted, diminishing an important source of revenue for most African countries.
- The same effect holds for aid flows, which developed countries have reduced during past downturns.

However, the main entry gate of the crisis into Africa has been international trade. U.S. trade statistics for 2008–09 provide one indication of how vulnerable African countries are on the trade side. Following the crisis, U.S. imports from Sub-Saharan African countries have fallen more dramatically than U.S.

imports from the rest of the world. This is especially true for African manufacturing exports, suggesting that the fall in African exports is not only a composition effect due to the importance of primary goods and the fall in primary goods prices.

What is behind this sharp fall of African exports to a country that, during this period, experienced an exceptional financial crisis by historical standards? What does the fall in exports reveal about the vulnerability of African exporters to financial crises in partner (importing) countries? And what are the mechanisms through which a financial crisis in a partner country affects African exports?

An earlier attempt to partially answer these questions analyzed the impact of past financial crises on bilateral trade flows (Berman and Martin 2010). According to a large sectoral database of bilateral trade and financial crises during the 1976–2002 period and a gravity equation approach, the deviation of exports from their "natural" level was quantified.

This chapter distinguishes two mechanisms through which a financial crisis in one country affects the exports of partner countries:

- *The first is an income effect* because financial crises are typically associated with sharp recessions (Reinhart and Rogoff 2008; Claessens, Kose, and Terrones 2009), which cause consumption and imports to fall. The elasticity of trade to income has increased in the past 40 years (Freund 2009).
- *Second, a disruption effect* may cause a financial crisis to adversely hit African exports. The disruption may take direct or more subtle forms.

The most direct disruption effect, one widely discussed in policy circles, is the fall in trade credit. Among the subtler disruption effects, although difficult to measure, is increased risk aversion among bankers and traders, which may more severely affect countries or groups of countries that are viewed as riskier.

As explained further in relation to figure 9.1 (in the section titled "Results"), the disruption effect on trade is more important (about 20 percent larger) for African countries than for exporting countries in other regions. Again, this disruption effect comes in addition to the fall of exports due to the fall of income and consumption. This sharp difference applies to both primary products and manufactured goods. In addition, for African countries, the largest disruption effect comes when the destination country hit by a financial crisis is industrialized.

Importance of Trade Finance to African Exporters

A banking crisis, by tightening financial constraints, may affect trade patterns in important ways. The difference between African and other countries may lie in the type of financing used by exporters. While firms operating in countries with relatively developed financial markets can use the banking system to finance trading operations, African exporters rely on other sources, particularly trade finance provided by institutions in the destination countries.

Trade can be disrupted by a financial crisis that affects banks, heightens risk aversion, and reduces trust in both the importing and exporting countries. Letters of credit (LCs) are among the forms of trade finance most affected. Importers use LCs issued by their banks (the issuing banks) as a means of assuring exporters that they will be paid. If the exporter submits the required documentation (for example, invoices or bills of lading) to its bank (the advising or confirming bank), payment is made to the exporter. LCs require both confidence and liquidity to provide finance and assurance of payment to the exporter. If confidence or liquidity is missing at any point along the chain from importer to exporter, the mechanism will not function: the importer's creditworthiness may be undermined, the issuing bank may have insufficient funds to extend credit to the importer, and the confirming bank may also lack confidence in the issuing bank.

In addition, under Basel II rules, when market conditions tighten, capital requirements for trade finance instruments tend to increase more than proportionally to the risk when the counterpart is in a developing country (Auboin 2009). Interfirm trade credit may also be deficient during a financial crisis because of the perceived increase in nonpayment risk. Indeed, trade finance fell sharply during the most important emerging markets' financial crises of the 1990s (Ronci 2005).

In the aftermath of the 2008–09 financial crisis, a burgeoning literature has attempted to analyze the sources of the trade collapse. This chapter is clearly part of this literature, although it focuses on African countries and on the greater issue of the transmission of financial crises to the developing world.

Regarding the recent crisis, the respective roles of financial conditions and trade credit have been in dispute. The World Trade Organization has pushed the idea that the trade collapse was partly due to the collapse in trade credit. Auboin (2009) reports a 2008 increase in spreads on 90-day LCs—from 10–16 basis points in normal times to 250–500 basis points for letters issued by developing countries. The African Development Bank noted that "paradoxically, although African commercial banks are ready to provide financing for trade operations, they are unable to do so because the global credit crisis has caused many international confirming banks to be forced to temporarily withdraw their credit support from the market. This has led to a growing gap between supply and demand for trade financing" (AfDB 2009).

Another study that surveyed several banks in developed and emerging markets reported a sharp increase in the cost of trade finance: 70 percent of the banks reported that the price for LCs had risen (IMF 2009). One possible explanation given by the International Monetary Fund (IMF) for the collapse of trade from emerging and developing countries is that rising trade finance costs and increased risk perception had a severe impact on low-margin products: the inability of importers to afford LCs. One issue is that these contrasting views are based on surveys rather than on comprehensive trade finance statistics. The series of trade finance statistics derived from balance of payments and Bank for International Settlements (BIS) banking statistics was discontinued in 2004 (Auboin 2009).

Recent papers find evidence that the credit conditions observed during the crisis affect export performance. For example, Chor and Manova (2009), who used data on the evolution of trade volumes during the crisis months, find that adverse credit conditions were an important channel through which the crisis affected trade flows. Iacovone and Zavacka (2009) and Amiti and Weinstein (2009) also find evidence on the negative effects of financial crises on exports. The latter argue that exporters typically turn to banks and other financial firms to handle payments because international trade is typically riskier than domestic trade. Collecting payments in foreign countries is more difficult than doing so domestically. Also, the added shipping times associated with international trade often mean that international transactions take two months longer than domestic transactions. The shipping lag imposes additional working capital requirements on exporters.

Using Japanese data, Amiti and Weinstein (2009) find that, of the 10.5 percent decline in Japanese exports following the 1997 banking crisis, the direct effect of declining negotiating bank health on exports caused about one-third of the decline. Another study, using French firm-level data, finds that firms in sectors structurally more dependent on external finance were the most affected by the crisis (Bricongne et al. 2009). Yet Levchenko, Lewis, and Tesar (2010), using U.S. data, find no support for the hypothesis that trade credit played a role in the trade collapse.

Methodology and Data

This section presents the empirical approach and the data used to assess the effect of financial crises on trade—and specifically on African exports.

Empirical Methodology

The econometric specification presented is based on the gravity equation. A large literature now addresses the difficulties of estimating a gravity equation (for example, Baldwin and Taglioni 2006). The aim here is to understand how a financial crisis in year t and country i (the importer country) affects the exports of country j (the exporter country).

A financial crisis in the importer country potentially affects several standard determinants of the gravity equation that a monopolistic competition trade model would typically generate:

- *The income of the importer country Y_{it}.* This is the direct income effect. As the financial crisis hits the income of the importer country, it also leads to lower consumption and therefore lower imports.
- *The bilateral trade costs between countries i and j.* Broadly speaking, if a financial or banking crisis hits the importer country, this may affect its imports over and above the direct effect on income. In particular, if importers or exporters rely heavily on credit for their trading relationship, the effect may be more important than the income effect. We call this the trade disruption effect.
- *The price index of the importer country i, P_{it}.* If prices fall in the importer country, this has a negative impact on the country's imports. Although this price index is not observed, the empirical strategy controls for it.

It is also important to control for the other standard gravity determinants that may or may not be affected by a financial crisis in country i, such as the income of the exporter country Y_{jt}; a country pair × sector fixed effect to control for all time-independent determinants of the bilateral trade relation in the sector (η_{ijh}); and a year-fixed effect (ξ_t) that controls for all determinants of trade that are common to all countries during a year (for example, changes in commodity prices).

Following Martin, Mayer, and Thoenig (2008), the following equation links financial crises to trade from countries i and j (m_{ijht}), relative to trade between i and a benchmark country b (m_{ijbht}):

$$\log\frac{m_{ijht}}{m_{ibht}} = \alpha_1\log\frac{Y_{jt}}{Y_{bt}} + \alpha_1\log\frac{p_{jt}}{p_{bt}} + \sum_{k=a}^{K}\beta_k\Delta_b FC_{it-k}$$

$$\times SSA_j + \Omega X_{ijt} + \eta\frac{i}{ij} + \xi_t + \varepsilon_{ijht} \tag{9.1}$$

where h denotes the industry,

p_{jt} is the producer price of country j,

FC_{it} is a binary variable, which equals 1 if country i had a financial crisis in year t,

SSA_j is a dummy, which equals 1 if country j is in Sub-Saharan Africa.

Finally, the shortcut Δ_b designates that all variables are in difference with respect to the base country b, and X_{ijt} is a vector including regional trade agreements and currency crises. The coefficients β represent the additional disruption effect of financial crises in Sub-Saharan African countries.

The main advantage of this methodology is that it controls for changes in the unobserved price index of the importer countries (or multilateral resistance index; see Anderson and Van Wincoop 2004), therefore solving the omitted variable bias.[1]

The following estimations use the United States as the benchmark country; robustness checks have been made using other benchmark countries. Finally, the specification includes two leads and seven lags of the FC_i variable; a modification of the number of lags leaves the results qualitatively unchanged.

Data Sources

A large sectoral database of bilateral trade is used that combines data from the United Nations Commodity Trade Statistics Database (Comtrade) and the CEPII Trade Production and Bilateral Protection Database (TradeProd) of the Centre d'Etudes Prospectives et d'Informations Internationales (Center for Research on the International Economy, or CEPII) for 26 International Standard Industrial Classification (ISIC) three-digit industries between 1976 and 2002.[2] For a study of the effect of financial crises on primary goods sectors as well, this database is completed using Comtrade for five different primary goods sectors.

The relative prices are captured by the price levels of gross domestic product (GDP); prices and GDP data come from the Penn World Tables v.6.1 (Heston, Summers, and Aten 2002). Sector-specific prices are not available for lack of data. Robustness checks included industry × year dummies to control for sector-specific price changes. Finally, the data on banking crises come from Caprio and Klingebiel (2003), primarily the systemic crises they define as events—possibly lasting several years—when much or all bank capital was exhausted.

Together, the database covers 76 countries and 27 three-digit ISIC manufacturing sectors and five primary sectors over the 1976–2002 period.

Results

In this section, we quantify the disruption effect of financial crises on trade and analyze the specific role of trade finance.

The Disruption Effect

The main result, shown in figure 9.1, is based on the estimated coefficients and confidence intervals of equation 9.1.[3]

Figure 9.1 African Exports after Financial Crisis in Partner Country

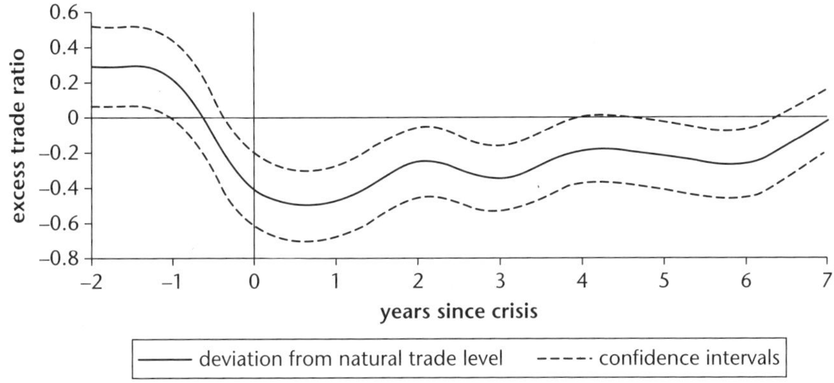

Source: Authors' computations.

More precisely, figure 9.1 shows the deviation of African exports before and after a financial crisis that takes place in year $t = 0$, with respect to the average disruption effect of other exporters. The x-axis represents the "natural trade" level as given by the gravity equation, and the figure can therefore be interpreted as the deviation from this level. The 5 percent confidence intervals are depicted by dotted lines around the estimated effect. The remaining figures in this chapter are constructed similarly, even though all of the associated regressions are not reported here.

Clearly, the disruption effect is stronger for African countries. The year the importer country is hit by a financial crisis, the additional effect for African exports is around 30 percent. Note again that this number measures the disruption of trade that comes from the financial crisis, not from the fall of income of the crisis-hit country, because this is controlled for. The fall is also long-lasting; it disappears only four years after the crisis in the partner country.

Again, remember that these regressions control for the common effect that the change in the income of the importer country has on all imports

• for all determinants of sectoral bilateral trade that are time-invariant (through the inclusion of country pair × sector fixed effects);
• for yearly changes in trade that are common to all countries (through the inclusion of year fixed effects); and
• for the effects of currency crises in the destination countries.

The robustness checks controlled for exporter × year or for sector × year dummies. This allows, in particular, controls for country- or sector-specific price changes, which the relative price variable does not properly capture. These controls are important because African exports are dependent on world prices in primary goods. Whatever the specification, African exports are found to be much more negatively affected than other countries by a crisis in the destination country.

What is the reason behind this sensitivity of African exports? The first possibility is that African countries are specialized in sectors that are particularly vulnerable to a financial crisis. However, when running separate regressions for (a) exports of primary goods and raw materials and (b) manufactured goods, we get similar results: whatever the sample, African exports are much more negatively affected than exports from other regions by a financial crisis in the partner countries.

The Role of Trade Finance

Another explanation for the drop in African exports when trading partners face financial crises relates to the disruption of trade finance. If low financial system development forces African firms to rely more heavily on trade finance from the importing country, and if financial crises hit this type of financing particularly hard (Ronci 2005), exports of African countries may also be hit harder, whatever the sector considered.

As a proxy for trade finance, following Ronci (2005), the estimate uses the level of outstanding short-term credit in U.S. dollars as reported in the World Bank's *Global Development Finance* dataset, which includes short-term credit for trade in dollars as reported by the Organisation for Economic Co-operation and Development and the international banks' short-term claims as reported by BIS. As Ronci (2005) points out, this variable has several limitations, in particular because it excludes trade finance associated with intrafirm trade by multinational corporations or trade related to foreign direct investment.

For each country, the average ratio of trade credit over total exports over the period is constructed. African countries clearly display greater dependence upon trade finance: the median (mean) of the ratio is 0.74 (0.95) for African countries and only 0.47 (0.60) for the rest of the sample.

Can dependence on trade finance explain the vulnerability of African trade to crises in partner countries? To answer this question, we compare the effect of the financial crisis on African exporters that are more dependent on trade finance with the effect on those that are less dependent. The results are represented in figure 9.2. African countries that display a higher level of trade finance clearly experience a larger drop of their exports to countries hit by a financial crisis in the first years.

Figure 9.2 African Exports after Financial Crisis

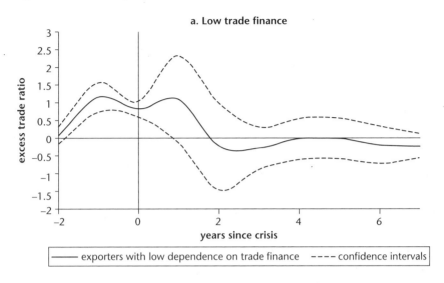

a. Low trade finance

— exporters with low dependence on trade finance ---- confidence intervals

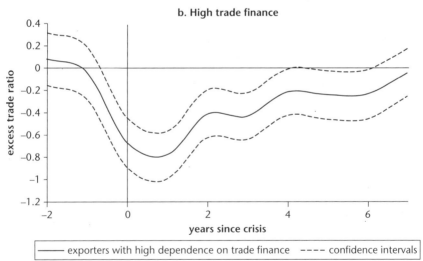

b. High trade finance

— exporters with high dependence on trade finance ---- confidence intervals

Source: Authors' computations.

Of course, these results should be interpreted with caution because only a proxy for trade finance has been used here. The results suggest, however, that this particular type of financing may play an important role in Africa in the aftermath of financial crises and, more generally, in the transmission of financial crises through international trade links.

Conclusions

The main conclusion is that, contrary to some arguments heard early in the 2008–09 financial crisis, the crisis may have hit Sub-Saharan African countries harder through its effect on the region's exports. Even though the direct effects of the crisis may be weaker due to the relative insulation and underdevelopment of the financial system in most Sub-Saharan African countries, the indirect effect through trade may be stronger. In the past, African exports have been hit harder by financial crises in the countries they export to. This is not only the result of the composition of African exports and the concentration on primary goods.

The higher dependence of African exports on trade finance may explain African exporters' particular fragility to financial crises in importer countries. One interpretation is that during a financial crisis, when uncertainty and risk are high and trust and liquidity are low, banks and firms in the importer country first cut exposure and credit to the particular countries they see as more risky. This response would, in particular, affect trade finance through LCs, by which the importer pays the exporting firm in advance.

It is also likely that during financial crises, financial institutions "renationalize" their operations and reduce their exposure to foreign banks and firms. Exporters in countries with strong financial systems may be able to better resist such retrenchment of foreign banks. Clearly, for African firms that are more dependent on foreign finance, this option may not be feasible. At this stage, these interpretations of the results are only tentative, and more research must be done to better understand the origin of the particular fragility of African exports to financial crises in industrialized countries.

Notes

1. For a more complete explanation of this methodology, see Martin, Mayer, and Thoenig (2008).
2. More information about Comtrade (the United Nations Commodity Trade Statistics Database) is available at http://comtrade.un.org/db. A more detailed description of the CEPII Trade, Production and Bilateral Protection Database (TradeProd) is available on the CEPII website at http://www.cepii.fr/anglaisgraph/bdd/TradeProd.htm.
3. Complete regression results can be found in Berman and Martin (2010).

References

AfDB (African Development Bank). 2009. "The African Development Bank Group Response to the Economic Impact of the Financial Crisis." Discussion paper, AfDB, Abidjan, Côte d'Ivoire.

Amiti, M., and D. Weinstein. 2009. "Exports and Financial Shocks." Discussion Paper 7590, Centre for Economic Policy Research, London.

Anderson, J., and E. Van Wincoop. 2004. "Trade Costs." *Journal of Economic Literature* 42 (3): 691–751.

Auboin, M. 2009. "Boosting the Availability of Trade Finance in the Current Crisis: Background Analysis for a Substantial G20 Package." Policy Insight 35, Centre for Economic Policy Research, London.

Baldwin, R., and D. Taglioni. 2006. "Gravity for Dummies and Dummies for Gravity Equations." Working Paper 12516, National Bureau of Economic Research, Cambridge, MA.

Berman, N., and P. Martin. 2010. "The Vulnerability of Sub-Saharan African Countries to Financial Crises: The Case of Trade." Discussion Paper 7765, Centre for Economic Policy Research, London.

Bricongne J-C., L. Fontagné, G. Gaulier, D. Taglioni, and V. Vicard. 2009. "Firms and the Global Crisis: French Exports in the Turmoil." Working Paper 265, Banque de France, Paris.

Caprio, G., and D. Klingebiel. 2003. "Episodes of Systemic and Borderline Banking Crises." Data set, World Bank, Washington, DC.

Chor, D., and K. Manova. 2009. "Off the Cliff and Back? Credit Conditions and International Trade during the Global Financial Crisis." Working Paper 16174, National Bureau of Economic Research, Cambridge, MA.

Claessens S., A. Kose, and M. Terrones. 2009. "What Happens During Recessions, Crunches and Busts?" Paper presented at the Forty-Ninth Economic Policy Panel Meeting, Brussels, April 24–25.

Freund, C. 2009. "The Trade Response to Global Crises: Historical Evidence." Working paper, World Bank, Washington, DC.

Heston, Alan, Robert Summers, and Bettina Aten. 2002. Penn World Table Version 6.1, Center for International Comparisons of Production, Income and Prices, University of Pennsylvania, Philadelphia. http://pwt.econ.upenn.edu/php_site/pwt_index.php.

Iacovone, L., and V. Zavacka. 2009. "Banking Crises and Exports: Lessons from the Past." Policy Research Working Paper 5016, World Bank, Washington, DC.

IMF (International Monetary Fund). 2009. "Impact of the Global Financial Crisis on Sub-Saharan Africa." African Department Note, IMF, Washington, DC.

Levchenko, Andrei A., Logan T. Lewis, and Linda L. Tesar. 2010. "The Collapse of International Trade during the 2008–2009 Crisis: In Search of the Smoking Gun." *IMF Economic Review* 58 (2): 214–53.

Martin P., T. Mayer, and M. Mathias Thoenig. 2008. "Make Trade Not War?" *Review of Economic Studies* 75 (3): 865–900.

Reinhart, C., and K. Rogoff. 2008. "This Time Is Different: A Panoramic View of Eight Centuries of Financial Crises." Working Paper 13882, National Bureau of Economic Research, Cambridge, MA.

Ronci, Marcio. 2005. "Trade Credit and Financial Flows: Panel Data Evidence from 10 Crises." In *Access to Trade Finance in Times of Crisis*, ed. Jian-Ye Wang and Marcio Ronci, 24–38. Washington, DC: International Monetary Fund.

WORLD BANK FIRM AND BANK SURVEYS IN 14 DEVELOPING COUNTRIES, 2009 AND 2010

Mariem Malouche

This chapter updates the findings of the 2009 World Bank firm and bank survey to assess the impact of the 2008–09 financial crisis on trade and trade finance in 14 developing countries (Malouche 2009). The follow-up survey used the same sample of firms and banks as in 2009, in 12 out of the original 14 countries.[1]

The findings of these surveys are particularly informative because of the general lack of data on trade finance. To the author's knowledge, no other firm and bank surveys had been conducted across a number of developing countries to assess the impact of the 2008–09 financial crisis on trade finance.

The 2010 survey resulted in these main findings:

- *In all surveyed countries, trade growth picked up after bottoming out in spring 2009.* Firms' exports became less constrained after the economic recovery began. The crisis does not appear to have led to immediate market shifts, although some firms reported looking for new market opportunities to diversify away from the developed-countries' markets that were hit hardest by the financial crisis.
- *Trade finance value and volume—in particular, interfirm trade credit—also bounced back.* Firms' revenues picked up along with the economic recovery and, thus, also interfirm trade finance. However, banks remained relatively risk averse because they needed to deleverage and reassess underwriting risks. As a

result, prices of trade finance instruments and spreads, although narrowing, remained higher than precrisis levels. Small firms and financially weaker exporters have faced particular difficulties in accessing trade finance, as the first survey already suggested.

• *Lack of trade finance may not have proven as critical as initially thought.* However, the expansion of trade finance programs and liquidity injection by governments and multilateral institutions have helped to mitigate the impact of the crisis and restore confidence. With the economic recovery and adequate liquidity, many governments have been backing off from policy measures aimed at adding liquidity in the financial market.

The main sections of this chapter provide an update on trade developments in the surveyed countries; discuss the role of trade-finance constraints on trade flows; report on country-level trade finance data; and provide an update on the policy actions of governments and multilateral institutions.

Trade Recovery without Major Structural Changes

Trade flows followed a V-curve in middle-income countries that export mainly light manufacturing and consumer goods, reflecting changes in global demand. Among commodity exporters, the flows fluctuated in more of a seesaw in response to price changes.

Monthly data for most of the surveyed countries indicate a sharp decline in exports and imports in late 2008 to early 2009, followed by a strong recovery in the second half of 2009 and first half of 2010, as figure 10.1 shows.[2]

The year-on-year growth rate trends followed a V-shaped curve for most countries, particularly middle-income countries such as India, the Philippines, South Africa, Tunisia, and Ukraine. Trade bottomed out around April 2009 and started to recover in the second half of 2010, but most countries had not yet recovered their precrisis levels by the first quarter of 2010. These results confirm the demand side of the crisis because the surveyed middle-income economies are mostly intensive exporters of merchandise goods and integrated into global supply chains in sectors that have been the most affected by the crisis and the slow economy (such as textiles and clothing and electronics).

The monthly trade growth trend was a bit more mixed for low-income countries and commodity exporters, whose trade fluctuations were more frequent and followed various patterns. For instance, in Kenya, despite large fluctuations in import and export growth rates, seasonally adjusted monthly export volumes hovered around $300 million. In Chile and Peru, imports were directly affected by the economic turmoil and posted negative growth mostly in the first half of 2009.

Figure 10.1 Export and Import Growth in Surveyed Countries

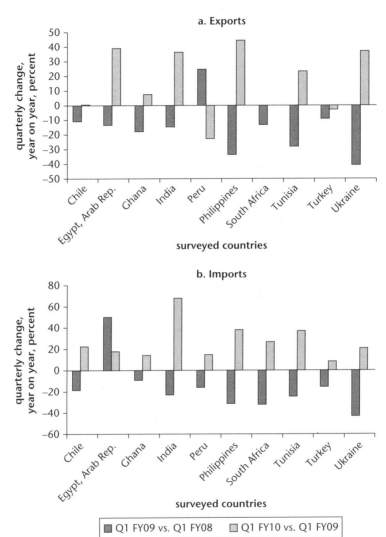

Source: World Bank data and author's calculations.

As of June 2010, import levels had returned to precrisis levels in Chile but not in Peru. Export growth was more directly affected by the trend in commodity prices than by the crisis.

The improvement in the country-level data was also reflected in surveyed firms' responses. Nearly 60 percent of the export firms claimed that their export levels had either improved or remained about the same as in the last quarter of 2008, as figure 10.2, panel a, illustrates. The firms' perceptions of constraints varied across regions, as figure 10.2, panel b, shows.

Firms in East Asia (the Philippines) still felt constrained as a consequence of the crisis, as did firms in North Africa (the Arab Republic of Egypt and Tunisia), Eastern Europe, and South Asia (India). In contrast, exporters in Latin America (Chile and Peru) and Sub-Saharan Africa felt the least constrained directly by the crisis. These differences are driven mainly by the nature of the goods exported. As indicated above, manufacturers of light manufacturing and consumer goods and firms integrated in supply chains have suffered the most, while commodity exporters such as in Chile, Ghana, Kenya, Peru, and Sierra Leone have been less directly affected by the crisis, being more vulnerable to commodity prices.

Figure 10.2 Postcrisis Export Growth and Constraints among Surveyed Firms

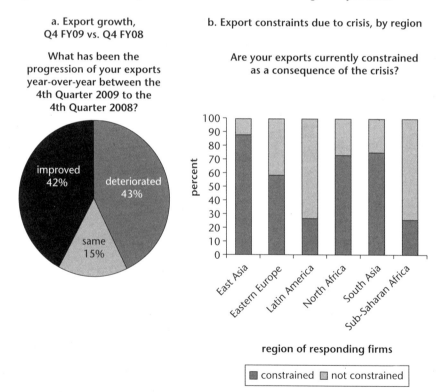

a. Export growth,
Q4 FY09 vs. Q4 FY08

b. Export constraints due to crisis, by region

Source: Author's data from April 2010 firm survey.
Note: Total respondents = 221.

Most of the respondents claimed they had not changed their export destinations as a consequence of the crisis for two main reasons: (a) the firms valued their current business relationships, and (b) they were mainly adopting a wait-and-see attitude, hoping the economy and their business would pick up. This attitude also reflected the global dimension of the crisis, with no obvious alternative markets that were easy to tap into.

Interestingly, though, about half of the respondents declared they were exploring new markets to diversify from advanced economies' markets, as figure 10.3 shows. This was particularly the case for firms that have traditionally relied on the European Union (EU) and the United States and therefore suffered more from the crisis, such as firms in Egypt, Tunisia, Turkey, and South Africa. Firms considering market diversification mostly mentioned regional and neighboring countries. Turkish and Ukrainian firms mentioned markets in Europe, Central Asia, the Middle East, and North Africa; Tunisian firms cited African and Maghreb countries; Philippine firms mentioned Malaysia, Mexico, and Middle East and

Figure 10.3 New Market Exploration in Developing Countries

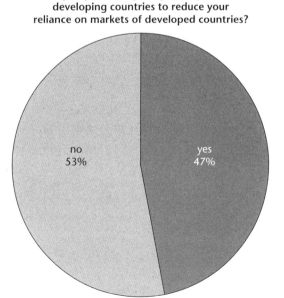

Do you plan to expand your exports to
developing countries to reduce your
reliance on markets of developed countries?

no
53%

yes
47%

Source: Author's data from April 2010 firm survey.

North African countries; and Indian firms mentioned African markets. These results corroborate the overall belief that this crisis is likely to translate into the emergence of new growth poles in the South.

The results are also consistent with empirical analyses of the trade collapse. Evidence from U.S. and French firm-level data suggests that the crisis has mostly affected trade on the intensive margin (Bricongne et al. 2009; Haddad, Harrison, and Hausman 2010).[3] These findings suggest that a global or regional economic recovery could happen faster than expected because ramping quantities back up with existing partners for goods already exchanged would be less costly and easier. Although establishing new export relationships or reestablishing dropped relationships would take longer, such expansion would also help reduce countries' vulnerability to external shocks in the long term.

Trade Finance Constraints and Trade Collapse

At the peak of the financial crisis, a number of articles and official statements from the heads of international organizations suggested that credit constraints were a significant contributing factor to the global decline in trade (Auboin 2009). Because financial intermediaries were at the epicenter of the global crisis, financial constraints could be particularly important for firms engaged in international trade because they must extend trade credit to their foreign counterparties before the shipment of goods. If these lines of credit were suspended, importing firms would cancel their orders for foreign goods, and foreign firms would reduce production. This fear triggered many governments and development institutions to act immediately to make liquidity available and facilitate trade.

A year into the crisis, several empirical studies, either at the macro level or at the firm level, looked at the role of trade finance constraints in the trade collapse. Most of them concluded that a drop in world demand played a major role and that frictions in the financial market had a marginal negative impact (Mora and Powers 2009; Bricongne et al. 2010; Chor and Manova 2010). These global results, however, disguise the fact that certain countries and market segments may have been seriously constrained and undersupplied, even if the global situation was not necessarily as tight as feared at the onset of the crisis.

Export Firm Survey Findings

The firm survey results confirm these general findings. Three-fourths of the respondents declared that their exports have been severely or moderately constrained by the financial crisis, as figure 10.4 illustrates.

Figure 10.4 Severity of Export Constraints due to 2008–09 Crisis, by Country

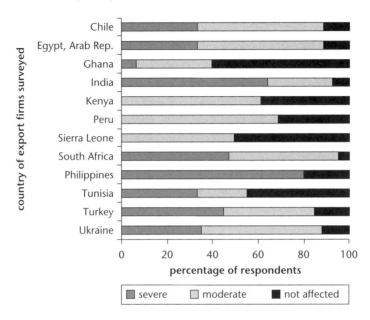

Source: Author's data from April 2010 firm survey.

Most respondents also reported that lack of orders and the related lack of finance—on the part of both buyers (trade credit) and their own companies—explained the market constraints, as figure 10.5 shows. Lack of finance from banks played a lesser constraining role.

Moreover, most firms did not cancel or postpone an activity because of trade finance constraints—the firm's activity, size, or location notwithstanding. Interestingly, the least-constrained exporters were those in Peru and the three low-income African countries and commodity exporters (Ghana, Kenya, and Sierra Leone). This result corroborates earlier findings that exporters in low-income African countries were insulated from the financial crisis because of the combination of (a) low development of the domestic financial sector and its limited exposure to international banks, (b) macroeconomic volatility, and (c) dedicated international credit lines for some commodity exporters.

These results were confirmed when firms were directly asked whether lack of trade finance or higher prices had affected their export plans. As shown in figure 10.6, panel a, more than 80 percent of respondents said they had neither canceled nor postponed a planned transaction because of lack of trade finance, or even because of higher-than-usual pricing of trade finance.

Figure 10.5 Sources of Export Market Constraints

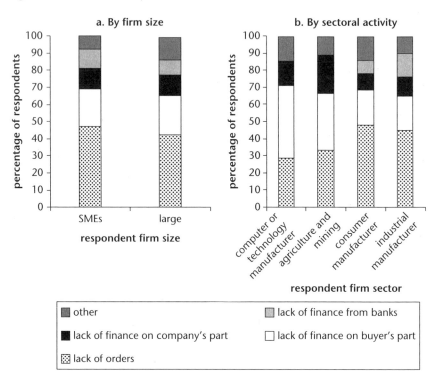

Source: Author's data from 2010 firm survey.
Note: SMEs = small and medium enterprises. Number of respondents = 257. "SMEs" have up to 250 employees; "large" firms have more than 250 employees.

Trade finance prices are reportedly still high and have even increased since the economic recovery started. As figure 10.6, panel b, shows, 42 percent of the respondents declared that prices had further increased by the last quarter of 2009 over the last quarter of 2008, when prices had been presumably at their crisis peak. A similar portion of respondents said prices remained the same, while a minority noted that prices decreased over the same period.

Although firms felt fewer trade-credit constraints from suppliers or buyers after global demand picked up, in particular from emerging markets, many respondents complained about the lack of access to bank-intermediated trade finance. Many firms—especially in Egypt and the Philippines, where banking intermediation is important—claimed that banks were still imposing stringent eligibility criteria for trade finance transactions, and 45 percent of firms reported

Figure 10.6 Trade Finance Changes and Effects on Export Firms

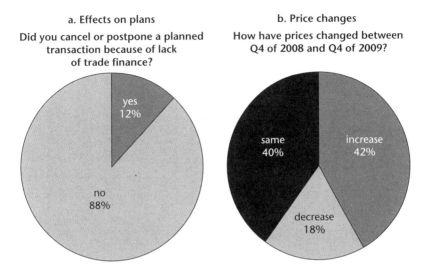

a. Effects on plans

Did you cancel or postpone a planned transaction because of lack of trade finance?

yes 12%

no 88%

b. Price changes

How have prices changed between Q4 of 2008 and Q4 of 2009?

same 40%

increase 42%

decrease 18%

Source: Author's data from April 2010 firm survey.
Note: Number of respondents = 257.

that banks remained as risk averse in the fourth quarter of 2009 as they had been in the fourth quarter of 2008.

Small and medium enterprises (SMEs) and firms operating in the sectors most affected by the slower demand (such as in Egypt, the Philippines, and South Africa) were those most often reporting that banks were still risk averse, as figure 10.7 shows. Financially weaker exporters, for which letters of credit (LCs) and documentary collection are the common payment method, were also finding it harder to access bank-intermediated trade finance.

Access to bank trade finance remained problematic because of heightened risk and the overall deterioration of traders' creditworthiness. It is worth noting that liquidity has not been identified as a constraint. Surveyed banks, even in low-income African countries, reported that liquidity was not an issue and that they could meet increased demand for short-term credit. These reports converge with those from the World Trade Organization (WTO) Expert Meeting on Trade Finance in April 2010, where participants noted that liquidity has returned to the trade finance market.

However, the cost of trade finance remained high in some markets. And the prices of trade finance instruments and spreads, although narrowing, remained higher than precrisis levels, even in macroeconomically sound economies such

Figure 10.7 Constraints on Bank-Intermediated Trade Finance, by Country

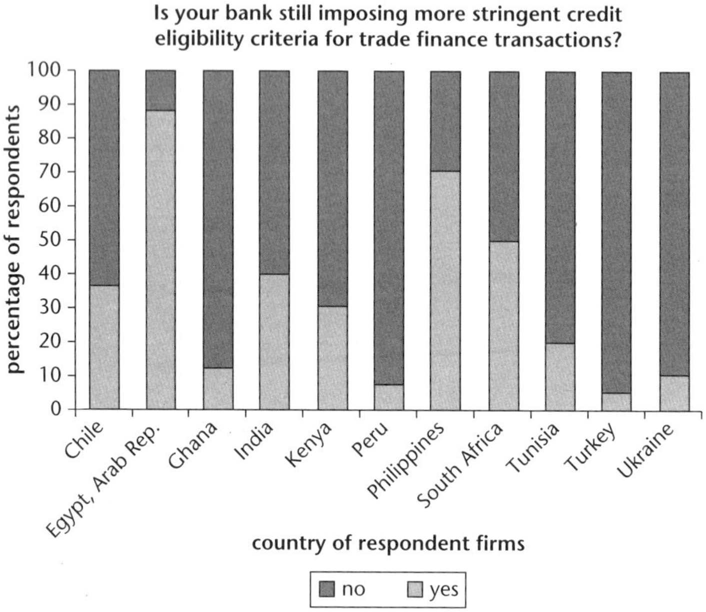

Source: Author's data from April 2010 firm survey.
Note: Number of respondents = 223.

as Chile. Regulatory issues—such as Basel II—remain a concern and have reportedly affected the degree of exposure banks can assume in a given transaction.

Other Bank and Firm Survey Findings

Other recent bank and firm surveys indicate a recovery in the trade finance market as a result of the recovery in trade, but access to bank trade finance remains difficult for small firms. An April 2010 survey of 93 major banks in 53 countries indicated an improvement in the trade finance market compared with previous surveys conducted in March and July 2009 (IMF-BAFT 2009; IMF and BAFT–IFSA 2010).

The results of an April 2010 International Chamber of Commerce (ICC) survey of 161 banks in 75 countries were somewhat less sanguine. It reported that the supply of trade finance remained constrained in both value and volume: 60 percent of respondents indicated that the value of trade finance activity had decreased between 2008 and 2009; 43 percent of respondents noted a decrease in export LC volume (ICC 2010). Trade finance pricing remained higher than precrisis levels, raising the problem of affordability for exporters. Banks had also intensified due diligence processes and scrutiny of documents, leading to more refusals and court injunctions. The survey noted that existing regulations placed low-risk trade finance instruments in the same category as higher-risk balance sheet items, constraining the trade finance market.

Overall survey findings suggest that trade finance was not the primary culprit; global demand was. Moreover, interfirm trade credit has been more resilient than bank trade credit. However, trade finance constraints were not insignificant in some instances: in countries where bank intermediation is predominant, for small and financially vulnerable firms, and for new firms without established business partners.

Indeed, trade dropped mainly because of the spillover to the real economy, drop in economic activity and global demand, decline in export revenues, delays in payment terms by buyers, and shorter payment terms by suppliers. The trade decline, in turn, squeezed exporters' and importers' capital base, working capital, and capacity to self-finance their transactions.

Although interfirm trade credit picked up with the economic recovery, banks remained risk averse and continued to apply more stringent requirements, and prices remained higher than precrisis levels. That interfirm trade credit has been more resilient than bank trade finance is consistent with the determinants of trade credit. The latter can be a superior option to trade finance when suppliers have an advantage over banks because of their access to information on the financial health of clients and because providers can more easily liquidate the goods in the event of nonpayment.

Country-Level Trade Finance Trends

One of the side objectives of this follow-up survey was to collect country-level data on trade finance value and volume because global and country-level data on trade finance have become illustrious for their scarcity. The dearth of data has seriously constrained policy makers in establishing an informed analysis of the impact of the financial crisis on trade finance.

An indication of the seriousness of this problem is that the WTO Expert Group on Trade Finance agreed to improve data collection through surveys under ICC leadership. The ICC and the Asian Development Bank (ADB) also established the ICC-ADB Register on Trade & Finance to collect performance data on trade finance products so that banks have better information on trade finance transactions and may treat them preferentially to riskier short-term transactions.[4]

'Some countries do publish trade finance-related data, although under different formats and covering different aspects of trade finance (value of LCs, short-term suppliers, credit, and so on). The data for India and South Africa (shown in figure 10.8) and for Turkey (in figure 10.10 later in this chapter) show a drop in trade finance value starting in fall 2008, bottoming out in the second quarter of 2009, and picking up in the second half of 2009.

Figure 10.8 Export and Import Trade Finance, India and South Africa

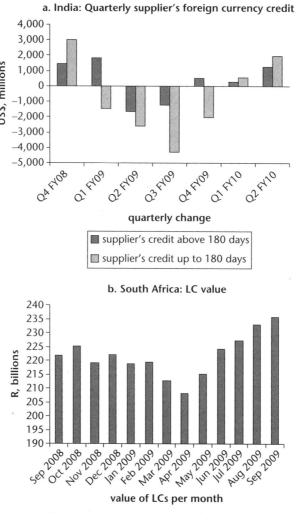

Sources: Reserve Bank of India; South African Reserve Bank.
Note: LC = letter of credit. R = South African rand.

Trade Finance Data from Africa

Data for low-income African countries are of greater interest because concerns about liquidity constraints in these countries drew particular attention from policy makers and development institutions. The data indicated that trade finance increased in both Ghana and Kenya, as figure 10.9 shows.

However, the financial crisis has exacerbated the fragility of these economies' economic growth. In Ghana, banks increased import and export finance during the financial crisis, possibly reflecting the increased capital base in line with the new capital requirements, which also led to improved buffer for risk absorption in the banking sector. However, credit conditions tightened somewhat throughout the year because of the high interest rates and deterioration in the quality of banks' lending books.

In Kenya, commercial banks delayed credit in general, particularly export and import credit, with credit volume increasing sharply during the peak of the crisis but then stabilizing around an average value in 2009. In addition to domestic factors such as postelection violence and drought, external shocks (high commodity prices, the global financial crisis, and the subsequent global economic slowdown) exacerbated Kenya's negative economic performance and resulted in low demand for, and supply of, bank credit.

Liquidity was reportedly not a constraint in Sierra Leone, where bank finance remained available to creditworthy borrowers, the larger established banks still tend to be underlent, and the influx of new banks has increased competition to book credit facilities.

Trade Finance Data from Turkey

A closer look at the Turkish data—the most detailed in terms of trade finance instruments and available monthly from January 2008 to December 2009—indicates a drastic dive in trade finance value across most instruments, primarily for the most-used ones, as shown in figure 10.10. Export finance using cash against goods and cash on delivery (the riskiest methods of payment) and LCs dropped the most. The import finance decline was more proportional across instruments, although advance payment methods, followed by cash against goods and on delivery and LCs, are the most-used instruments.

Turkish trade finance value picked up starting in January 2009 and remained on a positive trend until December 2009. These developments tend to support the idea that demand played a more important role than trade credit constraints. Moreover, it is worth noting that the value of trade finance increased in the months before the crisis, for exports more than imports.

Figure 10.9 Export and Import Trade Finance, Ghana and Kenya

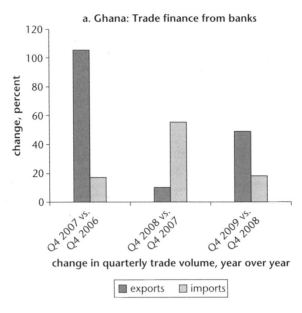

a. Ghana: Trade finance from banks

change in quarterly trade volume, year over year

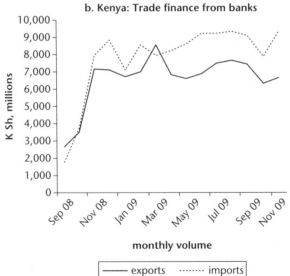

b. Kenya: Trade finance from banks

monthly volume

Sources: Bank of Ghana Research Department; Central Bank of Kenya.
Note: K Sh = Kenya shilling.

Figure 10.10 Export and Import Trade Finance in Turkey, by Instrument

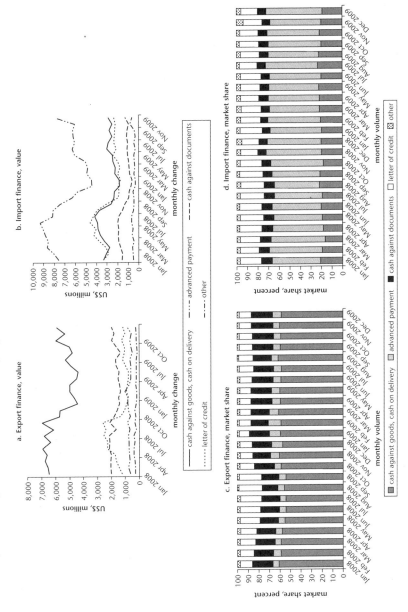

Source: TURKSTAT.

The share of LCs increased significantly, in particular for exports, leading to a compositional shift: the share of LCs reached 22 percent in August 2008, up from 12 percent in January 2008. This shift disappeared with the crisis, however, and the share of LCs hovered around 12 percent during the last quarter of 2009. Although it not clear why Turkish exporters relied to a larger extent on LCs in the months before the crisis, one possible explanation is that traders observed signs of an impending banking crisis and were already switching toward safer methods of payments.

Governmental and Institutional Interventions

Most governments implemented measures to support exporters during the financial turmoil, including fiscal stimuli, public spending, and making more funds available for lending. However, some governments are already withdrawing some of these measures (see Malouche 2009 for a list and box 10.1 for an update)—in particular, those aimed at increasing the liquidity in the financial sector, mainly because of (a) currently adequate liquidity in the banking system (for example, in India and the Philippines), or (b) some measures' ineffectiveness in adding liquidity in the real sector (for example, in Chile and Kenya). However, other countries (Ghana, for example) did not implement any direct measures to mitigate the impact of the crisis.

More specifically, government measures (or lack thereof) to support exporters in the surveyed countries included the following:

- *In Chile*, increased funding for commercial banks proved unnecessary because the situation never turned so critical, funds were not used significantly, and the program was discontinued soon after it began.
- *In Ghana*, the government took no direct steps to directly address the financial crisis's impact on trade finance. However, the Bank of Ghana's decision to increase its stated capital to ₵60 million (US$42 million) by 2010 helped improve the banking sector liquidity to undertake more trade financing. Also, the government's effort to stabilize the economy helped slow the increase in prices of trade finance instruments. This result could also be attributed to increased competition among the banks for trade finance provision.
- *In Kenya*, the Central Bank's efforts to increase bank credit to the private sector were hindered by inefficiencies in the transmission of monetary policy impulses from short-term to long-term lending interest rates. While interbank rates decreased considerably—from 6.66 percent in December 2008 to 2.95 percent in December 2009—commercial bank lending rates increased from 13.66 percent in September 2008 to 15.1 percent in June 2009, mainly because of higher risk perception by commercial banks.

Box 10.1 Policy Update on Selected Countries and Multilateral Initiatives

India

A year into the crisis, the Reserve Bank of India (RBI) announced the following policy changes with regard to export finance:

- Given the adequate liquidity within the banking system, the eligible limit of the Export Credit Refinance facility has been reduced from the level of 50 percent of the outstanding rupee export credit eligible for refinance to 15 percent.
- Interest subvention of 2 percent has been extended for one more year for exports covering sectors such as handicrafts, carpets, handlooms, and SMEs.
- The ceiling rate on export credit in foreign currency by banks has been reduced to London interbank offered rate (LIBOR) plus 200 basis points from the earlier ceiling rate of LIBOR plus 350 basis points.
- The RBI is in the process of replacing the existing Benchmark Prime Lending Rate (BPLR) system with a new system in which banks will be asked to announce a base rate below which they cannot extend loans to any borrowers. However, it has not yet announced the stipulations for export credit under the proposed system. Given that the interest rate on rupee export credit is now capped at BPLR minus 2.5 percent, it is unclear how the RBI will continue to support export credit under the new base rate system.

Kenya

The Central Bank has pursued an accommodative monetary policy to help cushion the economy from the negative effects of the global financial crisis, taking the following measures:

- Reduction of the cash reserve ratio from 6 percent to 4.5 percent (100 basis points in December 2008 and 50 basis points in July 2009) released an equivalent of K Sh 12.5 billion for lending to the economy.
- Consecutive reduction of the central bank rate from 8.75 percent to 7.75 percent was as a signal to banks to reduce lending rates.
- Allowing a reduction in foreign exchange reserves to less than three months reduced pressure on the depreciation of the Kenya shilling relative to hard currencies. Otherwise, the inflationary effect of the shilling's depreciation would have been worse in terms of intermediate imports, oil prices, and so on.

Peru

The government of Peru announced a stimulus plan in January 2009, listing around $3 billion in activities and financial resources to promote employment and continue economic growth. The first stage was to implement a stimulus package of $1.45 billion aimed at boosting economic activity, enhancing social protection, and increasing investments in infrastructure. The stimulus package was never fully implemented, and the government has debated whether to eliminate the temporary increase of 3 percent of the drawback to the exporters of nontraditional (noncommodities) products and return to 5 percent.

Multilateral Initiatives

Regional development banks and global institutions also put in place or ramped up their trade finance programs. The trade finance programs of the World Bank's private arm, the International Finance Corporation (IFC), have also been expanding in

(continued next page)

Box 10.1 *continued*

response to the financial crisis. The IFC's Global Trade Finance Program (GTFP) currently covers 183 emerging-market banks in 82 countries. As of May 2010, the GTFP had issued $3 billion in trade guarantees, of which 84 percent supported SMEs in IFC's client countries—52 percent in countries of the Bank's International Development Association (IDA) and 32 percent in Africa.

The IFC's Global Trade Liquidity Program (GTLP) is also on track to finance up to $15 billion of trade volume per year. As of March 2011, GTLP had mobilized $3 billion from development finance institutions and governments, significantly leveraging IFC funds of $1 billion allocated to this program. It also has supported $11.2 billion in trade volume without any default, mainly supporting SMEs, almost half of them in IDA countries and almost 30 percent in Africa. In response to a strong demand for GTLP solutions and to market priorities, the IFC is launching the program's second phase with GTLP Guarantee (portfolio-based, unfunded risk sharing) and GTLP Agri (food and agriculture sector–focused funding lines), with implementation first in regions that need it most: Europe and Central Asia, Africa, and Latin America and the Caribbean.

- *In the Philippines*, the Monetary Board decided in April 2010 to withdraw crisis-relief measures—in particular, reducing the peso rediscounting budget from ₱60 billion back to the original ₱20 billion.
- *In Tunisia*, the global crisis had limited first-round effects on the banking sector because of its limited exposure to financial assets and restrictions on capital transactions. However, the economy was hit hard because of its exposure to the EU business cycle. With slower pickup in the EU economies, the 2010 Budget Law maintained a supportive fiscal policy to ensure that the economic recovery would not be undermined by an early withdrawal of the fiscal stimulus measures introduced in 2009.

The firm and bank survey also aimed to shed light on how the private sector perceived the trade finance measures implemented by their respective governments and the multilateral development banks. Firms and banks were specifically asked whether they knew about these measures and, if so, how they viewed them.

The results indicate that a large majority of firms reported being unaware of any of these actions. Banks seemed slightly more informed than firms, and their feedback was positive about the credit lines made available by the International Finance Corporation (IFC), particularly in Africa. For example, a South African bank reported the IFC program bank was able to confirm LCs from countries and banks that it otherwise would not have had full credit appetite for. A Kenyan bank was in favor of programs such as the IFC's Global Trade Finance Program (GTFP) that help reduce the country risk for Africa. In Sierra Leone, surveyed banks used IFC credit lines, although these lines seemed small relative to total trade value.

Three factors might explain this poor overall awareness of governmental and institutional trade finance initiatives:

- The crisis was short-lived, while policy actions take time to become effective and observable.
- The measures taken either had not had an impact on the real economy yet or were not needed, as illustrated above.
- The governments and multilateral development banks did not communicate well enough with the private sector about these measures at the country level.

Conclusions

The firm and bank surveys have been valuable sources of information on trade and trade finance in developing countries during the global financial crisis. The 2009 survey showed that the financial crisis spilled over to the real economy and dampened firms' trade volumes and access to trade finance. The follow-up survey conducted in April 2010 indicates that trade and interfirm trade credit have picked up with the economic recovery.

This result indicates that trade finance is less of a constraint for firms in sectors affected by the crisis and the drop in global demand, as well as those integrated in global value supply chains and relying to a large extent on interfirm trade credit. However, banks were still risk averse and continued to impose stringent requirements; prices also remained higher than precrisis levels. These findings suggest that access to bank trade finance remains a source of concern for small firms, financially vulnerable firms, and new firms—implying that interventions targeting these firms remain crucial.

Findings from the latest firm and bank survey also point to a demand-driven trade crisis. However, the results should not suggest that trade finance constraints were not important or that governments' interventions were unnecessary. Given the magnitude and the scope of the crisis as well as the lack of data on trade finance, policy activism and coordination among governments and international organizations have been important to restore confidence and mitigate the impact of the crisis in the short term. International coordination successfully led to quick reaction, and most governments reacted swiftly in support of their domestic economies.

Policies implemented by developing-countries' governments have had mixed results so far. For example, injection of liquidity has not necessarily proven effective because banks remained risk averse, demand was low, and uncertainty about the soundness of the financial sector prevailed. Many governments dropped these measures within a year. More important, the financial crisis has proven that macroeconomic stability and fiscal consolidation are crucial in times of crisis so that governments have the option to implement counter-cyclical measures.

Annex 10.1 Key Findings from the 2009 Survey

The 2009 survey findings confirmed that the global financial crisis constrained trade finance for exporters and importers in developing countries. Yet drop in demand emerged as firms' top concern. The lack of export revenues was putting pressure on firms' cash flow and, therefore, on their capacity to fund their export and import transactions. The survey revealed some stylized facts at the firm, bank, and country-income levels.

Firm-Level Findings

Firms that rely to a large extent on the banking system for trade finance suffered from more risk averse and selective local banks. In contrast, firms that rely mostly on interfirm financing and self-financing were most affected by the slowing global economy, the lack and cancellation of orders, delays in buyers' payments, and shorter maturity imposed by suppliers.

SMEs were more affected than large firms because of a weaker capital base and bargaining power in relation to global buyers as well as banks. Also, SMEs have been more subject to high increases in the cost of trade finance instruments. Many SMEs operating in global supply chains or in the sectors most affected by the slow global economy, such as in the auto industry, reported being constrained both by the banking system and by the drop in export revenues and buyers' liquidity.

Bank-Level Findings

The drastic reduction in global financial liquidity and in the number of intermediary players pushed banks in developing countries to become more cautious, risk averse, and selective, and therefore more likely to tighten trade finance conditions.

Interviews with banks confirmed the increase in pricing and drop in trade credit volume. Yet the drop in volume seemed to reflect lack of demand due to the global recession rather than the increase in pricing. Moreover, lack of liquidity in local currency did not appear to be an issue.

Region-Level Findings

The three low-income African countries where the survey was conducted (Ghana, Kenya, and Sierra Leone) seemed relatively more insulated from the financial crisis as of March–April 2009. Their primary trade finance constraints originated from more structural problems, such as poorly developed banking systems and trade finance institutions as well as macroeconomic imbalances.

Many of the African exporters have traditionally relied on self-financing and cash-in-advance; therefore, they were also affected by the drop in commodity prices and global demand from their main export markets. The drop in their cash reserves further constrained their trade finance. The financial crisis also added strains on the countries' domestic financial systems and was unfavorable to SMEs and new firms seeking to diversify away from commodity exports.

Annex 10.2 Import and Export Growth, by Country

Figure 10A.1 Export and Import Growth, by Country

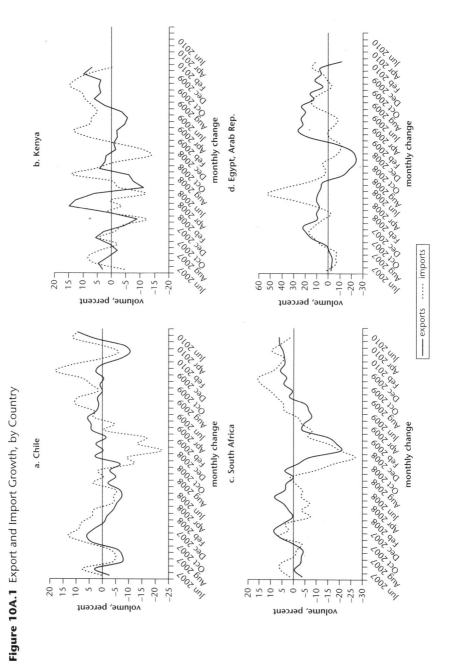

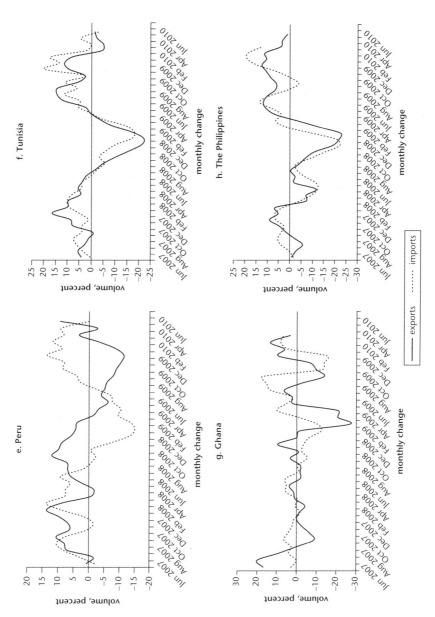

e. Peru

volume, percent

monthly change

f. Tunisia

volume, percent

monthly change

g. Ghana

volume, percent

monthly change

h. The Philippines

volume, percent

monthly change

—— exports ······ imports

(continued next page)

195

196

Figure 10A.1 *continued*

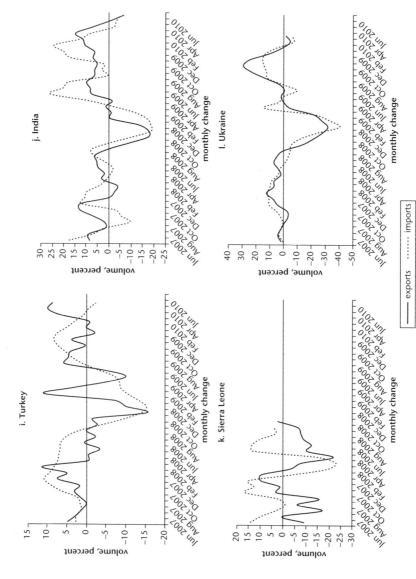

Source: Datastream and author calculations.

Notes

1. For the key findings of the 2009 survey, see annex 10.1 or Malouche (2009).
2. For country-level monthly import and export data, see annex 10.2.
3. The "intensive margin" of trade refers to changes in values of goods already being traded. The "extensive margin" refers to changes in the number of goods exported and in the number of destinations to which a country exports goods.
4. For more information about the ICC-ADB Register on Trade & Finance, see the announcement (http://www.iccwbo.org/policy/banking/index.html?id=39118) or "Findings of the ICC-ADB Register on Trade & Finance" (http://www.iccwbo.org/uploadedFiles/ICC/policy/banking_technique/Statements/1147%20Register%20Report%20ICC%20Final%20Draft%2021%20September%202010.pdf).

References

Auboin, Marc. 2009. "Boosting the Availability of Trade Finance in the Current Crisis: Background Analysis for a Substantial G-20 Package." Policy Insight 35, Centre for Economic Policy Research, London. http://www.cepr.org/pubs/policyinsights/PolicyInsight35.pdf.

Bricongne, Jean-Charles, Lionel Fontagné, Guillaume Gaulier, Daria Taglioni, and Vincent Vicard. 2009. "Firms and the Global Crisis: French Exports in the Turmoil." Working Paper 265, Banque de France, Paris.

Chor, David, and Kalina Manova. 2010. "Off the Cliff and Back? Credit Conditions and International Trade during the Global Financial Crisis." VoxEU.org article, Centre for Economic Policy Research, London. http://www.voxeu.org/index.php?q=node/4613.

Haddad, Mona, Ann Harrison, and Catherine Hausman. 2010. "Decomposing the Great Trade Collapse: Products, Prices, and Quantities in the 2008–2009 Crisis." Working Paper 16253, National Bureau of Economic Research, Cambridge, MA.

ICC (International Chamber of Commerce). 2010. "Rethinking Trade Finance 2010: An ICC Global Survey." ICC, Paris.

IMF-BAFT (International Monetary Fund-Bankers' Association for Finance and Trade). 2009. "IMF-BAFT Trade Finance Survey: A Survey among Banks Assessing the Current Trade Finance Environment." Report by FImetrix for IMF and BAFT, Washington, DC.

IMF and BAFT-IFSA (International Monetary Fund and Bankers' Association for Finance and Trade–International Financial Services Association). 2010. "Trade Finance Services: Current Environment & Recommendations: Wave 3. Report by FImetrix for IMF and BAFT, Washington, DC.

Malouche, Mariem. 2009. "Trade and Trade Finance Developments in 14 Developing Countries Post-September 2008." Policy Research Working Paper 5138, World Bank, Washington, DC.

Mora, Jesse, and William M. Powers. 2009. "Decline and Gradual Recovery of Global Trade Financing: U.S. and Global Perspectives." VoxEU.org article, Centre for Economic Policy Research, London. http://www.voxeu.org/index.php?q=node/4298.

PRIVATE TRADE CREDIT INSURERS DURING THE CRISIS: THE INVISIBLE BANKS

Koen J. M. van der Veer

This chapter deals with an explicit financial insurance market vital for domestic and international trade involving nonpayment risk: the market for trade credit insurance. After the Lehman Brothers' collapse, private trade credit insurers, too, were confronted with mounting risks calling for a quick and comprehensive reaction. Inevitably, they reduced their exposure substantially. Because private trade credit insurers have the right to reduce or cancel "credit limits" on buyers at any given time, they were able to react quickly to the increase in uncertainty.

The question is to what extent this reduction in the availability of trade credit insurance affected trade. In general, when suppliers are confronted with a loss of insurance cover on their buyer(s), they can (a) try to seek alternative means to avoid credit risk (bank letters of credit or factoring), (b) decide to take on the payment risk themselves, or (c) demand advance payment. If other instruments are available, trade might be unaffected. If one of the latter two options is chosen, the trade transaction need not be canceled, either, but negative side effects related to

This chapter is a revised and much-abridged version of an article that first appeared as DNB Working Paper 264 (van der Veer 2010). The use of the term *invisible banks* to characterize private trade credit insurers was introduced by Paul Becue, general manager at Euler Hermes Services Belgium, in his handbook on credit insurance, *Handboek kredietverzekering. De onzichtbare bank* (Becue 2009). The author would like to thank Gabriele Galati for carefully reading the manuscript. The findings, interpretations, and conclusions expressed in this chapter are entirely those of the author; they do not necessarily reflect views of De Nederlandsche Bank.

the balance sheet of the supplier or buyer could reduce the incentives to trade indirectly. When neither of the options is feasible, trade breaks down.

Van der Veer (2010) provides empirical evidence for the link between the supply of private trade credit insurance and trade, focusing on exports. The study exploits a unique bilateral dataset on worldwide activities of a leading private trade credit insurer and finds an average short-run multiplier for private trade credit insurance of 2.3. This multiplier implies that, on average, every €1 of insured exports generates €2.3 of total exports. Thus, the impact on trade of a change in the supply of private trade credit insurance is bigger than the change in the value of insured trade. One important reason that could explain this trade multiplier is that trade credit insurance improves a buyer's access to supplier credit.

In addition, van der Veer (2010) estimates the insurance supply elasticity of world and European exports. Extrapolating these estimates to the 2008–09 crisis period, the decline in the supply of private credit insurance in the last quarter of 2008 and the first half of 2009 can explain 5–9 percent of the collapse of world trade and 10–20 percent of the drop in European exports. Thus, even though private credit insurers cover only 6 percent and 12 percent, respectively, of world and European exports, the impact of changes in the supply of private credit insurance is economically relevant.

Within the literature on the role of trade finance during financial crises, the focus on private trade credit insurance is novel. More generally, van der Veer (2010) is the first empirical study to provide direct evidence on the link between the supply of a trade finance instrument and trade. Due to the lack of detailed trade finance data—that is, statistics on trade-related loans, trade credit insurance, and letters of credit—the literature thus far had either examined the link between trade finance and trade indirectly or relied on various proxy measures to study the role of the trade finance channel. The limitation of these proxy measures is that they include credits extended by other firms in addition to institutional finance or include credit for purchases other than trade. As a result, it is not always clear that changes in the supply of trade finance drive the results in these studies.

Moreover, while the literature shows convincingly that financial shocks affect trade, it does not fully address the extent to which trade finance frictions played a role in the 2008–09 global financial crisis. The results in van der Veer (2010) focus on just one aspect of the trade finance market—private trade credit insurance—and do not tackle this question, either. The outcome is indicative of a role for private trade credit insurance and can be interpreted as a minimum for the role of trade finance in the 2008–09 world trade collapse. For example, the market for letters of credit and short-term export working capital might have been an additional source of trade finance frictions, as surveys during the crisis seem to suggest.

The next section describes the general features of the private trade credit insurance market and how it differs from the better-known public counterpart. Subsequent sections provide

- a more detailed explanation of how a trade credit insurance policy works and how it compares to alternative instruments to cover nonpayment risk;
- an examination of the link between trade credit insurance and the provision of supplier credit and how this relates to the trade multiplier of credit insurance;
- a discussion of the results obtained in van der Veer (2010); and
- a preliminary evaluation of the policy response in European Union (EU) countries to support the availability of short-term export credit insurance during the 2008–09 financial crisis.

Private versus Public Trade Credit Insurance

The private trade credit insurance market differs in important ways from the guarantees provided by public export credit agencies (ECAs). In general, private trade credit insurers (a) cover short-term trade credits; (b) have a much higher exposure than ECAs; (c) cover domestic trade; and (d) are concentrated, although decreasingly, on trade involving Organisation for Economic Co-operation and Development (OECD) countries (European countries in particular). Because of these differences, relative changes in the supply of private trade credit insurance are likely to have a bigger and much faster impact on trade than changes in the supply of public insurance.[1]

Private trade credit insurers usually cover short-term credits with a tenor of 60 to 120 days, while medium- or long-term covers play only a minor role (Swiss Re 2006). Public guarantees, however, generally cover export projects with a duration of between two and five years. This difference in maturities is especially clear in Europe, where ECAs have been restricted from providing OECD core members with guarantees covering export risks with a maturity of less than two years. During the 2008–09 financial crisis, the ECAs' inexperience in the short-term credit insurance market, combined with the need for European Commission approval, delayed the implementation of public schemes to support the short-term export credit insurance market in Europe (see the final section for a fuller discussion).

Since the early 1990s, private trade credit insurance has registered strong growth. Private credit insurers provide substantially greater short-term credit insurance than ECAs do in all OECD countries except for Japan and Canada (Chauffour and Farole 2009). In 2008, an estimated €5.3 billion of global credit insurance premiums covered about €2.6 trillion of sales (Jones 2010). Based on Berne Union figures, the world share of private short-term insured exports to total exports was an estimated 6.1 percent in 2007. Likewise, for Europe, private trade credit insurers cover an estimated 12 percent of overall exports.[2] Exports covered by public credit insurance can be roughly estimated at €325 billion in 2008.[3]

Three private credit insurers—the so-called Big Three—now dominate the world market, covering a combined 87 percent: Euler Hermes (36 percent), Atradius (31 percent), and Coface (20 percent). These players are traditionally focused on Western Europe but have also expanded to Eastern Europe and the American and Asian markets. Still, in 2008, 59 percent of short-term credit limits covered exports destined for Europe (Morel 2010).[4]

How Private Trade Credit Insurance Works

The basics of trade credit insurance are quite straightforward, as figure 11.1 illustrates. A supplier selling goods on credit to a buyer can insure against the risk of nonpayment. The credit insurer indemnifies the seller if the buyer fails to pay for the goods or services. In turn, the credit insurer charges the supplier a premium. Crucially, the private credit insurer must have a credit limit on a buyer to enable the supplier to insure against nonpayment by that particular buyer. The credit limit is the maximum exposure specifically approved or otherwise authorized by the insurer with respect to a buyer.

Figure 11.1 How Private Trade Credit Insurance Works

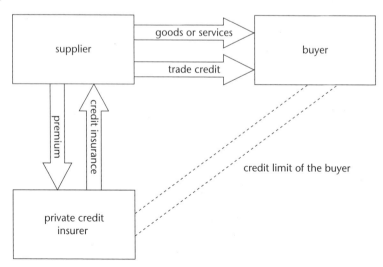

Source: Author.

A special feature of the credit insurance industry is that credit insurers have the right to reduce or cancel the credit limit on a buyer at any given time. Deliveries made after the date of the credit insurer's decision to cancel a credit limit are not covered by the insurance policy. This ability to dynamically manage credit limits allows credit insurers to react to a buyer's credit problems before they worsen. Thus, the mere expectation of rising claims can immediately affect exports through a reduction in the maximum exposure of credit insurers. Indeed, after the Lehman Brothers' collapse in September 2008, private credit insurers reduced their exposure substantially by reducing and canceling credit limits.

Credit insurers normally provide *whole turnover* policies that cover the insured suppliers' total trade receivables against the risk of nonpayment by their buyers. As a result, suppliers cannot select specific buyers for cover, even though the insurer can exclude or limit cover for buyers it considers not creditworthy. The whole turnover policies generally cover commercial and political risk—*commercial risk* referring to nonpayment due to default or insolvency and *political risk* relating to nonpayment as a result of action by the buyer's government (for example, intervention to prevent the transfer of payments, cancellation of a license, or acts of war or civil war).

Alternative Instruments: Letters of Credit and Factoring

Aside from trade credit insurance, suppliers can cover credit risk using letters of credit or factoring. Before the 2008–09 financial crisis, credit insurance also had some competition from capital market products such as credit default swaps and asset-backed commercial paper (Swiss Re 2006; Jones 2010). Nevertheless, these alternative bank services differ from trade credit insurance in important ways, making them imperfect substitutes.

Letters of Credit

A documentary letter of credit is a bank's agreement to guarantee payment by the buyer up to a stated amount for a specified period. They are most commonly used in international trade and cover about $700 billion to $1 trillion, or 10–15 percent, of global exports (Swiss Re 2006).

In general, letters of credit are more expensive than trade credit insurance for two reasons. First, unlike trade credit insurance, a letter of credit must be purchased by the buyer and reduces the buyer's available credit because it is charged against the overall credit limit set by the bank. Second, a letter of credit covers a single transaction for a single buyer, whereas trade credit insurance policies are usually whole turnover, that is, covering all sales.

Factoring

Factoring, another traditional instrument to deal with payment risk, allows a supplier that sells on credit to prefinance its receivables. Like trade credit insurance, factoring is used in domestic and international trade and had a transaction volume of $1.2 trillion in 2005 (Swiss Re 2006).

Factoring, too, is more expensive than trade credit insurance because the factor must also be compensated for prefinancing the receivables. Unlike letters of credit, factoring can be both a substitute and a complement to trade credit insurance. That is, factoring does not necessarily involve the transfer of credit risk to the factor (full-recourse factoring), in which case the factor has an interest in the client buying insurance to cover credit risk (Swiss Re 2006). Alternatively, under nonrecourse factoring, the factor does take on the risk of nonpayment by the buyer and may itself choose to purchase credit insurance cover.

Trade Credit Insurance, Supplier Credit, and the Trade Multiplier

Essentially, trade credit insurance stimulates trade with markets where a supplier would not sell otherwise. This follows immediately from the main reason for a supplier to buy trade credit insurance: the transfer of payment risk. Trade credit insurance also provides these benefits:

- Allowing suppliers to use the credit expertise of the credit insurer
- Facilitating access to receivables financing and improved credit terms from lending institutions
- Improving the buyer's access to supplier credit.

These benefits to both supplier and buyer provide the main rationale for the existence of a trade multiplier of credit insurance.

Supplier Credit

Even though buyers do not initiate trade credit insurance—often they do not even know that a private credit insurer has approved a credit limit until it is reduced or canceled—they are greatly affected by it. A trade credit insurance policy enables the supplier to extend credit to the buyer instead of requiring payment in advance. As a result, the buyer's working capital need is reduced, or the additional cash can be used for other purchases or investments.

Moreover, in practice, the news that a buyer's credit limit has been adjusted tends to travel fast among the buyer's suppliers, potentially influencing all of its trade transactions (Becue 2009); an upgrade generally improves the firm's access to supplier credit and vice versa. Private trade credit insurers can thus be seen as *invisible banks*; while they do not provide funding, their actions influence buyers' access to supplier credit.

The Trade Multiplier

The benefits of trade credit insurance for the supplier might also add to the trade multiplier, although less so than the benefits for the buyer. This is because most of the private trade credit insurance policies cover all of a supplier's sales (whole turnover), and the trade multiplier relates to additional trade generated on top of the value of insured trade.

Either way, these benefits can increase the insured supplier's sales for several reasons. First, an insurance policy gives the supplier access to professional credit-risk expertise. To illustrate how this could stimulate the insured supplier's sales, Jones (2010) gives a telling example: "A wholesale company's credit department has granted a credit line of €100,000 to a customer. They then purchased a trade credit insurance policy and the insurer approved a limit of €150,000 for that same customer. With a 15 percent margin and average turnover of 45 days, the wholesaler was able to increase its sales to realize an incremental annual gross profit of €60,000 on that one account. $[(150 - 100) \times 0.15 \times 360/45)]$"

Second, trade credit insurance might facilitate the supplier's access to bank credit and improved credit terms from lending institutions, some of which will insist on trade credit insurance before providing financing (Becue 2009; Jones 2010). Basically, suppliers can increase their collateral value by insuring their accounts receivable. Especially in the case of international trade, banks might see a supplier's trade partners as an extraordinary risk that reduces the value of the supplier's assets used as collateral.[5]

Another argument used to explain the trade multiplier of credit insurance comes from the studies focusing on public trade credit insurance (Funatsu 1986; Egger and Url 2006; Moser, Nestmann, and Wedow 2008). These studies argue that trade credit insurance allows suppliers to learn about the creditworthiness of their trade partners. Subsequently, after repeated transactions, the supplier may decide to export without costly export credit insurance.

Finally, a trade multiplier of private credit insurance could also follow from the information on foreign markets and firms that private insurers provide to noninsured firms. For example, private credit insurers publish their country ratings, which, in principle, prevail over their sector- and firm-level ratings when determining premiums and credit limits (Becue 2009). Also, the Big Three insurers all offer some kind of information service, allowing firms to get access to the insurers' detailed firm-level information about key customers, prospects, or competitors, even without buying insurance cover.

The Private Credit Insurance Effect on Trade

Van der Veer (2010) examines empirically whether private trade credit insurance stimulates trade. A unique bilateral dataset is used that covers the value of insured exports, premium income, and claims paid by one of the world's leading private credit insurers from 1992 to 2006.[6] The data include annual observations on 25 exporting economies (OECD countries and Hong Kong SAR, China) and 183 destination countries.

Estimating a variety of specifications of the gravity model, the study consistently finds a positive and statistically significant effect of private trade credit insurance on exports. Moreover, it finds an average multiplier of private trade credit insurance of 2.3, implying that every euro of insured exports generates €2.3 of total exports.

The Identification Strategy

The estimation of the private credit insurance effect on exports relies on the standard *gravity* model of bilateral trade, which models trade between a pair of countries as a function of their distance and their economic *masses*. Possible concerns about endogeneity are addressed by applying the method of instrumental variables. Hereto, the insurer's claim ratio (claim paid divided by premium income)—a primary determinant of the supply of credit insurance—is used as an instrument for insured exports. This approach allows establishment of a causal link between the supply of private trade credit insurance and exports.

The claim ratio proves to be a valid instrument for the value of insured exports according to various statistical tests and, notably, a causal story motivates this choice of instrument. The rationale is that an increase (or the expectation thereof) in the claim ratio reduces insured exports in two ways: first, through an increase in premiums (by lowering demand); and second, through the reduction or cancellation of credit limits (by lowering supply). The second channel is more direct and changes the supply of private trade credit insurance immediately. The impact of the premium increase on the value of insured exports evolves more slowly because the private insurer can only raise premiums of new contracts. The bulk of the contracts are fixed for one year, and about 25 percent of all contracts have a duration of two or three years.

In case of a shock, such as a credit crisis or sovereign default, claims increase. The claim ratio also increases because the general premium level takes longer to adjust. For example, during the 2008–09 credit crisis, total claims paid to insured customers by all Berne Union members more than doubled from 2008 to 2009 and reached $2.4 billion. As the total premium stayed roughly the same at an estimated $2.8 billion, the claim ratio jumped from 40 percent to 87 percent (ICC 2010).

Private Trade Credit Insurance and the 2008–09 World Trade Collapse

The deteriorating economic environment and (expected) rise in claim ratios at the end of 2008 resulted in a decline in the supply of private trade credit insurance. Private trade credit insurers reduced credit limits and raised premiums. Annual reports of the leading insurers mention a "substantial" reduction of exposure, but unfortunately, exact figures on the supply decline are not available.

Some EU countries, however, did provide estimates of the withdrawal of private credit insurance coverage. For example, Austria estimated a private supply decline of 15–30 percent; Denmark, of 0–40 percent; Lithuania, of 20–40 percent; and Sweden, of 20–30 percent.[7] In addition, the publicly available Berne Union figures on the world total of private and public insurance exposure, combined with information on their evolving shares (ICC 2010), give an idea of the size of the reduction in private insurance cover. For example, in the last quarter of 2008 and the first half of 2009, private short-term export credit insurance exposure declined by 16 percentage points more than public exposure. Although demand and price factors are likely to have contributed to the reported declines, the much larger decline in private insurance exposure might be a rough indication of the private supply reduction.

Either way, the actual decline in the supply of private credit insurance during the 2008–09 world trade collapse is unknown. Therefore, van der Veer (2010) calculates the contribution to the world trade collapse of a 10 percent, 15 percent, and 20 percent decline in the supply of private credit insurance and extrapolates the estimates of the insurance supply elasticity of exports to the crisis period.

The calculations show that the reduction in private trade credit insurance exposure during the 2008–09 world trade collapse can explain about 5–9 percent of the drop in world exports and 10–20 percent of the drop in European exports. Thus, while macroeconomic factors played an important role in the world trade collapse, these calculations suggest that the effect of private credit insurance on exports can account for part of the world trade decline.

EU Countries' Support of Short-Term Export Credit Insurance

Over the course of 2009 and 2010, 14 EU governments implemented state aid schemes to support their markets for short-term export credit insurance, as the overview in table 11.1 shows. In particular, these measures were set up to provide credit insurance cover for exports to other EU member states and OECD core members.

Under normal circumstances, credit risks on these countries are considered marketable, and EU law forbids official ECAs from providing insurance cover. The European Commission and these 14 EU authorities adequately recognized the

Table 11.1 EU Countries' State Aid to the Short-Term Export Credit Insurance Market

| | EC approval date | Maximum exposure (€ millions) | General eligibility restrictions | | | Premium (% of turnover) | | | | Basic market rates | Private credit insurer fee (% of premium income) |
| | | | Top-up only[a] | Maximum top-up | Buyers excluded | Credit terms up to 6 months | | Credit terms up to 12 months | | | |
						minimum	maximum	minimum	maximum		
Luxembourg	April 20, 2009	25	no	old credit limit	risk assessment by ECA	1.50	4.00	1.50	4.00	± 0.50	none
Denmark	May 6, 2009	no budgetary limitations	no	no	very high probability of default	1.00	2.00	1.00	2.00	0.25–0.30	25–35
Denmark (modification)	October 29, 2009	no budgetary limitations	no	100% of current credit limit	very high probability of default	0.50	2.00	0.50	2.00	0.25–0.30	25–35
Finland	June 22, 2009	no budgetary limitations	no	no	risk assessment by ECA	0.30	0.95	0.60	1.65	—	none
Germany	August 5, 2009	no budgetary limitations	no	no	risk assessment by ECA	0.49	0.64	0.73	0.82	—	none
Netherlands	October 2, 2009	1,500	yes	100% of current credit limit	within certain rating categories	1.50	1.50	1.50	1.50	0.10–0.60	35
Netherlands (modification)	February 5, 2010	1,500	yes	100% of current credit limit	less rating categories	1.00	1.00	1.00	1.00	0.10–0.60	25; set-up costs maximum €50,000
France	October 5, 2009	1,000 (cumulative)	no	100% of current credit limit	within certain rating categories	0.50	3.00	1.50	6.00	0.24	15–17
Belgium	November 6, 2009	300 per quarter	yes	100% of current credit limit but not exceeding old limit	no	1.00	1.00	2.00	2.00	0.30–0.70	20

Country	Date	Budget limit		Credit limit	Risk assessment						
Sweden	November 25, 2009	no budgetary limitations	no	no	risk assessment by ECA	0.26	2.20	1.36	3.96	—	none
Austria	December 17, 2009	no budgetary limitations	no	70–80% of total credit limit	risk assessment by ECA	0.13	2.50	1.50	5.00	—	27
Lithuania	December 21, 2009	29 (cumulative)	yes	100% of current credit limit	no	0.30	0.95	0.60	1.65	0.40–0.80	based on state-insured amount
Slovenia	March 16, 2010	no budgetary limitations	yes	old credit limit	risk assessment by ECA	—	—	—	—	—	33
Latvia	June 10, 2010	14 (cumulative)	no	no	risk assessment by state-owned guarantee institution	0.39	2.60	0.39	2.60	0.20–0.50	none
Hungary	July 5, 2010	183	no	100% of current credit limit	risk assessment by ECA	0.47	2.77	0.95	3.32	0.25–0.35	15–25
Portugal[b]	—	—	—	—	—	—	—	—	—	—	—

Source: National reports in the State Aid Register (by member state) of the European Commission, available at http://ec.europa.eu/competition/state_aid/register/ii/index .html#by_ms.

Note: EC = European Commission. ECA = export credit agency. — = not available. The following EU countries lack a state aid scheme to support the market for short-term export credit insurance: Bulgaria, Cyprus, the Czech Republic, Estonia, Greece, Ireland, Italy, Malta, Poland, Romania, the Slovak Republic, Spain, and the United Kingdom.
a. Top-up only: yes = scheme requiring exporter to hold a private credit insurance policy with a nonzero credit limit on the buyer(s) in question; no = scheme also available for completely withdrawn or newly rejected credit limits.
b. Portugal State Aid scheme has gained approval, but a public version of the EC decision was not available as of March 2011.

need to support the short-term export credit insurance market and thus use the escape clause within the European Community Treaty.[8] However, 13 EU countries did not intervene. Arguably, the trade credit insurance market is underdeveloped in some of these countries, but this is surely not the case for all of them. For example, no state aid schemes were set up in Italy, Spain, or the United Kingdom, even though these countries were among the top six markets with the highest value of claims paid on short-term export credit insurance (see Morel 2010).

Still, it is questionable whether the countries that did implement state aid schemes were effective in providing cover for export credit risks when private insurance was temporarily unavailable. A few observations can be made.

Delay in State Aid under EU Rules

First, for a number of reasons, public insurance through most of the state aid schemes became available only after the private insurers had reduced their supply. Thus, the state interventions did not mitigate the initial shock to suppliers following the reduction in the supply of private insurance.

As table 11.1 shows, all of the state aid schemes were implemented after the first quarter of 2009 and most of them in the second half of 2009. Understandably, some delay was unavoidable, but EU legislation also delayed the reaction because all state aid schemes needed approval by the European Commission. Given that the European Commission needed about two months to approve a scheme and assuming it took governments an additional month to gather the required information, overall, implementation of the schemes was delayed by about one fiscal quarter because of EU rules. Moreover, most EU governments also needed time to acquire knowledge on how to provide public insurance cover in the short-term trade credit insurance market. The reason is that, since the late 1990s, EU governments no longer provided cover for these "marketable" risks.

Problematical Role for Private Insurers

Second, a number of these schemes, the top-up only variants in particular, depended on implementation by private insurers. For example, the Dutch state aid scheme notes, "The decision whether to provide exporters with top-up cover on an individual basis is left to the discretion of credit insurers."[9]

At the same time, private insurers have stated clearly their concerns with respect to state interventions. In particular, they noted their worries about "[what] the short-term trade credit insurance landscape would look like after a protracted active involvement by governments and that it will be hard to reverse the role of the state once the crisis is over" (ICISA 2009).

All top-up schemes do include a fee for private insurers to cover administration and acquisition costs, but it is questionable whether these fees trigger private insurers to actively promote the availability of public insurance. For one thing, the fees do not compensate for the possible reputation costs to private insurers that might follow from state intervention. Moreover, some of the authorities noted their commitment to monitor the fees and costs incurred by the private insurers to ensure that the management fee does not provide revenues exceeding the costs incurred in running the scheme. In short, it seems somewhat problematic to build an effective state aid scheme that relies on the implementation by private insurers but does not allow them to make a profit.

Varied Effectiveness of State Aid Implementation

Last but not least, although little information is available at this moment, there are indications that the (initial) use of some of the state aid schemes was limited. For example, Denmark and the Netherlands modified their original schemes four months after implementation, arguing that the measure had proven insufficient to adequately provide exporters with the necessary coverage for their sound short-term export credit transactions. Both countries reduced the premium charge and eased other conditions to improve the functioning of the scheme (see table 11.1). The Dutch notification to the European Commission also stated that the total exposure of the scheme at the end of November 2009, two months after implementation, was (only) €5 million–€10 million.[10] In contrast, Germany experienced considerable demand from exporters for the coverage under the public scheme. On a cumulative basis, the total volume of approved limits under the measure amounted to €992 million (in the first seven months of the scheme), and the actual value of insured exports under these limits reached €465 million.

All in all, these preliminary observations call for a more comprehensive evaluation of the various state aid schemes to increase the effectiveness of such measures to support the short-term export credit insurance market in case of future crises. The evidence on the macroeconomic importance of trade credit insurance provided in van der Veer (2010) indicates that it will be worthwhile for governments and the European Commission to do so.

Notes

1. Egger and Url (2006) and Moser, Nestmann, and Wedow (2008) study the effect of public guarantees on Austrian and German exports, respectively, and find long-run multipliers of 2.8 and 1.7.

2. The world estimate is calculated using the 2007 world value of "short term new business insured" from the Berne Union *2010 Yearbook* (Berne Union 2010)—also available online at http://www.berneunion.org.uk/bu-total-data.html—and world exports from the world trade monitor of the CPB Netherlands Bureau for Economic Policy Analysis (http://www.cpb.nl/en/world-trade-monitor). Data from one of the Big Three private insurers reveals that 60 percent of the total value of its turnover on exports in 2007 related to exports from the Euro Area countries (excluding Cyprus, Malta, Portugal, and Slovenia). This share was used to calculate the value of private short-term insured exports from the Euro Area countries.

3. The Berne Union reports short-term export credit insurance new business covering $1.297 trillion in 2008. According to the International Chamber of Commerce, around 25 percent of this business ($324 billion) was covered by ECAs (ICC 2010). Medium- and long-term new business covered $154 billion of exports. Assuming that ECAs accounted for all medium- and long-term insurance (which is probably a slight overestimation), ECAs covered $478 (€325) billion of exports in 2008.

4. The Berne Union figures in Morel (2010) cover private and public short-term credit limits. A similar picture emerges from data from one of the Big Three private credit insurers.

5. Again, Jones (2010) gives a telling example of this link between trade credit insurance and access to bank credit.

6. This insurer is one of the Big Three private credit insurers. Company details are confidential.

7. This information was provided in the respective countries' State Aid Reports with respect to short-term export credit insurance, sent to the European Commission for approval. http://ec .europa.eu/competition/state_aid/register/ii/index.html#by_ms.

8. See point 4.4 of the "Communication of the Commission to the Member States pursuant to Article 93 (1) of the EC Treaty applying Articles 92 and 93 of the Treaty to short-term export-credit insurance." http://eur-lex.europa.eu/LexUriServ/LexUriServ.do?uri=CELEX:31997Y0917(01):EN:HTML.

9. See State Aid N 409/2009, the Netherlands "export credit insurance—reinsurance scheme," at http://ec.europa.eu/competition/state_aid/register/ii/by_case_nr_n2009_0390.html#409.

10. See State Aid N14/2010, the Netherlands "amendment to short term export credit insurance," at http://ec.europa.eu/competition/state_aid/register/ii/by_case_nr_n2010_0000.html#14.

References

Becue, P. 2009. *Handboek Kredietverzekering. De Onzichtbare Bank.* Antwerp: Intersentia.

Berne Union. 2010. *2010 Yearbook.* London: Berne Union. http://www.berneunion.org.uk/pdf/Berne %20Union%20Yearbook%202010.pdf.

Chauffour, J., and T. Farole. 2009. "Trade Finance in Crisis: Market Adjustment or Market Failure?" Policy Research Paper 5003, World Bank, Washington, DC.

Egger, P., and T. Url. 2006. "Public Export Credit Guarantees and Foreign Trade Structure: Evidence from Austria." *The World Economy* 29 (4): 399–418.

Funatsu, H. 1986. "Export Credit Insurance." *Journal of Risk and Insurance* 53 (4): 680–92.

ICC (International Chamber of Commerce). 2010. "Rethinking Trade Finance 2010: An ICC Global Survey." Banking Commission Market Intelligence Report, ICC, Paris.

ICISA (International Credit Insurance and Surety Association). 2009. "State Support Schemes for Short-Term Credit Insurance Business." Speech presented at the Organisation for Economic Co-operation and Development Export Credit Committee meetings, November 18.

Jones, P. M. 2010. "Trade Credit Insurance." Primer Series on Insurance Issue 15, World Bank, Washington, DC. http://siteresources.worldbank.org/FINANCIALSECTOR/Resources/Primer15 _TradeCreditInsurance_Final.pdf.

Morel, Fabrice. 2010. "Credit Insurance in Support of International Trade: Observations throughout the Crisis." Export credit insurance report, Berne Union, London. http://www.berneunion.org.uk/ pdf/Credit%20insurance%20in%20support%20of%20international%20trade.pdf.

Moser, C., T. Nestmann, and M. Wedow. 2008. "Political Risk and Export Promotion: Evidence from Germany." *The World Economy* 31 (6): 781–803.

Swiss Re. 2006. "Credit Insurance and Surety: Solidifying Commitments." *sigma* No. 6/2006, Zurich. http://media.swissre.com/documents/sigma6_2006_en.pdf.

Van der Veer, K. J. M. 2010. "The Private Credit Insurance Effect on Trade." DNB Working Paper 264, Netherlands Central Bank, Amsterdam.

TRADE FINANCE IN THE RECOVERY OF TRADE RELATIONS AFTER BANKING CRISES

Cosimo Beverelli, Madina Kukenova, and
Nadia Rocha

Trade finance may help explain not only the business cycle but also the eventual recovery of trade relations. The size of exports and exporting experience matter in the recovery of trade relations after banking crises. However, experience seems to matter more, especially in financially dependent sectors.

Using highly disaggregated U.S. import data, this chapter provides evidence on the impact of past and current banking crises on the duration of trade relations. It also investigates how product-level characteristics affect the recovery time of export relations after banking crises and whether such product characteristics affect recovery differently in long- and short-term financially dependent sectors.

International trade has been rapidly recovering after a 12.2 percent fall in 2009—the biggest fall in 70 years. The World Trade Organization forecast a 13.5 percent rise in 2010 over the previous year.[1] Additional evidence indicates that when recovery occurs, it occurs fast; most of the relations that recover after a banking crisis do so within two years, as table 12.1 shows.[2] Because recovery is well under way, it is as important as it is timely to draw lessons from past crises

---

The opinions expressed in this paper should be attributed to the authors. They are not meant to represent the positions or opinions of the World Trade Organization (WTO) and its members and are without prejudice to members' rights and obligations under the WTO.

Table 12.1 Recovery Time after Banking Crises, 1996–2009

Recovery time (years)	Number of products	% of products
1	3,640	49.48
2	1,193	16.22
3	695	9.45
4	444	6.04
5	387	5.26
6	278	3.78
7	220	2.99
8	199	2.70
9	132	1.79
10	90	1.22
11	57	0.77
12	22	0.30
Total	7,357	100.00

Source: Authors' calculations based on recovery dataset.
Note: The recovery dataset contains information only on export relations that exit during a banking crisis. The sample consists of 13,055 products, of which 7,357 reentered the U.S. export market and 5,698 did not. "Recovery time" is defined as the number of years it takes to reenter the U.S. export market after the banking crisis–induced exit.

about the factors that affect the probability of resuming trade relations that have been interrupted by the crisis.

The authors seek to answer the following questions: Which trade relations recover first? And what distinguishes these fast-recovering relations? Is it the level of financial dependence of the sector they belong to? Or do product-level characteristics matter?

Using data on product-level exports to the United States, this chapter analyzes how banking crises affect trade relations.[3] Several studies have highlighted the importance of product-, sector-, and country-level variables in determining survival rates (Besedes and Prusa 2006a, 2006b; Besedes 2007; Brenton, Saborowski, and von Uexkull 2009; Fugazza and Molina 2009; Volpe-Martincus and Carballo 2009).

The work presented here is innovative because it estimates how a banking crisis in an exporting country affects the survival of its export relations—which, to the best of the authors' knowledge, has not been addressed elsewhere. The study is related, though, to the firm-level literature that links credit access to export performance. Manova, Wei, and Zhang (2009) show that less-credit-constrained firms (foreign-owned firms and joint ventures) have better export performance than private domestic firms in China, and this effect is amplified in financially vulnerable sectors. Muûls (2008) shows that liquidity-constrained firms in Belgium are less likely to become exporters and, conditional on trading, they sell fewer products to fewer destinations. Also, Berman and Héricourt (2008) present similar results from a sample of 5,000 firms in nine developing and emerging economies.

Another original contribution of this work is the study of the determinants of recovery of trade relations that have been hit by a banking crisis. The novel result presented in this chapter is that, while both size and experience matter for recovery of trade relations after banking crises, experience has the greater significance, especially in financially dependent sectors. This outcome is consistent with some new empirical literature showing that not all exporting firms are the same and that firms that export for longer periods exhibit certain characteristics that differentiate them from sporadic exporters (Borgersen 2006; Álvarez 2007; Álvarez, Faruq, and López 2009). In this context, it is intuitive that, independent of size, those products that have been exported for longer periods are the ones that will have the least difficulty in recovering after a negative shock such as a banking crisis.

Trade Survival after Banking Crises

The authors collected annual product-level exports, disaggregated at the Harmonized System (HS) 10-digit level, from 157 countries to the United States between 1996 and 2009. The dataset provides information on the duration of each export relation, making it amenable to survival analysis. In this dataset, on average, 23 percent of trade relations were interrupted by a banking crisis between 1996 and 2008, as shown in table 12.2.

A simple graphical analysis confirms that banking crises negatively affect survival of trade. The Kaplan-Meier survival estimates shown in figure 12.1 suggest that trade relations hit by a banking crisis exhibit lower survival rates than trade relations not hit by a banking crisis.

The study also explores the effect of a banking crisis on the survival of export relations using a Cox proportional hazard model, as shown in table 12.3.

Estimates are expressed in terms of hazard ratios, with a hazard ratio greater than 1 indicating an increase in hazard and shorter duration, therefore meaning that an export relation is less likely to survive. The analysis indicates that a banking crisis raises the hazard ratio, thereby increasing the probability that a trade relation is interrupted by more than 11 percent (column [1], table 12.3). This outcome is in line with the stylized fact that banking crises negatively affect the survival of export relations.

In addition, control variables such as the total number of suppliers and the total value of product exports have a positive impact on the probability of survival. This result is consistent with the results of the literature of trade survival, in which both the extensive and the intensive margins of competition positively affect survival. Also, the coefficient on demand shock presents an expected sign, implying that positive demand shocks reduce the probability of exit (however, this

Table 12.2 Survival of Trade Relations after Banking Crises, 1996–2008

Country	Year of crisis[a]	Total relations (number)	Relations destroyed (number)[b]	Relations destroyed (%)
Argentina	2001	2,534	636	25
Belgium	2008	6,596	1,450	22
Bulgaria	1996	726	246	34
China	1998	9,382	949	10
Colombia	1998	2,239	573	26
Czech Republic	1996	2,382	610	26
Denmark	2008	11,116	1,128	10
Dominican Republic	2003	2,210	494	22
Ecuador	1998	1,059	321	30
United Kingdom	2008	10,585	1,350	13
Honduras	1998	573	180	31
Iceland	2008	610	235	39
Indonesia	1997	3,619	649	18
Ireland	2008	3,280	833	25
Jamaica	1996	786	245	31
Japan	1997	10,014	985	10
Korea, Rep.	1997	7,013	1,118	16
Malaysia	1997	3,420	721	21
Nicaragua	2000	386	96	25
Netherlands	2008	6,856	1,295	19
Philippines	1997	3,334	704	21
Russian Federation	1998	2,415	667	28
Slovak Republic	1998	807	263	33
Thailand	1997	4,632	870	19
Turkey	2000	3,323	693	21
Ukraine	1998	752	235	31
Uruguay	2002	715	171	24
Vietnam	1997	825	186	23
Yemen, Rep.	1996	23	5	22

Source: Authors' calculations based on survival dataset.
a. The data refer to systemic banking crises between 1995 and 2008 in countries exporting to the United States. "Banking crisis," as defined by Laeven and Valencia (2008), includes all the crises since 1996 from their dataset as well as the 2008 crisis episodes in Belgium, Germany, Iceland, Ireland, Luxembourg, the Netherlands, and the United Kingdom. Each of those countries has experienced the failure of an important banking institution, including Fortis Bank in the Benelux countries, Hypo in Germany, Icesafe in Iceland, Bank of Ireland in Ireland, and Northern Rock in the United Kingdom.
b. The survival analysis uses a database with a total of 921,960 spells. The dataset contains information on the dates of exit and reentry of products into the U.S. export market. Relations considered "destroyed" are all those that had been active the year before the crisis and turned inactive in the year of the crisis.

Figure 12.1 Survival of Trade Relations after Banking Crises

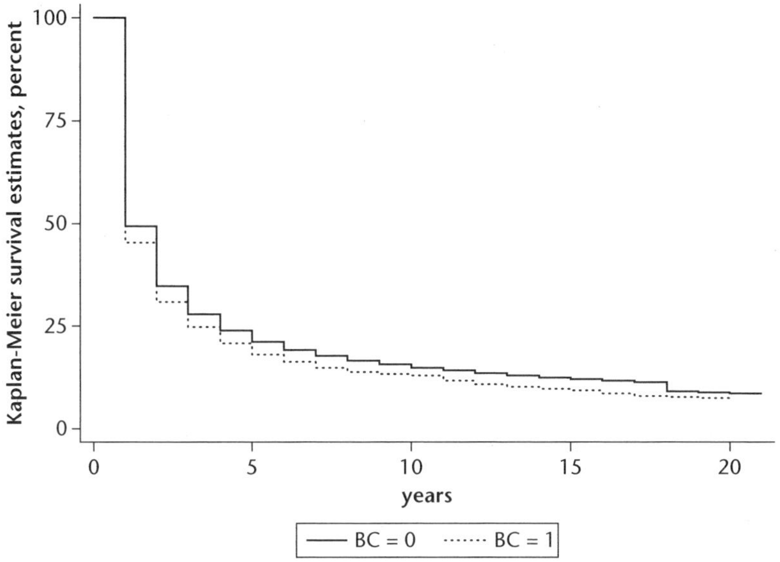

Source: Authors' calculations based on survival dataset.
Note: BC = banking crisis.

Table 12.3 Effect of Banking Crises on Trade Relations Survival
Cox proportional hazard estimates

Variables	BC (1-year length) (1)	BC (1-year length) (2)	BC (2-year length) (3)
Banking crisis	1.112*** [0.013]	1.133*** [0.013]	1.052*** [0.013]
Exports at spell end		0.906*** [0.001]	0.906*** [0.001]
Number of suppliers at spell end	0.990*** [0.000]	0.988*** [0.000]	0.988*** [0.000]
Total product exports at spell end	0.966*** [0.001]	0.992*** [0.001]	0.992*** [0.001]
Demand shock	0.991** [0.003]	0.993** [0.003]	0.994* [0.003]
Number of previous spells	0.951*** [0.002]	0.945*** [0.002]	0.944*** [0.002]
Observations	921,960	921,960	889,208

Source: Authors' calculations based on survival dataset.
Note: BC = banking crisis. Standard errors (in brackets) are clustered by country and by International Standard Industrial Classification (ISIC) three-digit industry. Sample is stratified by country, ISIC three-digit industry, and year.
***$p < 0.01$ **$p < 0.05$ *$p < 0.1$.

coefficient is not significant in most of the regressions). Size increases survival as well. However, its inclusion does not affect the banking crisis (BC) coefficient; to the contrary, it rises marginally.[4]

Neither the Laeven and Valencia (2008) dataset used for systemic banking crises nor other similar datasets provide systematic information on the final date of banking crises. Therefore, the previous regressions have assumed a common duration of one year for all banking crises. The replicated estimation considers that the effect of a banking crisis lasts two years instead of one year (column [3], table 12.3). The banking crisis coefficient is still positive and significant, although it is reduced by more than half. One intuition for this result is that, for a significant number of products, exports were resumed one year after a banking crisis (see table 12.1). Hence, the assumption that banking crises last for two years would suggest that those products never exited the export markets.

Alternative estimation techniques, such as linear probability and Probit models, have been used to check the validity of the previous results. In these models, the dependent variable is a dichotomous variable equal to 1 if an export relation is interrupted. Results, available under request, show that a banking crisis increases the probability of exit, as was found in the Cox regression. In addition, both size and experience reduce the probability of exit.[5] This outcome is in line with studies such as Brenton, Saborowski, and von Uexkull (2009), which show that initial size of an export flow, as well as exporting experience, positively affect survival.[6]

Time for Trade Recovery after Banking Crises

From the subsample of trade relations interrupted by a banking crisis in the exporting country, it is also observable that experience (defined as the number of years a relation was active before a banking crisis) unambiguously helps firms to recover faster. Specifically, 58 percent of the products exported for 18 years preceding the crisis reentered the export markets after 1 year, while only 17 percent of the products exported for 1 year reentered the market after 1 year, as table 12.4 shows.

Another way to visualize this is with Kaplan-Meier survival estimates. In figure 12.2, products have been ranked in three quantiles by experience level. The relations in the third quantile (more-experienced relations) recover faster than those in the second and first quantiles, respectively.

Size, however, does not matter as much as experience for recovery. In figure 12.3, products have been ranked in quantiles according to the size of the relation, measured as value of exports at the spell (that is, the time during which a product was exported) that ended with the crisis. This figure shows only limited evidence that bigger relations recover faster.

Table 12.4 Recovery Time, by Experience Level

Experience (years)	Total number of products	Product reentry after 1 year (number)	Product reentry after 1 year (%)
1	3,939	654	17
2	1,978	512	26
3	1,371	377	27
4	986	307	31
5	795	237	30
6	707	245	35
7	554	165	30
8	385	119	31
9	364	104	29
10	368	125	34
11	351	139	40
12	350	126	36
13	263	100	38
14	221	96	43
15	196	94	48
16	172	77	45
17	159	75	47
18	151	88	58

Source: Authors' calculations based on survival dataset.

Trade finance does not seem to affect the recovery of trade relations after a banking crisis. Put another way, different measures of short- and long-term sectoral financial dependence do not matter unconditionally for the recovery of trade relations.[7] A possible explanation for this result is the existence of significant product-level heterogeneity within sectors.[8]

Intuitively, even within sectors highly dependent on external finance, some products are likely to be affected more adversely than others by banking crises. Statistical analysis shows that measures of sectoral financial dependence have an experience-specific effect on the recovery of export relations. Consider, for instance, the unconditional survival estimates graphed in figure 12.4.[9]

Within the group of experienced relations (products with experience belonging to the third quantile), the survival function is lower in sectors of external financial dependence (EFD; EFD equal to 1) than in non-EFD sectors (EFD equal to 0). This implies that, in the former sector type, more-experienced trade relations reenter faster than those in the latter sector type. This pattern is reversed for less-experienced relations (products in the first and second quantiles). In fact, for this

Figure 12.2 Recovery of Trade Relations, by Experience Level

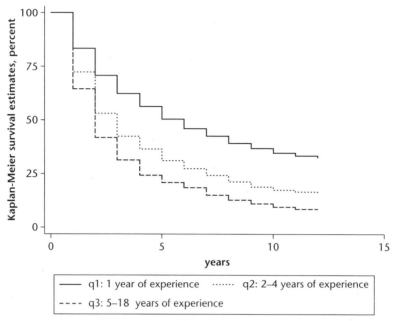

Source: Authors' calculations based on recovery dataset.
Note: q = quantile. In the graph, higher survival rates imply longer periods of inactivity, therefore a lower probability of reentry.

set of products, the survival function is higher in EFD sectors (EFD equal to 1) than in non-EFD sectors (EFD equal to 0). In contrast, as observable in figure 12.5, there is no clear descriptive evidence indicating effects of size heterogeneity, neither in financially dependent sectors nor in non-financially dependent ones.[10]

The effect of size and experience on time to recovery has been estimated using a duration model. In this case, duration refers to the time during which a trade relation has been inactive or, in other words, the number of years between the crisis-related exit and the restart of exporting (see annex 12.1 for details). Both experience and size increase the probability of recovering by 5.8 percent and 2.7 percent, respectively (columns [1] and [2], table 12.5).

The analysis also suggests that both the number of suppliers at reentry and the total exports of a certain product at reentry have a positive effect on the probability of recovery. These results indicate the presence of a pro-competitive effect at both the extensive and the intensive margins of competition. Finally, in all regressions, the higher the frequency with which a product has exited and entered the export market, the lower the probability of recovery.

Figure 12.3 Recovery of Trade Relations, by Size

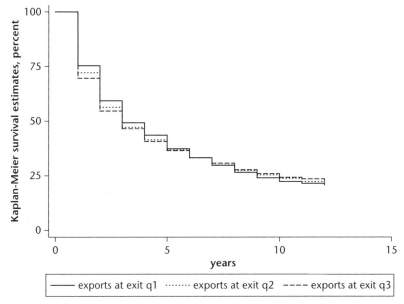

Source: Authors' calculations based on recovery dataset.
Note: q = quantile. In the graph, higher survival rates imply longer periods of inactivity, therefore a lower probability of reentry. From the graph, it might seem that the variable size is not constant across time. This is controlled for in the regressions by stratifying the sample (see annex 12.1).

A possible intuition for this result is as follows: relationships with multiple spells before the crisis might be low-productivity ones, with productivity levels close to the cutoff that makes exporting profitable. These trade flows will therefore tend to reenter later than single-spell flows after a banking crisis.

The previous regressions have been replicated, with the inclusion of a set of variables that capture sectoral financial dependence (table 12.6). The regressions do not show that the indicators of financial dependence have a significant effect.

Table 12.7 presents an examination of whether such variables, despite not being significant *per se*, have an experience-specific effect. To do this, the Cox proportional model has been reestimated separately for each of the three groups of export experience.

Reading across columns, it is possible to observe that the coefficients of both long-term EFD and trade credit dependence (TCD) change across quantiles, implying that there is indeed an experience-specific effect. Specifically, although for least-experienced products financial dependence has a negative impact on the

Figure 12.4 Experience, Trade Credit Dependence, and Recovery of Trade Relations

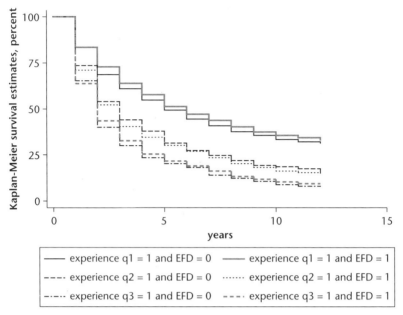

Source: Authors' calculations based on recovery database.
Note: q = quantile. EFD = external finance dependence. In the graph, higher survival rates imply longer periods of inactivity, therefore a lower probability of reentry.

time to recovery, more-experienced ones reenter faster in financially dependent sectors. The sign and the magnitude of the other explanatory variables do not vary significantly across different groups of export experience.[11]

An alternative approach—to investigate whether financial dependence has a product-specific effect—is presented in table 12.8. Both long-term financial dependence and trade credit variables are interacted with the two different groups of exporting experience and the size of exports, respectively. The results confirm that, in both long- and short-term financially dependent sectors, products with more experience recover faster than products with less experience (see columns [1] and [2]). In contrast, there is no clear evidence indicating the effects of size heterogeneity on the time to recover, neither in financially dependent sectors nor in non-financially dependent ones (see columns [3] and [4]).

Because the interpretation of interaction terms is not an easy task in Cox proportional models, similar regressions have been performed using both a linear probability model (LPM) and a Tobit model, as shown in table 12.9.

Figure 12.5 Size, Trade Credit Dependence, and Recovery of Trade Relations

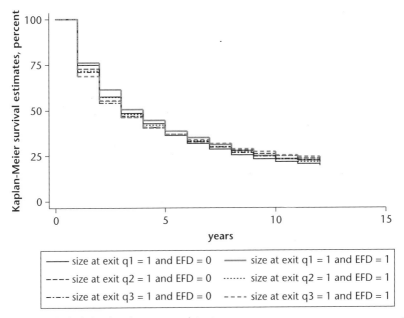

Source: Authors' calculations based on recovery dataset.
Note: q = quantile. EFD = external finance dependence. In the graph, higher survival rates imply longer periods of inactivity, therefore a lower probability of reentry.

Table 12.5 Recovery Time, by Exporter Characteristic
Cox proportional hazard estimates

Variables	(1)	(2)
Years of experience at exit	1.058***	
	[0.005]	
Exports at exit		1.027***
		[0.008]
Number of suppliers at reentry	1.032***	1.034***
	[0.002]	[0.002]
Total product exports at reentry	1.020**	1.019**
	[0.008]	[0.008]
Number of previous spells	1.032**	1.090***
	[0.013]	[0.015]
Observations	13,055	13,055

Source: Authors' calculations based on recovery dataset.
Note: q = quantile. Standard errors (in brackets) are clustered by country and by ISIC three-digit industry level. The sample is stratified by country and by ISIC three-digit industry level.
***$p < 0.01$ **$p < 0.05$ *$p < 0.1$.

Table 12.6 Recovery Time and Financial Dependence
Cox proportional hazard estimates

Variables	(1)	(2)
Years of experience at exit	1.064***	1.069***
	[0.004]	[0.005]
Exports at exit	1.023***	1.020***
	[0.007]	[0.007]
EFD	0.986	
	[0.034]	
TCD		0.953
		[0.033]
Observations	12,928	11,628

Source: Authors' calculations based on recovery dataset.
Note: EFD = external financial dependence. TCD = trade credit dependence. Standard errors (in brackets) are clustered by country and by ISIC three-digit industry level. The sample is stratified by country and by ISIC three-digit industry level. Other controls: total product exports at reentry, total number of suppliers at reentry, demand shock, and number of previous spells.
***$p < 0.01$ **$p < 0.05$ *$p < 0.1$.

Table 12.7 Recovery Time and Financial Dependence
Cox proportional hazard estimates with group varying characteristics

	Experience q_1	Experience q_2	Experience q_3	Experience q_1	Experience q_2	Experience q_3
Variables	(1)	(2)	(3)	(4)	(5)	(6)
Exports at exit	1.014	1.024**	1.022**	1.002	1.023**	1.024**
	[0.013]	[0.011]	[0.010]	[0.013]	[0.011]	[0.010]
EFD	0.893*	1.017	1.066*			
	[0.055]	[0.049]	[0.041]			
TCD				0.844***	0.987	1.053
				[0.053]	[0.050]	[0.043]
Observations	3,744	4,257	4,927	3,253	3,861	4,514

Source: Authors' calculations based on recovery dataset.
Note: EFD = external financial dependence. TCD = trade credit dependence. Standard errors (in brackets) are clustered by country and by ISIC three-digit industry level. The sample is stratified by country. Other controls: total product exports at reentry, total number of suppliers at reentry, demand shock, and number of previous spells.
***$p < 0.01$ **$p < 0.05$ *$p < 0.1$.

For both methodologies, the dependent variable is the number of years it takes for an export relation to reenter the foreign markets after a banking crisis. In addition, the latter model takes into account that some export relations are right censored and, hence, have not resumed yet.[12] As in the Cox proportional model, both experience and size decrease the time to recover. However, the effect of experience

Table 12.8 Financial Dependence, Exporter Characteristics, and Recovery
Cox proportional hazard estimates

Variables	FD = EFD (1)	FD = TCD (2)	FD = EFD (3)	FD = TCD (4)
Exports at exit	1.022*** [0.007]	1.020*** [0.007]		
Years of experience at exit q_2	1.322*** [0.060]	1.354*** [0.060]		
Years of experience at exit q_3	1.635*** [0.085]	1.693*** [0.093]		
FD	0.894** [0.051]	0.857*** [0.050]	0.98 [0.044]	0.977 [0.044]
Years of experience at exit $q_2 \times$ FD	1.129** [0.065]	1.135** [0.067]		
Years of experience at exit $q_3 \times$ FD	1.216*** [0.082]	1.256*** [0.091]		
Years of experience at exit			1.064*** [0.004]	1.069*** [0.005]
Exports at exit q_2			1.017 [0.041]	1.036 [0.040]
Exports at exit q_3			1.105** [0.046]	1.130*** [0.047]
Exports at exit $q_2 \times$ FD			1.034 [0.054]	0.994 [0.054]
Exports at exit $q_3 \times$ FD			0.993 [0.059]	0.931 [0.055]
Observations	12,928	11,628	12,928	11,628

Source: Authors' calculations based on recovery dataset.
Note: EFD = external financial dependence. FD = financial dependence. TCD = trade credit dependence. q = quantile. Standard errors (in brackets) are clustered by country and by ISIC three-digit industry level. The sample stratified by country. Other controls: total product exports at reentry, total number of suppliers at reentry, demand shock, number of previous spells, exports at exit (in columns [1] and [2]), and years of experience at exit (in columns [3] and [4]).
***$p < 0.01$ **$p < 0.05$ *$p < 0.1$.

is always higher. In addition, from columns (1)–(4), it is possible to conclude that more-experienced exporters enter first in financially dependent sectors. Once again, as shown in columns (5)–(8), the interaction between exports' size and long- and short-term financial dependence, respectively, is not significant.

From the previous results, it is possible to conclude that, independent of size, products with more years of experience might have a greater advantage in obtaining external finance, thereby recovering faster after a banking crisis.[13]

The results are in line with empirical studies on banks' lending behavior (for example, Petersen and Rajan 1994). They show that a firm's age and the duration

Table 12.9 Financial Dependence, Exporter Characteristics, and Recovery
OLS and Tobit estimates

Variables	OLS (1)	Tobit (2)	OLS (3)	Tobit (4)	OLS (5)	Tobit (6)	OLS (7)	Tobit (8)
Years of experience at exit	-0.208*** [0.024]	-0.443*** [0.044]	-0.230*** [0.025]	-0.488*** [0.046]	-0.266*** [0.020]	-0.542*** [0.036]	-0.289*** [0.021]	-0.590*** [0.039]
Exports at exit	-0.146*** [0.031]	-0.223*** [0.056]	-0.133*** [0.032]	-0.196*** [0.057]	-0.178*** [0.046]	-0.269*** [0.081]	-0.175*** [0.043]	-0.255*** [0.076]
EFD	0.311 [0.442]	0.626 [0.732]			-0.736 [0.748]	-0.958 [1.284]		
TCD			0.765*** [0.281]	1.177** [0.481]			-0.478 [0.622]	-0.681 [1.088]
Years of experience at exit × EFD	-0.104*** [0.030]	-0.178*** [0.050]						
Years of experience at exit × TCD			-0.117*** [0.030]	-0.197*** [0.049]				
Exports at exit × EFD					0.053 [0.062]	0.072 [0.107]		
Exports at exit × TCD							0.073 [0.062]	0.099 [0.109]
Observations	12,928	12,928	11,628	11,628	12,928	12,928	11,628	11,628
R-squared	0.283		0.284		0.282		0.282	

Source: Authors' calculations based on recovery dataset.
Note: OLS = ordinary least squares. EFD = external financial dependence. TCD = trade credit dependence. Standard errors (in brackets) are clustered by country and by ISIC three-digit industry level. The sample is stratified by country. All regressions include country and sector fixed effects (ISIC three-digit). Other controls: total product exports at reentry, total number of suppliers at reentry, demand shock, and number of previous spells.
***$p < 0.01$ **$p < 0.05$ *$p < 0.1$.

of its relationship with the financing bank are important determinants of the cost of financing. In light of this evidence, it is not surprising that after a banking crisis—when banks face a lack of liquidity, requiring them to restrict credit—only well-established and better-known firms are likely to get access to credit from the banks, being able to cover some of the cost of producing and exporting.

Policy Implications

The effect of a banking crisis on different export sectors and products is an important consideration for policy makers as they try to mitigate financial shocks. This chapter, based on disaggregated data at the product level, helps derive important implications relevant to policy makers.

First, banking crises seem to hit more-productive exporters less adversely than less-productive exporters. In line with expectations, small and less-experienced exporters may not be productive enough to overcome a sharp drop in foreign demand and, more important, they may also be more affected by short- or long-term credit restrictions. In the first case, small exporters might lack sufficient collateral or credit guarantees; in the second case, exporters with less experience have not yet built their reputations. In both cases, the policy implication is that if the objective is to reduce exit of trade relations, the target for policy support should be relatively small and inexperienced exporters.

Second, although on average size and experience have a significant impact on the recovery after banking crises, only the latter matters for the recovery of products belonging to industries that are highly dependent on external finance. Consistent with the idea that within-sector heterogeneity matters, this analysis finds that long- and short-term sectoral financial dependence has an experience-specific effect. In particular, more experienced exporters reenter faster in financially dependent sectors. This result has important policy implications: for instance, if the objective is to help trade recover faster after financial disruption, relatively inexperienced exporters should be targeted to restart foreign operations, independent of their size.

Annex 12.1: Methodology

The empirical analysis is divided in two main parts. First, the authors estimate a duration model à la Besedes and Prusa (2004) to study how trade relations are affected in times of crisis. Second, always using a duration model but this time only for those products that exited with a banking crisis, the authors analyze how certain exporter and sectoral characteristics affect the time to recover after banking crises.[14]

Except when otherwise indicated in the explanatory note below each table, the estimations are stratified by exporting country and three-digit International Standard Industrial Classification (ISIC) industry level[15]—this to allow for a different hazard function for each country and sector, respectively. In addition, standard errors are clustered by sector (ISIC three-digit) and country to allow for intraindustry and country correlation in the error terms.

The main explanatory variable for the survival analysis is a banking crisis dichotomous variable, which takes the value of 1 in those years in which a certain country has experienced a banking crisis. In addition, a common set of control variables is included in all regressions. First, variables such as the total number of countries exporting a certain product to the United States and the total value of product exports, respectively, serve as controls for the extensive and intensive margins of competition. Second, to control for the fact that the banking crisis variable might be capturing a deterioration of demand in the destination country, a product-specific measure of the growth of U.S. imports is introduced.

With respect to recovery, the authors test whether the size and experience of export relations at the time of exit affect the number of years it takes to reenter the export market. In addition, to analyze whether products that exit the export market during a crisis recover at different speeds, according to the sectors to which they belong, the authors also include an interaction term between long- and short-term financial dependence indicators and product characteristics. In this case, too, the total number of countries exporting a certain product to the United States and the total value of product exports are included as controls. Because it is not possible to compute these control variables for the subsample of products where exports have never resumed, their averages are calculated between the first year after the banking crisis and either the year of reentry or the last year of the sample, depending on whether exports have resumed.

Some econometric issues related to this empirical methodology are common to all duration models. First and most important, in the survival analysis, the authors do not want to artificially record a banking crisis that occurred during a trade relation as happening at the beginning or at the end of its duration. This problem is solved by splitting each export relationship at the time of the banking crisis and assuming that the crisis lasts for one year.

Second, for some export relations, it might be impossible to accurately observe their beginning or their ending. Whether an export relation that is first observed at time t actually started at time $s < t$ (left censoring) is unknown. Also unknown is whether an export relation that is last observed at time T was interrupted at T or continued after it (right censoring). To control for left censoring, variables are constructed using trade data from 1991 until 2009. However, the spells that started in the initial five years of the dataset (1991–95) are excluded from estimations. The Cox model controls for right censoring.

Third, there are products that exit more than once (multiple spells). The general approach of the literature to control for multiple spells in duration models is to include in the regressions a multiple spell dummy equal to 1 if the relation has at least one exit during the sample period. However, to control for the fact that multiple spells are time-varying within a relation, a different definition of multiple spell is considered, with the construction of a variable equal to the number of spells before time t. This approach, the authors believe, is theoretically more correct than the standard approach of the literature because it does not consider a relation to be characterized by multiple spells until its first observed reentry, but only after it.[16]

Due to the high level of disaggregation of the dataset, throughout all the analysis the assumption is that there is a representative firm for each trade relation. This allows the analysis to refer to "experience" and "size" as two measures of heterogeneity among exporters. Because size and experience are not the same (in the sample, the correlation is 0.19), they capture different characteristics of exporters.

Notes

1. The World Bank's forecast is 15.7 percent, and the Organisation for Economic Co-operation and Development's forecast is 12.3 percent.

2. Using data on U.S. imports at the Harmonized System (HS) 10-digit level of disaggregation from 157 countries between 1995 and 2009, the authors have extrapolated all relations that were interrupted at the occurrence of a banking crisis in the exporting country.

3. The authors chose the United States as the destination country because the original trade data used (from the Global Trade Atlas and the Center of International Data at the University of California, Davis) contains information at the 10-digit level of disaggregation only for trade flows in and out the United States.

4. After inclusion in the regression of the market share of a product to control for product heterogeneity, results do not change.

5. The variable experience cannot be included in a Cox regression because it is highly correlated with the duration of a spell, which is the conditioning variable in duration models.

6. The effect of experience should be interpreted with caution, since it captures both the negative duration effect (the fact that the probability of exit decreases the longer a product has been in the market) and the presence effect (learning by exporting). The authors are only interested in the latter effect, which has an economic interpretation.

7. The indicator of long-term external financial dependence (EFD) comes from Rajan & Zingales (1998) and is computed at International Standard Industrial Classification (ISIC) three-digit industry level. For short-term financial dependence, we use trade credit dependence (TCD) from Levchenko, Lewis, and Tesar (2009), computed at the North American Industry Classification System (NAICS) four-digit level (the original measure is from Fisman and Love [2003]). In the data, the correlation between EFD and TCD is very high and equal to 0.7.

8. For a similar approach, see Besedes (2007), section 3.3.2.

9. Similar results can be shown when using trade credit dependence (TCD).

10. From figure 12.5, it might seem that the variable size is not constant across time. This is controlled for in the regressions by stratifying the sample (see annex 12.1).

11. A Cox regression was also estimated for different groups of export size. The results, available under request, show that neither the financial dependence variable nor the other control variables have a size-specific effect.

12. In the sample, the maximum value of time to recover is 12 years. The assumption is that the products that have not reentered the export market yet will enter after 15 years. Another assumption is that they enter after 20 or 30 years and results do not change.

13. To sharpen these conclusions, the authors are planning to perform the same analysis using firm-level data.

14. The estimated regression is a stratified Cox proportional hazard model of the form $h_c(t, x, \beta)$ = $h_{c0}(t) \exp(x'\beta)$, where x denotes a series of explanatory variables and β is the vector of coefficients to be estimated. The baseline hazard $h_{c0}(t)$ represents how the hazard function changes with time and differs for each strata of the sample.

15. When sector-specific variables are included in the regression, the sample is not stratified by sector.

16. Alternatively, a multiple spell dummy equal to 1 if the relation that is interrupted at time t has at least one exit at time $s < t$ has been included. Results are qualitatively the same.

References

Álvarez, Roberto. 2007. "Explaining Export Success: Firm Characteristics and Spillover Effects." *World Development* 35 (3): 377–93.

Álvarez, R., Hasan Faruq, and Ricardo López. 2009. "New Products in Export Markets: Learning from Experience and Learning from Others." Unpublished manuscript, Indiana University, Indianapolis. https://editorialexpress.com/cgi-bin/conference/download.cgi?db_name=MWM2009&paper_id=153.

Berman, Nicolas, and Jérôme Héricourt. 2008. "Financial Factors and the Margins of Trade: Evidence from Cross-Country Firm-Level Data." Postprint and working papers, Université Paris1 Panthéon-Sorbonne, Paris.

Besedes, Tibor. 2007. "A Search Cost Perspective on Duration of Trade." Departmental Working Paper 2006-12, Department of Economics, Louisiana State University, Baton Rouge.

Besedes, Tibor, and Thomas J. Prusa. 2004. "Surviving the U.S. Import Market: The Role of Product Differentiation." Working Paper 10319, National Bureau of Economic Research, Cambridge, MA.

———. 2006a. "Ins, Outs, and the Duration of Trade." *Canadian Journal of Economics* 39 (1): 266–95.

———. 2006b. "Product Differentiation and Duration of U.S. Import Trade." *Journal of International Economics* 70 (2): 339–58.

Borgersen, T-A. 2006. "When Experience Matters: The Export Performance of Developing Countries' SMEs." *Journal of Sustainable Development in Africa* 8 (1): 106–18.

Brenton, Paul, Christian Saborowski, and Erik von Uexkull. 2009. "What Explains the Low Survival Rate of Developing Country Export Flows?" Policy Research Working Paper 4951, World Bank, Washington, DC.

Center for International Data. Import and Export databases. University of California, Davis. http://cid.econ.ucdavis.edu.

Fisman, Raymond, and Inessa Love. 2003. "Financial Dependence and Growth Revisited." Working Paper 9582, National Bureau of Economic Research, Cambridge, MA.

Fugazza, Marco, and Ana Cristina Molina. 2009. "The Determinants of Trade Survival." Working Paper 05-2009, Graduate Institute, Geneva.

Global Trade Atlas (database). Global Trade Information Services, Columbia, SC. http://www.gtis.com/GTA.

Laeven, Luc, and Fabian Valencia. 2008. "Systemic Banking Crises: A New Database." Working Paper 08/224, International Monetary Fund, Washington, DC.

Levchenko, Andrei A., Logan Lewis, and Linda L. Tesar. 2009. "The Collapse of International Trade during the 2008–2009 Crisis: In Search of the Smoking Gun." Working Paper 592, Research Seminar in International Economics, University of Michigan, Ann Arbor.

Manova, Kalina, Shang-Jin Wei, and Zhiwei Zhang. 2009. "Firm Exports and Multinational Activity under Credit Constraints." Unpublished working paper, Stanford University, Palo Alto, CA.

Muûls, Mirabelle. 2008. "Exporters and Credit Constraints: A Firm-Level Approach." Research series 200809-22, National Bank of Belgium, Brussels.

Petersen, Mitchell A., and Raghuram G. Rajan. 1994. "The Effect of Credit Market Competition on Lending Relationships." Working Paper 4921, National Bureau of Economic Research, Cambridge, MA.

Rajan, Raghuram G., and Luigi Zingales. 1998. "Financial Dependence and Growth." *American Economic Review* 88 (3): 559–86.

Volpe-Martincus, Christian, and Jerónimo Carballo. 2009. "Survival of New Exporters in Developing Countries: Does It Matter How They Diversify?" Working Paper 140, Inter-American Development Bank, Washington, DC.

UNDERPINNINGS OF TRADE FINANCE INTERVENTION DURING FINANCIAL CRISES

THE THEORETICAL CASE FOR TRADE FINANCE IN A LIQUIDITY CRISIS

Tore Ellingsen and Jonas Vlachos

The economic crisis of 2008 was characterized by a severe contraction of credit, and the contraction appeared to hit the trade finance sector particularly hard. Is there a theoretical case for policy intervention to boost trade finance in such a liquidity crisis?[1]

The main argument presented here in favor of trade finance intervention during a liquidity crisis is that it mitigates the problems that arise when firms hoard cash. When cash hoarding occurs, funding for interfirm transactions has greater social value than other funding because borrowers cannot hoard trade finance. Thus, the reasons for promoting trade finance are stronger than for promoting credit in general.

Although these arguments pertain to both domestic and international trade finance, they are arguably stronger in the international context. Because international loan enforcement is weaker than domestic enforcement, sellers are less willing to keep international loans on their books, and it is the seller's insistence on immediate payment that creates the demand for liquidity in the first place.

The authors thank Jean-Pierre Chauffour, Tom Farole, and Leora Klapper for very helpful comments. This text was previously published as T. Ellingsen, and J. Vlachos "Trade Finance in a Liquidity Crisis" (Policy Research Working Paper 5136, World Bank, Washington, DC).

A Theory of Trade Finance

Trade finance, broadly defined, is any financial arrangement connected to interfirm commercial transactions. By this definition, extension of ordinary trade credit is an example of trade finance. A narrow definition of trade finance is the funding of individual international commercial transactions by financial intermediaries.

Even under the broader definition, trade finance phenomenon is puzzling at first glance. Why do firms that do not specialize in financial intermediation extend credit to other firms? A common explanation is that firms in a business relationship acquire information about each other that would be expensive (or even impossible) for banks to obtain. Although plausible, the basic monitoring rationale does not explain why trade finance is provided almost exclusively in-kind; if the monitoring advantage is so great, why don't firms also lend cash to each other?

One explanation for this pattern is that firms with access to funding to buy illiquid assets are less tempted to engage in activities that are undesirable from the investors' point of view (Burkart and Ellingsen 2004). Because in-kind credit is expensive to divert to other uses, potential moral hazard problems on the borrower's side are reduced when trade credit is extended. The important implication here is that trade credit and other types of credit are complements rather than substitutes, a prediction supported by evidence in Giannetti, Burkart, and Ellingsen (2008). Such complementarities suggest that alternative sources of funding cannot fill the gap when trade credit dries up. Instead, reduced trade credit will reduce the access to other types of credit as well.[2]

The narrow definition of trade finance restricts attention to international transactions that are directly funded by intermediaries. Of course, not all international transactions are intermediated; sometimes the seller keeps the receivable on its own books, as is common for domestic trade credit. However, the more significant role of intermediaries in international trade informs us that there are often greater obstacles to international trade credit transactions than to domestic ones.

The authors' favored interpretation is that sellers are typically more worried about strategic default in the case of foreign buyers.[3] Thus, sellers tend to insist on up-front payment from foreigners. When the foreign buyer needs funding, a natural arrangement is to borrow from a bank in the buyer's own country. That bank, in turn, for the reasons discussed above, is more willing to provide specific loans for input purchases than to provide general cash loans. Hence, the obvious solution is for the buyer's bank to verify the shipment and pay upon delivery to the seller's bank while providing a loan to the buyer. In brief, this is the authors' theory of international trade finance.

The Case for Policy Intervention

If this theory is correct, what are the arguments for giving priority to trade finance programs rather than to more general programs aimed at easing credit conditions?

Before answering the question, the authors note that the markets for corporate funding differ from many other markets. In particular, corporate credit markets do not have market-clearing prices. Many borrowers would like to have additional funds at prevailing interest rates, but if their pledgeable returns are smaller than their full returns, lenders will rationally lend less than the borrowers desire. When credit constraints bind, it is sometimes (but far from always) justified to intervene in financial markets (Tirole 2005; Holmstrom and Tirole 2011). At the core of this argument in favor of an international trade finance program is the insight that it is more difficult to make credible pledges across borders than within borders.

Benefits of Financial Market Intervention

When a financial crisis turns into a recession, interventions in financial markets have two beneficial effects. The first direct effect is the value of additional funds to the financially constrained firms themselves. The second effect, an indirect one, is the value to the constrained firms' trading partners of the additional activity in the constrained firm. For example, when the constrained firm increases its production, it needs more inputs, and the input suppliers' profit goes up.

Policies to deal with the current crisis ought to focus on the indirect effect rather than the direct effect for two reasons. First, the indirect effects are large during a crisis because of excess capacity. Second, an increase of general credit provision may not lead to an immediate expansion of production at all because borrowers are so afraid of being even more heavily constrained in the future that they simply hoard the additional funds.

A final, and crucial, building block of this argument is that prices are downwardly rigid in the short term. For some reason, sellers cannot or will not immediately reduce their prices despite a high premium on liquidity.[4]

The assumption here is not that prices are stuck at a level that the buyer is unwilling to pay, but rather that they are so high that the buyer is unwilling to pay cash immediately, in view of the high opportunity cost of liquidity. Because of limited pledgeability, the seller, however, is unwilling to extend the necessary credit. Also, the opportunity cost of liquidity implies that a general loan to either party will be hoarded rather than spent on the transaction because the buyer does not internalize the seller's benefit when deciding whether to trade. However—and this is the main point—targeted trade finance loans cannot be used for another purpose and will thus be used to fund the transaction.

International Considerations

Next, consider how the argument works in a richer context where banks are involved in the funding of international transactions. Clearly, the pledgeability problem is again the central reason why international trade finance involves intermediaries. Sellers frequently do not extend trade credit to foreign buyers directly, but instead leave the lending to a domestic bank, which in turn contracts with the buyer's bank. Usually, these transactions leave the actual credit on the balance sheet of either of the banks rather than on the seller's. That is, the banks transfer liquidity to the seller. It is straightforward to see why the liquidity shock will disrupt such bank lending in the same way it disrupts spot transactions: if banks have the same opportunity cost of liquidity as the firms do, the firms will no longer be able to compensate the banks for the kind of liquidity service they have previously been offering.

The problem is most severe when there is less trust across borders than within them. Then, there is less trust between the two banks than between the buyer and the buyer's bank. In this case, the inability to pledge future returns is transferred from the buyer to the buyer's bank. In normal times, trade credit will typically be left on the books of the buyer's bank—with the seller's bank being paid off at the transaction date. Because nobody wants to make transaction-date payments when liquidity is scarce, the situation goes back to the original problem facing the two firms. (With complete cross-border trust between banks, the seller can hold a claim on the domestic bank, the domestic bank can hold a claim of the foreign bank, the foreign bank can hold a claim on the buyer, and all the claims can last until the buyer obtains cash.)

To the extent that sellers and buyers are in the same country, there is reason to expect domestic support for trade credit funding. However, when they are in separate countries, the most appropriate intervention is to provide selective funds to the buyer's bank, whereas the benefits to a large extent flow to the seller's country. This, then, is an argument for international policy coordination.

Annex 13.1 provides a simple formal model that articulates this argument more precisely. Annex 13.2 provides a model of short-term price rigidity and long-term price deflation, based on the assumption that buyers have private information about their financial position following a liquidity shock. The model demonstrates that it is optimal for sellers of durable goods to reduce their prices gradually over time. This model could be combined with the model in annex 13.1 to provide a rigorous justification for the assumption of nominal price rigidity.

As shown in Ellingsen and Vlachos (2009), asymmetric information about financial positions, as brought about by financial turmoil, could also affect prices and quantities in perishable-goods markets. However, according to this rudimentary analysis, the case for trade finance subsidies—as opposed to general interventions in financial markets—appears to be weaker in the case of perishable goods.

Conclusions

In summary, sponsoring trade finance is desirable during a liquidity squeeze primarily because the extension of credit is tied to actual current transactions. Thus, the additional credit cannot be hoarded. The above discussion shows that these problems are particularly severe in international transactions because it is more difficult to make credible pledges across borders than within borders.

A second reason why multilateral organizations ought to support trade finance specifically, rather than providing funding more broadly, is that domestic policy initiatives are likely to place a relatively low weight on foreigners' gains (*Economist* 2009). Because the support of trade finance typically involves supplying funds to the buyer's bank while primarily benefiting the seller, it is easy to see how these transactions will suffer under purely domestic policies.[5]

Annex 13.1: A Simple Formal Model

Here is a simple model that formalizes the logic of the main argument.

A seller has a resource that a buyer may purchase and refine. Refining takes two periods. For simplicity, assume that the process is costless. It increases the value of the resource from c to v. Traditionally, the seller and the buyer have been trading at a price $\bar{p} = (c + v)/2$ that splits the gains from trade equally. For reasons alluded to above (and further expanded upon below), suppose that this price is rigid in the short run.

However, due to an imminent liquidity shock, both the seller and the buyer face a one-period return to holding cash of r. That is, from the date 0 perspective, the two parties know they can trade to generate a surplus at date 2 of $v - c$, but also that any cash held at the beginning of period 0 earns an expected return r if held until date 1. Note that r may reflect either the expected return on investments made at date 1 or the drop in input prices between date 0 and date 1 but not the nominal one-period return on holding cash—which is typically close to zero.

Consequently, the buyer is only willing to pay a price of p if $v \geq p(1 + r)$, or equivalently if $p \leq v/(1 + r)$. The seller, on the other hand, is willing to accept any price p satisfying $p \geq c/(1 + r)$. If the price for one reason or another is rigid at p, then trade is disrupted if $p > v/(1 + r)$, or equivalently if $r > (v - c)/(v + c)$. In other words, if the liquidity shock is sufficiently large relative to the return to trading, then it disrupts trade at the price $\bar{p}$.

So far, only spot payments at date 0 have been considered. What if the buyer could credibly promise to pay at date 2? In this case, the problem evaporates because both parties are willing to trade at $\bar{p}$ as long as they do not have to forgo the date 1 return on liquidity.[6.] In other words, the buyer's inability to credibly pledge future payments to the seller is at the heart of the problem. For simplicity, assume that the buyer cannot make any credible long-term promises about future payments to the seller.

Observe that this problem cannot be resolved by just extending more credit to the buyer because these funds are more profitably invested to earn the liquidity return r than by paying $\bar{p}$ at date 0. However, here comes the main point: extending specific trade finance to the buyer does work if the interest rate is smaller than $(v - \bar{p})/\bar{p}$. Because such funds have no alternative use, they will be used to facilitate transactions. Of course, liquidity is increased by the same amount as a general credit facility, but the liquidity benefits now accrue to the seller rather than to the buyer. Thus, funding of trade credit generates benefits over and above those generated by general credit facilities.

As indicated above, the presence of banks does not make a substantial difference to the argument. In normal times, outstanding credit will typically be left on the books of the buyer's bank—with the seller's bank being paid off at date 0. Because the date 0 payments are infeasible when liquidity is scarce, the two firms are essentially back to the original problem, at least as long as there is insufficient trust between the two banks.

Clearly, a general increase of credit to the buyer's bank will not solve the problem because the buyer's bank will prefer to earn the liquidity return r over any interest rate that can be economically offered in return for a date 0 payment. However, if the buyer's bank is instead offered a selective facility for trade credit extension, it will use it as long as it earns a positive return, even if that return is below r. Thus, the argument in favor of trade credit is the same whether banks are involved or not.

Annex 13.2: Durable Goods and Endogenous Deflation

The argument above rested on two key assumptions: rigid prices and financial frictions. One feature of the crisis is the fear of falling prices, especially in durable goods markets. What is the relationship between financial frictions and price deflation? Is there a channel from financial frictions to temporary downward price rigidity? These are big questions, but here is a small contribution to answering them.

Specifically, consider the following scenario, adapted from Stokey (1979).[7] A seller produces a durable good. For simplicity, suppose that production costs are zero and that the good is infinitely lived. Let time be discrete, and let buyers value the good at v per period. Due to impatience as well as financial constraints, buyers discount future utility at a rate r per period. Let $\delta = 1/(1 + r)$ denote the corresponding discount factor.

If all buyers are identical, the optimal pricing strategy is for the seller to extract all the buyers' surplus by setting the price

$$p^\star = \frac{v}{1-\delta}. \tag{13A.1}$$

Suppose now that the shock to the financial sector hits buyers differently. One group of buyers gets hit hard and now faces an interest rate r_H. The other group gets hit less and faces the interest rate $r_L < r_H$. Let δ_L and δ_H denote the corresponding discount factors. Ideally, the seller would now want to set different prices for the two types of buyer. However, such "third-degree" price discrimination may be impossible, either because of arbitrage or because the seller cannot observe buyers' financial constraints. To extract as much surplus as possible, the seller may therefore engage in intertemporal price discrimination instead.

Rather than deriving the optimal intertemporal price discrimination scheme, the argument is illustrated by considering the strategy to sell immediately to type L and wait one period to sell to type H. Obviously, if type L has bought already, the optimal price next period is

$$p_H^\star = \frac{v}{1-\delta_H}. \tag{13A.2}$$

To induce type L to buy immediately instead of waiting, the initial price must give a utility that is at least as high. That is,

$$\frac{v}{1-\delta_L} - p_L \geq \delta_L \left(\frac{v}{1-\delta_L} - p_H^\star \right). \tag{13A.3}$$

Let $p_L^\star$ denote the largest p_L that is consistent with the above condition:

$$p_L^\star = \frac{v}{1-\delta_H} \left(1 + \delta_L - \delta_H \right). \tag{13A.4}$$

Let h be the fraction of type H buyer types, and let δ denote the seller's discount factor. The profit associated with intertemporal price discrimination can then be written as

$$\pi \left(p_L^\star, p_H^\star \right) = (1-h) p_L^\star + \delta h p_H^\star. \tag{13A.5}$$

Without intertemporal price discrimination, the seller can, in principle, choose between two options: (a) sell only to type L at a price $v/(1 - \delta_L)$, or (b) sell to both types at price $v/(1 - \delta_H)$. Note that the first option relies on the problematic assumption that the seller can credibly commit not to reduce the price in the next period. In a comparison of intertemporal price discrimination with the uniform price strategy (option b), it is straightforward to check that price discrimination is preferable if

$$h < \frac{\delta_L - \delta_H}{1 - \delta + \delta_L - \delta_H}. \tag{13A.6}$$

At first sight, it appears that intertemporal price discrimination is more likely to be profitable when δ is large. However, if $\delta > \delta_L$, it would pay for the seller to lend to the most constrained buyers. On the other hand, if $\delta < \delta_H$, such a financial transaction is unprofitable. Thus, the likelihood of intertemporal price discrimination is highest when the seller is neither so unconstrained as to offer trade credit to fund immediate purchase by all buyers nor so constrained as to prefer all revenues immediately to larger revenues gradually.

Under intertemporal price discrimination, the winners from the financial shock are the buyers that are hit less hard; they now pay less than their reservation value. The relatively better financial position turns into a net gain. The other buyer group is indifferent, whereas the seller loses. Due to the inefficient delay of trade, the seller's loss is greater than the favored buyers' gain. Thus, there is a welfare loss, even if it is smaller than in the model with exogenous price rigidity.

Note that the durable goods model can produce a prolonged period of price deflation even if there is no exogenously imposed price rigidity. Moreover, if funds are being made available at interest rate r_L specifically for the purchases of durable goods, price deflation would end and purchases would be made immediately. Trade finance subsidies are one way to offer such targeted support.

Notes

1. During the crisis, the main piece of advice offered to firms by Boston Consulting Group was "Hoard your cash" (Rhodes et al. 2008).

2. While this general argument seems to favor targeting trade finance over other types of interventions, that conclusion is premature. Because the value of the additional bank credit could, in principle, be extracted by the trade credit provider, it is not clear that the trade credit multiplier effect justifies specific trade credit subsidies. Rather, it is an argument for relaxing the sellers' access to finance by improving the workings of the financial sector in general.

3. Numerous studies demonstrate the importance of strategic-default fears by documenting that international contract enforcement is a serious concern for firms involved in international trade (Rauch 2001). Indeed, much of the recent theoretical work on international trade builds on the assumption of imperfect contract enforcement (Antrás and Rossi-Hansberg 2009). See also Anderson and Marcouiller (2002), who find that poor contract enforcement is a major impediment to international trade. Similarly, cross-border trust is an important determinant of international trade and investment (Guiso, Sapienza, and Zingales 2009).

4. There is a large and rapidly growing literature on the causes of price rigidity. The authors' argument is valid under many of these causes, but perhaps not under all of them. Below, a specific and new argument is provided for price rigidity under financial turmoil.

5. Sponsoring trade finance may also, in general, help to alleviate insufficient trade due to incomplete information among nonfinancial firms, but unless there is a liquidity squeeze, trade finance

subsidies have no obvious advantage over general financial measures. For a fuller discussion of this point, including a formal model, see Ellingsen and Vlachos (2009).

6. Large buyers in industrialized countries sometimes unilaterally initiate delayed payments to domestic suppliers. In terms of this model, this is a rational response to liquidity shocks if the pledge to pay later is credible.

7. Stokey's main point is actually that intertemporal price discrimination does not occur when buyers have identical discount factors. The point here is that with different discount factors, it occurs under reasonable additional assumptions.

References

Anderson, J. E., and D. Marcouiller. 2002. "Insecurity and the Pattern of Trade: An Empirical Investigation." *The Review of Economics and Statistics* 84 (2): 342–52.

Antrás, P., and E. Rossi-Hansberg. 2009. "Organizations and Trade." *Annual Review of Economics* 1 (1): 43–64.

Burkart, M., and T. Ellingsen. 2004. "In-Kind Finance: A Theory of Trade Credit." *American Economic Review* 94 (3): 569–90.

Economist. 2009. "Homeward Bound." February 7–13: 69–70.

Ellingsen, T., and J. Vlachos. 2009. "Trade Finance in a Liquidity Crisis." Policy Research Working Paper 5136, World Bank, Washington, DC.

Giannetti, M., M. Burkart, and T. Ellingsen. 2008. "What You Sell Is What You Lend? Explaining Trade Credit Contracts." *Review of Financial Economics* (online). http://rfs.oxfordjournals.org/content/early/2007/12/31/rfs.hhn096.extract.

Guiso, L., P. Sapienza, and L. Zingales. 2009. "Cultural Biases in Economic Exchange." *The Quarterly Journal of Economics* 124 (3): 1095–131.

Holmstrom, B., and J. Tirole. 2011. *Inside and Outside Liquidity.* Cambridge, MA: The MIT Press.

Rauch, J. 2001. "Business and Social Networks in International Trade." *Journal of Economic Literature* 69 (December): 1177–203.

Rhodes, David, Daniel Stelter, Shubh Saumya, and André Kronimus. 2008. "Collateral Damage, Part I: What the Crisis in Credit Markets Means for Everyone Else." Collateral Damage Series paper, Boston Consulting Group, Boston. http://www.bcg.com/documents/file15356.pdf.

Stokey, N. 1979. "Intertemporal Price Discrimination." *The Quarterly Journal of Economics* 93 (3): 355–71.

Tirole, J. 2005. *The Theory of Corporate Finance.* Princeton: Princeton University Press.

WHY BOOSTING THE AVAILABILITY OF TRADE FINANCE BECAME A PRIORITY DURING THE 2008–09 CRISIS

Jean-Jacques Hallaert

Economists disagree on the role trade finance played in the recent collapse in world trade. In contrast, policy makers seem to have reached a consensus. In a nutshell, their reasoning is that trade finance is the lifeline of international trade. The decline in trade is larger than what would be expected given the drop in global output. So part of the fall in trade reflects a shortage of trade finance, which could amplify and extend the plunge in trade and make the financial and economic crisis worse. Hence, boosting the availability of trade finance has to be part of the international response to the crisis. This chapter examines the claims underpinning this storyline and highlights the uncertainties on the role trade finance played in the current crisis.

How Big Is the Trade Finance Shortfall?

International trade presents many risks that trade finance can mitigate. The risk of nonpayment may be limited with the use of instruments such as letters of credit. The credit risk can be reduced with the use of export credit insurance. Trade finance also provides liquidity because some exporters may need loans if they lack

---

This chapter updates an article published initially in 2009 as "Boosting the Availability of Trade Finance: A Priority in the Current Crisis?" *Intereconomics* 44 (5): 273–78.

sufficient liquidity to process and acquire goods and services to fulfill export orders. However, a large part of trade finance does not involve financial institutions because trade partners often extend trade credit to each other.[1]

How much does international trade depend on trade finance? There is no solid statistical answer to this basic question. It is often reported that 90 percent of world trade relies on trade finance (WTO 2007). This estimate is of questionable quality and appears too high given the sharp increase over the past two decades in intrafirm trade, which is unlikely to use external financing. If the widely circulated numbers of trade finance reaching $10 trillion and world trade flows reaching $14 trillion are accurate, the share is closer to 70 percent.[2] The precise share of trade relying on trade finance does not matter much because, indisputably, trade finance is essential to trade. However, these uncertainties illustrate the poor quality of data on trade finance.

If it is so hard to measure total trade finance, estimating a shortfall cannot be more than a best guess. According to the World Trade Organization (WTO), a shortfall, albeit limited, existed before the 2008–09 crisis. In March 2007—on the eve of the financial crisis and more than a year before the bankruptcy of a major participant in trade finance (Lehman Brothers) and the collapse in trade—the WTO reported a transaction gap of less than $200,000 (WTO 2007). By the time of the WTO's Expert Group Meeting on Trade Finance in November 2008, market participants' broad estimate of the shortfall in trade finance had increased to $25 billion.[3] Four months later, in March 2009, at another WTO Expert Group Meeting, the estimate was revised to $100 billion–$300 billion, but it seemed that there was no consensus: "On the current market situation, *most* participants agreed that although trade flows were decreasing sharply, constraints to trade finance still existed" (WTO 2009, emphasis added).[4] In May 2010, participants in another Expert Group Meeting indicated that liquidity had returned to the trade market, although some regions (notably Sub-Saharan Africa) continued to face constraints (WTO 2010).

Jumping the Gun or Jumping on the Bandwagon?

Despite the lack of reliable data and the fact that the then-estimated shortfall accounted for only 0.25 percent of trade finance and less than 0.2 percent of world trade, the WTO put trade finance in the spotlight and marshaled strong support to trade finance by as early as the end of 2008.

Initiatives mushroomed. International and government-backed institutions were mobilized and responded quickly. The capacity of export credit agencies as well as regional and multilateral development banks was increased, new products were launched, and cofinancing with the private sector was encouraged, among other efforts (Chauffour and Farole 2009). Moreover, several countries used their official reserves to supply banks and importers with foreign currencies. The international effort to support trade finance culminated in April 2009 when the G-20 pledged to "ensure availability of $250 billion over the next two years to support trade finance" (G-20 2009) and the World Bank announced the Global Trade Liquidity Program, which could support up to $50 billion of trade.

The response was unusual not only in strength, but also in speed. It started as early as October 2008 (arguably even before then), when the magnitude of the collapse in trade was not even known! Initially there were concerns that the financial crisis (more precisely the credit crunch) that started in 2007 could spread to trade finance. However, at least until the first half of 2008, trade finance "was stable with volumes and rates at normal levels."[5] Signs of possible tension appeared only when the financial crisis morphed into a full-blown economic crisis.

At that time, the political economy was ripe to boost the availability of trade finance. Long before the crisis, many countries had been lobbying at the WTO to find ways to increase the availability of trade finance for developing countries. The Aid for Trade initiative, whose scope explicitly includes trade finance (WTO 2006), was seen as providing leverage (Auboin 2007). The 50 percent increase in the ceiling of the International Finance Corporation's (World Bank Group) trade finance guarantee in October 2008 was welcomed by the head of the WTO as "Aid for Trade in action."[6]

The economic crisis provided extra leverage. Boosting the availability of trade finance was seen not only as an answer to the concerns of developing countries but also as a means to address the global crisis. Lessons were evoked from the Great Depression and the role played by trade finance in recent financial crises (such as in Asia and in Argentina and Brazil).[7] Supporting trade finance was also branded as part of the international fiscal stimulus. With a high political profile and no strong interest to oppose it, the policy response could only be strong and swift.[8]

An Overestimated Problem?

Precautionary action against anticipated problems has some merit. Nonetheless, the problem with trade finance may have been overestimated. It has been claimed that the shortage in trade finance could account for 10–15 percent of the decline in trade (*Financial Times* 2009). However, available econometric estimates suggest that the shortfall would need to be much larger than the one reported to contribute that much to the drop in trade flows (Ronci 2004; Thomas 2009; Korinek, Le Cocguic, and Sourdin 2010).

Some econometric studies on the mechanism of the trade collapse fail to find any support for the idea that trade credit played a role (Levchenko, Lewis, and

Tesar 2010). Moreover, from October 2008 to January 2009, when the drop in trade took place, trade volume declined much more than trade finance (possibly four times more, according to Chauffour and Farole [2009]), suggesting that the drop in demand explains the contraction in trade finance.

The perception that the supply of trade finance played a significant role in the crisis stems from the fact that the collapse in trade has been so sharp and so much larger than the contraction in global output (Levchenko, Lewis, and Tesar 2010) that it left the impression that something other than the drop in demand must have hampered trade. Because financial problems triggered the crisis, disruption in trade finance was seen as a possible culprit. However, there is no need to invoke a trade finance shortfall to explain the recent plunge in trade.

First, the rise in the fragmentation of production increased the elasticity of trade to income from under 2 percent in the 1960s and 1970s to about 3.5 percent in recent years (Irwin 2002; Freund 2009). As a result, trade flows reacted more in 2008–09 than in past crises to changes in global output. Supporting this view are these facts: (a) East Asia, the region most involved in the international supply chains (and thus the region exhibiting the largest elasticity of trade to income), is the region that suffered from the largest fall in trade, and (b) the 2008–09 collapse in U.S. trade was exceptional by historical standards but was driven by the drop in trade in intermediate goods (Levchenko, Lewis, and Tesar 2010).[9]

Second, the collapse in trade in goods, which attracts attention, is larger than the drop in total trade because trade in services has been much more resilient than trade in goods. This supports the idea that the initial drop in trade in goods was amplified by a destocking effect (which cannot affect trade in services because services cannot be stored). Firms, anticipating a slowdown in growth, drew down inventories, thus magnifying the drop in trade. A close analysis of the timing as well as the sectoral and regional patterns of trade flows supports this interpretation (*Economist* 2009).

Third, the plunge in trade is often calculated in nominal terms on a year-on-year basis. This calculation overestimates the decline in *real* trade because commodity prices had fallen dramatically since their historically high level of mid-2008. For example, Levchenko, Lewis, and Tesar (2010) calculate that price explains 40 percent of the collapse in U.S. imports and about 27 percent of the collapse in U.S. exports.

All these points do not negate the potential role of a trade finance shortage in the plunge in world trade. Rather, they highlight that the decline in trade is not necessarily much larger than the slowdown in global output would suggest. Thus, the importance of the collapse in trade does not suggest that "something else"—like a disruption in trade finance—has *necessarily* played a *significant* role.

In sum, the lack of reliable data is so dire that there is no certainty that the decline in trade finance contributed significantly to the decline in trade. This lack prevents observers from solving the familiar causality problem: did the drop in trade cause trade finance to contract (a demand shock), or did a shortfall in trade finance contribute to the drop in trade (a supply shock)?

Surveys to Fill the Information Gap

To remedy the lack of data, several organizations came to the rescue with surveys in early 2009:

- *The International Chamber of Commerce* (ICC) surveyed 122 banks in 59 countries (ICC 2009).
- *The International Monetary Fund* (IMF) and the *Bankers' Association for Finance and Trade* (BAFT)—now merged with International Financial Services Association (BAFT-IFSA)—surveyed 44 banks from 23 countries (IMF-BAFT 2009).
- *The Institute of Development Studies* (IDS) surveyed 31 medium- and large-scale, export-oriented Sub-Saharan African firms (Humphrey 2009).
- *The Organisation for Economic Co-operation and Development* (OECD) surveyed its members about measures taken at the national level regarding officially support export credit (OECD 2009).
- *The World Bank* surveyed 425 firms and 78 banks in 14 developing countries (Malouche 2009).

According to these surveys, the problem with trade finance was not its availability but its cost.

Trade finance was somewhat more difficult to get in some regions of the world (mostly in emerging markets), in some sectors (those perceived as more risky than others), and for some firms. Nonetheless, the surveys did not depict an overly dark picture. Few of the African firms surveyed by IDS faced any problems with availability of trade finance (Humphrey 2009). Firms surveyed by the World Bank indicated that "the drop in global demand was their top concern and that trade finance was not a major binding constraint" (Malouche 2009). The Australian government reported to OECD that it holds regular consultations with market practitioners and that "anecdotal evidence to-date suggest to us that the slowdown or contraction in international trade is leading the slowdown in trade finance and export credit insurance uptake rather than a financial crisis-induced tightening of trade credit and credit insurance preventing willing buyers and willing sellers from doing international trade deals" (OECD 2009).

Among the banks responding to the ICC survey, 47 percent reported a drop in the volume of letters of credit, while 32 percent reported an increase and 21 percent reported no change (ICC 2009). In the IMF and BAFT-IFSA survey, "banks in advanced countries reported roughly the same number of trade finance transactions in the final months of 2008 as occurred at the end of 2007. But emerging market banks reported an average 6 percent decline in trade finance transactions" (Dorsey 2009).[10]

This limited decline in transactions may reflect several factors and not necessarily a shortage. Tighter guidelines by banks in light of risk reassessment played a role, but the drop in transactions may have also reflected an increase in the cost of trade financing and a drop in the aggregate demand for trade financing because of the contraction of trade.[11] Although 57 percent of banks in the IMF and BAFT-IFSA survey explained the drop in the value of trade finance transactions between October 2008 and January 2009 as due to less credit availability, 73 percent mentioned a fall in the demand as a reason, and 43 percent cited the fall in transaction prices, which likely reflected the drop in commodity prices. In the World Bank survey, banks "confirmed the increase in pricing and a drop in volume of trade credit. Yet, the drop in volume seems to reflect lack of demand due to the global recession rather than a consequence of the increase in pricing" (Malouche 2009).

For some exporters, trade finance may have been available but unaffordable. Surveys clearly showed that the price of trade financing shot up. The main reasons for this price increase appear to have been a perceived increase in default risks, a rise in the banks' cost of funds, higher capital requirements, and a decline in the value of collateral (for example, linked to the drop in commodity prices).

In this context, a policy that targets only the quantity of trade finance would most likely fail. If banks are reluctant to lend because of perceived risks, boosting the availability of trade finance is unlikely to result in more lending. As Malcolm Stephens, a former secretary-general of the Berne Union, pointed out in his analysis of trade finance during the Asian crisis, "The traditional role of export credit agencies is to support trade and to facilitate trade. They are less effective in, somehow, trying to create or initiate trade, especially, in circumstances where neither importers nor exporters are really willing (or able) to trade with each other" (Stephens 1998).

A policy that targets the risks would have more impact. According to World Bank President Robert Zoellick, under its Global Trade Liquidity Program, the Bank "would underwrite the riskiest part of the lending, while private banks would provide the bulk of the less risky elements" (*Financial Times* 2009). Although likely to be more successful, this kind of initiative raises the potential issue of moral hazard.

Need for Regulatory Change?

Policy makers may also tackle the reasons for the increased risk aversion and cost of funds. According to some bankers, regulatory changes could help. They argue that Basel II has a pro-cyclical effect on the supply of credit and particularly affects trade finance, most notably trade finance with emerging markets.

This complaint is not new, but recently it has been voiced more forcefully, notably at the WTO expert meetings (Hopes 2008; WTO 2008a, 2008b, 2009, 2010). Moreover, it has been relayed by Robert Zoellick (who publicly complained about a regulation that tripled the amount of capital needed to back trade finance [*Financial Times* 2009]) and Pascal Lamy (who wrote to the general manager of the Bank for International Settlements and to the chairman of the Financial Stability Forum). However, only one-third of the 15 banks that responded to the IMF/BAFT-IFSA question about the impact of Basel II on their capacity to provide trade finance indicated that it had a negative impact; 27 percent reported it had a positive impact, and the remaining banks reported it had no impact.

Since the 2008–09 crisis, calls for changing the rules have been frequent. They go beyond the call by the Group of 20 (G-20) for "regulators to make use of available flexibility in capital requirements for trade finance" (G-20 2009). For example, in December 2008, the European Commission introduced temporary changes in the Commission State Aid Guidelines on short-term export credits. It increased the flexibility of an existing escape clause so that official export credit agencies can cover short-term transactions in the OECD if the private market fails to do so (OECD 2009). In January 2009, the participants in the OECD's Arrangement on Officially Supported Export Credits decided to adjust some of the disciplines of the Arrangement to facilitate the financing of projects. These modifications allow signatories to provide officially supported export credit at more favorable terms and to increase the limit of the share of officially supported export credit in intra-OECD project finance. Then, in June 2009, OECD countries agreed to boost official backing for exports of renewable energy and nuclear power equipment by offering more generous terms.[12]

These changes are rather limited, but a lesson from past crises is that pressures to use officially backed export credit to protect or stimulate national exports are considerable during a worldwide recession. This was the case during the Great Depression—an experience that led to the creation of the Berne Union and "apparently convinced the GATT [General Agreement on Tariffs and Trade] founders that export subsidies exacerbate international political tensions and should be eliminated" (Baldwin 1980).[13]

During the 1970s crisis, world leaders pledged to refrain from resorting to protectionism. Today's leaders do the same. However, they do not follow their predecessors who also pledged to avoid competition in official trade credit. The concern about competition in official trade credit was so great in the 1970s that, to prevent it, OECD countries negotiated an Arrangement on Officially Supported Export Credit (Ray 1986). When international trade faced another contraction in the early 1980s, export subsidies came back in the form of tied aid and mixed credit (Byatt 1984; Messerlin 1986; Ray 1986).[14]

The rules currently in place were designed to prevent the mistakes of previous crises, namely competitions in export subsidies (through favorable terms) that not only distorted international trade and domestic protection but also proved to be fiscally expensive. They act as a safeguard, and no race for export subsidies has taken place in the current crisis. However, agricultural export subsidies and the lingering Airbus-Boeing dispute are reminders that the temptation to help domestic firms' exports is not a thing of the past. Moreover, pressures on policy makers to help domestic firms may increase if the recovery is not vibrant enough to rapidly reverse the rise in unemployment. The system may need more flexibility, but the lessons from history should not be forgotten.

Conclusions

Panic stemming from a sharp and sudden decline in trade flows, memories of the Great Depression, and the role of trade finance in recent financial crises, as well as a favorable political economy, explain why policy makers strongly and rapidly supported trade finance in response to the 2008–09 global financial crisis.

However, the trade finance shortfall and its contribution to the fall in trade flows are likely to be overestimated. Lack of reliable data is so dire that it is difficult to know whether a drop in the *supply* of trade finance contributed to the decline in trade or whether the decline was only due to the drop in *demand* for trade finance. In 2008–09, trade finance was somewhat harder to get in some parts of the world or for some firms but, in aggregate, available evidence suggests that a shortfall is unlikely to have contributed significantly to the plunge in international trade.

The cost of trade financing was more of a problem than its availability. If the rising cost was due to increased risk aversion, boosting the supply in trade finance is likely to be ineffective. Rather than trying to increase the supply of trade finance in particular, policy makers should help credit flows in general to return to normal. There are two main reasons to support this strategy. First, the access to intermediated trade finance appears to be less a constraint for exporters than preexport financing, which is similar to a working capital loan (Chauffour and Farole 2009; Humphrey 2009). Second, firms constrained in their access to institutional credit are likely to face difficulties in extending trade credit. Fixing the financial system will ease the credit constraint and help boost the interfirm trade credit that accounts for a large share of trade finance.[15]

Moreover, boosting the supply of trade finance is risky. Relaxing the rules limiting the competition of government-backed exports credit (on the grounds that more flexibility is needed to provide more trade financing) could make it more difficult to resist pressures to help domestic exporters. In addition, in many countries, the recession and large fiscal stimulus packages have led to ballooning fiscal deficits and public debts. In this context, boosting the availability of trade finance is probably not the best use of scarce public resources, and encouraging export credit agencies to take more risks could result in fiscal contingent liabilities.

Notes

1. Chauffour and Farole (2009) describe the various instruments. Petersen and Rajan (1997) discuss interfirm credit.

2. In 2008, trade finance reached $10 trillion–$12 trillion and trade flows reached $15 trillion (Auboin 2009). These numbers imply a share ranging from 67 percent to 80 percent.

3. It is interesting to note the precise nature of this estimate: "Market participants gave a broad estimate of the gap in the trade finance market of $25 billion, which was the amount of trade finance that banks kept on their books but could not off-load on the secondary market" (WTO 2009).

4. A caveat to this estimate: "this being roll-over finance, the gap would nevertheless need to be divided in terms of net flows by the average maturity of letters of credit, which could vary widely across areas of operation" (WTO 2009).

5. WTO Director-General Pascal Lamy's report to the WTO Trade Negotiations Committee in October 2008 (WTO 2008c).

6. WTO Director-General Pascal Lamy's report to the WTO General Council in November 2008 (WTO 2008c). The new ceiling would be doubled one month later to reach $3 billion.

7. Problems with trade finance were sometimes cited among the main risks for trade looking forward. For example, in his address at the WTO's Second Global Review of Aid for Trade in July 2009, Waleed Al-Wohaib of the Islamic Development Bank claimed that international trade was facing "the twin risks of rising protectionism and dwindling trade finance" (Wohaib 2009).

8. On the political economy of boosting trade finance, see also Baldwin (2009).

9. Levchenko, Lewis, and Tesar (2010) also note that although the drop in trade was exceptional by historical standards, it was comparable to the drop experienced during the 2001 recession when elasticity of trade to income was already very high.

10. There are signs that the situation deteriorated somewhat between October 2008 and January 2009.

11. It is difficult to untangle the reasons for the decline in demand for trade financing. The drop in demand due to lower trade flows can be offset by the increase in demand for the protection offered by trade finance in light of increased risks. In the ICC survey, banks reported such an increase in demand for protection.

12. See "Modifications to the Arrangement on Officially Support Export Credits" (http://www.oecd.org/document/40/0,3343,en_2649_34169_42168680_1_1_1_1,00.html) and "OECD Countries Boost Official Support for Renewable and Nuclear Energy Exports" (http://www.oecd.org/document/10/0,3343,en_2649_34169_43152266_1_1_1_37431,00.html).

13. Auboin (2007) discusses the WTO's agreement on subsidies and countervailing measures and their link with OECD rules.

14. Ray (1986) provides the history of the negotiations leading to the OECD Arrangement. The intense debates on export-credit subsidies that took place in the first half of the 1980s in both the United Kingdom and France are summarized in Byatt (1984) and Messerlin (1986).

15. For analyses of this mechanism, see Petersen and Rajan (1997) and Love, Preve, and Sarria-Allende (2007).

References

Auboin, Marc. 2007. "Boosting Trade Finance in Developing Countries: What Link with the WTO?" Staff Working Paper ERSD-2007-04, World Trade Organization, Geneva.

———. 2009. "Boosting the Availability of Trade Finance in the Current Crisis: Background Analysis for a Substantial G20 Package." Policy Insight 35, Centre for Economic Policy Research, London.

Baldwin, Richard. 2009. "Trade and the London Summit Outcome." Commentary, VoxEU.org, Centre for Economic Policy Research, London. http://www.voxeu.org/index.php?q=node/3417.

Baldwin, Robert. 1980. "The Economics of the GATT." In *Issues in International Economics*, ed. Peter Oppenheimer, 82–93. Boston: Oriel Press.

Byatt, I. C. R. 1984. "Byatt Report on Subsidies to British Export Credits." *World Economy* 7 (2): 163–78.

Chauffour, Jean-Pierre, and Thomas Farole. 2009. "Trade Finance in Crisis: Market Adjustment or Market Failure?" Policy Research Working Paper 5003, World Bank, Washington, DC.

Dorsey, Thomas. 2009. "Trade Finance Stumbles." *IMF Finance and Development* 46 (1): 18–19.

Economist. 2009. "Unpredictable Tides." July 23.

Financial Times. 2009. "Zoellick Urges Global Response." February 19.

Freund, Caroline. 2009. "Demystifying the Collapse in Trade." Article, VoxEU.org, Centre for Economic Policy Research, London. http://voxeu.org/index.php?q=node/3731.

G-20. 2009. "Leaders Statement: The Global Plan for Recovery and Reform." April 2, London.

Hopes, Andrew. 2008. "Basel II Has Become an Obstacle to Trade Flows." *Financial Times,* November 18.

Humphrey, John. 2009. "Are Exporters in Africa Facing Reduced Availability of Trade Finance?" Paper for the U.K. Department for International Development, Institute of Development Studies, Brighton, U.K. http://www.ids.ac.uk/index.cfm?objectid=C369D2D2-AEE3-EB77-A7847EA6F6FBF447.

ICC (International Chamber of Commerce). 2009. "Rethinking Trade Finance 2009: An ICC Global Survey." ICC Banking Commission Market Intelligence Report 470-1120 TS/WJ, ICC, Paris.

IMF-BAFT. (International Monetary Fund-Bankers' Association for Finance and Trade). 2009. "IMF-BAFT Trade Finance Survey: A Survey Among Banks Assessing the Current Trade Finance Environment." Survey presentation, IMF and BAFT, Washington, DC. http://www.aba.com/aba/documents/press/IMFBAFTSurveyResults20090331.ppt.

Irwin, Douglas A. 2002. "Long-Run Trends in World Trade and Income." *World Trade Review* 1 (1): 89–100.

Korinek, Jane, Jean Le Cocguic, and Patricia Sourdin. 2010. "The Availability and Cost of Short-Term Trade Finance and Its Impact on Trade." Trade Policy Working Paper 98, Organisation for Economic Co-operation and Development, Paris.

Levchenko, Andrei A., Logan T. Lewis, and Linda L. Tesar. 2010. "The Collapse of International Trade during the 2008–2009 Crisis: In Search of the Smoking Gun." Working Paper 16006, National Bureau of Economic Research, Cambridge, MA.

Love, Inessa, Lorenzo A. Preve, and Virginia Sarria-Allende. 2007. "Trade Credit and Bank Credit: Evidence from Recent Financial Crises." *Journal of Financial Economics* 83 (2): 453–69.

Messerlin, Patrick. 1986. "Export-Credit Mercantilism à la Française." *The World Economy* 9 (4): 385–408.

Malouche, Mariem. 2009. "Trade and Trade Finance Developments in 14 Developing Countries Post-September 2008: A World Bank Survey." Policy Research Working Paper 5138, World Bank, Washington, DC.

OECD (Organisation for Economic Co-operation and Development). 2009. "Officially Supported Export Credits and the Financial Crisis: Measures Taken at the National Level by the Participants to the Arrangement." Document TAD/PG(2009)4/FINAL, OECD, Paris. http://www.oecd.org/officialdocuments/publicdisplaydocumentpdf/?cote=TAD/PG(2009)4/FINAL&docLanguage=En.

Petersen, Mitchell A., and Raghuram G. Rajan. 1997. "Trade Credit: Theories and Evidence." *The Review of Financial Studies* 10 (3): 661–91.

Ray, John E. 1986. "The OECD 'Consensus' on Export Credit." *The World Economy* 9 (3): 295–310.

Ronci, Marcio. 2004. "Trade Finance and Trade Flows: Panel Data Evidence from 10 Crises." Working Paper WP/04/225, International Monetary Fund, Washington, DC.

Stephens, Malcolm. 1998. "Export Credit Agencies, Trade Finance, and South East Asia." Working Paper WP/98/175, International Monetary Fund, Washington, DC.

Thomas, Alun. 2009. "Financial Crisis and Emerging Market Trade." Staff Position Note SPN/09/04, International Monetary Fund, Washington, DC.

Wohaib, Waleed Al-. 2009. "Speech by Dr. Waleed Al Wohaib, CEO, International Islamic Trade Finance Corporation (ITFC)." Address at the WTO Second Global Review of Aid for Trade, Geneva, July 6–7. http://www.wto.org/english/tratop_e/devel_e/a4t_e/alwohaib_jul09_e.pdf.

WTO (World Trade Organization). 2006. "Recommendations of the Task Force on Aid for Trade." Task force report WT/AFT/1, WTO, Geneva.

———. 2007. "Aid for Trade: Boosting Trade Financing to Developing Countries and Economies in Transition." Note by the Secretariat WT/AFT/W/24, WTO, Geneva.

———. 2008a. "Expert Group Meeting on Trade Finance, 25 April 2008." Note by the Secretariat WT/WGTDF/W/38, WTO, Geneva.

———. 2008b. "Expert Group Meeting on Trade Finance, 12 November 2008." Note by the Secretariat WT/WGTDF/W/40, WTO, Geneva.

———. 2008c. "General Council, Minutes of the Meeting held in the Centre William Rappard on 14 October 2008." Meeting minutes WT/GC/M/116 WTO, Geneva.

———. 2009. "Expert Group Meeting on Trade Finance, 18 March 2009." Note by the Secretariat WT/WGTDF/W/44, WTO, Geneva.

———. 2010. "Expert Group Meeting on Trade Finance, 18 May 2010." Note by the Secretariat WT/WGTDF/W/48, WTO, Geneva.

MARKET ADJUSTMENT VERSUS MARKET FAILURE

Jean-Pierre Chauffour and Thomas Farole

As noted in preceding chapters, G-20 leaders agreed at their April 2009 London Summit to ensure $250 billion of support for trade finance to promote global trade and investment.[1] Notwithstanding this increased activism around trade finance, it remains largely unclear how much of the contraction in international trade may have been caused by restrictions in the supply of trade finance and to what degree this represents a legitimate target for intervention.

For intervention to be justified, at least three preconditions should be met:

- The scale of the supply gap should be significant.
- The shortfall in the provision of trade finance can be attributed to a structural or temporary market failure.
- Targeted interventions can achieve the desired response by market participants (that is, supplying trade credit at market-clearing prices) without creating unacceptable moral hazards or subsidizing credit that would have been provided in any case.

The authors would like to thank Olivier Cattaneo, Mona Haddad, Bernard Hoekman, Richard Newfarmer, and other participants in the joint World Bank-CEPR conference, "Trade Implications of Policy Responses to the Crisis" in Brussels, May 26–27, 2009, for their helpful comments and suggestions. An earlier version of this paper was published as Jean-Pierre Chauffour and Thomas Farole, "Trade Finance in Crisis: Market Adjustment or Market Failure?" in *Effective Crisis Response and Openness: Implications for the Trading System* (London: Centre for Economic Policy Research. 2009).

The views expressed in this chapter are those of the authors and do not necessarily represent those of the World Bank.

This chapter discusses these issues with a view to addressing the following questions: Is there a trade finance gap and, if so, what is its scale and nature? Is there a rationale for intervention to support trade finance? And what tools and policies are most appropriate to address the situation?

Is There a Trade Finance Gap?

By providing critical fluidity and security to enable the movement of goods and services, trade finance lies at the heart of the global trading system (Auboin and Meier-Ewert 2008). Some 80–90 percent of all trade transactions are said to be financed.[2] Trade finance mechanisms exist to support two fundamental aspects of the trading process: *risk mitigation* and *liquidity*.

Characteristics and Risks of Trade Finance

Trade finance differs from other forms of credit (for example, investment and working capital) in several ways that may have important economic consequences during periods of financial crisis.

Perhaps its most distinguishing characteristic is that it is offered and obtained not only through third-party financial institutions but also through interfirm transactions. That interfirm trade finance is so prevalent is typically explained by certain features that enable trade partners to better assess and mitigate risk than third parties, including an *informational advantage* and the advantage of trust, or *encapsulated interest* (Giannetti, Burkart, and Ellingsen 2008).

Relative to a standard credit line or working capital loan, trade finance—whether offered through banks or within the supply chain—is relatively illiquid, which means that it cannot easily be diverted for another purpose. It is also highly collateralized; credit and insurance are provided directly against the sale of specific products or services whose value can, by and large, be calculated and secured.[3] The illiquidity and collateralization of trade finance suggest that the risk of strategic default should be relatively low, as should be the scale of loss in the event of default.

However, the international nature of trade finance may imply greater potential risks, including the following:

- Higher macro-level or country risks, such as from exchange rate fluctuations, changes to policy, conflict, and political upheaval (Menichini 2009)
- Higher counterparty risk resulting from challenges of cross-border enforcement, which raises the risk of strategic default by suppliers, creating a problem of "credible commitment" across borders (Ellingsen and Vlachos 2009)

- Limited or nonexistent data by which to assess counterparty credit risk in many countries (for example, where public credit registry coverage or public access to accounts or court proceedings are limited).

These risks may be compounded in the case of supplier-extended credit because most suppliers operate in credit chains, which are vulnerable to shocks because they can quickly propagate problems across the chain (Kiyotaki and Moore 1997; Raddatz 2010).

Impact of Financial Crises on Trade Finance

Although trade finance was neither a proximate nor ultimate cause of the 2008–09 financial crisis, it quickly became collateral damage. As the crisis unfolded, the availability of trade finance tightened and its cost rose because of growing liquidity pressure in mature markets and a perception of heightened country and counterparty risks. However, with no comprehensive and reliable data on trade finance available, an overall assessment of trade finance developments in 2008–09 remains difficult. Historical precedents and selected information indicates that—along with global demand—trade finance flows declined in the last quarter of 2008.

Trade finance has tended to be highly vulnerable in times of economic crisis. During crisis episodes in the late 1990s and early 2000s in Argentina, Brazil, Indonesia, the Republic of Korea, Pakistan, Thailand, and other emerging economies, local banking systems encountered liquidity and solvency problems that made it difficult for local producers to get pre- and postshipment finance, open letters of credit (LCs), and obtain advance payment bonds and other forms of domestic trade finance. In 1997–98, for instance, bank-financed trade credits declined by about 50 percent and 80 percent in Korea and Indonesia, respectively. During the crisis in Latin America in the early 2000s, trade credits in Argentina and Brazil declined by as much as 30–50 percent (Allen 2003).

As noted in the next section, most banks reported a decline in the value of their LC business in 2008–09, and global buyers and suppliers indicated that foreign sales had been delayed or canceled due to both drops in new orders and difficulties in obtaining trade finance (Arvis and Shakya 2009). Evidence of liquidity pressure on trade finance was also reported by the banks participating in the Global Trade Finance Program of the World Bank Group's International Finance Corporation (IFC). Major international banks in the program have been unwilling to assume a portion of the risk in individual transactions, leaving the underlying risk to the IFC alone (International Financial Consulting 2009).

The firms most affected are generally those highly exposed to the international financial market (for example, in Brazil); small and medium enterprises (SMEs) that are crowded out by large firms in accessing trade finance (for example, in Chile and the Philippines); and firms that are highly integrated in global supply chains (for example, in India, Indonesia, Tunisia, and Turkey). The firms least affected are those in low-income countries with underdeveloped domestic banking systems, especially in Sub-Saharan Africa (for instance, Ghana).

However, a World Bank survey indicated that the biggest financing constraint—particularly for SMEs and firms operating in global supply chains (which generally work through open-account methods)—is not access to trade credit (for example, LCs) per se but rather preexport finance (Malouche 2009). It is here where banks have become particularly stringent in their risk evaluation, especially regarding emerging-market participants and SMEs. As the crisis forces exporters who normally self-finance to seek additional liquidity, constraints on preexport finance may become the most important inflection point of the trade finance gap.

Perhaps more important than supply alone, the price of trade finance and the need to secure transactions through guarantees and insurance have increased markedly. Tight credit conditions have allowed lenders to drive up interest rates for their loans in many countries, especially in emerging markets. By the end of 2008, trade finance deals were offered at 300–400 basis points over interbank refinance rates—two to three times more than the rate at the end of 2007. The cost of LCs reportedly doubled or tripled for buyers in emerging countries, including Argentina, Bangladesh, China, Pakistan, and Turkey. A joint International Monetary Fund (IMF) and Bankers' Association for Finance and Trade (BAFT)—now merged with International Financial Services Association (BAFT-IFSA)—survey confirmed this cost hike, finding widespread increases in pricing of all trade finance instruments relative to banks' costs of funds (IMF-BAFT 2009). A large majority of respondents indicated that the price of various types of LCs increased because of an increase in their own institutions' cost of funds (80 percent of respondents), an increase in capital requirements (60 percent of respondents), or both.

A recent attempt to disentangle the effects of trade finance from demand shocks—using disaggregated bilateral import and export data from Germany, Japan, and the United States—shows that in industries more dependent on interfirm financing, trade with countries more exposed to the crisis has not been affected more than trade overall (Freund and Klapper 2009). This finding suggests that trade finance has not been affected more adversely than other types of financing that firms rely on. However, Freund and Klapper also find some evidence that, in countries more affected by the crisis, trade has fallen more sharply in industries that depend more on short-term financing (broadly defined). This implies that financial needs have affected trade patterns during the crisis. However, the results do not necessarily suggest that a shortage of trade finance has constrained overall trade growth. Rather, in industries with high financial dependence, trade has shifted away from firms in the most-affected countries toward those in less-affected countries.

These findings show that bank-intermediated trade finance is only a small part of the story. Most exporters extend credit within the supply chain through open-account transactions and fund working capital or preexport finance through retained earnings. This means that in the short term most firms were not as badly constrained by restricted access to trade finance as anticipated. Yet, the massive drop in export orders from the end of 2008 through early 2009 means that the internal liquidity of these firms is likely to have dried up. And the survey evidence suggests that this type of financing (rather than necessarily LCs and other guarantees) pushed banks to be more selective and impose adverse conditions (such as greater collateral requirements and higher interest rates), particularly on SMEs. So although the interbank crisis of confidence was over by mid-2009, there was still danger of a second-round effect that could constrain trade and hinder the recovery.

Why Intervene to Address a Trade Finance Gap?

A critical question is whether the decline in trade finance supply resulted from market or government failures and, if so, whether there is a rationale for intervention or correction to address those failures. A precondition for answering this question is to understand what a trade finance gap is and what could contribute to its existence.

Trade Finance Gaps and How They Occur

First, a drop in trade finance could simply be the consequence of declining trade volumes. As long as those trade declines did not derive wholly and directly from *trade* finance constraints, a decline in demand for trade finance cannot be said to actually constitute a gap. In fact, the uncertainty brought about by the crisis might actually *increase* demand for trade finance (at preexisting price levels) as trading partners resort to more formal, bank-intermediated instruments to reduce the higher expected probability of default in open-account trade.[4]

Indeed, in a recent International Chamber of Commerce (ICC) survey, 48 percent of banks indicated they had experienced an increase in demand for issuance of bank undertakings between the last quarter of 2007 and the last quarter of 2008 despite stagnant trade volumes (ICC 2009). These developments are consistent with Berne Union data about export credit and investment insurance agencies, which indicate that, in the last quarter of 2008, total new insurance commitments fell by much less (7 percent) than trade volumes (20 percent), with medium- and long-term commitments remaining constant in volume (Berne Union 2009).

A real "gap" would emerge only when the supply of trade finance is insufficient to clear markets, either because it is not being supplied at all (missing markets) or because prices are temporarily too high to meet demand (overshooting markets).

Missing Markets: Insufficient Supply

Although trade finance transactions are dispersed globally, overall volumes are highly concentrated in a few major international banks, several of which (Lehman Brothers, for instance) went under in the latter part of 2008. Their business would be expected to be reallocated relatively quickly among other suppliers, at least in an efficiently functioning market. However, the severe liquidity constraints and a collective collapse of confidence may, in the short term, mean that alternative banks were unable or unwilling to take on this business. Thus, there might well be a need for transitory intervention to address this supply gap in the market.

There are a number of reasons that bank deleveraging and risk-adjustment processes in response to the financial crisis might unfairly restrict the supply of trade finance more than other forms of bank credit, even though trade finance should be a relatively low-risk product line.[5] Part of the problem may lie in the temporary inability of the market to properly calculate the risks; in other words, it is not a problem of risk per se, but of uncertainty.[6]

Uncertainty plagues trade finance (at least bank-intermediated trade finance) because of the number and nature of the parties involved. For example, in the case of LCs, the bank is reliant on three parties (the customer, the trade partner, and the partner's bank), two of which are in foreign countries. This may not have been perceived as a problem when banks were well capitalized and profits high. However, there is evidence to suggest that the 2008–09 economic crisis brought a systematic recalibration of international risk relative to domestic risk. Such a result stems from both real perceptions of higher macro-level risks and a herdlike "flight to safety" that works against international transactions.

Unique to this crisis is not just that developed-country banks lack confidence in their developing-country counterparts but also the other way around. This collective lack of confidence within the banking system may squeeze trade finance customers more than customers of traditional lines of credit because the most common forms of bank-intermediated trade finance, such as LCs, rely on *interbank* payments. This situation is particularly problematic for exporters in developing countries, who often lack access to other guarantees (for example, through export credit agencies [ECAs] and export-import banks) to cover the risks of nonpayment from developed-country importers. The problem of reduced interbank trust suggests a need for intervention—at the very least in emerging markets—either through the use of guarantees to restore confidence or through the imposition of institutions to ensure transparency and enforcement.

Exacerbating the uncertainty are information asymmetries in international markets, particularly acute in trade finance due to lack of transparency (Allen 2003; Auboin and Meier-Ewert 2008).[7] In the best of times, such informational problems raise the risk of adverse selection. But as Ellingsen and Vlachos (2009) point out, the problem of ensuring a credible commitment from borrowers becomes more severe in a liquidity crisis because of the increased incentive to hoard cash. Extending their argument to the current crisis—characterized by large lending spreads and low returns for most private investors—banks may react by substantially reducing the availability of trade credit and diverting it to credit lines in which the counterparty's incentive to hoard cash is relatively lower. Thus, the risk of strategic default is high, particularly so if there is less trust between banks operating across borders. This moral hazard might be contained through intervention to reduce the incentives to divert credit for other purposes.

The short-term nature of trade finance is also an issue. With the liquidity crisis forcing banks to recapitalize as quickly as possible, trade finance credit lines—most of which have terms of less than 180 days—are relatively easy to call in and so tend to be the first lines of credit that banks cut. Although banks may maximize their own gains by choosing liquidity over loans, in doing so they may fail to take into account the wider benefits to their customers of increased productivity, improved liquidity, and their subsequent spillovers to firms down the supply chain.[8]

Finally, strong political-economy factors may have contributed to the insufficient supply of trade finance during the financial crisis. Because much of the response to the crisis has taken place at the national level, through central banks providing liquidity to domestic banks, there is likely to be strong political pressure and moral suasion to use these funds to support domestic lending. Informal requirements for lending locally have been introduced in several countries. Interventions do create distortions, not only domestically but also across borders, affecting competition across segments of the credit system. This potential for distortionary effects suggests the possible need for further intervention to reestablish the level playing field and support collective action in this regard.

Interfirm trade finance may also face a problem of missing markets. When firms withhold credit for fear of default, buyers are forced to resort to the formal, bank-intermediated market. Similarly, because retained earnings that normally fund preexport working capital dry up in the face of recession, exporters may be forced to seek extended bank credit lines, exacerbating the gap between market demand and supply of trade finance.

Overshooting Markets: A Mismatch of Supply and Demand

The largest piece of the trade finance gap may result not from a lack of demand or supply, but from the two failing to meet—specifically, when the banks' trade finance supply is priced too high to meet market demand. Again, specific aspects of trade finance may make it relatively more prone to this form of market failure, particularly during a financial crisis.

On the supply side, systematic recalibration of risk has forced a downward shift in the supply curve for all kinds of credit. If risks were simply adjusting to new market realities, the cost of risks should at least in part be passed on to customers. Here, price rigidities may come into play. The current economic crisis appears to have brought with it strong deflationary pressure. As a result, market prices for most goods became sticky, giving traders little scope to pass these costs on to customers.

Changes in regulatory regimes (specifically Basel II) may also temporarily affect the efficient functioning of markets—specifically, setting the floor price above that which would clear the market. Although it is not specific to trade finance per se, Basel II characterizes risk (that is, focusing on counterparty risk—normally proxied simply by country risk—rather than on performance risk) in a way that penalizes trade finance because the risk premiums on international transactions tend to be relatively high despite the low performance risk of trade finance. The case is aggravated further for trade involving developing countries, which generally have the highest risk ratings.

Virtually all of the market failures discussed above derive from the severe crisis of confidence affecting markets, in turn leading to greater uncertainty, recalibration of risks, and changed lending behavior. Such a problem of confidence is generally a transitory phenomenon. Markets are already adjusting in terms of the view that risk is assessed and treated. In any adjustment, markets will probably overshoot the equilibrium for a time. In this case, the result is that where markets may have systematically underestimated risk in recent years, they may well be overestimating it in the short term. There may be a case for government intervention that can speed up the adjustment process or that compensates the short-term losers.

Additional Rationales for Intervention

Two final rationales for intervention in support of trade finance lie in the potential multiplier effects inherent in it. Because of the strong interaction between bank-intermediated credit and interfirm credit, a banking sector liquidity shock not only reverberates down supply chains, but also subsequently resonates back into the financial system as a result of increased defaults (Escaith and Gonguet 2009). Thus, trade finance may amplify and prolong the initial crisis, particularly in open economies that are integrated into global production networks. At the same time, an easing of the shock (for example, through the injection of liquidity or a demand stimulus) can also spread quickly across the chain. But because no individual seller is likely to fully take into account the cross-supply-chain gains of extending credit (including both demand and liquidity gains), there may be an insufficient provision of interfirm trade credit along a supply chain.

Second, the complementary nature of trade finance and other forms of firm financing (for example, investment and working capital) suggests that intervention to support trade finance could have a multiplier effect. Because trade credit cannot easily be diverted from production, it actually reduces the likelihood of default on other forms of firm-level financing (Ellingsen and Vlachos 2009). Thus, interventions to increase the flow of trade finance may reduce the cost of capital more generally or at least improve banks' liquidity positions.

Appropriate Intervention Approaches

The international community has had significant experience in dealing with financial crises recently as a result of the Asian crisis and further emerging-market crises in Latin America and in the Russian Federation and Turkey, among others. As such, a wide range of policies, tools, and programs have been implemented to address problems in trade finance markets—targeting specific issues such as liquidity, risk perception, and collective action.

Lessons Learned

Several important lessons can be drawn from the successes and failures of past interventions (Allen 2003):

- Interventions to support trade finance must be accompanied by macro and structural reforms.
- Where the domestic banking sector is weak, interventions that rely on the sector for intermediation are likely to fail.
- If the intervention doesn't target pre- and postexport liquidity, there may be no trade transaction to finance.
- The intervention must implement initiatives in a timely manner, including winding them down when markets begin to normalize.

- Interventions must be designed to ensure they are used by the specific parties being targeted.
- Interventions must ensure that pricing is appropriate, balancing between the risks of moral hazard and failing to complete markets.

Interventions to Date

Official interventions in support of trade finance multiplied in late 2008 and early 2009. As of April 2009, a number of economies and institutions (listed in annex 15.1) had launched domestic and multilateral interventions:

- National authorities have intervened to provide blanket liquidity to banks and targeted trade credit lines and guarantees for exporters that were cut off from trade finance.
- Governments have increased their support of ECAs to reflect substantial increases in demand after credit from traditional sources dried up.[9]
- Development institutions have taken actions to help ease access to trade finance.

For example, in response to the financial crisis, the IFC, among other actions, doubled its Global Trade Finance Program to $3 billion to facilitate trade by providing guarantees that cover the payment risk in trade transactions with local banks in emerging markets. To deal with the liquidity constraint, the IFC also introduced a Global Trade Liquidity Program, which, in collaboration with official and private partners, was designed to provide up to $50 billion of trade liquidity support in the three years following its launch in July 2009.[10]

Regional development banks such as the African Development Bank, the Asian Development Bank, the European Bank for Reconstruction and Development, and the Inter-American Development Bank also launched or expanded their trade finance programs.

Ten Principles for Intervention

Drawing on the lessons from past crises, the authors propose a set of 10 principles for effective public actions to support trade finance in the wake of the 2008–09 crisis.

Targeted interventions

One clear lesson that has already emerged from this crisis is that any money flowing into the banks—unless it is properly ring fenced and conditions are attached—is at risk of being used for recapitalization rather than lending. This risk can be overcome by asking the banks to set up special-purpose trade finance vehicles that would be required to use the new liquidity or risk capacity solely for financing trade with emerging markets.

Holistic response

Without corresponding measures to address wider liquidity issues of banks and to stimulate lending for investment and working capital purposes, neither the banks nor their customers who participate in the trade finance market will be healthy enough to do so.

Integration with existing institutions

Most trade finance operates within fairly well-established institutional relationships, using simple products such as LCs. Effective interventions in past crises have generally worked within these existing market practices and documentation and did not seek to reinvent mechanisms or to apply unduly complicated documentation or practices.

Collective action

The interdependencies in the financial system, more than ever, demand a coordinated effort to revive trade finance flows. Coordinating national interventions could send a powerful signal to market participants that could help restore confidence and eventually lower the overall cost of public intervention. Coordination at the regional level can also be effective. For example, the Asia-Pacific Economic Cooperation established the Asia-Pacific Trade Insurance Network at the end of 2008 to facilitate regional trade. The international community appears to have recognized the importance of such coordination, and initiatives coming out of the G-20 meeting in London have adhered to this approach.

Balance of risk and liquidity support

The current crisis requires interventions that address real liquidity constraints (for banks and firms) as well as those that perceived escalation of counterparty risk. A combination of ring-fenced funding to support trade finance loans as well partial guarantee programs (like the IFC's Global Trade Finance Program) that help offset the heightened risk premium in the current market may be effective to catalyze trade finance lending.

Importance of developed-market banks to emerging markets

Without attention to international banks' involvement in trade finance and acknowledgment of their huge distribution power and networks as fundamental to the global supply chain, initiatives that are devised to address the crisis may be too fragmented to have more than a marginal impact. Any new risk capacity should be distributed by institutions having the necessary processing capacity and technical expertise. As such, financial institutions in developed markets will be key players.

Promotion of interfirm credit

There is scope for financial institutions and enterprises to promote other sources of short-term financing, particularly for the large share of the market involved in integrated global supply chains. One such instrument that may be well suited to the heightened risk environment is factoring, which involves the outright purchase of an exporter's invoices at a discount rather than the collateralization of a loan. Although factoring is still a relatively small source of credit in emerging markets, the crisis affords an opportunity to expand factoring in both low-income and emerging countries.

Level playing field in terms of risk weight

As a result of Basel II, market dynamics, and domestic political pressures linked to bank bailouts, banks are increasingly going to give preference in their capital management processes and lending decisions to either domestic customers or those with a favorable risk profile. One way to offset the resulting risk handicap that trade finance counterparties in emerging markets incur is to provide partial risk guarantees from AAA-rated institutions, along the lines of the programs offered by the multilateral development banks. In the short term, at least, promotion of continued flexibility in the implementation of Basel II risk weighting may also help to give some relief to trade finance.

Improved transparency

The lack of available loss data for trade finance transactions—as well as participants' one-size-fits-all assumption that all trade is low-risk—are major factors in the specific problem of uncertainty in the trade finance market. This can be remedied only through a concerted collaboration of all the major trade finance banks to collate default and loss data so that appropriate relief can be argued with regulators and the Bank for International Standards. The creation of a Berne Union of banks as a forum for regular, confidential sharing of such data could be a potential long-term solution. In interfirm credit markets, extending public credit registers and voluntary exchange mechanisms to developing countries (where these systems are often still being designed) and promoting the sharing of this information across trading countries could be another important long-term solution.

Avoidance of moral hazards and wasteful subsidies

Achieving the desired aim of stimulating greater trade finance lending is a significant enough challenge. Doing so without creating substantial moral hazards or subsidizing "winners" is an even greater one. This challenge can be partly addressed through targeted programs that restrict program access to those banks and firms that really need them. However, experience has shown that achieving such restrictions often results in complicated programs that end up being too cumbersome and costly to be taken up in the market. Nonetheless, some practices have been shown to be effective in limiting moral hazards and wasteful subsidies—among them, limiting program time frames to avoid crowding out commercial banks and sharing rather than fully underwriting risk.

Annex 15.1 Governmental and Institutional Measures to Support Trade Finance, 2008–09

In the wake of the 2008–09 global financial crisis, governments have taken measures to make trade finance more accessible and affordable and also to support industries through potentially trade-distorting measures (table 15A.1).

With the liquidity crunch, international traders are requiring more secured means of payments than open accounts, increasing demand for documented transactions (for example, LCs) and guarantees. SMEs in developing countries are particularly challenged in coping with the rapidly changing risk landscape.

Table 15A.1 Governments and Multilateral Institutions that Took Trade Finance Measures, as of April 2009

Economy or institution	Trade Finance Measures
Argentina	√
Brazil	√
China	√
Ecuador	√
European Union	√
France	√
Finland	√
Germany	√
Italy	√
Netherlands	√
Portugal	√
Indonesia	√
India	√
Israel	√

(continued next page)

Table 15A.1 *continued*

Economy or institution	Trade Finance Measures
Japan	√
New Zealand	√
Norway	√
Korea, Rep.	√
Serbia	√
Taiwan, China	√
Thailand	√
United States	√
Vietnam	√
ASEAN, Japan, China, Korea, Rep.	√
Asian Development Bank	√
African Development Bank	√
G-20	√
Inter-American Development Bank	√
Islamic Development Bank	√
World Bank	√
International Monetary Bank	√
European Bank for Reconstruction and Development	√

Source: Authors' compilation.
Note: ASEAN = Association of Southeast Asian Nations. Trade finance includes loans and guarantees, foreign exchange allocations, subsidies, and other government financial support, including tax reductions and rebates.

Notes

1. "We will ensure availability of at least $250 billion over the next two years to support trade finance through our export credit and investment agencies and through the [multilateral development banks]. We also ask our regulators to make use of available flexibility in capital requirements for trade finance" (G-20 2009).

2. Although this range of 80–90 percent is widely reported, the source and evidence for the claim are unclear.

3. Of course, this is not true in all cases. Specific problems occur with products that are perishable (whose value erodes quickly or immediately), extremely differentiated (where there is little or no market value outside the intended buyer), and for services (which generally cannot be collateralized).

4. The economic crisis would be expected to threaten the viability of firms across supply chains and so would raise the overall probability of default in any interfirm financed exchange.

5. Bank deleveraging and risk adjustment is not in itself a reason for intervention. Indeed, it is a critical process to restore stability and confidence in the financial system over the medium and long term.

6. The reference here is to Knight's (1921) classic distinction between risk (where the probability of an outcome can be calculated mathematically) and uncertainty (where the probability of an outcome cannot be calculated, and so cannot be insured against).

7. It is normally difficult to get reliable information about the balance sheet of a foreign company (especially an SME) or a foreign bank.

8. This may be particularly relevant during a recessionary period, when spare capacity is likely to be high.

9. Economies that launched new programs include Chile, China, France, Germany, Hong Kong, the Nordic countries, and the United States. The programs include some specific bilateral agreements to provide targeted funding through export-import banks, including $20 billion between China and the United States and $3 billion between Korea and the United States.

10. For a more detailed discussion of the IFC Global Trade Finance Program and Global Trade Liquidity Program, see chapter 18 of this volume.

References

Allen, M. 2003. "Trade Finance in Financial Crises: Assessment of Key Issues." Paper prepared by the Policy Development and Review Department, International Monetary Fund, Washington, DC. http://www.imf.org/external/np/pdr/cr/2003/eng/120903.pdf.

Arvis, J-F. and M. Shakya. 2009. "Integration of Less Developed Countries in Global Supply Chains: A Global Buyers' and Producers' Perspective." Unpublished manuscript, World Bank, Washington, DC.

Auboin, M., and M. Meier-Ewert. 2008. "Improving the Availability of Trade Finance during Financial Crises." Discussion paper, World Trade Organization, Geneva.

Berne Union. 2009. Berne Union Statistics: Five-Year Trends (database). Berne Union, London. http://www.berneunion.org.uk/bu-total-data.html. Accessed July 2009.

Ellingsen, T., and J. Vlachos. 2009. "Trade Finance During Liquidity Crisis." Policy Research Working Paper 5136, World Bank, Washington, DC.

Escaith, H., and F. Gonguet. 2009. "International Trade and Real Transmission Channels of Financial Shocks in Globalized Production Networks." Final discussion draft for the Economic Research and Statistics Division, World Trade Organization, Geneva.

Freund, C., and L. Klapper. 2009. "Firm Financing and Trade in the Financial Crisis." Unpublished manuscript, World Bank, Washington, DC.

G-20 (Group of Twenty Finance Ministers and Central Bank Governors). 2009. "Leaders' Statement: The Global Plan for Recovery and Reform." Communique of 2009 G-20 London Summit, April 2.

Giannetti, Mariassunta, Mike Burkart, and Tore Ellingsen. 2008. "What You Sell Is What You Lend? Explaining Trade Credit Contracts." *The Review of Financial Studies* (online). http://rfs.oxfordjournals.org/content/early/2007/12/31/rfs.hhn096.full.pdf.

ICC (International Chamber of Commerce). 2009. "Rethinking Trade Finance 2009: An ICC Global Survey." Banking Commission Market Intelligence Report, ICC, Paris.

International Financial Consulting, Ltd. 2009. "Strategic Assessment of Trade Finance in Emerging Markets." Unpublished manuscript, World Bank, Washington, DC.

IMF-BAFT (International Monetary Fund – Bankers' Association for Finance and Trade). 2009. "Trade Finance Survey: A Survey among Banks Assessing the Current Trade Finance Environment." Report by FImetrix for IMF and BAFT, Washington, DC.

Kiyotaki, N., and J. Moore. 1997. Credit Cycles. *Journal of Political Economy* 105 (2): 211–48.

Knight, F. H. 1921. *Risk, Uncertainty, and Profit.* New York: August M. Kelley.

Malouche, M. 2009. "Trade and Trade Finance Developments in 14 Developing Countries Post-September 2008." Policy Research Working Paper 5138, World Bank, Washington, DC.

Menichini, A. 2009. "Inter-Firm Trade Finance in Times of Crisis." Policy Research Working Paper 5112, World Bank, Washington, DC.

Raddatz, C. 2010. "Credit Chains and Sectoral Comovement: Does the Use of Trade Credit Amplify Sectoral Shocks?" *The Review of Economics and Statistics* 92 (4): 985–1003.

SHOULD DEVELOPING COUNTRIES ESTABLISH EXPORT CREDIT AGENCIES?

Jean-Pierre Chauffour, Christian Saborowski, and Ahmet I. Soylemezoglu

International trade plunged in the latter half of 2008 and throughout 2009 (Baldwin 2009). The global financial meltdown not only led to a substantial drop in economic activity in both emerging markets and the developed world, but also made it increasingly difficult for potential trading partners to gain access to external finance. Although trade finance—due to its self-liquidating character—is generally on the low-risk, high-collateral side of the finance spectrum and underwritten by long-standing practices between banks and traders, developments have shown that it has not been spared by the credit crisis (Auboin 2009; Chauffour and Farole 2009).

The sharp drop in trade volumes was driven primarily by a contraction in global demand. Yet the decline in trade finance—itself driven mainly by the fall in the demand for trade activities but also, at least partly, by liquidity shortages—is likely to have further accelerated the slowdown. Reliable statistics on trade finance are scarce, but available evidence suggests that trade credit was the second-biggest cause of the trade collapse (Mora and Powers 2009). Anecdotal evidence from banks and traders reinforces this view, as do the sharp increase in short-term trade credit spreads and the sheer size of the trade volume decline.

Both bankers and the international community have since called upon state-backed export credit agencies (ECAs) to expand their operations to mitigate credit risk and keep trade finance markets from drying up. Given the renewed interest in

ECAs, the question arises whether a larger number of developing countries should follow suit and establish their own agencies to support exporting firms and to avoid severe trade finance shortages in times of crisis.

This chapter discusses some issues that require attention when deciding whether a country should establish an ECA as well as what shape, form, and modus operandi it should take. It also discusses why any decision to establish an ECA should be made only after a careful evaluation of the impact of such an institution on both the financial and real sectors of the economy. In addition, the choice of a sustainable business model for the ECA is crucial. The chapter does not seek to provide definitive answers as to whether, when, and how developing countries should establish ECAs. However, it tilts toward extreme caution in setting up such entities in low-income countries with weak institutions and highlights a range of factors that policy makers should consider in deciding whether an ECA should be established.

Export Credit Insurance and Guarantees: Public Agency Support?

Opening the discussion is an analysis of data from the International Union of Investment Insurers (the Berne Union) on the export credit insurance industry. The issuance of export credit insurance and guarantees is an aspect of trade finance that is of crucial importance, especially in a crisis environment of high systemic risk. In the context of a declining secondary market to offload loans, along with an increase in bank counterparty risk, demand is high for export credit insurance and guarantees.

The market for export credit insurance and guarantees comprises not only private but also public players, namely ECAs. Whereas the market for short-term insurance (credit terms of up to and including 12 months, for the purposes of this chapter) is dominated by private agencies (some 80 percent of overall business), ECAs underwrite the wider majority of medium- to long-term commitments.

The Berne Union is the leading association for export credit and investment insurance worldwide. Its members represent all aspects (private and public) of the export credit and investment insurance industry worldwide. The Berne Union made recent country-by-country data available to the World Bank's International Trade Department that span 2005 through the third quarter of 2009. The data cover 41 countries, 9 of which are classified as high-income countries, 22 as middle-income countries, and 10 as low-income countries. For a given country, the dataset includes information on the total value of insurance offers and insurance commitments on its imports.[1]

Figure 16.1 shows the evolution of both global trade and export credit insurance volumes from the first quarter of 2005 through the third of 2009. Mirroring

Figure 16.1 World Trade and Trade Insurance Volumes

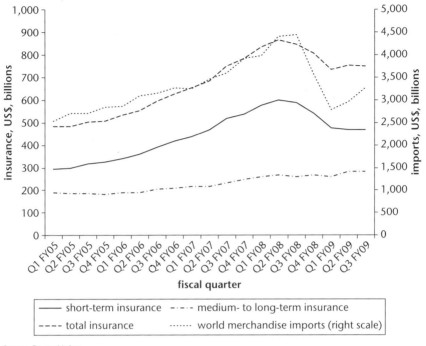

Source: Berne Union.

trade volumes, total insurance commitments of the Berne Union's members grew steadily during the past few years before dropping between the second quarter of 2008 and the first of 2009. Total insurance volumes have since recovered side by side with trade volumes. Intuitively, a growing volume of trade will increase the demand for trade finance, insurance, and guarantees independent of any change in the risk environment. This is likely the main reason why the export insurance business has grown steadily over the past years.

Similarly, the fall in trade volumes from the second quarter of 2008 through the first of 2009 can be seen as a proximate factor explaining the drop in overall insurance commitments. It is striking, however, that insurance volumes fell by much less (15 percent) than did global merchandise trade (36 percent) during this period. This observation is consistent with anecdotal evidence suggesting that trading partners resorted to more formal, bank-intermediated instruments to finance trade since the outbreak of the financial crisis to reduce the high probability of default in open-account financing. In addition, the increase in bank counterparty risk may have led to a substitution of export credit insurance for other trade finance products such as letters of credit. Such developments would lead to a greater relative demand for external credit insurance and guarantees despite the substantial increase in risk premiums and the cost of insurance, thus reflecting the increasingly important role of insurance and guarantees during times of crisis.

Figure 16.1 also illustrates how the composition of export credit insurance has evolved. Short-term insurance commitments almost doubled in value until the beginning of the financial crisis but dropped strongly (by 22 percent) between the second quarter of 2008 and the first of 2009 and kept falling at a slower pace thereafter (by 2 percent). Medium- to long-term commitments, however, remained almost constant in volume during the period of the strongest impact of the crisis (falling by 3 percent) and have recovered since then (increasing by 9 percent since the first quarter of 2009).

How may these findings be rationalized? Medium- to long-term insurance is typically used for large-scale transactions. The surge in longer-term relative to shorter-term commitments since the second quarter of 2008 was therefore likely because demand for insurance for large-scale transactions increases in an environment of high systemic risk. Given the need to recapitalize in a timely manner, supply-side factors may also have affected the composition of different maturities in insurance commitments. Indeed, with insurers and banks needing to recapitalize and offload their balance sheets from liabilities whose risk is difficult to assess, short-term commitments are more easily terminated on short notice.

However, given that insurance premiums for longer-term insurance are particularly expensive in an environment of high systemic risk and given that capital expenditures dropped rapidly during the crisis, the magnitude of the divergence between short-term and medium- to long-term volumes is difficult to explain solely based on the perspective of private market participants. Indeed, a likely factor that could explain these findings is the active intervention of the public sector. Whereas ECAs backed by state guarantees underwrite only about 10 percent of overall policies, this share is much higher for medium- to long-term insurance and historically accounts for most of the collected premiums and disbursed claims in export credit insurance. In other words, governments and multilateral institutions followed through on their pledges to boost trade finance programs.

It is interesting to consider the change in the composition of medium- to long-term commitments across income groups. Figure 16.2 shows that between the second quarter of 2008 and the first of 2009, medium- to long-term commitments grew by 6 percent for high-income economies, compared with decreases of 7 percent and 4 percent for low- and middle-income economies, respectively.

These numbers likely partly reflect the growing need for export insurance and guarantees for trade flows to industrialized economies that were previously at the low end of the risk spectrum. However, the figures may also indicate a shortage in

Figure 16.2 Medium- to Long-Term Export Credit Insurance

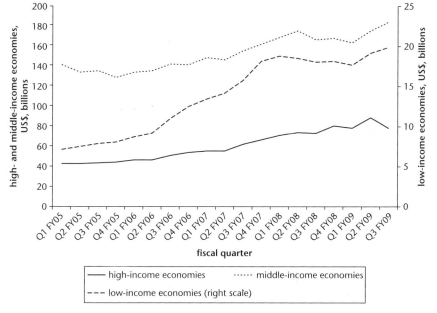

Source: Berne Union.

insurance supply for trade flows to developing, as opposed to developed, markets when the crisis reached its peak.[2] In the period after the first quarter of 2009, however, medium- to long-term insurance volumes rebounded strongly in both low- and middle-income economies (12 percent), suggesting that ECAs were more successful in supporting trade flows to developing countries during later stages of the crisis.

Key Issues When Setting Up an ECA

These findings suggest that ECAs, in line with recent pledges, may indeed have expanded their operations during the financial crisis to keep trade finance markets from drying up. The natural question to ask is whether more developing countries should follow suit and establish their own agencies to alleviate market frictions and support exporting firms. This section highlights specific issues that require attention when deciding whether to establish such an institution.

Many countries in both the developed and the developing worlds have set up ECAs to finance exports and alleviate market failures. However, it is difficult to make a generalized statement about the need for, and the most appropriate shape and form of, these institutions. Given that restructuring, reforming, or abolishing a public institution is more difficult than establishing one, the decision to set up an ECA should result from a comprehensive evaluation process.

Although the main motivation to establish an export finance institution may differ from one country to another, the creation of a public financial institution—the main task of which is to direct credit to a specific set of economic activities—always represents an intervention into the resource allocation process of the domestic economy. Whether such intervention is warranted or adds value should be carefully examined and satisfactorily answered during the decision process. The issues involved in this regard are complex and have been at the core of an ongoing debate.[3]

Any type of financial institution that aims to play a part in the financing of exports has an impact on two main dimensions in the country where it is located. First, the financial institution's activity changes the structure of the financial sector and influences the behavior of other financial institutions (financial sector dimension). Second, it changes the incentive framework in the real sector (real sector dimension). The net impact on the economy as a whole depends on many factors—ranging from the structure of the real economy and its competitive position to the overall governance environment in the country and the business model for the new institution (business model dimension).

Financial Sector Dimension

At least two questions should be addressed regarding the financial sector when considering the establishment of an ECA. The first question is whether the ECA can provide additionality through more trade finance-related products and services or greater volumes of such products, given conditions in the country's financial sector. The answer to this question will give a fairly good idea of whether such an institution is needed. The second question concerns the impact of an ECA on the equilibrium level of prices and quantities in financial markets as well as on the growth dynamics of the financial sector.[4]

Public intervention in financial markets, like any marketplace intervention, can be justified when significant and persistent externalities or market failures persist. The principles of effective intervention to support trade finance have been examined by Chauffour and Farole (2009). Ellingsen and Vlachos (2009), among others, argue that public support of trade finance volumes can be more effective than support for other types of credit. Menichini (2009) emphasizes the particular nature of interfirm trade finance and discusses policy options to support interfirm financing volumes during times of crisis.

Examination of the need for a specialized export finance institution needs to start with comprehensive analysis of the current conditions and trends in the domestic financial sector. The analysis of the financial system should aim to detect any market failures and imperfections that may adversely affect the volume of exports. In this regard, it is important to assess the financial system's capability of (a) attracting both domestic savings and foreign flows of capital and (b) carrying out its intermediary functions. In other words, the depth of the financial system and actual lending practices should be examined carefully. The lack of financial depth is an important factor and usually takes the form of a resource constraint for the financial sector and, in turn, inadequate supply of credit to the real sector.

To make an informed decision about whether sufficient externalities or market failures are present to justify intervention, one finds it instructive to pay close attention to the following issues:

- The levels and terms of working capital and investment finance
- The mechanisms to obtain working capital and investment finance
- The presence of any peculiar constraints for exporting firms to obtain finance
- The capacity of the banking system to handle cross-border transactions.

In addition to the analysis of the domestic financial sector, the financial systems in export markets as well as in competitor countries warrant closer attention. Because it is difficult to expand exports to markets where buyers face significant financial sector-related constraints—in terms of both the availability and the pricing of financial products (especially trade-related)—such market failure can have an impact on the domestic economy similar to a genuinely domestic market imperfection. Market failures in partner countries may thus equally require intervention by the domestic government. In fact, the origins of many export finance institutions lie in this argument.

Another important dimension of export financing is the availability of special financing schemes offered by other countries that supply investment goods and raw materials. The export sector can use these facilities for both working capital and investment finance. However, while these facilities can potentially be important sources of funding for exporting firms, especially for exporters of manufactured goods, the same institutions may work against the interest of the country's exporting firms if they support the competition in export markets.

Interventions into financial markets by way of funds earmarked for special purposes or specialized financial institutions, if they are not additional to the existing pool of funds within the financial sector, serve as mechanisms of credit directing and rationing.[5] This could have a considerable impact on the competitive pricing of credit. The magnitude of this impact depends on both the amount of the additional funds and the relative amount of credit demand.

Specialized financial institutions undoubtedly influence the composition of banks' loan books. The nature of this influence is highly dependent on the ECA's business model (Ascari 2007). For example, an ECA involved in retail lending and loans directed to final beneficiaries usually reduces lending by the rest of the financial sector to the targeted activities. However, the financial sector usually increases its lending to targeted activities if the ECA issues guarantees or acts as some sort of second-tier institution. Hence, following an intervention, the composition of final lending occurs either by choice of banks or by choice of borrowers. Which of these paths creates more distortion is an important question that must be answered.

ECAs can also potentially undermine the development of the financial sector. The presence of such institutions may discourage private banks from developing export-related financial products or may delink certain types of activities or borrowers from the commercial banking system if their influence becomes large. This result will limit the banking system's understanding and information about the activities and borrowers engaged in the export sector. In turn, the banking system may not only reduce its exposure to these activities but individual banks may also become hesitant to engage in additional business with the same borrowers because the system might not be able to properly assess underlying risks.

Likewise, a heavy reliance on ECAs primarily for borrowing may cause exporters to incur larger costs for other transactions. Commercial banks typically provide a wide array of services that an ECA cannot match in their entirety. A commercial bank may require higher fees from a client that maintains only limited business with the bank than it requires from a client that demands a variety of products and services. For example, a commercial bank may require higher fees for the opening of a letter of credit or the issuance of a performance bond from a customer that does not borrow from it and does not do business with it otherwise. To avoid such situations and to endorse close relations between exporters and the country's financial system, ECAs should channel their products to existing financial institutions as much as possible. The ECA's charter must, moreover, be clear enough to prevent competition between the ECA and the financial sector.

Real Sector Dimension

The main motivation behind the decision to establish an export finance institution is usually the judgment that a change in the behavior of the real sector toward export-related activities is warranted. In fact, an export finance institution is viewed as one of the main elements of a broader incentive framework to increase exports. It is therefore important to understand why policy makers desire an increase in export volumes and whether specific export products and markets are to be targeted. These questions are crucial in designing the broader incentive framework, including the financing element, and in determining the appropriate business model for the ECA.

ECAs typically support various types of firms operating in different sectors of the economy. However, driven by the same objectives that led to its founding, an ECA's activities are often biased toward a specific subset of sectors of the domestic economy. Consequently, export finance institutions may end up serving a narrow set of economic activities. If the broader incentive framework to boost exports (including the export finance element) is effective, the composition of both real sector activities and exports may change. Such changes will inevitably alter the structure of the economy and its macro balances in the long run.

Different policy objectives regarding the real economy point to different types of ECAs. For example, an ECA with wider reach may be preferable if balance-of-payment concerns are dominant. If, however, export-led growth policies are to be pursued, an export finance institution could be useful to promote economies of scale by dealing only with firms above a certain size threshold.

The financial products of an export finance institution should be shaped by the founding objectives. For example, providing credit to a cotton outgrower scheme for export purposes may require working capital loans with at least nine months' maturity, although a three-month facility would be sufficient for most manufacturing processes. If the country is mainly concerned with providing credit to buyers of its exports, the nature of the financial products needed would differ from those needed to support exporting firms with credit or guarantees directly. In particular, longer terms and lower interest rates may be necessary if the objective is to provide credit to purchasers of exports.

Finally, it should be kept in mind that real sector conditions evolve over time, both domestically and globally. Sufficient flexibility should be built into the product range and the ECA's objectives to allow it to adjust. For example, an ECA that starts out solely supporting the country's domestic export base can evolve into a global underwriter of trade risk or a facilitator of international projects that works with different suppliers from various countries, some of which may be competing with domestic firms.

Business Model Dimension

Specifying business models and governance structures as well as their implementation have proven to be important challenges for public sector entities. These challenges are especially formidable for financial institutions owned directly by the state.

A well-functioning financial sector is an important precondition to a sustainable path of economic development. Strong financial systems are built on good governance—of both the intermediaries and their regulators. An ECA is typically strongly linked with the government, although there are various options for the precise structure of the relationship. The institution is also designed to interact with many firms and financial institutions in the private sector. A satisfactory governance record is therefore crucial not only to efficient fulfillment of an ECA's role in the economy, but also to its influence on the quality of governance in the economy as a whole, given its tight relationships with both the government and the private sector (Beck and Honohan 2006). The stronger the ECA's position in the economy and the larger the resources dedicated to its business, arguably the more enhanced its role will be.

In the specification of an ECA business model, its governance structure should thus be among the most important considerations. In particular, the nature and quality of its board of directors deserve special attention because they could be potential destabilizing factors. Good governance cannot be achieved if the ECA's senior management and board of directors are not properly configured.

Care should also be taken in specifying a legal form for the ECA that is consistent with its business model. At least two interlinked quality characteristics, described below, are desirable in achieving efficient functioning of the institution as well as a strong governance record: operational independence and a sustainable mandate.

Operational independence

First, the ECA should be given operational independence. Good governance is difficult to achieve in the absence of an entity's operational independence and without a supporting legal form. In this respect—and because the independence of an export finance institution cannot realistically be achieved if the institution fails to generate enough income to meet its operational expenses and produce a surplus—it is important to equip the ECA with sufficiently large resources from the outset to efficiently fulfill its role in the economy.

The amount of operational expenses varies widely, depending on the ECA's specific business model. An institution involved in retail lending will need to have more staff, more branches, and a more expansive information technology (IT) platform than a second-tier organization would require. A small-guarantee scheme that underwrites specific portfolios of commercial banks could technically be operated by just a few people. If sufficient funds are not available, the potential outsourcing of some functions such as payroll and IT, using specialized consultancy services, should be considered as an option.

A sustainable mandate

Second, an ECA must be given a mandate that is both sustainable and compatible with the objectives of the institution. Sufficient financial resources are again important in fulfilling this condition. An export finance institution will likely fail to achieve its objectives if it cannot dispose of sufficient and sustainable resources from the outset. Many developing countries have established various export finance schemes and structures, but these institutions have failed to be relevant because of resource constraints. For the ECA to meet its objectives, it should be a relevant player in the country where it is located, in terms of both its resource base and its operational footprint.

A strong governance structure and the availability of a sufficiently large capital stock for the ECA to act independently and to have a strong enough operational footprint to achieve its objectives are two preconditions that are unlikely to be met in many low-income countries. Low-income countries often suffer from sovereign debt problems, weak institutional capacity, lack of good governance practices, and, more broadly, difficulties in applying the rule of law. These concerns are reminiscent of those related to the functioning of other types of public-backed institutions to support exports. For instance, export promotion agencies in developing countries have long been criticized for lacking strong leadership and client orientation, being inadequately funded, and suffering from government involvement (Lederman, Olarreaga, and Payton 2009).

A possible way to circumvent these issues may be the foundation of some form of a global ECA—in other words, an ECA designed as an international institution to support exporting firms in various low-income countries. The relative merits of establishing such an institution, however, would go beyond the scope of this chapter.

Conclusions

A number of issues require attention when deciding whether a country should establish an ECA as well as what shape, form, and modus operandi it should have. Any decision to establish such a specialized financial institution should be made only after a careful evaluation of its potential impact on both the financial and the real sectors of the economy.

In addition, the choice of a sustainable business model is crucial. A sustainable business model involves a strong governance structure as well as the availability of a sufficiently large capital stock for the institution to be capable of acting independently and to have a strong enough operational footprint to achieve its objectives. These are two preconditions that are seldom met in low-income economies, which often suffer from sovereign debt problems, weak institutional capacity, poor governance practices, and difficulties in applying the rule of law.

Notes

1. It is important to notice that the sample, albeit representative in its composition, does not cover all countries whose imports are insured by Berne Union members.

2. Insurance volumes had been growing strongly for low-income economies before the recent drop. Thus, an alternative explanation may be that volumes are returning to normal levels.

3. State intervention in financial markets has been discussed by many in the literature (addressing concerns such as principal-agent problems, information asymmetries, and regulation). Stiglitz (1994) and Besley (1994) provide good generalized discussions of state intervention in the financial sector. See also Zingales (2004) for a critique of endorsements of state intervention based on Coase's (1960) arguments applied to financial regulation.

4. The issues mentioned here are valid for a broader set of development finance institutions (DFIs) in developing countries, of which ECAs can be regarded a subset. DFIs are also the subject of many debates (Beck and Honohan 2006; De la Torre, Gozzi, and Schmukler 2007).

5. The impact of government intervention in financial markets on the equilibrium level of prices and quantities has been subject to close examination from a wide range of perspectives. For theoretical treatments of historical arguments, see Stiglitz (1994); Hoff and Stiglitz (2001); and Murphy, Shleifer, and Vishny (1989). For an empirical study of the impact of government-owned institutions, see Barth, Caprio, and Levine (2001) and Caprio and Honohan (2001).

References

Ascari, R. 2007. "Is Export Credit Agency a Misnomer? The ECA Response to a Changing World." Working Paper 02, SACE Group, Rome.

Auboin, M. 2009. "The Challenges of Trade Financing." Commentary, VoxEU.org, Centre for Economic Policy Research, London. http://www.voxeu.org/index.php?q=node/2905.

Baldwin, R. 2009. "The Great Trade Collapse: What Caused It, and What Does It Mean?" In *The Great Trade Collapse: Causes, Consequences and Prospects*, ed. R. Baldwin, 1–14. VoxEU.org e-book. London: Centre for Trade and Economic Integration. http://voxeu.org/index.php?q=node/4304.

Barth, J., G. Caprio, and R. Levine. 2001. "Banking Systems around the Globe: Do Regulation and Ownership Affect Performance and Stability?" In *Prudential Regulation and Supervision: Why Is It Important and What Are the Issues?*, ed. F. Mishkin, 31–96. Cambridge, MA: National Bureau for Economic Research.

Beck, T., and P. Honohan. 2006. *Making Finance Work for Africa*. Washington, DC: World Bank.

Besley, T. 1994. "How Do Market Failures Justify Interventions in Rural Credit Markets?" *The World Bank Research Observer* 9 (1): 27–47.

Caprio, G., and P. Honohan. 2001. *Finance for Growth: Policy Choices in a Volatile World*. World Bank Policy Research Report. New York: Oxford University Press.

Chauffour, J.-P., and T. Farole. 2009. "Trade Finance in Crisis: Market Adjustment or Market Failure?" Policy Research Working Paper 5003, World Bank, Washington, DC.

Coase, R. 1960. "The Problem of Social Cost." *The Journal of Law & Economics* 3 (October): 1–44.

De la Torre, A., J. Gozzi, and S. Schmukler. 2007. "Innovative Experiences in Access to Finance: Market Friendly Roles for the Visible Hand?" Policy Research Working Paper 4326, World Bank, Washington, DC.

Ellingsen, T., and J. Vlachos. 2009. "Trade Finance in a Liquidity Crisis." Policy Research Working Paper 5136, World Bank, Washington, DC.

Hoff, K., and J. Stiglitz. 2001. "Modern Economic Theory and Development." In *The Future of Development Economics in Perspective*, ed. G. Meier and J. Stiglitz, 389–459. Washington, DC: World Bank; New York: Oxford University Press.

Lederman, D., M. Olarreaga, and L. Payton. 2009. "Export Promotion Agencies Revisited." Policy Research Working Paper 5125, World Bank, Washington, DC.

Menichini, A. 2009. "Inter-Firm Trade Finance in Times of Crisis." Policy Research Working Paper 5112, World Bank, Washington, DC.

Mora, J., and W. Powers. 2009. "Decline and Gradual Recovery of Global Trade Financing: U.S. and Global Perspectives." VoxEU.org article, Centre for Economic Policy Research, London. http://www.voxeu.org/index.php?q=node/4298.

Murphy, K., A. Shleifer, and R. Vishny. 1989. "Industrialization and the Big Push." *Journal of Political Economy* 97 (5): 1003–26.

Stiglitz, J. 1994. "The Role of the State in Financial Markets." In *Proceedings of the World Bank Annual Conference on Development Economics 1993*, 41–46. Washington, DC: World Bank

Zingales, L. 2004. "The Costs and Benefits of Financial Market Regulation." Law Series Working Paper 21/2004, European Corporate Governance Institute, Brussels.

INSTITUTIONAL TRADE FINANCE SUPPORT DURING THE 2008–09 FINANCIAL CRISIS

WORLD TRADE ORGANIZATION RESPONSE TO THE CRISIS: A CONVENING POWER TO BOOST THE AVAILABILITY OF TRADE FINANCE

Marc Auboin

About 80–90 percent of world trade relies on some form of trade finance. Since the first half of 2008, there has been evidence of tightening market conditions for trade finance. As market participants expected, the situation worsened in the second half of the year and further declined in the first quarter of 2009. In market-based surveys, respondents indicated they expected the trade finance market to face difficult times through 2009. This situation had the potential to accelerate the great trade collapse due to a finance shortage—a direct spillover from the financial crisis. Policy intervention was required to avoid a disorganization of the trade finance market and a reduction of trade flows, particularly in the direction of developing countries.

Although public-backed institutions responded rapidly in 2008, their interventions were not enough to bridge the gap between supply and demand of trade finance worldwide at that time. As a result, the G-20 members, during their April 2009 London Summit, adopted a wider package for injecting some $250 billion in support of trade finance. This package greatly helped to restore confidence in world trade finance markets and, in particular, to secure international supply chains. In 2010, the global trade finance situation improved, but some gaps remain at the periphery of global trade flows.

This chapter lays out some recent facts and explains decisions made at the G-20 London Summit regarding what was potentially one of the main sources of contagion of the financial crisis from a trade perspective.

Why Trade Finance Matters

Part of the collapse of world trade, particularly in its early stage in late 2008, was due to problems with trade credit financing, but the policy response was rapid and prevented the problem from becoming worse. The global market for trade finance (credit and insurance) was estimated to be around $10 trillion–$12 trillion in 2008—roughly 80 percent of that year's trade flows.

The potential damage to the real economy from shrinking trade finance is enormous. International supply-chain arrangements have globalized not only production but also trade finance. Sophisticated supply-chain financing operations, including those for small and medium enterprises (SMEs), rely on a high level of trust and confidence that global suppliers will deliver their share of the value added and have the necessary financial means to produce and export it in a timely manner. Any disruption in the financial sector's ability to provide working capital, provide preshipment export finance, issue or endorse letters of credit, or deliver export credit insurance could create a gap in complex, outward-processing assembly operations and lead by itself to a contraction in trade and output.

WTO Involvement in Trade Finance Issues

The *institutional case* for the World Trade Organization (WTO) to be concerned about the scarcity of trade finance during periods of crisis is relatively clear. In situations of extreme financial crisis, the resulting credit crunch has the potential to reduce trade finance and hence trade. This happened already during the Asian financial crisis, when the collapse of the financial sector brought trade to a halt in some countries. In the immediate aftermath of the currency crisis, a large amount of outstanding trade credit lines had to be rescheduled on an emergency basis by creditors and debtors to reignite trade flows and hence the economy. Under the umbrella of the Marrakech Mandate on Coherence, the heads of the WTO, the International Monetary Fund (IMF), and the World Bank in 2003 convened an Expert Group on Trade Finance to examine what went wrong in the trade finance market and prepare contingencies.

The *economic case* for the involvement of international organizations, in particular the WTO, is based on the idea that trade finance is largely a secure, short-term, self-liquidating form of finance (Auboin and Meier-Ewert 2003). Even in some of the most acute periods of financial crisis (for example, in 1825 and 1930), international credit lines have never been cut off. For centuries, the expansion of trade has depended on (a) reliable and cost-effective sources of finance, backed by a deep, global secondary market of fluid and secured financing instruments; and (b) a wide range of credit insurance products provided by private and public sector institutions (including national export credit agencies [ECAs], regional development banks, and the International Finance Corporation [IFC] of the World Bank Group). Trade finance normally offers a high degree of security to the trade transaction and its payment. Such prime, secure corporate lending normally carries little risk and hence only a small fee (typically, a few basis points over the London interbank offered rate [LIBOR] for a prime borrower).

However, since the Asian crisis, the trade finance market has not been immune from general reassessments of risk, sharp squeezes in overall market liquidity, or herd behavior in the case of runs on currencies or repatriation of foreign assets. Such a situation happened again in the recent turmoil. Commercial risk in trade finance normally stems from the risk of nonpayment by the counterparty to the trade operation (either the client company or its bank). The perception of this risk obviously has changed along with exchange rate fluctuations, the rise in political risk, and bank failures, all of which undermine the profitability of trade. Such rapid change in risk perception happened again abruptly, for example, in fall 2008 regarding certain Eastern European countries. What aggravated the situation was that the secondary market also dried up. As much as lending was directly affected by the tight liquidity situation worldwide, the reinsurance market also suffered from the difficulties faced by AIG (American International Group, Inc.) and Lloyd's of London.

Of course, it can be argued that liquidity squeeze, exchange rate fluctuations, and other exogenous factors affecting risk are not specific to trade finance; they would likely affect any unhedged cross-border flow. Likewise, the credit supply would be affected by the greater scarcity of liquidity available to some banks in the interbank market. Yet because trade finance has to compete for an equal or reduced amount of liquidity, like any other segment of the credit market, the price of transactions increased sharply under the combined effects of scarce liquidity to back up loans and a reassessment of customer and country risks. Spreads on 90-day letters of credit soared in 2008 (from 10–16 basis points, on a normal basis, to 250–500 basis points for letters of credit issued by emerging and developing economies).

Even under stress, one finds it hard to believe that the safest and most self-liquidating form of finance, with strong receivables and marketable collaterals, could see its price increase by a factor of 10 to 50. Indeed, this segment of the credit market was by far one of the most resilient when the subprime crisis started in mid-2007, and signs of market gaps on a global scale appeared only in fall 2008.

This resilience can be partially attributed to facilitation devices developed by public-backed regional or multilateral financial institutions after the Asian financial crisis. Trade finance facilitation programs that provide for risk mitigation between banks issuing and receiving trade finance instruments have been developed into a worldwide network in which the IFC, the European Bank for Reconstruction and Development, the Asian Development Bank, and the Inter-American Development Bank participate. In addition, national ECAs have expanded short-term trade finance operations and added considerable liquidity to the markets in recent years, according to Berne Union statistics. Both types of institutions have developed a savoir-faire in recent years and could add further liquidity and expand the risk mitigation capacity if the need arose.

The Crisis Situation

Despite the resilience of the trade finance markets in 2007, the global liquidity situation became a major constraint in late 2008 for the largest suppliers, along with a general reassessment of counterparty risk and an expected increase in payment defaults on trade operations. The market gap initially appeared on Wall Street and in London when U.S.- and U.K.-based global banks, particularly those with deteriorated balance sheets, could not offload or refinance on the secondary market their excess exposure in trade credits. As a result, these banks could not meet customer demand for new trade operations, leaving a market gap estimated at around $25 billion in November 2008. That gap increased with the evaporation of the secondary market.

Some other large banks that used to roll over $20 billion per month of trade bills in the secondary market no longer found a counterparty. Demand for new trade credit could hence not be satisfied, and prices for opening letters of credit rose well above the levels required by a normal reassessment of risk. Large banks reported on several occasions that the lack of financing capacity made them unable to finance trade operations. The liquidity problem spread to other developing countries' money markets, with the poorer countries in Asia, Latin America, and Africa being particularly affected.

As discussed in chapter 5 of this volume, the joint IMF and Banker's Association for Finance and Trade (BAFT)—now merged with International Financial Services Association (BAFT-IFSA)—survey of commercial banks found that trade finance flows from developing-countries' banks fell by some 6 percent or more year on year (from the end of the third quarter of 2007 through the third of 2008).[1] That decline exceeded the reduction in trade flows from and to developing countries during the same period, implying that the lack in supply of trade finance was indeed an issue for these countries—and still is, for some of them. In late 2008, it was expected that trade finance flows for the same categories of banks would fall by another 10 percent in 2009 (IMF-BAFT 2009). If such numbers were confirmed (at least the surveyed local bankers seemed to agree), the market gap could be well over the $25 billion estimate mentioned above—between $100 billion and $300 billion. Such scarcity of trade finance likely accelerated the slowdown of world trade and output, at least during the peak of the crisis (end of 2008 and beginning of 2009).

Before the 2009 G-20 London Summit, the IMF and BAFT–IFSA provided a survey update that indicated the decrease in trade finance value had accelerated between October 2008 and January 2009 in almost all regions. Although more than 70 percent of the respondents attributed this further decline to the fall in demand for trade activities, 6 in 10 respondents attributed it also to restrained credit availability, thereby pointing to banks' increased difficulty in supplying trade credit because of the general liquidity squeeze and the increased risk aversion to finance cross-border trade operations (as chapter 5 also discusses further). Spreads (prices) on the opening of letters of credit had risen 10–15 basis points above LIBOR, up to 300 basis points in some emerging economies. Some banks even reported 600 basis points for particular destinations.

Results from an International Chamber of Commerce (ICC) survey (ICC 2009) broadly confirmed the conclusions of the IMF and BAFT–IFSA analysis, albeit relying on a wider panel of banks and countries (122 banks in 59 countries).[2] The results were also released for the WTO Expert Group meeting of March 18, 2009, and were further updated before the 2009 G-20 London Summit. It was obvious that tight credit conditions were affecting world trade. About half of the banks had confirmed a decrease in the volume and value of both letters of credit and aggregate transactions—a trend that was particularly clear when comparing data of the fourth quarter of 2007 with the fourth of 2008. This trend held particularly true for developed-countries' markets (and even more so for least-developing countries), with large-scale financing projects being deferred or having difficulty in obtaining finance.[3]

Apart from the reduction in the demand for trade, the main reasons provided by banks for the decrease in credit lines and increase in spreads[4] were the application of more stringent credit criteria, capital allocation restrictions, and reduced interbank lending. The ICC also pointed out that intense scrutiny of underlying guarantees by some banks led to higher rates of rejection of letters of credit. Prospects for trade finance in 2009 were negative, with the general view that "tight credit conditions may further reduce access to trade finance" (ICC 2009).

The Supply-Demand Mismatch

Because overall trade finance flows are unfortunately not subject to comprehensive statistical compilation but only to measurement by surveys, it is not possible to appropriately gauge changes in trade finance flows. However, the overall increase in spreads requested for opening letters of credit points to a supply shortage despite the reduced demand because of the overall decline in trade transactions.

Disagreement persists as to the causes of the trade finance shortage. Although the public sector in general maintains that trade finance gaps in extreme circumstances are a result of market failure, the private sector traditionally argues that they result from the cost of new rules—in this case, the implementation of the Basel II Accord (Auboin and Meier-Ewert 2003).

The market-failure argument rests on the inability of private sector operators to avoid herd behavior, in particular when credit risk and country risk are being confounded (for example, in cases of sovereign default rumors). Also, noncooperative games are played by global suppliers, with the best-run institutions refusing to refinance on the secondary-market letters of credit from banks in a less favorable liquidity situation.

On the regulatory side, commercial bankers have long complained about the implementation of Basel II rules, which are regarded as having a pro-cyclical effect on the supply of credit. When market conditions tighten, capital requirements for trade finance instruments tend to increase more than proportionally to the risk when the counterparty is in a developing country.

Both Western banks and developing countries have recently complained that ratings from international rating agencies maintain a bias against developing countries' risk. Several developing countries have made that point within the WTO Working Group on Trade, Debt and Finance, among other forums. They argue that they have neither been involved in the elaboration of recommendations of Basel II rules by the Basel Committee on Banking Supervision (BCBS) nor had any control over ratings by international rating agencies. Before and during the G-20 London Summit, it was agreed that all G-20 countries would become members of the Financial Stability Forum and its components, including the BCBS and other coordinating bodies on financial regulation. Therefore, they would be able to participate in the review of Basel II rules.

Recommendations by Business Associations

In the context of the current financial crisis, BAFT–IFSA, ICC, Business Europe, and individual commercial banks made recommendations to the G-20 London Summit in the following areas:

- *Reviewing Basel II rules.* Results from a survey conducted by the ICC United Kingdom in parallel with the ICC Global Survey (2009) indicate that implementation of the Basel II framework eroded banks' incentive to lend short-term for trade because capital weightings do not fully reflect the low risk level and short-term character of the activity. In a risk-weighted asset system, increases in minimum capital requirements had particularly adverse consequences on trade lending to SMEs and counterparties in developing countries.

- *Creating a ring-fenced liquidity pool for trade finance.* The general proposal was to design a small and targeted liquidity fund run by international financial institutions and useful for smaller segments of the market or new countries, in particular those most likely to be hit by the contraction of trade credit supply.
- *Increasing the cosharing of risk with public sector-backed institutions.* The idea would be to encourage cofinance between the various providers of trade finance. Public sector actors, such as ECAs and regional development banks, should be mobilized to shoulder some of the private sector risk.

One clear lesson from the Asian financial crisis is that, in periods prone to lack of trust and transparency as well as herd behavior, all actors—including private banks (which account for some 80 percent of the trade finance market by way of lending), ECAs, and regional development banks—should pool their resources to the extent practicable (IMF 2003). Cooperation among the various players is also important in the absence of a comprehensive, continuous dataset on trade finance flows. The main channel for reasonably assessing the market situation is through the collection of informed views and surveys from various institutions. Information collection has been a key objective of the WTO Expert Group chaired by the WTO director-general, particularly after the November 12, 2008, meeting.

The response of public sector–backed institutions since fall 2008 has been more than positive—in fact, of a magnitude unseen in recent history. Capacities in three types of activities were enhanced significantly as early as fall 2008:

- *All regional development banks and the IFC, on average, doubled their capacity under trade facilitation programs* between November 2008 and the G-20 meeting in London. Further enhancements of these programs were agreed on at the G-20 meeting, in particular the IFC's establishment of a liquidity pool allowing cofinancing operations with banks in developing countries, which would likely have a high leverage and multiplier effect on trade.
- *ECAs also stepped in with programs for short-term lending of working capital and credit guarantees aimed at SMEs.* For certain countries, the commitment is large (Germany and Japan). In other cases, large lines of credit have been granted to secure supplies with key trading partners (for example, the United States with China and the Republic of Korea). In still other countries, cooperation has developed to support regional trade, in particular supply-chain operations.

To this effect, the Asia-Pacific Economic Cooperation summit announced the establishment of an Asia-Pacific Trade Insurance Network to facilitate intra- and extraregional flows and investment through reinsurance cooperation among ECAs in the region. Japan's Nippon Export and Investment Insurance (NEXI) established itself as the leader and main underwriter of this collective reinsurance system.

- *Central banks with large foreign exchange reserves supplied foreign currency to local banks and importers,* generally through repurchase agreements. One problem often underestimated in developing countries is the difficulty for banks and importers of finding foreign exchange—for example, where the main currency of transactions (say, the euro or the U.S. dollar) has become scarce because of the depreciation of the local currency or because of the fall in receipts from remittances and exports. Since October 2008, Brazil's central bank has provided $10 billion to the local market. The Korean central bank pledged $10 billion of its foreign exchange reserves to do likewise. The central banks of Argentina, India, Indonesia, and South Africa are engaged in similar operations. However, many developing countries lack foreign exchange reserves and, unfortunately, cannot use similar facilities.

Why the Market Had Not Rebalanced Itself by Early 2009

The effort to mobilize public sector institutions to shoulder some of the risk carried by private sector banks has been, to an extent, a race against time. Although public institutions have provided more financing capacity, the private sector's ability to respond to importers' and exporters' demand for finance seemingly deteriorated even faster, particularly in developing countries in the last quarter of 2008 and the first of 2009. Also, BAFT–IFSA members (commercial banks) have complained that measures announced by ECAs and regional development banks were hard to track, so the banks lack information about who provided what and under which conditions. Filling this information gap was of one of the highest priorities of the WTO Expert Group meeting on March 18, 2009.

In this context, it is important that implementation and design of ECA programs are carried out cooperatively. Bankers have also raised the issue of financing both exports and imports because the survival of supply chains partly depends on the financing of both sides. Perhaps the Asian example of ECAs supporting both intra- and extraregional trade by working as a network should be examined by other regions.

As a result of the above factors, policy makers found that there was no quick fix to the trade finance problem but rather a need for quicker, more sequenced, cooperative implementation of measures mixing liquidity provision and risk mitigation. To that end, the WTO Expert Group on Trade, Debt, and Finance recommended the following:

- Accelerate implementation of IFC and regional development bank programs to enhance trade finance facilitation, which should open a liquidity window for cofinancing
- Fill the information gap about ECAs' activities by circulating a list of new programs and opening quick, user-friendly liquidity and reinsurance windows for both exporters and importers
- Encourage coordinated actions by ECAs (possibly regionally)
- Encourage liquidity pools by allowing rapid cofinancing between banks, ECAs, and international financial institutions (IFC proposal)
- Review Basel II regulation to better acknowledge the self-liquidating character of trade finance

In the meantime, the WTO and other institutions had to engage in intensive advocacy and mobilization work to explain why the trade finance collapse could be another source of economic contraction (Auboin 2009). Another role of multilateral agencies was to explain the rationale for a "trade finance"-specific package at a time when most of the liquidity provided by central banks to commercial banks was banked back at the central bank and not intermediated.

The G-20 Trade Finance Package

The Expert Group's recommendations were, to a large extent, reflected in the trade finance package of the G-20 London Summit's communiqué on April 2, 2009. Under the heading "Resisting protectionism and promoting global trade and investment," the communiqué says, "We will take, at the same time, whatever steps we can promote to facilitate trade and investment, and we will ensure availability of at least $250 billion over the next two years to support trade finance through our export credit and investment agencies and through the [multilateral development banks]. We also ask our regulators to make use of available flexibility in capital requirements for trade finance" (G-20 2009).

As indicated above, the trade finance package responds largely to the criteria developed by the WTO Expert Group: strengthened public-private sector partnerships in the context of existing trade finance facilitation programs, to be further enhanced with the opening and expansion of liquidity windows in these programs. The IFC showed the way by introducing a new global trade liquidity pool, allowing the IFC to immediately finance trade with commercial banks, on a 40–60 percent colending agreement. The IFC's scheme mobilized $5 billion in its own and donor funds, to be matched by $7.5 billion in commercial-bank funding, according to the colending formula. The total capacity of $12.5 billion, based on the rollover of a letter of credit every six months, would finance the targeted $50 billion in trade transactions over two years.

Another pillar of the package was to strengthen the existing capacities of ECAs within and outside the Organisation for Economic Co-operation and Development, allowing them to offer more finance and a wider spectrum of instruments (in particular, more short-term direct funding such as working capital and other forms of short-term direct support) and more capacity for short-term insurance, under state guarantees.

Conclusions

Markets have improved since fall 2009 although recovery patterns have been mixed across regions, and emerging markets have been leading the improvement. Consistent with the rapid recovery of trade in the Asian region, the high end of the market showed a large appetite for risk and ample liquidity to finance trade from China, India, and Korea, with a lowering of spreads. In Latin America, Brazilian authorities have been playing a significant role in the stabilization of the local market for trade finance; hence, with the recovery of trade and bank liquidity, spreads are returning to precrisis levels. The situation in other Latin American countries is more mixed. The same applies in the Middle East, where the situation is easing in some countries but remains a source of concern in others. Constraints on trade finance persist in Africa, particularly in Sub-Saharan Africa and in the financing of manufacturing imports and inputs.

The G-20 package is generally seen as having been instrumental in dealing with the 2009 crisis, in particular by helping to restore confidence and making available significant risk mitigation capacity to protect large supply-chain operators and buyers in regions such as Europe and Asia. In June 2010, the question was whether the remaining resources could be somewhat redirected toward the needs appearing in 2010. Thanks to the G-20 package, national ECAs and multilateral development banks have stepped up their activities, mobilizing some $190 billion in commitments in one year (and using $105 billion). The average utilization rate for additional capacity committed has declined from some 70 percent in the first half of 2009 to around 40 percent in the second half, reflecting the improvement in the global market situation. Given that some regions remain affected, there is currently little rush for a premature exit of the package, which remained valid until at least the end of 2010.

The assessment of the G-20 package points out that despite the G-20 London Summit's promise to mobilize $250 billion in additional short-term trade finance and guarantees within two years, the reality has been largely front-loaded. Large traders have been able to benefit from the rapid mobilization of their ECAs and risk-sharing mechanisms enhanced by international financial institutions. Within a year of implementation, the initiative helped mobilize $170 billion in additional capacity, mainly from ECAs, of which $130 billion had already been used. Therefore, at the November G-20 meeting, concerns were raised that the full impact of the G-20 package had not been felt by smaller exporters from Central America, Africa, Eastern Europe, and generally in low-income countries. These concerns motivated WTO Director-General Pascal Lamy to ask leaders at the 2010 G-20 Toronto Summit to ensure that remaining G-20 funds be focused on the users that need it the most and to commit to keeping the situation under close watch.

Notes

1. The IMF and BAFT–IFSA survey was undertaken in the context of the WTO Expert Group on Trade and Finance meeting on November 12, 2008, and was presented at the Expert Group meeting on March 18, 2009.
2. Chapter 21 of this volume discusses the ICC Global Surveys on Trade and Finance in greater detail.
3. Society for Worldwide Interbank Financial Telecommunication (SWIFT) data pointed to a deterioration that was particularly visible in the Asia and Pacific region.
4. Some 40 percent of the respondent banks indicated that spreads had increased over the previous year.

References

Auboin, Marc. 2009. "Restoring Trade Finance during a Period of Financial Crisis: Stock-Taking of Recent Initiatives." Working Paper ERSD-2009-16, World Trade Organization, Geneva. http://www.wto.org/english/res_e/reser_e/ersd200916_e.htm.

Auboin, Marc, and Moritz Meier-Ewert. 2003. "Improving the Availability of Trade Finance during Financial Crises." Discussion Paper 2, World Trade Organization, Geneva. http://www.wto.org/english/res_e/publications_e/disc_paper2_e.htm.

G-20 (Group of 20 Finance Ministers and Central Bank Governors). 2009. "Resisting Protectionism and Promoting Global Trade and Investment." In "Leaders' Statement: The Global Plan for Recovery and Reform," G-20, London, April 2. http://www.g20.org/pub_communiques.aspx.

ICC (International Chamber of Commerce). 2009. "Rethinking Trade Finance 2009: An ICC Global Survey." Banking Commission Market Intelligence Report, ICC, Paris. http://www.iccwbo.org/uploadedFiles/ICC_Trade_Finance_Report.pdf.

IMF (International Monetary Fund). 2003. "Trade Finance in Financial Crises: Assessment of Key Issues." Board Paper, IMF, Washington, DC. http://www.imf.org/external/np/pdr/cr/2003/eng/120903.pdf.

IMF-BAFT (International Monetary Fund–Bankers' Association for Finance and Trade). 2009. "IMF-BAFT Trade Finance Survey: A Survey among Banks Assessing the Current Trade Finance Environment." Report by FImetrix for IMF and BAFT, Washington, DC.

THE WORLD BANK GROUP'S RESPONSE TO THE CRISIS: EXPANDED CAPACITY FOR UNFUNDED AND FUNDED SUPPORT FOR TRADE WITH EMERGING MARKETS

Bonnie Galat and Hyung Ahn

Trade finance is the engine of an estimated $14 trillion in annual global commerce and is fundamental to the movement of goods at all stages of the supply chain, especially in emerging markets. Trade is recognized as a key driver of global integration and gross domestic product growth in many developing countries during the decade preceding the 2008–09 financial crisis.

The severe financial disruption witnessed internationally in late 2008 significantly curtailed trade flows, signaling potentially devastating effects on the economies of the developing world. The International Finance Corporation (IFC) of the World Bank Group immediately deepened its engagement with trade facilitation as one way to stimulate economic activity. Leveraging its experience from the Global Trade Finance Program (GTFP), launched in 2005, IFC sought to complement the program, which extends unfunded support through guarantees for individual trades.

The new IFC initiative, the Global Trade Liquidity Program (GTLP), was conceived to channel liquidity quickly to targeted markets by providing trade credit lines and refinancing portfolios of trade assets held by selected banks. GTLP also

The authors thank Michelle Abboud for her assistance.

was premised on leveraging the funding available from IFC by creating an historic collaboration with other international financial institutions (IFIs), which also contributed their financial resources when the GTLP began operations in 2009.

Both GTFP and GTLP successfully facilitated trade during the crisis period. This chapter presents the experience of each program.

The Global Trade Finance Program

Trade was an early victim of the deteriorating financial environment. The dramatic crisis of confidence among banks that brought the interbank market to a standstill in late 2008 severely affected the already fragile and contracted levels of liquidity among many major banks addressing their own portfolio pressures. Many banks quickly pulled or reduced short-term trade lines to ease pressures on the balance sheet. Risk mitigation from traditional sources such as private credit insurance also contracted and was further weakened by rating downgrades.

In late 2008, as a first step in responding to the unfolding crisis, IFC doubled GTFP's capacity to $3 billion (a revolving program ceiling) to enhance the countercyclical role that the World Bank Group was called upon to play. As a triple-A multilateral institution with a zero capital risk weighting under Basel rules, IFC experienced continued growth in demand for cover under GTFP.

In the context of a marked contraction of global trade volumes in 2009 by as much as 13 percent, banks made strategic decisions that ranged from reducing their trade books to exiting markets to building market share. Those banks that continued to intermediate trade sought risk mitigation arrangements with a stepped-up urgency. The market demand for 100 percent, as opposed to partial, coverage for guarantees issued under GTFP doubled in 2009 in contrast to the previous year. The full-cover accommodation permitted banks to continue to provide trade services and credit at a time when goods were reportedly languishing in ports because of lack of financing. Thus, the decline in global trade notwithstanding, GTFP's guarantee volume continued to grow from 2008 onward, meeting the demands comfortably under its larger program capacity and expanded coverage of markets and participating banks. With few exceptions, IFC maintained its original strategic focus on the smaller banks in emerging markets, the smaller trades, and the critical sectors such as agriculture.

2010 ushered in a recovery in global trade volumes—which, by year's end, had expanded by 15 percent for the year and exceeded precrisis levels for the first time (CPB 2011).

Despite the improved volume statistics and generally eased credit environment, the trends of bank retrenchment endured. Commercial banks' high priority on optimizing their capital resources led to a systematic requirement to incorporate risk mitigation as part of booking trade business, particularly for exposures in emerging markets. IFC's experience indicates that the recovery under way, largely driven by emerging markets, is not benefiting all markets evenly. There is evidence that low-volume markets, banks ranked below the top-tier institutions, and small and medium enterprise (SME) importers and exporters continue to struggle with limited access to bank financing.

Thus, the initial reduction in credit lines by major international banks in late 2008, although eased, was not uniformly reinstated due to several competing factors:

- Adoption of highly selective cross-border market strategies
- Persistent caution about the global credit environment
- Heightened sensitivity to counterparty bank risk
- Tightening effects of the Basel II and prospective Basel III regulations on capital for short-term trade
- Increasingly less favorable cost-return analysis of compliance with rigorous know-your-customer (KYC) requirements.

GTFP Operating Results

GTFP has grown consistently since its inception in 2005. With its principal focus on smaller, private-sector banks in the emerging markets, the program has helped such institutions establish relationships with an international network of potential financing partners. Before the crisis, when there was unprecedented liquidity in the global system, the program supported a strategy shift among many international banks to refocus on SMEs in emerging markets, where financing options were less available and pricing was more attractive.

Maintaining its focus during the crisis period but expanding its capacity and footprint, GTFP's issuance of guarantees continued to grow steadily—from $1.45 billion in fiscal year 2008 to $3.46 billion in fiscal year 2010, the later figure representing a 44 percent growth over the previous fiscal year. Notably, the number of guarantees issued in fiscal year 2009 grew at its fastest rate since the program began operations, evidencing the smaller shipments that were more typical during the period. To date, with more than 8,600 guarantees issued, no claims have been made under the trade program.

In concert with historical program trends, most of GTFP's guarantees (roughly two-thirds) have supported flows with underlying letters of credit as instrument of choice. However, given the need for funded support, the program also saw high-paced demand for IFC guarantees covering bank-to-bank promissory notes related to the extension of preexport and postimport loans, which grew from one-fourth of all 2008 guarantees to more than one-third in 2009–10.

GTFP now offers coverage for more than 200 banks in emerging markets, shown by geographic distribution in figure 18.1.

An additional 216 confirming banks from both developed- and emerging-market countries plus another 650 branches and subsidiaries worldwide are also GTFP participants, creating a vast network that has promoted trade across roughly 600 distinct trading routes, supported imports into more than 100 developing countries, and facilitated exports from 70 emerging markets.

Of the $3.46 billion of guarantees issued under GTFP in fiscal 2010, 36 percent supported flows between emerging markets, or South-South trade. Commitment volumes in International Development Association countries held steady at 51 percent throughout the crisis and recovery period. Figure 18.2 shows the regional shares of GTFP guarantee volume in 2010.

Regional Observations

GTFP is a global program, unique among the multilateral IFIs in its mandate to facilitate trade across all regions. Given that broad platform, GTFP provided a

Figure 18.1 Number of GTFP-Covered Banks in Emerging Markets, by Region

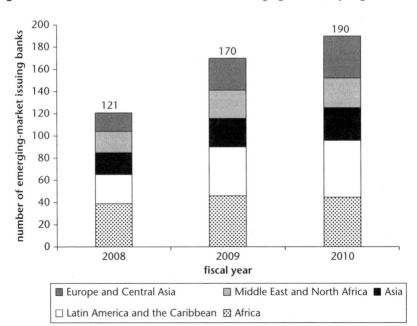

Source: IFC databases 2010.

Figure 18.2 Shares of GTFP-Issued Guarantees in 2010, by Region

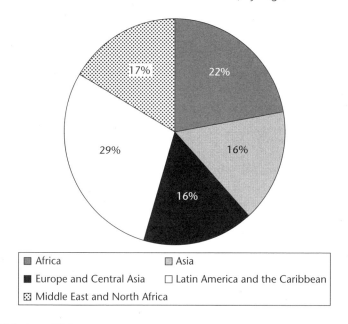

Source: IFC databases 2010.

window on how the crisis affected the 84 emerging markets it serves in the program.

GTFP in Africa

Banks in Sub-Saharan Africa were affected by the crisis but were somewhat shielded because of their relative lack of integration into the global banking system. The banks remained in fairly good condition and remained reasonably liquid because of both the cautious credit environment and the reduced corporate and consumer demand. Depressed commodity prices drove down the value of trade volumes, and a concomitant fall in remittances curtailed consumer consumption; both commodity prices and remittances had been steadily increasing before the crisis. Overall, GTFP data reveal that pricing for short-term, cross-border trade credit extended to IFC clients in Africa did not experience the dramatic swings witnessed in other markets worldwide.

In Nigeria, a domestic banking crisis, lower oil revenues, and political uncertainty caused a business slowdown that was reflected in a 22 percent drop in the value of guarantees issued for 2009. In response to the crisis, IFC extended guarantees to support trade-related cash advances, addressing liquidity constraints in countries such as Nigeria. By the second quarter of 2010, GTFP trade activity in Africa showed signs of a rebound, led by Nigeria.

Beyond Nigeria, IFC began working in close partnership with an African bank whose banking network spans several of the continent's poorest countries; the program was thus instrumental in leveraging the parent guarantees to support activities of its subsidiaries in weaker environments. This support facilitated trade in smaller African countries where banks had been even more affected by the global financial crisis.

GTFP in Asia

Given the relative strength of the Asian economies going into 2008 and the solid trends of intraregional trade driven by an economically robust China, Asia was largely unscathed by the crisis. From the time of its launch in 2005, GTFP's focus had been on the smaller economies and underserved banks in the region. Thus, the private banks in Bangladesh and Vietnam continued to be the most active beneficiaries of GTFP support. In fact, it was an intraregional shipment of steel from Malaysia to Vietnam that in December 2010 took the program over the $10 billion mark of guarantees issued since its operations began in 2005.

In keeping with industry trends elsewhere, Asian demand for risk mitigation through GTFP was significant, with guarantee dollar volume growing by as much as 175 percent in 2009. Pricing for short-term trade credit in the smaller economies rose but did not exhibit the dramatic swings seen in the large, high-volume markets of China, India, and the Republic of Korea. Those markets experienced significant supply-demand imbalances in credit capacity as market players urgently sought to recoup returns that had plummeted to meager levels in the months preceding the crisis.

GTFP in Europe and Central Asia

This Commonwealth of Independent States region was hard hit during the global financial crisis, with trade banks reporting drops in trade volume of 30–50 percent—a particularly harsh development for the import-reliant smaller economies such as Belarus and Ukraine. Despite the diminished aggregate of trade flows, the demand for risk mitigation was acute. GTFP asserted its support in the region in fiscal 2010 by approving 12 additional banks for trade lines and adding countries (Bosnia and Herzegovina and Romania) to the program. The GTFP trade volumes more than doubled in the region against the previous year, driven mainly by banks in Belarus, Kazakhstan, and the Russian Federation. Pricing generally rose with the perception of increased risk and, notably in the case of Russia, came down considerably in 2010.

With counterparty risk perceived to be untenable, IFC saw a migration from open-account transactions to GTFP-supported letter of credit issuance. Such instruments, available with postimport financing, provided much-needed financing to SMEs in the region. The general risk perception of Central Asia was severely affected by the protracted and controversial events surrounding the Kazakh restructuring. GTFP continued to lend support to two small, private sector banks there that emerged unscathed from the turmoil. In keeping with its strategic focus of supporting South-South trade and staying the course in challenging markets, the program recently issued a guarantee for a $3.4 million shipment of sugar from Brazil to Kazakhstan.

GTFP in Latin America

The decisive, well-timed intervention of the Brazilian government set the tone for the region, which emerged from the crisis early and avoided the depths experienced elsewhere. The challenge for the dynamic Brazilian market and particularly for the smaller economies in the region was the lack of liquidity available from the traditional international banks, which had been regular providers of finance to the real sector. The dearth of financing was most acute in the exporting countries such as Argentina, Brazil, Guatemala, Honduras, and Paraguay.

GTFP stepped up its capacity in the region by covering the risk of 51 banks and mining the GTFP network of banks for viable partners to channel funding to Latin American countries during the period. IFC maintained its focus on critical flows, with as much as 56 percent of its support representing agricultural goods. In addition, the program began to support energy-efficiency-related exports, which made up 14 percent of the $1.2 billion coverage extended in the region in fiscal 2010.

GTFP in the Middle East

Most of the banks in the Middle East and North Africa were not directly affected by the global financial crisis. The region's emerging markets were less exposed to the "toxic" assets affecting other banking systems, partly because of conservative central bank regulations and less integration into the global financial system. Nonetheless, banks assumed protective positions in the wake of the financial uncertainty, which made trade an indirect casualty of the resulting contraction in credit capacity. The eventual debt default and restructuring situations in Dubai and Saudi Arabia kept the region in a holding position.

As in other regions, the impact of the crisis varied from country to country. GTFP bank clients are drawn mostly from the region's non-oil-producing economies, which have a diversified export base and import needs highly reliant on the European and U.S. markets. Thus, the softening of these markets has put pressure on trade flows. For example, GTFP extended its guarantee in support of a bank in West Bank and Gaza, facilitating the shipment of critical medical imaging equipment to health centers there.

GTFP guarantees have historically been used in the region for unfunded risk mitigation related to letters of credit. In response to the onset of the crisis, the program increased the number of banks covered and enhanced the trade facilities for existing partner banks where it was most needed, notably in Pakistan. Assistance to Pakistan included a landmark trade transaction that brought together support from IFC, the Asian Development Bank, a global confirming bank, and a local Pakistani bank to provide trade finance coverage of up to €110 million in equipment for the textile industry, which accounts for more than 60 percent of the country's industrial activity.

GTFP Solutions Provided and Lessons Learned

In the wake of the crisis, IFC's responsiveness and ability to play its countercyclical role by taking more risk through the existing trade program and launching the complementary trade program proved critical to its success in supporting clients engaged in cross-border trade across all regions. IFC's ability to engage quickly and assume a leadership role among multilateral institutions was rooted in the experience and in-house expertise gained before the onset of the financial crisis, through three years of operating the GTFP platform.

Since GTFP's inception in 2005, the program has facilitated many first-time partnerships between banks looking for trade solutions on a transactional basis. Such "brokered" relationships have expanded correspondent banking opportunities for client banks, including bank lines of credit and released cash collateral requirements. Improved financing availability has enabled the client base of small local banks, largely SME importers and exporters, to reach new markets under competitive terms. Annually, roughly 80 percent of the guarantees issued have been for amounts less than $1 million, with the median at $155,000, reflecting support for shipment sizes consistent with small businesses.

As of late 2008, the crisis of confidence among banking institutions became a defining feature of the disruption to trade financing, which especially affected smaller banks, low-volume markets, and SME clients in the emerging markets. GTFP's mandate facilitates access to trade financing for underserved market segments. The program's ability to sustain partnerships among a broad number of banks from developed and developing markets helped to maintain trade across established corridors and to support nontraditional, nascent trade corridors—from exports of cashews from Côte d'Ivoire to Vietnam, to grain from Thailand to Mali, to cement from Turkey to Sierra Leone.

In addition to delivering access to trade credit, GTFP continued to provide trade advisory services to enhance the functioning of trade and the training of the trade professionals globally. During the crisis, the advisory program expanded its course offerings to respond to the heightened risk environment by adding modules in risk management and KYC compliance. In the midst of the crisis in 2009, the program provided its first training for Iraqi bankers to help this emerging nation rejoin international trade networks and promote growth of the Iraqi economy. In 2010, GTFP facilitated 58 trade training courses in 34 countries, reaching more than 1,880 bankers.

The Global Trade Liquidity Program

Against the backdrop of a world financial system in turmoil, IFC and development finance institutions, as part of the G-20 mandate, began exploratory discussions in early 2009 with global banks on how to work together to help keep trade flowing worldwide. These initial talks culminated in the GTLP initiative.

GTLP plays a stabilizing and catalytic role in trade finance. Phase 1 of this program—launched July 2009 at the second annual World Trade Organization (WTO) Aid for Trade Global Review in Geneva—has focused on a collaborative crisis response to rapidly mobilize and channel funding to support emerging markets' trade finance. GTLP is the first global solution of its kind in the trade finance business. It was implemented through a partnership among development finance institutions (DFIs), bilateral and multilateral organizations, and governments to mobilize temporary funding targeted to support trade finance in the developing world.

The IFIs, bilateral and multilateral organizations, and governments that have partnered with IFC for GTLP include the U.K. Department for International Development, the U.K. Commonwealth Development Corporation, the Japanese Bank for International Cooperation (JBIC), the Netherlands Ministry of Foreign Affairs, the African Development Bank, the Organization of Petroleum Exporting Countries' Fund for International Development (OFID), the Saudi Fund for Development, Canada's Department of Finance, the Swedish International Development Cooperation Agency (Sida), and China's Ministry of Finance (indirect support through private placement of IFC bonds).

IFC acts as agent on the program partners' behalf and partners with global, regional, or local banks (utilization banks, or UBs) to channel liquidity to the banks in two ways: (a) a 40 percent risk funded participation, and (b) short-term loans. The UBs that have partnered with GTLP include Standard Chartered Bank, Citibank, Commerzbank, JPMorgan Chase, Standard Bank South Africa, Afreximbank, and Rabobank.

A total of $1.7 billion in commitments from eight participants has been raised, along with an additional $1.5 billion parallel arrangement with JBIC under a memorandum of understanding. Since its official launch in July 2009, GTLP implemented a rapid-response approach to mobilize and channel funding to support emerging markets trade finance. This momentum has continued, supporting more than $12 billion in trade as of February 2011 and financing more than 8,500 trade investment instruments, with close to 40 percent of the program reaching low-income countries (LICs) and lower-middle-income countries (LMICs), and 81 percent supporting small and midsize businesses. The program's financial performance has been solid with no losses and an average net annualized yield of 1.96 percent. Three leading publications (*Global Trade Review*, *Trade Finance*, and *Finance Asia*) have recognized GTLP as "Deal of the Year" for its innovation, rapid deployment, and development impact.

GTLP Phase 2

As the financial crisis abated, the needs have evolved—turning from injecting liquidity to guaranteeing risk. Statistics show that global trade has picked up once again but with a slow recovery to different degrees across regions.

A survey of 88 banks by the International Monetary Fund (IMF) and the Bankers' Association for Finance and Trade (BAFT)—now merged with International Financial Services Association (BAFT-IFSA)—found that risk premiums for private trade finance continued to rise, although at a slower pace than during the peak of the crisis (IMF-BAFT 2009). The International Chamber of Commerce's Global Survey in April 2010 reported that banks continued to be risk-averse and selective in supplying trade finance (ICC 2010); 76 percent of the banks interviewed said more stringent credit criteria were being applied, and 24 percent cited capital allocation restrictions as a constraint on trade finance. One underlying reason for the overall constraint on trade finance is that the many countries' and banks' credit ratings were downgraded, which in turn also increased capital allocation requirements.

Although global trade recovery is encouraging, growth patterns have yet to stabilize across the globe. This instability is partly attributable to the temporary nature of some key drivers of the trade recovery. The IMF's *World Economic Outlook Update* reported that global exports, after growing at a 21 percent annualized rate in the first half of 2010, decelerated sharply, declining at an annualized pace of 1.65 percent in the third quarter of 2010 (IMF 2011). Other factors include high unemployment, limited consumer confidence, sovereign risks, spikes in food and fuel prices, and certainly recent turbulence in Europe, the Middle East, and North Africa, which are contributing to the slowing pace of global trade recovery. Therefore, since late 2010 as GTLP entered its first year anniversary, the initiative was implemented with mostly regionally-focused solutions to direct its resources where the needs were greatest—forming the foundation of GTLP Phase 2.

In L'Aquila, Italy, in 2009, the G-20 cited food security as a key priority for agriculture investments over the next three years. Trade was identified to play a role in the larger, comprehensive Global Food Initiative. As a complement, agriculture trade support is expected to help facilitate availability and movement of agricultural products. The leveraging of established vehicles such as GTLP offers one immediate and effective solution to help address the demand for greater action in addressing global food security.

In Phase 2 of GTLP, IFC will address these two challenges—mitigating risk and supporting agriculture trade—through two new products:

- *GTLP Guarantee.* IFC's proposed unfunded, risk-sharing solution aims to encourage banks to finance trade by helping to mitigate the credit risk of reentering, or expanding into, emerging markets.
- *GTLP Agri.* This program aims to support eligible export-oriented SMEs in the food and agribusiness sectors through banks. It provides a short-term loan solution to scale up lending to the agricultural export sector, thus supporting agriculture investments and food security over the next three years. GTLP Agri will help increase liquidity and stimulate trade flows in the agricultural sector, at the same time aiming to meet seasonal working capital needs to facilitate production and supply of agriculture commodities and food.

GTLP Design and Implementation

GTLP is structured to maximize each party's resources and network. The program has been implemented in phases, both on funding and use, to give the program partners a flexible platform to channel the aggregated funding to the UBs. The funding is allocated to each UB under a separate UB trade facility.

Phase 1 programs

Funds are channeled to the UBs through a risk-sharing structure. The setup maximizes leverage; program partners bear 40 percent of the funding and risk, and the UBs bear 60 percent. The risk sharing of funded trade financing is on a pro rata basis by purchasing up to 40 percent of short-term, self-liquidating trade assets. Trade assets are issued from a preapproved list of emerging-market issuing banks. These trade instruments go through a compliance check before they are deemed eligible. The estimated average size is up to $1.4 million and an average tenor of up to 140 days. Most of the facilities run for one year, with an option to extend for another year or two. GTLP and the UBs share returns on a pro rata basis.

Part of IFC's role as an agent is to supervise the portfolio to ensure that the UB uses funding for trade finance and meets the criteria. The UB also must demonstrate the developmental reach and incrementality of the trade assets. In the case of Standard Bank South Africa and Afreximbank, dedicated short-term loans are provided for trade financing to smaller or regional UBs without a risk-sharing scheme.

Specifically, GTLP comprises three basic interlinked components:

- Supply-side, or aggregate, funding from the program partners
- Demand-side funding, or individual UB trade facilities, whereby the program partners either (a) cofinance with the UB's pools of trade receivables under a risk-sharing scheme, or (b) provide fully funded, short-term loans to UBs, thus linking the supply and demand
- Handling of operational issues concerning IFC's role as agent on behalf of the program partners.

Supply-side funding

The program partners sign a GTLP Master Framework Agreement that governs the agreement among program partners, setting forth the

- guiding principles, capital contributions and cash flow management, regional and sectoral distribution, representations, and reporting requirements;
- criteria and guidelines to select the UB;
- role of IFC as agent for the program partners;
- establishment of a GTLP master account (for all cash flows) to be managed by a processing bank; and
- required information to be provided to program partners for each to endorse and to make credit decision (IFC is not the lender of record on behalf of other program partners).

The benefits of this structure to the program partners include

- increased deal flow through IFC's global origination capacity;
- access to IFC's due diligence, structuring skills, and global presence;
- efficiency in terms of time and costs; and
- equal rights and obligations among all program partners.

The benefits to the UBs include

- enhanced access to IFC and all program-partner funding while directly dealing only with IFC; and
- time and cost savings throughout the life of the facility.

Demand-side funding

The program partners together sign a UB Trade Facility Agreement with each of the UBs. IFC, acting as agent, undertakes the appraisal and negotiates on behalf of each of the program partners. Each agreement stipulates, among other things, the level of program partner funding, eligibility criteria, a list of preapproved issuing banks and their limits, and a regional diversification to meet the program partners' requirements.

Program partners are expected to cofund (their pro rata share of commitments) under the 40/60 risk-sharing investment structure. Under this approach, the program partners purchase up to 40 percent of pools of trade receivables confirmed by the UB and issued by preapproved issuing banks. Underlying trade receivables are self-liquidating and mature within 360 days.

. The risk sharing, among other features, ensures that the UBs retain a significant ownership interest in the trade assets, which mitigates the risk of cherry picking. Under the fully funded short-term loan, the program partners simply provide short-term (up to one year) loans to a UB, which would be renewable at the end of each year at the sole discretion of IFC. The flow chart in figure 18.3 shows an overview of the supply and demand structure.

Phase 2 programs

As summarized previously, IFC developed its GTLP Phase 2 programs to address two evolving needs: to mitigate risk and to support agriculture trade.

GTLP Guarantee

GTLP Guarantee envisions unfunded risk-participating arrangements that IFC and other program participants will provide to banks to facilitate trade across challenging markets. Consistent with the broader GTLP objectives, the GTLP Guarantee-supported portfolio will comprise funded and unfunded trade transactions where the obligor is an eligible emerging-market issuing bank (EMIB). GTLP Guarantee responds to an increasing demand for unfunded regional and multiregional solutions and also meets the needs of potential program participants that wish to join GTLP using guarantees instead of liquidity.

IFC and the program participants will provide credit guarantee coverage of up to 40 percent on portfolios of trade transactions (or 50 percent in Africa, to induce expansion in this region) originated by UBs through their networks of EMIBs. IFC will be the primary guarantor, with the program participants providing a pro rata counterguarantee in the countries they have agreed to support so that the net IFC exposure is capped at any given time.

Figure 18.3 GTLP Supply-Demand Overview

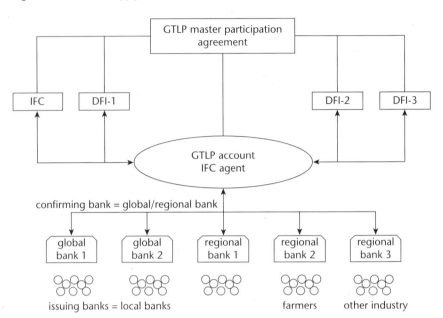

Source: IFC GTLP team.
Note: GTLP = Global Trade Liquidity Program. DFI = development finance institution. IFC = International Finance Corporation.

This structure allows IFC to fulfill its agency role to quickly mobilize and channel risk-sharing support from various mobilization sources to banks while also providing AAA guarantee coverage. In addition, it facilitates the ease of administration by the UB, which will interact with only one guarantor as opposed to several. The first projects under GTLP Guarantee are with Intesa Sanpaolo S.p.A (Italy), which provides a wide presence in Central and Eastern Europe, and Commerzbank for an Africa-focused portfolio.

GTLP Agri

GTLP Agri extends GTLP through its focus on the food and agribusiness industry. It complements the G-20 pledge to establish the Global Food Security Program to improve food security through support to the agribusiness sector and increased agriculture investments.

GTLP Agri, which provides mostly short-term funding, is designed to extend trade and working capital loans through regional banks in developing countries to eligible food and agribusiness farmers and SMEs in regions with an active food and agriculture export market to achieve a wider reach and greater development impact.

GTLP Solutions Provided and Lessons Learned

GTLP has shown that a successful program is not only about the raising of funds, but also about strategic placement of those funds. Partners will remember and assess such initiatives based on how effectively the funds were used to achieve their development and commercial objectives.

The program's approach of anticipating clients' needs and offering win-win solutions to build credibility for long-term partner-agent relationships has created a demonstration effect among IFIs, bilateral and multilateral organizations and governments, and banks. As a result, several GTLP partners and banks are keen to join Phase 2. GTLP has also been set up in a way that is not exclusive to IFC. Its flexible, market-based structure is designed for scalability and replicability. The GTLP Guarantee program, as an example, has provided an innovative, outside-the-box structure whereby IFC "fronts" DFIs' or governments' participation with counterguarantees.

Given that producers and exporters were hit hard by the economic crisis, GTLP was structured to seamlessly inject large amounts of funds in support of the world's trade system. The structure ensured that trade finance reached those in need without adding to the cost or administrative burden of the beneficiary companies—and without them even knowing how they were being supported "behind the scenes" and at no additional cost to them. Thousands of companies in key importing and exporting nations have benefited from GTLP, and the cases below are among the many that demonstrate how this extra capacity benefits the trading community.

Notwithstanding the overall success of GTLP, this initiative will be systematically wound up as originally planned beginning in 2012 given the temporary nature of this crisis response program. Despite this exit, GTLP provides IFC and its partners with a foundation of additional experience, partnership platform, and lessons that can be leveraged to develop future innovative solutions to tackle global strategic priorities such as SMEs and agriculture.

An award-winning cocoa financing deal in Nigeria[1]

As sole arranger and lender, Nigeria's Stanbic IBTC Bank, a member of the Standard Bank Group, successfully closed a $15 million cocoa financing for Agro Traders Ltd. (ATL) in November 2009. The transaction was one of the first applications of the Standard Bank Group's dedicated trade finance lines from the IFC to support trade to and from Sub-Saharan Africa. ATL is based in Akure, south-western Nigeria, and is one of the country's largest cocoa exporters, handling more than 15 percent of Nigeria's annual cocoa output.

The facility, structured as preexport finance, supported ATL's purchase of cocoa beans from the 2009–10 Nigerian cocoa harvest for export to Europe. Olu Ajayi, head of structured trade finance for Stanbic IBTC, called it arguably the first such "Made in Nigeria" transaction—provided in Nigeria by a local bank to a local exporter with documentation undertaken by a local legal counsel.

The transaction provided significant support to the Nigerian cocoa industry, which is undergoing regeneration as part of the Nigerian federal government's efforts to encourage the growth of the agricultural sector and to enhance the country's non-oil exports and revenues. The transaction also provided much-needed access to U.S. dollar funding and liquidity support to a local commodity trader at a time when a number of banks, both local and international, were with-drawing their U.S. dollar liquidity lines or applying punitive interest rates to Nigerian corporate borrowers because of the global financial crisis and the cur-rent crisis engulfing the Nigerian banking sector.

The transaction is particularly interesting in terms of the in-country Nigerian trade finance team supporting the local businesses rather than always transacting from outside the country. It also supports the bank's strategy of bringing experi-enced trade finance practitioners into the Nigerian market, thereby increasing the skills base in Lagos.

IFC's support, through a $400 million funding line for trade finance in Sub-Saharan Africa, enables Stanbic to originate transactions in West Africa, resulting in more deals in the continent.

The food producer in Vietnam

A mid-size Vietnamese food producer that exports to the East Asia region man-ages its working capital efficiently by obtaining discounts against its export receivables from Standard Chartered Bank through its local bank. Financing so channeled into the trade deal between these two parties happened swiftly and at a lower cost than they would have otherwise incurred. Their local banks, facing a liquidity crunch, would have charged much more for financing if not for the support of this GTLP program.

A garment manufacturer in Indonesia

A garment manufacturer based in Indonesia has a contract to supply to a buyer in Colombia. Typically, the exporter would prefer to be paid upon shipment, while the buyer can obtain the most favorable terms from the seller by paying cash on deliv-ery. Through the GTLP, the buyer could receive cost-effective import financing from its local bank, and the exporter received payment earlier in its working capital cycle, lowering costs and reducing risks for both parties.

Trade during postconflict reconstruction in Angola

Ango Rayan Group International is a company based in Luanda, Angola, that began operations toward the end of the country's decades-long civil war. It employs 700 staff members, and its business lines include food distribution, highway construction, and wholesaling electrical equipment, among others. With an annual income of about $4.8 million (in 2008), Ango Rayan's sales territory is 100 percent local, and its main customers are Angolan agencies, local stores, and outlets.

Early this year, with an export clean trade advance, Ango Rayan imported $500,000 worth of food products from Palmali Industrial de Alimentos Ltd., a meat exporter in Paraná, in south Brazil. The financing was extended by Brazil's Banco Bradesco, a GTLP issuing bank. It is companies like Ango Rayan that can contribute to the diversification of Angolan industries apart from the oil sector, preserve jobs, and contribute to reconstructing postconflict Angola.

Note

1. Summary of an article from *GTR* magazine, March 2010.

References

CPB (CPB Netherlands Bureau for Economic Policy Analysis). 2011. CPB, The Hague.

ICC (International Chamber of Commerce). 2010. "Rethinking Trade Finance 2010: An ICC Global Survey." ICC, Paris.

IMF (International Monetary Fund). 2011. *World Economic Outlook Update*. Washington, DC: IMF.

IMF-BAFT (International Monetary Fund and the Bankers' Association for Finance and Trade). 2009. "Trade Finance Survey: A Survey among Banks Assessing the Current Trade Finance Environment." Report by FImetrix for IMF-BAFT, Washington, DC.

REGIONAL DEVELOPMENT BANKS' RESPONSE TO THE CRISIS: SCALING UP THE TRADE FINANCE FACILITIES

Rudolf Putz, Ghazi Ben Ahmed, Steven Beck,
and Daniela Carrera

This chapter describes the impact of the 2008–09 financial crisis on regional trade and trade finance, the institutional response of four regional development banks—the European Bank for Reconstruction and Development (EBRD), the African Development Bank (AfDB), the Asian Development Bank (ADB), and the Inter-American Development Bank (IDB)—and the lessons learned from their trade finance programs.

As trade credit froze and trade volumes plummeted in most developing countries, regional development banks quickly recognized the need to ramp up their trade financing provisions. Their programs helped both to cover risks and to increase liquidity. They mainly targeted small local financial institutions and small and medium enterprises (SMEs). Moreover, cofinancing arrangements among development banks, export credit agencies (ECAs), foreign commercial banks, private insurance underwriters, and investment funds have been critical in times of both risk aversion and constrained availability of trade finance.

European Bank for Reconstruction and Development

During the 2008–09 financial crisis, most countries in Eastern Europe and participating countries in the Commonwealth of Independent States (CIS) where

---

This chapter has been put together by the editors Jean-Pierre Chauffour and Mariem Malouche based on original material submitted by the authors.

EBRD operates suffered deterioration in economic activities, which reflected negatively on trade finance volumes. These countries witnessed the worst crisis since the collapse of the centrally planned economy in the early 1990s as a consequence of accelerated economic decline in Western Europe, which led to a drop in foreign capital flows into the region as well as the decline of commodity prices.

Impact of the Crisis in Eastern Europe and Central Asia

Economic activity contracted rapidly, and by the end of 2008, many Eastern European and CIS countries were experiencing significant declines in industrial production. At the beginning of 2009, this was particularly noticeable as the crisis was spilling back from the real economy into the financial sector. Fears of bank credit losses triggered a new wave of currency pressures, coupled with an already ongoing depreciation of local currencies. The first quarter of 2009 saw levels of negative output even in the countries that had remained more resilient at the beginning, such as Bulgaria, Moldova, Mongolia, Romania, the Russian Federation, and the Slovak Republic.

The financial shock of September 2008 severely affected trade in the region. After years of developing trade integration in Eastern Europe and the CIS—within the region and with the rest of the world—and years of partially double-digit growth in export and import volumes, these countries faced a sharp fall in volumes. Even insulated countries in the Balkans or the Caucasus region were not immune and were eventually hit by the collapse of global trade. In Kazakhstan, Russia, and Ukraine, import and export volumes declined by approximately 50 percent in 2009 compared with 2008. Although trade volumes bottomed out in 2009 and improved over the course of 2010, there were no signs (as of the end of 2010) of swift recovery to the levels seen before the crisis.

Coupled with lower demand for investment and consumer goods, many local banks in Eastern Europe and the CIS region are still suffering from a high percentage of nonperforming loans. As a result, local banks had to stop lending to local exporters and importers to strengthen their capital base. Many local banks are now heavily engaged in restructuring their nonperforming loans and are cautious about taking on new risks. These banks perform stricter credit risk assessments of their clients, whether they are exporters or importers, and require good credit standing to give them access to trade finance; however, even a good credit standing does not guarantee the necessary support for these companies.

Although the liquidity crisis has eased and some banks are becoming more liquid again, there are no signs of granting more credit to companies engaged in export or import businesses. Especially for SMEs with low credit ratings, it is increasingly difficult to obtain the support they need to conduct international business. This is especially true in less-developed countries where local banks are restrictive in their business activity—further underlined by the fact that many Western commercial banks have reduced or completely closed their trade finance limits for many banks in Eastern Europe and the CIS region. In particular, this is the case in Kazakhstan and Ukraine, where the banking sector suffered enormously from well-known banking defaults.

EBRD Response to the Crisis

EBRD responded quickly to the crisis by increasing the overall program limit of its Trade Facilitation Program (TFP) from €800 million to €1.5 billion, which would have allowed the program to facilitate more trade. But, unexpectedly, TFP's overall use and volume fell sharply in 2009. After nine years of increased volumes year over year, the TFP turnover decreased by more than one-third—from €890 million in 2008 to €573 million in 2009. A major reason for the decline was the decrease in imports of investment goods (for example, machinery) that usually have a higher underlying value. Most TFP transactions were related only to essential goods such as foodstuffs and lower-value consumer goods, which continued to be imported to the region and were supported mainly by smaller local banks. In particular, foreign-owned subsidiary banks and larger local banks, which are usually involved in higher-value transactions with a special focus on the import of investment goods and machinery, were using TFP less because they had become more cautious about covering and financing large-scale transactions.

However, as the economies in many countries improved, EBRD saw an increased demand for TFP in the first half of 2010. Overall European Union (EU) industrial production began to recover in early 2010, with particular strength in Germany and France. Together with positive industrial confidence, data indicated a strong second quarter for the EU economy—with benefits accruing to those non-EU economies in EBRD's region that have strong trade links to the EU. Therefore, countries like Belarus also reported strong growth in the second quarter of 2010 when gross domestic product (GDP) grew faster than anticipated, led by a buoyant growth in exports and construction. These positive trends mirrored the increased demand for TFP support as more goods were being exported and imported into EBRD's countries of operation.

As of mid-2010, trade finance levels had stabilized but were unlikely to return quickly to the high-volume levels that preceded the financial crises. The TFP will continue its support, especially for small banks and banks in less-advanced countries, which will in turn allow those banks to manage the demand for trade finance from local SMEs needing support for their import and export businesses.

Lessons Learned

An important factor that enabled the EBRD to deal efficiently with the economic crisis was that TFP was already established and firmly in place, so it was well-developed and tested before the 2008–09 crisis. (See annex 19.1 for information about the history of TFP.) It was crucial to act swiftly, react, and adapt, implementing specific crisis-response measures during and after the crisis.

Because the latest economic crisis also encompassed a liquidity crisis, it became imperative not only to help cover risk but also to provide liquidity to the market. This was particularly the case for smaller banks and banks in less-developed countries where the general support was more directed toward a handful of large banks and international banking groups. TFP focused on supporting SMEs through smaller banks and banks in less-developed countries, often being the only source of support for their trade finance operations.

Because the program operates only through local banks, EBRD has implemented controls and monitoring measures jointly with its partner banks to develop a mechanism ensuring that only genuine trade finance transactions are guaranteed or financed. These control measures—such as checking the transactions and underlying documents to verify the cross-border movements of actual goods and services for quoted amounts—were introduced to provide security and to identify transactions that would not qualify as real trade finance. As a result of the crises and its subsequent losses, banks in EBRD countries of operation and foreign confirming banks are now more cautious and are checking transactions in more detail to ensure that their funds are actually used for trade finance and match the underlying trade finance cycle.

It has also been proven that cofinancing arrangements with other development agencies, export credit agencies, foreign commercial banks, private insurance underwriters, and investment funds is an advantage especially during times of risk aversion and constrained availability of trade finance. TFP has been in the forefront of such cofinancing arrangements and signed cofinancing arrangements with the Netherlands Development Finance Company (*Nederlandse Financierings-Maatschappij voor Ontwikkelingslanden, or* FMO), the Organization of Petroleum Exporting Countries' Fund for International Development (OFID), and private insurance underwriters. These institutions share EBRD's risk in TFP facilities for selected banks in Azerbaijan, Belarus, Georgia, Kazakhstan, Moldova, Russia, Tajikistan, and Ukraine. Without EBRD's involvement and expertise, private insurance underwriters in particular could not have continued their support and investments in many Eastern European and CIS countries because of the increased economic risks. The continuous involvement of risk-sharing partners allowed the TFP to maintain the limits for its issuing banks and provided the necessary support the banks in the region needed.

Another consequence of the crisis is that foreign exporters and commercial banks are more likely than before to decline new business, even with 100 percent EBRD risk cover under TFP guarantee facilities. The main reason is that they lack sufficient liquidity to finance these transactions, particularly in larger amounts and of longer tenors. If at all, foreign exporters are ready to accept payment by letters of credit (LCs) until delivery of the goods, but they can no longer grant longer payment terms to finance sales of machinery and equipment, storage, and distribution of the imported goods in EBRD countries of operation.

Importers and exporters in these countries, therefore, find it increasingly difficult to finance foreign trade transactions (particularly imports of machinery and equipment), exports from EBRD countries of operation, and intraregional trade transactions. As a result, EBRD not only offers up to 100 percent risk cover for LCs issued by TFP client banks in Eastern Europe and the CIS, but also provides the issuing banks with the necessary liquidity for preexport finance, postimport finance, and financing of local distribution of imported goods. EBRD often is the only institution that can still provide risk cover and liquidity to finance foreign trade with importers and exporters in this region.

African Development Bank

The adverse impacts of the financial crisis that hit the world in 2008 became evident in Africa toward the end of the same year. Its severity and detrimental impact on investment and trade required urgent, collective countercyclical actions by the international financial community, using creative and pragmatic approaches to support the recovery of trade flows as soon as possible. As many African commercial banks faced severe liquidity constraints, AfDB played an important role in helping the continent through the financial crisis.

Impact of the Crisis in Africa

Since the onset of the crisis, growth on the continent fell well below the 2006–08 trend line of 6 percent per year but remained positive overall. International Monetary Fund (IMF) Managing Director Dominique Strauss-Kahn expressed optimism about the continent's 2010 economic prospects, which have been strengthened by "good policies that had given Africa's governments the fiscal space to cope with the crisis" (Willson 2010).

The global economic crisis has given new impetus to domestic resource mobilization in Africa. However, it has also underlined Africa's lack of export diversification—that is, continued primary commodity dependence. Growth in the medium term will continue to depend largely on the recovery of global demand. The problem of import financing in Africa will likely fully materialize as demand picks up, and if not addressed adequately, it may hamper economic growth.

Furthermore, global commercial banks indicate that the high cost of information gathering on counterparty risk and the low profitability of small operations in the region are making the financing of imports in Africa, or the confirmation of LCs from local banks, unattractive. The impact of Basel II is preoccupying the market, and all major international players have become more selective in working with local counterparty banks—increasing requirements for documentation, cash collateral, and other forms of guarantees that are costly and cumbersome to fulfill. These conditions may lead to a shortage of international credit on affordable terms when consumer and investment demand pick up in Africa.

AfDB Response to the Crisis

In early 2009, AfDB assessed the activities of 74 African commercial banks and specialized financial institutions to develop an overview of the African trade market, its trends, and key actors and to determine how these have been affected by the global financial crisis. The assessment was updated in March 2010 to reexamine the situation and provide guidance. AfDB's primary concerns have been to ensure that its intervention meets the following objectives:

- Addresses the critical market constraints (that is, is effective)
- Responds to the crisis in a manner that is timely and that matches the AFDB's resource capacity
- Does not put AfDB's financial soundness at risk (that is, is prudent)
- Leverages the comparative advantages of partners while giving AfDB adequate visibility for its contribution (that is, garnering recognition that is both additional and complementary).

Following this assessment, AfDB established a Trade Finance Initiative (TFI) in January 2009 as part of a broader package of crisis response initiatives. The TFI responds to calls from its regional member countries and aims to help African commercial banks and development finance institutions (DFIs) to use AfDB resources to support and boost trade finance operations.

At the institutional level, while the largest pan-African banks have been able to support their clients on the financing of exports during the crisis (although at a higher cost and for a smaller size and tenor of transactions), smaller banks and banks in countries whose rating has been downgraded have suffered a loss of access to domestic and international inter-bank resources at acceptable terms. Like everywhere else in the world, smaller banks are suffering from the general re-assessment of "counterparty" risk. The response has therefore consisted in building a global network of DFIs that pool financial resources for maximum outreach and scale, broad risk diversification, and ability to leverage the economies of scale of partners already actively involved in the business. (Box 19.1 below summarizes the terms and conditions of TFI's credit products.)

Box 19.1 Terms and Conditions of TFI Credit Products

Eligibility

African financial institutions (commercial banks and DFIs) that are engaged in trade finance may apply for a trade finance line of credit (LOC) under the AfDB TFI. In reviewing credit applications, AfDB will use its standard selection criteria, including strategic alignment, commercial viability, development outcomes, additionality, and complementarity. All financial intermediaries must meet AfDB's credit standards (risk rating of 6 or better), and the risks of each transaction will be evaluated on a case-by-case basis. All applications will be subject to the AfDB's prescribed review and approval processes and procedures.

Use of Proceeds

The proceeds of a trade finance LOC will be used by the recipient financial intermediary for trade finance operations. This includes, but is not limited to, standard import and export finance operations including pre- and postshipment finance. Given the short-term nature of trade finance (90 percent is less than one year), the financial intermediary will be permitted to reuse or revolve the proceeds until the contractual repayment dates of the facility.

Maturity

Given the short-term nature of most trade finance operations, the standard final maturity of trade finance LOCs will be up to 3.5 years. Shorter final maturities can be expected.

Repayment Terms

Trade finance LOCs may have amortizing repayment terms with an agreed grace period on principal repayments (typically up to one year) or may be repaid in a single (bullet) installment at final maturity. In line with standard practices, AfDB may charge a prepayment fee for early repayment and a penalty for late repayment.

Disbursement Terms

Like standard LOCs, a trade finance LOC will usually disburse in two tranches. The first tranche (generally up to 50 percent) will be drawn after the conditions precedents have been met. The second tranche will be disbursed after AfDB has verified that the use of proceeds of the first tranche complies with the terms and conditions of the legal agreement.

Pricing

Like standard LOCs, a trade finance LOC will attract up-front fees of up to 1 percent of the committed amount and will be priced with a margin over a standard interest rate reference such as the London interbank offered rate (LIBOR) in the currency of the facility.

AfDB has allocated $1 billion for TFI, which has two main components: $500 million for trade finance lines of credit (LOCs) and $500 million allocated to the Global Trade Liquidity Program (GTLP) of the World Bank Group's International Finance Corporation.[1] AfDB's contribution to GTLP plays a key role in allowing the beneficiary banks to leverage their credit and cross-border limits and to significantly enhance trade credit availability across the continent. AfDB's involvement in the GTLP has also helped increase the share of GTLP resources targeted for Africa.

For the African component of the GTLP, the confirmed partner banks included Standard Bank of South Africa (SBSA), Afreximbank (to complement AfDB's trade finance LOC), and Citibank. The $250 million LOC facility to SBSA was the first GTLP transaction to be approved by AfDB and disbursed.

Initial demand for trade finance LOCs was strong. Cumulative trade finance requests to date amount to approximately $1 billion. This total includes requests from five regional banks, one DFI, one trade insurance agency, and three national banks. However, because the trade finance market has been improving in some African regions (North Africa, for example), some of the initial financing requests did not materialize.

In addition, AfDB helped secure the syndication for financing the purchase and export marketing of Ghana's 2009 cocoa harvest by the Cocoa Board of Ghana (Cocobod) because the diminished risk appetite of many international commercial lenders had initially indicated that a financing gap was threatening this vital trade transaction. For this transaction, AfDB and several commercial financiers raised a $1.2 billion preexport facility in September 2009. AfDB's endorsement of the feasibility of the transaction, with its $35 million participation in this globally syndicated trade finance operation, instilled confidence among commercial banks to successfully close the deal. Cocobod supports more than 2 million Ghanaians involved in the cocoa industry. In March 2010, AfDB sold $12.5 million (50 percent) of the remaining Cocobod exposure to Nedbank of South Africa, pricing it at par.

Although AfDB is a newcomer to the trade finance market, the urgent nature of the global financial crisis has forced it quickly up the learning curve. The learning process has been greatly facilitated by the sharing of experience with partner institutions including sister international financial institutions (IFIs) that have been active in the trade finance industry for many years. A recent roundtable discussion on trade finance cochaired by the AfDB president and World Trade Organization (WTO) Director-General Pascal Lamy concluded that, going forward, AfDB and other IFIs have an ongoing role to play in Africa's trade finance markets.

Lessons Learned

Local and international commercial banks active in Africa as well as DFIs acknowledged that AfDB still has an important role to play in supporting trade finance in the immediate postcrisis period.

First, several commercial banks indicate that the crisis is not over and that AfDB should maintain its TFI. Therefore, GTLP will continue to provide needed support and is expected to cease operations only after the markets have normalized and demand for its products is no longer sufficient to justify continuation of the program.

Second, access to trade finance facilities continues to be constrained by the small size of many African financial institutions. The liquidity problem has become a capital allocation problem based on a problem of risk appetite. In the short term, AfDB should therefore assess the additionality and impact of a guarantee program in partnership with a key trade finance player. This outsourcing would allow major partners active in trade finance to increase the scope of their programs (that is, include more banks) and to complement the existing program so existing banks can access increased trade lines.

Finally, African commercial banks reported increasing demand for facilities with importers and exporters in emerging Asia. However, the banks also reported that trade transactions are constrained by Asian banks' unfamiliarity with the continent and its financial institutions. Asian firms require LCs, and transactions are slow and difficult. African commercial banks suggested that AfDB could facilitate trade transactions by working with its counterpart financial institutions in Asian markets, especially China, India, the Republic of Korea, and Thailand.

Inter-American Development Bank

In the immediate aftermath of the crisis, the Latin American and the Caribbean region suffered many of the shocks experienced in other parts of the world: a fall in stock and bond prices, sharp currency depreciations, and recession, causing the productive asset values of the seven largest Latin American economies to collapse in the second half of 2008.

Impact of the Crisis in Latin America and the Caribbean

Because of an increase in the risk premium, the region experienced an increase in public sector borrowing costs and a leap in corporate costs. Risk perception also caused a significant outflow of capital, leaving the private sector with no access to external funding. In addition, Latin America experienced a significant decline in trade volumes, given that its major trading partners are the United States and the EU. The drop in prices of primary commodities such as oil had a dichotomous impact initially: oil exporting countries faced a detrimental period of trade shock while oil importing countries benefited, albeit only initially. Later, as the crisis unfolded through 2009, the general trend was downward for all the major economies in the region (Fernández-Arias and Montiel 2009).

However, unlike in previous periods of financial turmoil, Latin America faced neither bank runs nor currency and debt crises. Strong macroeconomic fundamentals of low inflation, twin current account and fiscal surpluses, considerable reserves, and increasingly flexible exchange rate regimes arguably cushioned the impact of the crisis (Izquierdo and Talvi 2010). Particular emphasis is placed by Izquierdo and Talvi on the role of the international community as a lender of last resort.

IDB Response to the Crisis

When the crisis hit, the IDB's Trade Finance Reactivation Program (TFRP) was in place to support IDB's fast response in Latin America and the Caribbean. Recognizing the countercyclical role that international trade plays to promote the exchange of goods and services, create jobs, enhance national production, and foster inclusive economies, the IDB's TFRP made a commitment to strengthen supply-side capacity and trade-related infrastructure in the region.

The TFRP includes the following tripartite offering of products and services that together seek to ensure stable and reliable sources of trade finance in the region:

- Trade Finance Facilitation Program (TFFP) guarantees and A/B loans
- Trade funds
- Specialized technical assistance and trade finance training

The TFFP implemented in 2005 proved an effective tool for not only mitigating the effects of the liquidity crisis, but also expanding trade finance for financial intermediaries (FIs) and their clients. The TFFP is a fast-delivery vehicle that provides guarantees and loans that allow importers and exporters to reduce systemic and transaction risks, access new capital sources, and strengthen competitiveness without subsidizing and distorting the market.

The TFFP A/B loans target the liquidity shortage by directly funding FI clients' trade-related activities, while guarantees continue to enable the region's network of issuing banks to access a broader number of international confirming banks.

The program issues standby LCs to cover confirming banks' trade finance risk and provide trade finance loans to issuing banks in Latin America and the Caribbean so that they can continue to finance export and import clients. In response to the global economic crisis in late 2008, the IDB increased its TFFP limit from $400 million to $1 billion. Currently, the TFFP has more than $1.2 billion in approved credit lines and issued guarantees and loans for more than $800 million. These funds supported more than 1,100 individual international trade transactions. The TFFP has built a network of 72 issuing banks in 19 Latin American and Caribbean countries. Through the network of international confirming banks, the program is now present in 51 countries worldwide with 250 confirming banks belonging to 92 banking groups.

The Financial Markets Division also finances trade funds that mobilize equity investors to offer short-term trade finance for medium-size exporters through special-purpose trade vehicles. These innovative instruments provide access to finance to SME clients who would otherwise face unaffordable or limited financing from conventional outlets. In 2010 alone, IDB participated in trade funds that financed more than $914 million in trade activity, supporting more than 1,400 transactions in 12 different countries with 70 different companies. This engagement leads to a multiplier effect—stimulating the production, movement, and consumption of more goods and services across a range of countries and industries.

In 2007, IDB launched a technical assistance project targeting the participation of smaller FIs hitherto underserved in the TFFP. It focused on remedying the high fixed cost of identifying appropriate institutions, conducting credit analysis, and monitoring FIs' compliance with TFFP requirements. Using preliminary market research and bank-specific knowledge, the project identified FIs that would most benefit from TFFP integration but were outside its reach on a stand-alone basis. This was followed by credit analysis and technical consultations to integrate them into the TFFP as issuing banks and to use their trade finance capacity for the benefit of SME clients.

To further enhance the coverage of SMEs in the region, issuing banks and their SME clients have benefited from specialized trade finance training to address supply- and demand-side barriers, share knowledge, and create competitive advantages. The goal is to increase the FIs' trade finance skills and enable them to better identify and meet their exporting and importing clients' needs.[2]

Lessons Learned

IDB programs helped recognize the demands of small and medium FIs, which traditionally work with smaller importers and exporters, and quickly adapted

---

Box 19.2 IDB Trade Financing Increases Intraregional Transactions

A trend in IDB's trade financing is the emergence of intraregional transactions. In its initial stages, the Trade Finance Facilitation Program (TFFP) disseminated information and promoted collaboration within its participating bank network. (For more information about the TFFP network and the extent of both interregional and intraregional transactions, see annex 19.2.)

Gradually, contacts formed—first between banks, and then intraregional or South-South, trade deals transpired. In one such transaction, Ecuador's Banco de Guayaquil issued an eligible instrument for Banco de Comercio Exterior de Colombia (BANCOLDEX) to guarantee the export of trucks. IDB's TFFP provided BANCOLDEX with $4.1 million in coverage. According to Banco de Guayaquil's external trade manager, Luis Ceballos Córdova, "Intraregional trade is traditionally backed by reciprocal credit agreements under the Latin American Integration Association (ALADI). While numerous transactions have been closed under ALADI, its limits oftentimes prove insufficient. The IDB's TFFP offers an excellent alternative to not only complement the support provided by ALADI's Reciprocal Agreements but also to allow our transaction volume to grow significantly."

In similar deals, IDB has supported the import of Argentine hydroelectric turbines to Paraguay, export of Brazilian turbo generators to Peru, and import of Argentine automobiles to Honduras, among other transactions. Without the necessary support, trade would involve higher costs and levels of risk for Latin American and Caribbean economies that rely on such diversification to foster product specialization, technology transfer, competitiveness, and resistance to market volatility.

---

products and services to respond to clients' needs. These FIs have been targeted given their difficulty in accessing international markets, coupled with their critical role in stimulating employment, reducing poverty, deepening intraregional trade, and fostering a robust and inclusionary real sector—important countercyclical forces during economic downturns.

The IDB program has also helped foster intraregional trade. Intraregional transactions grew partly in response to the IDB network approach of supporting confirming and issuing banks through financing, technical assistance, and relationship building. The IDB is able to ensure a stable source of trade finance and in traditionally larger volumes while reducing dependency on international markets, which in turn furthers business alliances, generates jobs, and contributes to real sector growth in Latin America and the Caribbean.

Long-term relationships with issuing banks are critical to efficiency and agility. Although time and dedication are required up front to manage the short-term, dynamic nature of trade finance transactions, the IDB's implementation of the TFFP stressed the importance of maintaining close relationships with clients. As a result, it has been able to facilitate future transactions—especially important when exploring areas of high social impact such as housing, SME, and education financing. Similarly, the IDB recognized the added value it could bring by employing a more holistic approach to the trade finance loans and risk mitigation products. with a combination of financing with training, technical assistance, and enhanced networks, there is a positive impact in capacity, expertise, and access to new markets in Latin America and the Caribbean.

Finally, coordination and communication between international institutions seeking to support and promote international trade have proved essential throughout program implementation.

Asian Development Bank

There is a persistent private sector market gap for trade finance in the more challenging Asian emerging markets—Bangladesh, Mongolia, Nepal, Pakistan, Sri Lanka, and Tajikistan to name only a few—but the gap became wider in both relatively well-off Asian emerging markets and the more challenging ones during the crisis. The gap widened after the September 2008 collapse of Lehman Brothers, when

- financial institutions took major hits to their capital base, leaving fewer resources available to support business in general, including resources for trade finance;
- everyone was concerned about counterparty risk, which dried up the secondary market for trade finance;
- financial institutions were worried about country risks—the prospect that evaporating demand for Asia's exports, lower remittances, and high unemployment could lead to social and political unrest; and
- Basel II rules (requiring more capital to be set aside for trade finance compared with Basel I) removed capital that otherwise would have been available to support trade.

Although there are persistent market gaps in trade finance at the best of times in the more challenging Asian emerging markets, the confluence of these four elements had a significant impact on the availability of finance—loans and guarantees—to support trade during the financial crisis. The Asian Development Bank's TFP focuses on the more challenging markets. The five greatest users of ADB's TFP are Bangladesh, Nepal, Pakistan, Sri Lanka, and Vietnam. Because the TFP focuses its resources on the more challenging markets, it does not assume risk in relatively developed markets such as China, India, Malaysia, and Thailand.

Impact of the Crisis in the Asia

While American and European financial institutions suffered, most of Asia's financial institutions—with some exceptions in central Asia such as in Kazakhstan—were in relatively good condition. Banks in these countries were generally not dependent on capital markets for funding because they tended to be funded through deposits, and they were not exposed to the subprime mortgage investments and credit default swaps that hit many Western financial institutions particularly hard. But the real economy in many export-dependent Asian countries was hit as American and European markets fell into recession and required fewer Asian goods. Numerous companies were affected, and this led to a rise in nonperforming loans among Asian banks, notably in Bangladesh, Pakistan, and Vietnam.

Recovery in the global economy is driving a sharp rise in trade, particularly in Asia. The trade increase, in turn, is spurring a rising demand among exporters, importers, and their banks for finance to support their trading activities. Although the trend in intra-Asian trade was established several years ago, the crisis accelerated the trend. China has played a major role in this trend, buying parts from other Asian countries for assembly in China for export to Europe and North America. Increasingly, we see China not only as an assembler and exporter of Asian parts but also as a final consumer. Although this dynamic has helped fuel a rebound in Asian trade, there will be challenges ahead, and the recovery will be uneven. Developed nations are recovering from the effects of the downturn much more slowly than emerging Asia.

ADB expects Asia to continue leading the global economic recovery. It projects a sharper rise in trade volumes in Asia as the region produces more for local consumers whose incomes are gradually rising, as well as for customers elsewhere who are starting to rebuild the inventories they depleted during the crisis. Within Asia itself, some countries will have more trouble than others in accessing enough trade finance. Even during noncrisis times, there is limited appetite for risk among private sector IFIs in Bangladesh, Nepal, Pakistan, Sri Lanka, and other more-challenging developing Asian markets. SMEs will also continue to find it difficult to get pre- and postshipment financing. And in all the exuberance about the rise of Asia, ADB is focused on the more than 900 million Asians living on less than $1.25 a day.

ADB Response to the Crisis

In March 2009, ADB ramped up its TFP activities, which supported $2 billion in trade—an increase of more than 300 percent over 2008. In 2010, the program supported $2.8 billion in trade, up from $2 billion in 2009. In the first two months of 2011, volumes were up by more than 500 percent compared with the same period in 2010. These figures suggest that although the TFP plays an important role in a crisis, its noncrisis role of filling persistent market gaps in the more challenging Asian markets is extremely important and continues to grow.

TFP provides guarantees and loans to more than 200 banks in support of trade within 24 to 48 hours of application. The program has made a point of not assuming risk in China and India, preferring to focus resources on more-challenging Asian markets where the private sector is not very active. In 2010, the bulk of TFP's activities were in Bangladesh, Nepal, Pakistan, Sri Lanka, and Vietnam, but TFP was also active in Azerbaijan, Indonesia, Mongolia, and Uzbekistan as well as other markets.

The program delivers tangible and measurable development impact. For example, in 2009 and 2010, TFP provided trade support for more than 540 SMEs. Supporting SME growth is a priority for ADB because smaller firms employ the largest number of people in most Asian countries. Increased trading activities and cross-border relationships enabled by TFP are helping to boost economic integration and cooperation in challenging Asian markets, which should, in turn, spur faster economic growth and help reduce poverty. In 2009 and 2010, nearly half of the TFP portfolio supported trade between ADB's developing-member countries (south-south trade).

Clearly ADB has played a role, albeit a small one, in supporting trade in ADB's most challenging developing-member countries. In 2010, TFP continued its explosive growth in business volumes, driving the program more deeply in central and other parts of Asia. The program expanded in Azerbaijan, Bhutan, Mongolia, the Philippines, Tajikistan, and Uzbekistan. The TFP will also be expanded to Armenia, Georgia, Kazakhstan, the Kyrgyz Republic, Turkmenistan, and some Pacific island countries in 2011 and 2012.

Lessons Learned

Public institutions proved to be critical intermediaries through which governments implemented their interventions during the crisis. They will continue to play key roles in the future, too. Being part of the multilateral development banks' trade finance programs is an important element in preparing for crisis, for banks in both emerging markets and the developed world. If crisis strikes, for whatever reason—be it national, regional, or global in scope—the multilateral trade finance programs and ECA initiatives can provide ways in which institutions can continue to offer loans and guarantees to keep the wheels of trade running smoothly.

Another lesson learned through this crisis is that there is a serious lack of statistics in trade finance. When considering what interventions may abate the free fall in international trade, policy makers applied "guesstimates" about the role a lack of trade finance played in plummeting trade volumes—and the extent of that role.

To address the general lack of trade finance statistics and to work toward more appropriate capital requirements for trade finance in the Basel framework, ADB, in conjunction with the International Chamber of Commerce (ICC), created the ICC-ADB Trade Finance Default Register. The ICC-ADB Register collected data on more than 5.2 million transactions going back five years, which included the financial crisis period. Statistics on this data set show a 0.02 percent probability of default on trade finance transactions.

This information was presented to the Basel Secretariat in October 2010 to support the case that Basel III guidelines should treat trade finance as a separate asset class for capital treatment. To do otherwise would deplete resources that could support trade by billions of dollars. Those emerging markets that would be most affected are those where persistent market gaps in trade finance exist, crisis or no crisis. These statistics in trade finance will help the trade finance community, national and international regulators, and policy makers to make more informed decisions to support companies engaged in international trade, which is a strong engine for economic growth and job creation.

Annex 19.1: History of the EBRD Trade Facilitation Program

After the Russian banking crisis in the late 1990s, the European Bank for Reconstruction and Development (EBRD) developed the Trade Facilitation Program (TFP) in 1999 to deal with liquidity crises, making it the first IFI to tackle trade finance-related problems.

The TFP is designed to support primarily small local banks and banks in less-advanced countries by promoting foreign trade to, from, and within the EBRD countries of operations. Through this program, EBRD provides guarantees to international confirming banks—taking the political and commercial payment risk of international trade transactions undertaken by banks (the issuing banks). The program currently includes 109 issuing banks in 22 countries, with limits exceeding €2 billion. In addition, more than 700 confirming banks throughout the world have joined TFP since its inception, including 128 banks in 23 EBRD countries of operation. The program strengthens local banks' ability to provide trade financing and gives entrepreneurs in the Eastern Europe and CIS region the support they need to expand their import and export trade.

Originally, the program aimed to service mostly short-term transactions of up to 180 days' tenor to facilitate basic trade. However, the facility was later extended to accommodate longer-tenor transactions to accommodate purchase of equipment, construction, and other term payment guarantees for up to three years for selected banks and countries. This was particularly crucial during the current crisis when local banks struggled to receive trade finance limits for transactions with a tenor longer than six months.

Annex 19.2: IDB Trade Finance

The Inter-American Development Bank's (IDB) Trade Finance Facilitation Program (TFFP) has built a network of 72 issuing banks from 19 Latin American and Caribbean countries with lines amounting to $1.2 billion. Through the network of international confirming banks, the program is now present in 51 countries worldwide, with 250 confirming banks belonging to 92 banking groups. Banks that were already confirming banks are now rejoining as B lenders—furthering the virtuous cycle and maintaining a constant source of trade financing in otherwise uncertain times.

Figures 19A.1 and 19A.2 show the extent of TFFP's interregional and intraregional transactions since its inception in 2005.

Figure 19A.1 TFFP Transactions since 2005, by Number

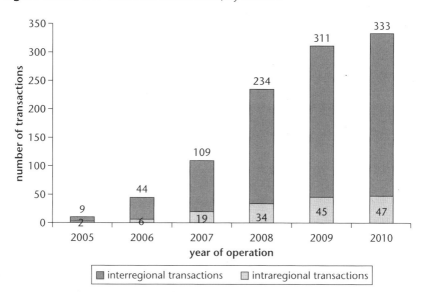

Source: Authors' compilation.
Note: TFFP = Trade Finance Facilitation Program.

Figure 19A.2 TFFP Transactions since 2005, by Value

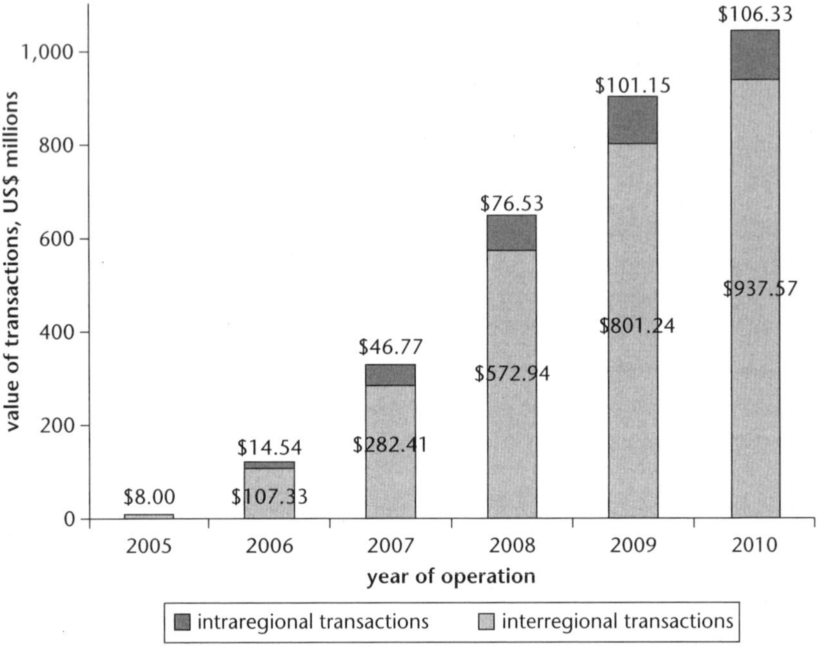

Source: Authors' compilation.
Note: TFFP = Trade Finance Facilitation Program.

Notes

1. Chapter 18 of this volume discusses the GTLP in greater detail as well as other World Bank programs in response to the crisis.

2. To complement training efforts, the IDB's beyondBanking program, launched in November 2009, highlights the catalytic role that FIs play in promoting large-scale economic growth and corporate change for IDB clients and the region. The program encourages FIs to recognize that financial operations that are more inclusive, environmentally friendly, and transparent translate into lower risk, access to new capital, and reputational advantages—as well as a tendency to produce higher financial and social returns than traditional operations. IDB, "beyondBanking: Banking on Global Sustainability." IDB, Washington, DC. http://www.iadb.org/es/recursos-para-empresas/ beyondbanking/beyond-banking-banking-on-global-sustainability,1961.html.

References

Fernández-Arias, Eduardo, and Peter J. Montiel. 2009. "Crisis Response in Latin America: Is the 'Rainy Day' at Hand?" Working Paper 686, Inter-American Development Bank, Washington, DC.

Izquierdo, Alejandro, and Ernesto Talvi, eds. 2010. *The Aftermath of the Crisis: Policy Lessons and Challenges Ahead for Latin America and the Caribbean.* Washington, DC: Inter-American Development Bank. http://idbdocs.iadb.org/wsdocs/getdocument.aspx?docnum=35121569.

Willson, Simon. 2010. "Africa Rebounding Almost in Line with World Recovery." *IMF Survey Magazine,* March 10. http://www.imf.org/external/pubs/ft/survey/so/2010/car031110a.htm.

CREDIT INSURANCE IN SUPPORT OF INTERNATIONAL TRADE: OBSERVATIONS THROUGHOUT THE CRISIS

Fabrice Morel

For decades, export credit insurers, public and private, have worked in the background oiling the wheels of international trade—largely unnoticed by the wider public or, indeed, by a large part of the community of exporters worldwide. This changed in mid-to-late 2008 when, in a deteriorating global economic environment, the crucial importance of trade finance and credit insurance to support international trade flows became apparent. Recognizing that international trade was a means of overcoming, or at least alleviating, the negative impact of the crisis, governments took initiatives in line with the call of the G-20 London Summit in April 2009 to support trade finance and trade flows through their official export credit agencies (ECAs) (G-20 2009). This chapter describes recent trends observed in export credit insurance, especially from 2008 to mid-2010.

The statistical background is provided by the Berne Union (BU), the International Union of Credit and Investment Insurers, which counts the major private credit insurers and most ECAs worldwide among its members. The BU collects

The views expressed are those of the author and cannot necessarily be attributed to the Berne Union or members of the Berne Union. Errors and omission remain the responsibility of the author. The author gratefully acknowledges guidance and advice from Lennart Skarp and Kimberly Wiehl, without whom this article would not have been written. Peter M. Jones reviewed the article and provided most helpful comments.

Box 20.1 Credit Insurance and How It Works

Credit insurance facilitates trade, allowing suppliers to sell goods and services without having to worry about not being paid by their customers. In simple terms, a credit insurer promises to indemnify a seller if a buyer fails to pay for the goods or services purchased. In return for accepting this default risk, the credit insurer charges the supplier a premium. Although credit insurance works for both domestic and international trade, international trade is, by definition, subject to a wider range of risks.

In addition to risks related to the buyer and its creditworthiness—the commercial risk, also called credit risk—international trade transactions are subject to political risks where an overseas buyer willing and able to pay might be prevented from doing so because of a political situation.

Export credit insurance allows exporters and trade banks to safely extend credit to buyers abroad, thus enabling trade transactions that would not happen otherwise. It is customary to define short-term export credit insurance (ST) as insurance for trade transactions with repayment terms of 1 year or less, while medium/long-term export credit insurance (MLT) covers trade transactions of more than 1 year (typically 3–5 years, occasionally up to 15 years). ST business is usually insured on a whole turnover basis whereby the credit insurer insures the exporter's entire portfolio of trade receivables—the "whole turnover." MLT business is usually insured on a transactional basis, covering sales of capital goods and services with repayment terms over several years.

---

data from its members on a quarterly basis. BU statistics show export sales that are credit insured. As such, they provide an indication of underlying trade flows. Altogether, BU members cover more than 10 percent of international trade, usually the riskier transactions for which exporters and banks decide to buy insurance to trade safely.

Short-Term Export Credit Insurance

This section briefly describes how credit insurers determine credit limits, and why the resulting volume of exports covered is typically higher or lower than those limits.

Credit Limits

Credit limits represent the amounts an insurer has committed to insure. These are credit limits on buyers, set by the insurer, that are influenced by various factors.

On the demand side, exporters request credit limits to protect their trade flows: To whom do exporters want to sell and in which countries? For which destination countries are exporters seeking insurance cover? In this respect, BU statistics are a proxy for international trade movements. The largest commitments by BU members in ST business (covering sales with credit periods of one year or less) are in destinations like the United States and countries in Western Europe. This is where most of the trade happens. These are the countries most goods are exported to.

On the supply side, credit limits set by the insurers reflect how much cover credit insurers are willing to provide. The constraints are the insurers' risk appetite and their capacity to offer the required coverage. Are the buyers creditworthy? What about political risk? Does an insurer have enough capital to support further risky business?

Credit insurers use their market intelligence regarding the financial situation of buyers and the economic and political situation in countries to "underwrite risks," which means to set credit limits and to accept or reject covering sales to a particular buyer. An additional piece of information is the actual payment behavior of a buyer: Did a certain buyer always pay on time in the past? This may point to a particularly diligent company that will strive to continue paying on time even if its financial situation is stretched. Or is a specific buyer usually late in paying for goods delivered? This may point to a buyer who will not necessarily strive to perform according to its obligations during hard times.

A deteriorating economic environment that puts more and more companies in difficulty prompts credit insurers to review the risks in their portfolios and to carefully scrutinize any new risk they are asked to cover. A credit insurer may reduce or cancel limits on buyers. In this case, any future sales to those buyers would not be insured and would be made at the exporter's own risk. Limit reductions or cancellations only apply to future sales. Shipments that have been made under an insurance policy before reduction or cancellation of a limit remain protected.

Covered Exports

In ST business, covered exports represent the turnover or the value of shipments made while being covered under a credit insurance policy. Covered exports are not identical with credit limits as described previously. Once an insurance policy and the respective credit limits are in place, actual exports may not take place for reasons that are independent from the credit insurance. Or, on the contrary, covered exports to a buyer during a year may be higher than the credit limit set. Indeed, once a shipment is delivered and paid for on time, the credit limit is freed up to support further shipments.

Although covered exports give a retrospective view of the trade flows that have actually been insured during a time period, credit limits give an indication of the insurer's commitment to insure at a given point in time.

Short-Term Export Credit Insurance during the Crisis

During the crisis, credit insurers were faced with a rapidly deteriorating risk environment and, at the same time, high demand from exporters who wanted credit insurance protection. The following describes the trends in export credit insurance during this period, taking into account the interplay of supply and demand.

Covered Exports

After several years of sustained growth, short-term exports covered by BU members declined by 13 percent, from $1.3 trillion in 2008 to $1.1 trillion in 2009 (Berne Union 2010). During the same time period, global trade contracted by around 23 percent in absolute terms, according to the United Nations Statistics Division (UNSD 2009).

Demand for ST export credit insurance experienced opposing influences from mid-2008 through a large part of 2009. On one hand, global trade was generally declining, as was the amount of international sales for which exporters could potentially seek insurance cover. On the other hand, the global crisis that followed the financial turmoil was showing its effects on the real economy, and companies around the world were defaulting on their obligations. Quite rapidly, exporters recognized the benefits of export credit insurance.

The worsening risk environment prompted those exporters who were willing to continue trade to turn to credit insurance to manage their receivables risks. Some decided to seek insurance for their entire receivables portfolios, where in the past they may have only insured a part of their risks. Other exporters who had never previously used credit insurance found the product was vital to protect their cash flows and to keep their business operations afloat.

Export credit insurers responded cautiously to the demand because they were feeling the impact of the crisis on a daily basis, with insured exporters filing more and more claims as a result of buyer defaults. Despite the challenging risk environment, the reduction of insured ST exports in 2009 was only around half the reduction in world trade in percentage terms. In the end, the total value of cross-border trade supported by BU members in 2009 was the same as in 2007, as figure 20.1 shows.

ST Credit Limits

Since 2005, BU members had continuously expanded their ST insurance, much in line with the growth of world trade. The peak in aggregate limits was reached in mid-2008 with a total amount of slightly more than $1 trillion for all BU members together.

Figure 20.1 ST Exports Covered, 2005–09

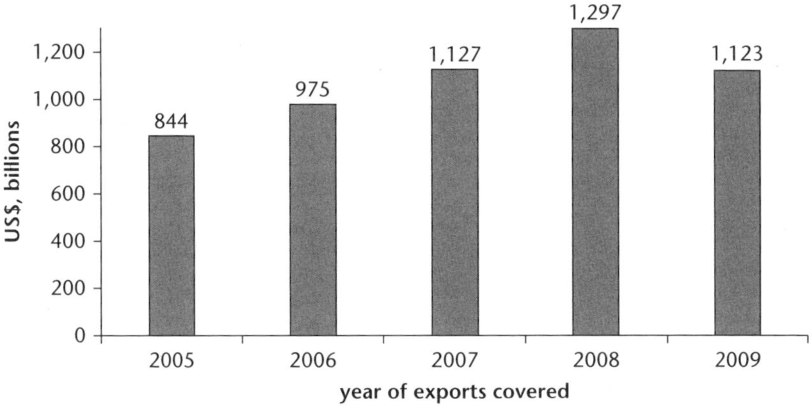

Source: Berne Union databases 2010.
Note: ST = short-term export credit insurance.

During the three quarters following the mid-2008 peak, overall limits quickly declined for two reasons: (a) lower underlying trade volumes due to reduced international economic activity; and (b) a more cautious risk assessment by private market insurers, which account for most of the ST business of the BU. When the crisis started to bite and claims notifications began to rise dramatically, several private insurers cut back limits—understandably so from their point of view, because buyer defaults had started to accumulate and insurers were hit by a wave of claims to pay. However, the cutbacks raised criticism in the exporters' community, and many claimed they could not sell without being covered by credit insurance. Private credit insurers countered the criticism, arguing that the risk environment had substantially changed from a previously benign economic environment to a challenging one, that they were adapting to the new circumstances, and that they were acting in the best interest of exporters by preventing them from entering into transactions with unsound buyers.

Since the second quarter of 2009, export credit limits seem to have stabilized, although further, smaller reductions were recorded at the end of the last quarter of 2009 and the first quarter of 2010. At the end of the second quarter of 2010, aggregate limits stood at $743 billion, a level last seen in early 2007, as figure 20.2 shows.

Private and Public Insurers

How did various players behave in the crisis, and what roles did they play? The Berne Union includes private market insurers that operate commercially to make

Figure 20.2 ST Credit Limits, Q1 CY05 to Q2 CY10

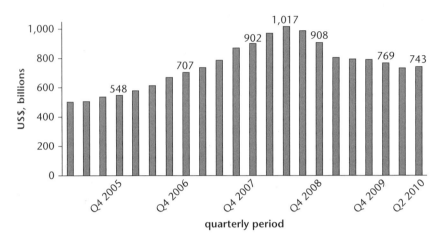

Source: Berne Union databases 2010.
Note: CY = calender year. ST = short-term export credit insurance. Figures represent end of calendar quarter.

a profit for their shareholders as well as public insurers, the official ECAs who are backed by their governments and whose mandate it is to support national interests. According to the World Trade Organization (WTO), ECAs are required to be self-sustaining and, therefore, have to break even in the long term (WTO 1995).

From the peak in credit limits in mid-2008 through the first quarter of 2009, all credit insurers felt the impact of the slowdown in world trade. With a few exceptions among ECAs, both public and private insurers recorded a drop in credit limits extended during that time.

From the second quarter of 2009, private market players as a group continued to reduce their credit limits. In contrast, the ECAs increased theirs because of government initiatives, in line with the call of the G-20, asking their ECAs to fill a perceived gap in export credit insurance supply (G-20 2009). As seen in BU statistics, the ECAs' share in global ST business increased in 2009 and 2010 compared with previous years.

The movement in market shares from private insurers to ECAs (as table 20.1 shows) was primarily due to a reduction in the volume of cover offered by private market players. To a smaller extent, it was also the result of some ECAs' real volume growth, particularly from East Asia and North America.

Much discussion has concerned the European Union (EU) Commission's temporary permission for ECAs from EU countries to be active in the so-called ST marketable risk business—coverage of ST exports to Organisation for Economic Co-operation and Development (OECD) countries, including those in the EU.

Table 20.1 Market Shares of Private and Public ST Credit Limits, 2006–10

	2006–08	2009	2010
Private insurers	85%	79%	72%
ECAs	15%	21%	28%

Source: Berne Union databases 2010.
Note: ST = short-term export credit insurance. ECA = export credit agency.

Under EU regulations, this was an area that EU ECAs had exited and left to the private market years ago. EU ECAs helped, and continue to help, thousands of European exporters, particularly small and medium enterprises (SMEs), by providing them with needed ST credit insurance during the crisis. The activity of EU ECAs in this field increased significantly, by around 50 percent as a group and more for some individual agencies. But their overall share of the ST business remains small, less than 2 percent of the overall volume, which is in line with their mandate to complement private market capacity in difficult times.

ST Credit Limits per Destination Region

Credit limits are the result of interplay between demand from exporters and supply considerations by insurers. Variations in credit limits on destination countries and regions give an indication of underlying trade flows (demand) and risk perception by the insurers (decision to supply cover).

The Berne Union tracks aggregate credit limits granted by its members for five destination regions: Africa, the Americas, Asia, Europe, and Oceania. The largest trade region is Europe, with around 60 percent of the total trade amounts covered by BU members, followed by Asia and the Americas, with Africa and Oceania being much smaller. Since 2005, as table 20.2 shows, the shares of ST credit limits for exports to the five regions have stayed relatively stable, with a slight indication of decline in the European share and a slight increase for Asia.

Most of the limits within the European region are for risks in Western European countries, which account for more than 70 percent of the European exposure. The biggest Asian destination country is China, with approximately 20 percent of the total credit limits for that region. Slightly more than 50 percent of the credit limits to the Americas is for cover on buyers in the United States.

In an analysis of the quarterly evolution of credit limits during the crisis for the largest destination regions—the Americas, Asia, and Europe—the first observation is that credit limits evolved in a similar fashion for all regions of the world

Table 20.2 Shares of ST Credit Limits, 2005–09, by Destination Region

	2005	2006	2007	2008	2009
Africa (percent)	3	3	3	3	4
Americas (percent)	15	15	14	15	15
Asia (percent)	18	18	19	21	21
Europe (percent)	63	63	62	59	59
Oceania (percent)	1	1	1	1	1
Total credit limits (US$, billions)	548	707	902	908	769

Source: Berne Union databases 2010.
Note: ST = short-term export credit insurance.

until the end of 2009. The trend shows a growth in limits until mid-2008 and then a sharp downturn until the first quarter of 2009, followed by a relative stabilization until the end of the year. This is in line with the fact that no decoupling between regions of the world was observed in the early phases of the crisis. Although the initial banking crisis began in the United States and extended to Europe soon after, the economic crisis that followed became widespread more or less simultaneously all over the globe. Consequently, variations of credit limits for different destination regions moved in line during 2008 and 2009.

The second observation is that the parallel movement did not continue in 2010. While credit limits on Asia and the Americas started to increase again, minimally during the first quarter and significantly by 8–10 percent during the second quarter of 2010, credit limits for exports to Europe continued to decrease, as figure 20.3 illustrates. Although this decrease slowed down in the second quarter of 2010, the figure is still negative. This suggests a looser connection of the big economies during the recovery, with Europe being less dynamic than Asia and the Americas. Whether this interpretation is substantiated will be shown as BU statistics continue to unfold for 2010 and beyond.

ST Claims Paid

If a buyer fails to pay for the goods purchased and the sale was covered by credit insurance, the exporter applies for indemnification for the loss under the insurance policy. The ability to make a valid claim and to be indemnified for a loss suffered is the fundamental reason why exporters buy export credit insurance.

ST claims paid by BU members to insured exporters more than doubled, from $1.1 billion in 2008 to $2.4 billion in 2009. Many claims were generated in late 2008 and were paid by insurers in 2009. The processing time explains why BU statistics for the year 2008 show a relatively low level of claims in figure 20.4.

Figure 20.3 Change in ST Credit Limits, Q4 2007–Q2 2010, by Region

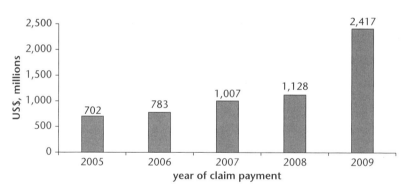

Source: Berne Union databases 2010.
Note: ST = short-term export credit insurance. Figures represent end of calendar quarter.

Figure 20.4 ST Export Insurance Claims Paid, 2005–09

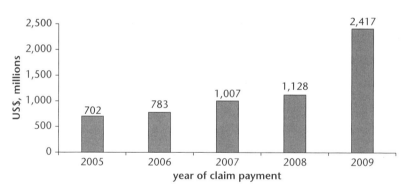

Source: Berne Union databases 2010.
Note: ST = short-term export credit insurance.

The jump in claims paid in 2009 pushed the loss ratio—claims paid in relation to premium income, a measure used by credit insurers to quantify the quality of the underwriting result—to 88 percent. Although this was a level at which insurers overall took an operational loss, the loss ratio did not reach the insurers' worst-case expectations at the beginning of the crisis. Notably, the years immediately preceding the crisis had been particularly beneficial for ST export credit insurers, with low loss ratios of 35–40 percent for BU members as a whole.

Overall, credit insurers coped with the extremely quick deterioration of the situation and the heavy volume of claims submitted in actual numbers and resulting value. Insurers paid claims promptly and supported their insured clients in the worst moments of the crisis.

The level of claims paid declined in the first two quarters of 2010. BU members also recorded a drop in obligor defaults and fewer notifications of buyer problems in general. These are signs that claims reached their peak in 2009 and that 2010 should be a better year for credit insurers. It remains to be seen at what level claims will stabilize and whether the situation will return to the particularly benign claims levels of the immediate precrisis years.

ST Claims Paid per Country

The global nature of the crisis was evident from the BU claims statistics. Buyer defaults, for which insurers had to pay claims, occurred and increased in every region and every country of the world.

The United States and Western European countries were among those with the highest volumes of claims. For defaults that occurred (from highest to lowest claim volume) in the United States, Italy, the United Kingdom, Spain, and Germany, BU members paid a total of nearly $800 million in claims in 2009, up from around $500 million the previous year, as shown in table 20.3.

Claims paid on exports to these five countries alone represented 32 percent of all ST claims paid globally by BU members in 2009. As mentioned previously, these countries are among the main destination countries for exports covered by BU members. They therefore account for a similar share of global

Table 20.3 ST Claims Paid, 2008–09, by Destination Country
US$, millions

	2008	2009
United States	183.8	294.0
Italy	107.6	152.1
United Kingdom	88.1	125.5
Spain	52.2	116.8
Germany	57.9	95.8
Total	500	800

Source: Berne Union databases 2010.
Note: ST = short-term export credit insurance.

insurance commitments—around 31 percent of all ST credit limits extended by BU members.

Credit insurers also suffered in emerging markets, where the total volume of claims in 2009 was of a magnitude similar to industrialized countries but with a much more dramatic increase over the previous year. For defaults that occurred (in order of highest to lowest claims) in the Russian Federation, Ukraine, Turkey, Brazil, and Mexico, for example, BU members paid a total of $550 million to insured exporters in 2009, up from around $100 million in 2008, as shown in table 20.4.

Claims paid in these five countries represented 23 percent of the total amount paid globally by BU members in 2009. But insurance commitments in these markets were much smaller, with only around 6 percent of total credit limits extended by BU members globally. This differs from industrialized countries, where the share of claims and credit limits was similar—around one-third of the totals. It was expected that claims would be paid because of defaults in emerging countries, but the speed and size of the increase in claims might not have been anticipated.

Year on year, claims in the five industrialized countries mentioned above (the United States, Italy, the United Kingdom, Spain, and Germany) increased by 60 percent. Among the five listed emerging countries (Russia, Ukraine, Turkey, Brazil, and Mexico), claims increased by 435 percent.

ST Outlook

The past two years have been unusually testing for ST credit insurers, private and public. However, despite unprecedented claims levels, no insurer defaulted and the industry paid claims promptly to insured exporters. Overall, the industry proved resilient.

Table 20.4 ST Claims Paid in Selected Emerging Markets, by Destination Country
US$, millions

	2008	2009
Russian Federation	22.5	188.2
Ukraine	2.9	128.0
Turkey	32.4	94.9
Brazil	26.8	91.3
Mexico	18.5	48.7
Total	100	550

Source: Berne Union databases 2010.
Note: ST = short-term export credit insurance.

Private market insurers reduced credit limits. This was understandable from their perspective because the risk environment had seriously deteriorated and they were affected by large amounts of claims to pay. Exporters argued that insurers made a difficult situation worse for many companies because the lack of coverage made it difficult to sell goods abroad. Insurers countered that they prevented exporters from trading unsafely, ultimately saving them from potential negative consequences. Without doubt, the measures taken helped to limit the losses of private market insurers, ensuring that they are still operating today and that they are in a position to further insure trade.

To continue to support ST trade, ECAs had to respond to multiple challenges. At a time when they were paying claims as well, they were able to quickly implement measures, as asked by their governments and the G-20, to supplement private market capacity. These measures helped to alleviate the impact of limit reductions by private players.

The level of claims paid declined in the first two quarters of 2010, and BU members also noticed a drop in obligor defaults and resulting claims notifications. Insurers now report cautious optimism that claims are leveling off and that confidence is returning to the market, which would be in line with early signs of a global recovery. However, insurers are aware of the volatile risk environment and continue to monitor their portfolios of risks closely.

Medium/Long-Term Export Credit Insurance during the Crisis

Most medium/long-term export credit insurance (MLT) worldwide (covering sales with credit periods of one year or more) is provided by official ECAs with the backing of their governments. BU statistics show MLT cover offered by ECAs only, and the following analysis does not include cover provided by private market insurers.

The MLT situation is quite different from the ST business, where different types of players reacted differently to the challenges posed by the global economic environment. In contrast, the behavior of BU members regarding MLT export credit insurance was generally consistent because, in the MLT field, BU members are all public insurers—that is, ECAs with similar mandates to support national exports and national interests.

After the Lehman shock in September 2008, bank financing almost dried up for a few months into early 2009. Activity then picked up during the year, particularly in sectors such as aircraft financing, telecom and satellite financing, infrastructure, and oil and gas. During this period, ECAs were instrumental in keeping the trade flows going. Indeed, in many cases, ECA insurance coverage had become a condition of lending without which banks could not finance MLT transactions.

New Exports and Total Exports Covered

Two parameters should be looked at to analyze the amount of insurance provided by ECAs in the MLT field: (a) new exports covered during a year, and (b) the total stock of export credits under cover at the end of a year. Because MLT transactions are repaid over a number of years and stay on insurers' books as "insured exposure" for a significant time period, both figures are important measures and give slightly different indications of recent and historic business activity.

MLT new exports

New exports covered show the volume of transactions for which an insurance contract has been signed during the year. Although an insurance policy comes into effect during a particular year, it is the result of work that has been performed before signature. In that respect, "new business" more often than not reflects the work of a time period that is much longer than the current year. This is particularly the case when a credit insurer underwrites large, complex projects that can take years to come to fruition.

MLT exports insured by BU-member ECAs had healthy growth in recent years, despite a seemingly benign risk environment. But when the crisis started in 2008, it gave exporters and banks an extra reminder of the volatility of the global economic environment. Banks, whose business is primarily to provide financing and which might have taken some risk in the benign precrisis years, were not prepared to do so in the higher-risk environment. Although insurance is not a source of liquidity in itself, it enhances the creditworthiness of the buyer. ECAs had a crucial role in this respect because they carry the full faith and credit of their respective governments, a security that was sought after, especially during the crisis. ECA cover was therefore able to ensure that bank liquidity continued to be available for MLT lending.

Consequently, ECAs, particularly those in developed countries, saw a huge increase in demand for their MLT cover in 2009. After a first quarter with relatively low business levels, new MLT exports covered increased steadily in each quarter to reach a full-year total of $191 billion, the highest level ever recorded, as shown in figure 20.5. The 2009 growth rate was 25 percent, almost double the compound annual growth rate of 13.7 percent from 2005 to 2008.

The largest destination countries for new MLT exports covered in 2009 were the United States, Brazil, the United Arab Emirates, Russia, Canada, Indonesia,

Figure 20.5 MLT New Exports Covered, 2005–09

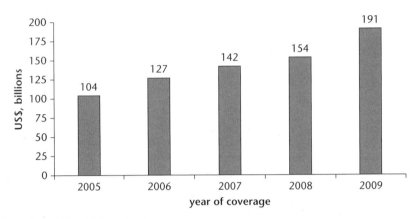

Source: Berne Union databases 2010.
Note: MLT = medium/long-term export credit insurance.

and India. New exports covered to these countries totaled $87 billion, close to half of the total global amount.

MLT Total Exports

Total exports under cover show the amount that credit insurers are exposed to under the insurance policies that are currently in force. For each policy, this would be the amount of credit covered at the beginning of the insured transaction, less any repayments made. In other words, it is the maximum amount that BU-member ECAs all together would have to pay to insured exporters in the unlikely event that all buyers under all current transactions would default on their obligations at the same time. Of course, such a situation would not happen in reality, but it shows the financial exposure that ECAs incur due to these transactions.

Figure 20.6 shows the total amount of MLT export credits under cover by BU-member ECAs at the end of a given year. This exposure includes deals that have been underwritten during the year as well as transactions where insurance cover started in previous years and where repayments are still due. The total MLT exposure on ECAs' books at the end of 2009 stood at $511 billion, 14 percent higher than in 2008. This was a record, as well as for the new exports covered.

Growth in insured MLT exports has been continuous and sustained since 2005. As table 20.5 shows, it was similar in all regions except for the biggest destination region, Asia, to which covered MLT exports have remained stable since

Figure 20.6 MLT Exports Covered, 2005–09

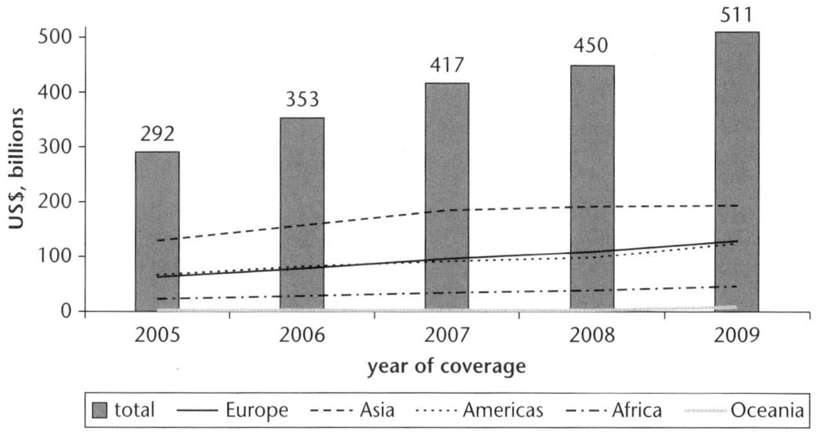

Source: Berne Union databases 2010.
Note: MLT = medium/long-term export credit insurance.

Table 20.5 Shares of MLT Exports Covered, 2005–09, by Destination Region

	2005	2006	2007	2008	2009
Africa (percent)	9	8	9	9	9
Americas (percent)	23	24	22	22	25
Asia (percent)	45	45	45	43	38
Europe (percent)	22	23	23	25	25
Oceania (percent)	1	1	1	1	2
Total exports under cover (US$, billions)	292	353	417	450	511

Source: Berne Union databases 2010.
Note: MLT = medium/long-term export credit insurance.

2007. Consequently, the Asian share has somewhat declined as a percentage relative to other regions.

With the exception of the United States (the largest-exposure country in MLT insurance), the big-exposure countries in this field are all in emerging markets: Russia, Brazil, India, China, the United Arab Emirates, Turkey, Saudi Arabia, and Mexico. This is a contrast to the ST market, which is dominated by industrialized Western European destination countries and the United States.

Both new business covered during the year by BU ECAs and the total amounts under cover at year's end reached an all-time high in 2009. This was also the case for insurance offers—transactions in which the export contract is not yet concluded. MLT offers increased even more than the two other indicators, by 32 percent, to $168 billion.

The MLT story is therefore very much a success story "from peak to peak" and is a testimony to ECAs' ability to support banks and exporters through the crisis and to prevent a potentially drastic reduction of MLT transactions.

MLT Claims Paid

Claims paid by BU-member ECAs to customers in 2009 nearly tripled compared with the previous year to reach $3.1 billion, as shown in figure 20.7. The 66 percent loss ratio was high relative to both 2008 and 2007, when it had been 29 percent and 35 percent, respectively. However, the 2009 level was not exceptional because similar levels had been recorded in 2005 and 2006. Historically, even much higher loss ratios had prevailed for more than a decade, from the early 1980s to the mid-1990s.

Two-thirds of the MLT claims paid by BU members in 2009, amounting to $2 billion, originated in commercial buyer defaults. The remaining one-third, slightly more than $1 billion, was due to defaults for political reasons. The country with the largest amount of commercial defaults was the United States, followed by Canada, Mexico, Brazil, Russia, and Kazakhstan. For claims paid due to political risks, the countries with the largest defaults were the United Arab Emirates, Serbia, Iraq, Angola, Sudan, and Argentina.

Figure 20.7 MLT Claims Paid, 2005–09

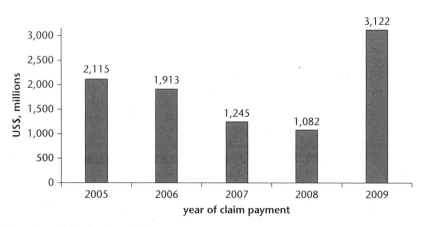

Source: Berne Union databases 2010.
Note: MLT = medium/long-term export credit insurance.

MLT export credit insurance is dominated by relatively few large—sometimes very large—transactions, which is why it is called a "lumpy" business. Compared with ST business, it does not have the same broad spread among thousands of smaller risks in many countries. In MLT business, a single large claim can have a noticeable impact on the loss ratio of the whole industry.

Even if a loss ratio of 66 percent is not unusual in MLT, several claims paid in 2009 were the result of the global financial crisis. The crisis put private buyers in a position where they were unable to pay their creditors (the commercial defaults) or prompted governments to decide not to honor their obligations or to interfere with private transactions (the political risk defaults).

MLT Outlook

Throughout the crisis, the ECAs' support of exporters and banks proved crucial in helping attract the necessary financing for MLT export transactions and therefore in sustaining international trade.

The question can be asked whether the 2009 losses indicated the beginning of a period of generally increased defaults due to the deteriorated financial and economic conditions worldwide. It is too early to tell, as it will depend on the speed of global recovery and future economic conditions for private companies and governments.

ECAs are used to dealing with risk and are familiar with the challenges of the global economic environment. They have therefore been able to run their business on a steady course since the start of the crisis in late 2008. The biggest challenge was a particularly high demand resulting in a busy operational activity that stretched their resources. With the support of their governments, ECAs took initiatives to pursue and expand their mandates to support national exports and national interests. ECAs also paid claims at a high but not exceptionally high level, and they have been commended by exporters and the banking community for the role they played during the crisis.

From a historical perspective, ECAs have usually recovered the largest part of the claims they have paid in the past. Recoveries might take a long time, but in the long run, the business of ECAs has been self-sustaining. With a satisfactory financial situation and with their governments behind them, ECAs can take a long-term view of the business that allows them to operate successfully in the MLT field.

Conclusions

The challenges posed during the crisis by a deteriorated economic environment and the resulting risks have highlighted the importance of risk management,

---

Box 20.2 The Berne Union

The International Union of Credit and Investment Insurers was founded in Berne in 1934. Known as "The Berne Union," it is the international trade association for credit and investment insurers promoting stability and cooperation in cross-border trade. Its membership includes the major private credit insurers and most national ECAs worldwide. Berne Union members support international trade and foreign direct investment by providing risk mitigation products to exporters, investors, and banks.

The Berne Union facilitates professional exchange among its members and with external stakeholders. It promotes the adoption of best practices and sound principles in export credit and investment insurance.

In 2010, the Berne Union had 49 members and 33 members in the Berne Union Prague Club, a group of credit and investment insurers in emerging and transition markets.

Information about the Berne Union can be found at www.berneunion.org.uk.

---

which has become a priority for companies and financial institutions all over the world.

As the global crisis moves on and signs of economic recovery are seen in some regions of the world, the indications for the credit insurance industry are positive:

- The value of credit insurance as a risk mitigation tool in cross-border trade has gained in global recognition, leading to increased demand for the product. Higher risk awareness and product awareness will bring opportunities for existing credit insurers, public and private, and for new market entrants.
- The solidity of the credit insurance industry has been demonstrated in light of an unprecedented global situation. Credit insurers met their obligations and paid claims—at a high level in MLT and at an unprecedented level in ST.
- Although credit insurance is not a source of liquidity in itself, it helped to unlock bank financing during the crisis and was able to ensure that liquidity was available for ST and MLT finance.
- The crisis also showed that both private and public credit insurers have a role to play and that ECAs are a vital part of the industry, complementing the private market as they demonstrate the ability to offer risk capacity even during difficult times.

This is a time where regulatory changes in the financial industry, especially concerning capital requirements, are being discussed and considered by various governments and regulatory bodies. Because such changes could affect trade and export finance, export credit insurers are carefully watching the developments.

With the lessons from the 2008–09 crisis, the credit insurance industry is well equipped to support international trade in the future. As they have done since 1934, Berne Union members, whether public or private credit insurers, will continue to offer risk capacity to facilitate trade transactions worldwide.

References

Berne Union. 2010. *Berne Union Annual Review 2010.* London: Berne Union.

G-20 (Group of Twenty Finance Ministers and Central Bank Governors). 2009. "Leaders Statement: The Global Plan for Recovery and Reform." April 2 summit communiqué, G-20, London. http://www.g20.org/pub_communiques.aspx.

UNSD (United Nations Statistics Division). 2009. "Analytical Trade Tables of the International Merchandise Trade Statistics Section (IMTSS)." UNSD, New York. http://unstats.un.org/unsd/trade/imts/analyticaltradetables.htm.

WTO (World Trade Organization). 1995. Article 3.1 (a) and Annex 1 (j) in "WTO Agreement on Subsidies and Countervailing Measures." WTO, Geneva. http://www.wto.org/english/tratop_e/scm_e/scm_e.htm.

BUSINESS RESPONDING TO THE FINANCIAL CRISIS: SETTING UP A POLICY AGENDA FOR TRADE FINANCE

Thierry J. Senechal

How do financial institutions and policy makers respond to the worst financial crisis in decades and develop policy actions to restore trade to normal levels? One answer to this question focuses on improving market intelligence so that future financial decisions can be based on solid evidence. To that end, the International Chamber of Commerce (ICC) over the past three years has developed intelligence gathering initiatives in trade finance to promote a banking model that would continue to finance a sustained expansion of international trade, even in difficult times. At the same time, the ICC has argued for the application of fair capital adequacy requirements for trade finance in view of its safe, essentially short-term, and self-liquidating nature.

This chapter explains how the ICC has addressed the lack of reliable information in trade finance and mobilized resources to engage in a constructive dialogue with regulators to bridge the information gap. It first reviews measures undertaken by ICC in the midst of the financial crisis, then discusses the market intelligence projects developed by the ICC Banking Commission—in particular, its reports on the Global Surveys on Trade and Finance titled "Rethinking Trade Finance" (ICC 2009c, 2010c, 2011). It also discusses key findings of ICC research contained in its Trade Finance Register and concludes by discussing future patterns of international cooperation and the need to establish a new set of regulations to supervise banks.

The World Trade Contraction during the Crisis

Substantial research has been conducted concerning the causes of the financial crisis. Some leading economists, apart from looking at the macro patterns and causes, have also looked into the role of trade finance to explain how recent events have affected different countries. The global financial downturn of 2007 was unique in many ways. It was the worst since World War II and pushed the issue of trade into the spotlight. Among its effects were unprecedented limits on the access to trade finance, an impediment that continued for more than two years (2007–09) and significantly curbed import and export trade, one of the principal drivers of economic growth worldwide.

The ICC has provided key information to document the contraction process. In the absence of a comprehensive set of international data and statistics on trade finance, the ICC Banking Commission, taking advantage of its international membership, undertook major market intelligence and research work.[1] At the outbreak of the crisis, the commission was ready to demonstrate that international trade in goods and services—supported by trade finance—remained a cornerstone of the financial system, facilitating economic expansion as well as international cooperation and development. When the crisis developed in 2007, the commission expressed concern to policy makers and regulators that trade finance had been severely affected and therefore that specific measures would be needed to bolster it to restore liquidity and trust in the markets. Early on, the ICC also pointed out that the capital requirements for trade finance under Basel II could exacerbate the crisis. Indeed, the ICC maintained that, after many years of rapid growth, the hard-earned gains of global trade seemed to hang precariously in the balance.

ICC Global Surveys: Gathering Market Intelligence

More than ever, our increasingly interconnected and interdependent world faces far-reaching uncertainties. The 2008–09 financial crisis has demonstrated, if it were necessary, that localized or isolated events could have systemic global consequences. The current fragile recovery must be sustained by informed financial decisions. In particular, the recovery of the banking sector requires that operators be better informed about the risks of their activities.

The ICC surveys have become an important information source enabling bankers, traders, and government officials to gain an accurate snapshot of the trends prevailing in the markets and to gauge future expectations for global trade.

Scope and Purpose

Global trade was plummeting to levels not seen since the 1930s, with all of the attendant social, economic, and political consequences. The ICC, recognizing that well-informed decision making at policy levels depended on the reliability of market information and data, decided to play a leadership role in gathering market intelligence.

In 2008, there was an absence of any knowledge management tool at the aggregate industry level that would provide an overview of the needs for adequate trade finance and could clarify the links between trade finance and economic growth. Apart from the piecemeal data available for some market segments or for particular regions, no global aggregates were available. Nor did the industry formally document information or experience that could be useful to others, especially during periods of crisis.

The ICC Global Surveys on Trade and Finance were made possible when the World Trade Organization (WTO) asked the ICC to provide data for the G-20 meeting of world leaders at their first economic summit, held in 2008 in Washington, DC. The WTO Expert Group on Trade Finance became an important forum during the crisis, holding regular meetings with partners from the commercial banks, the Berne Union, regional development banks, and other multilateral export credit and specialized agencies. The group, of which the ICC was a member, was instrumental in understanding the causes of the trade finance shortage and in devising cooperative solutions through which public institutions would help private sector financial institutions shoulder the risk of operating in an unstable financial environment.

The purpose of the ICC Global Surveys was to gain an accurate snapshot of the trends prevailing in the markets and to gauge future expectations for global trade and traditional trade finance. When planning the survey series in 2008, the ICC foresaw that the work would be most beneficial when acquired from the greatest number of sources and disseminated to the widest possible audience. Because the organization also planned to develop more substantial knowledge and research in the future, it convened high-level roundtable meetings of leading trade negotiators, WTO officials, academics, and business representatives.

Key Survey Findings

In early 2008, the ICC warned that the current environment was creating a risk-averse culture among both banks and traders. A special ICC report was sent to WTO on November 11, 2008: "Trade Finance in the Current Financial Crisis: Preliminary Assessment of Key Issues" (ICC 2008). The report contended that the credit crunch was entering a new phase, one in which it was becoming increasingly difficult to predict the timing and magnitude of events. Clearly the world was facing a period when it would be even more difficult to raise money to finance trade. The ICC was also keen to demonstrate that the logic of trade finance—to promote trade through accessible and affordable credit facilities—was being challenged in many ways.

Starting in 2008, tight credit conditions led lenders to drive up interest rates for their loans in many countries, especially in emerging markets. The increase in trade pricing in turn increased the reluctance of some banks to take on new trade assets, lest they miss an opportunity to price higher in the future. With banks having constrained balance sheets, global currency volatility, and more rigorous risk assessment, it was not surprising that the cost of trade finance soared. The tension in the market was also reflected in the Baltic Exchange's Dry Index, a measure of the cost of moving raw materials by sea (the means of transport for more than 80 percent of international trade in goods), which fell to a nine-year low on November 4, 2009, having plummeted 11-fold from its record high in May 2008.

The ICC Global Surveys highlighted a few key issues emerging from the 2008–09 crisis (ICC 2009a, 2009c, 2010c):

The global economy contracted sharply in 2009, and signs of recovery remained uncertain. Global gross domestic product declined by 2.2 percent in 2009, while the rate of growth in developing countries decelerated from 5.6 percent in 2008 to 1.2 percent in 2009. World trade, a casualty of the financial crisis, contracted in volume by around 12 percent in 2009, according to the WTO. Compounding the fall in demand from developed countries, developing countries became more vulnerable in 2009 because of a decline in foreign direct investment and remittance inflows. In aggregate, the crisis prompted a narrowing of global imbalances because of an overall decline in the volume of trade, falling oil prices, and a narrowing of the trade imbalance between China and the United States.

The 2008–09 supply of trade finance remained constrained in both value and volume. The constraint on supply raised fears that the lack of trade finance could prolong the recession. The trade messaging figures provided by the Society for Worldwide Interbank Financial Telecommunication (SWIFT) showed that the 2008 downward trend in volumes continued in 2009 (falling from about 46 million messages in 2008 to 42 million in 2009).

The weaker emerging economies—such as Bangladesh, Pakistan, and Vietnam—were being hit first. Based on a 2007 survey of its 92 offices worldwide, the ICC could point to considerable evidence that, at the inception of the crisis, ICC members reported an important decline in the syndicated loan market targeting most emerging markets. They noted that these syndications were an important means of backing international trade transactions for these countries. Fast-growing developing economies such as India and the Russian Federation were also suffering from the contraction, although Brazil and China were less vulnerable. Countries such as Argentina, Hungary, and Romania also had become vulnerable. Although low-value letter of credit (LC) business remained relatively unaffected, problems were reported in some Central and Eastern European countries and in the smaller, export-oriented economies in Southeast Asia.

However, some regions and sectors were more resilient than others. The 2010 survey showed that the trade slump was less marked in some regions, particularly in Asian countries (ICC 2010c). SWIFT data showed that the Asia and Pacific region continued to register far greater volumes of both sent (import) and received (export) messages. Most Chinese trade partners benefited from a fiscal stimulus and the rebound in Chinese imports.

During the crisis, exports of durable goods were the most affected. Meanwhile, trade in nondurable consumer goods such as clothing and food declined the least because basic demand for these products cannot be put off as long. In general, services trade was more resilient than merchandise trade.

Demand remained high in 2008–09, but access to affordable trade finance was still constrained. Demand for bank undertakings was sustained in 2009, with 50 percent of survey respondents indicating that demand was increasing for traditional trade finance instruments that helped substantially reduce risks for both exporters and importers. However, trade finance costs remained substantially higher than their precrisis levels, raising the problem of affordability for exporters. The widespread increase in pricing was said to reflect higher funding costs, increased capital constraints, and greater counterparty risk.

Over the 2008–10 period, there was more intense scrutiny of documents, leading to increases in refusals and court injunctions. In 2009, discrepancies cited in documents increased. The 2010 survey results showed that 34 percent of respondents had seen an increase in the number of refusals in 2010, up from 30 percent in 2009 (ICC 2010c). The number of respondents that had seen an increase in spurious or doubtful discrepancies remained high at 44 percent (albeit slightly down from 48 percent in 2009). This trend toward claiming discrepancies that have little or no foundation was worrisome and may prove damaging to the integrity of the documentary credit as a viable means for settlement in international trade.

The most recent ICC survey, in 2011, showed that trade flows had rebounded in many regions, and most experts agreed that business had significantly improved since the final quarter of 2009. Markets in several advanced economies were quickly returning to normal trading conditions, in terms of liquidity and the availability of trade finance. Similar improvements were seen in the acceptance of risk and in pricing. One positive development is that the average price for LCs in large emerging economies fell from 150–250 basis points in 2009 to 70–150 basis points in 2010. On the whole, the recovery was being driven by increased trade within North America, Europe, and Asia, and between Asia and the rest of the world.

However, the recovery has been uneven, particularly in Africa, where the market remains under stress. Moreover, traders in many low-income countries still have considerable difficulty accessing trade finance at an affordable cost, particularly for import finance.

In Asia and Latin America, liquidity has returned, but there is still a market gap resulting from a general deterioration in the creditworthiness of traders, coupled with greater risk aversion by commercial banks. As a result, the cost of trade finance in these regions remains disturbingly high.

According to the ICC 2011survey respondents, both the volumes and the overall value of trade finance transactions increased in 2010. The percentage of trade credit lines that were cut for corporate and financial institution customers fell markedly. Fees for bank undertakings and LC confirmations appear to have settled down and mainly flattened during the course of 2010. Respondents reporting an increase outpaced those reporting a decrease by about a 3-to-1 ratio. Of the financial institutions responding, some 58 percent reported an increase in export LC volume and 66 percent reported an increase in import LC volume. Considerable increases were also reported for guarantees.

Moreover, many respondent banks continued to report an increase in demand for documentary credits, which are considered to substantially reduce risks for both exporter and importer. Not surprisingly, therefore, the LC is considered today to be the classic form of international export payment, especially in trade between distant partners.

In terms of affordability of trade finance, around 75 percent of respondents indicated that their fees for issuing bank undertakings had not changed in 2010. And 78 percent of respondents anticipated that their fees for the issuance of bank undertakings would not rise in 2011. Still, as noted in 2009, there was intense scrutiny of documents in 2010, leading to a large number of refusals. Levels of court injunctions also increased.

Survey Impacts

The ICC Global Surveys were important for many reasons. To begin with, they were conducted at a crucial time for the global economy—a time of uncertainty about the course of economic recovery and one during which major economic policy and financial regulatory reforms were at the center of the G-20 summit discussions. These conditions rendered the surveys particularly influential in several ways:

- *They collected feedback on the timing and the calibration of reforms, helping policy makers achieve the right balance between stability and growth.* In fact, the information was used to formulate coordinated and targeted measures to stimulate trade finance markets and to prioritize the direction of available support. WTO Director-General Pascal Lamy confirmed that ICC research submitted in advance of the 2009 G-20 London Summit "contributed to help leaders make informed decisions on a support package for trade finance" (ICC 2010c).

- *In their comprehensiveness, the surveys ensured full industry representation and coverage.* For instance, the 2010 survey received responses from representatives of 161 banks in 75 countries—representing a 32 percent increase over the 2009 survey. The 2011 survey attained even better levels of responses, from 210 banks from 94 countries. More important, the 2011 survey was conducted in partnership with leading industry actors, including the World Bank, SWIFT, the Berne Union, the European Bank for Reconstruction and Development (EBRD), the International Finance Corporation (IFC) of the World Bank Group, the Asian Development Bank (ADB), the Inter-American Development Bank (IDB), the African Development Bank (AfDB), and Coastline Solutions.

- *The surveys, collectively, were a powerful instrument enabling the ICC to propose specific mitigation measures to policy makers and to engage in a dialogue with regulators.* The issues involved in financial regulation and the elements of policy change are highly complex and require an understanding on all sides. The ICC focused on collecting relevant market intelligence so that any decisions could be evidence-based. By collecting information from the private sector, governments, multilateral financial institutions, and official bilateral credit agencies, the surveys were unique in encouraging the parties to develop a mutual understanding of the issues with a view to reaching a consensus on processes and hence on a new regulatory framework.

The Changing Regulatory Environment and ICC Responses

ICC has welcomed the strengthening of the banking supervision framework. The recent crisis signaled the need to review the global financial regulatory framework to reinforce the banking sector's ability to absorb economic shocks and to build a stronger, safer international financial structure. ICC has also consistently voiced strong public support for the stated goals of the Basel Committee on Banking Supervision (BCBS) to improve the resilience of the banking sector.

Adequate and affordable trade finance is fundamental to economic recovery and growth. Most trade in developing countries is financed using traditional trade finance products such as LCs. In these countries, the shortage of available trade finance is critical, as it is for small and medium enterprises (SMEs) in developed countries, which often rely on smaller banks as their source of financing.

However, as ICC conveyed to the BCBS, some of the new regulatory measures will deter international banks and financial institutions from doing business in important ways. The most severe impacts are likely to be felt by SMEs in developing countries. The unintended effects of the regulatory reforms may defeat the G-20 goals of providing readily available short-term, trade-related funding at lower costs to businesses in these countries.

ICC Seeking Concessions on Basel II

The 2009 G-20 London Summit came up with a substantial package of measures to support trade finance—specifically, $250 billion of funding to be made available through multilateral banks and export credit agencies as well as a mandate for regulators to "make use of available flexibility in capital requirements for trade finance" (G-20 2009). The ICC had been actively promoting these two measures in the months preceding the summit. Regarding the latter, unfortunately, there has been limited follow-up from regulators concerning the impact of Basel II on trade finance.

To follow through on the trade finance data gleaned from its research, the ICC has pressed the case for further capital relief for traditional trade transactions. The 2009 and 2010 ICC surveys, for instance, highlighted the impact of the Basel II capital adequacy requirements on the provision of trade finance. The surveys found that implementation of the Basel II charter had significantly increased the capital intensity of trade finance lending, thereby constraining the ability of banks to provide short-term trade credit. The ICC clearly indicated that these increases had particularly adverse consequences on trade finance for SMEs and counterparties in developing economies.

The relatively favorable treatment received by trade finance under the previous international capital adequacy framework (Basel I) was reflected in the moderate rate of capitalization for cross-border trade credit during the 1980s and 1990s. However, as the banking and regulatory communities moved toward "internal-rating based" and "risk-weighted assets" systems under Basel II, a number of concerns emerged about the treatment of trade credit, particularly during periods of economic crisis. These trends could be ascribed to three primary factors:

- *Basel II's focus on counterparty risk rather than product or performance risk.* Basel II makes capital requirements an increasing function of banks' estimates of their loans' "probability of default" and "loss given default." However, insufficient mitigating consideration is given to the inherent strengths of trade finance products—for example, their short-term, self-liquidating nature and the tendency of companies to avoid defaulting on trade finance facilities. As a result, the anomaly is that trade is treated as having almost the same kind of risk as other unsecured lending, such as overdrafts.

- *Rigidities in the maturity cycle applied to short-term trade financing.* Although trade financing is usually short-term, based on 0–180 days' maturity, the Basel II framework applies a one-year maturity floor for all lending facilities. Because capital requirements naturally increase with maturity length, the capital costs of trade financing are artificially inflated as a result. All regulators have the national discretion to waive this floor. Although the U.K. Financial Services Authority did so at the end of 2008, several regulators have chosen not to take this step.
- *A lack of historical and performance data to assist in validating risk attributes.* Many banks face difficulties identifying and isolating sufficient data to estimate risk attributes for trade financing that can be validated. The factors causing this lack of data are many and varied, but particular problems include (a) migration of facilities (that is, when a trade loss results in an exposure on another facility, such as an overdraft), (b) customer-centric data collection practices, and (c) inherent biases in the data collected.

By increasing the amount of capital that banks are required to hold against trade finance lending, each of the above factors significantly restricted the ability of banks to provide essential short-term credit to businesses, particularly in the capital-constrained environment that prevailed in 2008 and 2009. In this context, the ICC Banking Commission issued a recommendations paper in advance of the 2009 G-20 London Summit, calling on the international community to address the impact of Basel II on the provision of trade credit (ICC 2009b).

ICC Comments on the Basel III Proposals

At its December 2009 meeting, BCBS approved for consultation a package of proposals to strengthen global capital and liquidity regulations, with the goal of promoting a more resilient banking sector. The consultation document includes proposals to introduce a new framework to limit the buildup of excessive leverage in the banking system, referred to as a "leverage ratio constraint."

Without commenting on the appropriateness of a new mechanism to limit bank leverage, the ICC has been concerned that the proposals would group trade products with other instruments that exhibit significantly different characteristics, effectively categorizing some trade products (such as LCs) as "risky" asset classes. The ICC sought to demonstrate that this approach was unjustified. Moreover, if implemented, it would potentially lead to an overall reduction in the supply of trade finance, which would conflict with the 2009 G-20 London

Summit agenda to promote international trade as a key component of economic recovery.

Summary of the proposals and ICC concerns[2]

Under the current Basel II framework, Credit Conversion Factors (CCFs) are used to calculate the potential future credit exposure for off-balance-sheet (that is, contingent) items. The most frequently used CCF values for contingent trade products are 20 percent for LCs and 50 percent for performance guarantees. These values reflect the fact that an off-balance-sheet exposure for a contingent trade product will not necessarily fully crystallize to become a credit exposure for the bank. The Basel Committee proposed, however, to increase the CCF for all off-balance-sheet exposures (including trade products) to 100 percent for the purposes of calculating a leverage ratio constraint. This proposal was based on the view that (a) all off-balance-sheet items are a significant source of leverage within the financial system, and (b) the failure to include off-balance-sheet items in measuring exposure creates an "incentive to shift items off the balance sheet to avoid the leverage ratio constraint."

The ICC considers this blanket approach to off-balance-sheet items under the proposed leverage ratio to be based on a fundamental misunderstanding of both the operational context and the mechanics of trade financing. Specifically, it is difficult to maintain that trade-related exposures are a source of significant leverage because the underlying transactions are driven by genuine economic activity—for example, the sale of goods or services. Furthermore, because trade transactions originate at the request of a client, these types of facilities are unlikely to be written as a way of avoiding leverage constraints.

What is more, the conversion of off-balance-sheet trade exposures is not driven by counterparty default but is performance-related (for example, performance guarantees) or dependent on documentary requirements (for example, LCs). Regarding the latter, for example, a bank has no obligation to pay an exporter under an import LC unless a range of documentation is submitted in compliance with the requirements of the instrument. In this connection, if the bank is not comfortable with the creditworthiness of the transaction, it has no obligation to waive the documentary discrepancies and make payment.

Increasing the CCF to 100 percent for trade-related contingencies to calculate a leverage ratio could significantly disadvantage trade finance-focused banks. When the leverage ratio becomes the binding constraint, the bank may choose to increase the cost of providing trade products or only selectively offer these products to customers. It is the fundamental concern of the surveyed ICC members that this cycle will adversely affect the supply of cost-effective trade credit to businesses, thereby compounding existing market constraints.

In this context, the ICC recommended that, if a leverage ratio is to be adopted, a framework should be developed to allow trade finance products to retain the CCF values used under the current Basel II framework. It is the ICC's view that such an approach would be consistent with the G-20 agenda to promote trade finance without compromising the overall objective of the Basel Committee proposals.

Views of 2011 ICC global survey respondents

In the 2011 survey, 81 percent of respondents indicated that their financial institutions were aware of the new regulatory regime imposing new capital, liquidity, and leverage requirements on all banking activities. The survey asked this question: "Do you anticipate that the Basel III requirements will cause your bank to reassess its trade finance strategy and products?" Thirty-four percent of the respondents said yes. Altogether, 31 percent of respondents also indicated that regulatory constraints had negatively affected their businesses in 2010.

An alarming 57 percent of respondents said they lacked sufficient information about new regulatory requirements at this stage—indicating an information gap between the industry and policy makers. Some 35 percent of respondents said they expected the Basel III requirements to "negatively" or "very negatively" impact their trade finance business.

Not surprisingly, ICC respondents have been seriously concerned about the unintended consequences that could arise from the new regulatory regime, which indiscriminately puts trade finance in the same risk class as other high-risk financial instruments. According to the respondents, the increase in the leverage ratio under the new regime would significantly curtail their banks' ability to provide affordable financing to businesses in developing countries and to SMEs in developed countries. Banks are now likely to be required to set aside 100 percent of capital for any off-balance-sheet trade finance instruments such as commercial LCs (against 20 percent under Basel II), which are commonly used in developing and low-income countries to secure trade transactions.

Specifically, survey respondents expressed the following concerns:

- *Banks could move away from trade finance.* There is a risk that small- to medium-size banks will move away from the trade finance market, significantly reducing market liquidity and the availability of trade finance.
- *The timing of implementation could have unintended consequences in different regions.* Considerable uncertainty persists about the impact of Basel III because of the role of regional regulators in deciding the local form of the rules. At this point, under the new regime, the movement of contingent liabilities onto balance sheets, financial institution counterparty risk weighting, and the weighting of export credit agency exposure could vary by country.

- *Trade finance costs could rise.* Those who remain in trade finance could raise their prices as a result of the more stringent regulatory requirements. There are already examples of what can happen when liquidity is reduced.
- *SMEs and banks in emerging markets would be the most constrained.* A reduction in the supply of trade financing and an increase in pricing would most severely affect SMEs in the developing world, where trade financing is needed most to create jobs and alleviate poverty.
- *Trade assets could gravitate toward nonregulated sectors.* Banks will be encouraged to move high-quality trade assets and contingents into nonbank sectors such as hedge funds. For instance, banks may likely decide to securitize their trade assets—pushing them into higher-risk, unregulated markets—contrary to the purpose of Basel III, which is being implemented to prevent another financial crisis.

The ICC-ADB Register on Trade & Finance: An Instrument for Regulators

To further advance the ICC research agenda and demonstrate to policy makers that trade finance merits some flexibility under the new regulatory framework, the ICC and ADB decided in 2009 to establish a project, the ICC-ADB Register on Trade & Finance, to collect performance data on trade finance products. This initiative aims to help the industry develop a pool of data to substantiate the argument that trade finance is, relatively speaking, a low-risk form of financing. At the same time, it seeks to provide the much-needed empirical basis for discussions regarding the treatment of trade financing under the Basel framework.

Notable features of the dataset

In the initial phase of the ICC-ADB project, a group of leading international banks provided portfolio-level data comprising 5,223,357 transactions, with a total throughput of $2.5 trillion between 2005 and 2009. Given the short business cycle, five years of data is considered sufficient to produce meaningful data. The data pooled within the register supported the view that trade finance is a relatively low-risk asset class, including the following findings (ICC 2010b):

- *Short tenor of trade transactions.* The average tenor of all products in the dataset is 115 days; the off-balance-sheet products covered by the register (import LCs, export confirmed LCs, and standby LCs and guarantees) exhibit average tenors of less than 80 days.
- *Low default across all product types.* Fewer than 1,200 defaults were observed in the full dataset of 5.2 million transactions. Default rates for off-balance-sheet trade products were especially low, with only 110 defaults in a sample

of 2.4 million transactions. Using a standard calculation, the ICC estimated the following average default rates within each product type over five years: import LCs, 0.058 percent; export confirmed LCs, 0.282 percent; standbys and guarantees, 0.01 percent; import loans, 0.124 percent (corporate risk) and 0.293 percent (bank risk); export loans, 0.168 percent (corporate) and 0.023 percent (bank). These low rates of default are consistent with the ICC's theoretical understanding of the mechanics and context of trade financing.

- *Relatively few defaults through the global economic downturn.* Fewer than 500 defaults were recorded out of more than 2.8 million transactions in 2008 and 2009. Indeed, the number of defaults on some products (for example, import loans, guarantees, and standby LCs) remained negligible through this period despite prevailing economic conditions and higher transaction volumes.
- *Good average recovery rates for all product types over the five years.* Looking at recoveries from written-off transactions, the ICC observed from the dataset an average recovery rate of around 60 percent across all product types, albeit with significant variance year on year.
- *Limited credit conversion from off- to on-balance-sheet.* Counterparty default—unlike, for instance, credit default swaps—does not in itself automatically result in the conversion of contingent trade products from off- to on-balance-sheet. From the data, the ICC found the documentary and (implied) performance contingencies inherent in trade products, which mitigated potential defaults for on-balance-sheet exposures. In the case of import LCs, for instance, an average of 50 percent of document sets presented to banks to make drawings under import LCs contained discrepancies on first presentation. In these cases, the bank has no obligation to waive the documentary discrepancies and make payment unless it provides reimbursement or the discrepancies are corrected within the validity period of the LC.

Evidence-based recommendations

Given the overarching economic imperative of promoting international trade as an engine of global economic recovery, the ICC-ADB Register on Trade & Finance is a powerful instrument that can provide a basis for reconsidering the mitigation of risk inherent in trade instruments and their correlation with mitigating credit risk under the Basel framework. The ICC recommended these particular steps:

- Implementation of the waiver of the one-year maturity floor for trade products on an international basis
- Reevaluation of the basis for calculating risk-weighted assets for trade facilities, in view of observed rates of recovery and demonstrated contingencies related to payment and default

- Consideration of appropriate uniform credit conversion factors for off-balance-sheet trade products under the proposed leverage ratio, in view of the data showing that the conversion of contingent trade products from off- to on-balance-sheet is not automatic and is separate from default.

Conclusions

The ICC Banking Commission, a leading international forum for the banking industry, has demonstrated its willingness to build on the solid groundwork of its day-to-day experience in trade and finance. In recent years, the commission has been at the forefront of market intelligence work to provide a clearer picture of conditions in the trade finance market, given concerns about the ability of companies to access this finance during the financial crisis. In pursuing that objective, the ICC Banking Commission has consistently advocated a fair and rules-based multilateral trading system that would work to the benefit of nations at all levels of development.

It is important that professionals in trade finance and regulators meet as often as possible in open and transparent discussions to share their experience with new and current forms of financing. Coordination among the parties regarding the issues highlighted in this chapter can assist in developing user-friendly intelligence for both the public and private sectors. Meanwhile, the ICC Banking Commission will continue its own efforts to collect market intelligence data to ensure that trade finance continues to benefit from the best available information. As a framework, however, governments need to take measures to make trade finance more accessible and affordable and, at the same time, avoid taking actions that distort trade.

Notes

1. The ICC Banking Commission is a leading global rule-making body for the banking industry, producing universally accepted rules and guidelines for international banking practice, notably letters of credit, demand guarantees, and bank-to-bank reimbursement. The ICC rules on documentary credits—the Uniform Customs and Practice for Documentary Credits (UCP)—are the most successful privately drafted rules for trade ever developed and are estimated to be the basis of trade transactions involving more than $1 trillion per year. With more than 500 members in 85 countries, many of which are emerging economies, the Banking Commission is one of the ICC's largest commissions. The ICC's voluntary, market-based approaches developed by the Banking Commission have often been praised for leveling the playing field in trade finance practices.

2. A full technical analysis is contained in the "ICC Response to the Basel Committee Consultative Document on 'Strengthening the Resilience of the Banking System'" (ICC 2010a).

References

G-20 (Group of Twenty Finance Ministers and Central Bank Governors). 2009. "Leaders Statement: The Global Plan for Recovery and Reform." Communiqué of 2009 G-20 London Summit, April 2.

ICC (International Chamber of Commerce). 2008. "Trade Finance in the Current Financial Crisis: Preliminary Assessment of Key Issues." Special report to the World Trade Organization, Secretariat of the ICC Banking Commission, Paris.

———. 2009a. "An ICC Global Survey for the WTO Group of Experts Meeting on March 18, 2009." Document 470-1118 WJ, ICC, Paris.

———. 2009b. "Banking Commission Recommendations on the Impact of Basel II on Trade Finance." Document 470-1119, ICC, Paris.

———. 2009c. "Rethinking Trade Finance 2009: An ICC Global Survey." Document 470-1120 TS/WJ, ICC, Paris. http://www.iccwbo.org/uploadedFiles/ICC_Trade_Finance_Report.pdf.

———. 2010a. "ICC Response to the Basel Committee Consultative Document on 'Strengthening the Resilience of the Banking System.'" Position paper of the ICC Commission on Banking Technique and Practice, ICC, Paris. http://www.iccwbo.org/uploadedFiles/ICC/policy/banking_technique/Statements/1139%20ICC%20Position%20Paper_Basel%20Committee%20Consultation.pdf.

———. 2010b. "Report on Findings of ICC-ADB Register on Trade & Finance." Document 470/1147 (Rev), ICC Commission on Banking Technique and Practice, Paris.

———. 2010c. "Rethinking Trade Finance 2010: An ICC Global Survey." ICC Banking Commission Market Intelligence Report, ICC, Paris. http://www.iccwbo.org//uploadedFiles/Rethinking_Trade_Finance_2010.pdf.

———. 2011. "Rethinking Trade and Finance 2011: ICC Global Survey on Trade and Finance." ICC Banking Commission Market Intelligence Report, ICC, Paris. http://www.iccwbo.org//uploadedFiles/Rethinking_Trade_Finance_2010.pdf.

PRIVATE BANKERS' RESPONSE TO THE CRISIS: WARNINGS ABOUT CHANGES TO BASEL REGULATORY TREATMENT OF TRADE FINANCE

Donna K. Alexander, Tan Kah Chye, Adnan Ghani, and Jean-François Lambert

In this chapter, representatives of the Bankers' Association for Finance and Trade–International Financial Services Association (BAFT-IFSA) and of three global banks—Standard Chartered Bank, Royal Bank of Scotland, and HSBC—present their assessment of how the 2008–09 crisis affected trade finance, their response to the crisis itself, and their concerns about the effect of the Basel Committee on Banking Supervision (BCBS) regulations on trade finance.

The authors agree that the global economic crisis seriously disrupted the trade finance market in 2008–09 and that the regulations under Basel II further constrained the supply of trade finance during the crisis. They echo the broader view of the banking and trade community (as expressed by 18 banking, services, and trade industry associations around the globe in a November 2010 letter to BCBS) about the unintentional consequences of the BCBS recommendations to increase capital requirements for trade finance. Although the signatories strongly support the BCBS's stated goal to improve the resilience of the banking sector, they also

---

This chapter has been put together by the editors Jean-Pierre Chauffour and Mariem Malouche based on original material submitted by the authors.

believe that the proposed recommendations neither reflect the risk profile of trade finance assets nor take into account the adverse effects of the proposed changes on global trade and growth.

The BAFT-IFSA Response

BAFT-IFSA[1] and the International Monetary Fund (IMF) were among the first institutions to join forces to help fill the information gap concerning trade finance developments during the 2008–09 financial crisis. BAFT-IFSA and the IMF collaborated on global trade finance surveys to gauge the magnitude of market dislocations around the globe and to benchmark key trends.[2]

Global Trade Finance Surveys

The first survey, conducted in late 2008, found a drop in the banks' ability to provide trade credit in fall 2008 (IMF 2009). The third survey conducted in July–August 2009 (IMF–BAFT 2009) showed that the capital and liquidity crisis mutually fueled the crisis in confidence and that the value of total trade finance activity dropped by 11 percent. Credit markets froze, transnational movement of goods fell, and protectionist measures gained footing, threatening to slow recovery. Banks also reported that the implementation of Basel II, concomitant with the global recession, added liquidity pressure because global risk deterioration had a dynamic effect on bank capital requirements. As global banks rushed to improve their capital positions to avoid losses in the crisis, trade finance credit lines suffered from heavy cuts. Global trade took a corresponding hit—hurting economic growth, triggering job losses, and depressing consumption.

The results of this joint survey served as an important reference, enabling all stakeholders to clearly understand the magnitude of the problem. Since then, BAFT-IFSA has conducted three more surveys with the IMF. The fourth, conducted in March–April 2010, found that the trade finance situation had started to stabilize (IMF and BAFT–IFSA 2010). Trade finance activities fell by 1 percent on average between the fourth quarter of 2008 and the fourth quarter of 2009—an improvement over the 11 percent decline noted above. Yet, given the global economic contraction, international banks continued to be exposed to heightened risks on a broad scale. Between the retrenchments in the markets and decreased access to private-sector risk mitigation providers, the effect was felt by both trade and non-trade-related clients.

These survey results have been regularly provided to Group of 20 (G-20) finance ministers, central bank governors, and other key regulators. The surveys and position papers gave policy makers tools for considering solutions to the crisis—including (a) a $250 billion pledge for multilateral development banks and export credit agencies (ECAs) to launch programs addressing trade finance market dislocations and (b) G-20 recognition that waivers by national jurisdictions of Basel II's one-year maturity floor for trade finance would help mitigate the crisis.

Other Collaborations

Throughout the crisis, BAFT-IFSA engaged on several fronts through its global convening power, its involvement in country-specific and regional matters, and its broad advocacy for fairer treatment of trade finance by the Basel Committee.

Global trade finance summits

BAFT-IFSA hosted the first of four global trade finance summits in London in January 2009. For the first time since the crisis hit, all major stakeholders in the trade finance crisis were gathered: banks from around the world, ECAs, public and private credit insurers, government officials responsible for trade and finance, the World Bank Group, the regional development banks, and other key multilateral institutions such as the World Trade Organization.

The first summit's aim was to promote a common understanding of trade finance among the gathered experts and stakeholders, to highlight the impact of the crisis on each region of the world, and to agree on recommended solutions. In preparation, BAFT-IFSA circulated a position paper that highlighted the low-risk, short-term nature of trade finance; its long history as "the oil to the wheels of commerce"; and BAFT-IFSA's recommended solutions to the crisis. Foremost was a warning against a retreat to protectionist measures. BAFT-IFSA recommended that governments form public-private partnerships to address the liquidity problems and revive the secondary markets for trade risk. It also advocated for ECA participation in, and creation of, short-term trade finance programs to ensure recovery.

Regional and country-specific efforts

A number of regional and country-specific trade finance difficulties had potentially broader systemic implications. BAFT-IFSA helped to address those difficulties—for instance, by collaborating with key banking associations, federations, and multilateral entities around the globe to ensure that Kazakhstan officials fully understood industry expectations of adherence to international practices for treatment of trade finance obligations during that country's banking sector crisis. It sensitized key policy makers to the perils of ignoring such practices, given that trade finance remains an integral tool for global recovery. Although this particular advocacy effort was country specific, it was a useful precedent for influencing the treatment of trade finance liabilities in similar restructuring exercises worldwide.

Response to Basel requirements

BAFT-IFSA has also played a key role in informing policy makers and regulators about the unintended consequences that the capital and liquidity requirement proposed in BCBS's consultative papers could have on trade finance. In BAFT-IFSA's view, implementation of the BCBS recommendations could result in decreased trade flows for trade-focused banks at a time when such flows are essential to supporting global economic recovery. Among the key arguments, BAFT-IFSA emphasized that the Basel II requirements disproportionately affect trade instruments and do not take into account the inherently safe nature of trade.

Because regulators have not fully addressed Basel II–related issues, BAFT-IFSA concerns are magnified by the pending BCBS capital and liquidity recommendations—collectively known as Basel III. These recommendations include proposals that could increase the risk weighting for trade finance instruments in a manner inconsistent with their short-term, low-risk nature. BAFT-IFSA is concerned that, given the crucial role of trade finance in global recovery, the Basel recommendations could ultimately limit trade activity. According to BAFT-IFSA, the BCBS recommendations fail to take into account that the movement of goods and services underpins trade finance, differentiating it from other forms of financial transaction in terms of lending security. In April 2010, BAFT-IFSA submitted comment letters to BCBS regarding these recommendations and their impact on trade and on transaction banking in general. It continues to work with other stakeholders in the international community to ensure that the Basel Committee and the G-20 are aware that, if adopted, the Basel Committee recommendations could ultimately result in decreased trade flows.

During the 2008–09 global economic crisis, BAFT-IFSA helped raise awareness about the key role of trade finance in sustaining the global trade recovery. It contends that a more appropriate treatment of trade finance under Basel II and III, alongside sustained public-private sector support and cooperation for trade finance, would help ensure the sustainability of the ongoing recovery.

Private Banks' Response to the Proposed Basel Regulations

This section describes how three private banks— Standard Chartered Bank, Royal Bank of Scotland, and HSBC—responded to the proposed Basel regulations.

Standard Chartered Bank

As a result of the global economic crisis, global trade fell some 23 percent, or $3.5 trillion, in value. Of this sum, Standard Chartered Bank estimates that 10–15 percent stemmed from lower trade finance liquidity. It is estimated that banks slashed their trade finance loans by 10 percent to shore up their capital positions. As a result, $350 billion to $525 billion of world trade, or up to 0.85 percent of global gross domestic product (GDP), may have been wiped out.

Financial support

Standard Chartered Bank took several steps to meet the markets' constraints, including signing an innovative $1.25 billion Global Trade Liquidity Program (GLTP) partnership with the World Bank Group's International Finance Corporation (IFC) to help support $50 billion of global trade. It also entered a $500 million risk-sharing program with the Organization of Petroleum Exporting Countries (OPEC) Fund for International Development to potentially fund more than $2 billion of trade.

Response to Basel requirements

In addition, Standard Chartered Bank actively helped foster sound banking regulation of trade finance activities. Although supportive of the Basel Committee's overall proposals in December 2009 to strengthen the resilience of the banking sector, Standard Chartered Bank considered that the proposed changes could have disproportionately adverse effects on banks' ability to provide trade financing at affordable costs to both importers and exporters.

In particular, the Basel proposals treat trade finance as a risky type of bank asset in the following ways:

- All trade contingents are subject to a 100 percent credit conversion factor (CCF) on the balance sheet in calculating the leverage ratio (compared with 10 percent for certain credit derivatives).
- Trade assets are not recognized as a high-quality liquid asset for the purpose of the liquid asset buffers.
- The proposed one-year maturity floor means that banks will have to hold more capital than is representative of the average trade tenor of 115 days.
- Basel makes no allowance for using real data to calculate the actual asset value correlation (AVC) and CCF of trade finance and instead imposes metrics that assume a much riskier profile than empirical evidence suggests is warranted.

As a result, the Basel proposals would lead to a significant increase in banks' cost of providing trade finance in terms of both capital and liquidity, which will lead to a lower supply or higher prices or both. Standard Chartered has taken the lead in highlighting the potential adverse effects that some of the proposed Basel regulations could have on world trade, supply, and trade finance costs:

- *Further drop in world trade.* If banks do not raise new capital (and if the consultation document is approved as drafted), banks could slash trade finance lending by as much as 6 percent a year, triggering a drop in international trade of up to $270 billion based on today's trade value. That would represent 1.8 percent of world trade or 0.5 percent of global GDP.

• *Decreased supply of trade finance.* A 25 percent increase in the AVC factor will require banks to hold as much as 10 percent more capital for banking and trading book exposures to large financial institutions worth more than $100 billion in assets. This requirement will erode 50 basis points from banks' capital adequacy ratio, limiting their ability to lend and negatively affecting their profile with investors and rating agencies. Banks will have two choices: raise more capital to preserve the market's confidence in their capital levels or lower their capital adequacy ratio to comply with the fledgling regulations, for all their negative consequences.

• *Increased pricing of trade finance.* As trade finance becomes more capital-intensive, its availability will decline, spurring higher prices. Trade finance banks lend to importers and exporters with funds from either other banks or clients' deposits. If a trade finance bank funds its lending through other banks, such borrowing will cost up to 37 percent more than it costs large financial institutions. These incremental costs may be passed on to the ultimate importers and exporters. If the trade finance bank's funding is from its deposits, the cost of its lending will rise by 15–25 percent for mid- to lower-rated importers and exporters in the emerging markets, which usually need trade finance the most.

Recommendations

Given trade finance's paramount importance in supporting international trade, Standard Chartered Bank recommends that the new regulations recognize that trade finance is different from the normal corporate or financial institution lending exposures. Standard Chartered has made concrete proposals to reduce the impact of the proposed Basel regulations on trade finance.

First, Standard Chartered proposes that the appropriate capital adequacy ratios be applied through the following means:

• *Mandatory extension of the maturity floor waiver to trade products* that are self-liquidating, short-term, nonrevolving, uncommitted, and do not form part of the ongoing financing of clients. BCBS should remove the national discretion given to regulators to waive the maturity floor rule and make it mandatory for banks to apply actual maturity tenor for trade finance and apply a minimum one-year tenor only on an exceptional basis.

• *Adoption of a separate AVC for trade finance* because trade finance is short-term and self-liquidating in nature, and such transactions are generally small, diverse, short-term, and self-liquidating—that is, inherently less risky.[3]

- *Permission for banks to use industry data* such as the Trade Finance Default Register of the International Chamber of Commerce (ICC) and the Asian Development Bank (ADB) rather than simply relying on internal estimates. Recent survey results from the ICC-ADB Register show that trade off-balance-sheet items (letters of credit [LCs] and guarantees) have low conversion rates into on-balance-sheet items that in turn require funding from the banks (ICC-ADB 2010).[4]

Second, Standard Chartered proposed recognizing the role of trade and financial institutions in providing liquidity through the following means:

- *Including trade of less than 30 days as a stable source of funding.* Short-term trade assets that will be paid off in less than 30 days should be considered as liquid assets. The attraction of trade finance as a class of assets is its ability to generate cash flow even during economic stress due to its self-liquidating nature.
- *Prescribing a required stable funding ratio for off-balance-sheet trade exposures.* Trade is an international, cross-border business, and hence, there should be greater harmonization in the treatment of global trade finance transactions. As such, leaving the required stable funding ratio for each national regulator to decide as trade business will run the risk that regulators, naturally inclined toward conservatism, would apply a 100 percent ratio, thus creating a complicating mix of rules for a global business. It is recommended that this required stable funding ratio be determined by calculating the probability of an off-balance-sheet trade exposure being converted into an on-balance-sheet asset.

Royal Bank of Scotland

The Royal Bank of Scotland (RBS) experienced the same trade finance developments as other institutions in 2008–09: business volumes declined, and the cost of trade finance increased. Exporters were hit by reduced order books, a demand for extended credit terms, and a greater propensity for their buyers to default. Importers were also hit by declining order books and destocked significantly.

The more successful companies paid down debt; reduced their levels of restocking; and adopted prudent, secure methods of settling export transactions. However, those that struggled did not respond quickly enough, finding themselves with too much stock and no demand. As a consequence, their credit ratings deteriorated—in some cases, quite dramatically. However, given the transparent nature of trade finance (whereby all parties involved have full control and visibility of transactions), trade finance should have been the least-affected method of financing during that turbulent period.

Three factors affected the reduced appetite for trade finance facilities and conspired to drive up prices:

- *Credit quality deteriorated, affecting price.* However, before the crisis, many trade finance professionals felt pricing had become too fine. Price increases were driven by an element of price correction as well as by the deteriorating credit quality of counterparties.
- *Capital availability became more constrained and much more expensive.* The Revised International Capital Framework (Basel II) played a role here: being highly risk-sensitive, a relatively small deterioration in credit quality results in a disproportionately large increase in the amount of capital required to support exposures.
- *The collapse of the interbank funding market led to a shortage of liquidity.* During the crisis, financial institutions found it difficult to fund their customers, but the downturn in demand mitigated this impact to an extent.

Notably, the impact on companies' behavior varied. In the United Kingdom, for example, small and medium enterprises (SMEs) tend to use overdraft facilities to finance international trade. Such facilities until recently were relatively cheap and flexible and were typically supported by a tangible security (such as property or shares). During the crisis, the value of the security underpinning the overdraft diminished and was worth less relative to the level of exposure. As a result, lenders scaled back overdraft facilities. (Lending on this basis is never a good way of supporting international trade because it does not link the finance to the underlying trade cycle.)

Financial support

RBS continued to provide trade finance solutions to importers and exporters. In the United Kingdom, for example, the bank offers export finance support to companies through packaged solutions that include export LCs, invoice discounting, and guarantees and bonds. RBS also plays a role in encouraging companies, particularly SMEs that have not exported in the past, to consider new markets by offering financial tools that fund credit periods and mitigate risk. RBS has also entered into risk-sharing arrangements designed to encourage exports. The bank participates in the LC guarantee scheme operated by the United Kingdom's official ECA, the Export Credits Guarantee Department (ECGD). Under the scheme, the ECGD shares the credit risks associated with confirmed LCs. The ECGD is also engaged in U.K. government schemes launched in 2011 to support exporters in accessing facilities for bonds, guarantees, or working capital related to export contracts.

For major importers in the North American and European markets, supply chain finance (SCF) open-account solutions—which introduce liquidity and security into the supply chain—have continued to grow. Before the crisis, many large importers believed the benefit of these solutions was all on the suppliers' side; however, the downturn highlighted the risk to buyers of failures in their supply chain. Buyers now see SCF as a way to ensure certainty of supply. Suppliers can reduce their Days Sales Outstanding from 90-day credit periods to seven days or less, and buyers can improve Days Payable Outstanding, taking longer deferred credit while remaining on commercial terms.

The adoption of SCF is blurring the boundaries between traditional trade finance and international cash management. Further developments include initiatives such as the Society for Worldwide Interbank Financial Telecommunication (SWIFT) Trade Services Utility and related Bank Payment Obligation, which provide many of the risk and finance benefits of traditional trade instruments but in a digitized environment, using data from the trading partners' supply chains.

Response to Basel requirements

As noted above, Basel II requirements contributed to capital constraints during the crisis. Under the Basel III proposals, measures such as the leverage ratio—aimed at preventing banks from using off-balance-sheet structures to leverage their balance sheets—will cause off-balance-sheet trade obligations to be treated in the same manner as on-balance-sheet items. LCs, bonds, and guarantees may therefore become less attractive options for banks that are capital constrained. Trade finance instruments, though off-balance-sheet in nature, directly reflect the value of customers' underlying commercial transactions; they are not a method banks can use to leverage their balance sheets.

The financial crisis showed that trade finance, which links funding to a customer's cash conversion cycle, is the most effective way of supporting international trade. A more prudent and risk-averse approach to trade finance will emerge as a result of the crisis. The trend toward open-account trade, in which export credit insurance and factoring were used to finance the trade, has been temporarily reversed in many cases. As the economic recovery takes hold, traditional LCs, which enable companies and their financial institutions to collaborate within a robust framework, will continue to play a role in risk mitigation, finance, and settlement of international trade.

HSBC

Trade has traditionally grown faster than GDP and, as such, is a key driving factor of the world economy. When the 2008–09 crisis hit, trade flows were rapidly affected, and it became clear that one of the governments' priorities was to foster trade to re-create the proper background for world growth to resume as early as possible. The 2009 G-20 London Summit was mainly dedicated to this subject. Then the availability of finance for trade activities became a key focus.

Trade finance became scarcer for a number of reasons, and, although none of those reasons can be held solely responsible for the overall squeeze, together they created the following significant negative impacts:

- *Increased distrust among banks.* Pursuant to Lehman Brothers' demise, the general level of distrust in the bank-to-bank market gathered momentum, first in developed economies and then in some developing economies. Toxic assets were hard to locate, and the general suspicion surrounding the presence of such assets in banks' balance sheets around the world triggered a general reassessment of risk among banks. Trade finance, being largely reliant on bank intermediation, was therefore gradually affected.
- *Scarcer liquidity.* Liquidity became scarce in developed countries. Banks, therefore, focused their support on their domestic markets. Gradually, this shift started to affect developing-market banks that received less hard-currency funding and, thus, faced growing difficulties in supporting their customers' international trade requirements.
- *Higher capital requirements.* The reassessment of country risks (as the crisis spread) and of bank-to-bank risks led to higher capital requirements for banks, affecting all of their lending activities. This phenomenon was amplified by the concomitant implementation of Basel II regulations in most parts of the world, with the noteworthy exception of the United States. Basel II, by putting more emphasis on the counterparty risk than on the instrument of lending, created a more challenging environment for trade finance in the context of the spreading crisis than would have existed during the previous regulatory environment.

The rebound of trade since mid-2009 is an encouraging sign that the crisis has diminished in intensity. In HSBC's May 2010 Trade Confidence Index, more than 50 percent of the respondents were bullish about trade outlooks, and they expected trade volumes to rise over the following six months. This optimism was confirmed in the September survey. However, the effect of the crisis on world economies was deep, hence recovery is still fragile. In this context, it is important that all pro-trade measures taken at the height of the crisis be maintained.

Financial support

HSBC has been an active provider of trade financing. It views international trade as a key driver of its development. Beyond its history, its raison d'être is its ability to serve its customers' businesses along their supply chains throughout the extensive HSBC global network. It takes a different view on trade risk than other financiers: because it has relationships on both sides of a global trade transaction, HSBC understands the business intimately and can weigh the risks associated with trade transactions accordingly.

During the crisis, HSBC continued to support its customers in financing their businesses for trade. Early on, decisions were made to direct financing to the corporate sector and notably to SMEs. HSBC announced a global $5 billion fund for the express purpose of lending to fundamentally sound SMEs and mid-market enterprises to supply working capital and to support businesses that trade or aspire to trade internationally. Furthermore, HSBC has been working closely with ECAs to help them devise financial packages to support trade finance, notably in the United Kingdom.

Recommendations

Trade finance never appeared more strategic than it did in the midst of the crisis. The 2008–09 financial crisis revealed that the trade finance industry was not organized and structured enough to assess its sheer weight and to face the challenges posed by the regulators. Banks have since taken measures to build a common base of information and organized dialogue.

In particular, the ICC-ADB Trade Finance Register represents a significant step forward because it will create a living database of the trade finance market that will help to demonstrate the resilience of this business (ICC-ADB 2010). The database will then enable the industry to objectively claim more favorable regulatory treatment of trade finance and thereby create the necessary incentive for banks to increase their commitment to international trade.

More generally, a closer dialogue between the banking industry and regulators over the treatment of trade finance in the Basel II and III frameworks is paramount to avoid unintended negative consequences over the financing of trade flows. HSBC welcomes the recent progress made in that respect.

HSBC has been closely involved in helping the industry to devise propositions to provide trade finance with a better regulatory environment and is committed to remaining at the forefront of such initiatives. HSBC obtained, together with other institutions, the lifting of the penalizing one-year maturity threshold by the U.K. Financial Services Authority. This action freed significant capital and created more space for banks to finance their customers' trade requirements. HSBC would advocate that such simple yet effective measures be replicated in all jurisdictions.

Trade financing has evidenced its low-risk nature, thanks to its unique features (self-liquidating, fast-turning, and linked to trade of goods and services): At the height of the biggest crisis since 1929 and as shown by the ICC-ADB Register, trade default rates remained at insignificant levels. The exchange of goods and services is the most powerful tool to create growth and prosperity. If there is one positive outcome the crisis has created, it is the awareness of the importance of trade and the availability of trade financing—a lesson that has resonated with HSBC's culture since its founding in 1865.

Notes

1. BAFT-IFSA is an international financial services association formed by the 2010 merger of the Bankers' Association for Finance and Trade and the International Financial Services Association, whose members include a broad range of financial institutions and suppliers around the globe.

2. Chapter 5 of this volume provides an in-depth discussion of the IMF and BAFT-IFSA global trade finance surveys.

3. For consumer banking, there is separate AVC for retail mortgage, credit cards, and other retail exposure because they vary in behavioral and payment factors and also react differently to macroeconomic factors. However, for corporate banking, there is only one AVC for all corporate products (lending, overdraft, derivatives, swaps and trade finance, and so forth).

4. We would recommend that the current CCF rule be refined such that off-balance-sheet trade will attract a CCF that matches its conversion level to on-balance-sheet items. Alternatively, BCBS could allow banks to adopt a CCF based on their internal methodology.

References

ICC-ADB (International Chamber of Commerce–Asian Development Bank). 2010. "Report on Findings of ICC-ADB Register on Trade & Finance." Final public report by the ICC Commission on Banking Technique and Practice, ICC, Paris.

IMF (International Monetary Fund). 2009. "Survey of Private Sector Trade Credit Developments." Report of IMF-BAFT 2008 trade finance survey results, IMF, Washington, DC. http://www.imf.org/external/np/pp/eng/2009/022709.pdf.

IMF-BAFT (International Monetary Fund–Bankers' Association for Finance and Trade). 2009. "Global Finance Markets: The Road to Recovery." Report by FImetrix for IMF and BAFT, Washington, DC.

IMF and BAFT-IFSA (International Monetary Fund and Bankers' Association for Finance and Trade–International Financial Services Association). 2010. "Trade Finance Survey," Report by FImetrix for IMF and BAFT-IFSA, Washington, DC.

TRADE FINANCE UNDER THE CURRENT BASEL REGULATORY FRAMEWORK: WHAT ARE THE ISSUES?

Marc Auboin

This chapter discusses issues related to the treatment of trade credit by international regulators. Although trade finance traditionally received preferential treatment regarding capital adequacy ratios on grounds that it was one of the safest, most collateralized, and most self-liquidating forms of finance, the introduction of the Basel II framework led to complaints inside and outside the World Trade Organization (WTO) about its potential adverse effect on the supply of trade finance during financial crises.

With the collapse of trade and trade finance in late 2008 and 2009, the regulatory treatment of trade credit under Basel II became a public issue, and a sentence in support of trade finance made its way into the communiqué of G-20 leaders following the April 2009 London Summit, calling on regulators to exercise some flexibility in the application of prevailing rules (G-20 2009). As the removal of obstacles to the supply of trade finance became a priority in the context of the WTO and of the G-20, new proposals on capital adequacy by the Basel Committee on Banking Supervision (BCBS), in the context of the making of Basel III, have spurred new policy discussions. The trade finance community hopes that the debate will lead to a better understanding of the two (trade and regulatory) communities' objectives and processes, eventually resulting in a set of regulations that is right and fair.

Basel I and Basel II: Apparently Similar but Different

Traditionally, short-term trade finance has been considered one of the safest, most collateralized, and most self-liquidating forms of finance. In the Basel I framework, assets are risk weighted based on the borrower's risk of default, ranging from the lowest risk weight (0 percent for the world's best government bonds) to a 100 percent risk weight (or more, in successor arrangements) for standard corporate loans. A 100 percent risk weight meant that the capital to be set aside for such loans had to be no less than 8 percent (minimum capital ratio to assets) of its notional value. The logic of this regulatory system—as well as its successor arrangement—was to protect financial institutions against risks of insolvency in case of default on their assets by accumulating enough capital to cover possible losses in difficult times, each category of asset being weighted in relation to estimated, historical risk.

The low-risk character of trade finance was reflected in the moderate rate of capitalization for cross-border trade credit in the form of letters of credit (LCs) and similar securitized instruments under the Basel I regulatory framework put in place in the late 1980s and early 1990s. The Basel I text indicates that "short-term self-liquidating trade-related contingencies (such as documentary credits collateralised by the underlying shipments)" would be subject to a credit conversion factor equal or superior to 20 percent under the standard approach. This meant that for unrated trade credit of $1 million to a corporation carrying a normal risk weight of 100 percent and hence a capital requirement of 8 percent, the application of a credit conversion factor (CCF) of 20 percent would "cost" the bank $16,000 in capital.

The basic text and CCF value for trade finance was kept largely unchanged under the Basel II framework. In particular, short-term, self-liquidating, trade-related contingencies (such as LCs) remained subject to an unchanged 20 percent CCF. However, issues of pro-cyclicality, maturity structure, and credit risk have arisen under the Basel II framework. In an internal-rating-based and risk-weighted assets system, the amount of capitalization to back up lending depends on the estimated risk at a particular time and for a particular borrower. For financial institutions without the resources to operate their own models of credit risk estimation, the standardized approach would provide guidelines of how to manage risk and allocate capital according to the wider proposed set of economic risk categories.

External credit ratings for cross-border lending under Basel II are based on benchmarks provided by international commercial agencies. More sophisticated financial institutions rely on an "advanced internal rating-based" approach to estimate such credit risk themselves, taking into account a number of compulsory criteria. Among the most-contested criteria is that, under Basel II, the country risk cannot be worse than any counterparty risk in that country; therefore, any deterioration of the country risk during a recession, for example, will automatically and negatively affect the country risk regardless of the underlying creditworthiness of that counterparty. The subordination of the risk weighting of end borrowers to that of the country risk is one reason why there are still 30 to 40 countries in the world in which access to trade finance at affordable rates is difficult—because recent sovereign defaults in Eastern Europe, Central Asia, or Africa still have a negative effect on the rating of individual counterparties.

Although even regulators acknowledge that the Basel II framework is inherently pro-cyclical in design (with capital requirements increasing in low cycle), trade finance professionals consider that banks face higher capital requirements for their trade assets relative to other forms of potentially riskier domestic assets, notably during crises. The reason is the high intensity of the banks' trade lending to midmarket companies and customers in developing countries. As the International Chamber of Commerce (ICC) indicates, "The capital intensity of lending to mid-market companies under Basel II is four to five times higher than for equivalent transactions under Basel I" (ICC 2009).

Regulators generally temper the professionals' remarks with the following arguments. First, the 20 percent CCF recognizes that trade credits are normally less risky than ordinary loans. Second, acknowledging that the bulk of the trade finance business is in the hands of large international banks, the regulators also suggest that, under the advanced internal rating-based approach, these institutions can determine their own estimates of the appropriate CCF to apply to a trade finance commitment when calculating the required amount of capital to back it up. Depending on historical loss experience, particularly if it is low, the capital required under the advanced internal rating-based approach could be lower than under the standardized approach.

Finally, perhaps the most difficult issue now facing trade financiers is the maturity cycle applied to regulation of short-term trade lending. Although trade finance lending is usually short-term in nature (markets indicate that more than two-thirds of lending is 60–90 days), the Basel II framework applies a de facto one-year maturity floor for all lending facilities. Because capital requirements increase with maturity length, the capital costs of trade finance are felt to be artificially inflated. If capital costs were instead to be applied for the exact maturity of self-liquidating instruments, considerable amounts of capital could be freed for trade finance.

Although the U.K. Financial Services Authority waived the one-year maturity floor, no other authority followed through immediately after the G-20 London Summit, when the Leaders Statement asked regulators to support trade finance by applying the rules more flexibly (G-20 2009). The Basel Committee responds that, subject to supervision discretion, the floor does not apply, for example, to short-term, self-liquidating trade transactions; import and export credit; and similar transactions. So the issue was not so much related to the rules of Basel II, but rather to how jurisdictions have implemented them.

At least, there might be a need for clarification within the competent regulatory circles. When one looks at the text of paragraphs 321 and 322 of the Basel II framework (BCBS 2006), the drafting clearly poses the principle of application of the one-year maturity floor to lending assets (Article 321) but indicates

> short-term exposures with an original maturity of less than one year that are not part of a bank's ongoing financing of an obligor may be eligible for exemption from the one-year floor. After a careful review of the particular circumstance of their jurisdictions, national supervisors should define the types of short-term exposures that might be considered eligible for that treatment. The results of these reviews might, for example, include some transactions such as: . . . some short-term self-liquidating transactions. Import and export letters of credit and similar transactions could be accounted for at their actual remaining maturity.

One the one hand, the text can be read as applying the one-year maturity principle unless some categories of short-term assets are exempted after review. On the other hand, the text could be read as clearly defining the exemptions to the rules and advising regulators to perform due diligence when providing for such exemptions. However, no regulator to date has conducted reviews apart from the U.K. Financial Services Authority.

Basel III Proposals

Notwithstanding the treatment of trade finance in the Basel II framework, on January 10, 2010, BCBS made new proposals to the Committee of Governors of Central Banks and Heads of Supervision of the Bank for International Settlements (BIS). These proposals, contained in a Consultative Document ("Strengthening the Resilience of the Banking Sector"), were opened for public comments in spring 2010 (BCBS 2010). The 279 comments from financial institutions, including commercial banks and export credit agencies, were published on the BIS website (www.bis.org). After an ongoing process of consultation, BCBS was scheduled to propose final recommendations by the end of 2010.

One of the Basel Committee's key proposals to reduce systemic risk is to supplement risk-based capital requirements with a leverage ratio to reduce incentives for leveraging. The intention of reducing such incentives is relatively consensual and has been shared by economists, regulators, and bankers. The idea, under paragraphs 24–27 of the BCBS draft proposals, is to impose such a leverage ratio, in the form of a flat 100 percent CCF to certain off-balance-sheet items (BCBS 2010).

The WTO's view is certainly not to challenge the well-founded principle of creating a leverage ratio to discourage the accumulation of off-balance-sheet items that could potentially become toxic for the financial system as a whole. On the contrary, its director-general has been on the record in calling for a strong, rules-based international cooperation on financial regulatory matters, not least because in the 1995 ministerial Decision on Coherence in Global Economic Policy Making, WTO ministers called for a stable financial environment. The current efforts of BIS and the Basel Committee are undoubtedly strengthening the international economic architecture as a whole.

Under paragraph 232 of the new Basel proposal, though, the leverage ratio would apply to "unconditionally cancellable commitments, direct credit substitutes, acceptances, standby letters of credit, trade letters of credit, failed transactions and unsettled securities" (BCBS 2010). The trade finance industry must examine the implication of this provision. Clearly trade credit exposures have never been used as a source of leverage, in particular given that they are supported by an underlying transaction that involves either movement of goods or the provision of a service.

The question of why off-balance-sheet trade exposures are not being automatically incorporated into the balance sheet (to avoid the leverage ratio) is one of process. The processing of LCs, which are highly documented for the financial transactions' own security, involve off-balance-sheet treatment at least until the verification of the documentation is finalized—a process that has existed for a long time. The financial crisis has resulted in even greater scrutiny of such documentation. The rigor of the document verification process is at the very heart of what an LC is, and it concurs to its safety. Given the high rejection rate of poorly documented LCs (up to 75 percent for first submissions) and the fact that, if definitively rejected, the LC might not even enter the balance sheet, it is argued that the off-balance-sheet management of these exposures is necessary and usually only a temporary treatment of what would eventually become an on-balance-sheet commitment.

The banking community argues that the application of the leverage ratio to off-balance-sheet LCs would increase banks' cost to offer such risk mitigation products. That cost will either be passed on to customers, making it even more difficult for smaller businesses to trade internationally, or, absent incentives to issue LCs, customers may simply choose to use on-balance-sheet products such as overdrafts to import goods (because these carry less-stringent documentary requirements) that may be far riskier for the banking sector in general.

Finally, the issue has some importance for developing-countries' trade. Open-account financing is not as appreciated by developing countries as by developed countries. Traditional LCs bring more security and are more appreciated. Given that world trade is likely to be driven by South-South trade in the future, the prudential treatment (and cost) of LCs is critical for developing- and emerging-market economies.

BCBS representatives argue that the adoption of a leverage ratio would have the effect of placing a floor under the risk-based measure and thereby help contain the buildup of excessive leverage in the banking system, one of the sources of the recent financial crisis. A leverage ratio per se is not risk-based. For example, cash items and AAA-rated government bonds would also be included at face value, although they are not subject to capital requirements under the risk-based measures. Conceptually, the leverage ratio also implies that all off-balance-sheet items would be included in the calculation using a flat 100 percent CCF, and hence, trade finance would not necessarily be at a disadvantage relative to other high-quality assets. But it is clear to regulators that the leverage ratio would help contain banks' building of an excessive, systemic position even in what appear to be low-risk activities, but that could pose severe risks in periods of systemwide stress. BCBS is nonetheless prepared to take account of the quantitative impact of its proposals based on the results of a comprehensive study it is conducting.

What is important at this stage is that the trade finance community and regulators speak based on facts and figures, not only on principles. The Basel II framework requires a minimum of historical data to establish the maturity structure and the safe character of specific financial instruments, but it has not always been easy for banks to isolate trade finance data from other credit exposure. For this purpose, under the sponsorship of the WTO Expert Group on Trade Finance, the Asian Development Bank and the ICC launched in November 2009 a pilot project to create an International Trade Finance Loan Default Registry, aimed at collecting data on trade finance operations and showing that the default rate for such business is one of the lowest in the industry (ICC 2010). The database has been operational since spring 2010, and the data are likely to be most instrumental in the discussion between the trade finance community and regulators on some of the regulatory aspects of both Basel II and the making of Basel III. On June 1, 2010, a first official and direct meeting took place to discuss some of these issues, with a view to reach a fair and just regulation for trade finance.

Conclusions

In the economics of regulation, there can be doubts about the ability of public authorities to adopt fully independent points of view. A recent paper argues that the Basel II framework did not fail because it was too ambitious but rather because creators fell short of their aim of improving the safety of the international banking system (Lall 2009). Intense and successful lobbying by the banking sector was, according to the paper, largely responsible for the failure of regulators and supervisors to impose sufficiently stringent standards.

For the same reason, Lall believes that recent proposals to reregulate the international banking system are likely to meet a similar fate. Drawing on recent work on global regulatory capture, the paper presents an interesting theoretical framework, emphasizing the importance of timing and sequencing in determining the outcome of rule making for international finance (Lall 2009). Lately, though, G-20 leaders have shown great resolve in amending international prudential regulation to strengthen the international financial system and avoid the repetition of past regulatory failures. To this aim, the Financial Stability Board has been reinforced in its mission to present important reforms, commensurate to the magnitude of the recent financial crisis.

The matters involved in financial regulation are inherently complex and require the understanding of all sides. In matters that are at the crossroads of trade and financial regulation, there should be a thorough examination of both cultures and instruments. In this regard, there should certainly be some middle ground in attempting, on the one hand, to prevent toxic assets from spreading throughout the financial system and harming its transparency through off-balance-sheet vehicles and, on the other hand, seriously disrupting a long-standing process for securing trade credit instruments.

For this reason, the trade finance and the regulatory communities should understand one another's processes and objectives; they are not necessarily at odds. The trade finance community believes it promotes a cautious model of banking that has clearly been financing the sustained expansion of international trade without major hurdles until the recent crisis. The two communities should be encouraged to develop a mutual understanding and to meet regularly during the comment period to reach a consensus on processes and, hence, on a new regulatory framework that can be both right and fair.

References

BCBS (Basel Committee on Banking Supervision). 2006. "International Convergence of Capital Measurement and Capital Standards: A Revised Framework." Comprehensive version, June 2006, Bank for International Settlements, Basel, Switzerland. http://www.bis.org/publ/bcbs128.pdf.

———. 2010. "Strengthening the Resilience of the Banking Sector." Consultative Document, Bank for International Settlements, Basel, Switzerland. http://www.bis.org/publ/bcbs164.pdf.

G-20 (Group of Twenty Finance Ministers and Central Bank Governors). 2009. "Leaders Statement: The Global Plan for Recovery and Reform." April 2 summit communiqué, G-20, London. http://www.g20.org/pub_communiques.aspx.

ICC (International Chamber of Commerce). 2009. "Recommendations on the Impact of Basel II on Trade Finance." Banking Commission Document 470/1119, ICC, Paris.

———. 2010. "Report on Findings of ICC-ADB Register on Trade & Finance." Final public report by the ICC Commission on Banking Technique and Practice, ICC, Paris.

Lall, Ranjit. 2009. "Why Basel II Failed and Why Any Basel III Is Doomed." Working Paper 2009/52, Global Economic Governance Programme, Oxford University.

INDEX

Boxes, figures, notes, and tables are indicated by *b, f, n,* and *t* following page numbers.

First published 2021
by Routledge
2 Park Square, Milton Park, Abingdon, Oxon OX14 4RN

and by Routledge
52 Vanderbilt Avenue, New York, NY 10017

Routledge is an imprint of the Taylor & Francis Group, an informa business

British Library Cataloguing-in-Publication Data
A catalogue record for this book is available from the British Library

Library of Congress Cataloging-in-Publication Data
Names: Yağcı, Mustafa, editor.
Title: The political economy of central banking in emerging economies / edited by Mustafa Yağcı.
Description: 1 Edition. | New York : Routledge, 2020. | Series: Routledge critical studies in finance and stability | Includes bibliographical references and index.
Identifiers: LCCN 2020012496 (print) | LCCN 2020012497 (ebook) | ISBN 9780367420994 (hardback) | ISBN 9780367823054 (ebook)
Subjects: LCSH: Banks and banking, Central—Developing countries. | Fiscal policy—Developing countries. | Developing countries—Economic policy.
Classification: LCC HG3550 .P65 2020 (print) | LCC HG3550 (ebook) | DDC 332.1/1091724—dc23
LC record available at https://lccn.loc.gov/2020012496
LC ebook record available at https://lccn.loc.gov/2020012497

ISBN: 978-0-367-42099-4 (hbk)
ISBN: 978-0-367-82305-4 (ebk)

Typeset in Bembo
by Apex CoVantage, LLC

The Political Economy of Central Banking in Emerging Economies

Edited by Mustafa Yağcı

Routledge
Taylor & Francis Group

LONDON AND NEW YORK

Contents

Contributors

Folajimi Ashiru lectures in business and strategy modules at Coventry University, UK. His core area of research is corporate governance. His research has been presented at major international conferences. He is a seasoned financial expert with extensive financial industry working experience. In 2009, he obtained an MBA from Aston University, UK, following which he established an entrepreneurial venture in the entertainment industry (TV shows and documentary production). He also has significant professional experience in the transportation industry.

Ioannis Glinavos is Senior Lecturer in Law at Westminster Law School. He studied at Essex (LLB) and Kent (LLM, PhD) before taking a Teaching Fellowship at SOAS (Contract Law). He then held lectureships at Kingston (Contract Law) and Reading (Company and Commercial Law). Ioannis has published two books with Routledge (2010, 2013) and a series of articles on law and development, law and economics, and investment arbitration. He is currently researching foreign investor rights in the context of economic crises and Brexit.

Christopher A. Hartwell is Professor of Financial Systems Resilience at Bournemouth University, Professor of International Management at Kozminski University in Poland, Visiting Professor at the Russian Presidential Academy of National Economy and Public Administration (RANEPA), and Fellow and former President of the Center for Social and Economic Research (CASE) in Warsaw. A leading scholar on the evolution of economic institutions, Dr Hartwell's interests are in institutional development, especially the interplay between financial institutions and other political and economic institutions and how firms deal with institutional volatility. Over his career, Professor Hartwell has advised governments in Kazakhstan, Armenia, Russia, Poland, Tonga, Kosovo, and numerous other countries around the world, and has published in journals such as *Regional Studies*. Dr Hartwell holds a PhD in economics from the Warsaw School of Economics, a master's in public policy from Harvard, and a BA in political science and economics from the University of Pennsylvania.

Tatjana Jovanić is Associate Professor and Vice Dean at the University of Belgrade, Faculty of Law, where she obtained an LLB in 2001, master's degree in 2004, and PhD in 2009. She also holds an LLM/Finance from the Institute for Law and Finance of the Johann Wolfgang Goethe University in Frankfurt am Main, obtained in 2005. During the academic year 2009/2010 she was a visiting scholar at the University of Pennsylvania Law School, Penn Program on Regulation.

Max Nagel is currently a PhD candidate in political science and sociology at Scuola Normale Superiore and has degrees in financial sociology (Goethe University Frankfurt) and international economics (Bayreuth University). His interest revolves around institutional change as well as global monetary and financial governance. In his dissertation he focuses on the relation between technocrats and politicians, particularly how it affects institutional change. He argues that the role of knowledge and ideas is central to explain the variety in change driven by technocrats as opposed to politicians. Using the cases of Argentina, Chile, South Korea, and Japan, he shows how both power balance between politicians and central bankers as well as the ideas informing monetary policy affect the stability of the monetary and financial system as well as economic performance.

Franklin Nakpodia is a Lecturer at Leeds University Business School, The University of Leeds, UK. He teaches on a number of modules within the accounting and finance undergraduate and postgraduate programmes. His areas of research are corporate governance and corporate social responsibility, focusing on institutional frameworks in developing economies. His research has been published in globally renowned academic journals such as *Accounting Forum*, among others. He actively engages with academics examining a variety of corporate governance issues in sub-Saharan Africa.

Nikolay Nenovsky is a Professor of monetary and international economics at the University of Picardie, France, and at Peoples' Friendship University of Russia (RUDN) in Moscow. He has published widely in the areas of Currency Boards and central banking, especially of post-communist countries. He has broad practical experience as a researcher and later as a member of the Governing Council of the Bulgarian Central Bank and different EU institutions.

Titilayo Ogunyemi is a Lecturer at Oxford Brookes Business School, Oxford Brookes University, UK. She has considerable industry knowledge and the experience of teaching a number of modules within the business and management undergraduate and postgraduate programmes. Her areas of research are corporate social responsibility and supply chain sustainability. She is an active researcher examining a variety of corporate social responsibility issues in the supply chain process of businesses. Her research has been presented at major international conferences. She has received a bursary award from the Chartered Institute of Purchasing and Supply (CIPS) for her research projects.

Vishnu Padayachee is Distinguished Professor and Derek Schrier and Cecily Cameron Chair in Development Economics in the School of Economic and Business Sciences at Wits. He is a lifetime Fellow of the Johns Hopkins University 'Society of Scholars'. He served nearly 12 years as a state-appointed non-executive director of the SARB from 1996 and was an economics advisor to the ANC and the Congress of South African Trade Unions (COSATU) during the years of the South African transition to democracy.

Jannie Rossouw is Head of School of Economic and Business Sciences at the University of the Witwatersrand (Wits) with an academic appointment at professorial level. He joined Wits after his retirement as a Deputy General Manager of the SA Reserve Bank. His publications include a book on the SA Reserve Bank, a number of book chapters, and more than 30 papers in accredited academic journals. His research focuses on containing inflation, ownership structures of central banks with private shareholders, and fiscal sustainability in South Africa.

Cornelia Sahling graduated from the Technical University of Dresden, Germany, and with a PhD in economics from RUDN in Moscow. She is currently teaching at the Department of International Economic Relations at RUDN in Moscow and is working and publishing on monetary policy, financial stability, European integration, and Russian economy.

Mario G. Schapiro is Professor of Law at the Fundação Getulio Vargas (FGV) and an associate researcher at the Center of Public Sector Politics and Economy (CEPESP–FGV). He has written widely on the developmental state and development banks, and is currently completing a book on central banking.

Matthew M. Taylor is an Associate Professor at the School of International Service at American University. Among other works, he published an analysis of the institutional evolution of the Brazilian Central Bank in *World Politics* (2009) and is currently completing a book manuscript on the political economy of Brazil under democracy.

Guillaume Vallet is Associate Professor of Economics at the University of Grenoble Alpes, France, Research fellow at Centre de Recherche en Economie de Grenoble, Research Centre, and associate researcher at the Institute of Sociological Research in Geneva, Switzerland. He holds two PhDs, one in economics earned from the University Pierre Mendès-France (Grenoble, France) and the other in sociology obtained from the University of Geneva (Switzerland) and at the Ecole des Hautes Etudes en Sciences Sociales (Paris, France). In his research, he studies monetary economics, the political economy of gender, and the history of economy thought during the Progressive Era. He has published in several distinguished academic journals (*Economy and Society*), especially on Albion W. Small (*Business History*), and he has been invited to give talks by prestigious institutions such as the New School for Social Research (New York, United States), the Bank of Ecuador, the Bank of Hungary, the Bank of Israel, the Swiss National Bank, and the United Nations in Geneva.

Mustafa Yağcı is Assistant Professor of International Political Economy at İstinye University, İstanbul, Turkey. His research interests lie at the intersection of comparative and international political economy, political economy of development, central banking, and public policy. He has published articles and book chapters on political economy of central banking, public policy, and international political economy. His research has appeared in journals such as *South European Society and Politics* and *Policy and Society*. He is the co-editor of the book "The China Puzzle: The Economic Rise of China, Transformation in International Relations, and Turkey" published by Koç University Press in Turkish.

Orhan H. Yazar is Associate Professor of International Business at Dongbei University of Finance and Economics located in Dalian, China. He received his PhD from the University of Sydney's Department of Government and International Relations and master's degree from the London School of Economics in the field of international political economy. Based in China, Dr Yazar has been teaching and researching on Chinese political economy and business. Alongside his post in China, Dr Yazar spent three semesters in New York as a visiting scholar at Frank Zarb Business School of the Hofstra University teaching courses on Chinese economy and finance between 2015 and 2018. His research interests are financial regulation, central banking, state-market relations, business negotiations, organizational justice, and more recently China's Belt and Road Initiative.

Ayca Zayim is Assistant Professor of Sociology at Mount Holyoke College. She completed her PhD in sociology at the University of Wisconsin–Madison. Her current research focuses on the economic and political sociology of financial globalization and central banking in emerging economies. Zayim earned research grants and fellowships from organizations such as the Center for Engaged Scholarship, the Horowitz Foundation for Social Policy, and the Mellon-Wisconsin Fellowship.

Preface

'Central banking is our topic, why are you studying it?'
An economist, responding to my PhD thesis topic on the political economy of
central banking

Central banks are at the heart of contemporary economies. Especially since the
onset of the global financial crisis in 2008, the centrality of the central banks
was intensified due to their extraordinary unconventional measures in advanced
industrialized countries. While the spotlight has still been on advanced economy central banks, the central banks in emerging economies play a crucial
role as significant as their advanced economy counterparts. While this has been
the case for a long time, academic literature has concentrated considerably
on the advanced economy central banks since the global financial crisis, whereas
there has been much less focus on emerging economy central banks. Moreover,
the scholarship on emerging economy central banks is mostly ignored in the
academic literature, intentionally or not. We cannot have a compelling understanding of central banking at the global level if we focus on a few central banks
in advanced industrialized countries. This book is a collective effort to examine
the political economy of central banking in emerging economies so that we can
be closer to reaching a global comprehension of central banks —well, at least a
step towards this ultimate objective. Thus, this volume aims to bring the emerging economy central banks back to the debates on central banking.

Political economy studies the interactions between political and economic
forces and presupposes the inseparability of economics from politics and vice
versa. Central banks are at the core of contemporary political and economic
debates, and it is high time to examine their activities with a political economy dimension. If you have ever attended a central bank conference, you have
likely heard the phrase 'putting political economy considerations aside'. Central bankers or orthodox economists may prefer not to talk about 'political
economy considerations', but academics cannot turn a blind eye on a theme
so central in our age, such as the political economy of central banking. In the
words of Susan Strange, the 'mutual neglect' between international economics
and international politics should be abolished to consider both domestic and

international dimensions of the political economy of central banking. In other words, we need to contextualize central banking activity within the temporal and spatial political economy to bridge macro- and micro-level analysis and to unravel how local and global forces are translated into monetary policy practices.

The volume's overarching theme is how the political economy context influences central banking in emerging economies and, in turn, how central banks do influence the political economy context. Central banks do not exist in a vacuum, and the political economy context within which they are embedded has a critical influence on central bank operations. The historical legacies, nature of the political system, organization of bureaucracy, structure of the financial system, state-business relations, exchange and capital account regimes, economic growth model, and the influence of international organizations and established norms such as central bank independence can all be considered as different dimensions of the political economy context. We need to consider in which countries and periods some of these variables are prominent, and why and how these variables are not consequential in others. This is what we mean by 'contextualizing' the central banking activity. On the other hand, scrutinizing the political economy context should not lead us to establish rigid, deterministic causal relations. The crucial role of individual agency and the specificity of the period under investigation may be highlighted in our quest to establish causal relations and improve theoretical development.

In the preparation of the book, we tried to reach scholars from diverse backgrounds studying various emerging economies with distinctive theoretical and methodological approaches. The chapters we compiled study central banking in four continents of Africa, Asia, Europe, and Latin America. A few contributors retracted their chapters during the process because of several reasons. Relatedly, in the introductory chapter, I included a section on the political economy of central banking in emerging economies with a focus on some countries that could not be covered in the book. Hopefully, with novel theoretical approaches and diverse empirical evidence from a variety of emerging economies, this book appeals to academics, central bankers, practitioners in the public and private sector, students at both undergraduate and graduate levels and anyone interested in understanding the functioning of the modern economies from the lens of the central banks around the world.

The completion of a project like this, which includes the contributions of about 20 authors from different parts of the world, started with an email from Andy Humphries of Routledge. He asked me if I would be interested in a project like this. I was thrilled and, of course, I accepted the challenge. I thank Andy for suggesting that I work on a project like this and encouraging me during the process. I thank Emma Morley, Autumn Spalding, and Megan Hiatt for their editorial assistance during the completion of the project. I thank my PhD advisors Caner Bakır and Ziya Öniş, who always encouraged me to pursue 'unconventional research topics' with an interdisciplinary orientation. Without their support during my graduate studies, I would not have had the chance to take part in this project. I thank all the contributors to this volume who enrich our understanding of central banking in diverse contexts. I thank my family, and especially my wife Çiçek, who has always been supportive of my research efforts. Finally, I would like to thank the economist who told me, 'Central banking is our topic, why are you studying it?', when I told her that I was writing my PhD thesis on the political economy of central banking. Her remarks have motivated me to first complete my PhD, publish related journal articles, and then to start a book project on the political economy of central banking. I hope this volume helps her and other sceptical people to recognize the value of political economy analysis applied to central banking.

1 Introduction

Political economy of central banking in emerging economies

Mustafa Yağcı

After the onset of the global financial crisis, central banks have taken over the policy debates with their unprecedented and unconventional measures. 'Quantitative easing' (QE), which refers to policies that expand the monetary base with asset purchases and lending programs, became a buzzword (Fawley & Neely 2013) in central banking jargon. With these measures, the central banks in advanced industrialized countries aimed to lessen the negative impact stemming from the global financial crisis and to stimulate economic growth in crisis affected advanced countries. The then Managing Director of the International Monetary Fund (IMF), and currently the President of the European Central Bank, Christina Lagarde hailed the central banks in advanced economies as 'heroes' because, with their unconventional policies, the world economy avoided another Great Depression (Lagarde 2013). The transformation in central banking activities and the dominance of monetary policy in economic policymaking started the debates that central banking became the 'only game in town' in advanced industrialized countries (El-Erian 2016). It is with this background that we witness populist backlash to central bank policies in both advanced and emerging economies (Canepa & Koranyi 2018).

Notwithstanding the critical role major central banks played in the aftermath of the global financial crisis, to have a global comprehension of central banking in the world, we need to understand the conditions under which central banks in emerging economies operate, why and how they take specific policy decisions, and how their policies create social, political, and economic repercussions. Accordingly, this volume aims to bring the emerging economy central banks back to the debates on central banking and monetary policy so that we can have a global understanding of the central banking phenomenon. In doing so, we hope to enrich our theoretical, empirical, and methodological understanding of central banking. Some of the questions we aim to answer in this volume include, but are not limited to, under what conditions emerging economy central banks take specific policy actions, how the political economy context influences their operations and vice versa, how global dynamics influence them and whether they have an influence on other policy domains.

We tackle these and other questions with an interdisciplinary perspective to highlight that we need a multidimensional perspective to understand central banking behavior and its reciprocal relationship with economic well-being, political struggles, and overall social welfare. With our political economy emphasis, we not only examine the interactions between politics and economics but also identify the winners and losers from central bank policies. Furthermore, in our volume, we aim to emphasize the political economy context within which central banks operate. Central banks do not operate in a vacuum, and we need to contextualize their activities within relevant constraints and enablers. Without a clear understanding of international and domestic political economy forces at play and the resulting historical specificities, we cannot make sense of why and how central banks take specific policy decisions and how their activities influence social, political, and economic dynamics. In this respect, the characteristics of political regimes, the structure of the financial system, the organization of bureaucracy, the macroeconomic framework with critical components of the exchange rate and capital account regimes, external relations with other states and international organizations, state–business relations, and the nature of the economic growth model adopted in different historical periods constitute some of the critical political economy dynamics that can be studied in our contextualization efforts.

This introductory chapter sets the stage for our volume and gives a short comparative historical background on central banking in emerging economies. The next section briefly analyzes the history of central banking with major shifts in the central banking paradigm. The second section examines the earlier literature on the political economy of central banking in emerging economies, and the third section delves into the central bank independence debate with comparative analysis of central banks in different regions of the world. The fourth and the last section provides a synopsis of the chapters in this volume.

A brief history of central banking

The foundation of early central banks took place for different reasons. The earliest of central banks such as the central bank of Sweden (Sveriges Riksbank was founded in 1668), the United Kingdom (Bank of England was founded in 1694), and Spain (Banco de Espana was founded in 1782) were founded mainly to finance wars (Schenk & Straumann 2016, p. 325). Early central banks in France, Finland, the Netherlands, Austria, Denmark, Portugal, Germany, Italy, Japan, and the United States were founded for economic or political reasons. Economic reasons included managing public debt, promoting economic growth, ensuring macroeconomic stability, regulating the financial system, and acting as the lender of last resort. Some of the political reasons for the establishment of central banks were ensuring monetary sovereignty, consolidating note-issuing authorities to become a single note-issuing entity, and modernizing the political and economic system (Schenk & Straumann 2016, p. 325).

During the early 20th century, international organizations such as the League of Nations and established central banks such as the Bank of England and Federal Reserve (Fed) were instrumental in the foundation of other central banks. For instance, the League of Nations was instrumental in the establishment of central banks in Austria, Poland, Hungary, Czechoslovakia, Estonia, Bulgaria, Greece; Bank of England advisers played critical roles in founding the central banks of South Africa, Australia, New Zealand, Brazil, Canada, India, El Salvador, Argentina, and Egypt; and Fed officials played an advisory role in the establishment of central banks in Colombia, Chile, Ecuador, Bolivia, and Peru (Schenk & Straumann 2016, pp. 332–334).

One of the essential critical junctures for the trajectory of the central banking paradigms is the Great Depression experience. The Real Bills doctrine was the most prominent central banking doctrine during the Great Depression era. According to this doctrine, the ultimate objective of monetary policy should be to provide sufficient credit for trade. Resultingly, during economic expansion periods money stock and credit increased, whereas during recessions they declined (Meltzer 1976, p. 455). Friedman and Schwartz ([1963], 2008) asserted that the overreliance on the Real Bills doctrine during the Great Depression turned a financial crisis into a depression because the Fed let the stock of money in the economy to decline and did not provide the desperately needed liquidity to the financial markets. This novel explanation of the Great Depression was influential in the rise of the 'monetarist' central banking paradigm and led to the adoption of unconventional measures in the aftermath of the global financial crisis (Bernanke 2002).

The world economy experienced a surge of inflation rates starting from the 1960s. There was a pursuit of finding remedies to the high inflation rates, and Milton Friedman proposed a simple remedy to solving the inflation problem with his famous quote 'inflation is always and everywhere a monetary phenomenon' (Friedman 1970, p. 11). In other words, only monetary policy could tackle the surging inflation rates, and central banks should be the primary organizations for conducting monetary policy. This simple prescription and the diffusion of other neoliberal ideas since the 1970s led to the emergence of the monetarist central banking paradigm. Friedman (1982, p. 100) himself acknowledges that the broad consensus on the monetary policy strategy emerged as a result of experiences rather than theoretical developments. Thus, the dictum of the monetarist paradigm that 'the long-run objective of monetary policy must be price stability' started to significantly influence central banking practices around the world (Friedman 1982, p. 100).

The rise of the monetarist paradigm and the decisive role central banks play in the conduct of monetary policy paved the way for the adoption of central banking independence around the world. Nevertheless, Friedman advocated a constant money growth principle in monetary policy, in contrast to central bank independence (Friedman 1962; Nelson 2008). Consequently, central bank independence has become a global norm in conducting monetary policy since the late 1980s and early 1990s (Forder 2005). According to Maxfield (1998), during the 1990s, legislations in favor of central bank independence passed in 30 countries, while this number was six during the 1960s, eight during the 1970s, and three during the 1980s.

The international monetary regime also had a significant influence on the conduct of central banks. Helleiner (1996) explicates that during the prevalence of the Bretton Woods system, states were allowed to adopt fixed exchange rate regimes and extensive capital controls. The liberal international financial system after the end of the Bretton Woods system allowed free capital movements in large scales, flexible exchange rate regimes, and a new international financial system with more volatility and uncertainty (Chwieroth 2009). This new non–system enabled central banks to play a more influential role in the conduct of monetary policy and central banks such as Bank of England and Fed have contributed to the 'financialization' of the global economy by making markets more susceptible to their policy implementation methods (Walter & Wansleben 2019).

Schenk and Straumann (2016) classify international monetary regimes in terms of their sustainability and suggest that the interwar gold standard, the Bretton Woods system, and the floating exchange rate regime from 1973 to 1979 were not sustainable because either the leading economic powers pursued divergent economic policies or the lack of central bank independence was insufficient to deal with exogenous shocks. On the other hand, they classify the classical gold standard and the floating exchange rate regime from 1979 to the present as stable regimes, because either there was an international consensus on economic policy, such as the classical gold standard, or the central banks had gained independence so that they had their tools to utilize (Schenk & Straumann 2016, p. 322). These international dynamics influenced the tools central banks possessed to achieve their objectives.

Krampf (2013) reviews the historically dominant policy norms in central banking and suggests that the liberal and developmental norms were prominent during the 20th century. The liberal norm prioritizes liberalized financial systems, free capital flow, full exchange convertibility, and price stability seeking independent central banks. On the other hand, the developmental central banking norm emphasizes managed exchange rates, capital controls, and preferential credit allocation for development objectives. Under the influence of developmental central banking norm, central banks are supposed to have extensive administrative instruments to control the banking system and manage the allocation of resources. The liberal central banking norm emerged in Europe and spread throughout the world with the critical role played by the Bank of England, Bank for International Settlements, the Bundesbank, the Organization for Economic Cooperation and Development (OECD), and the International Monetary Fund (IMF). The developmental central banking norm, in contrast, emerged in Latin America and diffused to East Asia with the help of Fed officials but ultimately lost its appeal with the dominance of the liberal norm since the late 1970s. Cobham (2018) classifies the monetary policy frameworks in advanced and emerging economies and finds that through time the emphasis of central bankers in both groups of countries has shifted more towards inflation targeting with less focus on exchange rates and monetary aggregates. Despite this shift, Wong and Chong (2019) find no positive effect of inflation targeting on growth.

There are different explanations on the prominence of central bank independence. Maxfield (1998) argued that the governments in emerging economies were interested in attracting foreign investment, and a concern to send a credit worthiness signal to international investors led them to implement central bank independence reforms. McNamara (2002) asserted that the delegation of independence to central banks emanated from legitimacy concerns and symbolic properties during times of uncertainty or economic distress. Burnham (2001) suggested that the central bank independence was an attempt by the politicians to shield themselves from economy-related criticisms and political risk. The global consensus on central bank independence started debates about the democratic oversight problem (Elgie 1998; Berman & McNamara 1999). The dominance of monetary policy in economic policymaking has also stirred debates around the rise of financial dominance, in addition to the fiscal dominance argument, which favors central bank independence over fiscal policy (Diessner & Lisi 2019).

In the aftermath of the global financial crisis, central banks in advanced industrialized economies implemented unconventional monetary policy measures such as reducing interest rates to zero or below zero levels and engaging in quantitative easing (Borio & Disyatat 2010; Borio & Zabai 2016). Financial stability became a critical objective for the central banks in addition to the price stability mandate, and central banks started to actively use macroprudential measures (Baker 2013; Galati & Moessner 2013). Despite the prominence of the financial stability mandate in the central banking community, there is also evidence showing that there is no consensus on formally adopting financial stability or a dual mandate in terms of adding employment or growth objective to price stability (Gnan et al. 2018). The central bank activism in this context spurred debates around central bank independence and the social and economic impact of monetary policy (Binder & Spindel 2017, 2018; Jacobs & King 2016; Adolph 2013). The dominance of monetary policy in economic policymaking and the overreliance on central banking practices led to the controversies of the politicization of central banks (Tortola 2019). With their focus on advanced economies, McPhilemy and Moschella (2019) highlight that expanded mandates brought extensive burdens on central banks' reputation, accountability, and regulatory roles.

Despite the similarities in the unconventional monetary policy measures adopted in advanced industrialized countries, there are also some divergences. For instance, Reisenbichler (2020) contends that the Fed implemented trillion dollars of bond-buying programs for the housing sector to support the US growth model consisting of credit allocation, demand, and consumption. Nevertheless, the European Central Bank (ECB) neither purchased housing-related bonds in an extensive scale as part of its QE nor aimed to stimulate the European housing market because of the divergent growth models in the Eurozone countries and their fragmented housing markets. This article is part of the broader academic literature, which shows how monetary policy has distributive consequences and contributes to the rising inequality debates.

This raises normative questions such as should central banks be concerned about distributional consequences of monetary policy, the rising inequality (Dietsch 2017), and recently environmental challenges such as climate change (Campiglio et al. 2018).

The unconventional monetary policies of central banks in advanced economies raised questions about international organizations' ability to guide central banks during turbulent times. There is a broad consensus on the critical role played by the Basel based Bank for International Settlements (BIS), especially for the introduction of macroprudential measures (Baker 2013; Westermeier 2018). IMF, on the other hand, could not play an instrumental role in the operation of central banks in the aftermath of the global financial crisis. This is reflected in the 'IMF Advice on Unconventional Monetary Policies' evaluation report of the IMF's Independent Evaluation Office (IEO). This report posits that IMF's limited depth of expertise on monetary policy issues hindered its capacity to make persuasive, cutting-edge advice relevant for country circumstances, IMF could have done more by proposing alternative policy mixes that would limit the side effects of unconventional monetary policy measures, and some emerging economies expect IMF to give more focus on the challenges they face from volatile capital flows (IEO of IMF 2019).

Thus, the post-global financial crisis context resulted in the proliferation of academic scrutiny on central banking. Nevertheless, most of the focus has been on advanced industrialized countries, and there is a tendency to avoid academic research on emerging economy central banks. This creates islands of research on central banking, but there is very little theoretical connection between them. To have a global understanding of central banking and to acknowledge context-dependent variables, there need to be more interlinkages between research on advanced and emerging economies. This would enrich our theoretical, methodological, and empirical knowledge of central banking as a global phenomenon. In this respect, it would be elucidatory and guiding to the rest of the book to look at some of the earlier work on the political economy of central banking in emerging economies from a comparative historical perspective.

Earlier studies on the political economy of central banking in emerging economies: a short review

Historically, there has been significant scholarship on the political economy of finance and central banking in emerging economies. With a comprehensive volume on the political economy of finance in emerging economies, Haggard et al. (1993) point out that the economic development trajectory and the accompanying financial sector reforms with compatible macroeconomic and industrial policies have a critical influence in shaping the roles of central banks in emerging economies. This has led the central banks in emerging economies to assume diverse roles depending on the political economy context in which they are embedded. Accordingly, there is a need to contextualize the central banking activities within the political economy context and historical specificities of various nations. Otherwise, it would be a challenge to establish verifiable causal relations with theoretical propositions.

Furthermore, the effort to posit generalizable propositions by contextualizing the central banks activities can be achieved with comparative historical studies. The selection of cases in these studies with proper validations and justifications would facilitate making causal claims for theory development. The theoretical and methodological roadmap for future research is further highlighted in the final chapter of our volume. We now turn to the review of earlier studies on the political economy of central banking in emerging economies.

Hamilton-Hart (2002) examines the rise of central banking in Southeast Asia and mentions that none of the central banks in the region could be described as legally 'independent' until the late 1990s. She brings the concept of 'governing capacity' to explain the different degrees Southeast Asian states managed to establish effective regulatory functions concerning money and finance. Governing capacity is described as 'the ability to implement policy in a consistent and rule-abiding' manner that reflects the aspirations of state officials, the political economy context, and the relative power of certain individuals and groups within these circumstances (Hamilton-Hart 2002, p. 9). Accordingly, the foundation of state organizations, structures, routines, and norms they have built through time are reflections of the governing capacity. Varying degrees of governing capacity reflects how states regulate finance, achieve financial mobilization, and resolve the financial crisis. Relatedly, an examination of central banks in Southeast Asia delineates the varying degrees of governing capacity the countries in the region had.

Reflecting the political economy context upon which they were founded and the norms and routines they have built through time, we can deduce the governing capacities of central banks in Southeast Asia. Monetary Authority of Singapore assumed a high governing capacity with an interventionist role in the financial system by regulating the banks and managing financial assets, indicating the disciplined, hierarchical state organizations found in Singapore. Malaysian central bank, Bank Negara Malaysia, at times had to compromise its governing capacity because of conflating public goals and private interests. Bank Indonesia had low governing capacity due to the mutually inconsistent routines, norms, personalized informal hierarchies, and vague disciplinary systems showing the characteristics of personalized organizations in Indonesia.

The governing capacities of central banks also reflect the broader political economy context within which they operate. For instance, up until the Asian crisis in the late 1990s, Indonesia did not have a comprehensive capital flow monitoring mechanism because the central bank capacity and the intricacies of the state-business relations did not allow this instrument to function. On the other hand, Malaysia and Singapore had instituted a comprehensive capital monitoring regime before the Asian crisis. This, to some extent, insulated the negative ramifications of the crisis in these countries. The bridge Hamilton-Hart (2002) builds between the broader political economy context within which central banks operate and the organizational characteristics they demonstrate in their routine operations is illustrative to connect both macro- and micro-level analysis in the study of central banks.

Some Asian economies such as South Korea, Taiwan, and Singapore are categorized as 'developmental states' because of their success in sustaining high economic growth levels for an extended period and being only a handful of countries in the world, graduating from low- to high-income levels (Woo-Cumings 1999). Nevertheless, we need to contextualize the economic development experience of these countries within specific historical periods and their unique political economy context. Each developmental state has peculiar political economy conditions, and this resulted in the variation of state-business relations, the development of the financial sector, and the central banking activity. For instance, Singapore took advantage of its existing domestic and international banking institutions in its development, Taiwan relegated more autonomy to its central bank because of a hyperinflation experience, and in South Korea the Ministry of Finance took control of the central bank after the military coup in 1961 and used it as a source of credit allocation and financial mobilization (Yeung 2017). Thus, central banks in developmental states had divergent mandates and roles in the economic development trajectory of these countries. These examples accentuate that we need to situate central banking within the broader political economy and historical context to make meaningful comparisons between countries.

South Korean central bank, Bank of Korea (BOK), played a crucial role in the economic development success of the country. Documenting the pivotal place of the central bank in the emergence of the South Korean developmental state, Woo (1991) asserts that starting from late 1950s BOK implemented a very elaborate system of selective discount policy whereby loans to the private sector were divided into three groups: eligible for rediscount, eligible only under particular conditions, and ineligible (Woo 1991, p. 63). In this system, manufacturing industries such as chemicals, textiles, machinery, metal mining, and food were identified as eligible for discount, whereas the services and consumer goods sectors of beverages, finished textile goods, furniture, fixtures, cosmetics, and retail trade were designated as 'nonproductive' activities and became ineligible for discount. In addition to the discount loans, the state promoted exports and heavy industries in a state-controlled financial system. Consequently, between 1974 and 1980, the average cost of bank loans to the export and heavy industries was almost always cheaper than the cost of loans for domestic consumption and light industries (Woo 1991, pp. 165–167).

Maxfield (1994) provides a comparative historical analysis of emerging economy central banks and posits that the legal measures of central bank independence are not conclusive in terms of revealing the aims, capacities, and authorities of central banks. The legal independence of central banks in Thailand, South Korea, Brazil, and Mexico is very similar between the 1950s and early 1980s, but their effectiveness in the economy and financial system varies significantly. Thus, the financial interests of government politicians and private banks are critical in instituting the limits of central banking operations. Maxfield (1994) also brings a methodological novelty for case selection and justification in her analysis. She relies on central bank governor turnover metric to assign low (South Korea and Brazil) and high authority (Mexico and Thailand) to the central banks and follows Mill's 'indirect method of difference' to compare most similar pairs with low and high authority. This methodological novelty is a good example for the future direction of comparative case studies in central banking.

Zhang (2005) provides a meticulous comparative analysis of central banking in Taiwan and Thailand and explains that in Taiwan, the central bank has enjoyed considerable autonomy from political and social groups and could prove its competency by prioritizing price stability and prudent financial regulation. The central bank of Thailand enjoyed a similar position until the 1980s. However, since then, the political shifts brought about a significant transformation in central banking practices, and the central bank became subject to political interference. The evolving capacity of these central banks and their contrasting levels of authority over the monetary policy and the financial system were reflected during the Asian crisis in the late 1990s. Before and after the Asian crisis, the Thai central bank did not have the proper instruments nor the authority to conduct effective monetary, financial, and regulatory policies, whereas the Taiwanese central bank could implement active and decisive exchange rate policy and took a leading role in the restructuring of the financial system. With an illuminating comparative historical study, Zhang (2005) shows decisively that it is not easy to draw strong correlations between political democratization or economic, financial liberalization on the one hand and central bank autonomy and effectiveness on the other. In other words, we need to contextualize central banking activity within international and domestic social, political, economic boundaries, and take into account political shifts, state-business relations, and bureaucratic interlinkages to draw conclusions.

Takagi (2014, 2016) provides a thorough analysis of the development of the central bank in the Philippines and asserts that the colonial past of the country had a decisive impact on the establishment of the central bank. Nevertheless, Filipino officers put their mark in the establishment of the central bank with their nationalist views, and the central bank played an indispensable role in state-building after independence. This study is a very good example of the fact that the central banks may occupy a much more critical political position in addition to their economic and financial roles. Moreover, the individual agency can have a much broader and decisive impact in a political economy than envisaged in most of the structural and institutional explanations.

Johnson (2016) examines the evolution and transformation of central banking in post-communism Hungary, the Czech Republic, Slovakia, Russia, and Kyrgyzstan and illustrates how the implementation of central bank independence reform required both external impetus through various international actors and domestic socialization. Nevertheless, the implementation of central bank legislation and de facto conformity to the Western model of central banking varied remarkably in the cases under examination. In other words, under the influence of similar international forces, the domestic context had a considerable influence on the central banking model being adopted through time. This underlines that the interactions between the international and domestic forces shape the political economy conditions under which central banking activity takes place.

Similar to Maxfield (1994), Dafe (2019) postulates that in African countries of Kenya, Nigeria, and Uganda, major providers of investible resources have a significant influence on the operating model of the central banks. In other words, countries dependent on natural resources are more likely to have central bank policies which reflect government preferences for financial expansion. In contrast, countries that rely on foreign aid are more likely to experience central bank policies ensuring macroeconomic stability, in line with the preferences of donors. Relatedly, central banks in countries dependent on private businesses are more likely to implement policies incommensurate with the preferences of major business groups. Dafe's (2019) single case study on Nigeria provides further evidence that the government's access to natural resources can curtail the power of financiers. Accordingly, governments can pursue central bank policies in line with their political objective of easing access to finance when they have access to higher oil revenues. This conflicts with the interests of private financiers. These papers offer an insight into the rarely studies case studies of central banking in Africa.

Berg and Portillo (2018) examine the macroeconomic context within which Sub-Saharan African country central banks have operated since their independence. One critical institutional variable these political economies have shared historically is that currency boards dominated their exchange rate regimes, and their currencies were pegged to sterling, the French franc, and the South African Rand (Berg & Portillo 2018, p. 2). After independence, many African countries maintained this institutional setting and the Rand Monetary Area and the CFA (Communauté Financière Africaine – African Financial Community) franc zone. These mechanisms limit the distinctive role central banks can play in national economies.

The central banks were instrumental in the post-independence national development programs in African countries, but increasing pressure to finance fiscal deficits limited the ability of the central banks to ensure macroeconomic stability (Berg & Portillo 2018, pp. 3–4). With the end of the Bretton Woods system, fixed exchange rate regimes shifted to managed and flexible regimes where some countries such as Ghana, Nigeria, Uganda, Kenya, Zambia, and Tanzania started to enjoy macroeconomic stability. Thus, institutional factors such as exchange rate regimes and other macroeconomic variables play a crucial role in the functioning of African central banks, in addition to political factors.

The next section revisits the debate on central bank independence with a comparative perspective and suggests that the concepts of de jure and de facto independence should be considered for proper analysis of central bank legal status.

Central bank independence debate revisited

As discussed in the previous sections, the central bank independence is a contentious topic. The level of independence a central bank achieves depends on several factors such as the type of the political regime, the significance of international influences, and the overall political economy context in terms of the exchange rate, capital account regime, the openness of the economy, the structure of the financial system, interests, and preferences of both economic and political elites and the type of state-business relations that is prevalent in the country. Notwithstanding the difficulty of examining all these factors for so many countries, there are attempts to quantify the independence of central banks and bring a comparative perspective to central bank independence. In this section, we aim to present evidence in terms of the divergent patterns of central bank independence in different parts of the world and explain the crucial difference between de jure (legal state) and de facto (actual state) central bank independence (Crowe & Meade 2008; Taylor 2013).

Central bank independence refers to instrument or policy independence so that the central bank can choose its instruments and policies to achieve its objectives. However, policy independence does not include policy goal independence. Monetary policy objectives should be determined in consultation with the political authority so that the central bank is accountable for policy outcomes, not policy inputs (Kohn 2013). We can identify four key characteristics of an independent central bank: central bank cannot lend to the government, central bank senior management is insulated from political pressure by secure tenure, political authority cannot decide or overturn central bank decisions, and the central bank has a clearly defined monetary policy objective (Crowe & Meade 2007, p. 70). The last feature of central bank independence, a clear monetary policy objective, is mostly interpreted that price stability should be the single monetary policy objective. These legal features reflect de jure independence of central banks.

Garriga (2016) provides one of the most comprehensive central bank de jure independence indices for 182 countries between 1970 and 2012. She relies on four components and 16 indicators of central bank independence in terms of central bank governor's characteristics (appointment, dismissal, term of office), policy formulation features (who formulates and has the final decision in monetary policy), central bank's mandate, and limitations on lending to the government (Garriga 2016, p. 854). These indicators are combined into a weighted index between 0 (lowest independence score) and 1 (highest independence score). These scores are reported in Figures 1.1–1.5, indicating the divergent trajectories of central bank independence in different regions of the world.

In her extensive analysis, Garriga (2016, pp. 859–861) finds that 72% of central banking reforms increased central bank independence in 182 countries between 1970 and 2012, whereas about 15% of reforms reduced central bank independence. Regionally, central bank independence increased most dramatically in postcommunist countries starting from the 1990s until the mid-2000s, followed by the Western European countries; in Latin America and Asia central bank independence increased gradually in a much more extended period with some exceptions of decline in independence, and in Africa and the Pacific central bank independence scores did not change much since the 1970s even

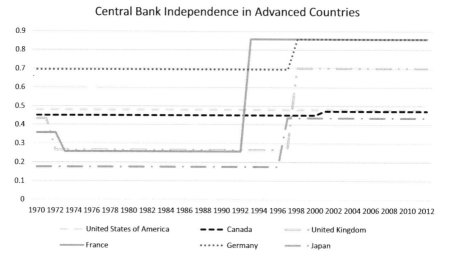

Figure 1.1 Central bank independence in advanced countries

Source: Garriga (2016)

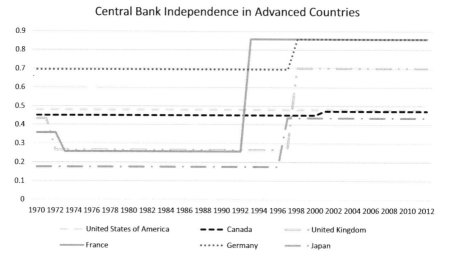

Figure 1.2 Central bank independence in Latin America

Source: Garriga (2016)

though these countries had very similar central bank independence rates compared to Western Europe during the 1970s.

Figure 1.1 shows high levels of central bank independence in the core Eurozone countries such as France and Germany, which are under ECB's jurisdiction. The United Kingdom achieves a relatively high score of 0.7, but other countries such as the United States, Canada, and Japan receive consistently low scores of central bank independence.

In Latin America, Chile, Argentina, and Mexico receive central bank independence scores higher than 0.6, and Brazil consistently receives a low score, whereas in Ecuador, the independence score drops from 0.9 to less than 0.5 in the late 2000s.

In the European periphery, Bosnia and Herzegovina received a very high central bank independence rate despite the institutional weaknesses in its overall economy. This high independence score is due to the Dayton Peace Accords, which was signed after the end of the Bosnian War in 1995. This agreement ensured central bank independence in the country's constitution (Article VII, Annex 4), and the central bank was required to implement monetary policy via a currency board (Crowe & Meade 2007, p. 74). This arrangement aimed to implement a hard fixed exchange rate regime whereby the monetary liabilities of the central bank could not exceed its net foreign exchange reserves, and the violation of this rule would lead to the dismissal of the central bank senior management (Crowe & Meade 2007, p. 74). Russia receives the lowest central bank independence score in Figure 1.3, and the other countries receive a score higher than 0.8.

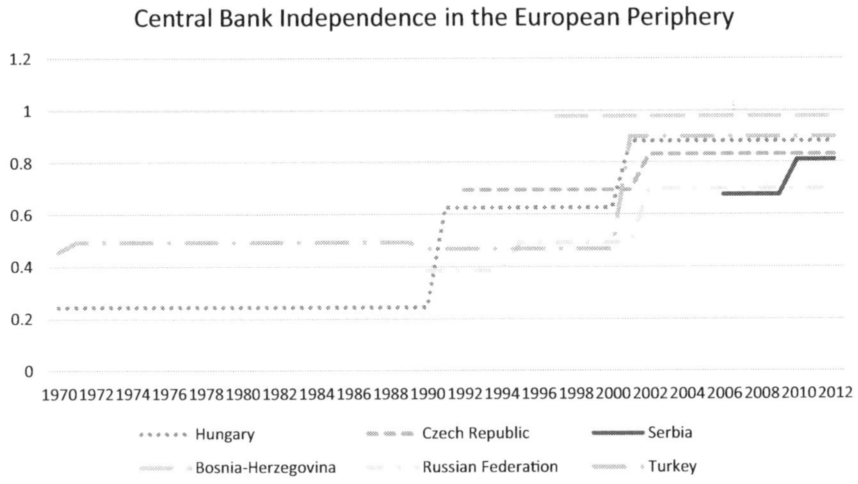

Central Bank Independence in the European Periphery

Legend: Hungary, Czech Republic, Serbia, Bosnia-Herzegovina, Russian Federation, Turkey

Figure 1.3 Central bank independence in the European periphery

Source: Garriga (2016)

The Turkish central bank has a high de jure independence rate in Figure 1.3, but the reality, de facto independence of the central bank, is much more complicated. The central banking reform of Turkey was enacted under an IMF program following the 2000–2001 twin economic crises (Bakir 2009). The central bank was successful in terms of reducing the inflation rates until the global financial crisis and maintained its autonomy during this period. In the aftermath of the crisis, the central bank actively pursued the financial stability objective and implemented unconventional measures for this purpose (Yağcı 2017). Nevertheless, these measures resulted in harsh criticisms from the ruling party and political pressure on the central bank because of allegedly increasing interest rates and slowing down economic growth (Yağcı 2018). Under the parliamentary system, these criticisms did not lead to the removal of the governor. However, after Turkey shifted to a presidential system, the executive powers of the president allowed him to remove the new governor because he was not willing to reduce interest rates (Coskun 2019). This episode of political struggles and the contestation of central bank independence in Turkey reveals the limits of de jure independence indices and how de facto independence is reflected in central bank operations.

In Asia, Indonesia receives the highest central bank independence score, which reflects the central bank reform adopted in the country following the Asian crisis. India has a consistently low score of 0.3, and the remaining countries receive scores below 0.6.

In Africa, Morocco and Nigeria receive scores higher than 0.6, and other countries are placed between the range of 0.3 and 0.5.

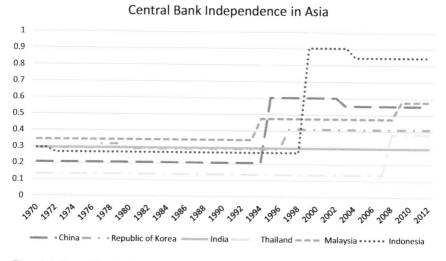

Figure 1.4 Central bank independence in Asia

Source: Garriga (2016)

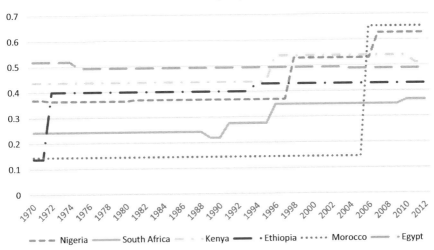

Figure 1.5 Central bank independence in Africa

Source: Garriga (2016)

There is almost a consensus among scholars that central bank independence should be reconciled with institutional and personal accountability under a democratic regime (Crowe & Meade 2007, p. 78). Relatedly, central bank independence should be supported with transparency in monetary policy conduct. A transparent central bank should reduce public uncertainty about its objectives and future orientation, regularly publish its economic data, models, forecasts that inform its policy decisions, communicate the policy strategy and decision-making processes, share and explain its policy actions on time, and openly discuss economic disturbances and policy errors in the transmission mechanism (Crowe & Meade 2007, p. 79). According to Crowe and Meade's (2007) analysis on central bank transparency, China, India, and Singapore score lowest transparency score of 0.15, the United Kingdom achieves the highest transparency score of 1.0, and interestingly the transparency score of the European Central Bank is quite low compared to the average level of transparency for inflation-targeting central banks.

International organizations started to formulate codes for central banks, and the IMF drafted a Central Bank Transparency code of five 'Transparency Pillars' (IMF 2019). This code underlines that central bank autonomy should involve transparency and accountability so that central bank operations and activities strengthen their credibility and effectiveness. Relatedly, IMF's proposal for central bank transparency consists of transparency in governance, policies, operations, outcomes, and official relations. Thus, central bank independence should involve transparency and accountability on the part of the central bankers to ensure that their activities are under public scrutiny to serve social welfare.

Political economy of central banking in emerging economies: a synopsis

The volume consists of five parts and 13 chapters, including the introduction and conclusion chapters. Part 1 investigates the global forces that influence the political economy of central banking in emerging economies. In Chapter 2, Glinavos articulates how the populist backlash against central bank independence in the West has profound implications for the emerging economies. He argues that because of this assault, emerging economies lose a critical impetus to modernize their economies, and autocratic leaders in these countries are emboldened. Hartwell's study in Chapter 3 examines the economic and financial reforms in Central and Eastern Europe (CEE) countries during the transition from communism to capitalism. He suggests that central banking reform in these countries had a significant influence on the development of political and economic institutions. Subsequently, these institutional transformations sowed the seeds of anti-market backlashes and populist threats to the rule of law. Zayim's Chapter 4 demonstrates how central banks of South Africa and Turkey use private meetings and roadshows to influence international financial investors, shape their market expectations, and try to promote investments in their economies. She acknowledges that the monetary policy of South Africa and Turkey is also susceptible to change as a result of these encounters. Nagel, in Chapter 5, tries to answer the question of how emerging economies structure their financial and monetary governance to insulate themselves from the financial crises and promote economic growth. He argues that forming a pragmatic political-technocratic consensus on objectives and conduct of monetary and financial policies is critical for a stable governance regime to ensue. He develops his theory with a comparative historical study on Chile and Argentina.

The rest of the chapters are divided into regional sections on the European periphery in Part 2, Africa in Part 3, Latin America in Part 4, and Asia in Part 5. Jovanic, in Chapter 6 of Part 2, adopts a novel methodology to evaluate both de jure and de facto independence of the Serbian central bank and suggests that the European System of Central Banks as an external impetus had a crucial role in introducing central bank independence to Serbia. Chapter 7 of Part 3 by Nakpodia, Ogunyemi, and Ashiru brings corporate governance perspective of resource dependence to study central banking in Nigeria. They assert that for the central bank of Nigeria to insulate itself from political interference, it needs to implement an incentive-based executive remuneration strategy with specific performance targets, and the directors of the central bank should be appointed separately from the traditional civil service regulations of Nigeria. Rossouw and Padayachee's Chapter 8 in Part 3 articulates the journey of the South African Reserve Bank from the apartheid system to the post-apartheid transition period. They suggest that the contentious central bank independence issue during the apartheid negotiations is on the table again. This time, the ruling party is in favor of nationalizing the central bank, and the debate on central bank independence is expected to persist and be a central part of political struggles in the country.

In Part 4 on central banking in Latin America, Chapter 9 by Vallet contributes to the volume with a gender perspective and expresses that with more women in senior positions, gender diversity in central banks is anticipated to bring the ability to accomplish new objectives, improve internal cooperation, deal with complexity of information and promote the culture and legitimacy of the central banks within the society. His propositions are articulated from his research on the Central Bank of Ecuador. In Chapter 10 of Part 4, Schapiro and Taylor situate the central bank of Brazil within the Brazilian developmental state and argue that despite the low level of central bank independence, the regulatory functions of the monetary authority have been resilient to ensure prudent financial regulation. According to the authors, this framework is a result of institutional complementarities within the developmental state of Brazil.

Nenovsky and Sahling examine the monetary policy regime of the natural resource-dependent Russian economy in Chapter 11 of Part 5. They posit that the rentier economy and natural resource rents in the economy of Russia have a significant influence on monetary policy conduct. Relatedly, in different periods monetary policy has reflected particular features of the monetary regime as a result of distinct resource allocation mechanisms. Yazar's Chapter 12 in Part 5 explores the central banking activities in China with a focus on the transformation of the Chinese political economy. He contends that the Chinese central bank is deeply embedded in the domestic political economy and its policies reflect the preferences of the Chinese Communist Party leadership. Accordingly, the weak capacity of the central bank is a challenge for the Chinese economy to transform, liberalize its financial system, and integrate into the global financial system. The last chapter of the volume reflects on the previous chapters and suggests new avenues of research on the political economy of central banking in emerging economies.

References

Adolph, C 2013, *Bankers, bureaucrats, and central bank politics: the myth of neutrality*, Cambridge University Press, Cambridge, UK.

Baker, A 2013, 'The new political economy of the macroprudential ideational shift', *New Political Economy*, vol. 18, no. 1, pp. 112–139.

Bakir, C 2009, 'Policy entrepreneurship and institutional change: multilevel governance of central banking reform', *Governance*, vol. 22, no. 4, pp. 571–598.

Berg, A & Portillo, R 2018, 'Monetary policy in Sub-Saharan Africa', in A Berg & R Portillo (eds.) *Monetary policy in Sub-Saharan Africa*, pp. 1–32, Oxford University Press, Oxford, UK.

Berman, S & McNamara, KR 1999, 'Bank on democracy: why central banks need public oversight', *Foreign Affairs*, vol. 78, no. 2, pp. 2–8.

Bernanke, BS 2002, 'On Milton Friedman's ninetieth birthday', in *In remarks at the conference to honor Milton Friedman*, University of Chicago, www.federalreserve.gov/BOARDDOCS/SPEECHES/2002/20021108/#fn1.

Binder, S & Spindel, M 2017, *The myth of independence: how congress governs the Federal Reserve*, Princeton University Press, Princeton, NJ.

Binder, S & Spindel, M 2018, 'Why study monetary politics?', *PS: Political Science & Politics*, vol. 51, no. 4, pp. 732–736.

Borio, C & Disyatat, P 2010, 'Unconventional monetary policies: an appraisal', *The Manchester School*, vol. 78, no. 1, pp. 53–89.

Borio, C & Zabai, A 2016, 'Unconventional monetary policies: a re-appraisal', *BIS Working Paper No. 570*.

Burnham, P 2001, 'New labour and the politics of depoliticization', *The British Journal of Politics & International Relations*, vol. 3, no. 2, pp. 127–149.

Campiglio, E, Dafermos, Y, Monnin, P, Ryan-Collins, J, Schotten, G & Tanaka, M 2018, 'Climate change challenges for central banks and financial regulators', *Nature Climate Change*, vol. 8, no. 6, pp. 462–468.

Canepa, F & Koranyi, B 2018, 'World's central bankers feel the heat as populists demand easy fix', *Reuters Business News*, 13 October, viewed 10 December 2019, www.reuters.com/article/us-imf-worldbank-cenbank/worlds-central-bankers-feel-the-heat-as-populists-demand-easy-fix-idUSKCN1MN0J0.

Chwieroth, JM 2009, *Capital ideas: the IMF and the rise of financial liberalization*, Princeton University Press, Princeton, NJ.

Cobham, D 2018, 'A comprehensive classification of monetary policy frameworks for advanced and emerging economies', *MPRA Paper No. 84737*, https://mpra.ub.uni-muenchen.de/84737/.

Coskun, O 2019, 'Turkey's central bank governor was sacked after resisting 300 point rate cut: sources', *Reuters Business News*, 22 July, viewed 17 December 2019, www.reuters.com/article/us-turkey-cenbank-governor/turkeys-central-bank-governor-was-sacked-after-resisting-300-point-rate-cut-sources-idUSKCN1UH142.

Crowe, C & Meade, EE 2007, 'The evolution of central bank governance around the world', *Journal of Economic Perspectives*, vol. 21, no. 4, pp. 69–90.

Crowe, C & Meade, EE 2008, 'Central bank independence and transparency: evolution and effectiveness', *European Journal of Political Economy*, vol. 24, no. 4, pp. 763–777.

Dafe, F 2019, 'The politics of finance: how capital sways African central banks', *The Journal of Development Studies*, vol. 55, no. 2, pp. 311–327.

Diessner, S & Lisi, G 2019, 'Masters of the "masters of the universe"? Monetary, fiscal and financial dominance in the Eurozone', *Socio-Economic Review*, https://doi.org/10.1093/ser/mwz017.

Dietsch, P 2017, 'Normative dimensions of central banking: how the guardians of financial markets affect justice', in L Herzog (ed.) *Just financial markets?: finance in a just society*, pp. 231–249, Oxford University Press, Oxford, UK.

El-Erian, MA 2016, *The only game in town: central banks, instability, and avoiding the next collapse*, Yale University Press, New Haven, CT.

Elgie, R 1998, 'Democratic accountability and central bank independence: historical and contemporary, national and European perspectives', *West European Politics*, vol. 21, no. 3, pp. 53–76.

Fawley, BW & Neely, CJ 2013, 'Four stories of quantitative easing', *Federal Reserve Bank of St. Louis Review*, vol. 95, pp. 51–88.

Forder, J 2005, 'Why is central bank independence so widely approved?', *Journal of Economic Issues*, vol. 39, no. 4, pp. 843–865.

Friedman, M 1962, 'Should there be an independent monetary authority?', in LB Yeager (ed.) *In search of a monetary constitution*, Harvard University Press, Cambridge, MA.

Friedman, M 1970, 'The counter-revolution in monetary theory', First Wincott Memorial Lecture, delivered at the Senate House, University of London, 16 September 1970. Institute of Economic Affairs, no. 33.

Friedman, M 1982, 'Monetary policy: theory and practice', *Journal of Money, Credit and Banking*, vol. 14, no. 1, pp. 98–118.

Friedman, M & Schwartz AJ [1963] 2008, *A monetary history of the United States, 1867–1960*, Princeton University Press, Princeton, NJ.

Galati, G & Moessner, R 2013, 'Macroprudential policy – a literature review', *Journal of Economic Surveys*, vol. 27, no. 5, pp. 846–878.

Garriga, AC 2016, 'Central bank independence in the world: a new data set', *International Interactions*, vol. 42, no. 5, pp. 849–868.

Gnan, E, Kwapil, C & Valderrama, MT 2018, 'Monetary policy after the crisis: mandates, targets, and international linkages', *Monetary Policy & the Economy*, Oesterreichische Nationalbank (Austrian Central Bank), no. Q2/18, pp. 8–33.

Haggard, S, Maxfield, S & Lee, CH (eds.) 1993, *The politics of finance in developing countries*, Cornell University Press, Ithaca, NY.

Hamilton-Hart, N 2002, *Asian states, Asian bankers: central banking in Southeast Asia*, Cornell University Press, Ithaca, NY.

Helleiner, E 1996, *States and the reemergence of global finance: from Bretton Woods to the 1990s*, Cornell University Press, Ithaca, NY.

IEO of IMF 2019, *IMF advice on unconventional monetary policies*, 24 April, viewed 15 December 2019, https://ieo.imf.org/en/our-work/Evaluations/Completed/2019-0614-unconventional-monetary-policy.

IMF 2019, *Policy paper: staff proposal to update the monetary and financial policies transparency code*, 13 May, viewed 12 December 2019, www.imf.org/en/Publications/Policy-Papers/Issues/2019/05/13/Update-The-Monetary-AndFinancial-Policies-Transparency-Code-46885.

Jacobs, LR & King, DS 2016, *Fed power: how finance wins*, Oxford University Press, Oxford, UK.

Johnson, J 2016, *Priests of prosperity: how central bankers transformed the postcommunist world*, Cornell University Press, Ithaca, NY.

Kohn, D 2013, 'Federal Reserve independence in the aftermath of the financial crisis: should we be worried?', *Business Economics*, vol. 48, no. 2, pp. 104–107.

Krampf, A 2013, 'The life cycles of competing policy norms: localizing European and developmental central banking ideas', *KFG Working Paper Series, No. 49*, April 2013, Kolleg-Forschergruppe (KFG) 'The Transformative Power of Europe' Freie Universität Berlin, http://userpage.fu-berlin.de/kfgeu/kfgwp/wpseries/WorkingPaperKFG_49.pdf.

Lagarde, C 2013, 'The global calculus of unconventional monetary policies', *Proceedings-Economic Policy Symposium-Jackson Hole*, Federal Reserve Bank of Kansas City.

Maxfield, S 1994, 'Financial incentives and central bank authority in industrializing nations', *World Politics*, vol. 46, no. 4, pp. 556–588.

Maxfield, S 1998, *Gatekeepers of growth: the international political economy of central banking in developing countries*, Princeton University Press, Princeton, NJ.

McNamara, K 2002, 'Rational fictions: central bank independence and the social logic of delegation', *West European Politics*, vol. 25, no. 1, pp. 47–76.

McPhilemy, S & Moschella, M 2019, 'Central banks under stress: reputation, accountability and regulatory coherence', *Public Administration*, https://doi.org/10.1111/padm.12606.

Meltzer, AH 1976, 'Monetary and other explanations of the start of the Great Depression', *Journal of Monetary Economics*, vol. 2, no. 4, pp. 455–471.

Nelson, E 2008, 'Friedman and Taylor on monetary policy rules: a comparison', *Review – Federal Reserve Bank of Saint Louis*, vol. 90, no. 2, pp. 95–116.

Reisenbichler, A 2020, 'The politics of quantitative easing and housing stimulus by the Federal Reserve and European Central Bank, 2008-2018', *West European Politics*, vol. 43, no. 2, pp. 464–484.

Schenk, C & Straumann, T 2016, 'Central banks and the stability of the international monetary regime', in MD Bordo, Ø Eitrheim, M Flandreau & JF Qvigstad (eds.) *Central banks at a crossroads: what can we learn from history?* pp. 319–355, Cambridge University Press, Cambridge, UK.

Takagi, Y 2014, 'Beyond the colonial state: central bank making as state building in the 1930s', *Southeast Asian Studies*, vol. 3, no. 1, pp. 85–117.

Takagi, Y 2016, *Central banking as state building: policymakers and their nationalism in the Philippines, 1933–1964* (Vol. 17), National University of Singapore Press, Singapore.

Taylor, JB 2013, 'The effectiveness of central bank independence vs. policy rules', *Business Economics*, vol. 48. no. 3, pp. 155–162.

Tortola, PD 2019, 'The politicisation of the European central bank: what is it, and how to study it?', *JCMS: Journal of Common Market Studies*, https://doi.org/10.1111/jcms.12973.

Walter, T & Wansleben, L 2019, 'How central bankers learned to love financialization: the fed, the bank, and the enlisting of unfettered markets in the conduct of monetary policy', *Socio-Economic Review*, https://doi.org/10.1093/ser/mwz011.

Westermeier, C 2018, 'The bank of international settlements as a think tank for financial policy-making', *Policy and Society*, vol. 37, no. 2, pp. 170–187.

Wong, KM & Chong, TTL 2019, 'Monetary policy regimes and growth revisited: evidence from a de facto classification', *Oxford Economic Papers*, vol. 71, no. 4, pp. 908–929.

Woo, J 1991, *Race to the swift: State and finance in Korean industrialization*, Columbia University Press, New York, NY.

Woo-Cumings, M (ed.) 1999, *The developmental state*, Cornell University Press, Ithaca, NY.

Yağcı, M 2017, 'Institutional entrepreneurship and organisational learning: financial stability policy design in Turkey', *Policy and Society*, vol. 36, no. 4, pp. 539–555.

Yağcı, M 2018, 'The political economy of central banking in Turkey: the macroprudential policy regime and self-undermining feedback', *South European Society and Politics*, vol. 23, no. 4, pp. 525–545.

Yeung, HWC 2017, 'Rethinking the East Asian developmental state in its historical context: finance, geopolitics and bureaucracy', *Area Development and Policy*, vol. 2, no. 1, pp. 1–23.

Zhang, X 2005, 'The changing politics of central banking in Taiwan and Thailand', *Pacific Affairs*, vol. 78, no. 3, pp. 377–401.

Part 1

Global influences on central banking in emerging economies

Debates on central bank independence and institutional evolution in national economies

2 Institutional metamorphosis

The backlash against independent central banking

Ioannis Glinavos

Introduction

The second decade of the 21st century has blessed us to live in interesting times. One of the ways this finds expression is through a historic change in our perception of institutions and state behaviour. The predominance of technocracy and institutional independence that underpinned our understanding of the market–state relationship since the end of the Cold War is being upended by renewed calls for re-politicisation from across the political spectrum. This is particularly evident in the area of central banking. The prime examples of this change of attitude towards independent institutions are of course the actions of President Trump in the United States and the proposed policies of the Labour Party leadership in Britain. Other examples from emerging economies include pressures on central banks ranging from President Erdogan of Turkey to tensions in India. The focus on the desirability (or not) of maintaining the technocratic status of central banks is a significant development for two reasons. Firstly, it points to a different, state-centric model of accountability and legitimacy for the operation of institutions. Secondly, it is significant because it is unfolding in an environment where a critique of institutional independence, based on issues like democratic accountability, is being overtaken – one could argue even hijacked – by a reactionary (extreme-left or hard-right nationalistic) critique that is at its base paternalistic (suggesting a leader-knows-best approach). Such critique has little to do with the literature on empowerment and greater accountability that was developed at the time of (and since) the financial crisis. What we are dealing with now is a metamorphosis of a debate on economic management towards undemocratic, capricious and state-centric directions. A political economy context such as the one described in this chapter influences central banking, particularly in emerging economies. As a result, in a sharp reversal to what had become orthodox thinking at the end of the 20th and the beginning of the 21st century, partisan politics is back on the driving seat of debates about central banks and their operations.

This chapter starts by explaining how institutional independence (and central bank independence in particular) represented a meeting point between market freedom and state support for economic development. It explains through the lens of institutional economics how legal and political initiatives led to the development of a stable equilibrium between democracy and the policy predictability needed for markets to flourish. The chapter then investigates how the idea of central bank independence took root and became the orthodoxy of macroeconomic policy. The discussion moves on to the critique of central bank independence and the consequences of a sustained attack from the left (but also the right) of the political spectrum on eroding the consensus in favour of institutional independence. The chapter concludes by highlighting the potentially destabilising effects for emerging market economies of a populist-driven retreat from independence in the West and reflects on how to preserve the core benefits of central bank independence for emerging economies.

Where we were

The purpose of this chapter is to present how the changing political economy of central banking is affecting and will affect the future of central banks in emerging economies. In order to do this, the chapter begins with a presentation of the orthodox view of the state–market relationship as it operated from the fall of communism in the early 1990s till the financial crisis of 2008. The legacy of the 1990s and the collapse of centrally planned economies have had a profound effect on our understanding of the state–market relationship (Glinavos 2013). We no longer view it as a relationship of opposition (in which the market stands against the state) but as a coexistent relationship in which state and market are mutually supportive. Institutional economists like Douglass North and Oliver Williamson have helped us understand the connections by offering a framework for explaining how state action and a foundation of law are complementary to successful market institutions (Groenewegen et al. 2010). An associated development has been increased recognition of the fact that democratic regimes are essential to the development of transparent and accountable states, within which the market is the ultimate good. This is because through market promotion policymakers believe that economic and social rights are guaranteed (Anghie 2000). Binding democratic politics with law-based policymaking (consistent with market respecting boundaries) is best achieved via politically independent institutions that both place checks on politicians' interpretations of the popular will and protect the public from possible arbitrariness, unpredictability or capriciousness of political leaderships. Independent central banks have been a key example of such independent institutions, forming the core of the contemporary (orthodox) understanding of economic processes and the state–market relationship.

An integral part of the way the state–market relationship has found balance in the last 20 years is through this idea of institutional independence from political control, with the most prominent expression of the promotion of institutional independence being central bank independence. Central bank independence ensures that macroeconomic policy is determined solely by 'economic' concerns. This promotes the pursuit of policies deemed good for the 'investment climate'. It also, however, limits governmental discretion, and this has led to popular consternation and significant political critique. States are less able to control their economy or to pursue expansionary economic policies to achieve policy objectives (Watson 2002). We will now consider the provenance of the doctrine of central bank independence in some more depth.

The core of the intellectual case for central bank independence revolves around the assumption of a persistent inflationary bias built into politicians' monetary policy preferences (Glinavos 2013, p. 50). It is argued that this bias can only be negated by vesting authority in policymakers who can be trusted to choose a policy rule that is non-accommodating of inflationary tendencies; namely central bankers. Central bankers are assumed to be better placed than politicians to enforce such a rule, because there is no clear symmetry of interest between the central bank and the labour market in the way that there is between the government and the labour market (Watson 2002, p. 184). Put in a simpler way, there is an assumption that political control over monetary policy makes the business cycle dependent on the political-election timetable, with politicians trying to manipulate economic performance to gain short-term political gain. Research (King 2005) suggests that in Britain, for instance, the Conservative governments that preceded Labour prior to 1997 engaged actively in trying to manipulate economic indicators for political purposes. There is also supportive evidence of political manipulation from the United States (Nordhaus 1975). Accepting this argument (as to the perverse incentives of politicians and their effects in distorting the economic cycle) was a key precondition to allowing the idea of independence to take root as a positive policy innovation.

The notion of central bank independence has a much longer pedigree, however, than debates on specific countries' electoral politics. It was introduced by David Ricardo in 1824 (Nika 2018). While Ricardo did not use the term 'independence' himself, he highlighted the dangers that might be created when elected representatives are entrusted to issue paper money. Ricardo also argued against having central banks financing directly their governments' deficits. In Ricardo's words (McCulloch 1888, p. 506):

> It is said that Government could not be safely entrusted with the power of issuing paper money; that it would most certainly abuse it; and that, on any occasion when it was pressed for money to carry on a war, it would cease to pay coin, on demand, for its notes; and from that moment the currency would become a forced Government paper.

King assessed the ascendency of the idea in the 1990s that monetary policy ought to be determined by technocratic criteria through independent central banks. Historically, attempts to depoliticise banking rested on distrust of both politicians and the public to behave in a way conducive to the country's best interests (Glinavos 2013, p. 48). Thomas Hutchinson, an 18th-century governor of Massachusetts, for instance, declared that 'the great cause of paper money evil was democratic government. The ignorant majority, when unrestrained by a superior class, always sought to temper with sound money' (Coggan 2011, p. 36). According to Chernow (1994, pp. 132–140), the Federal Reserve was created, in a rather clandestine manner, in 1913 to implement banking and currency reforms to prevent periodic banking crises. According to Das (2011, p. 130), central bank authority focused on ensuring that the value of money was not undermined by inflation, an idea consistent with Friedrich von Hayek's (1944) argument that mechanistic rules ought to limit the central bank's discretion (and as a consequence the influence of political process over central bank policies). Technocracy however suggested a distancing from democracy. According to Lastra and Miller (Kleineman 2001, p. 159):

> Central banks are not majoritarian, democratic institutions. Central banks are, instead, technocratic bureaucracies, staffed by career employees and, typically, a few leaders elected by the political authorities. It might be said that any bureaucratic agency is non-majoritarian. . . . But the problem is greatly exacerbated in the case of central banks as compared with typical bureaucracies. Central banks do not simply administer a technical regulatory scheme affecting discrete industries or interests. They regulate price levels, which is one of the most fundamental powers of government, and one of the most important practical concerns of the public at large.

There have been various descriptions of the meaning and forms of central bank independence (Nika 2018). For example, Cukierman (2008) provided four criteria for determining central bank independence: the ability of the central bank to appoint and dismiss all of its members, including the members of governing board; the freedom of the central bank to determine and decide on the goals of its monetary policy mandate; price stability as the main goal of monetary policy and whether there are lending restrictions imposed to the central bank's operation. Later, de Haan and Eijffinger (2016) incorporated two more dimensions into the notion of central bank independence: personnel independence, which involves the capacity of the central bank to have the final authority for the appointment and dismissal of its members, and financial independence, which refers to the central bank's autonomy of any kind of credit relation with the state, either directly or indirectly.

Ideas matter

Economic policy is influenced by ideological positioning to a greater degree than that assumed by traditional economic models (Rodrik 2014), and in the context of institutional independence, ideas matter more than in other areas of policymaking. North (1981) in his analysis of institutions shows the influence of a country's political economy on the evolution of economic systems. This can help explain the discrepancy between theoretical models and real life. In a fictional world of minimal transaction costs, North suggests, the market would indeed take care of itself, but in the real world, where transaction costs are considerable, he argues that much more is needed. Institutions are formed to reduce the uncertainties that would otherwise hinder economic exchange. By introducing the realities of actual markets – such as lack of information, political factors and ideology – into his theoretical model, North tries to elaborate why a functioning market needs much more than merely a bedrock of property rights and contract laws (Glinavos 2010, p. 111).

Describing the political economy that gave credence to the idea of central bank independence in Britain, King claims that New Labour's decision to give the Bank of England (BoE) operational independence was a political decision, not an economic one. It established New Labour's anti-inflationary credentials and delivered on the party's campaign promise to depoliticise the setting of interest rates (King 2005, p. 94). In fact, BoE independence forms part of a global trend during the 1990s, when more than 30 countries passed legislation acknowledging and increasing the legal independence of their central banks (Maxfield 1997). This trend represents one of the most dramatic changes in monetary frameworks since the deconstruction of the Bretton Woods regime. BoE reform came a decade after the start of the trend in central bank independence, which began with the 1989 reform of the Reserve Bank of New Zealand. The British decision however was not linked to changes in Britain's exchange rate regime, the collapse of the former Soviet Union, the adoption of an IMF programme or a decision to join the Euro area – explanations that cover most cases of central bank reform in the 1990s (Cukierman 1994, p. 1446), but it was motivated by the internalisation of the idea of independence by the Labour leadership (King 2005, pp. 95–96).

A similar political explanation can be found for the German Bundesbank's independent structure. According to Bernhard (1998, p. 322), the German bank's independence resulted from the balance of power politics in Western Germany that could only be maintained by detaching the government from the setting of monetary policy. It needs to be stated here that for politicians, academic discussions of economic gains are not enough; there also need to be clear electoral gains for the party in question, in order for them to champion such an institutional change. In a similar fashion, when the electoral costs exceed the electoral gains, politicians will have an incentive to retain the status quo (Glinavos 2013, p. 50). In the case of the BoE, independence provided electoral gains for Tony Blair's New Labour by making the party appear economically prudent and consequently more attractive to voters. By contrast, the Conservatives saw only electoral costs from this reform as it limited their ability to set interest rates strategically. In short, the political salience of institutional reform proposals explains patterns of adoption or rejection (King 2005, p. 115).

This is not to suggest, however, that everyone is convinced of the depoliticising effects of independence. Debelle and Fischer (1994) appear unconvinced with what they see as the three foundations of the idea of central bank independence. These foundations, they argue, are the success of the Bundesbank and the German economy, the academic literature on the assumed inflationary bias of politicians and the literature on the effects of central bank independence. They argue instead that the Bundesbank's unwavering inflation targeting has been very costly on German growth. One could make the same argument about the European Central Bank (ECB) in its pre-quantitative easing, stimulus-prone state. It should also be noted that inflation targeting, as a goal of monetary policy, does not automatically require independence for the central bank and further that the causal relationship between strict monetary policies and independence is not one directional. It could be, for instance, that countries have independent central banks because they have chosen monetarist policies and not the other way around, as commonly assumed (Glinavos 2013, p. 51).

The depoliticisation of central banking and the transfer of control over interest rates to independent central banks was also a key consequence of the success of the argument that Keynesian demand management was illegitimate. This was largely achieved by Friedman (Brittan 1982) when he sought to demonstrate that a market economy would tend to gravitate towards a natural state of unemployment determined crucially by the cost of productivity and the distribution of labour (Callinicos 2010, p. 15). For this reason, governments, Friedman and Schwartz (1963) argued, could not affect the rate of unemployment in the long term, unless they increased spending and cut taxes, which would result in an expansion of the money supply, and thus inflation. Friedman's imperative to maintain monetary and fiscal stability could only be maintained, therefore, if the economy was run on an autopilot for regulating the quantity of money. This autopilot was achieved via institutionally independent central banks and, one could argue, inadvertently led to a re-naturalisation of economic relations. Such re-naturalisation of economic relations suggests a return to the view that market processes need no state direction, which last held sway prior to the Great Depression (Glinavos 2013, p. 50). What can be done through achieving political consensus, however, can also be undone when the consensus fractures. It is precisely at this point of fracture that we turn now, examining how a change of perception first on the left and second on the right of the political spectrum has altered the political economy supporting central bank independence in the years since the financial crisis.

Leftist critique

Is it true that institutional independence, and more specifically central bank independence, results in apolitical economic governance, especially in the area of monetary policy? Those approaching the question from a critical standpoint (usually leftwing) argue that independence does not in fact 'depoliticise', but it only cements a particular ideology as the perpetual background to economic decision-making. McNamara argues (2002) that the advocacy of central bank independence relies on a series of contestable arguments including its purported depoliticising effects. Delegation of economic decision-making to politically independent institutions does not in and of itself eliminate partisan politics and interests, and monetary policy of any type (especially one with a strong anti-inflationary bias) has specific distributional consequences that raise important questions about legitimacy and account-ability. While control of inflation is currently the standard priority of all cen-tral banks (Fed, BoE, ECB), this does not mean that it is a policy without political content. There is indeed a trade-off between low inflation, growth and employment outcomes (Bernanke & Mishkin 1997), which leads one to ask: why is it political meddling to allow higher inflation and keep interest rates low as part of a policy aiming to promote employment and growth (or to eat away at public debt), while it is not political interference to maintain a strict inflation targeting regime in an economic climate (like the one post-financial crisis, for example) where the target arguably suppresses growth and employment? Callinicos (2010) argues that the effect of the financial crisis has been to broaden political horizons and to allow citizens to question a distinctive feature of economic orthodoxy, which he calls the 'naturalisation' of economic relations. State intervention in the economy in the form of Keynesian policies or bailouts (such as those experienced in response to the financial crisis post-2008) relegitimises the idea of political involvement in the economy. The lesson of the Phillips curve, which posits a trade-off between inflation and unemployment (Callinicos 2010, p. 14), was that governments could choose the mix of inflation and unemployment that best suited their values and priorities. This ability of governments implies that economic rela-tions are not governed by autonomous mechanisms resembling those driving physical processes (Glinavos 2013, p. 53). Consequently, a central bank run on an inflation-obsessed autopilot may not be offering the best service to the nation it operates in.

One could also legitimately ask, for instance, why is it political to run a monetary policy with an eye on social consequences for the worse off, while it is apolitical and technically sound to run such a policy (with price stability as an imperative) when it happens to benefit the already well-off? Joseph Stiglitz noted in an article to the *Economist* (1998, p. 216) that decisions made by cen-tral bankers are not just technical decisions, they involve trade-offs, judgements about whether the risks of inflation are worth the benefits of lower unem-ployment, and these trade-offs involve value judgements. Stiglitz returned to this theme in fact in *Freefall* (2010) by arguing that it is not so much the details of regulatory policy that we ought to be considering in the wake of the financial crisis but the ultimate goals: what is the role of regulation and what type of economy we want? These are key political questions and cannot indeed be answered by institutions independent from politics and, one could argue, detached from democratic legitimacy. In the words of McNamara (2002, p. 53), severing the direct institutional ties to elected officials appears to create an apolitical environment for policymaking, while central banks continue to make policies which have important, identifiable distributional effects and thus remain resolutely political and therefore partisan institutions. This is true with-out even beginning to consider the wealth of literature suggesting (as noted earlier) that inflation targeting in itself has dubious beneficial consequences on the economy (Bruno & Easterly 1996).

The independence of the BoE is a recent example of contemporary controversy generated by the left of the political spectrum. Jeremy Corbyn, Leader of the Labour Party (the Opposition in the House of Commons), proposed at the time of the British general election in 2015 a so-called People's Quantitative Easing (PQE) policy (Bootle 2015), which would require the BoE to print money in order to finance government investment. This was to be achieved (Yates 2015) through purchasing bonds issued by a state-owned National Investment Bank. Then this National Investment Bank would use the money to fund public infrastructure projects, including housing and public transport. This, apart from being a highly politically controversial topic, raised questions as to the possible threat that the proposed policies might pose to the independent status of the BoE, as a PQE would be materially different from the quantitative easing policies pursued after the financial crisis with the aim of injecting liquidity in the private sectors of the economy.

One could argue, however, that any policy mix should be at the discretion of the government and that in a democratic polity it is the legislator, empowered by citizens, that gives institutions, like central banks, their independence to begin with. Consequently, a future Labour government could legislate to instruct the BoE to pursue policies, including PQE. Mishkin (1998, p. 56) argued that having a central bank with a legislated mandate and goal dependence are basic democratic principles. The public is able to exercise control over government actions, and as by extension the goals of monetary policy are set by the elected government through legislation, the link of accountability is maintained. If the institutional commitment to price stability comes from the government in the form of an explicit, legislated mandate for the central bank to pursue price stability as its overriding, long-run goal, there is no tension between popular mandates and institutional independence. Indeed, central bank independence does not mean lack of accountability, as a higher degree of independence must be accompanied by greater accountability and judicial control to ensure equilibrium in policymaking.

Accountability is naturally linked with central bank independence (Nika 2018), because an independent central bank allows for the delegation of responsibilities to unelected monetary policymakers. Thus, in order to legitimise the role of a central bank within a given constitutional system, a substantial degree of accountability is required to insure against any perception of democratic deficit (Briault et al. 1996). Therefore, the main role of accountability is to ensure appropriate democratic control and good governance in the delegation of monetary policy powers to technocratic officials. Accountability in this context means that institutions with the power to affect the lives of people are subject to scrutiny by the elected representatives of these people. As such, accountability of institutions is an essential and constituent element of a political economy (Padoa-Schioppa 2004, p. 33). Critiques of central bank independence, however, may adopt the language of democracy and accountability, while having other goals. It is to these we turn to now, by considering attempts to bring central bankers to heel, following the wishes of political strong men (Rees 2019) and autocrats in developed and emerging economy contexts.

Populist challenges

With monetary policy being expansionary at a time of sluggish growth since the end of the financial crisis and little inflation in the majority of developed economies, one might have expected few criticisms of central bank policy from the right of the political spectrum. But that has not generally been the case. Some of the criticisms aimed at central banks have related to the slow tempo of the recovery; others to the possibility that one aspect of the unconventional economic recovery measures (such as negative nominal interest rates) may have had unintended effects (for example, weakening commercial bank profitability, impairing lending). Perhaps the main general criticism is that the unprecedented low level of nominal and real interest rates has been stimulating over-borrowing, creating a debt overhang, which may encourage present expenditures, but at the expense of fuelling future fragility and storing potential crises. The main reasons for such attacks though have related to their distributional and directional effects (Goodhart & Lastra 2018, p. 52). The assumption is that if politicians were in charge, they would have done things differently, with better outcomes for − what everyone likes to call − 'ordinary working people'.

This critique isn't new. In the United States, concerns about the role of the Federal Reserve (Fed) and its detachment from political processes predate the election of President Trump. For example, in 2016 the Senate rejected the controversial 'Audit the Fed' legislation, proposed by Republican Senator Rand Paul's calling for tougher audits of the Fed. The legislation aimed at eliminating restrictions on the US Government Accountability Office (GAO) audits of the Fed and mandated that the Fed's credit facilities, securities purchases and quantitative easing activities be subject to congressional oversight. In Paul's words (2016), 'nowhere else but in Washington, D.C., would you find an institution with so much unchecked power'. The Obama White House called Paul's proposal dangerous, and as Jason Furman, Chairman of President Obama's Council of Economic Advisers, highlighted (Sainato 2016): 'Congress shouldn't be telling the Fed what to do with monetary policy.' This episode also raised questions regarding the independent status of the Fed, with Ben Bernake (the then Chairman) stressing (Garver 2016) that this would result in a direct involvement of the government in monetary policy decisions, calling into question the Fed's independence.

Populist leaders (primarily, but not exclusively) have led criticism of independent central banks in the last few years. Highlights include the firing of the Turkish monetary policymaker Murat Cetinkaya by President Recep Tayyip Erdogan, who claimed the power to appoint rate-setters and put his son-in-law in charge of economic policy after winning the reelection in 2018, and US President Donald Trump's attacks on new Federal Reserve Chairman Jerome Powell (and incessant criticism of his predecessors) for raising interest rates. Reports suggested (Amaro 2019) that the US President has also looked at ways to legally demote the Federal Reserve Chairman. Appointment and dismissal procedures are important indicators of legal and de facto central bank independence (Cargill 2016). In 1965, President Lyndon Johnson had also considered firing then Fed Chairman William McChesney Martin, but upon learning that he lacked the legal powers to do so, he opted instead to complaining privately (Murphy 2018). Even the ECB, which is generally viewed as the institution most isolated from politics, saw the head of Germany's ruling Christian Democratic party urging incoming ECB Chief Christine Lagarde to shift monetary policy to make it comply with the bank's inflation-targeting mandate, while Italy's Deputy Premier Luigi Di Maio accused the ECB incumbent Mario Draghi of 'poisoning the climate' by weighing into the debate about Italy's budget (Koc et al. 2019). In Britain, BoE Governor Mark Carney has long faced accusations of bias from pro-Brexit politicians, who say he is overly negative about Britain's future outside the European Union. MP Jacob Rees-Mogg, for instance, dubbed him the 'high priest of project fear'. Carney denies the charge but was confronted with hostile comments after the BoE published scenarios showing that a no-deal Brexit could unleash a savage recession and a collapse in the pound. UK Prime Minister Theresa May had herself criticised the 'bad side effects' of BoE policies at the Conservative Party conference in October 2016, prompting Carney to respond that he would not take instruction from politicians on how to do his job (Bruce & Hobson 2016).

We should take a moment to reflect, however, on whether it is correct to taint the politicians mentioned previously with the label 'populist'. The chapter uses the word 'populism' to denote the policies of any political party of the right, or left, that does not share the main economic tenets of an 'orthodox' liberal, central establishment. Adopting the definition of Goodhart and Lastra (2018, p. 50), we can describe 'populism' as involving a major disagreement with the central liberal tenet that allowing the free movement of labour, capital goods and services between nations would be both generally beneficial and desirable in almost all circumstances. A populist therefore is someone wanting to restrict the movements of people, capital, goods and services between nation states. Further, linking to an earlier designation of 'autocratic' leaders, a populist would be a politician who, once having been democratically elected, would then seek to remove the checks and balances generally applied in a democratic state, in order to achieve the objectives upon which he (or she) was originally elected. This dual definition, therefore, combines the control of the movement of factors of production and products across national borders and a desire to achieve autocratic control over all executive powers of government, once having initially been democratically elected. Not all national populist movements are necessarily antidemocratic, or totalitarian, or 'fascist' in nature (Eatwell & Goodwin 2018). Often their challenge is a direct assault on the institutions of liberal democracy that populists consider cut-off from democratic processes, or more broadly (and vaguely) 'the popular will'. This is most evident in the area of economic institutions. The implications of populism on central banking specifically are a challenge to the exclusive focus of central banks on price stability, pitting a deflationary bias of economic policy against employment generation and growth (Rodrik 2018). This, of course, could be a legitimate challenge (as discussed elsewhere in this chapter), yet a populist narrative has negative consequences on the nations' political economy. This is because while the problems identified by populist leaders (for example, with respect to central banks) are real, their solutions are irrelevant, wrong or in many cases non-existent (Merler 2018).

Pressures on central banks are of course not limited to the developed world (Condon 2019). In South Africa, since an attempt by the country's anti-graft ombudsman in 2017 to have the Reserve Bank's mandate altered, it's Governor Lesetja Kganyago felt the need to continuously make the case for central bank independence (Kganyago 2019). India's new central bank governor, Shaktikanta Das, is seen as someone more amenable to government requests to relax tough regulations imposed on banks and is likely to ease monetary policy in an attempt to boost growth. Mr Das succeeded Urjit Patel, who resigned after a public row with Prime Minister Narendra Modi's government. In what is perceived as a related development, Deputy Governor Viral Acharya, one of the central bank's most outspoken officials, unexpectedly announced in June 2019 that he was standing down (Shastry 2019). The Pakistani central bank's independence has also come into question after Prime Minister Imran Khan replaced the governor in May 2019 as part of an overhaul of his economic team to address the nation's poor economic performance. In late 2018, he announced plans to make the central bank report any currency adjustments to a committee after successive devaluations of the national currency (Mangi & Dilawar 2018). Central banks in Russia, Nigeria, Greece and Thailand have also been subject to pressures by politicians in recent years.

Central banks have traditionally justified their powers with a mix of intellectual rationales for institutional independence – aimed at what are identified by many as 'elites' – combined with the cultivation of a mystique of economic success to win over the general public. This set of communication strategies left a critical void, according to Adolph (2018). As economic prowess since the financial crisis has fallen away and the success of monetary policy became less visible, the long-term cost of silence on issues such as inequality has come into focus, something that we touched upon earlier when discussing criticisms of central banking from a critical (left) perspective. One could argue that intellectually and rhetorically, the US Fed and other central banks are poorly situated to defend the legal powers of their institutions or the process by which they develop policy. The delay in nurturing an informed debate grounded in the real effects of monetary and fiscal policy has led to the populist hysteria against independent institutions (central banks first amongst them) that we are experiencing today.

But what is it that so many leaders of the world wish to achieve that is undermined by central banks? At the beginning of the chapter we discussed how inflation targeting has been the primary aim of monetary policy and the core objective of central banking in the modern era. We also discussed how such focus on inflation can have consequences on the growth balance of the economy in a number of areas, including on employment. The latter has been the focus of much critique of central banking coming from the left of the political spectrum, as already described. The critique from current leaders (belonging mostly to the right wing of politics) may have to do more with the balance between debt and inflation than effects on employment and growth. President Trump appears to be focused on interest rates but not on inflation. A looser monetary policy would allow the US government to finance debt more easily by letting the resulting higher inflation to erode the value of the currency in circulation and, if a spike in inflation surprises markets, to eat away at the value of pre-existing debt. There is actually good precedent on using inflation as a tool for debt relief, as former US presidents regularly sought to enlarge the budget deficit while persuading the central bank to keep interest rates low. Economists call that practice 'monetizing the budget deficit', and it tends to be part and parcel of rising inflation (Blinder 2019). As discussed earlier, in the 1970s, before the institutionalisation of central bank independence, it was normal for politicians to manipulate interest rates to boost their own popularity (*Economist* 2019). This, however, led a number of nations to experience a plague of inflation, and in extreme cases, which the United States has thus far managed to avoid, monetising deficits can lead to hyperinflation, seriously degrading the economic power and prospects of a country. One only needs to look at Zimbabwe and Venezuela as contemporary examples of the effects of unchecked inflation. While one could argue that developed economies are more in danger of deflation (than inflation), at the moment, there is still legitimate concern about using interest rates as a means of suppressing debt burdens.

Conclusion

Popular perceptions of independent institutions and of the legitimacy of state behaviour are currently changing. The model of central banking prevailing before the financial crisis was the result of a century-long quest for a monetary technology that would achieve two important objectives: firstly, to be more efficient than the gold standard, and to avoid the sustained inflation and deflation episodes that affected that arrangement; secondly, it sought to avoid the prolonged and acute price instability that had characterised the period after the gold standard was abandoned around the time of the First World War. From an institutional perspective, the technical and non-political task of identifying the best tools to achieve price stability fits well with the attribution, within a democratic policy, of this task to an independent agency (Papadia & Välimäki 2018, p. 256). The predominance of technocracy and institutional independence that underpinned our understanding of the market–state relationship since the end of the Cold War is being upended, however, by renewed calls for re-politicisation from across the political spectrum.

The chapter has discussed how President Trump in the United States and the Labour Party leadership in Britain as well as several prominent leaders in emerging economies have transcended ideological, national and class divides in order to stake a populist challenge to the idea of central bank independence. We are witnessing calls for a return to political-institutional environments long extinct in the West and (up until recently) in retreat in the developing world. The chapter has argued that this populism–fuelled critique is divergent from the literature on empowerment and greater accountability that was developed in response to the 2008 financial crisis. We are faced therefore with a metamorphosis of a debate towards undemocratic, capricious, populist and state-centric directions. This phenomenon has profound implications for emerging economies where efforts to build a pro-market institutional and legal framework have focused on the promotion of independent institutions. What this contemporary environment means for emerging economies is that a new vulnerability is revealed. Emerging economies looked to the Western capitalist states for leadership and best practice examples on institutional development. This is not meant to convey the idea that Western influence is always benign or always correct; see, for example, misguided efforts to promote capitalism in post-Soviet transition economies during the 1990s (Glinavos 2010). Nonetheless, one can be critical of the negative aspects of capitalism and the consequences of Western domination, while still accepting institutional innovation as a source of progress.

Governance problems in developing nations and emerging economies are real. Issues with inefficiency, politicisation and corruption are live concerns for millions of people. Missed opportunities and lacklustre growth aren't only the result of Western domination, predatory multinationals and unfair world trade rules. The former fits well a populist narrative that tries to blame 'others', usually foreigners, for any and all problems. National economic problems are to a significant proportion the results of domestic failures, inadequate technologies and political machinations. The promotion of independent apolitical institutions is meant to deal precisely with these types of weaknesses experienced by emerging economies. Detaching the setting of interest rates and monetary policy from the political timetables of frequently self-serving politicians sounds undemocratic but may be a necessary component of a strategy to set a nation on a sustainable growth trajectory. After all, by the same measure that one can decry 'capitalist' institutions for being undemocratic, one could condemn the politicisation that subjects economic rationalism to political calculation for personal gain.

What is the central message of this chapter on the changing political economy around central bank independence? The material presented here demonstrates that the populist assault on institutional independence in the West robs the developing world from the external impetus for reform. If America and

Britain (to take two key examples) abandon their ethical leadership, retreat from a defence of liberal values, free trade and even capitalism itself, what incentive is there for developing nations to continue along the path of reform? And it is to such a path that they should remain committed, as it represents the most likely avenue to an improved future life for their citizens. A collapse of confidence in liberal values in the West strengthens traditionalist, nativist politicians in emerging economies. It weakens those who advocate for reform if the 'shining city upon a hill' (Reagan 1989) is no longer a bright beacon to follow. Independent institutions are a bulwark against autocracy, not a threat to democratic governance. Policymakers in emerging economies would do a service to their nations to think of them as such.

References

Adolph, C 2018, 'The missing politics of central banks', *American Political Science Association*, vol. 51, no. 4, pp. 737–742.

Amaro, S 2019, 'These central banks' independence are "in crisis" as governments fight for control', *CNBC*, 21 June, viewed 31 July 2019, www.cnbc.com/2019/06/21/central-banks-independence-are-in-crisis-as-governments-interfere.html.

Anghie, A 1999–2000, 'Time present and time past: globalization IFIs and the third world', *NYU Journal of International Law and Politics*, vol. 32, p. 243.

Bernanke, B & Mishkin, F 1997, 'Inflation targeting: a new framework for monetary policy?', *Journal of Economic Perspectives*, vol. 11, no. 2, pp. 97–116.

Bernhard, W 1998, 'A political explanation of variations in central bank independence', *The American Political Science Review*, vol. 92, no. 2, pp. 311–327.

Blinder, S 2019, 'Why trump should leave the fed alone; in defense of central bank independence', *Foreign Affairs*, 23 April, viewed 31 July 2019, www.foreignaffairs.com/articles/2019-04-23/why-trump-should-leave-fed-alone.

Bootle, R 2015, 'What are we to think of Jeremy Corbyn's "people's QE"?', *The Telegraph*, 13 September, viewed 30 July 2019, www.telegraph.co.uk/finance/economics/11862318/What-are-we-to-think-of-Jeremy-Corbyns-peoples-QE.html.

Briault, C, Haldane, A & King, M 1996, 'Independence and accountability', *Bank of England Working Paper, No. 49*, The Bank of England.

Brittan, S 1982, *How to end the monetarist controversy*, Institute of Economic Affairs, London.

Bruce, A & Hobson, P 2016, 'BoE's Carney pushes back against criticism from PM May', *Reuters*, 14 October, viewed 31 July 2019, https://uk.reuters.com/article/uk-britain-eu-boe-idUKKBN12E0V0.

Bruno, M & Easterly, W 1996, 'Inflation and growth: in search of a stable relationship', *Federal Reserve Bank of St Louis Review*, vol. 78, pp. 139–146.

Callinicos, A 2010, *Bonfire of illusions: the twin crises of the liberal world*, Polity, London.

Cargill, T 2016, 'The myth of central Bank independence', *Mercatus Working Paper*, 31 October, George Mason University.

Chernow, R 1994, *The warburgs: the twentieth-century odyssey of a remarkable Jewish family*, Vintage, New York.

Coggan, P 2011, *Paper promises: money, debt and the new world order*, Allen Lane.

Condon, C 2019, 'Central bank independence', *Bloomberg*, 8 July, viewed 31 July 2019, www.washingtonpost.com/business/central-bank-independence/2019/07/08/cc0ea590-a19e-11e9-a767-d7ab84aef3e9_story.html?noredirect=on&utm_term=.72a01b58585a.

Cukierman, A 1994, 'Central bank independence and monetary control', *The Economic Journal*, vol. 104, pp. 1437–1448.

Cukierman, A 2008, 'Central bank independence and monetary policymaking institutions: past, present and future', *European Journal of Political Economy*, vol. 24, no. 4. p. 722.

Das, S 2011, *Extreme money: the masters of the universe and the cult of risk*, Financial Times/Prentice Hall, Harlow, UK.

Debelle, G & Fischer, S 1994, 'How independent should a central bank be?', *Conference Series; [Proceedings]*, Federal Reserve Bank of Boston, pp. 195–225.

de Haan, J & Eijffinger, S 2016, 'The politics of central bank independence', *CentER Discussion Paper Series, No. 2016–047*.

Eatwell, R & Goodwin, M 2018, *National populism: the revolt against liberal democracy*, Pelican Books, London.

Editor 2019, 'The independence of central banks is under threat from politics', *The Economist*, 13 April, viewed 31 July 2019, www.economist.com/leaders/2019/04/13/the-independence-of-central-banks-is-under-threat-from-politics.

"The Federal Reserve Transparency Act of 2015" (S. 2232, 114th congress 1st session, 12 January 2016) *commonly referred to as "Audit the Fed"*.

Friedman, M & Schwartz, A 1963, *A monetary history of the United States, 1867–1960*, Princeton University Press, Princeton, NJ.

Garver, Rob 2016, 'Why the controversial "Audit the Fed" bill is really a power grab', *The Fiscal Times*, 11 January, viewed 31 July 2019, www.thefiscaltimes.com/2016/01/11/Why-Controversial-Audit-Fed-Bill-Really-Power-Grab.

Glinavos, I 2010, *Neoliberalism and the law in post communist transition*, Routledge, London.

Glinavos, I 2013, *Redefining the market state relationship*, Routledge, London.

Goodhart, C & Lastra, R 2018, 'Populism and central bank independence', *Open Economies Review*, vol. 29, no. 1, pp. 49–68.

Groenewegen, J, Spithoven, A & Van den Berg, A 2010, *Institutional economics: an introduction*, Palgrave Macmillan, Basingstoke.

Hayek, F 1944, *The road to serfdom*, G. Routledge & Sons, London.

Kganyago, L 2019, 'Multilateralism and central bank independence', *Central Bank Speech*, Bank for International Settlements, 13 June, viewed 5 September 2019, www.bis.org/review/r190613e.htm.

King, M 2005, 'Epistemic communities and the diffusion of ideas: central bank reform in the United Kingdom', *West European Politics*, vol. 28, no. 1, pp. 94–123.

Kleineman, J 2001, *Central bank independence. The economic foundations, the constitutional implications and democratic accountability*, Kluwer Law International, The Hague, Boston.

Koc, C, Cattan, N & Bull, A 2019, 'Trump and Turkey threaten heyday of central bank independence', *Bloomberg*, 8 July, viewed 31 July 2019, www.bloomberg.com/news/articles/2019-07-08/trump-and-turkey-threaten-heyday-of-central-bank-independence.

Mangi, F & Dilawar, I 2018, 'Pakistan plans to curb central bank's power to manage currency', *Bloomberg*, 3 December, viewed 5 September 2019, www.bloomberg.com/news/articles/2018-12-03/fifth-devaluation-spurs-pakistan-to-mull-new-currency-management.

Maxfield, S 1997, *Gatekeepers of growth: the international political economy of central banking in developing countries*, Princeton University Press, Princeton, NJ.

McCulloch, JR 1888, *The works of David Ricardo. With a notice of the life and writings of the author*, John Murray, London.

McNamara, K 2002 January, 'Rational fictions: Central bank independence and the social logic of delegation', *West European Politics*, vol. 25, no. 1, pp. 47–76.

Merler, S 2018, 'Central banks in the age of populism', *Bruegel Blog Post*, 19 March, viewed 5 September 2019, https://bruegel.org/2018/03/central-banks-in-the-age-of-populism/.

Mishkin, F 1998, 'Central banking in a democratic society: implications for transition countries', *Zagreb Journal of Economics*, vol. 3, no. 3, p. 51.

Murphy, R 2018, 'The idea that the fed is "Independent" is absurd', *The Fiscal Times*, 30 August, viewed 31 July 2019, www.thefiscaltimes.com/Columns/2018/08/30/Idea-Fed-Independent-Absurd.

Nika, P 2018, 'ECB monetary policy and supervisory powers: competing objectives and policy conflicts', PhD thesis, University of Reading.

Nordhaus, W 1975, 'The political business cycle', *The Review of Economic Studies*, vol. 42, no. 2, pp. 169–190.

North, D 1981, *Structure and change in economic history*, W.W. Norton and Company, New York.

Padoa-Schioppa, T 2004, *The Euro and its central bank, getting united after the union*, MIT Press, Cambridge, MA.

Papadia, F & Välimäki, T 2018, *Central banking in turbulent times*, Oxford University Press, Oxford, UK.

Paul, R 2016, *Transcript of Rand Paul speech in the US 114 congress*, 12 January, viewed 31 July 2019, www.paul.senate.gov/news/senate-holds-vote-sen-rand-paul's-"audit-fed".

Reagan, R 1989, 'Farewell address to the nation', *The American Presidency Project*, 11 January, viewed 31 July 2019, www.presidency.ucsb.edu/documents/farewell-address-the-nation.

Rees, T 2019, 'Why populism and strong-arm leaders threaten the end for central bank independence', *The Telegraph*, 14 July, viewed 30 July 2019, www.telegraph.co.uk/business/2019/07/14/populism-strong-arm-leaders-threaten-end-central-bank-independence/.

Rodrik, D 2014, 'When ideas trump interests: preferences, worldviews, and policy innovations', *Journal of Economic Perspectives*, vol. 28, no. 1, pp. 189–208.

Rodrik, D 2018, 'In defense of economic populism', *Project Syndicate*, 9 January, viewed 5 September 2019, www.project-syndicate.org/commentary/defense-of-economic-populism-by-dani-rodrik-2018-01.

Sainato, M 2016, 'What Bernie Sanders' vote to audit the fed says about his devotion to bipartisanship', *The Observer*, 13 January, viewed 31 July 2019, http://observer.com/2016/01/what-bernie-sanders-vote-to-audit-the-fed-says-about-his-devotion-to-bipartisanship/.

Shastry, V 2019, 'Asian central banks face political capture', *Chatham House*, 20 March, viewed 5 September 2019, www.chathamhouse.org/expert/comment/asian-central-banks-face-political-capture#.

Stiglitz, J 1998, 'Central banking in a democratic society', *The Economist*, vol. 142, no. 2, pp. 199–226.

Stiglitz, J 2010, *Freefall*, Penguin, London.

Watson, M 2002, 'The institutional paradoxes of monetary orthodoxy: reflections on the political economy of central bank independence', *Review of International Political Economy*, vol. 9, no. 1, pp. 183–196.

Yates, T 2015, 'Corbyn's QE for the people jeopardises the Bank of England's independence', *The Guardian*, 22 September, viewed 30 July 2019, www.theguardian.com/business/economics-blog/2015/sep/22/jeremy-corbyn-qe-for-the-people-jeopardises-bank-of-england-independence.

3 Central banks and institutional evolution in transition

Christopher A. Hartwell

Introduction

Over the past 40 years, a consensus has formed internationally around the idea that monetary policy is best executed by an "independent" central bank, unpressured by political cycles and elections and comprised of technicians left alone to fine tune the economy. In perhaps an odd turn, the policy of central bank independence (CBI) far outpaced the economic theory behind it, with CBI being implemented as a policy and institutional experiment first and fully developed theories supporting it coming later (building on the backs of Kydland and Prescott 1977, Barro and Gordon 1983, and Rogoff 1985). By the beginning of the 1990s, the economics profession had belatedly joined the CBI party, with papers such as Cukierman et al. (1992), De Haan and Sturm (1992), and Alesina and Summers (1993) confirming that the institutional arrangement was correlated with better outcomes in monetary policy, especially in terms of fighting inflation.

The CBI revolution in the OECD economies was gathering steam just as a much more consequential revolution was taking place across the Iron Curtain, as the fall of the Berlin Wall in 1989, followed by the sweeping aside of communist parties across Central and Eastern Europe (CEE) and the soon-to-be former Soviet Union (FSU) led to a massive economic transformation. Although the economic reforms proceeded at different paces in different countries (and in some stalwarts such as Belarus and Turkmenistan, not at all), accompanying the change in *policies* was an emphasis on a change in *institutions*; in particular, new governance institutions were necessary to mediate, rather than plan, the market economy. In an example of two intellectual revolutions combining and reinforcing each other, the transition countries across the region adopted the prevailing wisdom of the West and began to create their own independent central banks as the new centralized monetary authority of their transformation.

From the vantage point of Warsaw, Prague, Kyiv, or Bishkek, the allure of an independent central bank was manifold: firstly, as noted, the international vogue for creating an independent central bank had elevated this institutional arrangement to international best practice, and the transition economies saw their transformation as a chance to leapfrog slow or evolutionary institutional change and go straight to the "best' model. Beyond the desire to have the shiniest toy, however, there were other imperatives for an independent central bank, the most important being, for countries in line for EU accession, that such a bank was a necessity to satisfy the EU and its conditionalities. Not only was CBI best practice, but it was actually a pre-condition for the countries with a hope of accession to complete the Acquis Communautaire. Finally, the exigencies of the transition process itself meant that monetary overhang and massive price adjustments needed to be tamed quickly so that growth could resume and the price system could send appropriate signals. With economic theory and empirical evidence on CBI showing it was associated with lower inflation, transition economies looked to this institutional model as a way to minimize political interference in monetary policy (Maliszewski 2000).

The purpose of this chapter is to examine the political economy of central banking in CEE and the countries of the FSU, with an eye towards understanding the interlinkages between this implementation of the independent central bank model and its effect on other economic and political institutions in transition. As Gabor (2011, p. 3) notes, "the political economy of central banking must pay equal attention to policy argumentation and institutional configurations." However, for far too long there has been neglect of the institutional side in understanding the central bank as essentially a monetary policy institution enmeshed in a country's institutional fabric (Hartwell 2018a). Indeed, as noted earlier, central banking started as an institutional experiment driven by institutional forces, but which has taken on a life of its own; part of this is due to the immense power accorded to central banks in modern governments, but part of it is due to the reality of complex interrelations between money and other institutions (Hartwell 2019).

This chapter attempts to rectify this oversight somewhat by focusing on the effects of central banks and monetary policy on the broader institutional development in transition. After all, it was not only monetary institutions which were in flux during transition, it was the entire political and economic institutional system. The main conclusion of this analysis is that central banks – even while being modeled on the modern, Western conception of independence – and monetary policies undertaken in the region exerted a far stronger influence on institutional development than previously realized. In particular, while institutional constraints and rules transfer helped to embed central banks in a restrictive milieu in the EU accession CEE countries, the lack of such constraints in the FSU meant that central banking enabled additional economic and especially political malaise. In both instances, however, the policies pursued by the central banks in transition, those same policies advocated in Western capitals, also aided the rise of financialization and the concomitant political issues associated with the dominance of the financial sector (Gabor 2012). By making themselves so important to the functioning of the market economy, central banks have created the conditions for anti-market backlashes and populist threats to the rule of law.

Central banks in transition

Although several authors have (and continue to) claimed that institutions were "neglected" in transition (Kolodko 1999; Stiglitz 2000), this argument has been thoroughly debunked (Hartwell 2013), with central banks being a prime exhibit of how institutions were central to transition economies. Indeed, one of the earliest institutional reforms to come about was the change from a communist mono-bank to an "independent" central bank modeled on Western economies. This section explains this transformation under a framework in which transition countries faced both exogenous pressure (from the EU and technical assistance donors) and endogenous desires (status conferred by an independent central bank, need to handle the exigencies of transition) for creating the institutional arrangement of the central bank.

With regard to exogenous pressure, it if fair to say that the entire modern idea of a central bank – that is, a centralized monetary authority which monitors the economy and adjusts monetary policy in accordance with current and forecasted conditions – was foreign to the communist countries of Central and Eastern Europe. Under communism, central banking did not exist per se, even as the institution of a central bank did; in reality, the central monetary authorities in communism were merely accountants overseeing the use of money as units to allocate resources across the plan. Money itself was never part of the utopian communist dream, as hyperinflation and other means of debauching the currency were explicitly utilized at the outset of communist regimes to both take over power and to consolidate it by destroying economic rivals (although not necessarily planned, hyperinflation played an effective role in pulling down capitalism, as shown in both Carr 1952 and Hartwell 2019). Once the idea of sound money was decimated, the Communist Party would then create a monobank to direct investment and credit in pursuit of development of the economy (Garvy 1977). In this sense, the central bank was also explicitly a part of the government's apparatus, a blunt tool rather than a calibrating instrument.

This is not to say that the institutional memory of central banking did not exist in much of the transition space. Indeed, countries such as Poland, Hungary, and the Czech Republic (Czechoslovakia) had proud traditions of central banking going back to the interwar period and their first tastes of (or, in Poland's case, reacquaintance with) independence. However, even these early experiences with central banking did not follow a "modern" model concerned with inflation targeting and, more importantly, independence from the rest of government. For much of the interwar period, central banks in Central Europe did not even have an independent monetary policy to follow, as much of the region was on the gold standard (Wolf 2008). Thus, the idea of an independent central bank, not subjected (at least formally) to political pressures from the Ministry of Finance and undertaking new forms of economic surveillance and monitoring was indeed a foreign idea.

This foreign idea was, unsurprisingly, propagated by foreigners during the transition. Technical assistance programs from USAID, the World Bank, the

International Monetary Fund (IMF), the European Union, and other donors helped to set up and staff central banks throughout the region. The ultimate goal of these programs was to create a bank modeled on the Western example, mainly an impartial technical body to oversee monetary policy but also an oversight mechanism to shepherd the development of the banking sector while preserving financial stability (Koch 2007). Rodlauer (1995), speaking on behalf of the IMF, noted that the transition to central banking was one of the Fund's successes in the region even as the development of commercial banking was more problematic, a point that Maliszewski (2000, p. 753) noted was due to the conflicting goals of monetary control and financial stability: "central banks, legally responsible for financial stability, were forced to bail out insolvent banks, in order to avoid financial crises and to provide quasi-fiscal subsidies to the public sector. Higher inflation was the price for the rescue operations."

Despite these contradictory mandates, for the most part the transition to a new central bank proceeded apace in the CEE and FSU countries, with the CEE economies seeing an additional exogenous pressure for adopting this institution, namely the prospect of EU accession. Hochreiter and Kowalski (2000, p. 48) noted that legislation in the countries "who seek EU membership will have to be compatible with the Treaty of Maastricht, which, in Protocol No. 3, contains the statute of the European System of Central Banks (ESCB) and that of the European Central Bank (ECB). Thus, the statutes of the ESCB already served as the benchmark" for these countries, a benchmark which had been reinforced by social contacts between Western central banks and their counterparts in the east (Epstein 2005). With EU and IMF assistance flowing in to help achieve this goal, and with founding legislation in the CEE countries based on a combination of the Bundesbank Act and (more prominently) the Austrian National Bank Act (Siklos 1994), the transition economies had both external funding and an exogenously set goal to guide the transition of their own monetary authorities.

However, it is fallacious to say that modern central banking in the region came about solely due to foreign influence, as before the transition even occurred some of the leading reformers in the region were quietly shifting their monetary governance; Hungary, for example, had discarded the communist monobank as early as 1987 and created a two-tier system with the National Bank of Hungary assuming the reins as a modern central bank (Hasan and Marton 2003). Even Epstein (2005), much more sympathetic to the idea of "rule transfer" as the determining factor for adopting independent central banks, notes that the move in Poland to a very independent National Bank (NBP) was defended by a broad societal coalition against left-wing attempts to create a more politicized authority.

Part of the motivation for creating central banks on the Western model, beyond the technical assistance or conditionality from the EU or IMF, was the sense that independent central banks were the (pardon the ironic pun) gold standard of monetary institutions. Indeed, as Marcussen (2005, p. 911) notes, "states have adopted certain organizational structures and legal standards because, in world society, these structures and standards are considered as examples of modernity, progress, civilization and excellence," and none was so powerful as the idea of an independent central bank. This allure of the best and latest model for monetary governance could be precisely why the countries of Central and Eastern Europe actually exceeded targets set by the EU; while they may have had an externally imposed objective, in many instances the banks set up during the 1990s exceeded Western models (Loungani and Sheets 1997) in terms of their independence, surpassing that of countries such as the United Kingdom (Cukierman et al. 2002). Indeed, the independence of the central banks in the region did not stop at conducting monetary policy, but also in decisions related to broader monetary integration, as witnessed by the resistance to the euro (Epstein and Johnson 2010).

A similar proof of endogenous desire can be found in the FSU countries, which saw comparatively less funding spent on technical assistance and less of a focus on (or prospect of) EU accession, but where modern central banking still flourished (albeit not uniformly across the region). In fact, the collapse of a common currency (the ruble zone) in the early years of transition meant that former republics other than Russia had to institute central banks, many of whom had no institutional memory with independent governance, let alone modern conceptions of central banking. Despite coming from a common (recent) institutional history, the diverging historical legacies and cultural precepts across the Soviet space meant that central banks were built along the spectrum of independence, with countries such as Kyrgyzstan, Georgia, and Moldova having highly independent central banks modeled on Western tenets (and saw lower inflationary outcomes); at the other end of the spectrum, Ukraine, Belarus, and Tajikistan had far less independent monetary authorities, in line with their general lack of reform (Lybek 1999). But for those who *did* want to reform institutionally, there was demand for an independent central bank to oversee the process, even in the absence of aid money. Perhaps blessed by history and the fact that it was the center of the USSR, the most successful central bank in the former Soviet Union is undoubtedly the Central Bank of Russia (CBR), which has maintained independence in a highly politically charged atmosphere and had to deal with a series of poor policy choices by the Russian government. Almost alone among the former Soviet republics (with the exception of the Baltics), the CBR's development has come about as an iterative process, done somewhat in spite of rather than because of IMF assistance (for an unintended account of the IMF's unhelpful hand in Russia, see Gilman 2010).

The sum of these pressures – both external and internal – was to propel the transition economies to a supercharged version of the central banks prevailing in the Western world in the 1980s, with a higher-than-average level of independence and an institutional arrangement that could only be described as cutting-edge. How this institutional arrangement was to impact the rest of transition is the subject of the next section.

The influence of central banks on the institutional transition

As seen from this overview of the genesis of central banks in the aftermath of communism, the modern institutional form of central banking was both imposed from external forces and created by internal actors during the transition. Given this interplay of interests, the exact influence that the central bank was to have on the economic transition was never assured, and was always going to be dependent upon the prevailing political institutions, public attitudes towards transition, and the personalities of those involved. Moreover, the transition to independent central banks in Central and Eastern Europe and the former Soviet Union, unlike in the West, did not occur in a vacuum but in a volatile environment in flux, and so the influence of the monetary authority in this unstable institutional ecosystem could have been either outsized or minimized, depending upon the institutional changes occurring around the bank. This section attempts to examine what effects the transition to a modern, independent central bank had on transition economies by looking at both the economic effects and the political ones.

Economic effects

As Loungani and Sheets (1997), Lybek (1999), and Cukierman et al. (2002) noted regarding the first decade of independent central banks in the transition economies, the same relationship between independence and inflation held as in the OECD countries: higher independence led to lower inflation overall, even when taking into account the various changes and initial conditions experienced across the region. Achieving price stability in an orderly fashion, quickly working through the changes which needed to be implemented as repressed prices were freed and the monetary overhang was cleared, was the sine qua non of transition. Simply put, without a functioning price system, a market economy could never spring into being, as the information imparted in prices makes transactions (both current and future) possible. Moreover, disorderly monetary effects, such as hyperinflation, could impede the development of other economic institutions within a country, such as trade, property rights, or even government agencies such as tax administration. Thus, the fact that independent central banks were able to quickly bring down inflation in what was necessarily an inflationary environment gave these countries a head start on successfully completing their transition to capitalism.

Given that price stability was paramount for completing the transition successfully, it should have been prioritized in any monetary policy moves made by the new governments of transition economies. However, it appears that countries which created central banks more interested in monetizing government debt and spending than focusing on price stability saw much worse economic outcomes overall but especially in inflation (see Figure 3.1 for a comparison in the former Soviet Union). This, in turn, had reverberations for the real

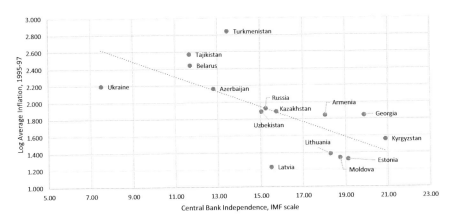

Figure 3.1 Inflation versus CBI in the Former Soviet Union as of 1998

Source: Based on data from Lybek (1999) and the IMF World Economic Outlook, October 1998

economy and (as we will see later) for institutional development. Ukraine is a key example of this dynamic, for, as Sochan (1998, p. 72) noted at the time,

> the legal status of the National Bank, its authority and the legal authority of the legislative and executive branches of government were poorly defined and often misunderstood in 1991 and 1992. It was clear that Parliament intended that the National Bank should report to and be subservient to the will of Parliament.

Before the passage of a new Law on the National Bank in 1999, the National Bank of Ukraine (NBU) was permitted to lend directly to the government, and did so with gusto: "up to 1997 direct credits to state budget were granted regularly and in large volumes. In particular, in 1995 the Bank's direct credits (advances, overdrafts, credits with fixed rate, etc.) accounted for about 70% of state budget deficit financing" (Schwödiauer et al. 2006, pp. 15–16). As a result, inflation remained high throughout the 1990s, from a hyperinflation in 1993 (the first in history not a direct result of a war) to elevated levels connected with half-hearted reforms (liberalization reversals) and the Russian crisis of 1998. It was not until the passage of the new Law in 1999 and the aftermath of the crisis that inflation levels began to settle, and Ukraine was able to see some (unspectacular) growth in the early 2000s.

Of course, an important argument needs to be raised here, one noted by both Mas (1995) and Hayo (1998), and that is that the correlation between an independent central bank in transition and low inflation does not mean causation, as there may be deeper cultural and institutional variables responsible for the behavior of the bank beyond its independence. In particular, in the transition context, perhaps it was not the delegation of independence to a new monetary authority which delivered lower inflationary outcomes, but the reality that inflationary preferences within that country were already low due to other reasons (for example, interwar experience with hyperinflation, as in Poland). Mas (1995) noted that, in such a situation, the institutional form of the independent central bank is redundant, as the conditions for low inflation and/or fiscal rectitude are already present (this is not entirely correct, however, as governance mechanisms can go against the will of the majority and even culture if personalities involved are strong enough). In this sense, the differences between Ukraine and Poland were not just about the independence of the central bank, it was the cultural and political imperatives which led to the central bank being fashioned in one way rather than the other in the first place.

While the argument on the causal nexus of CBI still rages, it is not the place of this chapter to dwell on it for too long. More important is to see what effect the new central banks in CEE and FSU had on economic development after the stabilization of prices was completed. Hartwell (2013) noted that countries which proceeded fastest in stabilization also saw institutional development move along most quickly, meaning that central bank reforms (as part of a package of rapid transformation) tended to be correlated with other favorable institutional changes such as in trade or property rights (perhaps also vindicating the Hayo [1998] view on cultural currents). In the realm of broader economic change, it thus appears that the move to central banks on the Western model was an important move for the outset of transition which had few deleterious consequences on economic institutions going forward.

However, while central banks may have had a positive impact on economic change, if we look more closely to the areas of the economy which central banks in transition were directly concerned with, a more nuanced picture emerges. Perhaps unsurprisingly, central banks played a key role in influencing the development of transition economies via their financial systems, an area which central banks were given suzerainty as part of their mandate (in relation to the aforementioned focus on "financial stability"). As Gabor (2011, 2012) has noted, the main issue which has come about via the adoption of independent central banks has been a spread in "financialization," or the growth of importance of the financial sector vis-à-vis the real economy.[1] Bohle (2018, p. 197) states plainly that "the availability of ample and cheap credit has induced a trajectory of financialization" in countries as diverse as Hungary and Latvia, and correctly traces this phenomenon to central bank policies both in these countries and in the ECB. The collapse of lending in the wake of the global financial crisis, afflicting domestic banks even in business lines where they were not active, led to undue hardship for consumers and businesses in transition but brought little ramifications for finance in the countries of CEE (due to their isolation and less competitive sectors, the FSU has been proportionally less affected by financialization). More importantly, financialization has not abated in the post-global financial crisis world, as the size of the financial sector (and the returns associated with the financial sector) has not diminished in any transition country, a situation which could lead to reduced growth in the medium-term (Arcand et al. 2015). Whereas transition economies may have leapfrogged intermediate institutional arrangements with independent central banks, they may have adopted far too soon the sort of advanced country malaise associated with financialization.

Political effects

The economic effects of central bank independence have been a centerpiece of the literature reviewing CBI, and in the transition case it appears that broader institutional evolution may have been aided by the institution of the central bank while financial sector development was skewed in one direction. A much more contentious area to examine is the effect of CBI and the newly designed central banks in transition on political institutions. Unfortunately, the economics literature has only begun to grapple with the reality that macroeconomic policy can have a real and direct effect on institutional development (Hartwell 2018b, 2019; Koyama and Johnson 2015), a point which the political science literature has touched upon but has been limited mostly to understanding electoral behavior (see Pacek [1994] on Central and Eastern Europe). Given the centrality of the independent monetary authority in modern market economies (along with the reality of the endogeneity of money), it is an egregious oversight to neglect what impact monetary policy will have on other economic and political institutions. In transition economies, where all institutions are in flux, the influence that an independent central bank could have may be even greater – and more immediate.

In the first instance, considering the lessons of Hartwell (2018b) and Koyama and Johnson (2015), it appears that monetary stability – and in particular the cessation of inflation occurring after transition – would be beneficial to the establishment of the rule of law and accessible political institutions. Indeed, countries which had higher levels of central bank independence/lower inflation had much higher levels of democracy, and it appears that the space afforded by macroeconomic stabilization allowed for the consolidation of democracy in a non-crisis atmosphere (Figure 3.2).

However important central banks were in helping to consolidate the transition to democracy by providing stable money, an important point regarding the relationship between independent central banking and democratic accountability has been heretofore overlooked. Post-Keynesians (perhaps rightly) decry the transfer of economic policy to central banks everywhere as creating a "democratic deficit" (Johnson 2006), a point which is less relevant in this region, given that the central banks of CEE and FSU remained influenced by political trends and societal preferences (making them never really "independent," see Hartwell 2018a). A democratic deficit of some magnitude does exist, however, via an institutional effect which came about from the move to independent central banking: in particular, the transfer of so much power to central banks meant that the central bank was the *only* guarantor of sound money and the key steward of the economy. With central banks as "the brains of modern capitalist economies, and their policies can affect prices and wages,

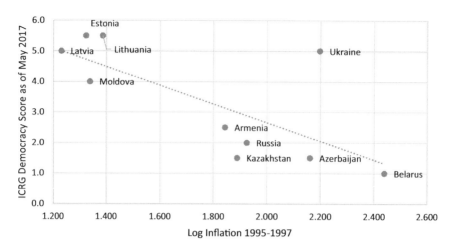

Figure 3.2 Early inflation versus later democracy in the FSU countries

Source: Author's calculations and International Crisis Risk Guide (ICRG). Democratic accountability indicator ranges from 0 to 6 with higher numbers meaning more democracy. ICRG does not have indicators for some FSU countries, including Georgia, Kyrgyzstan, Tajikistan, Turkmenistan, and Uzbekistan

determine whether an economy grows or stagnates, and influence who wins or loses financially" (Johnson 2006, p. 90), they had the ability to both save and destroy an economy.

The centrality of central banks in the transition brings up several issues related to political institutions which can be problematic. The first one is the reality that such an institution is highly susceptible to manipulation simply because of the power it wields (in particular in determining who wins and who loses), a trait which would undeniably attract political attention. Unlike the ECB, which has the strength to stand up to (or even dictate to) Member States, central bank governors in, say, Tajikistan or Turkmenistan have no such leeway even if the institution has statutory independence (a point made on Central Asia more generally by Arnone et al. [2009]). Indeed, despite having the trappings of independence, central banks in much of the former Soviet Union have been captured by political and financial interests, which, in most instances, are the same thing. If one looks at the distribution of politically connected oligarchs throughout the FSU countries, one thing is apparent: bank ownership is a necessary (but not sufficient) prerequisite for joining the oligarch club. With the most politically powerful agents in society also wielding economic clout, it would be suicidal (literally, in some countries) for a central banker to ignore this constituency, especially if financial stability is a mandate. In such a scenario, central bank policies favor the existing power structure and the "shadow principals" of the economy (Adolph 2018).

The more important issue related to the *primus inter pares* role of central banks is simply whether or not an institution, one which has such power, is desirable in a market economy; as Cochrane (2013) rightly stated, "an institution that relies on good leadership to avoid harm to the economy and the nation is not a good institution." However, this power is amplified in situations where there are relatively weak or new political institutions, as levers of protest and effecting change are not well-understood, checks and balances are not held in place by tradition, and political literacy may be low. In this situation, a dominant central bank which espouses its own "sectarian ideologies that take no account of the public interest" (Elster 1994, p. 66) can set off a backlash. But with no way to influence the central bank directly, the backlash must head towards political institutions and, usually, the political elite.

The key example of this can be seen where banks have veered from their original mandates for price stability and waded into propping up their respective economies with low/negative interest rates, easy money, and quantitative easing-type programs. Independent central banks in transition have undertaken all of these policies (to different extents) in pursuit of "rescuing" their economies from the deprivations of the twin shocks of global financial crisis and Eurozone crisis, dedicating themselves (along with the Western world) to negating the time value of money and pricing capital as if it were abundant. A glance at policy interest rates in a representative economy, the Czech Republic, will show how monetary policy has been in crisis mode for a decade, with interest rates hovering near zero (Figure 3.3). Much as with the ECB, who it tracks closely, the Federal Reserve, and other developed economy central banks, the Czech National Bank (CNB) has steadfastly refused to increase interest rates too quickly, believing the "recovery" to be too fragile. Mindful of the consequences of higher interest

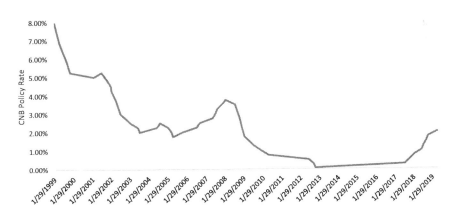

Figure 3.3 Policy interest rates from the Czech National Bank, 1999–present

Source: Czech National Bank

rates on both consumer spending and government debt, Czech politicians have only too eagerly supported this policy.

What effect has this pursuit of growth – or rather, bailing out the financial sector of the economy – had on the political system? Not coincidentally, the Czech Republic has also seen a strong strain of populism manifesting itself in the election of a populist President in 2013 (at the same time that interest rates flirted with zero), the election of a populist Prime Minister in 2017, and the re-election of the President in 2018. As Jarábik and Učeň (2018) noted, the Czech economy has indeed recovered, but populism remains popular because wages remain low; this is in one sense, a consequence of the very same integration with the West which has brought the Czechs a successful transition, as flexible labor markets and globalization have kept the bargaining power of Czech workers low (in addition to low labor productivity; see Figure 3.4). At the same time, low interest rates have increased the nominal stock of capital in the country, creating opportunities for firms to expand into new projects and take on new workers, without affecting levels of savings and without providing incentives for firms to increase wages. Concurrently, while wages for most of the country have stagnated post-global financial crisis, the financial sector has been reaping the benefit of easy money policies, with financial sector wages standing at approximately 84% higher than the Czech average by Q1 2019 (Figure 3.5). In such an environment, where the central bank appears to be protecting the financial sector, discontent has manifested itself in a populist

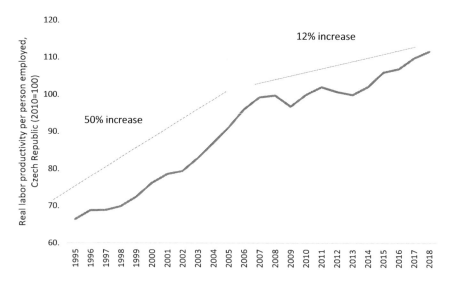

Figure 3.4 Labor productivity in the Czech Republic, 1995–2018 (2010 = 100)

Source: Eurostat and author's calculations

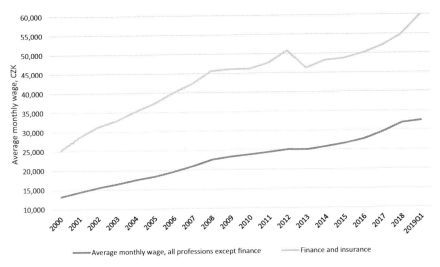

Figure 3.5 Real monthly wages, the Czech Republic, financial sector and all professions

Source: Author's calculations based on data from the Czech Statistical Office

backlash. The tale is similar elsewhere in Central and Eastern Europe, not to mention in the "core" Eurozone countries as well.

In sum, central banks may have helped with the consolidation of democracy in the fragile early years of transition, but their performance since has once again been focused on the financial sector (and political insiders) at the expense of the rest of the economy. This conduct of monetary policy, independent of bank independence, has translated into political pressures, populism, and threats to the rule of law. In this sense, in line with Cochrane's (2013) criticism, it is difficult to say that central banks have actively aided the development of political institutions in transition.

Conclusions

Our understanding of how monetary institutions influence the development of other segments of society, and in particular political and economic institutions, is still at a nascent stage. This chapter has attempted to advance our scholarship in this field by a small step, examining the effects of one institutional arrangement, an independent central bank, on the broader institutional evolution which was occurring in Central and Eastern Europe and the former Soviet Union. As shown, central banking in transition had similar economic effects, especially in relation to inflationary outcomes, as in the OECD countries in the 1980s, but it remains questionable whether it was simply the central bank which was the reason for this and not deeper societal and institutional currents. At the same time, the slice of the economy which the central bank was deeply enmeshed with, namely the financial sector, showed signs of over-financialization far beyond what was needed for the transition. With the financial sector playing an outsize role in transformation, it also influenced the development of political institutions, both by supporting certain interests and by sowing the seeds for backlash against the policies which actually completed the transition.

A final point, implicit in our analysis previously but not explicitly mentioned, is that the adoption of independent central banks in Central and Eastern Europe (especially) as an institutional arrangement did not last long at all. For many countries which acceded to the EU, the adoption of the euro meant that an independent national central bank was jettisoned in favor of perhaps the most independent central bank in the world, the European Central Bank. As of mid-2019, the euro area was comprised of several formerly communist countries, including Estonia, Latvia, Lithuania, Slovakia, Slovenia, with other countries having (at various points) been keen to join the club (including Hungary in the early 2000s and the Czech Republic in the mid-to-late 2000s). This reality, and the conditions that come with EU accession regarding eventual euro membership, means that the independent national central bank model was perhaps only ever a waystation to ever greater integration. Exploring this state of affairs, and how it may have influenced institutional development, is another avenue for research, especially because (as Beukers 2013 notes) the ECB may be independent but it has exhibited powerful interventionist tendencies towards EU Member States. This is particularly relevant for understanding the rise of populism in Central Europe, given the ECB's embrace of negative interest rates and perpetual easy money.

As in Hartwell (2018a), the real questions going forward are as follows: Is an independent central bank the best institution for monetary governance? Were they a necessary evil to help stabilize the macroeconomic situation in transition which then should have been discarded? Are there political institutions necessary to keep them in check? The reluctance of the economics profession to debate these questions is puzzling, but necessary if we are to understand the political economy of central banking.

Note

1 Other strands of the financialization literature focus on the shift in risk-seeking, from long-term "patient" finance to shorter-term searches for yields (Crotty 2003).

References

Adolph, C., 2018. The missing politics of central banks. *PS: Political Science & Politics*, *51*(4), pp. 737–742.

Alesina, A. and Summers, L.H., 1993. Central bank independence and macroeconomic performance: some comparative evidence. *Journal of Money, Credit and Banking, 25*(2), pp. 151–162.

Arcand, J.L., Berkes, E. and Panizza, U., 2015. Too much finance? *Journal of Economic Growth, 20*(2), pp. 105–148.

Arnone, M., Laurens, B.J., Segalotto, J.F. and Sommer, M., 2009. Central bank autonomy: lessons from global trends. *IMF Staff Papers, 56*(2), pp. 263–296.

Barro, R.J. and Gordon, D.B., 1983. Rules, discretion and reputation in a model of monetary policy. *Journal of Monetary Economics, 12*(1), pp. 101–121.

Beukers, T., 2013. The new ECB and its relationship with the Eurozone member states: between central bank independence and central bank intervention. *Common Market Law Review, 50*(6), pp. 1579–1620.

Bohle, D., 2018. Mortgaging Europe's periphery. *Studies in Comparative International Development, 53*(2), pp. 196–217.

Carr, E.H., 1952. *The Bolshevik Revolution 1917–1923*, Vol. II. The Macmillan Company, New York.

Cochrane, J.P., 2013. *Bernanke: A Tenure of Failure*. Mises Institute Daily Article, viewed July 25, 2019, https://mises.org/library/bernanke-tenure-failure.

Crotty, J., 2003. The neoliberal paradox: the impact of destructive product market competition and impatient finance on nonfinancial corporations in the neoliberal era. *Review of Radical Political Economics, 35*(3), pp. 271–279.

Cukierman, A., Miller, G.P. and Neyapti, B., 2002. Central bank reform, liberalization and inflation in transition economies – an international perspective. *Journal of Monetary Economics, 49*(2), pp. 237–264.

Cukierman, A., Web, S.B. and Neyapti, B., 1992. Measuring the independence of central banks and its effect on policy outcomes. *The World Bank Economic Review, 6*(3), pp. 353–398.

de Haan, J. and Sturm, J.E., 1992. The case for central bank independence. *Banca Nazionale del Lavoro Quarterly Review, 45*(182), pp. 305–327.

Elster, J., 1994. Constitutional courts and central banks: suicide prevention or suicide pact. *East European Constitutional Review, 3*, pp. 66–71.

Epstein, R.A., 2005. Diverging effects of social learning and external incentives in polish central banking and agriculture. In F. Schimmelfennig and U. Sedelmeier (eds.), *The Europeanization of Central and Eastern Europe*. Cornell University Press, Ithaca, NY, pp. 178–198.

Epstein, R.A. and Johnson, J., 2010. Uneven integration: economic and monetary union in central and eastern Europe. *JCMS: Journal of Common Market Studies, 48*(5), pp. 1237–1260.

Gabor, D.V., 2011. *Central Banking and Financialization: A Romanian Account of How Eastern Europe became Subprime*. Palgrave Macmillan, Basingstoke.

Gabor, D.V., 2012. The road to financialization in central and Eastern Europe: the early policies and politics of stabilizing transition. *Review of Political Economy, 24*(2), pp. 227–249.

Garvy, G., 1977. The origins and evolution of the soviet banking system: an historical perspective. In *Money, Financial Flows, and Credit in the Soviet Union* . NBER, Cambridge, MA, pp. 13–35.

Gilman, M., 2010. *No Precedent, No Plan: Inside Russia's 1998 Default*. MIT Press, Cambridge, MA.

Hartwell, C.A., 2013. *Institutional Barriers in the Transition to Market: Examining Performance and Divergence in Transition Economies*. Palgrave Macmillan, Basingstoke.

Hartwell, C.A., 2018a. On the impossibility of central bank independence: four decades of time-(and intellectual) inconsistency. *Cambridge Journal of Economics*, *43*(1), pp. 61–84.

Hartwell, C.A., 2018b. The "Hierarchy of Institutions" reconsidered: monetary policy and its effect on the rule of law in interwar Poland. *Explorations in Economic History*, *68*, pp. 37–70.

Hartwell, C.A., 2019. Short waves in Hungary, 1923 and 1946: persistence, chaos, and (lack of) control. *Journal of Economic Behavior & Organization*, *163*, pp. 532–550.

Hasan, I. and Marton, K., 2003. Development and efficiency of the banking sector in a transitional economy: Hungarian experience. *Journal of Banking & Finance*, *27*(12), pp. 2249–2271.

Hayo, B., 1998. Inflation culture, central bank independence and price stability. *European Journal of Political Economy*, *14*(2), pp. 241–263.

Hochreiter, E. and Kowalski, T., 2000. Central banks in European emerging market economies in the 1990s. *PSL Quarterly Review*, *53*(212), pp. 45–70.

Jarábik, B. and Učeň, P., 2018. *What's Driving Czech Populism?* Carnegie Europe Strategic Europe Blog, viewed July 14, 2019, https://carnegieeurope.eu/strategiceurope/?fa=75228.

Johnson, J.E., 2006. Postcommunist central banks: a democratic deficit? *Journal of Democracy*, *17*(1), pp. 90–103.

Koch, E.B., 2007. *Challenges at the Bank for International Settlements: An Economist's (Re)View*. Springer, Berlin.

Kolodko, G.W., 1999. Transition to a market economy and sustained growth. Implications for the post-Washington consensus. *Communist and Post-Communist Studies*, *32*(3), pp. 233–261.

Koyama, M. and Johnson, B., 2015. Monetary stability and the rule of law. *Journal of Financial Stability*, *17*, pp. 46–58.

Kydland, F.E. and Prescott, E.C., 1977. Rules rather than discretion: the inconsistency of optimal plans. *Journal of Political Economy*, *85*(3), pp. 473–491.

Loungani, P. and Sheets, N., 1997. Central bank independence, inflation, and growth in transition economies. *Journal of Money, Credit, and Banking*, pp. 381–399.

Lybek, T., 1999. Central bank autonomy, and inflation and output performance in the Baltic states, Russia, and other countries of the former Soviet Union, 1995–1997. *Russian & East European Finance & Trade*, *35*(6), pp. 7–44.

Maliszewski, W.S., 2000. Central bank independence in transition economies. *Economics of Transition*, *8*(3), pp. 749–789.

Marcussen, M., 2005. Central banks on the move. *Journal of European Public Policy*, *12*(5), pp. 903–923.

Mas, I., 1995. Central bank independence: a critical view from a developing country perspective. *World Development*, *23*(10), pp. 1639–1652.

Pacek, A.C., 1994. Macroeconomic conditions and electoral politics in East Central Europe. *American Journal of Political Science*, pp. 723–744.

Rodlauer, M., 1995. The experience with IMF-supported reform programs in central and eastern Europe. *Journal of Comparative Economics*, *20*(1), pp. 95–115.

Rogoff, K., 1985. The optimal degree of commitment to an intermediate monetary target. *The Quarterly Journal of Economics*, *100*(4), pp. 1169–1189.

Schwödiauer, G., Komarov, V. and Akimova, I., 2006. *Central Bank Independence, Accountability and Transparency: The Case of Ukraine*. FEMM Working Paper Series, University of Magdeburg, No. 30, December.

Siklos, P., 1994. Central bank independence in the transitional economics: a preliminary investigation of Hungary, Poland, the Czech and Slovak republics. In J.P. Bonin and

I.P. Székely (eds.), *The Development and Reform of Financial Systems in Central and Eastern Europe*. Edward Elgar, New York, pp. 71–98.

Sochan, P., 1998. The banking system in Ukraine. *Russian & East European Finance and Trade*, *34*(3), pp. 70–93.

Stiglitz, J.E., 2000. Whither reform? ten years of transition. In B. Pleskovic and J.E. Stiglitz (eds.), *Annual World Bank Conference on Economic Development*. World Bank, Washington DC, pp. 27–56.

Wolf, N., 2008. Scylla and Charybdis. explaining Europe's exit from gold, January 1928–December 1936. *Explorations in Economic History*, *45*(4), pp. 383–401.

4 Building confidence 'on the ground'

Encounters between finance and the central banks of South Africa and Turkey

Ayca Zayim

Introduction

The decline of the Bretton Woods system in 1973 has accompanied the rise of a new global order, based on unregulated capital markets, flexible exchange rates, and capital mobility across national borders. The predominant view in scholarship has been that heightened capital mobility under financial globalization accentuates the structural power of finance and constrains the policy space of national economies (Mosley 2000; Winters 1996). Accordingly, policy decisions that threaten or diverge from the interests of finance often lead to disinvestment, capital outflows and even full-blown crises (Block 1977; Culpepper 2015; Culpepper & Reinke 2014; Kalaitzake 2018; Offe 1975; Woll 2016). Policymakers' anticipation of the repercussions of any divergence from financial interests further disciplines economic decision-making, keeping divergent policy choices off the agenda (Fairfield 2015; Hacker & Pierson 2002). These disciplinary pressures push monetary policymakers to conform to the financial community's policy preferences, especially in those emerging economies such as South Africa and Turkey which depend on foreign capital inflows.[1]

South Africa and Turkey are both upper middle-income G-20 economies (World Bank 2017). They feature in several emerging market (EM) bond and equity market indices, such as the Morgan Stanley Capital International EM Index and the J.P. Morgan EM Bond Index, as well as several EM funds. Despite their macroeconomic differences in terms of natural resource base, GDP composition, and unemployment, financiers treat South Africa and Turkey as 'substitutes' in portfolio allocation decisions. Over the last decade, both countries have received significant foreign portfolio investment. For instance, in 2015 the share of foreign ownership in local currency debt amounted to over 30% in South Africa and just under 20% in Turkey (IMF 2016). Between 2011 and 2014, foreigners held around 30–40% of local currency government debt securities in South Africa and around 15–25% in Turkey (ibid.). In the Johannesburg and Istanbul stock exchanges, foreign ownership of companies was similarly around 30–35% and 60–70%, respectively, during the 2011–2014 period (Ozel et al. 2015; Thomas 2017). Furthermore, both South Africa and Turkey have had current account deficits that render them dependent on foreign capital inflows. For instance, between 2011 and 2014 South Africa's current account deficit amounted to 2.2, 5.1, 5.8 and 5.1% of its GDP (World Bank 2018). In Turkey, it was 8.9, 5.5, 6.7 and 4.7%, respectively (ibid.). In 2013, they were each dubbed one of the 'Fragile 5' countries, a grouping first coined by a Morgan Stanley analyst to describe the financial vulnerability of five economies to capital flight – Brazil, India, Indonesia, South Africa, and Turkey (BBC 2013). The dependence of South Africa and Turkey on foreign investment heightens the structural power of finance vis-a-vis these economies, putting pressure on and constraining monetary policy in similar ways.

This chapter explores how the Central Bank of the Republic of Turkey (CBRT) and the South African Reserve Bank (SARB) respond to these pressures 'on the ground'. It demonstrates how the two central banks rely on private meetings and 'roadshows' to manage the financial community's expectations – commonly dubbed 'market expectations' – and promote investments in their economies. The chapter studies private meetings and roadshows as the institutionalized spaces of the global financial infrastructure where central bankers and members of the financial community encounter one another. During these encounters, central bankers gauge investor sentiment and market expectations. They deploy carefully constructed narratives about economic data, monetary policy, and central bank independence. While central bankers use these venues strategically to influence investment decisions in favor of their economies, the chapter finds these encounters to be a two-way street. Roadshows and meetings also provide financial market actors with an opportunity to express their policy preferences, receive assurances from central bankers regarding future monetary policy, and gain an 'edge' vis-à-vis their competitors by discerning less publicized aspects of monetary decision-making. The chapter suggests these venues to also be a medium where power is exercised by finance to influence monetary policymaking in emerging economies.

An extensive political economy literature examines the rise of independent central banks since the 1990s and establishes their pivotal role in maintaining investor confidence and negotiating national economies' access to global financial markets. Scholars argue that central bank independence embodies the policy preference of the financial community for low and stable inflation and prioritizes the interests of creditors over those of debtors and workers (Arestis & Malcolm 1998; Epstein & Yeldan 2009; Fourcade-Gourinchas & Babb 2002; Goodman 1991; Maman & Rosenhek 2011; Posen 1995). By pursuing monetary policies that are focused on price stability, independent central banks are argued to instill business confidence, signal creditworthiness to the financial community, and attract capital flows (Maxfield 1997).[2] Importantly, they fill the 'credibility deficit' of developing economies (Grabel 2003).

This chapter contributes to the scholarship in two ways. First, the chapter goes beyond an analysis of the institutionalized roles of central banks as 'guardians of price stability' and provides a sociological account of the concrete processes by which investor confidence is built and maintained 'on the ground' through in-person encounters between financiers and central bankers. Second, the chapter reveals the heterogeneity within the financial community, and by doing so, highlights how and why global financial institutions emerge as the key constituency of central banking in emerging economies. By demonstrating how the CBRT and the SARB are particularly attuned to the interests of global financial institutions, the chapter suggests that EM central banks might be constrained in tailoring monetary policy to address domestic policy concerns such as unemployment and, thus, might have a strained relationship with their governments.

The chapter draws from over 15 months of fieldwork in South Africa, Turkey and London. As a global finance center, London is unique in that it hosts several financial institutions that mediate global investments in South Africa and Turkey. During 2013–2014, I conducted over 130 interviews with central bank officials in South Africa and Turkey and financiers in South Africa, Turkey, and London. The interviewees include 41 former and then-current CBRT officials and 22 SARB officials. They are comprised of monetary policy committee (MPC) members, directors, and deputy directors of several departments, and researchers. Additionally, I interviewed 19 financiers in Johannesburg, 31 in Istanbul, and 21 in London. These interviewees were primarily the chief economists and strategists at so-called 'sell-side' institutions and fund managers at asset management companies. The interviews ranged from 50 minutes to 3 hours, and some were recorded. I transcribed all recorded interviews word-for-word and translated them into English. As is common in qualitative research, I used the inductive coding approach to identify recurring significant themes in the interview transcripts and field notes (Boyatzis 1998; Corbin & Strauss 1990; Thomas 2006). I organized these themes into over 100 nodes and child-nodes such as 'roadshows', 'credibility', and 'constraints on monetary policymaking' using NVivo. Inductive coding was particularly well-suited to this research area 'with limited [prior] knowledge' (Chandra & Shang 2019, p. 92), as it allowed me to build theory from raw data 'without the restraints imposed by structured methodologies' (Thomas 2006, p. 238).

The next section briefly discusses the key actors and relations in the global financial system. By tracing where investments originate and how they are mediated into emerging economies, it demonstrates how and why global financial institutions emerge as the key constituency of the CBRT and the SARB. The third section examines the encounters between the two central banks and finance. The last section concludes by discussing the implications of the study for central banking in emerging economies.

Global financial institutions as a key constituency of monetary policy

The buy side and the sell side

The global financial system can be divided into two main groups of financial actors that are colloquially known as the 'buy side' and the 'sell side'. Buy-side financial actors source and control investments in emerging economies and typically include EM investment funds (e.g. mutual funds, pension funds, hedge funds), wealthy individuals, and asset management companies (e.g. PIMCO and Aberdeen Asset Management). The sell side involves investment banks (which fulfill brokerage functions), like Goldman Sachs and J.P. Morgan, and other brokerage firms. While these institutions might have a separate asset management arm akin to buy-side institutions (Naqvi 2019), they traditionally provide brokerage and other financial services for the buy side. The sell side executes trade orders, buying and selling assets in secondary markets in light of buy-side institutions' portfolio allocation decisions. In return for executing these trade orders, sell-side institutions charge a commission. Moreover, sell-side institutions produce knowledge about different economies and publicize profitable investment strategies in daily, weekly, bi-weekly or monthly research reports. These reports publicize the 'house view' of each institution. While reports differ in scope, topic, detail, and the region or country they specialize in, a 'research' team including economists, analysts and strategists typically prepares these reports.

Despite their apparent differences, the financial community often treats EMs as an asset class and invests in them as a group (Naqvi 2019, p. 764). While this has, in large part, been driven by large buy-side institutions such as institutional investors, it has increasingly led to the use of common EM bond and equity market indices in investment decisions (ibid.). Most buy-side institutions 'benchmark their performance to an EM index, either by being active (trying to produce a higher yield than the index for their clients), or passive (mimicking the index exactly)' (Naqvi 2019, p. 765). Different from passive investors, active fund managers take 'active bets against the index', strategically altering the allocation of portfolios among countries in order to be able to outperform the chosen benchmark (interview, portfolio manager, November 2014, London). This requires them to acquire some knowledge about individual countries in the benchmark, thereby rendering the research services of sell-side institutions valuable. A portfolio manager at an asset management company in London explains:

> We have our in-house research, but a sell-side broker hires ten men for one market. They all have their specialized areas and regions, et cetera. You, on the other hand, oversee ten countries by yourself . . . so you rely on their 'expert opinion' at some point.
>
> (Interview, December 2014, London)

Another fund manager similarly notes, 'They can point out things which we're simply missing . . . Our team altogether covers seventy countries' (interview, portfolio manager, November 2014, London).

Buy-side institutions typically work with several rival sell-side institutions. The brokers provide different, and even competing, research reports, all contributing to portfolio allocation decisions (interview with a portfolio manager, December 2014, London). Governing vast amounts of capital, funds and asset management companies pick and choose the brokers they will place their trades with, thus exercising immense economic power vis-à-vis sell-side institutions. Because brokerage firms depend on buy-side institutions for commissions, they fiercely compete with each other for new clients. As a SARB official with financial sector experience admits, 'If you're on the sell side, your interest is first of all to grab a greater share of transactions' (interview, September 2014, Pretoria). This requires publicity and advertising, which stands in contrast to the experience of buy-side research teams whose job is to discreetly support portfolio managers with their analyses and forecasts.

Sell-side institutions – specifically their research and sales teams – employ several strategies geared toward expanding their client base. Sales teams make cold calls and 'wine and dine' with existing and potential clients (interview with a sales employee, October 2014, Istanbul). Both research and sales personnel go on 'roadshows' where they 'market themselves' to buy-side institutions (interview, sell-side economist, October 2014, London). For publicity, sell-side economists appear on business and finance TV channels and participate in surveys regularly conducted by financial service providers like Reuters, CNBC, and Bloomberg. Reflective of the unequal power dynamic between the buy side and the sell side, a fund manager in South Africa likens self-promotion within the sell side to 'wearing a bikini on the beach' and adds, '[The sell side] is essentially selling a product or idea. . . . Why are the surveys only for sell-side people? Because that's the way they advertise. There you go in your bikini!' (interview, September 2014, Johannesburg).

Monetary policy occupies a pivotal place in communication between buy-side and sell-side institutions. Monetary policy decisions have immediate effects on financial profits through changes in interest rates and financial asset prices. More importantly, however, because financial investment decisions are based on expectations about the future – including future monetary policy – financiers on both the buy side and the sell side go to great lengths to predict future monetary policy decisions. They become 'central bank watchers', attuned to any comment or news that pertains to monetary policy. In efforts to expand their client base, almost all sell-side institutions release research reports following an MPC meeting and briefing notes after events such as governor speeches (interview, sell-side strategist, June 2014, Istanbul). Analyzing existing central bank decisions and predicting new ones in the future become 'a tool to get more business' for the sell side. As a SARB official notes, 'It's a commercial imperative for the sell side to talk about what the central bank does and use it as a tool to try to get more business' (interview, September 2014, Pretoria). This 'commercial imperative' also pressures sell-side economists to seek meetings with high-level monetary policymakers. Brokers hope that these meetings will provide them with new insights to publicize about monetary policy or to privately share with their existing and potential clients, as one sell-side economist in Johannesburg elaborates:

> If you're on the sell-side, you have to be more visible in the market. . . .
> Even when there wasn't much to do, you go and see the central bank. You

are to hype up almost every comment that the governor makes. . . . The analysts [research teams] are under pressure to tell a story so that they can gain market share, so they can convince clients to make transactions with the desk.

(Interview, July 2014, Johannesburg)

As part of their services, sell-side institutions also arrange private meetings for their clients. These meetings sometimes include one or two investors, other times a larger group. Similar to brokers, buy-side institutions view these in-person meetings as crucial venues where they might gather new information from monetary policymakers:

They [funds] speak to me, but as a different source of information they come down directly and see the SARB. . . . If I have five investors here from offshore, and we go see the governor, that will spread like wildfire through the markets. . . . Then I can assure you, before we've even seen her, I've had five other clients that haven't come on the trip, sitting in their offices in New York or London, saying to me 'Can we have a call with you straight after you've seen the governor?' Just in case I got a bit of inside information, or hints, hawkish or dovish, that she's alluded to that hasn't been put in public forum. Because that's how they obviously then get an edge.

(Interview, sell-side economist, August 2014, Johannesburg)

Because these encounters potentially allow meeting participants to outperform their competitors, securing one-on-one meetings becomes a rat race among financiers – especially for brokers trying to cater to their clients. The following section unpacks why central bankers concede to these meetings.

Expectation management and global financial institutions

Since the late 1990s, central banks have adopted greater transparency and communication with the financial community and the general public. This emphasis on central bank communication and expectation management in the conduct of monetary policy has led to the rise of what has sometimes been called 'performative' (Wansleben 2018), 'communicative' (Braun 2018), or 'discursive' (Gabor & Jessop 2014) central banking. According to neoclassical economic theory, central bank communication is valuable because (rational) expectations serve as a 'transmission channel' of monetary policy. By allowing central banks to influence market expectations about future monetary policy and economic parameters, greater transparency and communication increases the effectiveness and efficiency of monetary policy decisions (Blinder et al. 2008; Woodford 2005).

In contrast to the theory of rational expectations in economics, sociological literature rejects the existence of a 'true' model of the economy. It views expectations as 'fictional' – that is, as 'imaginaries of future situations' that 'orient decision-making despite the incalculability of outcomes' (Beckert 2016, p. 9). In this framework, expectation management becomes an act of governing financial markets through coordinating economic agents' 'conventions' (cf. Keynes 1937, p. 216; Blyth 2003), 'fictional expectations' (Beckert 2016), or 'intersubjective expectations' (Hall 2009). Through expectation management, the central bank aims to discipline market expectations, instill investor confidence, and govern the economy (Abolafia 2010; Braun 2015; Nelson & Katzenstein 2014).

The sociological approach contends that fictional expectations have 'performative' effects and can engender self-fulfilling prophecies (Braun 2015; Callon 1998; MacKenzie 2006). Expectations are also political. As Beckert (2016) argues, economic actors have an incentive to influence the expectations of others; yet, they have differential capacity to do so. In financial markets, those actors with economic power can more successfully influence the expectations of others. Moreover, by doing so, these same actors can 'caus[e] the event anticipated in the fictional depiction to transpire' (ibid., p. 84), realizing their anticipated profits. Thus, the 'accurateness' of expectations is not predetermined or given by economic fundamentals. It rests on existing power relations in the global financial system.

Global financial institutions are powerful actors in this regard, and their power renders them the key constituency of EM central banks. Due to the immense volume of capital they govern, both global buy-side and sell-side institutions 'move' the markets, causing the changes in economic parameters they expect to transpire:

> Why do big desks at funds make so much money? Because they can make the market; they can force a market change via their operations . . . because of their size. . . . It is to some extent an insider–outsider business. It is a big player versus a small player. . . . Some players have bigger pricing power than others do.
>
> (Interview, SARB official, September 2014, Pretoria)

A domestic sell-side strategist in Istanbul vividly describes how the expectations of global institutions engender self-fulfilling prophecies. The strategist calls these global institutions 'foreigners' because they are typically based outside of emerging economies:

> In financial markets if I say 'this is salt' [pointing at pepper on the coffee table] and everyone else says 'this is salt', pepper becomes salt. . . . If foreigners govern the majority of capital inflows and outflows, it is they who eventually decide whether this is salt or pepper!
>
> (Interview, December 2013, Istanbul)

While global buy-side institutions influence economic parameters directly through their investment decisions, sell-side institutions typically do so indirectly by influencing the expectations and investment decisions of their buy-side clients. In particular, brokerage houses (e.g. Goldman Sachs, J.P. Morgan, Citi) in major financial centers such as London and New York influence the movement of capital flows, asset prices, and the value of national currencies as a result of their large client case. These institutions have a dispersed global sales network that increases their visibility and directs potential clients to the firm. They can also produce comparative research across different countries and assets, and execute orders involving multiple countries (interview, chief EM economist, November 2014, London) faster than their domestic counterparts (interview, portfolio manager, December 2014, London). Consequently, global brokers attract global investors with 'deep pockets' (interview, SARB official, September 2014, Pretoria). This accrues global brokers economic power and puts them at an advantage vis-à-vis their local counterparts (interview, sell-side strategist, December 2013, Istanbul). One sell-side economist in Istanbul elaborates on the power differential between local and global brokers, although he continues to 'essentialize' the economy:

> The big brokers determine the market. For instance, think of J.P. Morgan. Even if its economist makes a wrong call, the market will follow it. Because they have such market power! For instance, I might give a [market] call that is true. What I say is true but I cannot direct the markets to the same extent. There are instances when I do, but I cannot beat him.
>
> (Interview, May 2014, Istanbul)

The power of global institutions produces a self-reinforcing dynamic. Due to the 'accurateness' of their market calls, global brokers attract new clients. Due to their capacity to influence market parameters, global buy-side institutions govern increasingly large sums of money. A CBRT official acknowledges the structural power of global institutions, saying, 'Foreign investors govern big sums. Hence, their negotiation power is enormous. They set the rules. They leave when there's a change in policy [they don't like]' (interview, January 2014, Ankara).

As a result of their structural power, global buy- and sell-side institutions emerge as the key constituency of central banks in emerging economies and the main target of their communication efforts. As Naqvi (2019, p. 765) argues, 'even small changes in the portfolio allocation of large investors can have a major impact on EM prices due to the massive scale of their investments relative to small and illiquid EM financial markets'. Thus, the expectations of global institutions about an emerging economy and its central bank have tangible consequences. These expectations need to be governed or managed by monetary policymakers. The following section explores how the CBRT and the SARB use private meetings and roadshows in this endeavor.

Encounters between the financial community and central banks

The rise of index-based investment – that is, the performance of an investment is benchmarked against an EM index – accelerates competition among countries for foreign investment. In the words of an Istanbul-based sell-side economist, this investment approach leads countries like South Africa and Turkey that are in the same EM indices to be 'evaluated in the same basket, [to be] compared to each other, [to be] traded against each other' (interview, June 2014, Istanbul). In effect, countries become 'substitutes' for each other, easily replaceable by a different country in the same sub-group when they 'underperform':

> If the same investor invests in both Turkey and South Africa, and buys the one which markets itself better and sells the other one, then these countries affect each other from the viewpoint of a portfolio manager. An organic relationship emerges between the two countries . . . like substitute goods. . . . I think one's overperformance is almost tied to the other's underperformance.
>
> (Interview, fund manager, November 2014, London)

One CBRT official describes the relationship among countries as 'a race' (interview, May 2014, Ankara). In this competitive environment, central bankers (along with finance ministers) take center stage in connecting with the financial community, promoting business confidence and attracting foreign investment. A fund manager in London describes central bankers' efforts as 'selling their country':

> Central bankers compare themselves to others. The goal is to ensure capital inflows. Hot money, direct inflow, whatever. Actually, central banks sell their countries . . . Why is our country better? '*We're moving to a better point in terms of macroeconomic conditions and you will profit if you invest in our country*'. . . . I think there's certainly competition among them. I've personally observed it at meetings.
>
> (Interview, November 2014, London)

As part of their efforts to attract capital flows, central bankers frequently hold face-to-face meetings with financiers. A senior SARB official, in fact, said, 'We see them all the time' (interview, August 2014, Pretoria). One common type of meeting is a regularly scheduled meeting following each MPC decision. These meetings target the research teams of sell-side and buy-side institutions and constitute a venue where the central bank announces the committee's decision and answers any emergent questions. A second type of meeting is a private meeting between central bankers and financiers. These meetings are held upon request of sell- and buy-side institutions and typically occur at the central bank. Oftentimes, local and global brokers organize them for their buy-side clients and accompany them to the meetings.

While financiers view face-to-face, private meetings as particularly useful in gaining an 'edge' vis-à-vis their competitors, these meetings also provide central bankers with a unique opportunity to gauge investor sentiment and influence market expectations. A SARB official is adamant about utilizing these meetings for the central bank's own goals:

> It mustn't be a one-way street. . . . As a central banker, you must be able to ask questions about their business and what they do. You must try to gather intelligence. A qualitative type of information you can use.
>
> (Interview, August 2014, Pretoria)

Another SARB official from the Financial Markets department details what 'qualitative information' can entail:

> The focus [is] on market intelligence. You need to understand more about who thinks what, who does what, who owns what. It's not just a matter of saying bond yields sold off yesterday because of negative market sentiment. You're trying to find out who was the seller. Was it one big player who dumped a position, or is there a broad tendency for many of the fund managers to sell at the same time? One has a more serious implication than the other . . . for a central bank. The challenge is. . . [to] understand better what is the micro-structure of the market that is driving the visible price moves.
>
> (Interview, September 2014, Pretoria)

Providing information about market movements, these meetings allow central bankers to tailor their communication with the financial community and align market expectations with the central bank's policy goals.

Extensive interviews suggest that the CBRT and the SARB pay greater attention to global financial institutions in their communication efforts. Several financiers in London attested to their differential access to economic policymakers including central bankers. For instance, a London-based sell-side economist at a major investment bank argued that he could meet with then Deputy Prime Minister for Economic and Financial Affairs of Turkey in person because they 'move the market':

> How many locals can meet with Babacan? [Not many] . . . I do, but why? Not because I am Brian Smith [pseudonym], but because I represent the A Bank [pseudonym]. We have breakfast in New York together. Why? Because if portfolio investment is coming to Turkey, who brings it? J.P., HSBC, Bank of America et cetera . . . Of course, you're a better platform

for him. These institutions move the market. Don't think of it as individuals, think of it as institutions. They have to take you seriously, because of your access to funds.

(Interview, November 2014, London)

Another London-based economist at a different investment bank similarly claimed that global brokers have better 'ability' to access central banks although local financial institutions might have more frequent interactions with central bankers given their proximity:

I think they [locals] definitely have much more frequency but I think in many cases their ability is lower. You come to the country a few times a year, you can actually go in and get senior meetings much more easily. For instance, most local analysts are still quite shocked that I can meet the central bank governor anytime I like, basically on my own. And that doesn't happen to locals. . . . I think you're accorded that status as a foreigner because they know your client base . . . the media tracks a lot more what I'm saying.

(Interview, November 2014, London)

As global brokers influence the global flow of capital, even top-level central bankers including governors and deputy governors feel pressured to engage with them and their clients. The pressure is especially paramount on those central banks whose economies depend on foreign investment. A London strategist gave the example of Turkey, which had a large current account deficit in 2013 and 2014:

Turkey runs a current account deficit . . . so to that extent, the Turkish central bank needs to spend more time with foreign investors. And to a certain extent, the local investors are stuck; they're there. If the central bank doesn't want to see you, fine. What the hell are you going to do anyway?

(Interview, sell-side strategist, November 2014, London)

Therefore, private meetings with global investors and brokers serve as a critical venue where access to foreign capital is negotiated and secured.

In addition to holding private meetings at the central bank, high-level central bankers undertake roadshows in major financial centers such as London and New York. These roadshows occur a few times a year, typically with the participation of the central bank governor, members of the MPC, and the finance minister. During roadshows, policymakers interact with sell-side research teams and their buy-side clients during mostly private meetings. Similar to financiers' visits to central banks, meetings during roadshows aim to portray the domestic economy in a favorable light and attract foreign investment. The significance of roadshows in this endeavor was most clearly revealed in March 2017, when the South African President Jacob Zuma instructed the Finance Minister Pravin Gordhan to return immediately from a roadshow in the United Kingdom and the United States. Calling the finance minister from his meetings with financiers caused an uproar. The financial community further interpreted Zuma's decision as an indication of a future political climate less favorable to finance. Following the news, the South African rand dropped abruptly by 3.2% against the US dollar (Mkokeli 2017). CNBC (2017) reported, 'Investors see Gordhan as a symbol of stability'. Reuters (2017) quoted a strategist in London, saying, 'He [Gordhan] knows investors like him and he likes us', to demonstrate the close relationships between him and financiers. Bloomberg cited Business Leadership South Africa's announcement that 'The damage to investor sentiment to South Africa as a result of the president's decision should not be underestimated' and it highlighted South Africa's 'tattered' credibility and the threat of significant rand devaluation as a result of capital outflows (Mkokeli 2017).

In a sense, roadshows provide an institutional space within the global financial infrastructure in which countries compete with one another and do finance's bidding. These encounters provide financiers with an additional opportunity to express their policy preferences and receive assurances from policymakers about the direction of future monetary policy. A London-based sell-side economist boasts about his better understanding of monetary policy due to his access to high-level policymakers during roadshows:

> Due to our access to funds, we can see the flows, the next move in Turkey before it actually happens. Because [high-level policymakers] know about this, they come and talk to our clients. And because we're also there, we can also ask them questions. I think we're in a better position to understand high-level policymaking.
>
> (Interview, December 2014, London)

Alongside unmatched access to high-level central bankers, some London-based financiers claim that they also receive higher quality information during roadshows. They assert a difference between the quality of information gathered at meetings held locally and in London. Some attribute this difference to questions posed in each location, positing that the London-based community can craft questions that reveal greater insights about future central bank policy:

> The questions posed [locally] and in London are different. Here, the guy knows the central bank's policy, wants to learn about the Bank's reaction function, his scenarios are very different. For instance, he says, 'in this scenario what would the central bank do?' When faced with such a question, the governor cannot say 'I will not say a word'. . . . Here everyone is highly qualified, well-equipped . . . It's like a chess game. I think all meetings are different.
>
> (Interview, EM sell-side economist, November 2014, London)

Others concede the structural power of London-based brokers and their clients, suggesting that central bankers are more willing to share high quality information about monetary policy in order to attract global investors to their economies. A Turkish economist at a global brokerage house in London says:

> It's about the client base, the money that is governed. The capacity of a local bank or broker to change the $/TL is drastically different than that of a Goldman Sachs, a Deutsche Bank. Eh, because [central bankers] know this very well, there emerges a difference between the quality of knowledge they share when they're here versus in Turkey.
>
> (Interview, December 2014, London)

When I probe 'quality', he notes, 'Let's say more in-depth, the same knowledge but more quality knowledge'. Similarly, an Istanbul-based strategist at a domestic brokerage firm contrasts the information locals receive at the meetings with what he believes the CBRT shares with global funds and brokers in London:

> I've heard that individual meetings were held in London. When that happens, you [pointing to himself] fall way behind in the competition. . . . I believe the central bank gives important information at those meetings, because if they beat around the bush like they do at the meetings in Ankara, it won't work. Because you need capital inflows.
>
> (Interview, June 2014, Istanbul)

While it is empirically difficult to ascertain the degree to which central bankers share more or different quality information about future monetary policy during roadshows, it is notable that a widespread perception exists that they do so. Such a perception demonstrates unequal power relations in the financial system between global and local financial institutions as well as between global institutions and central banks.

The post-2008 financial crisis period has demonstrated the significance of these encounters for EM central banks like the CBRT and the SARB that are heavily constrained by the structural power of finance. During the 2010–2014 period, the structural power of finance vis-à-vis emerging economies changed due to factors that are exogenous to these economies. During the 2010–2013 period, emerging economies witnessed a massive surge in short-term, volatile capital inflows known as 'hot money'. Advanced economies' quantitative easing policies and consequent interest rate differentials between advanced and developing economies were the primary push factor behind these flows, altering both risk perceptions and investment decisions of financiers regarding EMs (Koepke 2018; Naqvi 2019). Between 2010 and 2013, emerging economies received over half of all global capital inflows (Sahay et al. 2014, p. 7). Eight emerging economies, including Turkey, received 90% of net capital flows (ibid.).[3]

Consistent with recent literature (Campello 2015), the surge in capital inflows reduced the structural power of finance vis-à-vis emerging economies and expanded their room to maneuver. A CBRT official candidly explained how the central bank was not fighting for foreign investment:

> There is zero bound [in advanced economies]. That's the beauty. . . . You're quite free. . . . Normally the central bank needs to get along with the markets because investors can go to someplace else. But in this context you don't want a lot of investment anyway. So, you're so much more comfortable. That provides a wonderful thing to dominate the market. You say, 'don't invest if you don't want to, I don't care'.
>
> (Interview, February 2014, Ankara)

In this context, the CBRT abolished private meetings soon after Erdem Basci, then-governor of the CBRT, came into office in April 2011. The CBRT limited its communication with the financial community to formal publications, governor speeches, and the regular 'economist meetings' following the announcement of each MPC decision. While the CBRT's justification was to equalize access to the central bank, interviewees – particularly those based in London – criticized the CBRT's decision. Some even viewed the CBRT as intentionally limiting its communication with the markets in order to discourage hot money flows. One financier in London said, 'My theory is that their communication policy was deliberately bad' (interview, sell-side economist, December 2014, London).

By contrast, the SARB continued to pursue an 'open door' policy and have private meetings with financiers. The SARB MPC members frequently met with sell-side economists and their buy-side clients at their request, being 'remarkably accessible', as another sell-side economist noted (interview, August 2014, Johannesburg). According to a London-based economist with close ties to the SARB MPC, these encounters equipped the SARB with 'a global market related view' because monetary policymakers were 'close to the banking sector, to markets, to international investors. They talk[ed] to international investors more than anyone else in the public sphere' (interview, November 2014, London). By not holding private meetings, Turkish policymakers simultaneously removed one of the spaces where major global financial institutions exercise power to influence monetary policymaking in emerging economies. For instance, a London-based economist complained about the absence or low level of such influence in the case of the CBRT, saying, 'I think the central bank [CBRT] lacks *sensitivity* to the markets' (interview, December 2014, London). Another London-based financier confirmed:

> When you have these big meetings like the CBRT, you [as a central bank] actually isolate yourself from the rest of the world. . . . Central bankers get influenced by some people they listen to.
>
> (Interview, sell-side strategist, December 2014, London)

However, the CBRT resumed private meetings increasingly after May 2013. On 22 May 2013, then-Chairman of the US Federal Reserve Bernanke indicated that the Fed could begin reducing the pace of monthly asset purchases under its QE3 program (Eichengreen & Gupta 2015). His testimony, which later came to be known as the 'tapering talk', altered global risk sentiment. As capital moved to 'safe haven assets' in advanced economies, emerging economies witnessed significant portfolio capital outflows (Rai & Suchanek 2014). Capital scarcity accentuated the structural power of finance, once again rendering private meetings and roadshows as critical venues where investment is sought from global institutions. Thus, the divergent practices of the CBRT and the SARB were short-lived, attesting to the importance of these encounters in accessing global capital.

Conclusion

This chapter has shown that the dependence of South Africa and Turkey on foreign investment heightens the structural power of finance and constrains the actions of the CBRT and the SARB in similar ways. Monetary policymakers in both economies operate under intense pressures to govern market expectations and maintain investor confidence, and are less likely to have room to tailor monetary policy to address domestic policy concerns such as unemployment.

Based on extensive interviews with central bankers and financiers, the chapter has examined how the CBRT and the SARB respond to these pressures on the ground. Both central banks utilize private meetings and roadshows strategically to negotiate their respective economies' access to global capital. The fact that the divergent practices of the CBRT and the SARB after the 2008 financial crisis were short-lived not only attests to the common pressures the two central banks operate under, but also reveals the importance of these encounters for emerging economies in accessing global capital. Demonstrating the heterogeneity within the financial community, the chapter has also revealed global buy- and sell-side institutions as the main constituency of the CBRT and the SARB.

Private meetings and roadshows primarily constitute a *response* by emerging economies to the constraints imposed by financial globalization. However, the chapter has also suggested these venues to also be a medium where power is exercised by finance to influence monetary policymaking. Private meetings provide financiers with an opportunity to express their policy preferences and receive assurances from central bankers regarding the direction of future monetary policy. Beyond serving as a mechanism of direct influence, these encounters are also likely to alter the mindset of monetary policymakers, or at a minimum, make them more attuned to the policy preferences of finance. Thus, private meetings and roadshows might constitute an additional mechanism that conditions monetary policymaking to favor the interests of finance over those of the government or non-financial groups.

This raises serious questions about central bank accountability and independence. The literature on the politics of central bank independence has long raised the concern that central bank independence depoliticizes monetary policy, thereby reducing the accountability of central banks to the public. It has also underlined that central bank independence entails independence from the government, but *not* from financial markets. Consistent with this literature, the chapter suggests that encounters between EM central banks and finance deepen the relations of monetary policymakers with financiers. These private encounters exclude non-financial groups as legitimate constituencies, while rendering the influence of finance in monetary policymaking invisible. In sum, private meetings and roadshows crystalize the unequal access of different societal groups to central banks. Making these encounters known is a first step toward unmasking how the power of finance shapes monetary policymaking in emerging economies.

Notes

1 The chapter uses the terms 'the financial community', 'financiers', 'finance' and 'financial (market) actors' interchangeably.
2 In the post-2008 financial crisis period, the mandates of several central banks have expanded, incorporating financial stability as a secondary or complementary objective. However, price stability continues to remain the primary objective of monetary policy in emerging economies.
3 These countries are Brazil, China, India, Indonesia, Mexico, Peru, Poland, and Turkey.

References

Abolafia, MY 2010, 'Narrative construction as sensemaking: how a central bank thinks', *Organization Studies*, vol. 31, pp. 349–367.

Arestis, P & Malcolm, CS 1998, *The political economy of central banking*, Edward Elgar, Northampton, MA.

BBC 2013, *The fragile five*, viewed 5 June 2018, www.bbc.com/news/business-24280172.

Beckert, J 2016, *Imagined futures: fictional expectations and capitalist dynamics*, Harvard University Press, Cambridge, MA.

Blinder, AS, Ehrmann, M, Fratzscher, M, De Haan, J & Jansen, DJ 2008, 'Central bank communication and monetary policy: a survey of theory and evidence', *Journal of Economic Literature*, vol. 46, pp. 910–945.

Block, F 1977, 'The ruling class does not rule: notes on the marxist theory of the state', *Socialist Revolution*, vol. 7, no. 3, pp. 6–28.

Blyth, M 2003, 'The political power of financial ideas: transparency, risk, and distribution in global finance', in J Kirshner (ed.) *Monetary orders: ambiguous economics, ubiquitous politics*, Cornell University Press, Ithaca, NY.

Boyatzis, RE 1998, *Transforming qualitative information: thematic analysis and code development*, Sage, London.

Braun, B 2015, 'Governing the future: the european central bank's expectation management during the great moderation', *Economy and Society*, vol. 44, pp. 367–391.

Braun, B 2018, 'Central bank planning: unconventional monetary policy and the price of bending the yield curve', in J Beckert & R Bronk (eds.) *Uncertain futures: imaginaries, narratives, and calculation in the economy*, Oxford University Press, Oxford.

Callon, M (ed.) 1998, *The laws of the markets*, Blackwell, Malden, MA.

Campello, D 2015, *Globalization and democracy: the politics of market discipline in Latin America*, Cambridge University Press, New York.

Chandra, Y & Shang, L (eds.) 2019, *Qualitative research using R: a systematic approach*, viewed 27 November 2019, https://link.springer.com/chapter/10.1007%2F978-981-13-3170-1_8.

CNBC 2017, *South Africa's Zuma recalls Gordhan from international roadshow, rand falls*, 27 March, viewed 6 June 2018, www.cnbc.com/2017/03/27/south-africas-zuma-recalls-gordhan-from-international-roadshow.html.

Corbin, J & Strauss, A 1990, 'Grounded theory research: procedures, canons and evaluative criteria', *Zeitschrift für Soziologie*, vol. 19, no.6, pp. 418–427.

Culpepper, PD 2015, 'Structural power and political science in the post-crisis era', *Business and Politics*, vol. 17, no. 3, pp. 391–409.

Culpepper, PD & Reinke, R 2014, 'Structural power and bank bailouts in the United Kingdom and the United States', *Politics & Society*, vol. 42, no. 4, pp. 427–454.

Eichengreen, B & Gupta, P 2015, 'Tapering talk: the impact of expectations of reduced federal reserve security purchases on emerging markets', *Emerging Markets Review*, vol. 25, no. December, pp. 1–15.

Epstein, G & Yeldan, E (eds.) 2009, *Beyond inflation targeting: assessing the impacts and policy alternatives*. Edward Elgar, Northampton, MA.

Fairfield, T 2015, 'Structural power in comparative political economy: perspectives from policy formulation in Latin America', *Business and Politics*, vol. 17, no. 3, pp. 411–441.

Fourcade-Gourinchas, M & Babb, SL 2002, 'The rebirth of the liberal creed: paths to neo-liberalism in four countries', *American Journal of Sociology*, vol. 108, no. 3, pp. 533–579.

Gabor, D & Jessop, B 2014, 'Mark my words: discursive central banking in crisis', in B Jessop, B Young & C Scherrer (eds.) *Financial cultures and crisis dynamics*, Routledge, London.

Goodman, JG 1991, 'The politics of central bank independence', *Comparative Politics*, vol. 23, pp. 329–349.

Grabel, I 2003, 'Ideology, power, and the rise of independent monetary institutions in emerging economies', in J Kirshner (ed.) *Monetary orders: ambiguous economics, ubiquitous politics*, Cornell University Press, Ithaca, NY.

Hacker, JS & Pierson, P 2002, 'Business power and social policy: employers and the formation of the american welfare state', *Politics & Society*, vol. 30, no. 2, pp. 277–325.

Hall, RB 2009, *Central banking as global governance: constructing financial credibility*, Cambridge University Press, Cambridge.

IMF 2016, 'Development of local currency bond markets overview of recent developments and key themes', *Staff Note for the G20 IFAWG*, viewed 4 June 2016, www.imf.org/external/np/g20/pdf/2016/121416.pdf.

Kalaitzake, M 2018, 'Central banking and financial political power: an investigation into the European Central Bank', *Competition & Change*, doi:10.1177/1024529418812690.

Keynes, JM 1937, 'The general theory of employment', *The Quarterly Journal of Economics*, vol. 51, pp. 209–223.

Koepke, R 2018, 'FED policy expectations and portfolio flows to emerging markets', *Journal of International Financial Markets, Institutions and Money*, vol. 55, no. July, pp. 170–194.

MacKenzie, DA 2006, *An engine, not a camera: how financial models shape markets*, MIT Press, Cambridge, MA.

Maman, D & Rosenhek, Z 2011, *The Israeli central bank: political economy, global logics and local actors*, Routledge, New York.

Maxfield, S 1997, *Gatekeepers of growth the international political economy of central banking in developing countries*, Princeton University Press, Princeton.

Mkokeli, S 2017, 'Zuma pounds South Africa's credibility by ordering gordhan home', *Bloomberg*, 27 March, viewed 6 June 2018, www.bloomberg.com/news/articles/2017-03-27/zuma-said-to-order-gordhan-to-return-from-south-african-roadshow.

Mosley, L 2000, 'Room to move: international financial markets and national welfare states', *International Organization*, vol. 54, no. 4, pp. 737–773.

Naqvi, N 2019, 'Manias, panics and crashes in emerging markets: an empirical investigation of the post-2008 crisis period', *New Political Economy*, vol. 24, no. 6, pp. 759–779.

Nelson, S & Katzenstein, P 2014, 'Uncertainty, risk, and the financial crisis of 2008', *International Organization*, vol. 68, pp. 361–392.

Offe, C 1975, 'The capitalist state and the problem of policy formation', in LN Lindberg, R Alford, C Crouch & C Offe (eds.) *Stress and contradiction in contemporary capitalism*, Heath, Lexington, DC.

Ozel, O, Ozmen, U & Yilmaz, E 2015, 'Importance of foreign ownership and staggered adjustment of capital outflows', *CBRT Working Papers*, vol. 15/31, viewed 11 June 2017, https://ideas.repec.org/p/tcb/wpaper/1531.html.

Posen, AS 1995, 'Declarations are not enough: financial sector sources of central bank independence', *NBER Macroeconomics Annual*, vol. 10, pp. 253–274.

Rai, V & Suchanek, L 2014, 'The effect of the federal reserve's tapering announcements on emerging markets', *Bank of Canada Working Paper*, vol. 2014–50, viewed 10 June 2018, www.aeaweb.org/conference/2015/retrieve.php?pdfid=838.

Reuters 2017, *South Africa's zuma recalls Gordhan from international roadshow, rand falls*, viewed 6 June 2018, www.reuters.com/article/us-safrica-gordhan/south-africas-zuma-recalls-gordhan-from-international-roadshow-rand-falls-idUSKBN16Y0XM.

Sahay, R, Arora, V, Arvanitis, T, Faruqee, H & N'Diaye, P 2014, *IMF staff discussion note: emerging market volatility lessons from the taper tantrum*, viewed 7 June 2018, www.imf.org/external/pubs/ft/sdn/2014/sdn1409.pdf.

Thomas, DR 2006, 'A general inductive approach for analyzing qualitative evaluation data', *American Journal of Evaluation*, vol. 27, no. 2, pp. 237–246.

Thomas, L 2017, *Ownership of JSE-listed companies: research report for national treasury*, viewed 4 June 2018, www.treasury.gov.za/comm_media/press/2017/2017100301%20Ownership%20monitor%20-%20Sept%202017.pdf.

Wansleben, L 2018, 'How expectations became governable: institutional change and the performative power of central banks', *Theory and Society*, vol. 47, pp. 773–803.

Winters, JA 1996, *Power in motion: capital mobility and the indonesian state*, Cornell University Press, Ithaca, NY.

Woodford, M 2005, 'Central bank communication and policy effectiveness', *NBER Working Paper, No. 11898*, National Bureau of Economic Research, Cambridge.

Woll, C 2016, 'Politics in the interest of capital: a not-so-organized combat', *Politics & Society*, vol. 44, pp. 373–391.

World Bank 2017, *World Bank country and lending groups*, viewed 5 June 2018, https://datahelpdesk.worldbank.org/knowledgebase/articles/906519-world-bank-country-and-lending-groups.

World Bank 2018, *World development indicators: current account balance (% GDP)*, viewed 5 June 2018, http://databank.worldbank.org/data/home.aspx.

5 The impact of political-technocratic consensus on institutional stability and change

Monetary and financial governance in Argentina and Chile

Max Nagel

Introduction

The financial crisis 2007 was a forceful reminder that Western economies are not immune against adverse impacts originating from the international monetary and financial system. Insufficient microprudential regulation paired with monetary policy with a blind eye to financial instability was fueling the buildup of financial risks in the run-up to the crisis. Also emerging market and developing economies experienced a range of similar financial crises in the second half of the 20th century. Why could some of them successfully adjust their monetary and financial governance regime[1] to prevent a repetition, such as Chile and South Korea, while others like Argentina struggled to do so?

A twofold argument to help explain this divergence is advanced in this chapter. The presence of a political-technocratic consensus regarding objectives and conduct of monetary and financial policies is crucial for a stable governance regime. A consensus that is based on a pragmatic governance regime entailing the ability for making continuous adjustments against the background of a rapidly changing international monetary and financial system is more likely to prevent crises (see Grabel [2018]). It leads to relative institutional stability that is characterized by incremental change as opposed to punctuated change occurring under orthodox governance regimes.

A political-technocratic consensus is here understood as the alignment of central bankers and politicians regarding what they perceive as the best monetary and financial governance regime for the country. It results in a stabilization of their relation and a depoliticization of this policy issue. The political-technocratic consensus is therefore the flip-side of depoliticization, which is "the process of placing at one remove the political character of decision-making" (Burnham 2001, p. 128). It leads to a lock-in and a lack of potential of agency, choice, and political deliberation regarding the depoliticized policy issues (see Hay [2007]). To operationalize this political-technocratic consensus, the non-interference of the government in the duration of the central bank governor's term in office as well as the continuity in the academic formation of central bank governors since 1970 are analyzed to check for persistence in monetary and financial governance. It is expected that a consensus leads to non-interference into policymaking, no matter from which political spectrum the government originated, and a continuity in the academic formation of central bankers.

For making the case, a comparative case study of Chile and Argentina is conducted. Both countries followed similar trajectories of monetary and financial governance after World War II. First, structuralist economic ideas and import-substituting industrialization (ISI) shaped a state-based form of governance that was characterized by channeling financial flows to sectors that were considered to be beneficial for national economic development. Central banks were not independent and took orders to direct credit allocation and finance the government. In the early 1970s, brutal dictatorships in Argentina and Chile adopted orthodox neoliberal governance regimes, entailing flexibilization of financial flows and limiting the use of monetary policy (Zahler 1983). The 1982 debt crisis in Chile interrupted this common trajectory. Pinochet's dictatorship turned away from the market-led governance regime and changed to a pragmatic, hands-on approach that tightly regulated domestic and international financial flows. Simultaneously, monetary policy was allowed to be used more flexibly to support economic growth. Although Argentina experienced a range of similar financial crises, it could not adopt pragmatic governance regime that effectively regulates financial flows such as in Chile. Instead, constant disruptive change of rotating orthodox governance regimes, primarily neoliberal (1976–2001, 2015–9) but also nationalist-developmentalist (2007–2015), coincided with frequent eruptions of financial crises.

Chile adopted a pragmatic governance regime in the second half of Pinochet's dictatorship (1982–90) which is based on a political-technocratic consensus that was left almost unchanged during and after the democratic transition in 1990. Argentina could never reach such a consensus regarding monetary and financial governance during its civic–military dictatorship (1976–1983) and thereafter. Monetary and financial policy was continuously a politically contested issue with politicians and central bankers divided regarding the question of how to optimize the governance regime. A brief exception is Néstor Kirchner's presidency 2001–2007 that aimed at achieving a compromise between neoliberal and nationalist-developmentalist governance but was not transformed into a consensus. Monetary policy focused primarily on price stability, but with an implicit goal to control exchange rate movements to prevent financial instabilities and to promote economic growth. Simultaneously, financial regulation was tightened against the backdrop of the 2001–2 crisis.[2]

Considering the substance of the governance regimes, Chile's successful post-1982 regime is based on a macro-financial approach. It entails that monetary and financial policies are interconnected and need to be coordinated to safeguard the stability of the monetary and financial system. Financial markets are not perceived as self-stabilizing, making the regulation of financial flows necessary. Also the effect of monetary policy on financial stability is to be taken into account. Argentina, in contrast, repeatedly embraced regimes that entrusted governance largely to financial markets. This went so far that active monetary policy was suspended during the *Convertibilidad*, the 1:1 peg of the peso to the US dollar, while domestic and international financial flows were deregulated (1991–2002). Only during Cristina Kirchner's Presidency (2007–2015), the state was actively shaping monetary and financial policies, resulting in frictions with financial investors.

After discussing contributions of the literature, a comparative study of monetary and financial governance regimes in Chile and Argentina since the 1970s is conducted. Particular emphasis is put on the stability of governance regimes, the effect that political-technocratic consensus plays has on it, and what it can tell us about institutional change more broadly. The chapter concludes that convergence of governance regimes will be limited, particularly between Western and non–Western countries.

The missing link between monetary and financial governance

To what extent can the existing literature explain diverging trajectories of monetary and financial governance regimes? By analyzing these two realms largely isolated from each other, the effects of their interactions on the stability of the monetary and financial system as a whole and the consequential implication for the stability and change of governance regimes are largely left out. This shortcoming can be approached by offering an integrated perspective that identifies governance regimes and their trajectory as distinct outcomes of the relation between politicians and central bankers as well as the substance of knowledge that informs them.

On the one hand, the literature on monetary governance is primarily interested in the convergence of regimes across time and space. Institutionalist explanations focus on the convergence of central banks and monetary policy across cases, given isomorphic mechanisms (Polillo & Guillen 2005), the role of global financial markets (Maxfield 1997), cultural processes (McNamara 2002), or as a strategy for dictators to tie the hands of incoming democratic governments (Boylan 2001). From this perspective it is puzzling why there is a delay of convergence across cases.[3] Other contributions do identify divergences but do not offer explanations (for example, Marcussen 2005). Less effort is invested for explaining the variety of governance regimes. This is to a certain extent counterintuitive, given that there are new contributions on the politics of monetary policy after the recent financial crisis 2007, indicating how country-specific contingencies drive divergence (e.g., Moschella [2015]; Nagel and Thiemann [2019]).

The analysis of variety, on the other hand, is prominent in the literature on financial governance. Contributions identify interactions on and between domestic, international, and transnational levels as drivers of divergence (Moschella & Tsingou 2013b; Helleiner & Pagliari 2011; Thiemann 2018). The shift from microprudential to macroprudential regimes after 2007 received particular attention in the literature (Baker 2013; Moschella & Tsingou 2013a). Nevertheless, less focus is put on the question why countries like Chile and South Korea undertook a similar change already before the financial crisis 2007.

The benefit from accounting for the interactions between monetary and financial governance for explaining stability and success of governance regimes is that this integrated approach can explain the failure of governance regimes that cannot be identified by isolated analyses. When a consensus among central bankers and politicians entailing an integrative perspective on monetary and financial governance emerges, the regime can stabilize over time. However, it would be misleading to claim that there were no contributions entailing an integrated perspective before 2007. Particularly, the structuralist tradition in Latin American, which originated under Raul Prebisch's United Nations Economic Commission for Latin America and the Caribbean in the middle of the 20th century (Prebisch 1962; O'Connell 2001), accounts for the politics of and interactions between monetary and financial governance.[4] Although there exists a lack regarding attempts to explain the variety aside from the division between core and periphery, the structuralists pointed out early why a convergence of monetary and financial governance to Western standards could lead to crises and hinder economic development in less economically developed countries.

To explain the existing variety of monetary and financial governance regimes across cases and their success and failure, this chapter adopts a socio–historical approach (Mannheim 1959). Central to it is the understanding that knowledge which informs policymaking is determined by contingent social structures and processes at given points in time and space, delimiting convergence over time. From this venture point, the analysis of the conditions (the relation between politicians and central bankers and the substance of the knowledge they draw on) under which knowledge diffuses into governance regimes becomes focal for explaining the stability and success of the governance regime. Given the contingency of the social world, regimes drawing on orthodox knowledge are expected to be more susceptible to crisis and therefore will be more frequently changed. Those building on pragmatic knowledge are more self–reflective and avoid using taken-for-granted truths regarding the potential of either state or markets to solve governance problems. The flexibility gained from this pragmatic approach makes it easier to constantly adjust the governance regime to an evolving environment, particularly due to developments on financial markets.

Argentina's struggle for stability and Chile's success story

First, a brief historical overview of monetary and financial governance since the 1970s is presented for Argentina and Chile, followed by a more detailed account how both the relation between central bankers and politicians and knowledge they drew on at specific times was molded into governance regimes. The observed regimes are classified into state-based (the state as the main actor to solve governance problems), market-based (the market as the main actor to solve governance problems), and pragmatic ones (a middle ground between market and state-based regimes).

Argentina

A range of financial crises shook the Argentinian economic development since the 1970s, including the 1975 Rodrigazo crisis, the 1981 failure of Tablita plan, the 1982 exchange rate crisis, the 1989 hyperinflation/failure of Austral plan, the 1995 Tequila crisis and the 2001–2002 failure of the 1:1 peg of the peso to the US dollar and the subsequent default on sovereign debt (Frenkel 2002; Damill et al. 2016). Crises responses share the common characteristic that they are part of different attempts to find a monetary and financial governance regime that protects against the destabilizing impact from the international monetary and financial system. A range of governance regimes were implemented drawing on knowledge that was available at the specific time. Policymakers recurred repeatedly to orthodox ad-hoc solutions to adjust the governance regime, creating thereby the foundation for the subsequent crisis. Only in the period between 2003 and 2007, a time of monetary and financial stability is identified that coincides with the pragmatic governance regime implemented under Néstor Kirchner's government. N. Kirchner aimed at finding a compromise between those favoring more state interventions on the one hand and those favoring market solutions on the other. Cristina Kirchner, the subsequent president, discontinued this compromise approach and conducted an orthodox turn towards nationalist-developmentalism, including an increasing instrumentalization of the Central Bank of the Argentine Republic (BCRA) for political objectives that led to conflicts with global investors and stricter regulation of financial flows. A renewed turn to orthodox neoliberalism in 2015 by the incoming Macri government has promoted the renewed buildup of foreign debt, dismantling financial regulation and liberalizing the exchange rate.

Monetary and financial governance during the military dictatorship 1976–1983 (*Proceso de Reorganización Nacional*) followed the lead of Martínez de Hoz, Minister of Economy, who promoted anti-inflationary, exchange rate focused monetary policy and financial liberalization (Undurraga 2015; Calvo 1986). After the end of the dictatorship in 1983, the Unión Cívica Radical under the presidency of Raúl Alfonsín initially returned to developmentalist policies. But having to deal with the debt problem from the preceding government as well as renewed inflationary pressures, the government partly gave in to pressure by the International Monetary Fund to conduct neoliberal reforms that were combined with heterodox measures to fight inflation under the Austral Plan 1985 and Spring Plan 1988 (Veigel 2009, p. 150). Monetary policy remained tight and passive, with the high interest rates fueling renewed debt problems, resulting in a renewed hyperinflation in 1989/90.

During Carlos Menem's government (1989–1999), the neoliberal orientation of the governance regime increased. It was based on a 1:1 parity to the US dollar which effectively ended active monetary policy while domestic and international financial flows were liberalized. Inflation rates were reduced, but its flip side was a surge in foreign debt and increasing influence of global investors that could sanction unwanted policy decisions by reversing financial flows to Argentina. Given the exchange rate peg and fiscal imbalances in the late 1990s, the only perceived option to increase the competitiveness of Argentinian economy was to induce a deflation. This led to a further destabilization of the monetary and financial system, that was already under pressure due to capital outflows (Damill et al. 2016). The outcome was the severe crisis starting in 1998 and reaching its climax in December 2001 (Frenkel 2002).

The 1:1 peg was supposed to strictly delimit the politics of monetary policy by delegating it to financial markets (Expert interview, 20 September 2018) but it showed how the combination with financial liberalization endangered the stability of the system. The government believed that the peg could be sustained without a deterioration of monetary and financial stability when minimizing both the role of central bankers and politicians. High exit costs were to lend credibility to the governance regime (Expert interview, 20 September 2018) but the inherent risk that this regime may fail was not anticipated.

Pragmatic monetary and financial governance characterized a brief period of monetary and financial stability between 2003 and 2007, coinciding with the government of Néstor Kirchner. While reversing some of Menem's neoliberal policies, the aim was not to fundamentally overturn them. Instead, regulations were introduced that induce financial investors to conduct productive investments and thereby to foster economic development, resulting in an approach coined neo-developmentalism (see Wylde [2011] and Gezmis [2017]). The logic of market credibility informed monetary and financial governance, resulting in the appointment of Martín Redrado as the central bank governor in 2004 who, as a former investor, was recognized among financial actors (see Redrado [2010], p. 33). Monetary policy was not as restricted as during the 1:1 peg, although it remained largely passive with a focus on price stability. Exchange rate interventions and the buildup of foreign exchange reserves were introduced not only to support the stability of the monetary and financial system but also to sustain the core of an export-led growth strategy under the Stable and Competitive Real Exchange Rate (SCRER) (Frenkel & Rapetti 2007; Pesce 2008). At the same time, financial regulations were strengthened based on the 2001–2 crisis experience, including the reduction of currency mismatches (2003), the regulation of short-term capital flows (2005) and the implementation of capital controls (2007, 2011) (Damill et al. 2016; interview with former BCRA policymaker, 19 September 2018).

N. Kirchner's approach to monetary and financial governance was pragmatic and oriented towards a compromise between interests of global investors on the one hand and developmentalists on the other. This changed when Cristina Fernández de Kirchner took up the presidency as she stopped to continue the politics of compromise (Wylde 2016; Gezmis 2017), thereby diminishing the possibility for the stabilization of a political-technocratic consensus. She took up the presidency in 2007 and confirmed central bank governor Redrado in the same year. Nevertheless, their relationship soon deteriorated due to conflicting positions concerning the use of exchange reserves for the payment of foreign debt, which led Redrado to leave office in 2010 (Redrado 2010). A central reason for the appointment of his successor, Mercedes Marcó del Pont, was her commitment to support the use of reserves for political purposes (interview with former BCRA policymaker, 19 September 2018). Monetary policy was to be used more actively for national goals, qualifying the approach of her predecessor. Price stability was subordinated to promote the growth of demand (Damill et al. 2015). International financial flows were further regulated, including currency controls that were active from 2011 until the takeover of Macri as new president in 2015 (ibid.).

A major achievement during C. Kirchner's presidency was the introduction of a new central bank charter (Carta Orgánica) in 2012, although the idea for this dates back to 2005 (interview with former BCRA policymaker, 19 September 2018). By adopting these new statutes, monetary policy became more flexible and shifted the focus on supporting economic development.[5] This charter led to coordinated efforts with other state agencies that define financial regulation and economic policy (Vanoli 2018). It included multiple objectives which aimed to promote national development and put a temporary end to the self-regulation of capital markets. At the same time, the introduction of the new charter reflects an increased use of monetary policy for political objectives over the course of the 2000s (interview with former BCRA policymaker, 19 September 2018). It allows for more space for government financing, including the selling of reserves but also resulted in inflationary tendencies and the buildup of debt (expert interview, 14 September 2018).[6]

The 2015 election of Macri as the new president mirrors a renewed turn towards orthodox neoliberal governance regime. Financial regulations introduced by the two previous governments were reversed, including the immediate discontinuation of capital controls, which since then led to a doubling of foreign debt (see Vanoli [2018] and INDEC [2019]). A return to price-stability focused, passive monetary policy has accompanied this change, resulting in a return of a market-based governance regime.[7]

Chile

Chile, like Argentina, largely adhered to import-substituting industrialization (ISI) characterized by a state-led monetary and financial governance regime during the post–World War II period.[8] Allende's orthodox socialist turn in the early 1970s, entailing strong restrictions of capital account movements, as well as active credit allocation and unsustainable use of expansionary fiscal policy, coincided with a large current account deficit, hyperinflation that turned into public unrest. What followed was Pinochet's coup d'état in 1973 and a military dictatorship that lasted until 1990. Since then, Chile's trajectory of its monetary and financial governance regime did not follow a straight-forward path (see Ffrench-Davis [2010] and Caputo and Saravia [2018]). Orthodox neoliberalism, as informed by the infamous Chicago Boys, was directly informative for monetary and financial governance only in the first half of Pinochet's dictatorship. The 1982 debt crisis led to a punctuated change towards a pragmatic governance regime that allowed for countercyclical monetary policy and a relatively tight regulation of the financial system, particularly of international capital flows. Macro-financial knowledge that informed this pragmatic regime was shaped by the 1982 debt crisis and has been maintained until today (Expert interview, 9 October 2018). Even though economic and social policies were adjusted to counter economic and social inequalities, the transition to democracy in 1990 only led to small adjustments of monetary and financial governance. Contestations concerning this issue were missing. Instead, the dictatorship was able to institutionalize a political-technocratic consensus that did not allow for interference by the incoming democratic government to monetary and financial governance, not only institutionally as identified in the literature[9] but also ideologically. In the late 1990s, experts at the Chilean central bank increasingly pushed for orthodox neoliberal policy reforms, resulting in the flexibilization of the exchange rate regime in 1999 and capital account liberalization in 2001, gradually undermining the political-technocratic consensus.

In the first half of Pinochet's dictatorship, orthodox monetarist ideas were inserted by the Chicago Boys to guide monetary and financial governance. The dollar-peg and price stability orientation made monetary policy largely passive. Together with the liberalization of the financial system, first internally and then 1979 externally, this initially resulted in lower inflation rates, but it also induced a rapid buildup of foreign debt (Zahler 1983). In combination with a highly appreciated exchange rate this resulted in a massive economic and social crisis in 1982 when interest rates in the United States were increased and debt payments could not any longer be serviced (see Ffrench-Davis [2016]).

This crisis experience resulted in a swift and pragmatic turn away from the orthodox neoliberal governance regime. Financial regulations, including restrictions of international (short-term) capital flows and supervision with a systemic (macro-prudential) perspective, were combined with active, countercyclical monetary policy and exchange rate interventions to safeguard the stability of the monetary and financial system (see Ffrench-Davis [2010], Redrado [2010, p. 165], and Cox Edwards and Edwards [1992]).

Although plans for making the Chilean central bank independent to decrease political guidance of monetary policy existed already during the first half of Pinochet's dictatorship,[10] Pinochet was not convinced by this idea. As Boylan (2001) convincingly shows, it was the motivation to prevent the incoming democratic government from actively influencing monetary and financial governance leading to this outcome. As a corollary, expectations by global investors for less state interventions in financial markets could be satisfied, while pragmatic financial regulation prevented the buildup of financial risks such as happened in Argentina in the 1990s. This approach to monetary and financial governance is anchored in the central bank's constitutional mandate from 1989 which states that the central bank should "look after the stability of the currency and the normal functioning of internal and external payment systems," thereby explicitly framing monetary and financial stability jointly.

The incoming democratically elected government under President Aylwin (1990–4) reversed many policies of the dictatorship to reduce social and economic inequalities in Chile. At the same time, there was a puzzling continuity of monetary and financial governance (see for example Cox Edwards and Edwards [1992]). Alejandro Foxley, finance minister from 1990 to 1994 emphasized that the government will continue economic policies that were inserted by Pinochet, although strongly criticizing them before (ibid.). Montecinos (1998) traces a convergence of politicians and technocrats that smoothed out the transition by delimiting available policy options (see also Puryear [1994]). There was an adaption of the incoming democratic government to the established governance regime, after having called for more fundamental reforms of Pinochet's monetary and financial governance before 1990. With this being said, there was a punctual strengthening of countercyclical policies, particularly the introduction of unremunerated reserve requirements (1991–1998) as well as coordinated efforts between the Ministry of Finance and the Central Bank of Chile (CBC) to further regulate a surge in financial inflows in the first half of the 1990s. These were however offset by subsequent neoliberal reforms in the late 1990s and early 2000s (Ffrench-Davis 2016).

Since then, the general tendency is pointing to more market-based monetary and financial governance. Already since 1992 there was a gradual flexibilization of the exchange rate regime (Agosin & Ffrench-Davis 2001). In the second half of the 1990s and early 2000s, there was an incremental turn towards more neoliberal policies, driven by the CBC's aim for flexibilization of the exchange rate regime as well as the removal of barriers to capital account transactions (Ffrench-Davis 2016). Inflation targeting was already partially adopted in 1991, monetary policy was largely reduced to setting overnight interest rates in 1996/7, the exchange rate band was dropped in 1999 and the capital account was further liberalized in 2001 (see Carriere-Swallow et al. [2013] and Calvo and Mendoza [1999]). Also the institutionalization of the fiscal rule in 2000 to strengthen its coordination with monetary policy may hinder the use of countercyclical fiscal policies in times of crisis. The incremental turn towards neoliberalism was promoted by the CBC, as the combination of its increased independence with an inflow of US-educated economists as staff members since the 1980s (interview with former CBC policymaker II, 5 October 2018; expert interview, 9 October 2018) and its increased self-management promoted the gradual distancing of the CBC from the political-technocratic consensus (Expert interview, 4 October 2018). Nevertheless, there are still tight financial regulations in place which were updated after the Asia crisis 1997 (see Pesce [2008] and Marshall [2000]). In spite of the incremental changes towards a more neoliberal governance regime, (macro-)prudential financial regulation, particularly of short-term capital flows, helped Chile to overcome recent financial crises without further repercussions. What these developments show is how a pragmatic approach to monetary and financial governance was informed by knowledge shaped by the 1982 crisis experience and turned into a political-technocratic consensus in the late 1980s. Institutional change since then remained incremental and was increasingly driven by neoliberal knowledge in the independent CBC.

Discussion

The comparison lent evidence to the two arguments advanced in this chapter. The presence of a political-technocratic consensus supports the stabilization of a governance regime. A pragmatic approach is better suited to cope with a dynamic international monetary and financial system and therefore to prevent financial crises from occurring. These mechanisms are discussed in more detail.

Stability of the monetary and financial governance regime

Chile's attempts to implement a governance regime that safeguards the stability of the monetary and financial system were successful compared to other emerging market and developing countries. The core of Chile's governance regime originated from the 1982 crisis experience and subsequently changed only incrementally. It remains until today successful in terms of safeguarding the stability of the monetary and financial system. Monetary policy was deployed countercyclical and with a focus on the stability of the overall monetary and financial system. Financial regulation with a systemic perspective prevented the buildup of unsustainable risks such as large currency mismatches through short-term international capital flows.

Argentina, in contrast, did not adopt pragmatic macro-financial governance, as it separated monetary and financial stability. The division was so strong in some periods that the financial system was liberalized while active monetary policy was given up, as it happened in the 1990s. Based on the 2001 crises experience, regulatory tightening occurred during the presidencies of Néstor and Cristina Kirchner, while monetary policy was more actively deployed. Exchange rate interventions were conducted in a pragmatic, punctuated manner to stabilize the monetary and financial system while promoting export-led growth. This period was offset by the incoming Macri government, who discontinued exchange rate interventions and active monetary policy, while financial regulations were dismantled. The return to a strict separation between monetary and financial system indicates that financial instabilities are returning.

The question of a stable monetary and financial governance regime is linked to the degree of pragmatism it entails. Orthodox governance regimes that are either heavily state or market-based tend to be destabilizing (Table 5.1). Pragmatism implies a position between the two extremes in-the middle of the spectrum and is characterized by a macro-financial regime that does not

Table 5.1 Typology of governance regimes

	State-based governance	Pragmatic governance	Market-based governance
Monetary policy	Active, countercyclical, shaping credit allocation, subordinated to fiscal policy	Active, countercyclical, less shaping of credit allocation, financial stability-oriented	Passive, no shaping of credit allocation, subordinated to inflation target or exchange rate
Financial regulation	Strict financial regulation, including international capital flows	Micro and macro-prudential regulation, including international capital flows	Weak financial regulation, free international capital flows
Governance regime	Developmentalist: monetary and financial governance based on development objectives	Macro-financial: integrated monetary and financial governance	Neoliberal: strict division between monetary and financial governance

separate between monetary and financial stability. Financial flows are liberalized but tightly regulated with a systemic view that is supported by countercyclical, financial stability–oriented monetary policy.

Political-technocratic consensus

How did Chile achieve the period of institutional stability while Argentina could not perpetuate an emerging pragmatic governance regime over the 2000s? The presence of a political-technocratic consensus needs to be in place that allows for its depoliticization and the prevention of contestations from politicians or central bankers. Argentina did not adopt such a consensus. This lack of depoliticization combined with orthodox governance regimes made disruptive ad-hoc changes of the regime more likely. The major conflict lines that divide the country are between two extreme positions on how the monetary and financial system should be governed, either state-based or market-based.[11] The short period of a pragmatic governance regime during N. Kirchner's tenure aimed at drawing compromises between these positions.

Chile introduced a pragmatic governance regime after the 1982 crisis. A political-technocratic consensus emerged over the mid-/late-1980s, lending stability to this regime that even endured the democratic transition in 1989. Political contestations, even by the incoming democratic governments of Aylwin (1990–94) or the socialist Bachelet (2006–10, 2014–18) were missing. The convergence of perspectives between politicians and central bankers smoothed out the transition to democracy and delimited policy options. It seems unlikely that such institutional stability would have been possible without a consensus in place that prevents contestations.[12] It also seems unlikely that the regime remained largely unchanged in the transition to democracy if the pragmatic turn in the 1982 did not reinforce the institutional stability.

Central bank governors can be exchanged at free will during dictatorships, while this is different in democracies. Continuity of central bank governors with similar backgrounds along different governments reflects a political-technocratic consensus. In Chile, no central bank governor since the central bank's independence in 1989 was ousted by the government, no matter from which political spectrum the party in power was. Even Bachelet, president from the Socialist Party (2006–2010 and 2014–2018), had too much respect of the central bank to interfere in their policymaking (interview former minister, 16 October 2018). Only Carlos Massad had to leave office during his second term of office due to personal misconduct. All central bank governors are known economic experts, published in academic journals and received their PhDs at prestigious US universities (University of Chicago [2], MIT [2], Harvard University [1], Cambridge University [1]). Furthermore central bank governors and the governments did not question the governance regime from the 1980s. Even though the democratic challengers to the dictatorship discussed wider reforms to the monetary and financial governance regime, these were scraped to not putting economic stability at risk (Bianchi 2016).

Argentina, in contrast, had not a single central bank governor fulfilling her or his tenure since the transition to democracy in 1983, albeit its central bank was granted legal independence in 1992. Twenty-three governors during 12 governments after the end of the civic-military dictatorship in 1983, compared to Chile's seven governors during the seven governments after Pinochet's dictatorship, show a substantial difference in consensus among politicians and central bankers. Changes of governments frequently led to changes in central bank governors. Furthermore central bank governors came from different backgrounds. While neoliberal presidents Menem and Macri selected governors that received their PhDs in prestigious universities (University of Chicago, Columbia University, MIT), C. Kirchner selected governors that are close to her nationalist-developmentalist agenda, with Joan Fabrega (2013–4) not having an academic degree at all, while Marco Del Pont (2010–2013) and Alejandro Vanoli (2014–5) have only graduate degrees in Economics. N. Kirchner, reflecting his compromise approach, opted for credible governors that received their PhDs from Harvard and University of Pennsylvania and that are considered to be close to the financial system. The missing continuity and the different approaches to monetary and financial governance that were adopted reflect the lack of political-technocratic consensus.

Institutional stability and change

What are the implications of depoliticization and lack of contestation for the institutional change can be observe? The increased relevance of central bankers

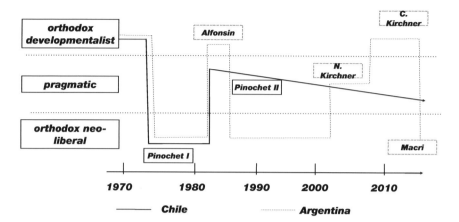

Figure 5.1 Diverging trajectories of institutional change in Argentina and Chile since 1970

for the development, conduct and change of policies is based on the political-technocratic consensus that lends legitimacy to them. The Chilean case illustrates how this results in a qualitative difference of institutional change in the 1990s. This takes the form of incremental changes shaped by the backgrounds of the central bankers conducting them that are not contested in public. Knowledge gained in economics programs at US universities that is promoting the idea of free market efficiency is increasingly deployed. Until today, this turn was not so pronounced that the core of the pragmatic, macro-financial governance regime was substantially altered. Even though Chile entered a time of institutional stability since 1983 there was incremental, less obvious change occurring (see Figure 5.1).

A missing political-technocratic consensus and depoliticization allows for political contestations. Governance regimes may change disruptively according to the availability of proposals for a contesting governance regime, as it recurrently happened in Argentina in the analyzed time frame. Politicized and punctuated institutional change allows for the adoption of different governance regimes, ranging from neoliberal to developmentalist. It reduces the leeway of central bankers to develop, conduct and change policies independently of the government. Given its integration in the international financial system, the constant potential of change caused financial investors to punish political decisions that reduce their profit outlook. This in turn increased the risk of financial crisis and a renewed change in governance regimes.

Conclusion

The comparison between the two countries indicates that a pragmatic monetary and financial governance regime which is stabilized via a political-technocratic consensus is beneficial in terms of preventing crises from occurring. It leads to relative institutional stability that is characterized by incremental change as opposed to only brief periods of stability and punctuated change such as occurring under orthodox governance regimes that lack depoliticization by a political–technocratic consensus.

On a theoretical level, the development of a political-technocratic consensus was identified as a necessary condition for the stabilization of a monetary and financial governance. Institutional change becomes qualitatively different when this occurs as the relation between politicians and experts is altered, with the latter gaining increasing leeway to implement incremental adjustments.

Instead of a global convergence towards one type of governance regime, a socio-historical analysis expects variety and different trajectories of monetary and financial policies across countries. Although the homogenization of economic knowledge tends to mold central bankers worldwide into an epistemic community, distinct relations between politicians and central bankers and the knowledge they draw on shape the governance regime and its trajectory. That Western central banks increasingly adopt a macro-financial approaches to monetary and financial governance after the financial crisis 2007 indicates furthermore that the diffusion of knowledge via the epistemic community is multidirectional, and does not only flow from advanced economies to less developed economies.

Acknowledgements

The author would like to thank for helpful comments by Mustafa Yagci, Manuela Moschella, Matthias Thiemann, and Mans Lundsted as well as by the participants at presentations at European University Institute in October 2019, Central European University in June 2019, the AFEP-IIPPE conference in July 2019.

Notes

1 Monetary and financial governance are jointly analyzed in this chapter since the interactions between monetary and financial systems affect both monetary and financial stability (see Borio [2014] and Borio and Disyatat [2010]).
2 There are several important differences between Argentina and Chile, such as the degree of federalism, the strength of the military, the role of natural resources or the Peronist ideology in Argentina (see also Undurraga [2015]). However, these factors were already present before the 1980s and can therefore not explain the subsequent divergence.
3 See, for example, Cukierman (1994) or Berger et al. (2001).
4 A more recent example is Prates (2005).
5 Section 3 of the Charter states: "The purpose of the Bank is to promote – within the framework of its powers and the policies set by the National Government – monetary and financial stability, employment, and economic development with social equality."
6 Nevertheless, it is formulated quite open, so that it allows for different approaches to monetary policy, even though it does allow the government to have a stronger say in monetary and financial policy.
7 Of high symbolic value was the acceptance of a ruling from a U.S. judge in 2012 that obliged Argentina to fully pay back vulture funds (which bought bonds the Argentinian government defaulted on in 2001) in 2016, thereby legitimizing and vindicating the interests of global finance as opposed to national goals.

8   The central bank's mandate by decree from 1953 was to "encourage the orderly and progressive development of the national economy through credit and monetary policy, avoiding any inflationary or depressive tendencies, and thus permitting the maximum use of the country's productive resources" (CBC 2019).

9   See, for example, Boylan (2001).

10   Some elements of the 1989 central bank reform stem back from the Chicago Boys (Boylan 2001, p. 88).

11   For example, the perspectives of two former central bank governors Vanoli and Redrado give evidence on how politicized monetary and financial issues are, blaming the other position for power abuses and poor policy choices (see Redrado [2010] and Vanoli [2018]).

12   Former CBC governor Roberto Zahler noted that

> [Pinochet's] regime intended to go far beyond technocratic and bureaucratic modernization; in fact, an attempt has been made to reshape the foundations of the Chilean society, its values, its structures and its behavioral patterns, which included as a main component a clear-cut economic model.
>
> (Zahler 1983, p. 510)

The stability of the political-technocratic consensus suggests that at least in the realm of monetary and financial governance this was successful.

References

Agosin, MR & Ffrench-Davis, R 2001, 'Managing capital inflows in Chile', in *Short-term capital flows and economic crises*, pp. 199–225, Oxford University Press, Oxford.

Baker, A 2013, 'The gradual transformation? The incremental dynamics of macroprudential regulation', *Regulation & Governance*, vol. 7, no. 4, pp. 417–434.

Berger, H, Haan, JD & Eijffinger, SC 2001, 'Central bank independence: an update of theory and evidence', *Journal of Economic Surveys*, vol. 15, no. 1, pp. 3–40.

Bianchi, A 2016, 'La independencia del Banco central de Chile: los años iniciales', in CBC (ed.) *25 Años de Autonomía del Banco Central de Chile*, pp. 13–29, Banco Central de Chile, Santiago.

Borio, C 2014, 'The financial cycle and macroeconomics: what have we learnt?', *Journal of Banking & Finance*, vol. 45, pp. 182–198.

Borio, C & Disyatat, P 2010, 'Global imbalances and the financial crisis: reassessing the role of international finance', *Asian Economic Policy Review*, vol. 5, no. 2, pp. 198–216.

Boylan, DM 2001, *Defusing democracy*, University of Michigan Press, Ann Arbor, MI.

Burnham, P 2001, 'New labour and the politics of depoliticization', *The British Journal of Politics and International Relations*, vol. 3, no. 2, pp. 127–149.

Calvo, GA 1986, 'Fractured liberalism: Argentina under Martínez de Hoz', *Economic Development and Cultural Change*, vol. 34, no. 3, pp. 511–533.

Calvo, GA & Mendoza, EG 1999, 'Empirical puzzles of chilean stabilization policy', in G Perry & DM Leipziger (eds.) *Chile: recent policy lessons and emerging challenges*, pp. 25–54, World Bank, Washington, DC.

Caputo, R & Saravia, D 2018, 'The monetary and fiscal history of Chile: 1960–2016', *Becker Friedman Institute for Economics Working Paper, No. 2018–62*.

Carriere-Swallow, Y & Garcia-Silva, P 2013, 'Capital account policies in Chile macrofinancial considerations along the path to liberalization', *IMF Working Papers, 13/107*.

CBC 2019, *Origin of the central bank of Chile*, Banco Central de Chile, Santiago, viewed 14 October 2019, www.bcentral.cl/documents/145129/150750/bcch_archivo_098936_en.pdf/ed55d433-fa42-e34e-a782-a8579b5bd71f.

Cox Edwards, A & Edwards, S 1992, 'Markets and democracy: lessons from Chile', *The World Economy*, vol. 15, no. 2, pp. 203–219.

Cukierman, A 1994, 'Central bank independence and monetary control', *The Economic Journal*, vol. 104, no. 427, pp. 1437–1448.

Damill, M, Frenkel, R & Rapetti, M 2015, 'Macroeconomic policy in Argentina during 2002–2013', *Comparative Economic Studies*, vol. 57, no. 3, pp. 369–400.

Damill, M, Frenkel, R & Simpson, L 2016, 'An unlikely phoenix: the recovery of Argentina's monetary and financial system from its ashes in the 2000s and its lessons', *Journal of Post Keynesian Economics*, vol. 39, no. 2, pp. 228–255.

Ffrench-Davis, R 2010, *Economic reforms in Chile*, Palgrave Macmillan UK, London.

Ffrench-Davis, R 2016, 'Is Chile a role model for development?', in A Calcagno, S Dullien, A Marquez-Velazquez, N Maystre & J Priewe (eds.) *Rethinking development strategies after the financial crisis – volume II: country studies and international comparisons*, pp. 81–92, United Nations Publications, New York.

Frenkel, R 2002, 'Argentina: a decade of the convertibility regime', *Challenge*, vol. 45, no. 4, pp. 41–59.

Frenkel, R & Rapetti, M 2007, 'Argentina's monetary and exchange rate policies after the convertibility regime collapse', *Center for Economic and Policy Research*, April.

Gezmis, H 2017, 'From neoliberalism to neo-developmentalism? The political economy of post-crisis Argentina (2002–2015)', *New Political Economy*, vol. 23, no. 1, pp. 66–87.

Grabel, I 2018, *When things don't fall apart: global financial governance and developmental finance in an age of productive incoherence*, The MIT Press, Cambridge, MA.

Hay, C 2007, *Why we hate politics*, Polity, Cambridge, UK.

Helleiner, E & Pagliari, S 2011, 'The end of an era in international financial regulation? A postcrisis research Agenda', *International Organization*, vol. 65, no. 1, pp. 169–200.

INDEC 2019, *Estadisticas integradas de balanza de pagos, posicion de inversion internacional y deuda externa, anos 2006–2019*, Instituto Nacional de Estadística y Censos, República Argentina, viewed 15 October 2019, www.indec.gob.ar/indec/web/Nivel4-Tema-3-35-45.

Mannheim, K 1959, *Ideology and Utopia*, Harvest Books, Eugene, OR.

Marcussen, M 2005, 'Central banks on the move', *Journal of European Public Policy*, vol. 12, no. 5, pp. 903–923.

Marshall, J 2000, 'Managing foreign debt and liquidity risks', *BIS Policy Papers*, vol. 8.

Maxfield, S 1997, *Gatekeepers of growth*, Princeton University Press, Princeton, NJ.

McNamara, K 2002, 'Rational fictions: central bank independence and the social logic of delegation', *West European Politics*, vol. 25, no. 1, pp. 47–76.

Montecinos, V 1998, 'Economists in party politics: Chilean democracy in the era of the markets', in *The politics of expertise in Latin America*, pp. 126–141, Palgrave Macmillan, London.

Moschella, M 2015, 'Currency wars in the advanced world: resisting appreciation at a time of change in central banking monetary consensus', *Review of International Political Economy*, vol. 22, no. 1, pp. 134–161.

Moschella, M & Tsingou, E (eds.) 2013a, *Great expectations, slow transformations: incremental change in post-crisis regulation*, ECPR Press, Colchester.

Moschella, M & Tsingou, E 2013b, 'Regulating finance after the crisis: unveiling the different dynamics of the regulatory process', *Regulation & Governance*, vol. 7, no. 4, pp. 407–416.

Nagel, M & Thiemann, M 2019, 'Shifting frames of the expert debate: quantitative easing, international macro-finance and the potential impact of post-Keynesian scholarship', in L-P Rochon & V Monvoisin (eds.) *Finance, growth and inequality: post-keynesian perspective*, pp. 235–256, Edward Elgar Publishing, Cheltenham.

O'Connell, A 2001, 'The return of "vulnerability" and Raul Prebisch's early thinking on the "Argentine business cycle"', *CEPAL Review*, vol. 2001, no. 75, pp. 51–65.

Pesce, MA 2008, 'Capital flows, economic performance and economic policy: Argentina's experience during the last decade', *BIS Papers*, vol. 44, pp. 89–101.

Polillo, S & Guillen, MF 2005, 'Globalization pressures and the state: the worldwide spread of central bank independence', *American Journal of Sociology*, vol. 110, no. 6, pp. 1764–1802.

Prates, DM 2005, 'As assimetrias do sistema monetário e financeiro internacional', *Revista de Economia Contemporânea*, vol. 9, no. 2, pp. 263–288.

Prebisch, R 1962, 'The economic development of Latin America and its principal problems', *Economic Bulletin for Latin America*, vol. 7, no. 1, pp. 1–22.

Puryear, JM 1994, *Thinking politics: intellectuals and democracy in Chile, 1973–1988*, Johns Hopkins University Press, Baltimore, MD.

Redrado, M 2010, *No reserve: the limit of absolute power*, Amazon Crossing, Seattle, WA.

Thiemann, M 2018, *The growth of shadow banking*, Cambridge University Press, Cambridge, UK.

Undurraga, T 2015, 'Neoliberalism in Argentina and Chile: common antecedents, divergent paths', *Revista de Sociologia e Política*, vol. 23, no. 55, pp. 11–34.

Vanoli, A 2018, 'Managing monetary policy and financial supervision in Argentina: historical analysis and present neoliberal challenges – A personal account', *International Journal of Political Economy*, vol. 47, no. 1, pp. 3–30.

Veigel, KF 2009, *Dictatorship, democracy, and globalization: Argentina and the cost of paralysis, 1973–2001*, Pennsylvania State University Press, University Park, PA.

Wylde, C 2011, 'State, society and markets in Argentina: the political economy of neodesarrollismo under Nestor Kirchner, 2003–2007', *Bulletin of Latin American Research*, vol. 30, no. 4, pp. 436–452.

Wylde, C 2016, 'Post-neoliberal developmental regimes in Latin America: Argentina under Cristina Fernandez de Kirchner', *New Political Economy*, vol. 21, no. 3, pp. 322–341.

Zahler, R 1983, 'Recent southern cone liberalization reforms and stabilization policies: the chilean case, 1974–1982', *Journal of Interamerican Studies and World Affairs*, vol. 25, no. 4, p. 509.

Part 2

Central banking in the European periphery

6 The impact of European economic governance and EU accession negotiations on the central banks in candidate countries

The case of the National Bank of Serbia

Tatjana Jovanić

Introduction

As a multilateral negotiation system which aims to align national economic policies that may have negative external effects (Heise 2008), European economic governance (EEG) has trickled down to the EU candidate countries and become an integral part of the EU accession process. Economic and financial dialogue between candidate countries and EU institutions and Member States is becoming more complex compared to the earlier accession of countries from Central and Eastern Europe, and the scope of obligations a candidate country should fulfil prior to accession has been continuously expanding. Legal, administrative and economic conditionality related to the conduct of economic policies, as external pressures on central banks in the Western Balkan (WB) region, have strengthened the importance of central banks within national economic coordination structures.

In the Western Balkan region, two countries have formally started accession negotiations: Montenegro opened accession negotiations in June 2012, whereas Serbia formally started accession negotiations in January 2014. Albania and the Republic of North Macedonia have the status of candidate countries. In this Chapter, Serbia is chosen as a positive example of the link between the economic conditionality imposed by the European integration process and the competences and capacities of the central bank. This is visible both at the level of national economic policy coordination and in structured dialogue within the relevant subcommittees established to monitor the stabilisation and association process and accession negotiations. The main hypothesis is that accession process requirements have reinforced the functional independence of the National Bank of Serbia (NBS) and its role in the coordination of macroeconomic policies. The conditionality set out in the accession process is harmonised with that of international financial institutions (IFIs), such as the International Monetary Fund (IMF). A comparison of Serbia with Montenegro and North Macedonia has led to the conclusion that the 'light' requirements of the EEG stipulated for WB economies and determinants of the legal independence of central banks within the European System of Central Banks (ESCB) have strengthened the de jure independence of central banks. In line with the main hypothesis, this strengthened independence is expected to positively correlate with the attempt to anchor inflation expectations.

In order to explain the impact of Europeanisation by the imposed conditionality, it is necessary to briefly present the main characteristics of the new approach to accession negotiations and the main channels and instruments through which requirements for adhesion to the EU influence the role of central banks in candidate countries. Evaluating the EU as the most influential source of external pressure, the Chapter examines how accession negotiations have strengthened the functional independence of the National Bank of Serbia in pursuing monetary and macroprudential policies, maintaining financial stability and contributing to economic reforms.

Comparing the values of the legal (de jure) independence of the NBS based on the Cuikerman index (CWN) (Cukierman et al. 1992) and modified Cuikerman index (Jacome & Vasquez 2005), with the values constructed for peer countries, as well as the independence indexes of central banks during the accession of new EU Member States, the result shows that the NBS ranks among the most independent central banks in the region in terms of the determinants of legal independence. Obviously, legal independence should be treated with a dose of reserve, as it may be jeopardised through indirect influence. In the absence of clear protocols on measuring the impact of informal factors, the final section of this Chapter attempts to measure the transparency of inflation targeting (IT) as the most objective measure of the de facto independence of Serbia's monetary authority. The result, based on methodology developed by Dincer and Eichengreen (2014), and Eijffinger and Geraats (2006), confirms the hypothesis that growing independence and transparency of the NBS has contributed to the greater anchoring of inflation expectations.

The new approach to accession negotiations and the main tools to monitor economic governance

Accession negotiations between a candidate country and the EU have been modified over the previous decades, from the accession of ten CEE (Central and Eastern European) countries in 2004, to the somewhat more complex subsequent accession process of Bulgaria, Romania and Croatia. With regard to Western Balkan applicants, apart from being more demanding in terms of the thoroughness of conditionality checks, the new approach to EU accession negotiations has brought some substantial changes in the very substance of accession conditionality and the framework for approximating national legal systems (Ćemalović 2015). By formulating an individual list of benchmarks for every negotiating chapter, the European Commission has introduced a more target-oriented approach in defining key conditionality (Gateva 2016, p. 131).

The European Commission has identified economic governance as one of the key challenges for the countries of the Western Balkans (European Commission 2016). The reformed European economic governance framework which affects the role of central banks has been trickling down to the EU accession process through two main channels (Miščević & Mrak 2017, p. 199). The first channel for strengthening economic governance in EU candidate countries which have commenced negotiations is a broadened scope for acquis harmonisation within Chapter 17 of EU accession negotiations entitled 'Economic and Monetary Policy' and is explicitly linked with fulfillment of the Copenhagen economic criteria. In contrast to the pre-crisis period, the acquis chapter on economic and monetary policy has become much broader. Among the most important requirements for the harmonisation of laws and practices are the determinants of central bank independence, as well as the implementation of budgetary policy with a view to stabilising public finances and overall macroeconomic stability. So far, the former have significantly strengthened the independence of central banks. This Chapter aims to outline the impact of legislative changes which strengthened the de jure independence of the central banks of Serbia, Montenegro and Northern Macedonia. Provisions of the Law on the NBS[1] are largely aligned with requirements relating to central bank independence under the Treaty on the Functioning of the EU (TFEU) and the Statute of the European System of Central Banks and of the European Central Bank (hereinafter: ESCB/ECB Statute). The remaining requirements, which should be fulfilled in order to strengthen independence in terms of accession to the ESCB, are identified in the National Programme for the adoption of the EU acquis (Government of the Republic of Serbia 2018) and relate to all aspects of central bank independence: institutional, personal, functional and financial independence. Amendments to the Law on the National Bank of Serbia aiming to further strengthen its independence are scheduled to be adopted by late 2021. Among other things, they are expected to include provisions that will be applied after the Republic of Serbia's accession to the EU (e.g., provisions on the NBS's position within the ESCB, tasks and functions of the NBS, subscription and payment of the NBS's capital to the ECB's capital, membership in ECB bodies, as well as provisions which will achieve full alignment with requirements regarding the independence of the NBS).

The second channel for strengthening economic governance is a broadened framework for consultations on economic policy coordination. The Stabilisation and Association Agreements established cooperation between the EU and the candidate countries in the area of economic policy to improve the exchange of information on macroeconomic results and help create the economic policy and tools for its implementation. In 2014, candidate countries were asked for the first time to produce a document entitled 'Economic Reform Programme' (ERP) which, in fact, represents a new generation of documents supporting economic policy dialogue between a candidate country and the European Union. The ERP is not a national strategic document, rather a benchmarking tool for the easier comparison of WB economies. It is a rolling programme, which means that each new development cycle needs to some extent to ensure continuity in the area of priorities. The cycle begins every June, when the European Commission issues detailed guidelines for the Western Balkans and Turkey, and ends in May the next year with the adoption of a strategic document entitled 'Joint Conclusions of the Economic and Financial Dialogue between the EU and the Western Balkans and Turkey' at a meeting of the Economic and Financial Affairs Council (ECOFIN Council). The ERPs are examined together with representatives of the EU, ministers of finance and economy, representatives of the central banks of EU Member States, and responsible European institutions. The meeting results in targeted policy guidance, which reflects shared views on the short-term policy measures that should be implemented to address macrofiscal vulnerabilities and structural obstacles to growth.

The tools used in the vertical process of diffusing the principles of economic governance for non-EU Member States include technical assistance, reports, training and the practice of conditionality with regard to third countries. The latter has a coercive pattern of diffusion as it is imposed via a number of tools such as annual progress reports, recommendations, conclusions, opinions, enlargement strategies, association agendas, and action plans (Lianos et al. 2016, p. 291). Acknowledging that central banks are a pillar of monetary and financial stability contributing to overall macroeconomic stability, the EU has supported central banks in candidate countries in harmonising regulations, pursuing policies and adjusting to ESCB standards and best international practices through a number of projects which have helped to strengthen institutional capacities. Project deliverables have been achieved in the form of draft laws, strategies, gap analyses, action plans, internal guidelines, manuals, and economic models, supported with a number of capacity-building activities.[2]

The abovementioned Joint Conclusions of the Economic and Financial Dialogue between the EU and the WB and Turkey are similar to country-specific recommendations adopted under the European Semester for EU Member States. The implementation of policy guidance is elaborated by the European Commission's Directorate-General for Economic and Financial Affairs, in annual reports analysing economic developments (European Commission 2019). The latest Joint Conclusions of the Economic and Financial Dialogue between the EU and the Western Balkans and Turkey, as of May 2019, address issues related to the tasks of central banks, and macroeconomic and monetary policy in Policy Guidance No. 3 (Joint Conclusions 2019). For instance, the central bank of Montenegro has been asked to conduct a comprehensive asset quality review of the financial sector in line with international best practices and to publish the results. North Macedonia was invited to legally clarify the national bank's mandate to set macroprudential policy and establish a framework for effective cooperation among all agencies involved in macroprudential supervision. The Central bank of Bosnia and Herzegovina was requested to enhance its analytical and forecasting capacities, and develop its macroprudential toolkit. Continued promotion of the local currency and implementing measures foreseen in the programme and action plan to resolve non-performing loans (NPLs) were some of the key recommendations for Serbia. Measuring success and establishing benchmarks of performance, Joint Conclusions and annual Progress Reports are a specific form of horizontal flexible integration, which may be interpreted as an 'alternative to conditionality' (Lavenex 2008).

Juxtaposing conditionalities and their impact on policy changes

The process of European integration has significantly enhanced the role of central banks in WB countries and has made them prominent players in the existing negotiation structures in areas related to policy reforms and the coordination of economic policies. Operating in similar environments where actors share similar organisational cultures and learn through interaction (Momani & Amand 2015), Europeanisation in the area of economic governance may be seen as an indirect mechanism of diffusion based on competition over meeting certain performance criteria to which WB states adjust their behaviour. Mechanisms imposed by international financial institutions (IFIs) and the EU, as external factors, may be interpreted as external incentives which aim to foster mimicry among WB states by promoting comparisons, setting benchmarks and performing regular peer reviews. Such mechanisms of the procedural and instrumental diffusion of good practices among Western Balkan central banks could better be explained as emulation or indirect influence (Börzel & Risse 2009, p. 9). Compared to the executive branch, central banks in WB countries have a strong internal capacity for organisational learning (Dibella et al. 1996), as they fulfil the key requirements necessary for it. In line with the findings of organisational learning literature (Goh & Richards 1997), clear goals and missions, a leadership role, and the ability to transfer knowledge are some of the key elements determining the practice of organisational learning. The objective of financial stability has significantly contributed to organisational learning within central banks (Yagci 2017). The process of Europeanisation is an influential institutional factor in policy changes, and could be interpreted as an exogenous impulse which facilitates the endogenous mechanism of institutional and policy change, especially in relation to pursuing the objective of financial stability and macroprudential tools. The juxtaposition of conditionalities imposed by the EU and IFIs has facilitated institutional and policy changes, as well as organisational learning within the peer group of central banks of Western Balkan countries (Tabaković & Mrak 2015).

In accession negotiations, Serbia's and Montenegro's central banks play a leading role under negotiation Chapter 17 on Economic and Monetary Policy and make a significant contribution to the preparation of strategic documents. The most important are the abovementioned National Programme for the Adoption of the EU Acquis and the Economic Reform Programme, as well as data related to the Annual Progress Report of the European Commission.

In addition to participating in ministerial conferences and annual meetings within the Economic and Financial Dialogue, Serbia's and Montenegro's central banks play an important role within bodies for the implementation of the Stabilisation and Association Agreement. These are the Subcommittee for the Internal Market and the Protection of Competition and the Subcommittee for Economic and Financial Affairs and Statistics. Central banks actively participate in the preparation of the macroeconomic outlook in the Economic Reform Programme, in a similar way in which they participated in negotiations with international financial institutions.

When comparing the assessments of ERPs, country progress reports in the part on Economic Reforms, the conclusions of the European Council, and screening reports, the reader might notice a striking similarity of approaches between the institutions of the EU and international financial institutions (International Monetary Fund and the World Bank). Moreover, in evaluating ERPs and Economic Criteria evaluations (Progress Reports), the European Commission often refers to IMF assessments, and even subcontracts the IMF to assess national economic programming documents. This corresponds with findings in the earlier Europeanisation literature that the thrust of the EU's economic agenda for former socialist countries was and still is neoliberal, emphasising privatisation, reduction in state involvement and further liberalisation (Grabbe 2002). There is a striking similarity between the EU and the IMF on domestic cutback management in EU Member States facing economic and fiscal crisis (Kickert & Ongaro 2019; Cepilovs & Török 2019). However, when juxtaposing traditional conditionalities imposed by international financial institutions (IFIs), and those formulated in the process of accession negotiations, the following three differences should be noted. Firstly, the accession conditions are less precise and are broken down in various documents. Secondly, the main benefit is accession to the EU and not financial gain. Thirdly, accession is a highly politicised process. In this context, fulfilling particular tasks and receiving benefits is much less clear than in IFI conditionality, because the tasks are complex and many of them cannot be measured by quantitative targets (Grabbe 2002, p. 252).

Serbia is a good example to examine the interplay between the International Monetary Fund (IMF) and the EU in formulating and monitoring the fulfillment of economic conditionality, as the IMF has been an external policy anchor for Serbia's Economic Reform Programme. Serbia is the second country with the so-called Policy Coordination Instrument (PCI), the new IMF mechanism for advisory and technical assistance to countries that have no need of external financing, to define and implement their economic program (IMF 2019). At the same time, the EU is scrutinising policy and economic governance in Serbia, as it is in other candidate and pre-candidate countries. The process of verifying the pace and strength of economic reforms and fulfillment of the economic and administrative conditionality the candidate countries must fulfil is concentrated in the tools of reporting. Serbia has periodic sustainability crosschecks that are conducted separately by the IMF and by the European

Commission. If their assessments of the progress made and measures to be taken, including structural reforms, differed significantly, it would be difficult to provide a consistent economic agenda. Both institutions share the assessment that Serbia has been maintaining macroeconomic and financial stability for quite some time, with a sustained macrofiscal framework, consistent economic policies and positive macroeconomic outlook.

Case study: the impact of Europeanisation on the objectives of the National Bank of Serbia

The impact of Europeanisation on prudential policy

Central bank responsibility for financial stability has become a worldwide trend for a number of reasons. In this context, central bank independence and transparency significantly influence the application of the policy regime and the path of macroprudential turn (Fernández-Albertos 2015; Horvath & Vaško 2016). This has triggered a wave of changes in central bank legislation to emphasise that the primary focus on price stability does not prevent a central bank from pursuing other goals (Lastra 2015, p. 58). In Serbia, monetary, microprudential and macroprudential policy is formulated under the roof of the National Bank of Serbia. The NBS mandate for prudential policies stems from Article 4(3) of the Law on the National Bank of Serbia. A 2010 amendment stipulated that the NBS shall determine and implement, within its scope of authority, the activities and measures aimed at maintaining and strengthening the stability of the financial system. This mandate enables the NBS, without prejudice to its primary objective – price stability, to contribute to maintaining and strengthening the financial system's stability, as set out in Article 3, par. 2 of the Law on the National Bank of Serbia.

The NBS mandate for macroprudential policy is harmonised with the European Systemic Risk Board's (ESRB) Recommendation 2011/3 of 22 December 2011 on the macroprudential mandate of national authorities. Furthermore, the ESRB Recommendation 2013/1 on intermediate objectives and instruments of macroprudential policy recognised the need to improve the coordination mechanism with relevant authorities at the national level with a view to monitoring and assessing financial risks and enhancing coordination between institutions involved in the supervisory and regulatory framework of the financial sector. In late 2013, the NBS set up the Financial Stability Committee. Besides representatives of the central bank, the Committee comprises representatives of the Ministry of Finance, Deposit Insurance Agency and Securities Commission. The NBS is represented by the Governor (chairing the Committee), the Vice-governor in charge of the Financial Stability Sector, and the Director General of the Banking Supervision Department. The Committee has established a system of regular dialogue among competent bodies and a line of communication regarding financial stability issues. In addition, the NBS published the Macroprudential Framework in March 2015 (National

Bank of Serbia 2015), setting out the objectives, instruments and decision-making process of macroprudential policy. The process is harmonised with the ESRB Recommendation 2013/1 and currently applied macroprudential measures and instruments in Serbia are fully harmonised with EU regulations and international best practices.

In addition to functions related to implementing monetary and foreign exchange policies and supervising the payment system, and functions related to maintaining and strengthening the stability of the financial system, the NBS supervises most financial institutions and is the banking resolution authority. With the primary objective of minimising the use of budgetary and other public funds in order to preserve financial stability, it undertakes preventive measures and carries out the resolution procedure. In this capacity, the NBS has established cooperation with the EU's Single Resolution Board and participates in the resolution colleges' exchanging information and aligning this function with international standards. Assessing the whole framework, harmonisation with the acquis of the European Union on Financial Services has increased the level of Europeanisation in the overall prudential policy context, including microprudential. On the road to the opening of Chapter 9, the legal framework regarding financial services went through changes. The opening of negotiations is the actual confirmation that the requirements for financial services prescribed by domestic legislation, including microprudential policy, are sufficiently aligned with European standards and rules for financial institutions.

In February 2015, the NBS implemented several reforms with respect to banking operations in Serbia, primarily through amendments to the Law on the National Bank of Serbia and the Law on Banks. The aim was to improve the framework for bank recovery and resolution in accordance with the principles and rules set out in the EU. Furthermore, the NBS adopted a set of regulations in December 2016 introducing *Basel III* standards into the regulatory framework of the Republic of Serbia. These regulations set out a reduction of the prescribed minimum capital adequacy ratio and simultaneously set capital buffers as of the starting date of the implementation of Basel III standards (30 June 2017).

As a result of the implementation, along with adequate supervision of the implementation, of regulations which are harmonised with the EU acquis, Serbia's banking sector is stable, highly capitalised and liquid, and all regulatory requirements are at a satisfactory level. The capital adequacy ratio was 23.23% at the end of June 2019 (the last available data), which is sufficiently above the regulatory minimum in Serbia (8%). The average monthly liquidity ratio amounted to 2.15 in August 2019 (the regulatory minimum is 1.0), which is double the regulatory prescribed threshold in the long run observed. The average narrow liquidity ratio was 1.77 in August 2019 (the regulatory minimum is 0.7). The most recently introduced liquidity coverage ratio (LCR) amounting to 216.23% also confirms the high liquidity of Serbia's banking sector. Regarding the NPLs as the main issue in the Republic of Serbia's banking sector in the previous period, by late August 2019, the NPL ratio stood at 4.90%, down by 17.35 pp compared with late August 2015.

The impact of Europeanisation on strengthening the role of Serbia's monetary authority in supporting other economic policy objectives

From 2000 to 2006, Serbia was de facto in a regime of discretionary monetary policy. During that time the exchange rate was a predominant target, similar to many other central banks in Central and Eastern Europe (Frömmel et al. 2011). The 2006 Memorandum on the Principles of a New Monetary Policy Framework officially marked a shift toward an inflation targeting regime. The discretionary monetary policy in the period 2000–2008 had been challenged by politically influenced goals. It produced high real appreciation of the dinar and increased the euroisation of Serbia's financial system, threatening to jeopardise financial stability (Šoškić 2015; Fabris 2015). In an effort to define a legal framework to implement the monetary policy, the National Bank of Serbia made a formal Agreement with the Government on targeting inflation.[3] Although the NBS opted to target inflation already in 2006, implicit targeting in the transitional period led to full inflation targeting as of 2009, when the inflation target was clearly defined as a numerical range with its central value for each month. Until 2012, inflation targeting coincided with the financial crisis which caused volatile inflation. During the second period, from 2013 onwards, the stabilisation of movements in the foreign exchange market helped maintain the inflation rate at low levels (Tabaković 2019).

Since 2012, communication with market participants and the general public has intensified. This has brought an additional mechanism to address temporary shocks and reinforce monetary policy flexibility at times of more volatile capital flows. In this way, the NBS has intensified several transmission channels. As a result, volatility of the dinar exchange rate has been reduced, inflation in Serbia since 2013 has been low and stable at around 2%, while inflation expectations have been reduced and stabilised. It also helped reduce the level of Non-Performing Loans (NPL), along with a Strategy for their resolution, adopted in August 2015 (Government of the RS 2015). The Strategy was supported by the strategic decision of the NBS to lower the medium-term inflation target to $3 \pm 1.5\%$ (down from $4 \pm 1.5\%$).

Having previously explained how the European integration process has influenced the macroprudential policy of the central bank and the achievement of its objective of financial stability, let us also shed light on the impact of this process on the central bank's role in other economic policy goals. Monetary policy conducted by a central bank cannot be viewed as being isolated from the government's economic policy. Its macroprudential mandate requires a policy regime which involves elements of fiscal and monetary policy, a regulatory regime of financial sector regulation and supervision, and capital control measures, evidently the tools of the executive (Galati & Moessner 2013). Modern monetary laws envisage a central bank's obligation to support other economic policy objectives (Lastra 2015). According to Article 127 of the Consolidated Treaty on the European Union (TEU) and Treaty of the Functioning of the EU (TFEU), 'without prejudice to the objective of price stability, the ESCB will support general economic policies in the Community'. This support should contribute to achieving objectives which, pursuant to Article 3 of the TEU, encompass sustainable and non-inflationary growth, respecting the environment, and high levels of employment and social protection. In a similar way, Article 3. par. 3 of the Law on the NBS stipulates that the National Bank shall, without jeopardising monetary and financial stability, support the economic policy of the Government, in line with the principles of a market economy.

Monetary and fiscal policy measures gradually began to converge through implementation of the fiscal consolidation programme aimed at achieving sustainable levels of fiscal deficit and public debt (Vujović 2015). Since 2015, when a programme of fiscal consolidation measures and structural reforms was put in place as a response to the requirements set out within a broadened framework for consultations on economic policy coordination, the NBS responded to fiscal restrictiveness with significant monetary policy easing. The full coordination of monetary and fiscal policies since 2015 seems to have played a determining role in strengthening macroeconomic fundamentals and minimising macroeconomic fluctuations over the past several years. Fiscal consolidation enabled Serbia to record a fiscal surplus in 2017 and 2018. This represents a huge difference compared to the deficit of 6.2% of GDP in 2014, and reduced the general government debt ratio by around 20 pp by mid-2019. Serbia's example therefore challenges many studies which questioned the prospects of inflation targeting in securing stable inflation in environments with decreasing parameters of economic activity facing macroeconomic and financial instability (Walsh 2009; Mishkin 2004). The predictability of inflation was preserved despite the fact that external conditions were highly volatile (primarily commodity prices and capital flows). Despite some recent findings that conventional monetary policy instruments have limited effects in times of crisis (Bucholz et al. 2019), the fact that the use of unconventional measures was not necessary has further strengthened the credibility of the NBS policy. The pursuit of this policy has placed the NBS among banks that use standard monetary policy measures. Both the ECB and the European Commission, as well as the IMF, have continuously assessed the monetary policy stance of the NBS as appropriate in terms of the inflation and growth framework.

Coordinated monetary and fiscal policy and a framework for structural reforms were supported and assessed by the IMF, and welcomed by European institutions and rating agencies.[4] Most of all, a consistent macroeconomic policy recognised by investors has accelerated economic growth on a sustainable basis, raised employment and wages in the private sector, and created a favourable growth outlook. It could also be interpreted as confirmation that Serbia is adjusting to practices accepted in the EU within the process of Serbia's accession to the EU, as recognised in the Economic Reform Programme. The findings of the annual economic policy dialogue stressed that Serbia's monetary policy was being well conducted and inflationary pressures kept in check (European Commission 2019). To quote Sem Fabrizi, the EU Ambassador to Serbia, 'It is very positive that Serbia maintained macroeconomic and fiscal stability in 2018, a result that is expected also in the future. The joint Economic Reform Programme conclusions stress that it is particularly important to lock in recent gains and give stronger impetus to structural reforms' (European Commission 2019).

Measuring the legal independence of Serbia's central bank

A high level of central bank independence is one of the prerequisites for macroeconomic stability, as confirmed by the results of numerous empirical studies showing a negative correlation between central bank independence and inflation. Independence analyses are predominantly calculated on the basis of its four components: personal, institutional, financial and functional. Since the early 1980s, researchers have strived to construct different indexes of independence to prove the argument that central bank independence affects the inflation rate (Bade & Parkin 1988). Although there are complex indexes which try to measure the economic independence of central banks (Grilli et al. 1991), most evaluations of central bank independence have been based on the comprehensive indexes of central bank independence, constructed by Cukierman, Webb and Neyapti (the CWN index). Along with other indexes, this index shows a correlation between a higher level of central bank independence and lower inflation. A number of studies have evaluated the impact of central bank independence in transition economies where it was calculated that the change in legislative framework, especially in new EU Member States, strengthened institutional independence (Cukierman et al. 2002; Freytag 2003; Bogoev & Petrevski 2015; Dvorsky 2008; Maliszewski 2000). The previous section provided insight into elements of the de facto independence of the National Bank of Serbia, which was also strengthened through harmonisation with the EU acquis and compliance with the good practices of EU Member States. It is reflected by operations related to the practice of inflation targeting, conducting open market operations, arrangements related to the exchange rate regime, as well as in the context of the central bank's broader role in fulfilling macroprudential and macroeconomic goals. This section focuses on the de jure independence of the National Bank of Serbia and compares the values of legal independence with those constructed for Montenegro and North Macedonia. In terms of the normative determinants of independence, the process of European integration has significantly contributed to strengthening the independence of the three central banks. In line with previous research findings (Dvorsky 2008), the level of independence in candidate countries largely corresponds to their level of EU integration.

The evaluation of the legal (de jure) independence of the NBS will be based on the Cuikerman (CWN) index (Cukierman et al. 1992), one of the most commonly used indexes in the empirical analysis of the normative determinants of central bank independence. The CWN index includes 16 variables grouped in 4 clusters, coded from 0 (lowest level of independence) to 1 (highest level of independence). The aggregate Cukierman index of independence is calculated as a weighted average of the values assigned to the individual variables. For the purpose of measuring the legal independence of Serbia's central bank, a modified Cuikerman index (Jacome & Vasquez 2005) will also be applied, as it incorporates some specific issues that are more relevant for small open emerging market economies.

The constructed Cuikerman index confirms that the level of legal independence of the NBS is high, amounting to 0.985. Looking back to the past, the level of independence of the NBS has increased over time, because it equalled 0.892 under the Law on the National Bank of Serbia adopted in 2003. Evaluating the 16 criteria within the four aspects of independence defined by the Cuikerman index – the governor (personal independence), monetary policy formulation (institutional independence), the objectives of the central bank (functional independence), and the limitations on central bank lending to the government (financial independence) – the most notable progress over the period observed was achieved in the aspect of financial independence, followed by higher personal independence, while objectives and policy formulation were already set high.

The contribution of personal independence criteria to the total index of independence according to the Cuikerman index increased from 0.154 to 0.167 today, because the governor's term of office has been extended from five to six years. The governor is appointed by Parliament, with the possibility of being re-elected. The NBS has full responsibility for conducting monetary policy in order to achieve its objectives. Full instrumental independence, which the NBS fulfils, is a very important precondition for an inflation targeting (IT) regime. Regarding the functional independence criteria, the NBS Law contains clearly defined price stability as the primary objective. In addition to its primary objective, the NBS also pursues the goal of financial stability. This group of criteria thus contributed 0.15 to the overall index. As for financial independence, it contributed 0.5 to the overall index, as the NBS Law strictly forbids monetary financing of the government (Table 6.1).

According to Radović et al. (2018), who calculated the Cuikerman index of central bank legal independence for Montenegro, the level of independence of the Central Bank of Montenegro (Centralna banka Crne Gore – CBCG) is high and amounts to 0.88 out. Prior to the introduction of the Law Amending the Law on the Central Bank of Montenegro of 2017, the CBCG's independence was set at 0.8665. This difference shows that reforming the legislative framework, mainly as a result of accession negotiations, contributed to a higher level of independence.

A paper exploring the level of independence of the National Bank of the Republic of Macedonia (NBRM) in late 2016 by Angelovska Bezhoska (2017) confirmed previous findings on the high level of legal independence of the NBRM (Jankoski 2010). The first law on the NBRM adopted in 1992 granted only a moderate level of independence with the value of the aggregate index being 0.60. The law adopted in 2002 strengthened the bank's mandate and independence (index of 0.70), and the most recent law adopted in late 2010 and subsequently amended contributed to a rise in the value of the index to 0.92.

The modified Cuikerman index tries to capture some specific issues relevant for transition countries, and therefore adds a new group of criteria to measure

Table 6.1 Index of the National Bank of Serbia's legal independence according to Cukierman et al. (1992)

Measurement of independence of National bank of Serbia according to Cukierman index

Description of variable	Max value of Index	Law on the NBS adopted in 2003 and amendments to the Law:				
		2003	2010	2012	2015	2018
1. CHIEF EXECUTIVE OFFICER (CEO)	**0.200**	**0.154**	**0.167**	**0.167**	**0.167**	**0.167**
a. Term of office	0.050	0.025	0.038	0.038	0.038	0.038
b. Who appoints CEO?	0.050	0.038	0.038	0.038	0.038	0.038
c. Dismissal	0.050	0.042	0.042	0.042	0.042	0.042
d. May CEO hold other offices in government?	0.050	0.050	0.050	0.050	0.050	0.050
2. POLICY FORMULATION	**0.150**	**0.150**	**0.150**	**0.150**	**0.150**	**0.150**
a. Who formulates monetary policy	0.038	0.038	0.038	0.038	0.038	0.038
b. Who has final word in resolution of conflict?	0.075	0.075	0.075	0.075	0.075	0.075
c. Role in the government's budgetary process	0.038	0.038	0.038	0.038	0.038	0.038
3. OBJECTIVES	**0.150**	**0.150**	**0.150**	**0.150**	**0.150**	**0.150**
4. LIMITATIONS ON LENDING TO THE GOVERNMENT	**0.500**	**0.373**	**0.500**	**0.500**	**0.500**	**0.500**
a. Advances (limitation on non-securitised lending)	0.150	0.100	0.150	0.150	0.150	0.150
b. Securitised lending	0.100	0.067	0.100	0.100	0.100	0.100
c. Terms of lending (maturity, interest, amount)	0.100	0.100	0.100	0.100	0.100	0.100
d. Potential borrowers from the bank	0.050	0.050	0.050	0.050	0.050	0.050
e. Limits on central bank lending defined in	0.025	0.008	0.025	0.025	0.025	0.025
f. Maturity of loans	0.025	0.017	0.025	0.025	0.025	0.025
g. Interest rates on loans must be	0.025	0.006	0.025	0.025	0.025	0.025
h. Central bank prohibited from buying or selling government securities in the primary market?	0.025	0.025	0.025	0.025	0.025	0.025
TOTAL INDEX VALUE	1	**0.827**	**0.967**	**0.967**	**0.967**	**0.967**

Source: Author's calculations

the accountability of the central bank. It focuses on the entire governing structure of the bank, not only the governor, and specifically evaluates the level of accountability of the central bank. Furthermore, it includes a criterion on the formulation of the exchange rate policy and tracks the involvement of the central bank in the public debt policy, rather than only in the budgetary process. The modified index captures the involvement of the central bank in managing banking crises and evaluates the role of the central bank in systemic liquidity management. The modified Cuikerman index comprises 18 criteria grouped in 5 aspects of independence (accountability is added to the original Cuikerman index) and resulted in the even higher legal independence of the National Bank of Serbia – of 0.985, that increased from 0.892 under the NBS Law of 2003 (Table 6.2).

Table 6.2 Index of the National Bank of Serbia's legal independence according to Jacome and Vasquez (2005)

Measurement of independence of National Bank of Serbia according to modified Cuikerman index

Description of variable	Max value of Index	Law on the NBS adopted in 2003 and amendments to the Law:				
		2003	2010	2012	2015	2018
1. CENTRAL BANK BOARD	**0.2000**	**0.177**	**0.200**	**0.200**	**0.200**	**0.200**
a. Term of office of governor	0.0400	0.027	0.040	0.040	0.040	0.040
b. Who appoints the Governor?	0.0400	0.040	0.040	0.040	0.040	0.040
c. Appointment and term of office rest of the Board	0.0400	0.030	0.040	0.040	0.040	0.040
d. Dismissal of Board members	0.0600	0.060	0.060	0.060	0.060	0.060
e. CEO allowed to hold another office in government	0.0200	0.020	0.020	0.020	0.020	0.020
2. CENTRAL BANK OBJECTIVES	**0.150**	**0.150**	**0.150**	**0.150**	**0.150**	**0.150**
a. Fundamental objective	0.15	0.150	0.150	0.150	0.150	0.150
3. POLICY FORMULATION	**0.15**	**0.135**	**0.135**	**0.135**	**0.135**	**0.135**
a. Who formulates monetary policy	0.075	0.075	0.075	0.075	0.075	0.075
b. Government directives and resolution of conflicts	0.045	0.045	0.045	0.045	0.045	0.045
c. Central bank involvement in debt approval	0.03	0.015	0.015	0.015	0.015	0.015
4. CENTRAL BANK LENDING	**0.400**	**0.330**	**0.400**	**0.400**	**0.400**	**0.400**
a. Limitations on advances	0.06	0.040	0.060	0.060	0.060	0.060
b. Lending to Government	0.12	0.090	0.120	0.120	0.120	0.120
c. Who decides financing conditions to government	0.04	0.040	0.040	0.040	0.040	0.040
d. Beneficiaries of Central bank financing	0.04	0.040	0.040	0.040	0.040	0.040
e. Interest rates in advances or lending	0.04	0.020	0.040	0.040	0.040	0.040
f. LOLR	0.06	0.060	0.060	0.060	0.060	0.060
g. Financial autonomy	0.04	0.040	0.040	0.040	0.040	0.040
5. ACCOUNTABILITY	**0.100**	**0.100**	**0.100**	**0.100**	**0.100**	**0.100**
a. Accountability of Central Banks	0.075	0.075	0.075	0.075	0.075	0.075
b. Central Bank transparency	0.025	0.025	0.025	0.025	0.025	0.025
TOTAL INDEX VALUE	**1.000**	**0.892**	**0.985**	**0.985**	**0.985**	**0.985**

Source: Author's calculations

In addition to legal independence, the turnover rate of central bank governors may be used as a proxy of practical independence. Cukierman (1992, p. 383) relied on the actual average terms of office of central bank governors. This indicator is based on the assumption that a more rapid turnover implies a lower degree of de facto independence. Based on this criterion, the turnover rate of NBS governors during the entire relevant period (2001–2019) is 0.26, close to the threshold of 0.25, which implies the appointment of one governor every 4 years. During the period observed, two different sub-periods can be identified. In the first sub-period (from 2001 to mid-2012) practical independence was rather low, with a turnover rate of 0.34, as 4 governors served during this period. In the second period (as of mid-2012), the turnover rate was 0.14, as one governor was appointed for 6 years and re-elected (see Table 6.3). This implies that along with institutional and operational independence, the NBS has ranked higher in terms of practical independence since 2012.

Throughout the period from March 2001 to May 2018, the CBCG had four governors, and the turnover rate of the governor for the given period was 0.23 (Radović et al. 2018). This means that the governor turnover rate in Montenegro was within the preferred interval (Table 6.4). The current high independence of the NBRM is complemented with a turnover rate of 0.17, which is roughly one governor every 6 years (Angelovska Bezhoska 2017).

Comparing the values of legal independence assessed by these two indexes for Serbia with the values for other candidate countries, as well as the indexes of central bank independence during the accession of new EU Member States, one may conclude that the NBS is among the most independent central banks

Table 6.3 Turnover rate of central bank governors according to Cukierman (1992)

Governors	Period	Reference period	Turnover rate
M. Dinkić	November 2000–July 2003	November 2000–August 2012	0.34
K. Udovički	July 2003–February 2004		
R. Jelašić	February 2004–July 2010		
D. Šoškić	July 2010–August 2012		
J. Tabaković	Since August 2012	August 2012–November 2019	0.13
		November 2000– November 2019	**0.26**

Source: Author's calculations

Table 6.4 Comparison of the turnover rates of central bank governors in Serbia, Montenegro and North Macedonia

Central bank	Reference period	Turnover rate
National Bank of Serbia	2000–2019	0.26
Central Bank of Montenegro	2001–2018	0.23
National Bank of the Republic of Macedonia	1992–2017	0.17

in the region. Empirical studies should be treated with a dose of reserve, as there may be a difference between legal and actual independence (Cargill 2013). The latter may be influenced by other factors, such as the indirect influence of the executive branch. Albeit attempts have been made to measure the impact of informal factors on the status and operational independence of central banks (Cukierman 2004), such interpretations should be taken with caution (Banaian 2008). Therefore, the next and final section of the Chapter focuses on transparency in pursuing the main goal of a monetary authority in Europe, as one of the most objective measures of de facto independence.

Measuring the transparency of inflation targeting (CBT-IT index)

Central bank transparency is influenced by the monetary policy regime. An inflation targeting regime often leads to a relatively higher level of transparency. This was confirmed by the methodology of Dincer and Eichengreen (2014), and Eijffinger and Geraats (2006). The assessment of central bank transparency was based on 5 aspects (political, economic, procedural, policy and operational) to an overall index of 11, out of a maximum 15 points. Compared with the results for some other central banks in the region (Dincer et al. 2014; Gattin Turkalj & Ljubaj 2017; Naszodi et al. 2016) the NBS ranks among the most transparent central banks, not only in the region, but among inflation targeters as well. The same questionnaire filled out before the introduction of an IT regime would have resulted in a transparency index of around 3 points, which clearly shows an improvement in transparency over time.

Regarding political transparency criteria as defined by the Memorandum on Inflation Targeting as Monetary Strategy,[5] the only numerical guideline for the NBS is the annual percentage change in the consumer price index (CPI). An important part of political transparency is the Agreement on Inflation Targeting between the NBS and the Government of the Republic of Serbia,[6] which declares that the NBS has instrumental independence. In November 2016, the NBS and the Government agreed to lower the inflation target by 1 p.p. to 3%±1.5 p.p. starting from 2017. In the meantime, an inflation target at this level was defined in the NBS Memorandum on Inflation Targets to 2021. The key policy rate (KPR), as an operational objective for short-term money market interest rates, has become the main policy instrument, and is supported in its role by a corridor of interest rates on lending and deposit facilities (±1.25 pp relative to the key policy rate) and also by other open market operations. KPR is set at regular meetings of the Executive Board, which aims to formulate its decisions in a predictable manner based on an analysis of the current economic situation, future developments and the medium–term inflation projection (Tabaković 2019).

The tenth anniversary of inflation targeting in Serbia has revealed several ideas which may improve policy considerations on the achievement of inflation targeting in small non-EU economies. The communication strategy of the NBS, based on a medium-term price stability strategy and focusing on transparency, strengthened its monetary policy credibility and helped to control inflation expectations. In the course of a decade, the following information was given to the public: (1) monetary policy objective(s); (2) monetary policy achievements and interaction with other policies; (3) numerical values for medium-term inflation targets; (4) reasons for the deviation of actual from targeted inflation; (5) tools and measures that are used or will be used to reach the target (Tabaković 2019). In accordance with the principles of transparency and accountability and with a view to anchoring inflation expectations around the target, the National Bank of Serbia communicates with the public through press releases, press conferences, monthly Inflation Reports, the annual Financial Stability Report, and various other publications. The content of the survey of inflation expectations (including medium-term expectations as of 2014) is clearly defined and distributed to the following four groups of respondents: the financial sector, corporate sector, households and trade unions.

Within economic transparency criteria, the NBS provides a broad range of information and analyses of various macroeconomic indicators. Since the introduction of an IT regime, the NBS has been using a quarterly projection model (QPM) as the main macroeconomic forecasting tool. This tool yields precise forecasts on the main macroeconomic variables and explains the transmission mechanisms of Serbia's economy. Quarterly inflation and GDP forecasts are regularly published in the Inflation Report. Each decision made on the key policy rate is explained via a press release following the Executive Board meeting. The Board gives its views on all relevant factors of inflation, as well as the inflation outlook. Medium-term inflation and GDP forecasts, including comments on deviations from previous forecasts, as well as monetary policy stances, are given at the quarterly Inflation Report presentation that is followed by a press conference, and broadcasted live on the NBS website (Table 6.5).

The strengthened independence and transparency of the NBS is expected to positively correlate with more anchored inflation expectations. When measuring the inflation expectations of economic participants in Serbia over the past ten years, two different periods were identified. The first refers to 2009–2012, and was marked by the high and volatile expectations of economic agents, exceeding the upper bound of the target range for consumer price growth

Table 6.5 Transparency index of the National Bank of Serbia (2019)

Type of Transparency	Dincer and Eichengreen (2014) methodology	Eijffinger and Geraats (2006) methodology
1. Political transparency	3	3
2. Economic transparency	3	3
3. Procedural transparency	1	1
4. Policy transparency	2	2
5. Operational transparency	2	2
Total	**11**	**11**

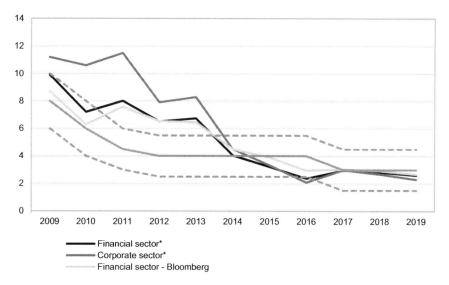

Figure 6.1 One-year inflation expectations of economic agents and inflation target

Source: National Bank of Serbia, Inflation Reports (2019)

despite subdued aggregate demand (Tabakovic 2019, p. 93). Curbing inflationary pressures on a sustainable basis and bringing inflation to a low and
stable level of around 2% on average thereafter, while intensively communicat-
ing with the general public, anchored inflation expectations. More concretely,
since 2014, both one-year and mid-term inflation expectations are within the
NBS inflation target tolerance band (Figure 6.1). This result has confirmed the
hypothesis that growing NBS independence and transparency has contributed
to the greater anchoring of inflation expectations.

Conclusion

This article has studied the political economy of central banking in Serbia,
with special focus on the impact of accession negotiations on the policy regime
of the National Bank of Serbia. The analysis focused on the impact of conditionality and procedures for 'light' economic coordination, which are the
founding pillars of the Economic Programmes of EU Member States. Central
bank independence is considered to be a crucial precondition for pursuing its
main goal of maintaining price stability. Measuring the legal independence
of the NBS based on the index of Cukierman et al. (1992) and the modified Cukierman index of Jacome and Vasquez (2005) indicated that the legal
independence of the NBS has increased over the years and the current legal
framework provides a high level of de jure independence. Progress has been
evident across all included parameters. Strengthening the bank's legal mandate,

the personal independence of the governor and other top bank personnel, institutional independence from the executive branch and strict limitations on government borrowing have helped the implementation of an adequate policy mix conducive to price stability. Serbia's example may offer solutions to policymakers in a small and open economy with a legacy of hyperinflation and consequent high level of euroisation. Despite such a legacy, the NBS ensured price stability, soundness of the financial system and contributed to reducing external and internal imbalances. The inflation targeting strategy chosen by the NBS has allowed greater flexibility in policymaking and the use of available tools, taking into account a new hierarchy of global risks and new interconnectedness between different economies.

The macroeconomic environment and structural reforms implemented on the road to the EU, albeit an external conditionality, have contributed to a shift from external factors toward the importance of domestic factors. The peer group of central banks in the Western Balkan region share a similar organisational culture and learn through the process of interaction. Mechanisms imposed by the EU represent external incentives which diffuse good practices among central banks, strengthening their capacities of organizational learning and facilitating endogenous mechanisms of institutional and policy changes.

Notes

1 Official Gazette of the Republic of Serbia, no. 72/2003, 55/2004, 85/2005 – other law, 44/2010, 76/2012, 106/2012, 14/2015, 40/2015 – Constitutional Court Decision and 44/2018.
2 For instance, IPA Project "Strengthening of the institutional capacities of the National Bank of Serbia" was managed by ECB from February 2011 until December 2013. Its extension, the Twinning Instrument "Strengthening of the institutional capacities of the National Bank of Serbia in the process of EU accession" managed by the ECB was launched in 2018. EuropeAid/158827/ID/ACT/RS
3 The Agreement between the National Bank of Serbia and the Government of the Republic of Serbia on targeting inflation, dated 19 December 2008.
4 This is confirmed by Serbia's progress on the Doing Business List of the World Bank by around 50 places during 2011–2019. In parallel, three leading global rating agencies (Standard & Poor's, Fitch Ratings and Moody's) upgraded Serbia's credit rating.
5 www.nbs.rs/internet/english/30/Memorandum_monetarna_strategija_122008_eng.pdf
6 www.nbs.rs/internet/english/30/Memorandum_gov_nbs_122008_eng.pdf

References

Angelovska Bezhoska, A 2017, 'Central bank independence – the case of the national bank of republic of Macedonia', *Journal of Central Banking Theory and Practice*, vol. 6, no. 3, pp. 35–65.

Bade, R & Parkin, T 1988, *Central bank laws and monetary policy*, Department of Economics, University of Western Ontario, Canada.

Banaian, K 2008, 'Measuring central bank independence: ordering, raking or scoring?', *Working Paper 3*, St. Cloud State University, Economics Faculty.

Bogoev, J & Petrevski, G 2015, 'Central bank independence in transition economies', in J Hölscher & H Tomann (eds.) *Palgrave dictionary of emerging markets and transition economics*, Palgrave, London.

Börzel, TA & Risse, T 2009, 'The transformative power of Europe: the european union and the diffusion of ideas', *KFG Working Papers 001*, Free University Berlin.

Bucholz, M, Schmidt, K & Tonzer, L 2019, 'Do conventional monetary policy instruments matter in unconventional times?', *Discussion Paper No. 27/2019*, Deutsche Bundesbank, Frankfurt am Main.

Cargill, T 2013, 'A critical assessment of measures of central bank independence', *Economic Inquiry*, vol. 51, no. 1, pp. 260–272.

Ćemalović, U 2015, 'Framework for the approximation of national legal systems with the European union's acquis: from a vague definition to jurisprudential implementation', *Croatian Yearbook of European Law and Policy*, vol. 11, pp. 241–258.

Cepilovs, A & Török, Z 2019, 'The politics of fiscal consolidation and reform under external constraints in the European periphery: comparative study of Hungary and Latvia', *Public Management Review*, vol. 21, no. 9, pp. 1287–1306.

Cukierman, A 1992, *Central bank strategy, credibility and independence: theory and evidence*, MIT Press, Cambridge.

Cukierman, A 2004, *Legal, actual and desirable independence: a case study of the bank of Israel*, viewed 10 August 2019, www.tau.ac.il/~alexcuk/pdf/boiactvslegl-4.pdf.

Cukierman, A, Miller, G & Neyapti, B 2002, 'Central bank reform, liberalization and inflation in transition economies – an international perspective', *Journal of Monetary Economics*, vol. 49, no. 2, pp. 237–264.

Cukierman, A, Webb, SB & Neyapti, B 1992, 'Measuring the independence of central banks and its effect on policy outcomes', *The World Bank Economic Review*, vol. 6, no. 3, pp. 353–398.

Dibella, AJ, Nevis, EC & Gould, JM 1996, 'Understanding organizational learning capability', *Journal of Management Studies*, vol. 33, no. 3, pp. 361–379.

Dincer, NN & Eichengreen, B 2014, 'Central bank transparency and independence: updates and new measures', *International Journal of Central Banking*, vol. 10, no. 1, pp. 189–253.

Dvorsky, S 2008, 'Central bank independence in Southeast Europe with a view to future EU accession', *International Journal of Monetary Economics and Finance*, vol. 1, no. 3, pp. 302–328.

Eijffinger, SC & Geraats, PM 2006, 'How transparent are central banks?', *European Journal of Political Economy*, vol. 22, no. 1, pp. 1–21.

European Commission 2016, *Communication on EU enlargement policy*, COM (2016) 715 final.

European Commission 2019, 'Economic reform programmes of Albania, Montenegro, North Macedonia, Serbia, Turkey, Bosnia and Herzegovina and Kosovo★, the commission's overview & country assessments', *Institutional Paper 107*, July 2019, Brussels, viewed 10 September 2019, https://europa.rs/ministerial-dialogue-with-the-western-balkans-and-turkey-eu-encourages-serbia-to-strengthen-the-institutional-framework-and-speed-up-structural-reforms/?lang=en.

European Systemic Risk Board, *Recommendation of 22 December 2011 on the macroprudential mandate of national authorities*, ESRB/2011/3.

European Systemic Risk Board, *Recommendation of 4 April 2013 on intermediate objectives and instruments of macroprudential policy*, ESRB/2013/1.

Fabris, J 2015, 'Inflation targeting in Serbia', *Journal of Central Banking Theory and Practice*, vol. 2, pp. 59–74.

Fernández-Albertos, J 2015, 'The politics of central bank independence', *Annual Review of Political Science*, vol. 18, pp. 217–237.

Freytag, A 2003, 'Central bank independence in central and Eastern Europe on the Eve of EU enlargement', *Occasional Paper No. 4*, Institute for Economic Research, Ljubljana.

Frömmel, M, Garabedian, G & Schobert, F 2011, 'Monetary policy rules in central and Eastern European countries: does the exchange rate matter?', *Journal of Macroeconomics*, vol. 33, no. 4, pp. 807–818.

Galati, G & Moessner, R 2013, 'Macroprudential policy – a literature review', *Journal of Economic Surveys*, vol. 27, no. 5, pp. 846–878.

Gateva, E 2016, *European union enlargement conditionality*, Springer, London.

Gattin Turkalj, K & Ljubaj, I 2017, *CNB transparency and monetary policy, surveys S-25*, viewed 10 September 2019, www.hnb.hr/documents/20182/1998425/s-025.pdf/555fadae-1bc1-4115-88ce-08f43e980ad6.

Goh, S & Richards, G 1997, 'Benchmarking the learning capability of organizations', *European Management Journal*, vol. 15, pp. 575–583.

Government of the Republic of Serbia 2015, 'NLP resolution strategy', *Official Gazette of the Republic of Serbia, No. 72/15.*

Government of the Republic of Serbia 2018, *National programme for the adoption of the acquis* (NPAA), Third Revision, Belgrade.

Grabbe, H 2002, 'European union conditionality and the acquis communautaire', *International Political Science Review*, vol. 23, no. 3, pp. 249–268.

Grilli, V, Masciandaro, D & Tabellini, G 1991, 'Political and monetary institutions and public financial policies in the industrial countries', *Economic Policy*, vol. 6, no. 13, pp. 341–392.

Heise, A 2008, 'European economic governance: what is it, where are we and where do we go?', *International Journal of Public Policy*, vol. 3, no.1/2, pp. 1–19.

Horvath, R & Vaško, D 2016, 'Central bank transparency and financial stability', *Journal of Financial Stability*, vol. 22, no. 1, pp. 45–56.

International Monetary Fund 2019, 'Republic of Serbia – staff report for the 2019 Article IV consultation and second review under the Policy Coordination Instrument', *IMF Country Report, No. 19/238*, July 2019, Washington DC.

Jacome, L & Vasquez, F 2005, 'Any link between legal central bank independence and inflation? Evidence from Latin America and the Caribbean', *IMF Working Paper, No.05/75*, Washington DC.

Jankoski, B 2010, *Trends and challenges of the contemporary central banking – a case study for national bank of the republic of Macedonia*, VDM Verlag Dr. Muller GmbH & Co.KG, Saarbrucken.

Joint Conclusions of the Economic and Financial Dialogue between the EU and the Western Balkans and Turkey 2019, *Economic and financial dialogue between the EU and the Western Balkans and Turkey*, 17 May, Brussels.

Kickert, W & Ongaro, E 2019, 'Influence of the EU (and the IMF) on domestic cutback management: a nine-country comparative analysis', *Public Management Review*, vol. 21, no. 9, pp. 1348–1367.

Lastra, R 2015, *International Financial and Monetary Law*, Oxford University Press, Oxford, UK.

Lavenex, S 2008, 'A governance perspective on the European neighbourhood policy: integration beyond conditionality?', *Journal of European Public Policy*, vol. 15, no. 6, pp. 938–955.

Lianos I, Fazekas, M & Kariluk, M 2016, 'Cross-national diffusion in Europe', in CA Dunlop & CM Radaelli (eds.) *The handbook of regulatory impact assessment*, Edward Elgar Publishing, Cheltenham.

Maliszewski, WS 2000, 'Central bank independence in transition economies', *Economics of Transition*, vol. 8, no. 3, pp. 749–789.

Miščević, T & Mrak, M 2017, 'The EU accession process: Western Balkans vs EU-10', *Croatian Political Science Review*, vol. 54, no. 4, pp. 185–204.

Mishkin, FS 2004, 'Can inflation targeting work in emerging market countries?', in *Festchrift in Honnor of Guillermo Calvo*, International Monetary Fund, Washington DC.

Momani, B & Amand, S 2015, 'Best practices in central bank organizational culture, learning and structure: the case of the Moroccan central bank', *Economic Notes*, vol. 44, no. 3, pp. 449–482.

Naszodi, A, Csavas, C, Erhart, S & Felcser, D 2016, 'Which aspects of central bank transparency matter? A comprehensive analysis of the effect of transparency on survey forecasts', *International Journal of Central Banking*, vol. 12, no. 4, pp. 147–192.

National Bank of Serbia 2015, *Macroprudential framework*, March, viewed 10 September 2019, www.nbs.rs/internet/english/18/macroprudential_framework_201503.pdf.

Radović, M, Radonjić, M & Đurašković, J 2018, 'Central bank independence – the case of the central bank of Montenegro', *Journal of Central Banking Theory and Practice*, vol. 3, pp. 25–40.

Šoškic, D 2015, 'Inflation targeting challenges of emerging market countries: case of Serbia', *Economic Annals*, vol. 60, no. 204, pp. 7–30.

Tabakovic, J 2019, 'A decade of full-fledged inflation targeting in Serbia', *Ekonomika Preduzeća*, vol. 67, no. 1–2, pp. 83–100.

Tabakovic, J & Mrak, M 2015, *Economic governance in Europe and EU accession process: what is the role of central banks*, Conference Proceedings, Belgrade.

Vujović, D 2015, 'Serbia: fiscal consolidation – program design and political economy issues', *Ekonomika preduzeća*, vol. 64, no. 1–2, pp. 1–13.

Walsh, CE 2009, 'Inflation targeting: what have we learned?', *International Finance*, vol. 12, no. 2, pp. 195–233.

Yağcı, M 2017, 'Institutional entrepreneurship and organisational learning: financial stability policy design in Turkey', *Policy and Society*, vol. 36, no. 4, pp. 539–555.

Part 3

Central Banking in Africa

7 The political economy of central banking in Nigeria

A resource dependence perspective

Franklin Nakpodia, Titilayo Ogunyemi, and Folajimi Ashiru

Introduction

The economic importance of a robust central banking system continues to attract considerable attention in the literature. This interest, especially in the last few centuries, demands that central banks consolidate their primary tasks, that is, its relationship with the government, its interaction with financial market participants, its internal management structure and decision-making process (Ugolini 2013). In addition to these responsibilities, a growing number of scholars (e.g., Crowe & Meade 2008; Alpanda & Honig 2014; Agoba et al. 2017) claim that the performance of central banks reflects its degree of independence. However, central to the independence retained by central banks is government and political institutions. Political interference can affect the independence of central banks. Nag et al. (2018) identified 17 central banks (in countries such as Turkey, New Zealand, the United States, the United Kingdom, India, Mexico, among others) that have experienced an unusual amount of political interference. The interference of political actors in central bank operations, according to Ugolini (2013), underpins the notion of political economy. As a feature of economics, Ugolini (2013) explains that political economy broadly describes how the interplay among different interest groups influences economic policymaking. The interaction implies that the performance of central banks embodies a degree of collective bargaining among a variety of interested parties.

While the literature (e.g., Epstein 1992; Crowe & Meade 2008; Agoba et al. 2017) admits that political influence alters the operations of central banks, a core feature in the literature is the inconsistent findings reported between developed and developing economies. Using the probability that a central bank governor will be replaced following a political change in power, Cukierman and Webb (1995) show that where there is a non-constitutional (e.g., military coup) change in government (typical in developing and emerging economies), the central bank governor is replaced about half the time within six months. In contrast, when there is a routine change in government, the central bank governor is less likely to be replaced within six months. This result is consistent with findings in a prior study (Cukierman et al. 1992), which indicates that the frequency of change of central banks' leadership is a valid proxy for central bank independence among developing countries. Balls et al. (2016) also suggest that, unlike in emerging and developing economies, central banks in advanced countries could afford to sacrifice some political independence without undermining its operational autonomy.

In contributing to the scholarship in this field, this chapter focuses on Africa's largest economy Nigeria to explore the link between the independence of the Central Bank of Nigeria (CBN) and the country's political institutions (i.e., the role of political elites). In doing this, the chapter employs the resource dependence theoretical notion to understand in what ways the external resources available to an organisation (specifically, political influence) affect the performance of the CBN. This chapter emphasises that the capacity of the CBN to support economic development in a developing economy is maximised when monetary and fiscal policies are shielded from the interference of political elites who lean towards seeking contradictory, albeit personal objectives. To minimise the impact of political institutions on CBN's independence, this chapter articulates some propositions. Among others, this chapter proposes that the CBN should implement an incentive approach for its executives that is characterised by specific performance targets. Also, this chapter recommends that the appointment of CBN executives should rely on criteria that depart from the country's civil service regulations.

The rest of the chapter proceeds by discussing the CBN, focusing on its evolution and its economic importance. Next, the chapter reviews the resource dependence perspective, exploring the impact of external resources on the independence of central banks. This chapter concludes by articulating proposals that enhance the CBN's autonomy, thereby allowing it to effectively support the economic and developmental goals of the Nigerian government, as stated in the CBN Act (2007).

Central banking in Nigeria

Contemporary central banking dates to 1668 with the establishment of the Swedish National Bank (Sveriges Riksbank) (Fregert 2018). Makanjuola (2015) informs that from the 17th century, the responsibilities, and objectives of central banks in a dynamic world have dominated debates among policymakers and economists. The frontrunners of central banking in Europe were instituted primarily for the acquisition of government debt, as a clearing house for business-related activities, and currency stability. Given the economic impact of central banks, virtually every country across the globe has invested in central banking. Nigeria also embraced the central bank concept with the establishment of the CBN, which commenced operations in 1959 (CBN 2019). A combination of factors which include the increasing call for political independence, the growing traction among indigenous banks and the need to incentivise the country's economic growth prompted the birth of the CBN.

The role of central banks in developing economies like Nigeria is multi-faceted. Makanjuola (2015) argues that given the unpredictable institutional environment among emerging economies, central banks in such countries aim to provide a sense of commitment, sternness, and sturdiness to its financial markets. A range of events in the Nigerian banking system alludes to this fact. In the late 1980s and early 1990s, the Nigerian banking sector experienced considerable uncertainty owing to widespread bank failures which impacted the capital market and stifled economic growth. The country also witnessed another systemic banking crisis in 2009/2010, culminating in a phased programme of reforms aimed at fortifying the country's banking sector and boosting its international competitiveness (Nakpodia 2018). The primary economic obligations of the CBN, which compares with the goals of central banks in many countries, are discussed as follows:

First, the CBN acts as the *monetary regulator*. The bank is responsible for designing and implementing monetary policies in Nigeria. The primary focus of this intervention is the maintenance of price stability and the management of inflation level. The apex bank executes the monetary policies of the government by navigating market interest rates (short-term) to accomplish predetermined targets. This is achieved by the strategic management of the supply of liquidity (the bank's deposits with the CBN) using open market instruments (Bahago et al. 2019). However, the monetary regulatory function of the CBN provides ample opportunities for political interference, as politicians wield their influence in promoting policies that might be inconsistent with broader economic expectations (Nakpodia et al. 2018).

Second, the CBN is the *banker to the government*. The CBN Act (2007) gives the central bank the overall administration and control of the financial policies of the federal government. In this instance, the CBN provides legal tender currency in the country, maintains external reserves to safeguard the international value of the legal tender; facilitates the emergence of a robust financial system, acts as banker and provides economic and financial advice to the Government. Taken as a whole, the CBN is responsible for implementing the Banks and Other Financial Institutions Act (BOFIA), enacted in 1991. BOFIA (1991) focuses on, among others, the establishment of an effective payment system in the country. Besides, the CBN, on behalf of the government, executes numerous developmental projects in the agricultural, industrial and financial sectors of the economy.

Third, the CBN acts as the *banker to other banks* in the country. In addition to its responsibility as banker to the government, the CBN is statutorily saddled with the regulation and supervision of banks in Nigeria. The CBN Act and BOFIA confer on the CBN the authority over banks. This authority allows the CBN to issue and withdraw banking licences, undertake bank examination, establish prudential guidelines, and ensure that banks comply with regulatory and statutory provisions (Adetunji 2009). The CBN also, as it deems necessary, introduces prudential regulations for licensed banks in addition to the statement of accounting standards and capital adequacy requirements. Typically, these guidelines indicate the benchmarks for banks in categorising non-performing loans (CBN 2019). Given the challenges in the banking environment in Nigeria in the last few decades, the CBN has consistently intervened in the sector. In 2005, for instance, the CBN increased the minimum share capital of Nigerian banks (Alajekwu & Obialor 2014). Furthermore, in 2009, the CBN sacked the headship of five (5) banks in the country due to unethical practices and poor management of their banks (Omoh & Komolafe 2009).

Despite the critical contributions of the CBN to the Nigerian economy and particularly, its banking sector, an assortment of issues such as institutional quality, systemic corruption, weak enforcement of regulations, poor infrastructure, illiquid capital market, among others (Okoh & Ebi 2013; Fagbemi & Ajibike 2018; Nakpodia & Adegbite 2018; Nakpodia et al. 2018) blend to frustrate its operations. It is also worth reporting that CBN's policies have been the subject of litigations. For instance, at the expiration of the banking consolidation deadline, announced in 2005, fourteen (14) banks failed to meet the requirements. One of such banks was Société Generale Bank of Nigeria (SGBN), resulting in the revocation of its banking licence. SGBN filed a court injunction against the CBN challenging the revocation. A Federal High Court favoured SGBN in its ruling, maintaining that the CBN's withdrawal of the licence was unconstitutional, unjustifiable, and null and void (Adetunji 2009).

Fundamental to these challenges is the role of political actors and their interference in CBN's operations. The CBN Act (2007) mandates that the CBN board must include a representative of the Ministry of Finance who typically represents the executive arm of government (a political appointee). Uche (1997) unpacks the challenges in such an arrangement, emphasising that a lack of operational independence emerges from the structure. There has been further evidence of political intrusions in CBN's operations. In 2012, for example, two bills were proposed in the Nigerian parliament (Rice 2012). The first bill sought to compel the CBN to submit its annual budget to the National Assembly to supposedly ensure fiscal transparency and accountability. The second bill demanded that parliament be allowed to replace board members of the CBN with political appointees. The CBN Governor (at the time), Sanusi Lamido insisted that passing such bills diminishes the power of the CBN and expose it to greater manipulation by politicians. Recently, Ohuocha (2018) noted a threat to CBN's independence following a standoff over the confirmation of new members of the CBN's interest rate committee. The confrontation involved the CBN, on one hand, and the executive and the legislative arms of government, on the other. This impasse led to a slump in the stock market index (Ohuocha 2018).

The seeming undesirable influence and interference of political actors in CBN operations notwithstanding, this chapter enriches the underlying debate by paying attention to the probable benefits which accrue to organisations like the CBN on account of its interaction with external influences, for example, politicians. Given its economic value, scholars (Goodman 1991; Lohmann 1998; Zhang 2005) suggest that the performance of central banks demands that they must necessarily explore and take advantage of opportunities offered by its external environment. In delving into this line of thought, this chapter embraces the resource dependence notion.

Resource dependence and central banking

The concept of political economy has been examined using a variety of theoretical lenses (Pagano & Volpin 2005; Haque et al. 2011), underlining the comprehensiveness of the subject. In embracing the resource dependence proposition, this chapter extends the intellectual horizon of the political economy, drawing traction to a previously overlooked theoretical option in the political economy scholarship.

The resource dependence theory thrives on two central themes (Hillman & Dalziel 2003; Hillman et al. 2009). First, the theory emphasises the relationship between an organisation and its environment, highlighting the significance of environmental linkages between corporations and external resources (Pfeffer & Salancik 2003). The second theme underpinning resource dependence theory is its capacity to draw attention to the power of corporate directors in ensuring that organisations benefit from the resources presented by its business environment (Agrawal & Knoeber 2001; Hillman 2005; Carter et al. 2010). In this instance, directors are primarily saddled with the task of connecting the firm with external factors that allow organisations to optimise the resources it needs to enhance the firm's ability to maximise the wealth of its shareholders.

The thrust of resource dependence, based on the interactions between the two themes identified, can be illustrated as follows – firms depend on resources to pursue and achieve their predetermined goals. These resources are accessed from or provided by the external environment. However, the environment is an agglomeration of other organisations. It could, therefore, be reasoned that the resources needed by an organisation are supplied by other organisations. Consequently, the ownership, control and search for resources trigger economic activities such as negotiation, interaction, interdependence and more importantly, the allocation of power across business environments (Kim et al. 2005). This is consistent with Shleifer and Vishny's (1997) narrative of corporate governance, as providers of finance seek to maximise their returns. In response, organisations, through its directors, must articulate a strategy that enhances its power to attract the resources it needs, at the least possible cost. This interaction informs Tricker's (2019) perspective of resource dependence, which stresses the role of corporate boards as the linchpin between organisations and the resources it needs to achieve its corporate goals.

Drawing from the first theme that focuses on the collaboration between businesses and its immediate environment, the relationship is defined by ownership and control of resources (Fama & Jensen 1983), and primarily moderated by the degree of institutional advancement (Aguilera & Jackson 2003). In developing and emerging economies, for example, many of the resources are directly or indirectly controlled by the government. As a result, the power of directors to attract resources correlates positively with their access to and relationship with key political actors (Hillman 2005). Shareholders are therefore encouraged to appoint directors that have access to key politicians and government officials. This expectation has become an important executive recruitment criterion among organisations. By leveraging on their knowledge, connections and reputation in their industry and society, executives can extract valuable resources in favour of their organisations. However, it is noteworthy to acknowledge that this relationship portends a variety of implications for corporate independence and autonomy.

With respect to central banking, independence and autonomy concerns have been examined using the resource dependence notion (Pfeffer & Salancik 2003; Boyd 1990; Jung & Moon 2007). Given that the resources of the central banks are typically domiciled in the hands of the government, the independence and autonomy of the central bank are characteristically impacted by external variables such as the government. Jung and Moon (2007) explain that as governments and organisations (such as central banks) build close relationships to drive economic performance, they become interdependent in many ways. They (Jung & Moon 2007) report that the use of public resources (as central banks rely on government funding) has a dual effect – it reduces managerial autonomy but creates a boost in institutional legitimacy. Relying on an earlier study by Boyd (1990), variations in institutional environments significantly impacts the interconnections between central bank independence, managerial performance and governments (as the provider of resources).

In many developing economies, the subject of independence, especially among government agencies (such as Central Banks), remains a concern. Taking into account the role of government in setting up these establishments, Hayo and Hefeker (2002) and Arnone and Romelli (2013) unearth cases where a vested political actor unduly influences government agencies. For this reason, such agencies are hindered from implementing policies that would benefit most of its stakeholders where such policies are inconsistent with the preference of political or government actors. As the government is the biggest economic agent in business exchanges in such countries, corporate directors are obliged to consent to sub-optimal corporate policies in order to access resources in the environment. These concerns have provoked a stream of (corporate governance) literature investigating the factors that impede organisational independence (Schnatterly & Johnson 2014; Velikonja 2014) and its impact on firm performance (Lefort & Urzúa 2008; García-Ramos & García-Olalla 2014). Interestingly, the scholarship has paid due attention to the autonomy of central banks.

The degree of central bank independence (CBI) is one of the four factors influencing the monetary policy of countries (Epstein 1992). Loungani and Sheets (1997) and Agoba et al. (2017) illustrate how the independence of central banks contributes to lowering long-run average inflation. Contrastingly, there is a strand of literature that reports a negative correlation between CBI and economic characteristics such as inflation (Brumm 2011; Arnone & Romelli

2013). The failure of CBI to incentivise the projected economic development rests on a mix of factors. In particular, the political system frustrates the independence of central banks. Though Ugolini (2013) contends that central banks would hardly survive in the absence of reliable political support, the political system is consistently perceived as the major impediment to the independence of central banks (Cukierman & Webb 1995). This concern assumes a more considerable significance in developing economies.

In weak institutional environments such as Nigeria, a range of elements characterise the performance of board members and their ability to deploy external resources in realising corporate objectives (Hermalin & Weisbach 1991; Kula 2005; Lefort & Urzua 2008). Whereas the research in this space converges predominantly around internal organisational variables such as board size, board independence, and board diversity, among others, exogenous firm considerations have equally attracted increased traction. The resource dependence theorising acknowledges that the gamut of resources accessible by organisations extends beyond the environment (Hillman et al. 2009; Drees & Heugens 2013). For instance, Chin et al. (2013) and Domadenik et al. (2016) analyse the role of political actors and their influence on organisational outcomes. In Nigeria, there is empirical evidence corroborating the relationship between the political system and corporate performance. Nakpodia and Adegbite (2018) report that political elites in the country engage three instruments (political influence, political authority, and political immunity) to retain control over corporate choices. The institutional and political arrangements in the country imply that the CBN has not been able to insulate itself from the problems initiated by corrupt political interventions.

Given the oppressive influence of political actors in the Nigerian business environment, a core challenge faced by the CBN is autonomy. There is an expectation that central banks should enjoy a high degree of independence from members of the political class (Hayo & Hefeker 2002). According to De Beaufort Wijnholds and Hoogduin (1994), the case for central bank autonomy has been made with considerable success validated by a global movement towards greater independence. The impact of CBN autonomy on the Nigerian economy is diverse. Okafor and Eyiuche (1999) showed that CBN autonomy is significantly and positively related to inflation but inversely related to economic growth and interest rates in the country. While this outcome stresses the economic importance of CBN's autonomy, Makanjuola (2015) contends that its operations and critical decisions tend to reflect the preferences of key political actors rather than the monetary and fiscal necessities of the economy. Indeed, this interaction has brought undue pressure on CBN officials to act as a conduit for achieving unethical and corrupt outcomes.

Yusuf (2015) cites the alleged misappropriation of public funds by the Nigerian government from May 2010 to May 2015 with the connivance of key officials of the CBN. This case prompted concerns relating to the approval procedure for release of funds in the organisation, the anticipation that the CBN acts in the public interest and the relative ease with the obligor limit of the bank was set aside to accommodate executive (political) fiat. Furthermore, in 2017, a former Minister for Finance in Nigeria called on federal legislators to strip the CBN of some of its powers to allow for greater executive oversight over the policies of the apex bank (Nwachukwu 2017). While the minister argued that the call was intended to stem the disconnect between monetary and fiscal policies of the government implemented by the CBN, it is essential to acknowledge that the independence of the CBN is designed to insulate monetary and fiscal policies from political actors seeking short term payoffs. Besides, given the numerous corruption allegations against politicians, it is contentious when politicians in Nigeria claim that they are acting in the public interest.

Further concerns regarding CBN autonomy rests in the operationalisation of its policies. In highlighting some problems of the CBN, Prof Charles Soludo (a former governor of the CBN) notes that there is little incentive for Nigerian banks to extend loans to riskier sectors at lower interest rates because riskless government instruments such as treasury bills are available at higher interest rates. While this exposes the incoherence between policies of the political class (the executive arm of government) and those of the CBN, it uncovers how the government may circumvent and frustrate the monetary and fiscal goals of the CBN. Such possibilities compel CBN executives to snuggle up to politicians, at the expense of their independence.

In the main, the literature suggests that the political class has invaded the autonomy of the CBN. This has led to sub-optimal results in the CBN as the (inconsistent) goals of political actors impact the capability of board members to harness their knowledge of the business environment for the benefit of CBN. These challenges, nonetheless, political actors desirous of economic growth must understand that the CBN is crucial to attempts at entrenching a robust economic architecture in the country. Counting on this expectation, this chapter proceeds by discussing some policy options that may enhance the political economy of the CBN.

Maximising the political economy of the CBN

Splitting of functions

In Nigeria, the CBN oversees wide-ranging responsibilities. Given the traditional nature of the country's institutional environment (Okike et al. 2015), the extensive remit of the CBN exposes it to manipulations by political elites. The spread of its responsibilities increases the likelihood of interactions and contact between CBN executives and the country's political leaders, allowing politicians to exert undue pressure on CBN directors (Oloni & Adewara 2013). Therefore, a course of action that streamlines the functions of the CBN would reduce the chances of politicians to wield excessive pressure over CBN officials.

Given that Nigeria is steeped in weak institutions (Adegbite 2015), a strategy for lowering the political impact on CBN's operations is to break up the functions of the CBN. In this instance, the CBN could be responsible for the monetary policies of the country, while a separate financial supervisory authority is established to oversee banking supervision. Indeed, considering the growing interest and investment by politicians in Nigerian mainstream banks, relieving the CBN from banking supervision responsibilities will not only help in addressing its workforce challenges, but it will also shield the apex bank from frequent engagement with and exposure to political officeholders. By breaking up the functions of the CBN, its leadership will become more professional and less politically inclined.

Performance-related compensation package

Attempts to improve corporate governance practices across the globe have emphasised the implementation of a performance-based remuneration strategy (Kirkpatrick 2009; Johnston 2014). Interestingly, virtually all the banks in Nigeria adopt this recommendation in remunerating its executives. In contrast, the CBN remuneration system pays very little attention to performance-related compensation, as a substantial element of the remuneration of the executives is fixed. This strategy creates a variety of problems. It impedes the motivation of the executives to commit optimally to the attainment of organisational (e.g., CBN) objectives (Agarwal 2010). This is evident in the apathetic and sluggish attitude of executives to their assigned responsibilities. Such attitude also denotes that executives lack the incentive to confront or challenge interference by politicians and other government officials. The motivation to challenge such interference is lost as it has little or no effect on their compensation package.

Besides, the CBN workforce continues to increase. Between 2015 and 2018, the staff strength has grown by 13% from 6955 (2015) to 7891 (2018) (CBN Annual Reports 2017, 2018). Consequently, the introduction of a performance-driven reward system could enable the bank to manage its staff strength as well as improve their effectiveness and efficiency. The proposal to implement a performance-related compensation package will also allow the CBN to focus on its core activities, reduce operational costs, and become more accountable. Moreover, such a policy can boost the professionalism of the CBN, as a performance-related pay structure could enable the bank to benchmark its staff performance with employees of similar organisations.

Disentangling the CBN from traditional civil service regulations

Nigeria, like many countries of the world, has an established civil service system. The civil service is organised around federal ministries. The ministries are headed by a minister, appointed by the president. Despite the various attempts to position the Nigerian civil service among the best organised and managed in the world, the establishment has remained stagnant and inefficient (Magbadelo 2016; Tom 2017). Various reform interventions aimed at improving the civil service have had little effect. While Ijewereme (2015) reports that corruption has impacted the effectiveness of Nigerian civil service, Eke (2016) clarified that weak institutional structures, cumbersome administrative processes, negative attitude of civil servants to work and the insatiable appetite for wealth at all cost fuel corruption in the Nigerian civil service.

Unfortunately, considerable elements of the structure and operations of the CBN draw from the country's civil service regulations. It is therefore unsurprising that many of the problems confronting the Nigerian civil service, particularly the intrusion by government officials and politicians manifest in the CBN. The traditional operational structure of the civil service does not allow for the emergence of a contemporary, forward-looking organisation (Beetseh 2014) that the CBN should represent. It is therefore critical that the CBN must be isolated from the restraints imposed by the Nigerian civil service regulation if it is to enhance its professionalism and contribute to the growth and development of the country.

CBN as an autonomous institution

Evidence shows that in developed countries, price stability and economic growth are achieved when central banks experience a relatively high degree of autonomy (Oluduro 2014). In Nigeria, the CBN manages and controls the exchange rate of the Naira (the local currency) through regular interventions in the foreign exchange market. The dollars which the CBN sells in the foreign exchange market are obtained mainly from crude oil sales by the Nigerian government. The reliance of the CBN on the government for its foreign currencies impedes its operational autonomy and exposes it to the dictates of the ruling government. A recent case exemplifies this concern. On August 9th, 2019, the Nigerian president directed that the CBN should not allocate forex to importers of food items that can be produced locally (Erezi 2019). While analysts and commentators support the idea of local food production, they criticised the president for issuing a directive to a supposedly autonomous CBN.

Given the foregoing, the autonomy of the CBN could be enhanced if the activities that compel the CBN to rely on the federal government are streamlined. This may be via a predetermined annual budget which eliminates the constant need for the CBN to look to the government for funding. Autonomy may also be achieved by adopting an open market foreign exchange system that will give the CBN more control in articulating and implementing its related policies. This would enable the CBN to attain more market stability and ultimately, less political interference.

Strengthening the capital base of the CBN

There is a deliberation in the Nigerian banking sector challenging the economic relevance of the existing capital base of banks. These calls have relied mostly on adverse foreign exchange movements. Based on the exchange rate of USD/132.85 in 2009 when the current thresholds were set, the capital base of banks is N15 billion (USD113 million) for a regional licence, N25 billion (US$188m) for a national licence and N100 billion (US$753m) for an international licence. However, at the current exchange rate of USD/305, the capital base of Nigerian banks, in real terms, has plummeted to USD49 million for regional licence, USD82 million for national licence and USD328 million for international licence.

While the discussion regarding an improved capitalisation among Nigerian banks gathers momentum, the capital base of the CBN, as the industry regulator, would benefit from a corresponding increase from its existing N100 billion (USD328 million). This is necessary bearing in mind that the current CBN capitalisation is similar to the capital requirements of banks seeking an international licence, which may impact the ability of the CBN to supervise such banks adequately. An increase in CBN's capital would provide the financial muscle necessary for the bank to effectively fulfil its lender of last resort function and improve its sectoral development roles. Furthermore, as noted in Hasse et al. (1990), the adequate capitalisation of the CBN would enhance its independence and insulate it from the overbearing influence of political elites, as this would translate to less reliance on the government for financial support.

Focus on core activities

An issue confronting many public institutions is the lack of focus. It is challenging to make a distinction between what the actual responsibilities of a central bank are, and the specific business that it has undertaken. For example, the CBN collects data on exports, imports and other trade-related activities to support local and foreign users. However, in Nigeria, there is a public authority, that is, the Nigerian Bureau of Statistics (NBS) whose primary activity is the collection and dissemination of statistical data. If the CBN transfers this responsibility to the NBS, it will free up resources that could help it to improve its overall efficiency. Moreover, this will help the bank to deepen its micro and macro supervision responsibilities. Heikensten (2003) shows that concentration on core activities among organisations is a prerequisite for sustainable performance. Refocusing CBN's operations could be extended to its non-core services, as it may consider outsourcing services such as cleaning, security and corporate social responsibility initiatives.

A strategic rationale for proposing increased concentration of CBN's operations lies in the possibility to alter the perception of stakeholders towards the bank. Political interference is possible where politicians identify structural and operational issues among central banks. A concentration on core businesses sends a signal to stakeholders that signify a more professional organisation. This signal, in the long term, discourages the motivation while limiting the opportunities for external political influences.

Monitoring manpower development

In developing economies, matters relating to the political economy of the central banks accentuate the concern regarding the level of professionalism of CBN executives. Critical to this development is the restricted attention directed at training and development, which means that CBN executives are deprived of adequate understanding and appreciation of contemporary, global best practices in central banking. Inadequate exposure to training and development programmes also implies that the dangers of political interference, among others, are not sufficiently understood or accounted for. These shortcomings provide further gaps for government officials to interfere and manipulate CBN appointees in pursuit of their economic preferences.

In Nigeria, the CBN has responded to this challenge by developing a framework to support the development of its executives. According to its Annual Report (2017), it has, in partnership with various training organisations, instituted soft skills training on leadership development, lean management, among others. However, an effective monitoring methodology enriches the effect of human development programmes. Consequently, a transparent monitoring system of the training programmes of CBN executives must be implemented. Monitoring the development of CBN directors provides the impetus to improve their productivity. It is critical that the monitoring activity is assigned to a reputable, independent, external body, whose report must be available in the public domain. A consciousness of this requirement among executives would improve their overall accountability, as well as increase their awareness of the impact of political interference in their decision-making and their future career prospects.

Conclusion and areas for further research

This chapter extends the frontiers of the political economy of central banking. Drawing insights from an under-researched political context, this chapter examines how the independence and the autonomy of the Central Bank of Nigeria react to the political institutions in the country. To deepen the discussion in this chapter, the resource dependence theory with a corporate governance perspective was employed to understand the need and incentive that embed the relationship between the CBN and its operating environment.

The basis of resource dependence thrives on the argument that organisations must explore resources presented by its operating environment to enhance their corporate output. Thus, the CBN is anticipated to identify such resources and take advantage accordingly. This expectation is evident in the appointment of the governor and board members, reliance on the government for funding, drawing from the expertise and knowledge provided by the banking community, among others. However, the weak institutional environment in Nigeria has been exploited by government agents and politicians to exert undue pressure on the CBN hierarchy. Consequently, the benefits and resources derived by the CBN on account of its association with the external business environment are diluted by the inappropriate and ill-advised interference from government bureaucrats.

In acknowledging these challenges, this chapter contends that the capacity of the CBN to fulfil its corporate goals demand strategic policies that would insulate the apex bank from the suffocating interests of political elites. Consequently, this chapter proposes an assemblage of interventions that include splitting the responsibilities of the CBN, implementing a performance-driven remuneration policy, and disentangling the CBN from the outdated modus operandi of the Nigerian civil service. This chapter further recommends improvement in the bank's capital base, a streamlining of its core activities and the establishment of a system that monitors the impact, on the bank's executives, of its various training and development programmes.

Besides, while a recommendation relating to the remuneration of central bank executives has been proposed, the concept of corporate governance offers additional opportunities for improving not only the independence of central banks but also their political economy. In particular, we look to stakeholder activism as a way of limiting government's interference in central banks' activities. It is imperative for the broader literature to examine how a wider combination of stakeholders can influence the actions of central banks when they insist on exercising their rights. This is particularly relevant in developing and emerging economies where the existence of such stakeholder groups is virtually non-existent. There are pieces of evidence where annual general meetings are deliberately held in locations that the majority of stakeholders may not find accessible. Atte (2015) and Nelson (2015) add that some shareholders receive notice of annual general meeting long after the date of the meeting.

In line with the foregoing, and given that the aforementioned proposals relied on minimal empirical input, future studies should aim to collect relevant data, bearing in mind the institutional peculiarities among varieties of capitalism, to investigate how the recommendations proposed in this chapter may enhance the independence of the CBN. Such empirical investigation would provide a robust understanding of the political economy of central banking as well as advance the literature in this research field.

References

Adegbite, E 2015, 'Good corporate governance in Nigeria: antecedents, propositions and peculiarities', *International Business Review*, vol. 24, pp. 319–330.

Adetunji, O 2009, 'Cracking a nut with a sledgehammer – has the central bank of Nigeria been too hasty in revoking banking licenses?', *Law and Financial Markets Review*, vol. 3, no. 1, pp. 49–53.

Agarwal, AS 2010, 'Motivation and executive compensation', *Journal of Corporate Governance*, vol. 9, no. 1/2, pp. 27–46.

Agoba, AM, Abor, J, Osei, KA & Sa-Aadu, J 2017, 'Central bank independence and inflation in Africa: the role of financial systems and institutional quality', *Central Bank Review*, vol. 17, no. 4, pp. 131–146.

Agrawal, A & Knoeber, CR 2001, 'Do some outside directors play a political role?', *The Journal of Law and Economics*, vol. 44, no. 1, pp. 179–198.

Aguilera, RV & Jackson, G 2003, 'The cross-national diversity of corporate governance: dimensions and determinants', *Academy of Management Review*, vol. 28, no. 3, pp. 447–465.

Alajekwu, UB & Obialor, MC 2014, 'Nigerian bank recapitalisation reforms: effect on the banks and the economy (2000–2012)', *International Journal of Managerial Studies and Research*, vol. 2, no. 2, pp. 48–56.

Alpanda, S & Honig, A 2014, 'The impact of central bank independence on the performance of inflation targeting regimes', *Journal of International Money and Finance*, vol. 44, pp. 118–135.

Arnone, M & Romelli, D 2013, 'Dynamic central bank independence indices and inflation rate: a new empirical exploration', *Journal of Financial Stability*, vol. 9, no. 3, pp. 385–398.

Atte, B 2015, 'Enhancing shareholder's participation in company meetings in Nigeria through application of information technology', *IOSR Journal of Humanities and Social Science*, vol. 20, no. 9, pp. 62–66.

Bahago, K, Jelilov, G & Celik, B 2019, 'Impact of banking supervision on liquidity risk and credit risk: evidence from Nigeria', *International Journal of Economics and Financial Issues*, vol. 9, no. 3, pp. 200–204.

Balls, E, Howat, J & Stansbury, A 2016, 'Central bank independence revisited: after the financial crisis, what should a model central bank look like?', *M-RCBG Associate Working Paper Series*, vol. 67, pp. 1–114.

Beetseh, K 2014, 'Challenges of ethics and accountability in Nigerian civil service', *Journal of Poverty, Investment and Development*, vol. 3, pp. 1–5.

BOFIA 1991, 'Banks and Other Financial Institutions Act', viewed 15 June 2019, https://www.cbn.gov.ng/OUT/PUBLICATIONS/BSD/1991/BOFIA.PDF.

Boyd, B 1990, 'Corporate linkages and organizational environment: a test of the resource dependence model', *Strategic Management Journal*, vol. 11, no. 6, pp. 419–430.

Brumm, HJ 2011, 'Inflation and central bank independence: two-way causality?', *Economics Letters*, vol. 111, no. 3, pp. 220–222.

Carter, DA, D'Souza, F, Simkins, BJ & Simpson, WG 2010, 'The gender and ethnic diversity of US boards and board committees and firm financial performance', *Corporate Governance: An International Review*, vol. 18, no. 5, pp. 396–414.

Central Bank of Nigeria 2007, 'Central Bank of Nigeria (CBN) Act', viewed 20 July 2019, www.cbn.gov.ng/OUT/PUBLICATIONS/BSD/2007/CBNACT.PDF.

Central Bank of Nigeria 2017, 'Annual report', viewed 12 June 2019, www.cbn.gov.ng/Out/2018/RSD/CBN%202017%20ANNUAL%20REPORT_WEB.pdf.

Central Bank of Nigeria 2018, 'Annual report', viewed 12 June 2019, https://www.cbn.gov.ng/Out/2019/RSD/2018%20AR%20KAMA1.pdf.

Central Bank of Nigeria 2019, 'Regulatory measures to improve lending to the real sector of the Nigerian economy', viewed 22 August 2019, https://www.cbn.gov.ng/Out/2019/BSD/CIRCULAR%20ON%20REGULATORY%20MEASURES%20TO%20IMPROVE%20BANK%20LENDING%20-October%202019.pdf.

Chin, M, Hambrick, DC & Treviño, LK 2013, 'Political ideologies of CEOs: the influence of executives' values on corporate social responsibility', *Administrative Science Quarterly*, vol. 58, no. 2, pp. 197–232.

Crowe, C & Meade, EE 2008, 'Central bank independence and transparency: evolution and effectiveness', *European Journal of Political Economy*, vol. 24, no. 4, pp. 763–777.

Cukierman, A & Webb, SB 1995, 'Political influence on the central bank: international evidence', *The World Bank Economic Review*, vol. 9, no. 3, pp. 397–423.

Cukierman, A, Webb, SB & Neyapti, B 1992, 'Measuring the independence of central banks and its effect on policy outcomes', *The World Bank Economic Review*, vol. 6, no. 3, pp. 353–398.

De Beaufort Wijnholds, JO & Hoogduin, LH 1994, 'Central bank autonomy: policy issues', in JO De Beaufort Wijnholds, SCW Eijffinger & LH Hoogduin (eds.) *A framework for monetary stability: financial and monetary policy studies*, Springer, Dordrecht, Netherlands.

Domadenik, P, Prašnikar, J & Svejnar, J 2016, 'Political connectedness, corporate governance, and firm performance', *Journal of Business Ethics*, vol. 139, no. 2, pp. 411–428.

Drees, JM & Heugens, P 2013, 'Synthesizing and extending resource dependence theory: a meta-analysis', *Journal of Management*, vol. 39, no. 6, pp. 1666–1698.

Eke, GF 2016, 'Corruption in the civil service: the dearth of effective service delivery', *International Journal of Arts and Humanities*, vol. 5, no. 2, pp. 285–295.

Epstein, G 1992, 'Political economy and comparative central banking', *Review of Radical Political Economics*, vol. 24, no. 1, pp. 1–30.

Erezi, D 2019, 'Buhari directs CBN to stop providing funds for food importation', *The Guardian*, viewed 7 September 2019, https://guardian.ng/news/buhari-directs-cbn-to-stop-providing-funds-for-food-importation/.

Fagbemi, F & Ajibike, JO 2018, 'Institutional quality and financial sector development: empirical evidence from Nigeria', *American Journal of Business and Management*, vol. 7, no. 1, pp. 1–13.

Fama, EF & Jensen, MC 1983, 'Separation of ownership and control', *Journal of Law and Economics*, vol. 26, no. 2, pp. 301–325.

Fregert, K 2018, 'Sveriges riksbank: 350 years in the making', in R Edvinsson, T Jacobson & D Waldenstrom (eds.) *Sveriges Riksbank and the history of central banking*, pp. 90–142. Cambridge University Press, Cambridge, UK.

García-Ramos, R & García-Olalla, M 2014, 'Board independence and firm performance in Southern Europe: a contextual and contingency approach', *Journal of Management & Organization*, vol. 20, no. 3, pp. 313–332.

Goodman, JB 1991, 'The politics of central bank independence', *Comparative Politics*, vol. 23, no. 3, pp. 329–349.

Haque, F, Arun, T & Kirkpatrick, C 2011, 'The political economy of corporate governance in developing economies: the case of Bangladesh', *Research in International Business and Finance*, vol. 25, no. 2, pp. 169–182.

Hasse, R, Weidenfeld, W & Biskup, R 1990, *The European central bank: perspectives for a further development of the European monetary system* (Vol. 2), Bertelsmann Foundation, Gütersloh, Germany.

Hayo, B & Hefeker, C 2002, 'Reconsidering central bank independence', *European Journal of Political Economy*, vol. 18, no. 4, pp. 653–674.

Heikensten, L 2003, 'How to promote and measure central bank efficiency', *BIS Review*, vol. 24, pp. 1–5.

Hermalin, BE & Weisbach, MS 1991, 'The effects of board composition and direct incentives on firm performance', *Financial Management*, vol. 20, no. 4, pp. 101–112.

Hillman, AJ 2005, 'Politicians on the board of directors: do connections affect the bottom line?', *Journal of Management*, vol. 31, no. 3, pp. 464–481.

Hillman, AJ & Dalziel, T 2003, 'Boards of directors and firm performance: integrating agency and resource dependence perspectives', *Academy of Management Review*, vol. 28, no. 3, pp. 383–396.

Hillman, AJ, Withers, MC & Collins, BJ 2009, 'Resource dependence theory: a review', *Journal of Management*, vol. 35, no. 6, pp. 1404–1427.

Ijewereme, OB 2015, 'Anatomy of corruption in the Nigerian public sector: theoretical perspectives and some empirical explanations, *SAGE Open*, vol. 5, no. 2, pp. 1–16.

Johnston, A 2014, 'Preventing the next financial crisis? Regulating bankers' pay in Europe', *Journal of Law and Society*, vol. 41, no. 1, pp. 6–27.

Jung, K & Moon, MJ 2007, 'The double-edged sword of public-resource dependence: the impact of public resources on autonomy and legitimacy in Korean cultural nonprofit organizations', *The Policy Studies Journal*, vol. 35, no. 2, pp. 205–226.

Kim, PH, Pinkley, RL & Fragale, AR 2005, 'Power dynamics in negotiation', *Academy of Management Review*, vol. 30, no. 4, pp. 799–822.

Kirkpatrick, G 2009, *Corporate governance lessons from the financial crisis* (Vol. 1), OECD Financial Market Trends.

Kula, V 2005, 'The impact of the roles, structure and process of boards on firm performance: evidence from Turkey', *Corporate Governance: An International Review*, vol. 13, no. 2, pp. 265–276.

Lefort, F & Urzúa, F 2008, 'Board independence, firm performance and ownership concentration: evidence from Chile', *Journal of Business Research*, vol. 61, no. 6, pp. 615–622.

Lohmann, S 1998, 'Federalism and central bank independence: the politics of German monetary policy, 1957–1992', *World Politics*, vol. 50, no. 3, pp. 401–446.

Loungani, P & Sheets, N 1997, 'Central bank independence, inflation, and growth in transition economies', *Journal of Money, Credit, and Banking*, vol. 29, no. 3, pp. 381–399.

Magbadelo, JO 2016, 'Reforming Nigeria's federal civil service: problems and prospects', *India Quarterly*, vol. 72, no. 1, pp. 75–92.

Makanjuola, Y 2015, *Banking reform in Nigeria: the aftermath of the 2009 financial crisis*, Palgrave Macmillan, New York.

Nag, A, Vollgraaff, R & Brandimarte, W 2018, *All around the world, central bank independence is under threat*, viewed 7 August 2019, www.bloomberg.com/news/articles/2018-12-07/the-political-heat-is-on-for-central-banks-from-u-s-to-europe.

Nakpodia, F 2018, 'Corporate governance in the Nigerian banking sector: a bounded rationality conundrum', in B Díaz Díaz, SO Idowu & P Molyneux (eds.) *Corporate governance in banking and investor protection: from theory to practice*, pp. 271–285, Springer International Publishing, Cham, Switzerland.

Nakpodia, F & Adegbite, E 2018, 'Corporate governance and elites', *Accounting Forum*, vol. 42, no. 1, pp. 17–31.

Nakpodia, F, Adegbite, E, Amaeshi, K & Owolabi, A 2018, 'Neither principles nor rules: making corporate governance work in Sub-Saharan Africa', *Journal of Business Ethics*, vol. 151, no. 2, pp. 391–408.

Nelson, D 2015, 'The dilemma of the shareholders under the Nigerian company law', *Journal of Law, Policy and Globalization*, vol. 37, pp. 89–106.

Nwachukwu, C 2017, *Adeosun wants national assembly to cut CBN governor's powers*, viewed 17 July 2019, https://guardian.ng/news/adeosun-wants-national-assembly-to-cut-cbn-governors-powers/.

Ohuocha, C 2018, *Nigerian political standoff threatens central bank independence*, viewed 2 May 2019, www.reuters.com/article/nigeria-cenbank-politics/nigerian-political-standoff-threatens-central-bank-independence-idUSL8N1PI4V8.

Okafor, SO & Eyiuche, AC 1999, 'Autonomy of Central Bank of Nigeria (CBN) under different governments: implications for Nigeria's economic development', *Journal of Economic Studies*, vol. 2, no. 1, pp. 61–69.

Okike, E, Adegbite, E, Nakpodia, F & Adegbite, S 2015, 'A review of internal and external influences on corporate governance and financial accountability in Nigeria', *International Journal of Business Governance and Ethics*, vol. 10, no. 2, pp. 165–185.

Okoh, AS & Ebi, BO 2013, 'Infrastructure investment, institutional quality, and economic growth in Nigeria: an interactive approach', *European Journal of Humanities and Social Sciences*, vol. 26, no. 1, pp. 1343–1358.

Oloni, EF & Adewara, SO 2013, 'Macroeconomic effects of central bank independence and transparency: the case of Nigeria', *Journal of Economics and Sustainable Development*, vol. 4, no. 9, pp. 18–27.

Oluduro, OF 2014, 'The central bank of Nigeria: a critical appraisal', *Academia Arena*, vol. 6, no. 12, pp. 7–13.

Omoh, G & Komolafe, B 2009, *CBN sacks 5 banks' CEOs, appoints acting MD/CEOs*, viewed 14 August, 2019, www.vanguardngr.com/2009/08/cbn-sacks-5-banks-directors/.

Pagano, M & Volpin, PF 2005, 'The political economy of corporate governance', *American Economic Review*, vol. 95, no. 4, pp. 1005–1030.

Pfeffer, J & Salancik, GR 2003, *The external control of organizations: a resource dependence perspective*, Stanford University Press, Stanford, CA.

Rice, X 2012, *Nigeria's central bank warns on autonomy*, viewed 19 July 2019, www.ft.com/content/42d7dc52-afec-11e1-b737-00144feabdc0.

Schnatterly, K & Johnson, SG 2014, 'Independent boards and the institutional investors that prefer them: drivers of institutional investor heterogeneity in governance preferences', *Strategic Management Journal*, vol. 35, no. 10, pp. 1552–1563.

Shleifer, A & Vishny, RW 1997, 'A survey of corporate governance', *The Journal of Finance*, vol. 52, no. 2, pp. 737–783.

Tom, EJ 2017, 'Reengineering the Nigerian civil service for optimum performance: the path not taken', *Global Journal of Political Science and Administration*, vol. 5, no. 4, pp. 1–11.

Tricker, B 2019, *Corporate governance: principles, policies and practices* (4th ed.), Oxford University Press, Oxford, UK.

Uche, CU 1997, 'Does Nigeria need an independent central bank?', *African Review of Money, Finance and Banking*, vol. 1/2, pp. 141–158.

Ugolini, S 2013, 'The political economy of central banking: historical perspectives. A changing role for central banks?', *41st Economics Conference*, pp. 52–58.

Velikonja, U 2014, 'The political economy of board independence', *North Carolina Law Review*, vol. 92, no. 3, pp. 855–916.

Yusuf, IA 2015, *How autonomous in CBN?* viewed 28 August 2019, https://thenationonlineng.net/how-autonomous-is-cbn/.

Zhang, X 2005, 'The changing politics of central banking in Taiwan and Thailand', *Pacific Affairs*, vol. 78, no. 3, pp. 377–401.

8 The independence of the South African Reserve Bank

Coming full circle in 25 years?

Jannie Rossouw and Vishnu Padayachee

Introduction

Monetary policy implementation and the conduct of the SA Reserve Bank in the 1980s were subjects of considerable controversy at that time and are still treated as such in policy assessments. These assessments show that the autonomy and independence of the central bank were eroded in the 1980s (Rossouw 2018). This chapter goes beyond those criticisms of the central bank by focusing attention on the restoration of its autonomy and independence in the 1990s.

Despite any legal requirements or prescripts, it is necessary to make the point at the outset that there is no such thing in practice as total central bank independence. Nominally, independent central banks in modern economies have to operate and interact in complex ways with a variety of stakeholders, including business, government, trade unions and the public at large. This interaction creates both invisible and overt relationships of some sort with sectoral, regional, political or ethnic agents over concerns that cannot be fully suppressed when operational decisions over monetary policy are exercised. Such concerns hum away constantly in the background.

That has certainly been the case in the close on 100 years of the existence of the SA Reserve Bank. A whole variety of institutions and characters were in fact involved in the debate about whether or not the [then] Union of South Africa should establish a central bank. These included the Bank of England, as South Africa was still an integral part of the British Empire, local political parties and political movements such as the Afrikaner Bond, private commercial banks, which had been issuers of their own bank notes, and sectoral constituencies such as local businesses and farmers (see Rossouw [2011]).

It is both useful to our narrative and to a proper appreciation of the import of the issues raised here to situate our new evidence in the context of the power relations in the lead up to and in the negotiations itself (referred to as CODESA).[1] The story of the economics of the transition, as it were, is fully explored in a book co-authored by one of the authors of this chapter, and which has recently been published (see Padayachee and van Niekerk 2019).

These authors argue that the 'balance of capabilities' between the main negotiating parties at CODESA differed in the economics front compared to the political front. Most commentators on the South African transition would agree that the ANC prevailed in most areas of the political settlement and delivered South Africa's celebrated democracy partly because the organisation was the bearer of the democratic dream and through the 'Madiba factor'.[2]

While the nature of the negotiations over a political settlement appeared well organised with all major parties being well prepared, this was not the case in respect of negotiations over economic issues. The negotiations over crucial economic issues, such as the matter of the independence of the SARB were in contrast marginalised and occurred in the periphery. Dr Chris Stals, Governor of the SA Reserve Bank during the transition period, makes the very valid observation that far more direct attention should have been placed on the economics of the transition by both major sides (Stals, telephone conversation with Padayachee, 23 November 2017). Debate continues to this day about the need for an 'economics' CODESA suggesting clearly that this was a missing element in the transition.

In respect of the few economic policy debates that did occur (such as the debate over central bank independence), Padayachee and van Niekerk show that both inside and outside formal negotiating forums the National Party was able to turn to well-resourced economic institutions and experienced individuals. These well-trained and experienced state bureaucrats had decades of experience in economics and had since the day of former President P.W. Botha been at the forefront of the development of market-friendly economic policy reforms. This chapter in fact begins precisely then, in the last few years of the Botha administration and in the ascendancy to power of former President FW de Klerk, who succeeded Mr Botha. In particular, we examine the way in which these two leaders viewed the role, power and autonomy of the South African Reserve Bank and how this all impacted on the constitutional debates that followed from 1992.

This chapter is organised as follows: By means of an eclectic literature review, the following section elucidates the erosion of the central bank's autonomy and independence in the 1980s. The next section highlights critical elements of the subsequent restoration of this autonomy and independence from a political perspective. The fourth section sets out the impact of these developments on ANC thinking in respect of central bank independence. The assessment and conclusions follow in the final section.

Eclectic literature review

The major pieces of enabling legislation governing the SA Reserve Bank since its inception in 1921 include the Currency and Banking Act, No 31 of 1920; the South African Reserve Bank Act, No 29 of 1944; the South African

Reserve Bank Act, No 90 of 1989; and the constitutional clauses dealing with the central bank (Sections 222 to 225 of the 1996 Constitution of South Africa). Apart from the last mentioned relevant Sections of the Constitution, all these pieces of enabling legislation were amended many times through their existence.

Like most other central banks formed in the inter-war years, the SA Reserve Bank was established with private shareholders. Ownership structures of central banks with private shareholders started changing after the Great Depression, with the nationalisation of the Danish and New Zealand central banks introducing this trend. Most recently, the Austrian central bank was nationalised in 2010. The SA Reserve Bank is indeed an exception and it remains one of eight central banks having private shareholders and is fully owned by these private shareholders (see Rossouw and Breytenbach [2011] on the matter of central banks with private shareholders).

The question of the *autonomy* and/or *independence* of the SA Reserve Bank, like most other central banks, hardly ever arose for most of the 20th century. Central banks operated with varying degrees of practical autonomy within the ambit of the state, with their executives being 'sub-ordinate' in one way or the other to the government of the day, reporting to government via the Minister responsible for financial matters (the Minister of Finance).

At a theoretical level, rapidly followed by practice, central bank independence became a matter of debate in the context of the demise of Keynesianism, and the sidelining of old style monetarism and the rise to dominance of the new neoclassical school of economics under leading US academics such as Robert Lucas Jr, Edward Prescott, Robert Barro and Thomas Sergant, among others. Using the notion of 'dynamic time inconsistency' built around the fear of government interference in central bank decision-making for populist or electoral reasons, these academics pushed the debate onto the practical policy level, after the election of conservatives such as Mr Ronald Reagan in the United States, Ms Margaret Thatcher in the United Kingdom and Mr Helmut Kohl in West Germany around 1980. Their impact was to prove irresistible, and during the course of the 1980s and 1990s, many central banks acquired one or other form of *independence*, at least at an operational level (instrumental independence).

The SA Reserve Bank followed different monetary policy approaches in the 1980s, but there was no clear notion of *autonomy* or *independence* in South Africa as it is understood today, despite the international environment after 1980. After the abolition of credit ceilings and credit control in September 1980 (De Jongh 1980) and the concomitant movement from direct controls to a market-oriented monetary policy, no policy anchor or policy target was initially used (Nel 1993, p. 120). Although this has been described as a period of market-oriented conservative Keynesian demand management policies and monetarism, the important point is that policy was set in a discretionary fashion without any nominal anchor (Gidlow 1995, p. 4).

Even in terms of goals, the SA Reserve Bank in the 1980s under Governor Gerhard de Kock did not follow a 'monetary rule'. Rather as Goedhuys points out 'the Bank followed a more discretionary path and allowed the primary objective of price stability to be modified or even overridden temporarily by exchange rate and economic growth objectives' (1994, p. 153)

Later this was followed by the use of a money supply target (M) as an anchor for monetary policy. The use of a monetary policy anchor was announced by the (then) Minister of Finance in the Budget speech of 17 March 1986 (Du Plessis 1986). The operationalisation of the monetary policy anchor was explained in a statement issued by Dr de Kock as Governor of the central bank (De Kock 1986). A monetary policy target serves as a monetary policy anchor. An acceleration in money supply growth should result in policy tightening and a deceleration in policy easing.

M3 money supply targeting was neither well understood, nor well communicated. In the annual explanation of the achievement (or otherwise) of the M3 target for a particular period of time and the implications for monetary policy and the level of interest rates, considerable focus was placed on the velocity of circulation of money (V), with MV-growth, rather than M3-growth, used as a motivation that the target was achieved (see for instance De Kock [1987], p. 5). The implication is that money supply adjusted for velocity of circulation (MV) rather than money supply (M) became the effective monetary policy target (see also De Kock [1988] and De Kock [1989] on this matter).

In practice, the SA Reserve Bank nominally followed an M3 money supply growth target but paid considerable attention to the growth rate in money supply adjusted for velocity of circulation, which is effectively a target for GDP growth, without announcing estimates of potential, nominal and real GDP growth (see Bernanke, Laubach, Mishkin and Posen [1999], p. 306 on this matter). The SA Reserve Bank simply equated a growth target announced for M3 to MV and used growth in MV to justify achievement of the target. As growth in M3 and growth in MV cannot be equated to one-another, the rationale for interest rate adjustments was not well understood by businesses and the general public. This contributed to the criticism of monetary policy implementation in the 1980s.

This lack of general understanding of the monetary policy framework and the rationale for interest rate decisions was exacerbated by a lack of autonomy and independence in monetary policy application in the 1980s. At the same time, the highest annual average rate of inflation in South Africa was recorded in the 1980s. The annual average rate of inflation amounted to 14.7% between 1980 and 1990. The ability of the SA Reserve Bank to contain inflation was impeded by its inability to adjust or retain rates without political interference.

The best-known example of political interference in monetary policy occurred in November 1984, when the SA Reserve Bank dropped interest rates ten days before a by-election in the Primrose constituency. This drop in interest rates, subsequently known as the 'Primrose Prime' incident, alleviated pressure on the Government and the governing party at the time (the National Party) in an attempt to increase electoral support (see for instance *Finweek* [2006], p. 8, or Goedhuys [1994], p. 155). The *Financial Mail* stated at the time that

> there is no escaping the fact that. . . (the) . . . cut in prime interest rates was most likely the opportunity cost of the National Party winning the Primrose by-election. Despite Reserve Bank Governor Gerhard de Kock's firm denial, this obvious political manoeuvre has all the signs of a quick fix.
>
> (Financial Mail 1984, p. 35)

Goedhuys (1994, p. 155) refers to the dropping of interest rates before the Primrose by-election as one of ' . . . two instances of political pressure on the Bank stand(ing) out from the record'. It is worth quoting Goedhuys on this, noting in particular his usage of the term 'induced' to refer to the political pressure faced by the Governor.

> In February 1983,[3] when the ruling National Party faced a serious challenge from the Conservative Party in the by-election in the Primrose district of Germiston,[4] the Bank was *induced to lower its discount rate from 12.81 to 10.06 per cent. The following month it raised the rate again to 12.04 percent. This temporarily low discount rate, reflected also in the prime rate, came to be known as the 'Primrose prime', and it helped to retain the Primrose seat for the National Party.*
>
> (1994, p. 155; our emphasis)

This statement of Goedhuys is of particular historic importance, as Goedhuys served as an Advisor of the Governor of the SA Reserve Bank at the time of the Primrose Prime interest rate decision.

The reduction in rates before the by-election was followed by a quick succession of rate increases, bringing rates to the previous level by 8 January 1985 (SA Reserve Bank 1985, p. 16). Any doubt about possible economic justification for the reduction in rates before the by-election is indeed eradicated by the subsequent increase in rates to their previous level.

In an assessment of the autonomy and independence of the SA Reserve Bank in the 1980s, a much more serious incident occurred in 1988. Gidlow, who also served as an advisor to the governor in the 1980s, states that the SA Reserve Bank was unable to raise interest rates in 1988 despite the fact that market-oriented monetary policy

> kan op die mees doeltreffende wyse toegepas word in 'n milieu waar die sentrale bank volkome onafhanklik is. Dit was in 1988 byvoorbeeld nie die geval nie toe die owerhede moeilikheid ondervind het om rentekoerse hoër op te stoot op 'n tydstip toe die betalingsbalansposisie en inflasionistiese druk versleg het [can be applied most effectively if the central bank has complete autonomy. This was for instance not the case in 1988 when

the authorities experienced difficulty to increase interest rates at a time when the balance-of-payments position deteriorated and inflationary pressures increased].

(Gidlow 1995, p. 9)

Goedhuys (1994, p. 155) is much more critical of the events of 1988, stating that

> (a) notable clash over interest policy occurred early in 1988. During the preceding two years the Reserve Bank had advisedly adopted a low interest policy, because under the foreign financial and trade sanctions business was so depressed that the risk of overstimulating the economy was remote. By 1988, however, continued inflation, some business revival, and the low foreign reserves urgently demanded higher interest rates, but the State President absolutely forbade it.

The autonomy and independence of the SA Reserve Bank in the conduct of monetary policy was indeed in a precarious position by the end of the 1980s, as is evident, inter alia, from the abovementioned examples. Padayachee (2001, p. 753) refers to the fact that the SA Reserve Bank had no real autonomy before 1989 and also states that the central bank ' . . . was largely subservient to political agendas' (Padayachee 2000, p. 500). A different approach to monetary policy was indeed necessary, as South Africa's inflation rate in the 1980s remained stubbornly high.

In 1989 the Governor Stals[5] stated shortly after his appointment to the position that

> [a]t a time when most of the industrial countries of the world pursued strong anti-inflationary policies, South Africa was pre-occupied with short-term economic problems. . . [and] . . . [i]nflation was at that stage not regarded as South Africa's main economic problem. . . [but] . . . the main emphasis of monetary policy has. . . [now] . . . been switched to the curtailment of inflation. . . . In the circumstances it can no longer be regarded as appropriate to continue to accommodate price increases through large increases in SA Reserve Bank credit and in the monetary policy
>
> (Stals 1989, p. 10).

The firm belief held by Stals in the responsibility of the central bank to protect the value of the currency was confirmed in a Mission Statement issued by the Bank in 1990:

> The South African Reserve Bank is the central bank of South Africa. It regards as its primary goal in the South African economic system the protection of the domestic and external value of the rand. In the pursuit of its mission, the Reserve Bank believes it is essential that South Africa has a

vigorous economy based on the principles of a free market system, private initiative and effective competition. It recognises, in the performance of its duties, the need to pursue balanced economic growth.

This mission statement was later revised to 'the protection of the value of the rand' and the mission statement also forms the basis of the subsequent wording used in the Constitution for the autonomy and independence of the central bank.

Naturally, a renewed focus on containing inflation in a market-oriented monetary policy requires what Gidlow (1995, p. 9) describes as a framework of complete central bank autonomy. The SA Reserve Bank indeed managed to restore its autonomy and independence in the conduct of monetary policy after 1989, as is shown by the analysis in the next section.

Critical political elements of the institution of central bank autonomy and independence in South Africa

The announcement in 1989 of a renewed commitment to contain inflation caused a 'time inconsistency' problem in South Africa. After nearly two decades of double-digit inflation commencing in 1974 and numerous abortive commitments to contain inflation, the public simply did not believe the Governor's announcement.

As a result, the central bank had two challenges on its hands. On the one hand, autonomy and independence had to be restored to support a policy of containing inflation, while on the other hand the public had to be convinced of the central bank's commitment to contain inflation. This policy approach started bearing fruit with the rate of inflation declining to single digits in 1992.

Although an M3 money supply growth target lost some usefulness as a money policy anchor by the end of the 1980s (Casteleijn 2001, p. 6; see also Rossouw 2005), it was still used for some time by the SA Reserve Bank. It was replaced by money supply growth guidelines in the early 1990s and by eclectic monetary policy in 1996. The important points, however, are that (i) monetary policy achieved its objective, namely low inflation and (ii) the autonomy and independence of the SA Reserve Bank were restored. This chapter focuses on this latter aspect.

When Dr Stals assumed the position of Governor of the SA Reserve Bank, he inherited a system of historic liaison between the State President and the Governor (respectively, Mr P W Botha and Dr G P C de Kock), somewhat to the exclusion of the Minister of Finance.

However, Dr Stals' appointment was followed by political change, with Botha being replaced by Mr de Klerk as President on 14 August 1989. Dr Stals therefore had to manoeuvre a new political environment. From the outset, he guarded against the exclusion of the Minister of Finance in any interaction with the executive.

Dr Stals inherited a tradition of the Governor addressing the Cabinet on monetary policy and interest rate decisions. At least two such meetings occurred each year according to Dr Jannie Roux, the Chief of Staff in the Office of President PW Botha, who also served as Cabinet Secretary under Mr Botha (Personal interview, 18 February 2019). On monetary policy in general the Cabinet had to agree to the annual setting of the M3 money supply growth target, while Cabinet ministers were seemingly under the impression that they had a right of veto over interest rate decisions.

This practice was changed in phases with the support of Mr de Klerk whose overall approach was that the state should not interfere in monetary policy matters (Personal interview with Mr de Klerk, 28 January 2019). In a first step, Dr Stals and Mr de Klerk agreed that it would no longer be required from the Governor to submit the annual M3 money supply growth target (later the growth guideline) to Cabinet or to Mr de Klerk personally for approval.

More dramatically, however, was a particular presentation to the Cabinet, on which occasion Dr Stals made it clear that interest rates had to increase. He was attacked on this matter by several Cabinet Ministers who vehemently opposed such an increase. The matter was brought to finality by Mr de Klerk, who closed the discussion by informing the Governor that ' . . . Cabinet members will read with interest in the newspapers the decision of the Governor on interest rates. . . .' The accuracy of this statement was confirmed in separate personal interviews held by the authors with Mr de Klerk (Personal interview, 28 January 2019) and Dr Stals (Personal interview, 18 February 2019). Indeed this remark set the record straight: The Governor had the final say in interest rate decisions, thus confirming the effective autonomy and independence of the SA Reserve Bank in conducting monetary policy. Despite these positive developments aimed at underpinning a degree of independence for SARB, the situation remained contingent of course. It could have been argued that its maintenance rested (unsatisfactorily) on upon who was the President and who was the Governor. In other words there was in the period c1990–93 no statutory revisions to buttress this 'shift' instigated by Mr de Klerk and much turned at that time on the political support of Mr de Klerk and his government. That changed only in 1994 through the adoption of the Interim Constitution of the Republic of South Africa, in which clauses 223–225 guaranteed both the independence of the SARB and its price stability mandate. The Interim Constitution was debated at a Constituent Assembly after democratic elections in 1994 and made final in 1996.

This remark confirms the important role of Mr de Klerk in the restoration of central bank independence in South Africa. With this single remark, Mr de Klerk removed monetary policy from the (political) realm of the Cabinet to the control of the central bank. His role in central bank autonomy and independence in South Africa has previously been unrecorded and unreported.

His remark also set the South African Reserve Bank on a trajectory of autonomy and independence which culminated in the constitutional provisions of 1996. The Constitution (1996) requires the SA Reserve Bank to act 'independently', subject only to the requirement of regular consultation between the central bank and the Minister responsible for financial matters

(Sections 222–225). The restoration of the central bank's autonomy and independency made it possible to include this aspect in The Constitution.

The global financial crisis of 2008 (continuing) threw a massive shadow over central bank operations and independence, as the crisis demonstrated painfully that traditional instruments of central bank practice such as manipulation of short-term interest rates were simply useless in the face of the severity, depth and length of the crisis. As argued by Padayachee (2014), the SA Reserve Bank did fairly well in this cauldron of global chaos and uncertainty.[6] Former Reserve Bank Governor Tito Mboweni pointed out in early 2009 that South African banks had improved their capital ratios in the past year, noting that the country's banks were 'strong and healthy' and that the capital adequacy ratio was increased from 11.8 percent in January 2008 to 13percent in December 2008 (Business Day: 2 March 2009).

The 2008 SARB banking supervision annual report highlighted the buffers that have protected the local banking industry: including that banks had not been allowed to use hybrid structures in their capital base (like US/UK); banks had not relied on derivative structures for funding; banks were required to increase capital adequacy in good times; and capital adequacy requirements were raised on home loans when banks granted more than 80 percent of the value of the property, a factor which limited banks from giving loans simply to fund high lifestyles.

To the question 'what protected South Africa during this period of extreme global turbulence', the SARB's senior deputy Head of the Research Department, Brian Kahn responded as follows:

> It turns out that we were protected to some extent by prudent regulation by the Bank regulators, but more importantly, and perhaps ironically, from controls on capital movements of banks. Despite strong pressure to liberalise exchange controls completely, the Treasury has adopted a policy of gradual relaxation over the years. . . . With respect to banks, there are restrictions in terms of the exchange control act, on the types of assets or asset classes they may get involved in (cross-border). These include leveraged products and certain hedging and derivative instruments. For example banks cannot hedge transactions that are not SA linked. Effectively it meant that our banks could not get involved in the toxic assets floating that others were scrambling into. They would have needed exchange control approval which would not have been granted, as they did not satisfy certain criteria. The regulators were often criticised for being behind the times, while others have argued that they don't understand the products, but it seems there may be advantages to that!
>
> (2008, p. 1).

However, local banks did experience some stresses, especially in their earnings as credit growth to the private sector fell to 2.34 per cent year on year in September 2009, the weakest growth since October 1966 (see Business Report 1 October 2009).

So in what ways, if at all, has the SARB responded in terms of its operations and mandate?

The South African Reserve Bank's response, within the limits of its current constitutional mandate, focused on the following interventions:

- successively but gradually lowering the repo rate (so influencing onward lending rates).
- further improving banking regulation and supervision, improving its institutional capacity to ensure financial stability, while avoiding the dangers of over-regulation.
- using moral suasion to get the banks to tighten their lending criteria, while letting credit to flow.

Even notable critics of the Bank's policy stance such as Hassan Comert and Jerry Epstein argue that the Bank reacted fairly well. They point out (2011, p. S9) that 'the SARB policy regime as well as its rhetoric about monetary policy significantly changed in response to the crisis of 2008' (2011, p. S94). In essence flexibility and pragmatism have characterised its approach.

It was an extraordinary time and all over the world, including in the United States, the United Kingdom and Europe, the old certainties, rules and traditions established with such mathematical nicety and precision in the 1980s and 1990s, disappeared out of the windows. Syll (2016) invoking William Buiter (https://voxeu.org/article/macroeconomics-crisis-irrelevance) has argued that:

> I believe that the Bank [of England] has by now shed the conventional wisdom of the typical macroeconomics training of the past few decades. In its place is an intellectual potpourri of factoids, partial theories, empirical regularities without firm theoretical foundations, hunches, intuitions and half-developed insights. It is not much, but knowing that you know nothing is the beginning of wisdom.

Much has recently been written about the debate over central bank independence in South Africa (see, for instance, Padayachee [2014], Padayachee, Valodia and van Niekerk [2019, forthcoming] and Hickel [2016]). In this chapter and based on some recent new evidence arising out of discussions with former President de Klek, former Governor Stals and former Cabinet Secretary Roux, it is necessary to revisit the nature of this debate in the period running up to democratic elections in 1994 and ending with the adoption of the new democratic constitution in 1996.

Impact on ANC thinking on central bank independence and later developments

It is useful at the outset to make the point that the independence or non-independence of the South African Reserve Bank was located by both the outgoing

National Party (NP) and the incoming ANC in a wider policy agenda aimed either at supporting the market driven status quo in the case of the former, or (at least notionally) supporting a re–distributive imperative that addressed the apartheid era's devastating economic and social legacy on blacks in the case of the latter. Independence of the South African Reserve Bank was not a debate in and for itself.

Jason Hickel has argued that:

> Knowing that the ANC were going to assume political power, the National Party wished to insulate economic policy as much as possible from their control. . . . An independent Reserve Bank with a low inflation mandate was central to this strategy. The National Party had presided over a state-controlled central bank for decades and knew how powerful it could be: they did not trust the ANC to wield this power, probably fearing that the latter would engage in 'loose' monetary policy for populist ends which would undermine creditors, people with accumulated wealth and businesses seeking foreign finance – all of which were disproportionately represented in the white community whose interests the National Party sought to secure. This move to tie the hands of its successor government is recognised in the literature as a classic motive for enshrining central bank independence
>
> (Hickel 2016, pp. 4–5).

As noted in his biography, Mr De Klerk was clear that he wished to influence ANC thinking on economic policy, including on central bank independence, so as to wean the ANC under the leadership of Mr Nelson Mandela away from what he considered its socialist leanings (also confirmed in the personal interview of 28 January 2019). At the dawn of the negotiations between the apartheid state and the ANC, the latter did not stand for central bank independence. The ANC's Macroeconomic Research Group (MERG) called for greater autonomy for the central bank (compared to the situation in the 1980s), but not for full constitutional independence. Leading figures in the ANC's Department of Economic Policy gradually changed their view in the light of interactions with Western governments (notably Germany), international financial institutions and local capital.

This culminated in an agreement on the inclusion of the independence of the SA Reserve Bank in the Constitution of South Africa adopted in 1996, with Sections 223 to 225 dealing with this independence. The wording of the independence clause was based on the existing Mission Statement of the Reserve Bank already issued in 1990. This status quo still prevails, despite voices challenging from time to time the mandate of the SA Reserve Bank, namely containing inflation.

At the Constituent Assembly (CA) after 1994 set up to approve the Interim Constitution, the matter of SARB independence came up again for final ratification. Mr Jeremy Cronin, then a member of the Central Committee of the

South African Communist Party (SACP) and a member of the ANC's National Executive Committee (NEC), informed Padayachee, Valodia and van Niekerk (2019) that Dr Rob Davies, also then a senior party member, argued that the SARB should only be granted operational independence and not full independence (Cronin, interview, 25 July 2017). He lost that argument, of course (Padayachee, Valodia and van Niekerk 2019).

For most of the period following the advent of democracy and government led by the African National Congress (initially under a Government of National Unity and then on its own) the ANC maintained a strong and unambiguous policy of not interfering with the independence of the SARB. Relations between the SARB and the ANC government were sound, and there were no signs within the ANC alliance of any major discontent with the status quo as far as SARB was concerned. But as the economy began to experience serious distress after c2015 with growth slowing and unemployment rising sharply some sections of the alliance including its trade union ally (the Congress of South African Trade Unions or COSATU) and in a growing populist section of the ANC itself, began to agitate about the continuing private ownership of the SARB, and in a clumsy way also about its independence and mandate. That gained momentum as the ANC removed President Zuma as President of the country, after his term as President of the party lapsed in December 2017.

The role, institutional structure, mandate and independence of the SA Reserve Bank are again the topic of renewed debate in South Africa 25 years after the democratic elections of 1994, as the ANC has adopted a resolution for the nationalisation of the central bank at its National Conference on 19 December 2017 (Hunter 2017). Central banks with private shareholders are indeed an exception, with only eight such instances. The nationalisation of the central bank will thus not be out of order, with the nationalisation of the Austrian central bank in 2010 as the most-recent example of nationalisation (see, for instance, Rossouw and Rossouw [2017]).

The real issue is the matter of the autonomy and independence of the central bank, not its nationalisation, as the shareholders of the SA Reserve Bank have limited powers in any case (see for instance Rossouw and Breytenbach [2011]). After 25 years, central bank independence might have come full circle, with the current ANC government's stated objective as agreed at its National Conference in December 2018 to 'nationalise' the SA Reserve Bank. It is not clear whether this is merely an amendment to an institutional structure to bring it into line with global trends, or indeed whether it is an insidious move to interfere with the operations of the Bank, possibly the first step in taking the South African Reserve Bank under executive control again, as was the case in the 1980s.

Assessment and conclusions

The assessment in this chapter highlights some of the problems experienced with sustained high inflation and challenges to the autonomy and independence of the SA Reserve Bank in the 1980s. This lack of autonomy and independence is evidenced by the Primrose prime incident and the State President forbading an interest rate increase in 1988.

Given the subsequent level of understanding central bank independence today, the notion of a central bank 'asking permission', 'not being granted permission' or being 'induced' by the government of the day on the matter of monetary policy and interest rate decisions is indeed a strange one. In the 1980s, however, the notion of an independent central bank was not as pronounced as it is today.

The subsequent restoration of autonomy and independence of the SA Reserve Bank is indeed of particular importance, as this autonomy and independence contributed to lower inflation in South Africa. In this restoration of the autonomy and independence of the SA Reserve Bank, the role of the State President at the time, Mr de Klerk, is not recorded. Mr de Klerk was indeed a joint facilitator of this restoration with Dr Stals.

The restoration of central bank independence under the joint leadership of Mr de Klerk and Dr Stals changed thinking on this topic among the ANC leadership. This change culminated in the provision for the independence of the SA Reserve Bank in the Constitution of South Africa.

After 25 years, central bank independence might have come full circle, with the current ANC government's stated objective as agreed at its National Conference in December 2017 to 'nationalise' the SA Reserve Bank. It is not clear whether this is merely an amendment to an institutional structure to bring it into line with global trends, or indeed whether it is an insidious move to interfere with the operations of the Bank, possibly the first step in taking the South African Reserve Bank under executive control again, as was the case in the 1980s.

Notes

1   CODESA was the acronym for the Congress for a Democratic South Africa.
2   The first President of democratic South Africa, Mr Nelson Mandela, is often referred to as *Madiba*, the clan or family (tribal) name representing a person's ancestry, in this instance the Mandela family.
3   The reference to February 1983 is incorrect. The Primrose prime incident occurred in November 1984.
4   The voting district constituted mainly white industrial workers many of whom held current mortgage bonds.
5   Dr C L Stals was appointed as Governor of the SA Reserve Bank on 8 August 1989.
6   This section draws heavily on Padayachee (2014)

References

Bernanke, B. S., Laubach, T., Mishkin, F. S. & Posen, A. S. 1999. *Inflation Targeting – Lessons from the International Experience*. Princeton University Press, Princeton, NJ.
Casteleijn, A. 2001. *South Africa's Monetary Policy Framework*. Paper prepared for the Conference On Monetary Policy Frameworks in Africa, 17–19 September. SA Reserve Bank, Pretoria.

Comert, Hassan & Gerald, Epstein. 2011. Inflation Targeting in South Africa: Friend or Foe of Development? *Economic History of Developing Regions*, 26(Suppl. #1).

Constitution of the Republic of South Africa. 1996. Available at www.gov.za/documents/constitution-republic-south-africa-1996 [Accessed on 13 March 2019].

De Jongh, T. W. 1980. *Governor's Address*. Address at the Sixtieth Ordinary General Meeting of Stockholders, 26 August.

De Kock, G. P. C. 1986. *Money Supply Targets for 1986. Statement by Dr Gerhard de Kock, Governor of the SA Reserve Bank*. SA Reserve Bank, Pretoria, 17 March.

De Kock, G. P. C. 1987. *Money Supply Targets for 1987. Statement by Dr Gerhard de Kock, Governor of the SA Reserve Bank*. SA Reserve Bank, Pretoria, 10 March.

De Kock, G. P. C. 1988. *Money Supply Targets for 1988. Statement by Dr Gerhard de Kock, Governor of the SA Reserve Bank*. SA Reserve Bank, Pretoria, 22 February.

De Kock, G. P. C. 1989. *Money Supply Targets for 1989. Statement by Dr Gerhard de Kock, Governor of the SA Reserve Bank*. SA Reserve Bank, Pretoria, 7 March.

Du Plessis, B. J. 1986. *Budget Speech*. National Treasury, Pretoria, 17 March.

Financial Mail. 1984. *Hallucinations now, Reality Later*, 23 November.

Finweek. 2006. *Bylae Oor Die Suid-Afrikaanse Reserwebank*, 21 September.

Gidlow, R. M. 1995. *Monetary Policy Under Dr Gerhard de Kock, 1981–1989*. South African Reserve Bank, Pretoria.

Goedhuys, D.W. 1994. Monetary Policy in the 1980s: Years of Reform and Foreign Financial Aggression. *South African Journal of Economic History*, 9(2), September.

Hickel, J. 2016. *The (Anti) Politics of Central Banking: Monetary Policy and Class Conflict in South Africa*. Paper presented at the Conference on Capitalism in the Global South, London School of Economics, April 2016.

Hunter, Q. 2017. ANC Instructs Government to Start Nationalising Reserve Bank. *Times-Live*. Available at www.timeslive.co.za/sunday-times/business/2017-12-20-anc-instructs-government-to-start-nationalising-reserve-bank/ [Accessed on 13 March 2019].

Kahn, B. 2008. Challenges of Inflation Targeting for Emerging-Market Economies: The South African case. In *Challenges for Monetary Policy-Makers in Emerging Markets*. South African Reserve Bank, Conference Series.

Nel, H. 1993. *Die monetêre beheermeganisme in Suid-Afrika*. Unpublished D Com thesis, University of Port Elizabeth.

Padayachee, V. 2000. Independence in an Era of Globalisation: Central Banking in Developing Countries. *International Review of Applied Economics*, 14(4), October.

Padayachee, V. 2001. Central Bank Transformation in a Globalized World: The Reserve Bank in Post-Apartheid South Africa. *Journal of International Development*, 13(6), August.

Padayachee, V. 2014. Central Banking after the Global Financial Crisis: the South African case. In Bhorat, H, Hirsch, A, Kanbur, R & Ncube, M (eds.), *The Oxford Companion to the Economics of South Africa*. Oxford University Press, Cape Town.

Padayachee, V., & van Niekerk, R. 2019. Shadow of Liberation, contestation and compromise in the economic and social policy of the African National Congress, 1943–1996. Johannesburg: Wits University.

Rossouw, J. 2005. Monetêre beleid in Suid-Afrika sedert 1965: die vordering vanaf direkte beheer tot inflasieteikens. *Tydskrif vir Geesteswetenskappe*, Jaargang 45(2), Junie.

Rossouw, J. 2011. *South African Reserve Bank: Commemorative Publication, 2011*. SA Reserve Bank, Pretoria.

Rossouw, J. 2018. Politics and Policies: Determinants of South Africa's Monerary Policy Problems in the 1980s. *Economic History of Developing Regions*, 33(1).

Rossouw, J. & Breytenbach, A. 2011. Identifying Central Banks with Shareholding: A Review of Available Literature. *Economic History of Developing Regions*, 26(Suppl. #1).

Rossouw, J. & Rossouw, C. 2017. Forcing the Few: Issues from the South African Reserve Bank's Legal Action Against its Delinquent Shareholders. *SA Business Review*, 21.

SA Reserve Bank. 1985. *Quarterly Bulletin*. SA Reserve Bank, Pretoria, March.

SA Reserve Bank. 1988. *Quarterly Bulletin*. SA Reserve Bank, Pretoria, December.

Stals, C. L. 1989. *Governor's Address*. Address at the Sixty-Ninth Ordinary General Meeting of Shareholders.

Syll, L. P. 2016. *'Modern' macroeconomics — a costly waste of time*. Available at https://larsp-syll.wordpress.com/2016/09/22/modern-macroeconomics-a-costly-waste-of-time/ [Accessed on various dates].

Newspapers Cited: *Business Day* (Johannesburg), 29 August.

Interviews

Personal interviews and discussions with Dr C L Stals on 30 July 2015, 8 December 2015, 26 October 2018 and 18 February 2019. Pretoria. (with Jannie Rossouw, the last with Jannie Rossouw and Vishnu Padayachee).

Personal interview with former President FW de Klerk, 28 January 2019. Cape Town. (with Jannie Rossouw and Vishnu Padayachee).

Personal interview with Dr Jannie Roux, former Chief of Staff in the Office of former President PW Botha and Cabinet Secretary under Botha. Pretoria. (with Jannie Rossouw and Vishnu Padayachee).

Part 4

Central Banking in Latin America

9 Gender diversity as a tool to make central banks progressive institutions

The case of the Central Bank of Ecuador

*Guillaume Vallet**

Introduction

In the aftermath of the 2008 crisis, central banks were criticized for their failure to fulfill their missions and maintain social legitimacy. The 2008 crisis resulted in calls on central banks to redefine and broaden their missions in a way that better reflects the social consequences of their actions in an increasingly complex economic context. Indeed, central banks as institutions perform the social mission of producing a public good – macroeconomic stability and prosperity – by achieving their targeted macroeconomic objectives. Central banks are the "agent" of a "principal" (society) and its political representatives (generally politicians). However, central bankers are not democratically elected, instead being appointed by politicians on the basis of their competencies, namely, their ability to reach the targets defined by the "principal" (Walsh 1995; Alesina & Tabellini 2008). Thus, central banks should ensure that people have confidence in their actions, and central bankers must demonstrate that they are not elites disconnected from the will of people.

Reciprocal trust between central banks and society is the cornerstone of central banks' performance, and of their broader social legitimacy. Through their performance, central banks must redefine their relations with society in order to be perceived as legitimate and reliable. As Janet Yellen, the former Governor of the American Federal Reserve System, stressed "in every phase of our work and decision-making, we consider the well-being of the American people and the prosperity of our nation" (Yellen, quoted in Dietsche et al. 2018, p. 1).

Therefore, central banks can no longer be seen as "black boxes" (Adolph 2013), which provide a purely "technical," disembodied image of their operations, actions and missions: as institutions embodying the will of the people, their internal structures must really embody what society is.

Similarly, central bankers should change their reputation as a closed-off group (Johnson 2016). They are often seen as a clique of experts disconnected from the needs of the people (Pixley 2018; Riles 2018).

* *This work is supported by the French National Research Agency in the framework of the "Investissements d'avenir" program (ANR-15-IDEX-02).*

Hence, central banks need to change as public institutions, and they must rely on new tools and types of expertise. Specifically, because central banks have increasingly been asked to cope with new objectives such as environment or income distribution in order to reach the aforementioned macroeconomic stability and prosperity, they should turn to new staff. In that sense, central banks would mutate into progressive institutions, namely, more "embedded" institutions explicitly seeking to improve the economic and social global welfare of societies.

Indeed, it should be borne in mind that central banks are not neutral with respect to the consequences of their policies. Conversely, central banks wield significant societal power through the definition and implementation of monetary policy about the economy and society: central banks exercise "structural power" (Strange 1994) on societies, influencing their structures and dynamics through the regulation of credit growth and inflation in particular. Central bankers' expertise gives them power, because they are able to control information related to the central banks, a type of information that most people do not fully understand (Pixley 2018). To put it in another way, central bankers exert a kind of technocratic power, one of the concrete forms of their "structural power," which could "clash" with their societal mission if such power merely served central bankers' own interests or were not legitimate in the eyes of the people. Changing the internal structure and organization of central banks through an increase in staff diversity would be a paramount step to changing the exercise of their "structural power," and to transforming them into more progressive institutions.

To that end, the aim of this chapter is to demonstrate that an increase in gender diversity – understood here as an increase in the feminization rate (proportion of women) and participation rate (high occupancy of senior positions by women) in central banks, but also as a socio-demographic variable taken into account in central banks' decision-making – will bring about a new "vision" and a new paradigm in the world of central banking. In an increasingly complex economic world, which puts greater demands on central banks to exercise social responsibility, gender provides a vital new instrument for expanding our understanding of how central banks function. Resting specifically on the case of the Central Bank of Ecuador – which I have been investigating for one year (interviews, direct observations, internal survey, interviews with the governor and the staff) – which recently decided to address the issue of gender to implement its monetary policy, I propose that gender diversity could be a good way to promote progressivism. Specifically, I attempt to argue that gender diversity could help to promote:

(1) The ability to reach new central bank objectives.
(2) The ability to improve cooperation within the internal organization of the central bank, in order to deal more efficiently with the management of the complexity of information.
(3) The ability to promote the culture of the institution, which is of the utmost importance in the creation of the legitimized national models of central banks, especially in emerging countries.

The remainder of the chapter is as follows. The second section explains why central banking is a man's world. Elaborating on that feature, the third section deals with the specific case of the Central Bank of Ecuador. The fourth section attempts to draw lessons from the Ecuadorian case. Finally, the fifth section concludes.

This is a man's world: central banks as bearers of gender

Among many characteristics, one of the striking features of the structures and organizations of central banks is the relative lack of women, on two levels. The proportion of women is very low, and women working in central banks generally do not have roles with high responsibilities (Vallet 2019). Therefore, gender is an extremely relevant category in the world of central banking, as men outnumber women by far and occupy more senior posts than women. At present, among the world's central bank governors (173), only around 6% are women. Up to the 2008 crisis, there were only 10 female governors world-wide (Davies & Green 2010; Adolph 2013; Diouf & Pépin 2017). Today, still only 15 central banks are chaired by women: Aruba, Belize, Cuba, Curaçao & Saint-Martin, Cyprus, Ecuador, European Central Bank, Lesotho, Republic of Macedonia, Malaysia, Russia, Samoa, San Marin, Serbia and the Seychelles.

The recent nomination of Christine Lagarde as Governor of the European Central Bank does not hide the gendered reality that central banks are male-dominated institutions. If we follow the figures of the General Balance Index Score (O.M.F.I.F. 2019), taking into account both the number of female governors and the number of women as deputy governors, the situation is alarming (see Table 9.1):

Table 9.1 General balance index score, 2017–2019 (in percent)

Geographic Area	2017	2018	2019
Africa	23	19	21
North America	68	24	36
Latin America–Caribbean Islands	5	11	19
Pacific–Asia	8	6	9
Europe	28	35	38
Middle-East	11	12	10

Source: O.M.F.I.F. Analysis 2018, 2019

The index identifies the presence of women and men in the governing bodies of central banks, by weighting their number by their hierarchical importance in the institution. Thus, we find the following coefficients according to the positions: governor (7), deputy governor (5), member of the executive committees (3), member of the monetary policy committees (1). Individuals in more than one category are counted in the one with the highest coefficient. The Global Score Index of each zone thus calculates the ratio of women to men weighted by the aforementioned coefficients. Note that the scores are also weighted by the size of the economies corresponding to the institutions concerned. In total, a score of 100% would mean a perfectly gender-balanced institution. Considering the methodology chosen, caution should be exercised when interpreting certain figures: for example, Yellen's departure from the leadership of the US Federal Reserve in 2018 had a very negative impact on the index for North America.

Likewise, an overview of the gendered distribution of "central banks chairs" (CBC) (including governors and deputy governors), in relation to the major currencies of the International Monetary System,[1] reveals the absence of women in the main decision-making organs of the central banks (Table 9.2).

According to recent research, central banking is a man's world, mostly because there is a discrepancy between power and authority, in favor of male domination (Vallet 2019). Specifically, as the previous figures indicate, such a discrepancy means that, first, it is difficult for women to exercise the "structural

Table 9.2 Gendered distribution of the main decision-making organs of central banks

Central banks	Governor	Vice-Governor	Decision-making organs	Other committees
European Central Bank	C. Lagarde	L. de Guindos	**Council of governors:** 4 men + 2 women (directoire) 18 men + 1 woman (governors of national central banks)	**General council:** 29 men + 1 woman **Prudential supervision council:** 21 men + 7 women
Swiss National Bank	T. Jordan	F. Zürbrugg	**General direction:** 2 men + 1 woman; Bank's council: 8 men + 3 women	
Federal Reserve	J. Powell	R.K Quarles (for supervision)	**Board of Governors:** 2 men + 1 woman; **Federal Open Market Committee:** 9 men + 3 women	
Bank of Japan	H. Kuroda		**Policy board:** 8 men + 1 woman	**Monetary affairs department:** 3 men; **Financial system and bank examination:** 14 men; **Payment and Settlement System Department:** 4 men; **Financial Market Department:** 2 men (only the "Officials")
Bank of England	M. Carney		**Court of directors:** 8 men + 4 women; **Monetary Policy Committee:** 8 men + 1 woman	**Financial Policy Committee:** 12 men + 1 woman; **Prudential Regulation Committee:** 9 men + 2 women
Bank of China	Y. Gang		**Management team:** 7 men	

Source: Author, from central banks' websites

Normally, there are seven members.

power" of central banks because they are not often found among the "CBC" Second, even when they are among the "CBC" and then have the opportunity to exercise such power, their authority is not legitimate. Indeed, following Weber (1971), power and authority converge on the condition that authority is viewed as a legitimate power. In central banking, this relationship exists at the expense of women.

Such a situation is clearly a loss for both women and society: indeed, increasing gender diversity, as we have defined it in the introduction, could bring about a new vision in central banking, being part of rendering central banks more progressive institutions. Focusing on the case of Ecuador, which is relevant to this perspective, we explain why this is the case in the next section.

The Ecuadorian case: gender matters

Before focusing on the issue of gender, let us mention some facts about the Central Bank of Ecuador (CBE). The CBE came into existence after the "Revolution Juliana" occurred on July 9, 1925. Throughout its history, the CBE has had to deal with exchange rate movements, because Ecuador is a small, open economy. This has sometimes led to inflationist pressures, which is one of the reasons[2] that compelled the country to abandon its currency, the *sucre*, during a severe economic crisis in 2000. Ecuadorian authorities chose to adopt the US dollar as the official currency instead, which has been used ever since. This is called "dollarization," referring to the situation in which one country officially adopts the currency of another for all monetary and financial transactions. Generally, the main objective of dollarization is to reduce high inflation, especially through the elimination of the risk of a sudden devaluation of the country's currency. As a result, dollarized economies are likely to attract capital inflows and then to enjoy a higher degree of confidence among international investors. However, dollarization prevents the country from implementing an independent monetary policy, and compels the country to rest on current account surplus in order to increase its reserves in the foreign currency used as legal tender.

In spite of doubts regarding such a choice – among some Ecuadorian leaders, such as R. Correa, who came into power trying to develop a parallel electronic currency in 2014, for instance (Correa et al. 2019) – the US dollar remains the official currency today.

It is true that such a monetary regime raised fundamental issues regarding both the macroeconomic stability and the economic and political sovereignty of Ecuador (Correa et al. 2019). Regarding macroeconomic stability, dollarization has helped to stabilize the economy with respect to some macroeconomic variables (low inflation, in particular). Similarly, this monetary regime successfully has faced many shocks, including the recent "Great recession" crisis. The CBE has increasingly been involved in developing policies aimed at promoting financial and banking stability. The Constitution implemented in 2008 also ensures strong regulation of the existing monetary and financial operations and institutions, including the CBE.

Actually, dollarization has accelerated and strengthened such changes rather than creating them *ex nihilo*: indeed, a paramount law came into force in May 1992 – the so-called Law of Monetary Regime and State Bank – enabling the CBE to intervene in the financial system through open market operations. The CBE was then authorized to play the role of lender of last resort, within strict financial parameters. However, such an evolution is evidence of the fact that the CBE has always been tied to the government, whatever its official status (independent or not). For this reason, the CBE's decisions must be assessed with respect to the aforementioned "principal–agent" framework, the Ecuadorian Government representing the principal in the name of Ecuadorian society.

Consequently, the CBE also has in its hands the fate of Ecuador's economic and political sovereignty. To that end, the central bank seeks to promote specific objectives strengthening Ecuadorian society, beyond mere price and banking and financial stability. For instance, since 2012 the CBE has been committed to a new type of policy designed to support financial inclusion, in connection with the Maya Declaration (launched in 2011). The Maya Declaration refers to a global initiative for responsible and sustainable financial inclusion that aims to reduce poverty and ensure financial stability for the benefit of all. It includes roughly a hundred central banks – including the CBE – and other financial regulatory institutions from nearly ninety emerging and developing countries.

In fact, the CBE's policies are part of a broader context of reforms in Ecuadorian society, implemented under R. Correa's presidency. Correa has implemented economic but also political reforms that have led to an improvement in the well-being of the population and in citizen participation. As Correa states, the main objective of such reforms was to fight inequalities and to promote development in Ecuador (Correa et al. 2019). These reforms gave very good results, with respect to the decrease in income inequalities and poverty in particular (Table 9.3):

Table 9.3 Indicators of income inequalities and of poverty in Ecuador (2001–2017)

Years	Gini Index (related to income distribution)	Theil Index (related to income distribution)	People living with less than 50 percent of median income (in percent of total population)
2001	0,538	0,643	18,1
2008	0,493	0,458	18,6
2012	0,464	0,393	19,0
2014	0,449	0,400	16,3
2016	0,445	0,391	16,2
2017	0,440	0,375	17,0

Source: Author from Cepal 2018

Overall, in order to promote development, Correa was convinced that the key factor was to rest on solid institutions capable of carrying out a development strategy and for Ecuadorians to be organized collectively (Correa et al. 2019).

This is against this backdrop that the CBE increasingly turned to the issue of gender, especially with the nomination of Veronica Artola as governor in 2017. Specifically, governor Artola has sought to support gender diversity in its institution in two main ways: first, recruiting policies; and, second, new types of monetary policy.

(1) With respect to recruiting policies, from the beginning of her tenure, Artola's aim was to hire more women. Now, among roughly a thousand persons working in the institution, approximately 40% are women. In comparison to the aforementioned figures of the Global Score Index, this percentage is high. Moreover, women working in the CBE have high-skilled tenures such as general managers, second managers, planners or directors of departments. In Artola's view, such diversity helps to make the CBE a more committed institution, because it entails new types of leadership and new types of organization. In other words, gender diversity and organizational change go hand in hand, and their association improves the whole functioning of the institution. For instance, the CBE has a room for lactating women and it proposes to change office hours for staff members to accommodate personnel taking care of their children.

According to Artola, being able to rely on such internal services for staff (women and men) is important because the possibility to reconcile professional and family lives lies at the core of gender relations, and of the inequalities between men and women (Vallet 2018a). Artola claims that she has experienced situations in which the impossibility of balancing both lives was a burden for women:

> I have been to conferences with other female leaders, especially in the private sector. Sometimes you have this invisible threshold that women don't want to cross. I am talking how combining family and work, that is a complicated issue. I have cases where very good women, I offered them high posts and they don't accept. Why? Because it was too much sacrifice for them and their family.
>
> (Artola with Vallet 2018b)

More broadly, the will to enhance gender diversity has encouraged the CBE to create new internal organs or increase the degree of decentralization of its decisions. Hence, according to Artola, the internal organization of the CBE has become more creative:

> There is an innovation department that we are trying to strengthen over the coming years and it's called [the] 'innovation process department.' The idea is to make staff generate better ideas and how to make things. This is how we try to promote staff creativity.
>
> (Artola with Vallet 2018b)

The organization has also become more "collectively inclusive," and Artola states that "I never take a decision alone. Of course it depends on the decision,

I could trust on a bigger, wider or smaller staff team but I always ask someone" (Artola with Vallet 2018b).

Overall, gender diversity has provided Governor Artola with incentives to change her leadership in order to be more open-minded and to listen to different points of view: "We combine men and women's visions, and this generates better policies" (Artola with Vallet 2018b). Her aim is summarized as follows:

> I try to reach people right, I try to understand their worries and their needs. I think that people have recognized that, that they feel good, and what I want of course, I want my legacy to be this memory, that I was able to improve the work conditions of my staff, and they feel that the central bank is the most important institution. Because I leave tomorrow and I say, price stability is the most important, maybe the next manager would probably have done the same. But if I add these things, I think it is the most important. All these topics might not be noticeable, but they change people's lives. This probably makes a difference between central banks, and they should be more involved in these issues. Also gender equality is very important for the whole economy.
>
> (Artola with Vallet 2018b)

(2) This first way of empowering women discussed previously is related to the second one, namely, implementing new types of monetary policy. Indeed, on the one hand, the enlargement of central banks' mandate to include the gender issue is a good opportunity to create wealthier and more inclusive societies. Specifically, because the issue of gender deals with the articulation between professional work, domestic work and grey economy, collecting data on such an articulation facilitates sustainable economic growth. Artola really believes in this necessity for central banks, which exert the aforementioned "structural power" on the fate of societies (Artola with Vallet 2018b).

Likewise, the CBE implements specific policies dedicated to women in order to develop their inclusiveness and their capabilities in Ecuadorian society. For instance, it is promoting a special credit for women who have been victims of gender violence. This is a truly original progressive policy of the CBE, because "no one has seen this before" (Artola with Vallet 2018b). Such policies favor both a higher level of productivity, because women can find a job that is consistent with their skills, and a higher degree of cohesive wholeness for Ecuadorian society. Similarly, such a policy of supporting credit for women is paramount to helping women become entrepreneurs. As some papers have emphasized, access to credit is very often the "bottleneck" preventing women from empowerment in economic activities (Leclaire 2015).

To a greater extent, such policies implemented by the CBE are important because they demonstrate that women are able to occupy high-ranking positions in the professional sphere. In other words, such policies support the "role models" criterion, which plays a significant role in female empowerment. The "role models" criterion means that every woman in a given society is able to identify with the example of women who have achieved high-ranking positions in several fields. Obviously, such "role models" are efficient only on the condition that it triggers a global improvement in the situations of women, not just of the "happy few." This could be a trap in central banking (Vallet 2019). For this reason, in order to improve the situation of women in central banking, it is also important to empower women in other public institutions. Governor Artola, who is extremely aware of this, agrees: "This should be replicated in other instances of different institutions and with other women that are in the same situations" (Artola with Vallet 2018b).

Eventually, through its monetary policies, the CBE exemplifies a key feature of central banking, as highlighted in the introduction, namely, that a central bank should be more "embedded" in society vis-à-vis what it is accountable for. Specifically, the CBE wants to be committed to global projects designed to improve Ecuadorian society, including the lives of women, but more broadly the global welfare of Ecuadorians. To this end, it must be in charge of holding and promoting the history, culture and identity of Ecuador ("culture" generally). In the case of Ecuador, we believe that it is even more important that the country is dollarized. Since money is a "total institution" (Vallet 2017), there is a loss of sovereignty induced by the domestic use of the US dollar, particularly from a social and political perspective. Therefore, promoting the "culture" of Ecuador through monetary policies of a different kind, albeit dollarization, is of the utmost relevance. Such cultural empowerment will help Ecuadorian people, especially the "weak," to be aware of what they are and what they could do in Ecuadorian society.

Artola has been pursuing this objective since her nomination, creating new organs dedicated to this purpose:

> But I think there is another area not related to human resources, it is the institutional cultural change direction. It is a direction oriented specifically to change the culture of the institution. That direction there is a lot of issues and approaches, there are not related to the technical issues, but on how people feel at work.
>
> (Artola with Vallet 2018b)

Similarly, such policies are key to enhancing the social legitimacy of the central bank:

> I think that's also an important issue to make the staff feel at ease at work and give as much as they can give to the institution. It does make the difference. We as a central bank, and this is also a government policy, we measure working environment. One of the topics that are measured is staff empowerment. If they understand the institution, if they like the institution and if they know what that means working for the central bank, we rely on this particular matter and we have a good assessment: we have monthly dynamics or activities to make people know about the institution values, our history, the main topics they are working on. Here in Ecuador,

for example in Economics school, they have the feeling that working in the central bank is the top institution to work in for economists. And we try to promote the same thinking with our staff, that they feel that it is truly the best institution to work in. Maybe this is because personally I started my career here in the central bank, so I am very very attached to this institution. So I make an effort that the staff feel the same way.

(Artola with Vallet 2018b)

What does the Ecuadorian case tell us?

The Ecuadorian case is especially relevant with respect to the issue of transforming central banks into progressive institutions through gender diversity. It is true that it is difficult to strictly "transplant" the Ecuadorian model onto other cases, either because the latter also have shortcomings or, more importantly, because each case is specific. Indeed, since we have emphasized that gender diversity should be related to each context within which the central bank implements its monetary policy – the focus on culture exemplifying it – the central bank in each country or monetary zone should define what best fits the treatment of gender-balanced central banks.

Nonetheless, we believe that the Ecuadorian case is likely to be a source of inspiration for other central banks in two ways, which are intertwined. We elaborate on each of them, also quoting other female central bankers who have expressed their viewpoint on this situation.

(1) First, we believe that the time is ripe to hire more women in central banks. This should be an objective per se – it is neither normal nor fair in a democracy that institutions embodying the system are not gender-balanced – and also for the benefit of the institution itself. To this end, changing the recruitment policies in central banks has become both urgent and mandatory. One solution could be to set up quotas in order to promote women in these institutions, in "CBC" positions in particular. This is what Jorgovanka Tabakovic, the current Governor of the Central Bank of Serbia, suggests:

"Over the past decade, some countries have introduced quotas to improve the representation of women in businesses. Some people feared that insufficiently experienced women would be appointed to boards, damaging company performance. This has not happened. Although quotas have not produced all the results that legislators promised, it is encouraging that their introduction did not precipitate the doom that many forecast. Quotas, I expect, will become an integral part of corporate culture.

(O.M.F.I.F. 2019, p. 7)

However, although quotas are a potential solution, they also raise other questions, such as the ideal number of women. As Artola reminds us, "there is no magical number, but they should be women, definitely. It is women in all areas" (Artola with Vallet 2018b). Empirical evidence on other types of institution, such as private companies, demonstrates that a minimum rate of 35% of women is required to trigger real change (Kanter 1977). With this threshold, women would be sufficiently numerous to feel confident enough to express their views and create coalitions.

That said, we argue that changing the culture of central banking to promote new types of attitude (Vallet 2016) in central banks in favor of women is more important. "Outsiders" will be accepted by the community only if "insiders" change their mind. Indeed, even though there are already women working in central banks, these women still encounter resistance from men. On the one hand, such resistance is related to the lack of women's connections with politicians, which is a prerequisite for central bankers to build an efficient network for their career, according to data (Diouf & Pépin 2017).

On the other hand, because there are still only a few women governors, women students in economics find a lack of examples to which they can aspire. For instance, our recent research shows that the mandates of female central bankers do not give rise to mandates for other women (Vallet 2019).

As a result, a decisive step in increasing gender diversity would be to create new conditions in the study of economics in order to encourage female students to choose a career in central banking. One central banker agrees with this proposal:

> Yes, in the sense that the pipeline is too small at the outset. Even at the undergraduate major level, women are underrepresented (about 1/3 of economics majors). Women are underrepresented in Ph.D. programs to an even greater extent, so the numbers who have the skills needed to hold top jobs are small.
>
> (CBA with Vallet 2018b[3])

Likewise, authors such as Coyle (2013) have stressed that giving incentives to female students in economics to follow more macroeconomics or finance studies – academic skills that are necessary to work in central banks – instead of what she calls "applied microeconomics," is required. A second central banker confirms this, emphasizing that the problem for female students in economics is not the lack of "technical skills" (econometrics, maths) but their ability to choose the "right" way:

> It is not the technicalization per se, in fact there has been a fast rise in the number of women in math and computer science in academia, but not a parallel rise in Economics, so it is clearly not the quantitative aspect which is an obstacle.
>
> (CBB with Vallet 2018b)

(2) Second, redesigning central banks' internal organizations based on gender diversity should be the next step. We believe that a more gender-balanced

internal organization could help central banks to improve the management of the complexity of information, which has become a key issue in central banking: "Problem is not of asymmetric information, but of complex information to be processed" (CBB with Vallet 2018b).

Therefore, gender diversity – and diversity generally – should be promoted by central banks, particularly because of their new missions and mandates, whether actual or forthcoming. From this perspective, creating new organs based on staff with new skills and promoting new programs of research on new topics are mandatory. Specifically, we propose hiring specialists from social sciences other than economics in which women are dominant, and ensuring that these specialists sit in the main decision-making organs of the central banks. Indeed, "economics (like all disciplines) ignores certain aspects of reality in order to focus on others. In particular, it lacks a framework for understanding the nature of politics, of culture, and of regulation. For this we need new tools" (Riles 2018, p. 68).

This would indirectly enhance the situation of women in central banking. As Governor Artola states,

> to have only economists does not let us see the reality as a whole. To have sociologists helps us to have clear policies communicators, to be able to communicate on many things that are happening. We as economists are (?) very technical and we are not able to transmit everything that it is worth saying or doing. This is important to have or to create new organs aiming at improving public policies. But not just in central bank, but maybe in other institutions, such as in ministries. So we can have a wider vision.
>
> (Artola with Vallet 2018b)

Likewise,

> for instance, the communication aspect of monetary policy has become central to the policy itself, so skills in that field have become more important perhaps than in the past. In addition, depending on the various roles taken by the specific central bank, a broader or narrower set of skills may be needed.
>
> (CBB with Vallet 2018b)

Such changes are important in terms of transforming the aforementioned culture of central banking, which is not currently in favor of female empowerment. Indeed, to be accepted by the community of central bankers, women governors must be able to follow the cultural rule of the field, which prioritizes combatting inflation. Women are sometimes accused of not having the right "attitude" regarding the culture of central banking, being either too risk-averse or too "lazy" toward inflation. Among the community of central bankers, "lazy" central bankers are associated with "doves" rather than "hawks" (Adolph 2013): "doves" central bankers would be more tolerant of inflation and would accord more importance to other variables than mere inflation (growth and unemployment for instance), while "hawks" would be more conservative and anti-inflationary central bankers. Therefore, women central bankers tend to over-conform for the "male models" in the field, entailing a kind of essentialization of the métier of the central banker (Vallet 2019).

More women in central banking, coming from more diverse social sciences, could promote new types of leadership and management, to the benefit of the whole institution. Indeed, central banks must change with respect to "regulatory" and "testimonial" expertise (Dietsche et al. 2018), but they should also consider the "managerial expertise" that they rely on. Indeed, the ability to manage the internal organizations to cope with the complexity of information is now of the utmost importance. As Artola states, "it is not a person that makes the institution, but the entire staff behind it" (Artola with Vallet 2018b). Likewise, this female central banker acknowledges this that

> managing a central bank team that includes experts with scientific authority is challenging and requires considerable managerial skill – not just technical expertise. It takes managerial skill to find policies that can command consensus and broad support. Individuals with strong technical skill may lack this ability.
>
> (CBA with Vallet 2018b)

Overall, we believe that increased gender diversity is likely to lead to new types of managerial expertise in central banks, enabling transformation of the central banks in "mobilization structures" (Joachim 2007), in that central banks are part of a process facilitating change (Nadler & Tushman 1997). In that sense, the internal organization associated with increased gender diversity is key to both enhancing the management of the complexity of information and enabling the central bank as an institution to reproduce itself over time. Indeed, information has little value in itself if it is disconnected from the organizational framework, because the latter allows it to be managed efficiently. Similarly, from the perspective of the personnel of central banks, the internal organization is paramount to their own "empowerment" as individuals. For this reason, it is worth applying the "social interactor/replicator" model (Hodgson & Knudsen 2010) to the more gender-balanced organizations of the central banks. A "social interactor" can be defined as "an entity that directly interacts as a cohesive whole with its environment in such a way that this interaction causes replication to be differential" (Hull 1988, p. 408).

A replicator is "a material structure hosted by the entity that is causally involved in the replication process [namely, in the production of a copy of the replicator] and carries the information [that makes the copy similar to its source]" (Hodgson & Knudsen 2010, pp. 240–241).

The organizations of central banks can be considered "social interactors," evolving structures founded on the social interactions created therein, which form a coherent and cohesive emerging system (Hodgson & Knudsen 2010).

Although the structure of central banks rests on bureaucratic, functional and centralized forms of organization (Weber 1971; Chandler 1977; Mintzberg 1979), they cannot simply be considered the incarnation of a bundle of contracts defined ex ante and complying with the bureaucratic nature of the organization. As it is essential to match the structure and means of coordination with the final objectives, the formal framework of the central bank only partially determines the means of coordination and cooperation; the informal elements must also be taken into consideration (Meyer & Rowan 1977). The aforementioned "social interactors" also operate according to informal rules, which give rise to complex coordination mechanisms and other forms of authority, both charismatic and traditional, on both vertical and horizontal levels (Goold & Campbell 2002). These informal aspects are key elements for analysis, as they represent the heart of organizational cultures and routines that are unfavorable to women.

Furthermore, these "social interactors" enable each central bank to reproduce itself as a specific entity in relation to a given context, and thus to become a replicator. Along with their structure, the organizations of central banks display properties that are more than the sum of the properties of their internal components. Including such properties in the analysis is crucial for managing the complexity of the information efficiently: the adhesion of central banks' members to these properties, embodied in the culture of the institution, is decisive for not only the efficiency of the institutional organization but also the institution itself. These replicators as "emerging properties" enable a central bank to reproduce itself over time as an institution, and to contribute to a culture and history that transcend the framework of the organization.

These replicators are also key to anchoring people's confidence in the central banks, and then to improving their legitimacy. Both the efficiency and legitimacy of organizations depend on not just the efficient coordination and control of activities. They also rely on the ability of the institution to be "isomorphic" with its environment (Meyer & Rowan 1977). Despite the convergence on a common objective and common means currently observed in most central banks, they are not strictly identical in their operations and organizations from one country to another. Each country must design its own model, with the central bank as the replicator. To this end, central banks could use gender diversity as a tool to become more "embedded" in social concerns, like the CBE does. As one female central banker recalls, "there is only one central bank per country, so when comparing central banks we are also of course comparing countries" (CBB with Vallet 2018b).

Conclusion

This chapter attempts to emphasize the extent to which the Central Bank of Ecuador (CBE) is a relevant example of central banks supporting the global development (monetary, economic and social) of the society that it is accountable for. Far from targeting inflation only, the CBE designs its monetary policy according to the needs of people, especially since the "citizen's revolution" promoted by R. Correa and V. Artola's governorship of the central bank. It clearly insists on the fact that its mandate must reconcile monetary and financial efficiency and democratic access to the system of payment and the whole inclusiveness of the nation to the economy. In that sense, the CBE can be considered a progressive institution. As mentioned on its website, the central bank seeks to be a central bank of the twenty-first century, but above all, *for* the 21st century. Among many tools and means to achieve this objective, the CBE affords high status to increased gender diversity, particularly since the nomination of Veronica Artola as Governor of the Central Bank in 2017.

As a result, the Ecuadorian case is insightful for the central banks of other countries, not for them to copy it but for it to be a source of inspiration to redesign their internal organizations to suit the culture of their countries. The issue of gender is a global issue concerning not only women but also men: gender diversity is a mean capable of enhancing the whole institution and the individuals working in it. Empowerment goes hand in hand with progressivism.

For this reason, we believe that central banks of developing and emerging countries should use the issue of gender diversity to become more connected each other, creating international networks of a new kind. Indeed, data shows that central banks from developing or emerging countries have often been leaders and even pioneers in recruiting women in central banks (Vallet 2019). Therefore, it comes as no surprise that female central bankers such as Artola state that "the alliances of central banks in the South could be important to promote, and to assess what benefits they could have if they promoted such a policy" (Artola with Vallet 2018b).

More broadly, the issue of gender diversity should be related to the analysis of the functioning of the current capitalism, as one female central banker underlines:

> Institutions (central banks, international organizations, etc.) reflect in their structures and functioning the tensions manifested in modern capitalism, the product of a long phase of financial globalization that has led to a shift in power between capital and job. The widening of inequality is a manifestation of this stage. Gender issues are another aspect of this tension. The unique discourse, the hegemony of the orthodox vision of the economy dominate and, with them, the presence and importance of men and, in some cases, women, those who express these same ideas, are reinforced. We need more men and women who integrate the dimension of equality as a decisive factor in decision-making. And for that, it is necessary to reinforce a current of thought alternative to the neoliberal hegemony.
>
> (CBC with Vallet 2018b)

In the future, changing gender relations would certainly mean changing the global functioning of capitalism.

Notes

1 With reference to the reserve currencies of the IMF.
2 The Ecuadorian banking sector had also serious problems.
3 The central bankers from central banks A, B, and C wanted to remain anonymous; they will be called CBA, CBB, and CBC respectively.

References

Adolph, C 2013, *Bankers, bureaucrats and central bank politics. The myth of neutrality*, Cambridge University Press, Cambridge, MA.

Alesina, A & Tabellini, G 2008, 'Bureaucrats or politicians? Part II: multiple policy tasks', *Journal of Public Economics*, vol. 92, pp. 426–447.

Cepal 2018, *Panorama Social de America Latina*, 233p.

Chandler, A 1977, *The visible hand*, Harvard University Press, Cambridge, MA.

Correa, R, Rocca, M & Ponsot, JF 2019, 'La fabrique de la politique économique équatorienne. Le point de vue d'un acteur clé', *Revue de la régulation*, vol. 25, no. 1.

Coyle, D 2013, 'Gender does matter in central banking', *Financial Times*, 10 October, viewed www.ft.com/content/c79884ae-319c-11e3-817c-00144feab7de.

Davies, H & Green D 2010, *Banking on the future: The fall and rise of central banking*, Princeton University Press, Princeton.

Dietsche, P, Claveau, F & Fontan, C 2018, *Do central banks serve the people?*, Polity Press, Cambridge, UK.

Diouf, I & Pépin, D 2017, 'Gender and central banking', *Economic Modelling*, vol. 61, pp. 193–206.

Goold, M & Campbell, A 2002, *Designing effective organizations. How to create structured networks*, Wiley, San Francisco.

Hodgson, GM & Knudsen, T 2010, *Darwin's conjecture: the search for general principles of social & economic evolution*, University of Chicago Press, Chicago.

Hull, DL 1988, *Science as a process: an evolutionary account of the social and conceptual development of science*, University of Chicago Press, Chicago.

Joachim, J 2007, *Agenda setting, the UN, and NGOs: gender violence and reproductive rights*, Georgetown University Press, Washington.

Johnson, J 2016, *Priests of prosperity, how central bankers transformed the postcommunist world*, Cornell University Press, Ithaca.

Kanter, R 1977, 'Some effects of proportion on group life: Skewed sex ratios and responses to token women', *American Journal of Sociology*, vol. 82, no. 5, pp. 965–990.

Leclaire, J 2015, 'Women and investment: the role of fiscal policy', *International Journal of Political Economy*, vol. 44, no. 4, pp. 296–310.

Meyer, JW & Rowan, B 1977, 'Institutionalized organizations: formal structure as myth and ceremony', *American Journal of Sociology*, vol. 83, no. 2, pp. 340–363.

Mintzberg, H 1979, *The structuring of organizations. A synthesis of the research*, Prenctice-Hall, Englewood Cliffs.

Nadler, DA & Tushman, ML 1997, *Competing by design: the power of organizational architecture*, Oxford University Press, New York.

Official Monetary and Financial Institution Forum (OMFIF) 2018, 'Gender balance index', *BulletinFocus*, March.

Official Monetary and Financial Institution Forum (OMFIF) 2019, 'Gender balance index', *BulletinFocus*, March.

Pixley, J 2018, *Central banks, democratic states and financial power*, Cambridge University Press, Cambridge, UK.

Riles, A 2018, *Financial citizenship*, Cornell University Press, Ithaca and London.

Strange, S 1994, 'The study of international political economy', in U. Lehmkuhl (ed.) *Theorien internationaler politik*, R. Oldenburg Verlag, München/Wien, pp. 310–330.

Vallet, G 2016, 'A local money to stabilize capitalism: the underestimated case of the WIR', *Economy and Society*, vol. 45, no. 3–4, pp. 479–504.

Vallet, G 2017, '"Think twice": using economics and sociology to understand monetary issues – the case of Switzerland', *International Review of Sociology*, vol. 27, no. 1, pp. 160–178.

Vallet, G 2018a, *Sociologie du genre*, Bréal, Paris.

Vallet, G 2018b, Interviews with Veronica Artola, CBA, CBB and CBC.

Vallet, G 2019, 'This is a man's world: autorité et pouvoir genrés dans le monde du central banking', *Revue de la régulation*, vol. 25, no. 1, doi:10.4000/regulation.14738.

Walsh, CE 1995, 'Optimal contracts for central bankers', *American Economic Review*, vol. 85, no. 1, pp. 150–167.

Weber, M 1971, *Économie et société, tome 1: Les catégories de la sociologie*, Plon, Paris [First published in 1922].

10 The political economy of Brazil's enigmatic Central Bank, 1988–2018

Mario G. Schapiro and Matthew M. Taylor

Monetary authority in Brazil's New Republic (1988–2018) has been marked by subordination to the executive branch, permissiveness with regard to the concentration of the banking sector, and the bifurcation of the banking sector between private and public oligopolies. One consequence is monetary policy that is more ineffective than might otherwise be thought desirable, controlling inflation only through record-breaking real interest rates. Somewhat paradoxically, however, the Brazilian Central Bank (BCB) has proven capable of undertaking stringent regulatory oversight, with a regulatory framework that is widely considered to meet and even exceed the prudential banking standards set out in the Basel accords.

This chapter seeks to explain the resilience of this odd institutional design. We argue that the durability of the BCB model is an outcome of institutional complementarities[1] that emerge from the unique political economy of the Brazilian "developmental state,"[2] understood as a bundle of state economic institutions designed to proactively tackle the market failures and coordination problems that plague late developing economies. The political and economic conditions of a democratic developmental state create the self-reinforcing complementarities that help to explain the enigmatic characteristics of Brazil's monetary authority.

Incomplete central bank independence

Central bank independence is assumed to resolve problems of intertemporal policy inconsistency, insulate long-term growth from short-term political pressures, enhance policy credibility and reduce inflationary bias (Rogoff 1985; Kydland and Prescott 1977). Although there is some debate about the size of the effects, empirical evaluations over time and across countries demonstrate that central bank independence contributes to lower inflation, lower variation in inflation and output, greater monetary policy credibility, and lower uncertainty among economic actors (Garriga 2016; Bodea and Hicks 2015; Cukierman 1992; Cukierman et al. 2002; Cukierman et al. 1992; Persson and Tabellini 1990; Rogoff 1985; Raposo and Kasahara 2010). International institutions recommend central bank independence, and the IMF and World Bank have explicitly recommended central bank independence since the late 1990s (Kern et al. 2019).

Yet, since the establishment of the BCB in 1964, the BCB has often been powerful, but never independent. In a cross-national dataset of 182 countries over the 1970 to 2012 period, the global mean score on weighted central bank independence[3] was 0.49; Brazil's weighted mean over the period was less than half this, at 0.21. Multiple initiatives were undertaken over the six decades from 1945 to the 2000s to enhance BCB independence, but most of these languished or proceeded only incrementally (Taylor 2009). The Bolsonaro government, inaugurated in 2019, has proposed legislation to make the BCB independent. As of the time of this writing, however, the Central Bank remains an agency within the executive branch, subject to presidential control. Why has the BCB failed to develop independence, despite evidence of the likely policy gains, despite the possibility of political gains from having an agency that can shoulder the political blame for slow growth, despite ongoing political rhetoric supporting greater independence, and despite the high costs of a subservient monetary authority?

First, there is the relationship between politics and regulation. As discussed later, the public sector plays a big role in Brazilian credit markets, and there have traditionally been important political gains from controlling the disbursement of credit. Such public sector lending might well run afoul of an independent bank regulator: an independent BCB might threaten the allocation of credit by politically controlled state entities. The political downside may be significant: there is no evidence of corruption, but scholars found a connection between campaign donations and policy choices, including the availability and size of BNDES disbursements and government contratcs (Claessens et al. 2008; Lazzarini et al. 2015; Bandeira de Mello 2015; Musacchio and Lazzarini 2014, p. 271; Boas et al. 2014). Furthermore, campaign donations from regulated banks have also been significant: until 2016, corporations were able to contribute to political campaigns, and banks figured among the largest corporate donors in most electoral cycles. These pressures all generate incentives against placing banking regulation in the hands of a body outside political control.

Second, although the 1988 Constitution prohibits the BCB from financing the public sector, given the heft of public sector banks in Brazil, financial transfers between public banks and the public sector have been significant. Related to this is the fact that there are efficiency gains from maintaining a dependent BCB in a "developmental state" (Haggard 2018). There has been some fluctuation over the years, with more developmentalist governments preferring less BCB autonomy and governments focused on stabilization preferring greater autonomy (Raposo and Kasahara 2010, p. 930). But overall, Brazil's political economy since 1988 has been marked by considerable continuity of the developmental state model, with the federal government taking a leading role in shaping economic activity through a variety of levers of state control: state-owned enterprises, including state-owned banks; subsidized state credit mechanisms;[4] cross-shareholding; and active industrial policies. Under these conditions, a dependent central bank provides the government with policy tools that may be needed either to push developmental objectives or simply to address the short-term contingencies of macroeconomic policymaking. A dependent BCB has given the government greater ability to manipulate interest rates, to adjust monetary policy to respond to fiscal pressure, and to manipulate exchange rates in favor of domestic industrial policy objectives. An independent BCB might threaten this policy maneuverability.

Regulatory bureaucracy alongside a hierarchical banking industry

The BCB's strong regulatory bureaucracy coexists with a hierarchical banking industry. The BCB's regulatory bureaucracy is coherent and meritocratic, with links to orthodox economic academic institutions and the financial markets. In other words, the bureaucracy is autonomous of the political system and has manifest incentives to regulate the financial system on a "technical" basis, using regulatory tools widely accepted in banking systems worldwide. However, despite being committed to market-based regulation and otherwise hostile to the developmental state model of intervention, the BCB regulatory bureaucracy's behaviors are quite different from what might be anticipated. Liberal values and market incentives coexist with a highly concentrated banking sector, in which five national players hold 80% of banking assets, there are lasting regulatory barriers to new entrants, and a long-standing rivalry between the BCB and the antitrust authority (CADE) has hindered the enforcement of antitrust law for banking mergers.

Since its establishment in 1964, the BCB has persistently refused to meddle in the financial sector. Throughout its history, BCB faced many judicial cases requesting that it regulate the cost of financial contracts. Yet the BCB has never imposed a regulatory cap on bank interest rates. This stance has been reinforced by the high court: the Supreme Federal Tribunal (STF) has been consistently deferential to the BCB on financial matters. A case in point that highlights this deference is Precedent 596, in which the Court decided that BCB regulations, and not the established usury law, would regulate the market. The BCB, in turn, has chosen to exercise its discretion by preserving bankers' freedom of contract, despite a number of statutory and constitutional clauses that might point in a more restrictive direction.

This liberal style of regulation has permitted the Brazilian banking sector to become one of the most concentrated in the middle and high-income countries, while also discouraging entry by small and foreign competitors. There is a high degree of concentration among three private sector and two public sector banks, which represent 80% of banking, by comparison to 20–30% in comparable middle-income countries (Taylor 2020). Market concentration has increased continuously since the 1960s, especially from the 1990s onwards, due to mergers and acquisitions that took place in both the state-owned and the private sectors.

In the public sector banks, market concentration resulted from the partial privatization process conducted in the 1990s. Until then, Brazil had federal public banks that belonged to the Federal Government and also public banks owned by the states. The states' public banks, in particular, had a track record of severe financial losses that derived from political mismanagement. Coupled with problems related to their soft budget constraints, local state banks were a permanent source of fiscal imbalance, because they enabled each governor to offer local subsidies and generous credit policies. All these issues represented a threat to the success of the stabilization plan known as the Real Plan, implemented in 1994, which required tight fiscal controls. Accordingly, as it implemented the stabilization plan, the BCB rescued some of those indebted state banks and privatized part of them under a program (PROES) designed to both reduce financial losses and recentralize economic policy in the hands of federal authorities. Notwithstanding the liberal conception of PROES, the outcome contributed to the hierarchical organization that the banking sector has assumed: private players bought the former state banks, thus increasing the concentration of financial assets in the hands of incumbent players.

A parallel wave of merger and acquisitions also took place among private banks, reinforcing concentration. Due to the interruption of the inflation float in 1994, some smaller banks had severe liquidity problems, which in several cases drove them into insolvency. During the inflationary period, a portion of these smaller banks were able to preserve artificially positive results because of their gains from overnight investments. Despite the fact that these banks had serious problems with financial losses and bad administration, they were able to camouflage those problems by profiting from the depreciation of their savers' assets. When the inflation float was interrupted by the stabilization engendered by the Real Plan, the banks' precarious situation became immediately apparent. The BCB came up with a regulatory remedy – PROER – to avoid a dangerous contagion of the whole financial system. PROER conceded tax incentives to banks that bought competitors facing economic hardship.

Lastly, in the aftermath of the 2008 turmoil, a new wave of mergers and acquisitions reduced foreign banks' market shares drastically. The foreigners in many cases entered the Brazilian market at the end of the 1990s as a result of a conscientious effort by the BCB to foster competition. The Brazilian Constitution imposes rigid restrictions against the internationalization on the banking sector. According to constitutional article 192, authorization for foreign banks' activities depends on the enactment of a special law that the Congress has never approved. Nevertheless, the Constitution offers a tiny exception to this general rule, according to which the authorization for foreign banks may be conceded if it is essential to diplomatic relations. The BCB used this loophole in an effort to attract foreign banks that might reduce market concentration and contribute to reducing the high cost of credit, without requiring a structural intervention in the banking market. Initially, the policy was quite successful, and the share of foreign banks increased substantially, with their market share increasing from 9% to 25% of all credit available (Schapiro 2009). Some of these banks partici- pated in PROES and PROER, acquiring local state-owned banks and regional private banks. After 2008, however, a new round of mergers and acquisitions restructured the banking market, and Brazilian incumbents bought a significant part of foreign banks' local assets. The only significant survivor of this effort to attract foreign institutions was the Spanish–owned Banco Santander.

The concentration of the financial sector contributes to high net interest margins (NIM) (IMF 2018). In 2018, the Brazilian average of NIM was 6.2%, and the most prominent private bank – Itaú – recorded a net margin of 5.11%. On average, banks in the United States had a net margin of 3.31% in the same year. Also, the sector operates under oligopolistic competition standards. A measure of this is the H–Statistic, which measures the elasticity of the bank- ing sector, comparing the variation of interest revenues to input prices. The scale ranges from 0 (complete monopoly) to 1 (competition). In a study of the Latin American banking sector, the World Bank and IMF found that the Brazilian H–Statistic was 0.60, by comparison to 0.81 in Chile, revealing severe limitations to competition in the Brazilian banking sector (World Bank and IMF 2017).

In sum, compared to other developing countries, the Brazilian financial sys- tem is unusual. First, it stands out the degree of market concentration, espe- cially when contrasted with China, India, or Singapore. Secondly, national players are dominant, which makes the Brazilian case an outlier even when compared to the Mexican economy. Though Mexico also has high levels of market concentration, the five largest Mexican banks are foreign–owned, and its concentration level declined in recent years. The Brazilian financial system has achieved a unique composition in which national financial institutions, whether private or state-owned, constitute a concentrated oligopoly. The posi- tive side of the banking sector's high concentration degree is financial stability. Economic crises had little effect on the banking system during the crises of the 1990s and 2000s. Financial bankruptcies are very rare in the country and the sector presents good indicators, as revealed by the World Bank and the Inter- national Monetary Fund joint assessment (2018) on the local implementation of Basel core principles. The system is highly capitalized, achieving a capital adequacy ratio around 17%; it is liquid, with a liquidity index above 200% (liquidity assets to short-term liabilities); and it is also profitable, with a return on equity equivalent to 14% (IMF 2018).

The negative side effect of market concentration's degree is the limited size of the credit market and, consequently, the high cost of credit. Data from the World Bank shows that Brazil and Mexico have a smaller credit market than China, South Korea, and Singapore.[5] While the Mexican market is around 35% of GDP and Brazilian is 60% of GDP, all these Asian countries have credit markets that exceed 100% of GDP. In terms of cost, the data drawn from BCB shows that the average price for a credit operation is around 40% a year, but some specific transactions go further than this and reach 400% a year, as in credit card interest rates.

The combination of oligopoly structure, imperfect competition, limited credit markets, and good banking performance lead to a second-best institutional arrangement. It is a second best because it implies a trade-off between concentration and stability, as if the price for stability were market concentration.

Political and market dominance with strong banking regulation

Brazil's economy is marked by an odd combination of political dominance in economic policy and high market concentration in the financial sector. Yet despite the incentives this establishes, the BCB has been able to regulate the financial system strictly, imposing standards that exceed those stipulated in the Basel accords. Standard political economy stories are likely to have a hard time explaining this outcome. Standard assumptions would assume that, given the opportunity, politicians would have some interest in enlarging banks' leverage in order to increase credit and, as a consequence, boost investments, income, and employment. Banks, meanwhile, might be expected to take advantage of the political benefits of a concentrated financial sector – most notably, fewer challenges of organizing collective action – to push for a lower regulatory burden. In other words, there would be incentives to follow the Asian experience of lax prudential regulation that implied only cosmetic compliance with Basel standards (Chey 2006; Walter 2008).

Politically, there are ample institutional venues by which the government could be pressured into driving the BCB to adopt a more flexible regulatory framework and a looser monetary policy. The principal regulatory authority for the financial system is the National Monetary Council (CMN), which is a political body constituted by the Finance Minister, the Planning Minister, and the BCB President. The CMN is in charge of defining all policies and regulatory frameworks under which BCB plays its operational role. Since the Finance Minister is politically accountable for the overall performance of the economy, there are strong incentives for the Finance Minister to play an active role in choosing the BCB governors and monitor their outcomes. A good proxy for this proximity between Finance Minister, the executive branch, and the BCB is the fact that all Brazilian presidents have altered the composition of BCB governors upon taking office.

The BCB, in turn, does not have the political independence to singlehandedly determine monetary policy or banking regulations. Even though BCB has operational autonomy, this is limited (Sola et al. 1998). Every time the BCB must regulate a financial matter, it has to request regulatory approval from the CMN, and only then, under CMN regulatory standards, can the BCB stipulate a new rule. Similarly, BCB does not have the autonomy to specify monetary policy itself. It is the CMN that defines the target inflation rate, assigning to the BCB the management of basic interest rates to meet the stipulated targets.

Thus, the executive branch retains vast control over economic policymaking and has the institutional controls to exercise its political influence.

On the market side, there are also institutional incentives for banks to act politically to avoid strict regulation and foster lax monetary policy. The literature on regulatory capture (e.g., Stigler, Buchanan) has long emphasized that interest groups move politically to capture policymakers and benefit themselves. Collective action arguments add detail to that claim, arguing that the smaller interest groups are, the better they will be able to advance their interests vis-à-vis the public administration (Olson 1982). Consequently, the Brazilian banking industry would seemingly be well positioned to become a powerful interest group that can shape policy interventions to its interests. The banking industry has substantial economic power and can lobby policymakers, through a combination of tools such as campaign finance donations and public advocacy using its ties to think tanks, the media, and academia. Moreover, due to high market concentration, there is a small number of players, which drastically reduces the cost of coordination.

In sum, not only do political authorities have the clear institutional wherewithal to pursue an agenda that privileges growth over stability, but market players would seemingly also be capable of working effectively in favor of a less rigid regulatory toolkit. There might be good reasons for them to do so: strong prudential regulations and tight monetary policies affect banks' bottom lines directly, limiting lending capacity and potential profitability.

Curiously, however, the institutional incentives available for both governmental authorities and market players have not resulted in lax regulation. In the domains of prudential norms and monetary policy, the BCB has implemented rules that go further than the requirements of international agencies' global standards.

In the case of Basel rules, the BCB diverges from other developing countries' central banks. The literature on Basel accords' enforcement notes that most developing countries oscillate between mock compliance, that is, a merely formal observance of the rules (Walter 2008), and selective compliance, that is, a strategy of observing some rules, but not others (Jones and Zeitz 2017). While some Asian countries, such South Korea, Thailand, and Malaysia, follow the mock compliance track (Walter 2008), Latin-Americans and Africans largely adopt the selective compliance strategy (Jones and Zeitz 2017).

Since Basel I, however, the BCB has complied substantively with rules on capital adequacy. While the accord required a minimum total regulatory capital ratio of 8%, the BCB has stipulated from 1997 onwards a minimum of 11% for all banks. The BCB also implemented the other Basel agreements without delay, having begun the implementation of Basel II in 2007, and Basel III in 2013, keeping up with the central banks of developed countries. For Basel analysts, the rules' timely implementation in Brazil has met the global frameworks in both letter and spirit (BIS 2013). The Basel's Regulatory Consistency Assessment Program (RCAP) "found Brazil to be an overall a 'compliant jurisdiction,' with its capital standards aligned with the international minimum requirements for Basel Committee members" (BIS 2013). Similarly, the IMF and the World Bank considered that Brazilian authorities comply with the Core Principles for Effective Banking Supervision, which includes 25 principles on capital adequacy, methods of financial supervision, and also corrective measures on the banking crisis. It is noteworthy that the IMF and the World Bank considered Brazil fully compliant in 23 out of the 25 principles, and for the two remaining criteria, the report designated Brazil as "largely compliant" (World Bank and IMF 2018).

Assessing the prudential norms more deeply, the BCB's toolkit also imposes significant regulatory costs. Though Basel II fosters banks' self-regulation, BCB favors a command and control sort of discipline and privileges standardized approaches over individual banks' internal models. The Basel II established three categories of capital adequacy, which are: (i) credit risk; (ii) market risk; (iii) operational risk. For each category, the Basel norms enable a range of regulatory options that encompass the standardized approaches and the banks' internal models. While in the standardized approaches Central Banks design and enforce the same pattern of rules for all kind of banks, in the internal model, banks might develop their regulatory policy, and the Central Banks would only check its consistency. In other words, the internal models are less costly than the standardized approach, because the amount of regulatory capital is not stipulated ex ante, and each bank can customize its capital level to its own risk exposure. Today, the three private largest banks, Bradesco, Itaú, and Santander employ internal models for market risk, but for the credit and the operational risk, they still follow the standardized pattern. The overall panorama, therefore, indicates substantive, but costly, compliance with Basel II.

In sum, Brazil's odd combination of executive dominance, market concentration, and strong regulation ensures the strict enforcement of regulatory standards and provides simultaneous gains to both political and market players. The causes of this odd coexistence are multiple. The developmental state, and especially state-owned banks and direct credit policies, give politicians leverage for a pro-growth agenda that offers rewards to politically connected sectors. The CMN not only sets target inflation rates, which is the main tool for inflation control, but it also sets discretionary policy-oriented interest rates for selected sectors, such as agriculture, manufacturing, and housing. These rates are typically lower than the basic interest rate. Moreover, state-owned banks are provided specific financial sources that make their funding partially independent from their capacity for deposit-taking. As a rule, the benefitted sectors (e.g., agriculture, industry) are able to draw on the services of a state-owned bank and a particular source of privileged funding, channeled from compulsory savings, that funds government investment priorities in that sector.

The developmental state also offers immense profit opportunities to private banks. The large Brazilian state is dependent on private financing due to long-standing and severe budgetary constraints. Private banks are the main financiers of public debt, and they profit on interest from sovereign bonds. The financing of public debt is massive in the Brazilian economy, so significant that it is bigger than the private debt market. Meanwhile, regulation imposes costs on leading financial institutions, but it also provides benefits to incumbents. Though rules on capital adequacy limit banks' leverage, they increase the barriers to new entrants in the market. The banking market offers several obstacles to newcomers, such as structurally concentrated economic power and the cost of reaching consumers in 5,500 geographically dispersed municipalities. Compliance with strict prudential regulations is an additional challenge to any new market challenger. Implementation of Basel rules, mainly through a standardized approach, may help the incumbents deter new entrants, and as the incumbents grow in market size, they have been able to pass along some of those regulatory costs to consumers.

Meanwhile, particularly for the state-owned banks, Basel rules provide a shield against over-politicization. The literature on state banks is fraught with cases of governance failure that compromised banks' success. Traditionally, such governance failures facilitated politicization of management and converted would-be developmental agencies into patronage-ridden, captured entities. In this context, Basel rules perform a useful function by empowering the leadership of state banks within the government. For this reason, the bureaucracy within Brazilian state banks supports the implementation of Basel rules, especially to the extent that they see them as an institutional buffer against political patronage.

Good regulation with tolerance of public banks

The Brazilian financial system is marked by the continued influence of state-owned banks (SOBs) in the economy. Although public state-owned enterprises (SOEs) have become less important than private firms over the past generation, the role of public banks remains as significant as that of private banks. SOBs accounted for 50% of all credit in the late 1960s; this figure rose to 70% by the early 1980s (Trebat 1983, p. 28), and although it has fallen somewhat, remains above half of all credit in the financial sector today. Together, three SOBs – the Banco do Brasil (BB), the national development bank (BNDES), and the Caixa Econômica Federal (CEF) – accounted for 53% of corporate lending between 2015 and 2017. The BB accounted for more than 50% of the outstanding credit to agriculture, and the BB and CEF jointly accounted for more than 75% of real estate lending during this period (Banco Central do Brasil 2018).

Why is it that the BCB has tolerated the ongoing presence of behemoth state-owned banks (SOBs), such as the BNDES, BB and CEF, despite BCB governors' general distaste for such state-run enterprises, and the fact that SOBs complicate monetary policymaking? Certainly, in light of potential moral hazard, there are arguments for breaking up or privatizing behemoth SOBs. There are also enormous costs to maintaining SOBs: efficiency costs, bureaucratic costs, and the opportunity costs of foregone investment elsewhere. There has been support for reform in the past: politicians from the center to center-right have frequently called for the privatization of SOBs when campaigning for office. Influential policymakers, including some public bank presidents, have also questioned the need for such public sector banks.[6]

Yet upon taking office, would-be reformers have usually lost interest in reform. Historical, political and economic reasons jointly help to explain this pattern. Historically, the BB harkens back to the early days of the 19th century and of the Emperor,[7] and the BNDES and CEF, founded in 1952 and 1961, are in some ways the very face of Brazil's developmental heyday. This creates reservoirs of goodwill and political power that contribute to SOB longevity. Politically, SOBs can provide sinecures for patronage appointments, and presidents use appointments in the SOBs as a way to hold together their legislative coalitions. There is some evidence of links between SOB activities, such as lending, and campaign contributions, as noted earlier. Further, the bureaucracy in these SOBs has been very powerful, either as a corporatist interest group defending its own privileges, as in the BB's pushback against BCB authority in the 1980s, or as a high-capacity island of excellence, as in the BNDES' long history of preeminence in economic policymaking, both during periods of liberalism and privatization (e.g., during the 1990s) and periods of state-led policymaking (e.g., during the 1970s and 2010s). Dismantling such large and lasting institutions would be a daunting and thorny political job.

Politically, also, the longstanding lobbying power of public sector bank employees and their sway over Congress has often served to foil reform (Nóbrega 2005). It has also complicated oversight: one prominent BCB president, Gustavo Franco, noted that one of the tensest moments of his time in office was when he decided to audit the public banks. He sent a team of 150 BCB staff to the BB, which refused them entry; they had to storm their way past the guards to do their jobs (Dieguez 2014, p. 211).

Perhaps less recognized is the economic logic for maintaining SOBs. At their most basic, SOBs serve as ready-made instruments for policymakers. They may provide presidents with policymaking muscle and expertise that is not readily available elsewhere. Second, as Mettenheim (2005) noted, Brazilian SOBs perform an essential function. They operate within a particular variety of financial system that is bank-centered, along the lines of the German and Italian systems, rather than market-centered, along the lines of the United States or the United Kingdom. In the former, stock market capitalization is hovers around 30% of GDP, by comparison to 90–110% in the latter. This forces firms to look for capital through borrowing and revenue, rather than stock market capitalization. A related chicken-or-egg problem arises from high spreads and low private sector credit, which mean that there is enormous pressure to keep up subsidized public lending. This in turn lessens the likelihood that private banks, even foreign entrants into the banking sector, will be able to develop viable private lending operations (Luna and Klein 2006, p. 99). The daily liquidity of federal debt, meanwhile, provides a highly profitable incentive for private sector banks to lend to the government, rather than to business, making SOBs the only feasible alternative for corporate finance (Luna and Klein 2006, p. 88). By way of example, in 2014, long-term loans at Brazil's largest private bank, Itau-Unibanco, accounted for 1.59% of its total loan portfolio, by contrast to 15% at BB and CEF, and 57% at BNDES (Rezende 2015).

Third, SOBs help to provide a functional solution to the fiscal constraint, serving as one of the most important fiscally opaque policy instruments for presidential administrations to accomplish their objectives in a constrained fiscal environment. They fill the gaps left by the private sector in long-term investment, housing and agricultural credit, regional development, microcredit, and banking availability in distant regions; serving as a lender of last resort; and acting as the key agent for implementation of federal social policies (Araujo and Cintra 2011; Mettenheim 2006). Within the spectrum of public institutions, SOBs also have a key comparative advantage that makes them valuable to cash-strapped policymakers: leverage. As of 2019, the BCB set reserve requirements on demand deposits at 21% and on savings at 20%.[8] This means that SOBs can lend out roughly five times the money entrusted to them, a source of funds that can be very significant in a constrained fiscal environment. Finally, SOBs have an essential counter-cyclical role, and in recent years, have increased lending at crucial moments when private banks pulled back from credit markets and BCB liquidity operations were either slow or anemic (Paula et al. 2013; Rezende 2015; Soihet and Cabral 2016).

Conclusion

Few central banks anywhere meet all the idealized objectives of a monetary authority independent of both political and market forces. This essay has shown, however, the enigma of central banking in Brazil, where both political and market dominance is strong, yet the central bank has managed to operate autonomously and rigorously both in establishing monetary policy as well as imposing a strong regulatory framework, even in a context of private oligopoly and behemoth public banks.

The reasons for this strange, "second-best" institutional model are multiple, including the efficiency gains to the developmental state from controlling monetary policy, the way in which state owned banks provide politicians access to useful policy instruments in a fiscally constrained environment, the general sourcing of corporate finance to banks rather than markets, and the path dependence of the relationship between public and private banks, whereby the longstanding involvement of public banks in development finance has led private banks away from long-term corporate lending and into shorter-term lending to the public sector.

Conversely, this "second-best" institutional model also carries some significant political and economic downsides. Politically, the Brazilian arrangement generates an accountability deficit. The relationship between the Central Bank, the government, and the banks is highly opaque and takes place far from public scrutiny. Congress performs only limited monitoring of monetary policymaking and regulatory design. Economically, the Brazilian "second-best" model contributes to the centralization of financial decisions in a few hands. The banking system is highly concentrated in a few players who have enormous leverage over the economy. The credit market is restricted, interest rates are prohibitively expensive, and long-term financing is still entirely dependent on state-owned banks.

State-owned banks, in turn, have weak governance and accountability mechanisms. First, SOB officials are still developing instruments for assessing cost-effectiveness, which means that throughout the period examined, they have frequently implemented lending policies without an adequate mechanism to evaluate the corresponding social gains and financial costs. Second, because these banks have an ample mandate, they are vulnerable to the Executive branch's political choices, and, as a consequence, their policies respond to the electoral cycle (Schapiro 2013, 2017). Because weak accountability and political vulnerability reinforce each other, state-owned banks have had strong incentives to pursue governmental policies even when there have not been clear long-term positive externalities.

Undoubtedly, the Brazilian financial system works. It is well regulated, stable, and keeps inflation under control. The lingering question, however, is at what economic and political cost this odd institutional design persists.

Notes

1 Institutional complementarity is understood as the interdependence between diverse institutions whereby "certain institutional forms, when jointly present, reinforce each other and contribute to improving the functioning, coherence or stability of specific institutional configurations, varieties or models of capitalism" (Amable 2016, p. 79). Such "institutional configurations create a particular contextual 'logic' or rationality of economic action" (Deeg and Jackson 2007).

2 Developmentalism "argues that the state can serve as a muscular engine of long-term development by consciously altering investment conditions, expanding human capabilities, and tackling the market failures and coordination problems that plague late developing economies" (Taylor 2020; Haggard 2018; Schneider 2015).

3 There are 16 weighted components to the CBI score calculated by Garriga (2016).

4 For example, the BNDES until 2018 offered credit to firms at the Long-Term Interest Rate (TJLP), which was below the government base lending rate, SELIC.

5 World Bank, "Domestic Credit to Private Sector," available at https://data.worldbank.org/indicator/FS.AST.PRVT.GD.ZS, accessed November 15, 2019.

6 Cuadros (2016, p. 172) notes that BNDES presidents Pérsio Arida and José Pio Borges, for example, questioned the need for the development bank.

7 The Banco do Brasil was founded in the early 1800s, collapsed in 1829, and was refounded in 1851 by Baron of Mauá.

8 www.bcb.gov.br/POM/SPB/Ing/ReserveRequirements_PrimaryRules.pdf, accessed May 24, 2019.

References

Amable, Bruno. Institutional Complementarities in the Dynamic Comparative Analysis of Capitalism. *Journal of Institutional Economics* 12, no. 1 (2016): 79–103.

Araújo, Victor L. and Marcos A.M. Cintra. *O Papel Dos Bancos Públicos Federais Na Economia Brasileira*. Instituto de Pesquisa Econômica Aplicada (IPEA), 2011.

Banco Central do Brasil. *Relatorio de Economia Bancaria*. 2018, available at: www.bcb.gov.br/publicacoes/relatorioeconomiabancaria

Bandeira de Mello, Rodrigo. Financiamento de Campanha não Esgota a Relação entre Empresas e Governo. *O Estado de S. Paulo.* April 8, 2015.

BIS, *Regulatory Consistency Assessment Programme (RCAP) Assessment of Basel III Regulations in Brazil.* 2013, available at: www.bis.org/bcbs/implementation/l2_br.pdf

Boas, Taylor, F. Daniel Hidalgo, and Neal P. Richardson. The Spoils of Victory: Campaign Donations and Government Contracts in Brazil. *The Journal of Politics* 76, no. 2 (2014): 415–429.

Bodea, Cristina and Raymond Hicks. Price Stability and Central Bank Independence: Discipline, Credibility, and Democratic Institutions. *International Organization* 69 (2015): 35–61.

Chey, Hyoung-kyu. *Compliance with International Regulatory Regimes: The Basel Capital Adequacy Accord in Japan, South Korea, and Taiwan, 1988–2003.* PhD Dissertation, London School of Economics, 2006.

Claessens, Stijn, Erik Feijen, and Luc Laeven. Political Connections and Access to Finance: The Role of Campaign Contributions. *Journal of Financial Economics* 88 (2008): 554–580.

Cuadros, Alex. *Brazillionaires: Wealth, Power, Decadence, and Hope in an American Country.* New York: Spiegel & Grau, 2016.

Cukierman, Alex. *Central Bank Strategy, Credibility and Independence: Theory and Evidence.* Cambridge, MA: The MIT Press, 1992.

Cukierman, Alex, Geoffrey P. Miller and Bilin Neyapti. Central Bank Reform, Liberalization, and Inflation in Transition Economies: An International Perspective. *Journal of Monetary Economics* 49 (2002): 237–264.

Cukierman, Alex, Steven B. Webb and Bilin Neyapti. Measuring the Independence of Central Banks and Its Effect on Policy Outcome. *The World Bank Economic Review* 6 (1992): 353–398.

Deeg, Richard and Gregory Jackson. The State of the Art: Toward a More Dynamic Theory of Capitalist Variety. *Socio-Economic Review* 5 (2007): 149–179.

Dieguez, Consuelo. *Bilhões E Lágrimas: A Economia Brasileira E Seus Atores.* São Paulo: Portfolio-Penguin, 2014.

Garriga, Ana Carolina. Central Bank Independence in the World: A New Dataset. *International Interactions* 42, no. 5 (2016): 849–868.

Haggard, Stephan. *Developmental States.* New York: Cambridge, 2018.

IMF. *Brazil – Financial System Stability Assessment.* Washington, DC, 2018, available at: www.imf.org/en/Publications/CR/Issues/2018/11/30/Brazil-Financial-System-Stability-Assessment-46411

Jones, Emily and Alexandra Zeitz. The Limits of Globalising Basel Banking Standards. *Journal of Financial Regulation* 3, no. 1 (2017): 89–124.

Kern, Andreas, Bernhard Reinsberg and Matthias Rau-Göhring. IMF Conditionality and Central Bank Independence. *European Journal of Political Economy*, available online 14 March 2019.

Kydland, Finn E. and Edward C. Prescott. Rules Rather than Discretion: The Inconsistency for Optimal Plans. *Journal of Political Economy* 85 (1977): 473–491.

Lazzarini, Sergio G., Aldo Musacchio, Rodrigo Bandeira-de- Mello and Rosilene Marcon. What Do Development Banks Do? Evidence from Brazil, 2002–2009. *World Development* 66 (2015): 237–253.

Luna, Francisco Vidal and Herbert S. Klein. *Brazil since 1980.* Cambridge: Cambridge University Press, 2006.

Mettenheim, Kurt von. Commanding Heights: Para Uma Sociologia Política Dos Bancos Federais Brasileiros. *Revista Brasileira de Ciencias Sociais* 20, no. 58 (2005): 47–66.

Mettenheim, Kurt von. Still the Century of Government Savings Banks? The Caixa Econômica Federal. *Brazilian Journal of Political Economy* 26, no. 1 (2006): 39–57.

Musacchio, Aldo and Sergio Lazzarini. *Reinventing State Capitalism: Leviathan in Business, Brazil and Beyond*. Cambridge: Harvard University Press, 2014.

Nóbrega, Mailson da. *O Futuro Chegou: Instituições e Desenvolvimento No Brasil [The Future has Arrived: Institutions and Development in Brazil]*. São Paulo: Editora Globo, 2005.

Olson, Mancur. *The Rise and Decline of Nations: Economic Growth, Stagflation, and Social Rigidities*. New Haven: Yale University Press, 1982.

Paula, Luiz Fernando de, José Luis Oreiro and Flavio A.C. Basilio. Estrutura Do Setor Bancário E O Ciclo Recente De Expansão Do Crédito: O Papel Dos Bancos Públicos Federais. *Nova Economia* 23, no. 3 (2013): 473–520.

Persson, Torsten and Guido Tabellini. *Macroeconomic Policy, Credibility and Politics*. London: Harwood Academic Publishers, 1990.

Raposo, Eduardo de Vasconcelos and Yuri Kasahara. Instituições Fortes, Moeda Estável E Banco Central Do Brasil Autônomo. *DADOS – Revista de Ciencias Sociais* 53, no. 4 (2010): 921–958.

Rezende, Felipe. Why Does Brazil's Banking Sector Need Public Banks? What Should the Bndes Do? *PSL Quarterly Review* 68, no. 274 (2015): 239–275.

Rogoff, Kenneth S. The Optimal Degree of Commitment to an Intermediate Monetary Target. *Quarterly Journal of Economics* 100 (1985): 1169–1189.

Schapiro, Mario G. *Novos Parametros para a Intervenção do Estado na Economia*. São Paulo: Saraiva, 2009.

Schapiro, Mario G. O Que a Política Industrial Pode Aprender Com a Política Monetária? *Novos Estudos CEBRAP* 96 (2013): 117–130.

Schapiro, Mario G. Legalidade ou Discricionariedade na Governança de Bancos Públicos: Uma Análise Aplicada oo Caso do Bndes. *Revista de Administração Pública* 51, no. 1 (2017): 105–128.

Schneider, Ben Ross. The Developmental State in Brazil: Comparative and Historical Perspectives. *Revista de Economia Política* 35, no. 1 (2015): 114–132.

Soihet, Elena and Cesar Murilo Nogueira Cabral. Insights on Monetary Policy and Public Banking in Brazil (2008–2012). *Nova Economia* 26, no. 1 (2016): 43–67.

Sola, Lourdes, Christopher Garman and Moisés Marques. Central Banking, Democratic Governance and Political Authority: The Case of Brazil in a Comparative Perspective. *Revista de Economia Política* 18, no. 2 (1998): 106–131.

Taylor, Matthew M. Institutional Development through Policymaking: A Case Study of the Brazilian Central Bank. *World Politics* 61, no. 3 (2009): 487–515.

Taylor, Matthew M. *Decadent Developmentalism: The Political Economy of Democratic Brazil*. Cambridge: Cambridge University Press, 2020.

Trebat, Thomas J. *Brazil's State-Owned Enterprises: A Case Study of the State as Entrepreneur*. Cambridge: Cambridge University Press, 1983.

Walter, Andrew. *Governing Finance: East Asia's Adoption of International Standards. Cornell Studies in Money*. Ithaca: Cornell University Press, 2008.

World Bank and International Monetary Fund. *Mexico – Financial Sector Assessment*. Washington DC, 2017, available at: http://documents.worldbank.org/curated/en/621671508177153708/pdf/Mexico-2016-FSAP-Update-FSA-03232017.pdf

World Bank and International Monetary Fund. *Brazil – Financial Sector Assessment Program Detailed Assessment Of Observance – Basel Core Principles for Effective Banking Supervision*. Washington, DC, 2018, available at: www.imf.org/en/Publications/CR/Issues/2018/11/30/Brazil-Financial-Sector-Assessment-Program-Detailed-Assessment-of-Observance-Basel-Core-46412

Part 5

Central Banking in Asia

11 Interpreting the evolution of the monetary regime in Russia

The political economy of rent seeking and central banking

Nikolay Nenovsky and Cornelia Sahling

Introduction

The specificities of the economic development in post-Soviet Russia have long been in the focus of attention of researchers who have united around the assertion that reforms in Russia have been unsuccessful and have not led to the development of a modern and efficient economy (see, e.g., Yakovlev 2014). The country's resource dependency is a central structural problem (Inozemtsev 2019). Much less attention has been devoted to the place of the monetary regime (MR) and the monetary policy (MP) in the political and economic dynamics of the post-Soviet system processes (Johnson 2018; Tompson 1998).[1] It is true that the MP has been the subject of analysis, especially its macroeconomic and technical aspects (see, e.g., Esanov et al. [2005] or Korhonen and Nuutilainen [2016]).

The formation and evolution of the MP have reflected the struggle of economic and power interests as well as of the balance of forces of the leading economic and political actors as regards the use and reproduction of the rent resources. The clash of interests has been accompanied by the struggle of ideas, ideology of the main actors as regards the place and role of money and the MP. To the interests and ideas, we could add an institutional momentum, specific dependence on the initial conditions and path dependence related to the moneyless and planned economy. All these factors, together with geopolitical considerations, have determined the MR for the last 30 years. We refer to the analysis of these processes as "the political economy of the MR."[2]

The political economy of the exchange rate regime is of importance within the frameworks of the political economy of the MR. Exchange rate is the link, the anchor binding the national economy with the global economy. It is noteworthy that two main features distinguish the Russian economy from the other emerging markets: (i) it inherited a 70-year-old planned economy, and (ii) subsequently, it was the result of an extremely rapid and unjust formation of a new capitalist class (in the years of President B. Yeltsin).

In this study we propose a theoretical approach which is the result of the studies of other researchers as well as of our personal observations and discussions with Russian and foreign economists. First, we offer a simplified working succinct model explaining the development of the MR as a function of the dynamics and structure of the main rent resources. In a nutshell, the nature and size of the rent determine the type of sources of money and the type of MR respectively (part two). Second, by using the proposed model and hypotheses we have reconstructed the MR development in Russia for the last 30 years (1990–2020) (part three). Three periods have been differentiated by financial, economic and political crises and instability. These are namely (i) the period up to 1998 – "an inflationary monetary regime," (ii) the 1999–2013 period – "a controlled exchange rate regime" divided into two sub-periods, and (iii) the post 2013 period – when it was proceeded overtly or covertly towards the liberalization of the ruble exchange rate and a switchover towards "inflation targeting (IT)" was declared.

Here we must make an important clarification. The ideas and statements set forth as well as the empirical illustrations reflect our standpoint of external observers of Russia's economic development. To this effect they are marked by the limitations and characteristics of the foreigner's viewpoint. This standpoint is also important for the theory and practice as is the viewpoint of a Russian observer and participant in the events.

The monetary regime and the rent reproduction: definitions, theoretical model, main hypotheses

We shall need a few preliminary working definitions before we proceed to the theoretical model.

Under *a monetary institution*, we shall understand the set of rules and the mechanisms for enforcing them that determine the monetary behavior of economic actors. The system of monetary institutions shall be referred to as a monetary system. When the rules are formal, we shall refer to them as Monetary regime (MR). Apart from the MR there are also informal rules and practices within the framework of the monetary system. In general, they have a national, cultural character and at certain times they are of major significance (e.g., the barter in the late 1990s in Russia, see Yakovlev [2000, 2001]). The new MR could be borrowed from outside or could be domestically constructed. They could also be the result of the formalization of informal practices. And vice versa it is possible to "deformalize" several rules and institutions related to monetary behavior. Such deformalization was characteristic of the self-organizing adaptation of economic agents and the population in the years of state disintegration between 1993 and 1995 (Radaev 2001). In the past in the countries of Eastern Europe and certainly in Russia, to the transfer of institutions from Western Europe was referred to as "forms without substance."

The MR (formal institutions) is above all related to the mechanisms of money supply and in part to the money demand processes (the motives of using money). The MR consists of two large components: external and internal. The external component is related mostly to the exchange rate regime. The internal component is related to the regime of the interest rate, credit and inflation (the relationship of money with the domestic assets, commodities and services). The first component shows the external sources of money supply while the second – the domestic ones (the two sources are interrelated).

The *Central bank* (CB) is a leading monetary organization, a collective monetary agent. Its main task is the creation, formalizing and enforcing of monetary rules, of formal monetary institutions, that is, the MR and the MP. The other players in the monetary and power field possess varying organizing capabilities and therefore varying opportunities to influence the overall dynamics. The least organized, dependent and losing actor among them is the population (households). Although unorganized the population is an important actor. This is so not only because it votes at elections but also because in the event of a lack of compensation for losses the population has the destructive power of social riots and could provoke uncontrollable political turmoil.

We must add a definition for the rent.[3] The rent represents a non–competitive source of material and non–material resources and incomes. The rent includes various elements such as (i) the material, tangible resources (leading resources in Russia are oil and gas which are exported) as well as (ii) non–material resources (intangible) – positioning within the network of power.

There is a consensus among Russian economists as regards the natural rent and its damaging effect for the long-term development of Russia[4] (e.g., Gaidar 2007, pp. 81–130; Inozemtsev 2019, ch. 3). Noteworthy is the second, intangible component of the rent. It includes the power, political and bureaucratic resources (their positioning within the party and the state network). The source of the power resource is of key importance for Russia in the long term. According to V. Inozemtsev:

> The reason is probably the rent character of our economy. . . . It is actually a matter of the entire domestic economy inherited by Russia from the Soviet Union. Privatization which started in the mid-1990s was carried out either without compensation or for symbolic money according to market rates. . . . That is why investments in new projects is often considered risky. . . . Moreover, as a result of this the state power has become the most profitable kind of business in Russia and its ideology has turned out to be the continuous redistribution of available profits.
>
> (Inozemtsev 2015, p. 190)

With a view to a theoretical simplification further on we shall refer to two groups of rents – "a natural resource rent" and "a power resource rent" and to respectively two types of MR – (i) for "an externally oriented MR" where the external sources of money supply dominate and in this case the main anchor is the exchange rate, and (ii) for "an internally oriented MR" where the domestic sources of money creation play the leading role and the intermediate and final objectives such as "volume of loans," "interest rate," "inflation," and so forth determine the MP. As a rule, a fixed exchange rate is applied for the former regime, while a floating exchange rate is applied for the latter regime.

The main theoretical hypotheses can be reduced to the following cause and effect relations and dependencies. First, in a rent economy, the type of MR is the result of the struggle of the leading groups concerned as regards the reproduction of the rent. The MR is an institutional compromise and a temporary balance reflecting the interests of the leading elites and groups and coalitions among them. The classifications of these groups and coalitions can be different – creditors/debtors, external/domestic, industry/finance, and so forth. To put it differently – the type and size of the rent determines the type of the MR. For its part the latter creates conditions for the reproduction of the rent, it serves for coordinating the behavior of the key actors as regards the rent, and so forth. The relations could be illustrated in a simplified form (Figure 11.1):

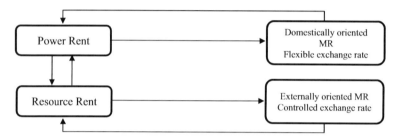

Figure 11.1 Rents and monetary regimes

When we refer to the circular dynamics illustrated in Figure 11.1, we must consider the entire institutional system of the economy where the MR is the structuring but not the only element. Apart from the MR the character of the balance of payments, public finances, labor market, corporate governance to mention but a few are also important.

Second, the dynamics of the MR reflects the changes in the size and nature of the rent, of the coherence of the different types of rent. It can be assumed that an internally oriented MR develops and is even hyperbolized in the presence of a power resource rent. Then it is advantageous for elites and leading groups to develop domestic sources for the creation of money and a floating rate is preferred. The floating rate (and possible exchange restrictions and capital control) makes it possible to reduce and even to put an end of the dependence on foreign countries. Conversely, when the sources of the rent are natural (export of resources), the elites strive to stabilize their relations with foreign countries. A controlled and fixed rate is the best way to create such a stability and predictability. It should be noted that the export of resources is not flexible because of the nature of international resource markets. It is influenced slightly by the manipulations of the rate, especially by its depreciation (Polterovich & Popov 2016). Moreover, the attraction of capital requires a stable or at least predictable exchange rate.

Finally, a third statement about the dynamics of the MR. The transition from one MR configuration to another occurs after an economic, financial or political crisis, when the source of the rent decreases or is exhausted and a new source is sought to replace it. The rent elite is generally preserved although there are redistributions within its frameworks (e.g., in the case of Russia – from oligarchs to government officials, Yakovlev 2006; Robinson 2013). The losers must be compensated in the transition to new MR and MP. Of particular importance to this effect are households (Nenovsky & Rizopoulos 2003). The new MR, which can also be regarded as a new equilibrium within the frameworks of a social game, reflects the new disposition of forces, which makes it possible to mobilize a new rent resource. This resource is reproduced until the emergence of another crisis, and so forth. The crises themselves are provoked by endogenous or exogenous shocks on the size and nature of the rent.

Armed with the aforementioned theoretical model it is possible to reconstruct the development of the MR in Russia for the last 30 years. We must reiterate that what we are proposing is only one of the possible political and economic interpretations.

The evolution of the rent and monetary regime in Russia during the 1990–2020 period

The evolution of post-Soviet Russia and its periodization have been well described in the literature and there is a consensus as regards their main characteristics. There is also a consensus as regards the endogenous logic in the economic and political system of contemporary Russia.[5] The periods follow logically one after the other – they are a manifestation of the life cycle of the system (e.g., Furman 2010; Kapeliushnikov 2016). There is a similar understanding as regards the MR and MP stages (Golovnin 2016; Gurvich 2016).

In general, the periods are reduced to three and two sub-periods defined within the frameworks of the second period (Table 11.1). The first period (1990–1998) covered the unprecedentedly rapid formation of capitalism and the core structures of the market economy. The power resource rent had a leading role during that period, and it was above all related to privatization. There was no established system of property rights during that period. The emergence of the new owners and the reproduction of the power resource rent happened through the credit emission and an inflationary MR. The financial and public debt crisis followed in August 1998.

The power resource rent shrank during the second period (1999–2013); it was internally restructured by being replaced by the rent related to the extraction and export of natural resources. Oil prices rose. The MR serving that process was externally oriented, that is, towards stability and exchange rate control. The sources of the money base and money supply were predominantly external. There were two sub-periods (1999–2008 and 2009–2013) within that period the dividing line of which was a function of reducing the sources of the natural resource rent and of some global and geopolitical shocks (global financial crisis of 2008).

Table 11.1 Periodization of Russian monetary regimes

	MR I	MR II		MR III
Period	1990/91–1998	1999 – September 2013		September 2013 – ongoing
		1999–2008	2009–2013	
MR orientation	Domestically oriented	Externally oriented		Domestically oriented
MR	Elements of credit and monetary targeting	Exchange rate targeting		Inflation targeting
Exchange rate regime	Various until mid-1993 – Ruble zone (common currency area) 1995–1998 – Exchange rate band	Managed floating Since 1999 – managed floating Since 2005 – dual-currency basket (USD and Euro) Increasing weight of the euro in the basket and since Feb 2007–0,55 USD and 0,45 Euro Floating operation Since Jan 2009 – fixed upper and lower borders of 41 and 26 Rub Since Feb 2009 – floating band at 2 Rub Since Oct 2010 – abandonment of the fixed band		Free floating July 2012– August 2014 – widening of the operational band (at 7 Rub and later 9 Rub) Nov 2014 – cancelling of the operational band and introduction of free floating
Crises	Difficult economic situation with different IMF lending agreements (1992 – SBA, 1993 – STF, 1994 – STF, 1995 – SBA, 1996 – EFF, 1998 – different)	1998 – financial crisis 1999 – SBA approval by the IMF	2008–2009 – global financial crisis	2014–2015 – currency crisis
MP	Growth in CB credit to government GKO Until mid-1992 multiple currency rate 1991–1992 – creation of commercial banks	Bank reserve requirements regulation (differentiated for rouble and foreign currency since Nov 2009)	Currency interventions Repo operations	Inflation targeting framework Interest rate corridor with the main elements – the key rate, standing facilities and Repo operations
CB governors	1990–92 – G. Matiukhin 1992–94 – V. Gerashchenko 1994–95 – T. Paramonova (acting chairperson) Nov 1995 – A. Khandruyev (acting chairperson) 1995–1998 – S. Dubinin	1998–2002 – V. Gerashchenko 2002–2013 – S. Ignatiev		Since 2013 – E. Nabiullina

Source: Authors' collection

The third period which is currently ongoing started after September 2013. Then the natural resource rent was increasingly depleted and oil prices dropped. The elites were forced to search for new sources within the state network, that is, again in the power resource rent. This resource rent was proceeded to MR and MP directed to domestic goals and anchors. The country was isolated, the currency reserves were safeguarded, and the exchange rate was liberalized.

The power resource rent, privatization, floating exchange rate and money emission (1990–1998)

That period was marked by the creation of private owners through privatization. The state property was privatized in lack of domestic savings, capital and in absence of market mechanisms and established property rights.[6] It is important to make a detour here.

It has often been underscored that not only in the former USSR but in CEE as well it is a matter of processes that can be defined as "primitive accumulation of capital" (PAC) (Nenovsky & Mihaylova-Borisova 2015). In fact, that was not actually the case. R. Simonyan (2016) was right to mention that we could not refer to the PAC (the way Marx interpreted it) – it was rather a matter of looting and giving away property and capital. To this effect P. J. Proudhon with his "Property is Theft" was much more accurate than Marx in the conditions of Russia. As G. Matiukhin, the first governor of the CB, noted that the PAC in the European countries in the 19th century was carried out not only for a long time but also in the conditions of deflation and shrinkage of the money supply (the price of gold rose) (Matiukhin 2017 [1993], p. 75). Savers and creditors dominated at the time. Inversely, in contemporary Russia (during 1992–1995/96 period) things were different. It was not a matter of accumulation of capital or of investments, but a matter of looting rather than of privatization where debtors and thieves predominated (Bunich 2006).[7]

In general participants in the privatization were related to the old party nomenclature who converted their power positions (power resource rent) into property and assets. As noted by numerous Russian observers however that freshly emerging private property being rent property by birth remained dependent, unstable as a status and was inefficiently used. A new rent bank and business elite[8] emerged which consisted of different types of oligarchs. That elite destroyed the state as an independent economic entity and as an institution creating and controlling impartially the rules of the game. The economic and political discourse of the elite was showy liberal and market one. The rent elite considered that independent civil servants and politicians would be a threat for them. The Russian state was practically falling apart, and its fiscal base disappeared. Public finances were in a disastrous state; in 1991 the deficit reached 31% of GDP (in 1994 it dropped to 10%). The only sources for money were external aid and the IMF and the World Bank tranches (see Camdessus 2014; Aleksashenko 1999).

Within the frameworks of that configuration which was unique as regards its scope and complexity the MR and the CB played a key role. That money was unimportant during socialism, the CB was subordinated to planning[9] and MP was non–existent (see Lavigne [1970]). The USSR disintegrated in December 1991 and a little later the monetary space of the Soviet ruble followed suit (the new Russian money was issued in July 1993, for details see Abdelal 2003). After a brief "war" between Gosbank of the USSR and the newly established Russian CB (in December 1990) a fresh tension occurred that time between the Russian CB and the power and political elites. The bank tried to develop an independent and conservative MP,[10] that is, to restrict the unsecured refinancing of the budget and banks. That encountered the fierce resistance of the main political authorities – the coalition composed by the Government, the Duma (Parliament) and the President's staff.[11] That coalition fought for the "unconditional and automatic" printing of money whenever the state institutions and enterprises needed funds. Actually they controlled that "automatic money emission" and channeled the money flows for serving their personal and corporate interests.[12] The automatic emission did not encounter any resistance (even from the liberal Y. Gaidar) thereby resulting in the consensus on the need of an inflationary MP.[13]

The attacks on the attempts at achieving the CB autonomy were extremely aggressive. In July 1992 the CB management was replaced and the old Soviet functionary Viktor Gerashchenko was appointed (since July 1992 acting chairperson/since November 1992 chairman). Gerashchenko cemented the inflationary MR in the country. Any request for refinancing from the budget (see Table 11.2) or from the banks was automatically granted. The money emission was carried out at a gigantic pace.

The inflationary MR reproducing the power resource rent was manifested not only in the large volumes of refinancing but also through the negative real interest rates. According to G. Matiukhin:

> The fact is that it was impossible to stabilize Russia's monetary system with a negative interest rate as a result of high inflation rates. The CB therefore began to raise that rate gradually: initially by 6% to 20%, then by

Table 11.2 Financing the budget deficit in 1993–1995

	1993		1994		1995	
	Trill of Rub	%	Trill of Rub	%	Trill of Rub	%
Budget deficit	16,7	100,0	60,5	100,0	73,2	100,0
CB credit	9,9	59,3	48,1	79,5	0	0
Domestic loans	0,2	1,2	6,9	11,4	50,1	68,4
Foreign loans	1,5	9,0	5,5	9,1	23,1	31,6
other	5,1	10,5	0	0	0	0

Source: Illarionov & Sachs 1995, p. 91, tab. 9

20% to 40%, then by 40% to 80%. After the second increase Hasbulatov (authors: Chairman of Parliament, Duma) called me on the phone and ordered that our decision be immediately cancelled. I disobeyed. After the third increase, he sent a letter to the CB requesting that the interest rate be kept at its previous level. I disobeyed again. Then Hasbulatov in a traditionally Bolshevik manner forbade me to go abroad: "He will run away somewhere!"

(Matiukhin 2017 [1993], p. 69)

In R. Simonian's words:

Thus, for instance in February 1993 a commercial bank with good connections could be granted a loan for 7% per month by the CB. The index of consumer commodities' prices rose by 25% during the same month. The result was – a net profit of 15% for a few weeks.

(Simonyan 2016, p. 71)

The issue of money continued to grow at a gigantic pace practically throughout the entire period (the famous statement by V. Gerashchenko that "the large-scale emission of money inevitably leads to a greater economic growth").[14] The velocity of money also rose. According to estimates from December 1992 to April 1994, the velocity of money more than doubled – from 5.4 to 11.4 (Illarionov & Sachs 1995, p. 47). Statistical studies showed that inflation had a strong correlation with the emission of money – in 1992 the correlation occurred with a lag of 4 months, in 1993–5 months, in 1994–6 months, and in 1995 it reached 8 months (see also Sachs [1994], p. 72). And because of the close link between the dynamics of money supply and the budget deficit, inflation moves in line with the development of the deficit and the state of public finances (see Sachs [1994], p. 87). According to another participant in the events:

The whole growth of the money supply and consequently the level of inflation are today determined by the sums received by the government from the Central Bank.

(Aleksashenko 1999, p. 18)[15]

Along with inflation (the initial leap came from the liberalization of prices on 2 January 1992 when 90% of retail prices and 80% of wholesale prices were liberalized), a strong depreciation of the ruble rate occurred. The volatility of the course reached its peak on October 11, 1994 when the depreciation to the dollar reached more than 20%, and the ruble price quickly rose[16] only a few days after that. V. Gerashchenko was immediately replaced but the existing MR continued to triumph up to the crisis in August 1998.[17] In a nutshell, the elites needed an inflationary MR.

A new factor, the emission of short-term state bonds (GKO) emerged at the end of the period. They were aimed at restricting the direct unsecured refinancing on the part of the CB, that is, the emission of money. The GKO were launched in 1993 in negligible quantities but gradually increased and reached 3 times per month[18] in 1995. The short-term debt of GKO helped the state cover its current expenses and pay the wages in the public sector. But its short-term character and avalanche-like growth resulted in grave impediments in its servicing. The greater part of that debt consisted of quarterly securities and the attempts at 6 and 12-month emissions failed. The CB often bought GKO on the primary market which ran contrary to market principles. Eventually GKO became a "debt pyramid" used for the enrichment of definite groups. The instability of the GKO was the result of the fact that between 30 and 50% of the GKO volumes were possessed by non-residents who not only speculated but also later withdrew their capital converting it into dollars.

In principle that debt implied a MR based on a predictable exchange rate especially the part of the debt held by non-residents and denominated in dollars (the latter was around 1/3 of the total). As it has already been indicated (unsuccessful) attempts at switching over to the anchor of the exchange rate were made in 1995 when the financing of the budget from the GKO reached 68.4% (11.4% in 1994 and 1.2% in 1993). It is noteworthy that during that same 1995 the banks were also offered a system of loans-for-shares-auctions aimed at "winning" their participation in the purchase of GKO. In a state of a huge economic and financial chaos and of political turmoil towards the end of the period the economic agents and the population spontaneously began to organize themselves and to resort to the use of informal barter and monetary practices and rules.[19]

Summing it up, we may underscore the following. During the first period the MR (until 1999) was a unity of two processes – on the one hand, it was a continuation of the practices, institutions and ideas that existed in the planned economy. On the other hand, the MR reflected the processes of appropriation of the power resource rent in building the new capitalist system. As an example, the easy and automatic crediting was both a technical result of the old institutions of planned economy as well as deliberately sought after because it served the interests and enrichment of leading groups and elites (related to the Duma, the Government, the President's group and the newly established banks).[20] Two groups (business elites and political elites) could be differentiated within the power elites related to the power resource rent. The first aimed at privatization because the political power was temporary for it – until it acquired the business. The second sought long-term power positions in the state apparatus guaranteeing a long-term power resource rent.

To a certain extent that corresponds to the classification of M. Olson of the availability of "roving" bandits and "stationary" bandits, Olson (2000). The second group gradually became emancipated from the first and at a certain point it began to control business. Political power became emancipated from the economic one. A. Yakovlev (2006) referred to a transition from "state capture" to "business capture," R. Simonyan (2016) referred to a transition from "oligarchic capitalism to clerical capitalism" (p. 234), and Gaidar and Chubais (2011) referred to dilemma "oligarchs or the state" (p. 93).

The regular end point of the dynamics thus set forth was the depletion of the power resource rent and the inflationary MR servicing it. The crisis and the default in August 1998 were the concrete result. At the same time inflation contributed to clearing the accumulated debts of the new elites and prepared the ground for the second stage.

Growing resource rent and the regime of a controlled exchange rate (1999–2013)

After the financial crisis and the political instability related to electing President B. Yeltsin's successor it was relatively quickly and logically proceeded to the second economic and political stage (Furman 2010). The main task was to safeguard the achievements of the elites in the first stage, the legitimacy of their property (overcoming the "property without legitimacy"[21] problem). The state had to recover by partially compensating the losing actors – above all the population and citizens (which were a dangerous "revolutionary force"). The depletion of the power resource rent related to privatization was almost automatically replaced by another important and traditional source for Russia – oil and gas exports (the main representatives of the natural resource rent). Russia's researchers had long since defined that rent as the main reason for the lack of economic modernization and for the reproduction of the political authoritarianism. According to V. Inozemtsev:

> Whenever Russia returned to the new turnabout in its history to the commodity specialization the traditional authoritarian state was revived. . . . In this "non-economy" the source of money were not natural resources created by the people. . .; the main objectives of their utilization were to enrich the ruling class as well as to ensure apathy and relative satisfaction (stability) of the masses.
>
> (Inozemtsev 2019, pp. 128, 140)

Since 2000 the natural resource rent recovered, and Russia returned to its long-term economic trajectory. The increase of production and of the export of oil products as well as the rapid rise of their prices on the international markets contributed to that effect. The MR had to adjust to the new conditions; it changed radically and focused on the balance of payments. The exchange rate became the main anchor of the MP, the link with the global economy.

As we have already pointed out within the frameworks of that period two sub-periods can be differentiated. They will be dwelt upon later.

Growing natural resource rent and a stable exchange rate (1999–2008)

The period from 1999 until the onset of the global crisis in 2008 was defined as "*exuberant decade*" (*tuchnoe desyatiletye*) (Simonyan 2016, p. 170). The crisis led to the restructuring of the composition of the leading elite in which the civil servants and the new political power (V. Putin) rapidly gained the upper hand. The state was restored, the so-called "vertical of power." That occurred relatively fast – after some resistance the oligarchs gave up part of their positions to the state administration (the famous clash for "Yukos" in 2007). According to many observers during that period and particularly up to 2004, there were relatively stable property rights and the rules of the game were respected (Aleksashenko 1999, pp. 21, 57).

Economic reforms started with a fiscal reform and above all with the introduction of a flat tax, low income taxes, and so forth. After the three-fold depreciation of the ruble during the crisis it began to stabilize. Foreign exchange reserves were accumulated partially due to the Law on the forced sale to the state of 75% of exporters' foreign currency revenues. At the same time oil prices rose (the 20-dollar for barrel limit was crossed in 1999 and on 5 July 2008 it reached 144 dollars, see Figure 11.2). The ruble rate became increasingly stable (Polterovich & Popov 2016, p. 194). All that led to the rapid imposition of new, externally orientated MR and MP. The exchange rate became the main anchor. In the years that followed the oil and gas rent grew at accelerated rates and the current account became the major source for money supply in Russia. Capital inflows were also significant. The foreign currency reserves of the CB and the net external assets of the banking system grew. The capital inflow was also significant. The foreign exchange reserves of the CB and the net foreign assets of the banking system grew.[22]

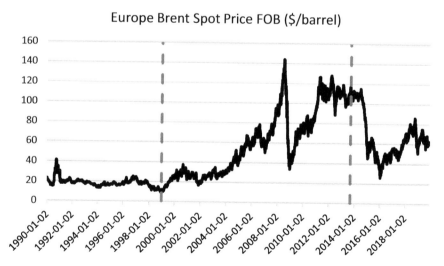

Figure 11.2 Oil price development

Note: The vertical lines represent the beginning of a new MR period.

Source: *EIA – U.S. Energy Information Administration, Europe* Brent Spot Price FOB, viewed 14 November 2019, www.eia.gov/dnav/pet/hist/RBRTED.htm

Still while the stable rate was advantageous for the reproduction of the oil, gas rent and its lobby, it held back the development of other sectors.[23] According to Polterovich and Popov:

> During the 2000s, the export of non-commodity goods became increasingly less profitable. Accumulating reserves, the CB prevented the rise of the nominal rate which from 1999 to September 2014 fluctuated within the 25% range. However, our prices rose 4.5 times since the end of 2013 while prices in the US and the euro zone increased by only 2–3% annually and rose about 1.5-fold during that period. So, the actual rate of the ruble more than doubled.
>
> (Polterovich & Popov 2016, p. 194)

Part of the natural resource rent was mobilized by the state by redirecting it to the public sector. Wages were increased significantly. Armaments were modernized which increased the military expenditure thereof after 2000. Eventually a certain amount was set aside in the newly established Stabilization Fund and the National Welfare Fund.[24] In general, the losers in the previous MR were partially compensated.

Let us dwell on the technical steps undertaken by the CB for the enforcement of the new MR. Those steps were formally set forth in a document of the CB.[25] Thus, until 2005 the CB had set an interval for intervention as regards the ruble/dollar rate (Figure 11.3). Since 2005, it proceeded to the operational goal "the value in rubles per basket of dollar and euro." The interventions were

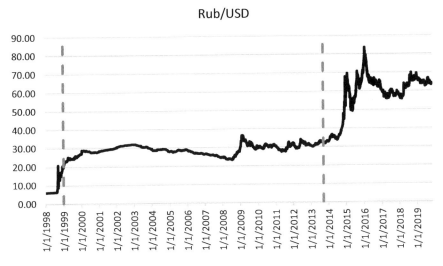

Rub/USD

Figure 11.3 Rate of the Ruble to the US Dollar

Note: The vertical lines represent the beginning of a new MR period.

Source: The Bank of Russia, *Dynamics of the official exchange rates*, viewed 14 November 2019, http://www.cbr.ru/eng/currency_base

already done in the two segments – ruble/dollar and ruble/euro and that was done on the stock exchange as well as on the foreign exchange market. Since February 2007 the weight of the euro increased – the dual currency basket contained 45-euro cents and 55 American cents. After the crisis in 2008 and in early 2009 the control over the exchange rate weakened and the CB discretion increased.

It is important to point out here that during that period as well as during previous ones and until 2014 banking supervision was at an extremely rudimentary level and according to some observers it was even nonexistent. That was an enormous failure which illustrated the power of social interests related to the banking sector triggered by privatization in the early years of post–communism.[26]

Natural resource rent and controlled exchange rate (2009–2013)

The end of 2008 was marked by a series of external shocks for the Russian economy which automatically affected the volume of the natural resource rent. That in turn triggered a change in the political and business strategies of the leading political and economic elites. The logical result of the adjustment of interests and strategies was the change in the MR. Slowly and gradually the MR began to reorient towards internal objectives and to serve the increasing influence of the "power resource rent" that started to recover its importance. In concrete terms shocks were associated above all with the onset of the global financial crisis which cut the volumes of international trade and consequently of Russian exports. At the same time prices of oil and gas products fell sharply and foreign exchange reserves melted.

In that situation initiatives were launched for changing the MR. First as regards the exchange rate – since January 2009 the CB had introduced a lower and upper limit for the value of the basket, 41 and 26 rubles respectively, and since February 2009 – a mechanism of the automatic correction of the limits of the range of permissible values of the basket. That range was set at 2 rubles and subsequently it was widened. In October 2010 the rate limits were abolished. From 24 July 2012 to 17 August 2014, the width of the range became 7 rubles, and since 18 August 2014 – 9 rubles.

It is noteworthy that from 1 October to 7 October 2013 the CB and the Ministry of Finance declared a new regulation for the replenishment and expenditure of the sovereign funds. Thus, the discretion regarding the exchange rate increased. The Treasury became particularly active. On 7 October 2013 a new technical detail was introduced – an additional "technical" internal range for non–intervention of the CB (0.1 ruble), and the "neutral" range was extended from 1 to 3 rubles. Hence two ranges emerged – "neutral" (3 rubles) and "technical" (0.1 ruble) whereas the total fluctuation became 3.1 ruble (within which range the CB did not intervene).

A particularly important component in the structuring of the MR which would be of major importance in the third period was the emergence of MP objectives and instruments related to restoring the active management of internal liquidity, that is, by building an internally oriented MP. It was about the restarting of the repo operations in late 2008 and their intensive utilization from 2011 to 2014 (see Golovnin [2016]). The repo right rate became the main instrument of the MP. The logical conclusion of that process was the adoption (on 13 September 2013) of the percentage of direct weekly repos for the CB's base interest rate. Therefore, we are justified in claiming that that date (certainly not automatically) marked the start of the next third stage. Inflation targeting (IT) was introduced at the third stage as well as the active management of the interest rate and the switchover to the floating exchange rate. The latter two components became structural ones for the new MR (IT) which was oriented towards internal objectives and power resource rent.

Falling natural resource rent, a floating exchange rate and inflation targeting (2013–present)

The 2008/2009 crisis (the crisis of the private corporate debt) was followed by other serious geopolitical shocks. A turning point was the annexation of Crimea in 2014 which resulted in the imposition of sanctions by the EU and the United States and in the imposition of counter sanctions by Russia. Russia was gradually isolated from the main trade and capital flows of the world economy. The prices of oil and gas products continued to decline and fluctuate on the international markets at levels marking the limit for maintaining Russian public finances and for servicing the private external debt. Foreign exchange reserves were increasingly melting as were the accumulated sovereign funds (Figure 11.4).[27] The late 2014 and early 2015 were marked by a distrust in the banking system, rapid devaluation of the ruble and a strong inflation (see Golovnin [2016], p. 171). The CB quickly increased the base interest rate (key rate) which reached 17% on 16 December 2014. The keeping of foreign exchange reserves became a major objective in the situation of isolation and international hostility.

Following the new internal and external configuration, the institutional components of the MR (objectives and instruments) continued to change. First the exchange rate continued to be liberalized and its free floating was announced in November 2014 in connection with the transition to IT. On 22 May and 17 June 2014, the volume of interventions in the exchange rate range was reduced by 100 million dollars and as of August 18, 2014 it was reduced to 0 dollars. The rule was reintroduced in late December 2013 that in the event of accumulated intervention of 350 million dollars the limits of the intervention range were automatically moved by 5 kopeiki.[28] The targeted interventions were discontinued on 13 January 2014 in connection with the transition to a floating rate.

Discretionary monetary instruments were developed as well. Today the mechanics of base interest rates approaches that of the developed countries' CBs. The main instrument is the interest rate on the daily basis of the weekly

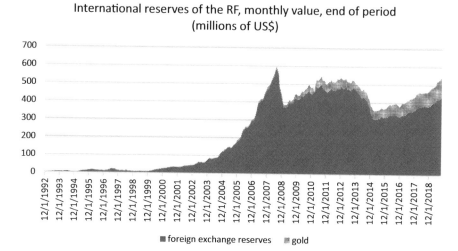

Figure 11.4 Dynamics of the foreign exchange reserves

Source: The Bank of Russia, *International Reserves of the Russian Federation (End of period)*, viewed 14 November 2019, www.cbr.ru/eng/hd_base/mrrf/mrrf_m/

auctions (repo transactions in injecting liquidity and deposit auctions in absorbing liquidity). The range of fluctuations of the interbank interest rates was determined by the two marginal interest rates on the overnight standing facilities (limit +/-1%). At the same time irregular auctions were held for "fine tuning" (period of 1 to 6 days), as well as for providing/absorbing liquidity for longer periods. Of interest were the bonds issued by the CB in order to reduce the high volume of liquidity in recent years. Those bonds could be traded on the secondary market and could in turn serve as collateral in the event of liquidity.

Since November 2014 and above all since early 2015 the official position of the CB had been the transition to the MR of IT (price target of 4%), and to the floating exchange rate. The website of the bank published the Russian translation of the Practical Guide for conducting IT by the Bank of England (Hammond 2012). In addition to price stability the CB's objective was also financial stability.[29] Like all modern banks it published a report on MP. As regards the floating ruble the motives of the CB were as follows:

> The floating exchange rate functions as an 'automatic stabiliser' for the economy, which is its main advantage compared with the managed exchange rate. It facilitates the economy's adjustment to changes in external conditions by mitigating the impact of external factors.
>
> By increasing the economy's dependence on external environment, the fixed or managed exchange rate also makes the monetary policy dependent on other countries' policies and external economic situation. Under the

managed exchange rate regime, in response to changing external conditions the CB is forced to intervene to influence the domestic currency, thus adversely affecting other economic parameters, including inflation rate. The floating exchange rate allows the Bank of Russia to conduct an independent monetary policy aimed at resolving domestic objectives, and primarily – at reducing inflation.[30]

Although in a vague form, the aforementioned quotation illustrates the assertion that the introduction of IT was rather a consequence of the desire to switch over to a floating exchange rate regime. That was in turn a function of the need to protect and even to raise foreign exchange reserves and to isolate the Russian economy from the global financial and political inflows. That is Russia's strategic objective was to switch over to developing its internal sources of development. Moreover, IT was a formal monetary rule, the MR, which was extremely useful from an "ideological point of view" because it brought the country closer the developed market economies. According to S. Aleksashenko:

> I am ready to suppose that neither in the Kremlin nor in the White House (the authors: the Government) or in Neglinnaya (the authors: the Central Bank) a possibility for en masse support of the ruble at the expense of spending the currency reserves was considered in earnest.
>
> (Aleksashenko 2019, p. 128)

Concluding remarks

In this chapter we have set forth a political economy interpretation of the development of the MR in post-Soviet Russia. Its nature and evolution have been dwelt upon as a result of a function of the struggle of the leading groups for the realigning, distribution, control and reproduction of the leading rent resources. The dynamics of the rent and its alternation – privatization, natural resource and power resource rent – have determined the nature of the MR and of the MP. For their part the MR and the MP have been considered to be major institutional mechanisms coordinating the distribution, reproduction and evolution of the rent. Against a historical background for the past 30 years we have established three main monetary regimes – (i) a vague one which can be referred to as an "issue or inflationary one," (ii) exchange rate targeting, and finally (iii) inflation targeting, related respectively to alternating various rent sources (consecutively – (i) power rent [privatization], (ii) natural rent, and (iii) again power rent).

The historical reconstruction set forth makes it possible to consider the place of the CB, its independence as well as the character of the monetary institutions (and the institutions as a whole) in post-soviet countries such as Russia. In brief, we may point out the following.

With small exceptions CB is not an independent institution, it is included within the common institutional framework of the Russian economy which as we have already pointed out has been directed at using definite rent resources. And despite the definite formal approximation with the formal rules of independence over the past years it is clear for everyone that CB is a politically subordinate institution.

The heaviest dependence was certainly evidenced during the first period when the new capitalist structure was developed and when the CB was entirely subordinated to the central government and to the president. A flagrant example of an interference was for instance the decree of Boris Yeltsin of May 22, 1996, according to which the CB had to transfer to the Ministry of Finance its profit of 1994 to the tune of 5 trillion rubles (see Aleksashenko [1999], p. 76).

During the second period of favorable conditions and particularly in the beginning (1999–2004), the CB was not subjected to strong pressure and pursued its policy relatively independently (above all that of sterilization of external money flows). According to many observers, it was no accident that the property rights were most stable and the general rules of the game were observed.

The third period after 2014 was a regime of sanctions. The CB was a function of Russia's strategy of self(isolation) from the world economy and of reducing its dependence on the international financial and trade markets. Currently, from a formal institutional viewpoint the MR in Russia – IT – is like that in the developed countries. Actually we consider that that regime was just a front screening other institutional objectives and rules. They were related to the fact that the exchange rate would not be defended because the CB had to accumulate currency reserves and to participate in mobilizing the internal rent sources. The property rights were again extremely unstable similarly to the first period. The total failure of the bank supervision in Russia which resulted in huge costs for the budget in tackling the bank crisis in 2014–2016 (about 4 and more % of the GDP according to some data) brought the nationalization of the banking sector (about ¾ of assets were state owned). That resulted in the total concentration of credit resources in the state and their potential channeling towards definite group interests.[31]

Against a general methodological background, the question of principle remains open – the extent to which the formal institutions in Russia have the same importance as those in the West. Actually, their content was radically different from that of the developed market economies (some Russian authors referred to a "deformalization of rules"). The political economy of the MR which we have presented here in a simple and hypothetical form aims precisely at providing food for thought and direction for future research.

Although the Bank of Russia managed to keep its target of 4% in late October 2019 the Bank of Russia reported a lower that envisaged forecast for inflation for 2019 (3.2–3.7%) and for 2020 (3.5–4.0%). It was announced that deflation risks were higher than inflation ones. There followed a decrease of the interest rate to 6.5% and a further decrease was announced for December 2019. At the same time in her statements the CB governor Elvira Nabiullina (e.g., her speech in the Duma on November 6, 2019[32]) has increasingly stressed the need for the state (by means of the budget and the fiscal policy) to increase its expenditures including those for investments (the lack of investments has long since been pointed out as a key problem[33]). All this is an evidence that the mechanisms of the third period of the development of internal resources follow their own logic.[34] In the long term that logic could result in the increase of domestic sources of the money supply and, at a definite stage in the choice between depreciation of the ruble or in the introduction of currency and capital control.[35]

Notes

1 Noteworthy is the extremely interesting literary and historical work of E. Pismennaya "On a large scale" ("Po bol'shomu schetu"), dedicated to the history of the Russian Central Bank since 1990 to date based on the personal stories of the bank's governors. This book offers a genuine political economy (Pismennaya 2019).

2 There is certainly extensive literature on international political economy of the monetary and exchange rate regimes (see Broz and Frieden [2008] and Cohen [2015]).

3 For an overview of economic consequences of rent seeking, see Tullock 1967 and Appelbaum & Katz 1987.

4 We should consider that in most transition countries high levels of rent-seeking were possible only in the first years after transition, but the energy sector offered greater possibilities (Treisman 2014, p. 284).

5 A serious research on the development of the political economy of Russia is presented in Vercueil (2019); especially Chapter 6 develops some similar ideas about the rent economy in Russia.

6 We must recall here that it is a matter of a privatization radically different in scope. The private sector in Russia developed from scratch. In the mid-1980s oil prices began to fall and the resource rent and the foreign currency proceeds melted. At the same time Russia was heavily dependent on imports of grain above all (the drama related to the foreign currency proceeds was described in detail by Illarionov and Sachs [1995], Gaidar [2007] and Gaidar and Chubais [2011]). The entire dynamics of processes during the first few years was analyzed in full in the report of the World Bank (1992). See also Petrakov (1998, especially pp. 88–286). Academician N. Petrakov has been an active participant in the discussions on reforms during this period.

7 As regards privatization and its mechanisms, see also Glinkina (2006) and Herrmann-Pillath (2017). The privatization's contribution to the budget was insignificant (it accounted for 0.13% of the total revenues for the 1992–1995 period). Gaidar & Chubais 2011 acknowledged the mistake related for the voucher funds and dwelt on his version of the "loans-for-shares auctions" (in 1995) when the banks were offered the deal of "a loan for the government against property namely shares of state enterprises".

8 A total of 1,400 banks emerged within an extremely short time.

9 There were six banks at the end of the communist period – Gosbank, Vnesheconombank, Sberbank, Promstroybank, Zhilsocbank, and Agroprombank.

10 The CB management under G. Matiukhin could be considered independent in a "western" manner and that openly resisted the attacks of politicians. Within a short time and in extremely difficult economic and political conditions that management succeeded in laying the foundations of a modern two-tier banking system.

11 According to Matiukhin 2017 [1993]:

> The government continued to consider the CB as a bottomless barrel of credit resources and the parliament now and then adopted decrees on soft loans to different sectors of the economy. . . . If in the first six months of 1992 the CB issued 561 billion rubles directly to the national economy it issued 858 billion rubles in the next 4 months. In addition, indirect lending to the national economy through sectoral ministries had increased several times. Thus, if such loans granted by the CB

amounted to 441 billion rubles for the first half of the year by November 1992, they rose to 1,366 billion rubles. Prices rose by 18% in July and by 25% in August and by 27% in September and 30% in October.

(Matiukhin 2017 [1993], pp. 57, 74)

12 There is much evidence to this effect in archived documents (Illarionov A 2013, "Why did Gaidar fire Matiukhin?," *LiveJournal*, web blog post, 5 March 2013, viewed 25 July 2019, https://aillarionov.livejournal.com/510963.html). Particularly illustrative is the documentary which can be seen in youtube (online video, viewed 14 November 2019, www.youtube.com/watch?v=qgu2hxVw7bI). Those years also saw the emergence of the proposals for the introduction of a Currency Board (see Hanke et al. [1993]), and later that system was also proposed by the IMF representatives.

13 According to A. Illarionov's testimonials, the real reformer and "hero" was the Finance Minister B. Fedorov, a principled man, not E. Gaidar, who, to the disappointment of the Liberals, does not differ significantly from other pro-inflation economists (Illarionov 2010).

14 What is interesting is that the behavior of the CB in those years reminds of the theoretical viewpoint of "issue economy" opposed to "tax economy" (promoted by S. Falkner, O. Schmidt), which was popular during the first years of Bolshevik power. As regards the model of "issue economy," the state could exist forever by emitting money without being hit by inflation.

15 During the 1993–1995 period an important role was played by the established "Credit Commission" which coordinated the standpoints of the government and of the CB as regards the volumes and limits of the credit emission.

16 In theory the depreciation of the ruble was prompted by the need to stop the actual overvaluation of the ruble. At the same time foreign exchange reserves reached a very low level.

17 Notwithstanding the claims that attempts were made in 1995 at switching over to a new regime, at restricting crediting, at a corridor of the exchange rate 4300–4900 rubles per dollar.

18 An exhaustive analytical material about the GKO market was provided by Illarionov and Sachs (1995), chapter 3.4 and the annexes. Most data have been taken from there. Generally, the Russian crisis of 1998 was deeply studied and exposed in different interpretation (see, e.g., Montes & Popov 1999; Aleksashenko 1999; Vavilov 2001).

19 See Yakovlev 2001; Volkov 2005; Barsukova 2017 [2015].

20 Thus, for instance, the pressure of Vice President A. Rutskoy in April 1992 for granting a credit to the tune of 7 billion rubles to Vozrozhdenie Bank which was close to him against the threat for governor G. Matyukhin and deputy governor V. Rasskazov to be fired in a week's time. That fact was announced publicly by Rasskazov himself in the presence of Rutskoy (Matiukhin 2017 [1993], 70).

> The monetary emission aimed at enriching the financial intermediaries standing between the 'monetary authorities' – Central Bank, Ministry of Finance and the State Property Committee – and the rest of society. During the 1992–1993 period they became fabulously rich by the distribution of cheap loans, by 'scrolling' funds between state-owned enterprises and the budget.
>
> (Simonyan 2016, p. 73).

According to Aleksashenko (1999), the main guilt for the failure of the monetary policy (despite the attempts of the CB and the IMF) during that period was to be sought in the failure of the fiscal base of the state and in the public finances as a whole. Aleksashenko did not go further to expose the actual driving forces behind the failure of public finances. Ilarionov, for his part, believes that the introduced exchange rate corridor (with the participation of S. Aleksashenko himself) is one of the leading factors leading to the 1998 crisis, Illarionov 2010.

21 See Kapeliushnikov 2016.

22 Still, according to observations two-thirds of the increased rent were due to prices, and only about one-third was the result of the efforts of enterprises engaged in exports.

23 That statement can be disputed.

24 It is noteworthy that profits in the natural resource sector were extremely high due to the low cost of the extraction. Thus, for instance according to reports for 2015 the cost of extraction for Rosneft was 2.6 dollars per barrel or 30-fold lower than market prices of oil. As regards Gasprom, prices were 13 dollars per cu m or 12.5–14-fold lower than market prices (Inozemtsev 2019, p. 124). As regards sovereign funds, see Kudrin (2006), Navoy and Shalunova (2014), and Dabrowska and Zweynert (2015).

25 See The Central Bank of Russia, *The History of the Bank of Russia FX policy*, viewed 10 August 2019, www.cbr.ru/eng/DKP/exchange_rate/fx_policy_hist/

26 We cannot but mention also the murder in September 2006 of the deputy-governor responsible for the banking supervision, A. Kozlov, who was among the few who tried to improve the control on banks.

27 On the dynamics of the balance of payments in the conditions of the 2014–2017 shocks, see Navoy (2017).

28 Consequently, with the rate fluctuations related to Crimea that sum rose to 1,500 mil for a short time.

29 According to Art. 3 of the Federal Law, "On the CB of the Russian Federation" the main goals of the CB are to ensure the stability of the ruble, strengthen the national banking system, ensure the stability of the national payment system and of the national financial market. As a consequence, maintaining financial stability can be regarded as an implicit goal.

30 The Central Bank of the Russian Federation, Exchange rate regime, viewed 2 August 2019, www.cbr.ru/eng/DKP/exchange_rate/

31 Without going into details, we must note that the IT in Russia has been repeatedly criticized as being inappropriate and intangible for the development of Russia and its financial structure (see, e.g., Vedev [2019], "I don't really understand this spill of free floating," Speech presented at the Moscow International currency association conference, 1 July, viewed 5 November 2019, www.iep.ru/ru/sobytiya/aleksey-vedev-ya-ne-ochen-ponimayu-etu-stepen-svobodnogo-plavaniya.html). For a deeper discussion about the limitations of IT in Russia, see our recent paper Nenovsky & Sahling 2019.

32 Statement by Bank of Russia governor E. Nabiullina at the Federation Council, 6 November, viewed 10 November 2019, www.youtube.com/watch?v=BMz7NwPpw9Q

33 See Aganbegyan (2019), as well as Aganbegyan (2018), in particular Chapter 5 "The Reduction of Investments – Ruin for the Economy, the Growth of Investments – a Path towards Its Growth" and Chapter 9 "The Investment Credit – a Key Form of Overcoming the Decline of the Socio-economic Development of Russia".

34 The work on this chapter was finished in November 2019 and later developments have not been considered. But the most recent events as for example the announcement of a new Government in Russia in January 2020, the recent monetary decisions and the sudden decline in oil prices in March 2020 confirm our views of the domestic orientation of the current monetary regime and the growing importance of internal resources for the country.

35 Aleksashenko's opinion is different, the ruble will remain stable in the long term is not so obvious because the Russian economy remains resource-dependent and lacks competitive markets.

References

Abdelal, R 2003, 'Contested Currency: Russia's Rouble in Domestic and International Politics', *Journal of Communist Studies and Transition Politics*, 19(2), pp. 55–76.

Aganbegyan, A 2018, *Finance, Budget and Banks in New Russia*, Delo Publishers, Moscow (in Russian).

Aganbegyan, A 2019, 'Crucial Growth. On the Protracted Stagnation in which the Country is Tied Up', *Ogonek*, 31, 12 August, p. 13 (in Russian).

Aleksashenko, S 1999, *Battle for the Ruble*, Alma Mater, Moscow (in Russian).

Aleksashenko, S 2019, *Russian Economic Miracle. What Went Wrong?* AST, Moscow (in Russian).

Appelbaum, E & Katz, E 1987, 'The Political Economy of Rent Seeking', *The Economic Journal*, 97(387), pp. 685–699.

Barsukova, S 2017 [2015], *An Essay on the Informal Economy, or 16 Shades of Grey*, National Research University Higher School of Economics, Moscow (in Russian).

Broz, JL & Frieden, JA 2008, 'The Political Economy of Exchange Rates', in DA Wittman & BR Weingast (ed.), *The Oxford Handbook of Political Economy*, pp. 587–598, Oxford University Press, Oxford, UK.

Bunich, A 2006, *Autumn of Oligarchs. The History of Grabbing (Privatisation) and the Future of Russia*, Eksmoed, Yauza (in Russian).

Camdessus, M 2014, *La scène de ce drame est le monde. Treize ans à la tête du FMI*, Editions des Arènes, Paris.

Cohen, B 2015, *Currency Power: Understanding Monetary Rivalry*, Princeton University Press, Princeton.

Dabrowska, E & Zweynert, J 2015, 'Economic Ideas and Institutional Change: The Case of the Russian Stabilisation Fund', *New Political Economy*, 20(4), pp. 518–544. doi:10.1080/13563467.2014.923828.

Esanov, A, Merkl, C & Vinhas de Souza, L 2005, 'Monetary Policy Rules for Russia', *Journal of Comparative Economics*, 33(3), pp. 484–499.

Furman, DE 2010, 'The Political System of Post-Soviet Russia', in *Russia-2010: Russian Transformations in the Context of World Development*, pp. 123–196, Logos, Moscow (in Russian).

Gaidar, E 2007, *Collapse of an Empire. Lessons for a Modern Russia*, Russian Political Encyclopedia, Moscow (in Russian).

Gaidar, E & Chubais, A 2011, *Bifurcations in Current Russian History*, OGI Publishing House, Moscow (in Russian).

Glinkina, SP 2006, *Privatization: Concepts, Realization and Efficiency*, Nauka, Moscow (in Russian).

Golovnin, MY 2016, 'Monetary Policy in Russia During the Crisis', *Journal of the New Economic Association*, 29(1), pp. 168–174 (in Russian).

Gurvich, ET 2016, 'Evolution of Russian Macroeconomic Policy in Three Crises', *Journal of the New Economic Association*, 29(1), pp. 174–181 (in Russian).

Hammond, G 2012, *State of the Art Inflation Targeting*, Centre for Central Banking Studies, Bank of England, viewed 10 August 2019, www.bankofengland.co.uk/-/media/boe/files/ccbs/resources/state-of-the-art-inflation-targeting.

Hanke, S, Jonung, L & Schuler, K 1993, *Russian Currency and Finance. A Currency Board Approach to Reform*, Routledge, London.

Herrmann-Pillath, C 2017, 'Modernisierungsblockaden 1917–2017. Utopische Eigentumsrevolutionen in Russland, 1917–2017', *Osteuropa*, 6–8, pp. 133–143.

Illarionov, A 2010, 'The Hard Way to Freedom', *Continent*, 145 (in Russian).

Illarionov, A 2013, 'Why did Gaidar fire Matiukhin?', *LiveJournal*, web blog post, 5 March 2013 (in Russian), viewed 25 July 2019, https://aillarionov.livejournal.com/510963.html

Illarionov, A & Sachs, J (eds.) 1995, *Financial Stabilization in Russia: June 1995*, Progress Academy, Moscow (in Russian).

Inozemtsev, VL 2015, 'Seven Domestic Political Constraints of Russian Modernization', *Journal of the New Economic Association*, 28(4), pp. 189–194 (in Russian).

Inozemtsev, V 2019, *Non-modern Country. Russia in the XXI Century World*, Alpina Publisher, Moscow (in Russian).

Johnson, J 2018, 'The Bank of Russia: From Central Planning to Inflation Targeting', in P Conti-Brown & RM Lastra (ed.), *Research Handbook on Central Banking*, pp. 94–116, Edward Elgar, Cheltenham and Northampton.

Kapeliushnikov, RI 2016, 'Where is the Beginning of that End? (to the Question of Ending the Transition Period in Russia)', in RI Kapeliushnikov (ed.), *Economic Essays: Methodology, Institutes, Human Capital*, pp. 343–389, National Research University Higher School of Economics, Moscow (in Russian). doi:10.17323/978-5-7598-1292-0.

Korhonen, I & Nuutilainen, R 2016, 'A Monetary Policy Rule for Russia, or Is it Rules?', *BOFIT Discussion Papers N° 2*.

Kudrin, A 2006, 'The Mechanisms of Forming of Russia's Non-Oil-and-Gas Budget Balance', *Voprosy Ekonomiki*, 8, pp. 4–16 (In Russian). doi:10.32609/0042-8736-2006-8-4-16.

Lavigne, M 1970, *Les économies socialistes soviétique et européennes*, Armand Colin, Paris.

Matiukhin, G 2017 [1993], *The Central Bank of Russia – the Beginning of the Road. Memories of the First Chairman* [first published as: 'I was the head banker of Russia'], URSS Publishers, Moscow (in Russian).

Montes, MV & Popov, VV 1999, *Asian Virus of Dutch Disease? Theory and Evidence of Currency Crises in Russia and Elsewhere*, Delo Publishers, Moscow (in Russian).

Navoy, AV 2017, 'Adaptation of the Balance of Payments of the Russian Federation to External Shocks in the 2014–2017', *Russian Journal of Money and Finance*, 11, pp. 3–13 (in Russian).

Navoy, AV & Shalunova, LI 2014, 'Reserve Fund and National Welfare Fund of Russia in the International System of Sovereign Wealth Funds', *Russian Journal of Money and Finance*, 2, pp. 26–33 (in Russian).

Nenovsky, N & Mihaylova-Borisova, G 2015, 'Debts, Ideas and Interests in the Balkans. Chronology of the Post-Communist Transformation, 1990–2013', *Économie et Institutions*, 23(2), pp. 121–145.

Nenovsky, N & Rizopoulos, Y 2003, 'Extreme Monetary Regime Change. Evidence from the Currency Board Introduction in Bulgaria', *Journal of Economic Issues*, 37(4), pp. 909–941.

Nenovsky, N & Sahling, C 2019, 'Monetary Targeting Versus Inflation Targeting: Empirical Evidence from Russian Monetary Policy (1998–2017)', Forthcoming. Paper presented at the XX April International Academic Conference "On Economic and social development", National Research University Higher School of Economics, Moscow, Russia.

Olson, M 2000, *Power and Prosperity. Outgrowing Communist and Capitalist Dictatorships*, Basic Books, New York.

Petrakov, N 1998, *Russian Roulette. An Economic Experiment at the Cost of 150 Million Lives*, Economics, Moscow (in Russian).

Pismennaya, E 2019, *On a Large Scale. The History of the Central Bank of Russia*, Mann, Ivanov and Ferber, Moscow (in Russian).

Polterovich, V & Popov, V 2016, 'Exchange Rate, Inflation and Industrial Policy', *Journal of the New Economic Association*, 29(1), 192–198 (in Russian).

Radaev, V 2001, 'Deformation of Rules and Tax Avoidance in Russian Economic Activity', *Voprosy Ekonomiki*, 6, pp. 60–79 (in Russian).

Robinson, N (ed.) 2013, *The Political Economy of Russia*, Rowman & Littlefield Publisher, Plymouth.

Sachs, J 1994, *Market Economy and Russia*, Economics, Moscow (in Russian).

Simonyan, R 2016, *Without Anger and Bias: The Economic Reforms of the 1990s and Their Consequences for Russia*, Economics, Moscow (in Russian).

Tompson, W 1998, 'The Politics of Central Bank Independence in Russia', *Europe-Asia Studies*, 50(7), pp. 1157–1182.

Treisman, D 2014, 'The Political Economy of Change after Communism', in A Aslund & S Djankov (ed.), *The Great Rebirth: Lessons from the Victory of Capitalism Over Communism*, pp. 273–296, Peterson Institute for International Economics, Washington, DC.

Tullock, G 1967, 'The Welfare Costs of Tariffs, Monopolies, and Theft', *Western Economic Journal*, 5(3), pp. 224–232.

Vavilov, A 2001, *Public Debt: Lessons of the Crisis and Principles of Management*, Institute for Financial Studies, Moscow (in Russian).

Vedev, A 2019, 'I Don't Really Understand This Spill of Free Floating', Speech presented at the Moscow International currency association conference (in Russian), 1 July, viewed 5 November 2019, https://www.iep.ru/ru/sobytiya/aleksey-vedev-ya-ne-ochen-ponim-ayu-etu-stepen-svobodnogo-plavaniya.html

Vercueil, J 2019, *Économie politique de la Russie (1918–2018)*. Le Seuil (Collection: Points. Économie), Paris.

Volkov, V 2005, *Violent Entrepreneurship. Economic and Sociological Analysis*, National Research University Higher School of Economics, Moscow (in Russian).

World Bank 1992, *Russian Economic Reform: Crossing the Threshold of Structural Change (English)*, A World Bank Country Study, Washington, DC.

Yakovlev, A 2000, 'Barter in the Russian Economy: Classifications and Implications (Evidence form Case Study Analyses)', *Post-Communist Economies*, 12(3), pp. 279–291.

Yakovlev, A 2001, 'Black Cash tax Evasion in Russia: Its Forms, Incentives and Consequences at the Firm Level', *Europe-Asia Studies*, 53(1), pp. 33–55.

Yakovlev, A 2006, 'The Evolution of Business – State Interaction in Russia: From State Capture to Business Capture?', *Europe-Asia Studies*, 58(7), pp. 1033–1056. doi:10.1080/09668130600926256.

Yakovlev, A 2014, 'Russian Modernization: Between the Need for New Players and the Fear of Losing Control of Rent Sources', *Journal of Eurasian Studies*, 5, pp. 10–20.

12 The PBOC in the "new era" of Chinese political economy

Orhan H. Yazar

The Chinese central bank, People's Bank of China (PBOC), has become one of the most watched financial authorities around the world by policymakers, investors and businesses. Any announcement by the PBOC regarding the credit allocation or the exchange rate moves financial markets across the world. The growing impact of the Chinese economy in the global economy elevates the PBOC as a signaling post for the direction of the world economy and thinking of China's leaders. A better understanding of the functioning of the PBOC would enable us to make better economic decisions either as policymakers or investors. Since the PBOC continues to evolve and it is embedded in the Chinese political economy, delving into its history, organizational capacity and mandate would be a useful first step towards that goal. The next step would be to unpack the PBOC's operating environment and focus on the "new era," which is the current institutional and political context emerged after the 18th Party Congress of the Chinese Communist Party in late 2012.

China has experienced an impressive economic development in the last four decades. Economic reforms since 1978 enabled the country to sustain economic growth levels that lifted millions out of poverty and improved living conditions for majority of the population. The post-1978 transition from a command economy to a relatively more efficient market economy brought significant changes to the organization of economic life and economic governance in the country. Reform and opening (*gaigekaifang*) entailed a process of marketization and greater integration with the world economy. In line with this agenda, many economic institutions had to be built from scratch and the existing ones, that were in forms only to assist the implementation of the country's economic plan, were revamped.

China's financial system was in the latter category. The functions of the financial system and the operations of the actors within were strictly determined by the Chinese state. Chinese central bank, People's Bank of China, was a mere accountant for the state allocation of credit to the state-owned enterprises and making sure that there were enough savings in the system (Cassou, 1974) before the reform. After the reforms, the role and functions of the Chinese central bank have evolved with the country's economic development and integration to the global markets. As China continues to calibrate its economic system and implement economic reforms in new areas, this evolution is expected to continue.

Chinese central bank operates within the context of the Chinese political economy and the dynamics of Chinese politics and ideology sets the boundaries of its actions. The Chinese Communist Party (CCP) is the main driver of all policy decisions in the country including the monetary policy, which is traditionally considered to be the domain of the central banks in other countries. Lastly, the Chinese economy's greater integration to the world economy largely with trade in goods and services, gained a new pace with cross-border investments and increasing capital flows in and out of the country. Increasing willingness of China to play a larger role in the global financial system necessitates the central bank to accept new challenges to its operational independence and seek influence in international norm setting.

Thus, the evolutionary political and global characteristics of the environment in which the PBOC functions affect its behavior and decision-making capacity. Having outlined the general political economy context within which PBOC operates, we can discuss its history, structure, functions and constraints.

A brief history of the PBOC

Before the economic reforms in 1978, People's Bank of China was a monobank functioning as a banker for the state and providing commercial banking services for the public (Ray Chaudhuri, 2018). Issuing currency, setting interest rates and controlling money supply were its central banking functions while collecting deposits and distributing short-term loans were its commercial banking functions (Han, 2016). The Bank was allocating credit through loans made to the state-owned enterprises directed by the central planning authorities and had thousands of branches across the country in order to allow people to access their deposits easily in an effort to encourage private savings. The bank kept the prices under control by tightly matching the money supply to the amount of goods (Cassou, 1974). However, it could not escape the excesses of political turmoil during the Mao years that weakened its ability to fulfill its functions as the central bank either because of excessive lending or purges of staff (Hsiao, 1982). The functions of managing country's trade and currency settlements were fulfilled by a separate bank; the Bank of China, and the People's Bank of China had no role in managing the exchange rate or country's external finances. Overall, PBOC was a "cashier" (Hsiao, 1982) for the state with no real say in monetary policy decisions.

The role of People's Bank of China has changed after the Third Plenary Session of the 11th Central Committee Meeting of the Chinese Communist Party, which instigated country's market reforms and opening up. In 1979, the monobank structure was deconstructed and PBOC assumed the role of the central bank in charge of managing money supply while its commercial banking responsibilities were dropped (Hsiao, 1982). The State Council policy announcements in 1982 and 1983 firmly established the PBOC as the central bank of the country with clear guidelines regarding its operations. The first years of the new central bank operations were quite bumpy as the PBOC had difficulty deciding the amount of currency in circulation causing inflationary pressures at times and industrial output decline on other occasions prompting government intervention for reversals (Yi, 1992). In the late 1993, the State Council defined the goals of the PBOC as "keeping the currency stable and promoting economic growth" and clarified its role in relation to other financial authorities (State Council, 1993). The Ministry of Finance was prohibited from borrowing from PBOC which was expected to increase the central bank's independence (Jun, 1996). While the PBOC was responsible for prudential supervision of the banking system in the 1990s, the securities regulation function was diverted from the PBOC to the newly established China Securities and Exchange Commission in 1992. The PBOC was also responsible for supervision and administration of the interbank bond market. These changes were codified in 1995 in the Law of People's Republic of China on the People's Bank of China. 2003 Amendment to the 1995 Law delegated the prudential supervision functions to the newly established China Banking Regulatory Commission (currently China Banking and Insurance Regulatory Commission) and strengthened its role in monetary policymaking in line with institutional reforms in the early 2000s. The Chinese economic reform process targeted developing an effective central bank from the start and gradually established a respected financial governance authority not only within the country but abroad as well.

The PBOC in the state apparatus

The Chinese state and its various departments are organized according to a strict hierarchy that places the Chinese Communist Party at the top. The ability of different government agencies to influence key decisions is determined by their assigned place in the hierarchy by the Party. It is important to understand PBOC's place in the apparatus of the Chinese state, specifically economic governance. In the pre-reform era, the PBOC was implementing the decisions of the Central Planning Committee and subjected to the authority of the Ministry of Finance. After the reforms, the PBOC was listed as a ministerial level organization under the State Council placing it at the same level with other ministries. Moreover, the PBOC governor is ranked higher than heads of state-owned commercial banks giving the PBOC an authoritative clout over the banks for implementing monetary policy.

The PBOC is also protected from the interference of other ministries, local governments and government agencies by the 2003 PBOC Law. Despite supplementary measures to emphasize PBOC's authority, the PBOC is not an independent central bank politically, financially or operationally and has to follow the guidelines set by the State Council. The governor of the central bank is nominated by the Premier and approved by the National People's Congress (NPC) or the Standing Committee of the NPC when the NPC is not in session. There are no term limits for the governor and as the case of former PBOC governor Zhou Xiaochuan (2002–2018) illustrates, it can extend beyond the terms of Chinese Presidents. Finally, the President can appoint or remove the governor of the PBOC while deputy governors can be appointed or removed by the Premier (Law of PBOC, 2003).

The strengthening of the PBOC in the state apparatus was accompanied by the centralization of the PBOC in 1998. The implementation of monetary policy was ineffective due to the collusion between local branches of the PBOC and local governments which were in favor of greater credit expansion envisioned by the PBOC's monetary policy at the center. To increase the effectiveness of the PBOC's policy execution, the number of regional branches were cut to nine from the previous thirty-one dispersed across China's thirty-one administrative provinces. However, when policy capture risk dissipated, PBOC unofficially continued to use sub-regional branches in provincial capitals to coordinate monetary policy in 2004. Today, the PBOC is considering returning to the provincial-based organization model in order to address the different needs of various provinces combined under one regional branch (Wu et al., 2018).

The functions of the PBOC

The main task of the PBOC is formulation and implementation of monetary policy. The formulation of the monetary policy in China is the result of a consultative process which takes place initially within the Monetary Policy Committee (MPC). The MPC devises policy according to economic priorities of the Party. The Committee has 14 members and consists of the central bank governor and deputies, top level officials from the State Council, National Development and Reform Commission, Ministry of Finance, heads of other regulatory and supervisory organizations, president of the banking association and academics. The members can be replaced by the State Council with a decree. Table 12.1 illustrates the latest members of the Committee which was reshuffled in June 2019.

The PBOC uses reserve ratios, interest rates, open-market operations, window guidance and direct lending to implement the monetary policy. Some of these instruments are very similar to the ones employed by other central banks but their weight and way of application in administering the policy differs due to China's economic structure and continuing evolution of its financial system. The main tool for controlling money supply in the economy was through credit allocation until the mid-1990s. There was a lack of commitment from the political authorities for interest rate liberalization as government-set interest rates were allowing financial repression and mobilization of cheap deposits to address short-term economic problems (Shih, 2011). This dependence on credit allocation as an easy fix to economic problems in a political economy which relies on good economic results for its continuity, prioritized the use of reserve ratios or window guidance as preferred tools of monetary policy.

Table 12.1 Members of the Monetary Policy Committee of the PBOC (2019)

Members of the Monetary Policy Committee of the PBOC:
Chairman: Yi Gang – Governor of the PBOC
Members: Ding Xuedong – Deputy Secretary General of the State Council
Lian Weiliang – Deputy Director of the National Development and Reform Commission
Zou Jiayi – Vice Minister of Finance
Chen Yulu- Deputy Governor of the PBOC
Liu Guoqing – Deputy Governor of the PBOC
Ning Jizhen – Director of the Bureau of Statistics
Guo Shuqing- Chairman of the Banking Regulatory Commission
Yi Huiman – Chairman of the China Securities and Regulatory Commission
Pan Gongsheng- Director of the Foreign Exchange Bureau
Tian Guoli- Chairman of the China Banking Association
Liu Shijin – Vice Chairman of the China Development Research Foundation
Liu Wei – President of the Renmin University
Ma Jun – Director of the Center for Finance and Development Studies Tsinghua University

Source: Caijing.com.cn

Recently, the PBOC accelerated its efforts to adopt a more market-based interest rate that will function close to benchmark interest rates in other countries.

The PBOC is also mandated for managing the stability of the financial system. In the early 2000s, China adopted "one bank three commissions" (*yihangsanhui*) system to manage financial risks. The regulation and supervision of the securities market, banking sector and insurance sector were delegated to three separate agencies and the PBOC has become an oversight authority for systemic risks with a mandate to coordinate regulation efforts. Following the 2008 Global Financial Crisis (GFC), China has put more emphasis on macro-prudential regulation and coordination among various regulatory agencies. However, the inadequate information sharing mechanisms and regulatory agency rivalry inhibit the level of coordination sought by the government especially with growing complexity of financial instruments in the market (He, 2018). Recently, China merged country's insurance and banking regulators. There is growing demand from the top-leadership for "financial security" in China and this policy objective is pulling various regulatory agencies to work closely together under a more hands-on Chinese leadership (Naughton, 2017). The establishment of the State Council Financial Stability and Development Committee (SCFSDC) is the pinnacle of these efforts and aims to monitor and prevent financial risks in a comprehensive and coordinated manner. The SCFSDC ensured that PBOC remains significant in regulatory efforts by appointing the PBOC governor as the vice-chair, however the new Committee also took away the chances of PBOC becoming an umbrella regulatory agency overseeing the whole financial system.

Lastly, the PBOC has a function in the sphere of currency exchange management as well. The role of PBOC in deciding the value of the Renminbi

(RMB) has been quite controversial as the value of the RMB has been a sour point in the discussions between China and its international economic partners. When the Chinese currency fell below the 2008 levels against the US dollar recently in reaction to a stalemate in the ongoing China – US trade talks, the US Treasury officially announced China as a "currency manipulator" (Smith, 2019). The extent of PBOC's intervention in the exchange rate market has declined since July 2005 when China decided to move from a US dollar pegged-exchange rate regime to a semi-floating exchange rate regime. However, it is the necessities of the Chinese economy that sets the broader strategy for the China's exchange rate regime and the PBOC is again a mere executer for the will of the state in regard to the desired exchange rate levels. It is important to include domestic political economy ramifications of exchange rate changes and the changing direction of the Chinese economic model into our analysis of China's policy directions in this area (Chin, 2013). As the current governor of the PBOC once pronounced in an academic article, the Chinese political economy unlike any other emerging market economies will be unwilling to give up its monetary policy independence (Yi, 2008). The state's ability to manage growth through monetary policy is paramount for managing the economy and the risk of losing this capacity with a haphazard capital account opening is undesirable. Hence, a complete withdrawal of the PBOC from exchange rate management is unthinkable at this stage of China's economic development. Even reversals from the market-oriented forms of exchange rate management is possible in times of need with a technical wild card like "counter-cyclical variable" (Bradsher, 2017). On the other hand, the reorientation of the economy towards domestic consumption, efforts to internationalize the use of RMB and greater opening of the financial markets to global capital inflows continue to push China towards a more flexible exchange rate regime in pursuit of greater efficiency. Nevertheless, the realization of these liberal reforms is gradual and contingent upon their utility to generate positive outcomes both domestically and for China's international stance.

The Chinese central bank in the New Era

The new era (*xinshidai*) is a reference to the start of the Xi–Li (Chinese President Xi Jinping and Premier Li Keqiang) leadership at the beginning of the 18th Party Congress at the end of 2012. The new era emphasizes the need to reevaluate socialism with Chinese characteristics and the kind of socialism that can benefit the country at its current phase of development. The key leader behind this concept is China's current President Xi Jinping. Xi formulated his vision under "Xi Jinping Thought on New Era Chinese Socialism" which has become a part of China's constitution at the 19th Party Congress in 2017. At first sight, the conceptualization of the new era may seem like a political propaganda tool to garner support around a new leadership however it's rather a grand vision with ramifications for China's economic development model, bureaucratic governance and international economic relations. Changes in these policy areas directly or indirectly impact the central bank and its operations since PBOC lacks independence and is a subordinate to the Party, and the political survival of the technocrats rely on their ability to accommodate the wishes of the top leadership.

New economy and challenges

The new leadership knew from the beginning that China's growth model that relied on low value-added exports and investment was no longer sustainable. Demographic changes, structural imbalances, greater inequality and environmental problems made the Chinese leadership to devise a new economic development model that emphasized quality economic growth at moderate levels. Relatedly, decelerating GDP growth, increasing consumption, expanding services sector and related job and overall economic growth fueled by technological innovation have become the "new normal" for China. The PBOC, which had a stabilization role following the GFC, was tasked with dealing with the excesses of credit expansion and acute debt levels. On the other hand, the PBOC had to manage deceleration in economic growth to avoid rising unemployment and social unrest which are governance red lines of the Party. Greater emphasis was put on bringing the shadow banking sector under control, supporting farmers and rural cooperatives through favorable monetary regulations in line with government's rural poverty alleviation efforts, enabling innovation and technology in real economy and finance.

The size of the shadow banking in China, credit intermediation activities outside the regular banking system (FSB, 2014), reached 28.5 % of total banking sector assets in 2016 (Moody's, 2017). Aside from the financial risks associated with the shadow banking industry, Chinese monetary policy to a large extent relies on credit controls and the rise of the shadow banking industry brought the ability of the PBOC to implement an effective monetary policy into question. The gradual financial liberalization in China generated regulatory arbitrage opportunities that allows financial market players to defy the PBOC (Brunnermeier et al., 2017; Lu et al., 2015). An illustration of this issue was presented by the increase in total new credit despite a decline in the new bank loans between 2010 and 2015 in line with PBOC's contractionary monetary direction (Chen et al., 2018). The involvement of local governments, commercial banks and credit-starved private firms allow the shadow banking activities to thrive and have adverse impact on the PBOC's contractionary efforts while compounding its expansionary efforts (Gabrieli et al., 2017). However, it is important to note that PBOC does not see shadow banking as an evil force to be crushed but, as Governor Yi suggested, an area that requires standardization and better regulation (China Banking News, 2018).

Starting with the second half of 2016, the Chinese government established a stricter regulatory and supervisory framework for the shadow banking industry in an effort to prevent financial risks which were one of the "three tough battles" (*sandagongjianzhan*) announced by the President Xi. In April 2018, the

PBOC announced a new set of asset management rules to be implemented by the end of 2020. These targeted implicit guarantees used for promotion of wealth management products, non-transparent nature of the financial products, excessive leveraging through asset management products and the regulatory supervision difficulties caused by these products distributed across various asset classes that goes beyond the jurisdiction of one regulator. The stock market crash in the summer of 2015, better economic growth prospects in 2016 compared to the previous couple of years or to reign in the local government officials may have prompted the Party to take stricter regulatory stance (Naughton, 2017) against the shadow banking. For the local governments, expansion of credit through shadow banking is a defiance of the financial repression devised by the central government. The actions of the local governments can be tolerated for economic growth considerations but once they reach a systemic risk threshold threatening the Party's legitimacy and political survival, intervention by the central government becomes inevitable.

One of the centennial objectives of the Chinese Communist Party, established in 1921, is to eradicate poverty in the country by 2020. According to the government reports by the end of 2015, there were 55.75 million Chinese citizens living below the nationally designated poverty line. The 13th Five-Year Plan (2016–2020), which is a guiding policy document for government agencies at all levels, has made significant commitments to poverty alleviation and development of rural communities (State Council Information Office, 2016). PBOC has a major responsibility for diverting more financial resources to rural areas and increase financial inclusiveness. In addition to the policy guidance, PBOC encourages more bank lending to small, micro-businesses and agricultural sector by offering preferential reserve-requirement-ratios (RRR) as an incentive to commercial banks which are willing to support those groups with their loans (PBOC Annual Report, 2018). The PBOC can also choose to directly precipitate more lending by decreasing the RRR for rural commercial banks as it did by lowering the RRR to 8% from 11.5% in May 2019 to increase more lending to the real economy rather hastily as guided by the State Council (Li, 2019).

The rural households have recently come to prominence in the CCP's economic strategy for several reasons. The urbanization has accelerated with China's economic reforms but also generated a huge chasm in rural-urban inequality. This is a pressing issue for Chinese leaders to address along with eradicating poverty. Secondly, the on-going trade war with the United States affects the job security of millions of migrant workers in the export industries and the livelihoods of their families, who rely on the remittances sent by the migrant workers. The Chinese government wishes to protect those families and rural communities from the impact of adverse economic swings by generating self-sustaining local ecosystems. Lastly, digitization of the Chinese economy has already reshaped China's consumerism in urban areas and the rural areas are fast catching-up. This is a blessing for the Party which is looking for transforming China to a consumption and services based economic model. Hence, PBOC again acts in service of the CCP and the goals set by the top leadership in the 18th Party Congress paving the way to the "new era."

The new era thinking also places great importance on technological development and innovation for "the great rejuvenation" of the country. Technology is considered to be a great enabler for economic development and receives huge support from the top leadership. Premier Li Keqiang's emphasis on internet technologies and their application to manufacturing, retail and finance has made the term "internet plus" (*hulianwangjia*) one of the most discussed in 2015 (State Council, 2015). With over 800 million internet users and state of the art telecom infrastructure soon to be running on 5G networks, the Chinese financial sector can potentially increase credit allocation efficiency with the use of big data and develop new financial instruments to increase inclusiveness of the financial system for millions of households (Hau et al., 2019). The peer to peer (P2P) lending platforms, online money market funds and third-party payments platforms are currently the most prominent forms of fintech applications in China and there is great interest for developing a local cryptocurrency. One of the factors that allowed Chinese fintech industry to grow rapidly was lax regulation. Despite the huge growth of the industry since 2012, no major regulation was introduced until risks built up (Xu, 2017) and were revealed with failing P2P lending platforms. The regulators tried to avoid the complications of reigning in an already messy industry (Chorzempa, 2018).

The PBOC has also watched the development of the industry on the sidelines until 2015. In 2015, with slower economic growth, the failures among the P2P platforms accelerated and caused a regulatory reaction. In July of 2015, the PBOC along with other regulatory agencies and ministries issued a guiding document for the healthy development of the industry and clarified the roles of each regulatory agency for regulation and supervision of the sector with the PBOC being responsible for supervising internet payment companies (Borst, 2015). In 2016, under the guidance of the State Council, a rectification process started to clean up the sector targeting bad apples and lawlessness (PBOC, 2017). As the industry continued to grow, the central bank has established a fintech committee in 2017 to study the impact of new technologies on the monetary policy, financial markets, financial stability, payments and clearing systems (PBOC Annual Report, 2018), signaling greater oversight. Soon after, the PBOC announced the inclusion of select financial products by P2P platforms to its macro-prudential assessment (Wu, 2017).

As indicated by the recently issued "FinTech Development Plan" (PBOC, 2019), the PBOC continues to try to develop a framework for the healthy development of the fintech industry but challenges remain ahead. The conduct of monetary policy and assessment of indicators like inflation can become more challenging in an algorithm driven marketplace. The dominance of China's internet giants in the fintech industry and the regulatory arbitrage that they are enjoying compared to the traditional banking industry can generate regulatory capture in a political environment that holds technological innovation dear to its development goals. The competition between local governments to attract greater financial resources to their provinces may also result in a regulatory race to the bottom. As local governments become customers for P2P lending themselves (Chorzempa, 2018), the PBOC's efforts may be diluted particularly at local levels.

Another area of fintech that the PBOC pays close attention to, is the cryptocurrencies. Cryptocurrencies are digital assets or electronic cash that requires no central management and authenticated by a digital computation process (Iwamura et al., 2019). For the central banks which are responsible for managing currency in circulation and money supply, cryptocurrencies may pose a serious challenge to their authority. An indication of such fears along with the European Central Bank and Bank of England, the PBOC was quick to state its reservations when the social networking giant, Facebook, announced its own cryptocurrency, Libra. The concerns raised by the Deputy Director of PBOC payments department Mu Changchun were about foreign exchange risk, monetary policy repercussions, non-traceability of illegal activities, and Libra's technical capacity to deal with high number of concurrent retail transactions (Bloomberg, 2019). Majority of the criticisms were concerning aspects of the proposal that would result in the PBOC's loss of control over China's financial system. Libra is not alone in attracting the ire of the PBOC in the cryptocurrency world.

The Chinese financial system accommodates mechanisms that allow the Party to control both domestic and international capital movements and the Party officials were surely rattled by the idea of a digital currency with the potential to endanger their control. When the most prominent cryptocurrency of the world, Bitcoin, became a tool for capital flights from the country, the PBOC was quick to ban all transactions by financial institutions and payments companies in 2013 (Ju, 2015). A complete ban on trading on the Bitcoin exchanges was introduced in late 2017. The acquisition of Bitcoins through mining, a process that allows miners to release new coins as a result of solving highly complicated mathematical puzzles, is also targeted by the government. As China hosts more than 70% of Bitcoin mining activities in the world, the authorities are seeking an orderly phasing out to avoid a major collapse in the Bitcoin market. Lastly, the possible use of cryptocurrency metadata to disseminate information about politically sensitive matters, as illustrated by the use of Ethereum blockchain network to share information about a vaccine scandal in 2018 (Liao, 2018), makes the use of cryptocurrency a lot more complicated for regulators.

The increase in the risks associated with an imminent rise of a third-party cryptocurrency gave the PBOC a strong incentive to expedite the development of a home grown alternative. PBOC has been working on a digital currency since 2014 and the central bank officials recently announced that they were very close to issuing their own "cryptocurrency" (Bloomberg News, 2019). However, to avoid the risks associated with the use of cryptocurrency, the central bank does not develop an algorithm based, decentralized cryptocurrency but a digital or virtual currency that will be backed by cash or M0 through the banking system (Yi, 2019). In addition to the challenges posed by the domestic political economy, the PBOC faces the dilemmas of any other central bank in developing a true cryptocurrency which will force them to ignore Know Your Customer (KYC) or Anti-Money Laundering (AML) provisions and adopts a second-best strategy with PBOC issued electronic money which has the appeal of eliminating any third party non-payment risk (Berentsen and Schär, 2018).

Bureaucratic reorganization

The new era conception indicated that politics as usual and "fragmented authoritarianism" was no longer acceptable in China. There was a push for radical change in the bureaucracy coupled with a demand for absolute loyalty to the new leadership (Pei, 2019). Anti-corruption campaigns and constant purges of cadres set the tone for non-compliance from the beginning. The bureaucratic fiefdoms were no longer tolerated and decision-making in many areas concentrated in the hands of few, with the expansion of leading small groups (LSGs). LSGs, traditionally coordinating mechanisms in areas where multiple bureaucratic organizations are involved, became drivers of policy and a tool for centralization for the new leadership (Johnson et al., 2017). After the 19th Party Congress, a reorganization of the LSGs transformed some into Central Commissions increasing their transparency and more openly signaling their significance in guiding policy.

The PBOC is as strong as its leadership within the Chinese bureaucratic system. The previous PBOC Governor, Zhou Xiaochuan, had served the bank for more than 15 years. His experience, professionalism and political wisdom made him an invaluable asset to several leaders. In addition to his position as the Governor of the PBOC, Zhou was the Party Secretary of the PBOC, making him the sole authority at the PBOC and allowing him to wield greater power in economic governance. His strength as an institutional entrepreneur allowed him to push for reforms regarding interest rates and exchange rate. Zhou's retirement and appointment of Yi Gang in 2018 opens a new era in central banking in China. Yi had been the deputy governor at the PBOC for ten years before his appointment and has established himself as a capable technocrat both within and outside the country. Yi is expected to lead China in an era of greater financial opening within the country and increasing influence of RMB internationally.

At the time of Yi's appointment as the Governor of PBOC, Guo Shu-qing, the head of the China Banking and Insurance Regulatory Commission, has become the Party Secretary of the PBOC to allow greater coordination between the central bank and regulators (Chen, 2018). However, this arrangement is likely to constrain Yi's power within the organization. Both Yi and Guo will also be closely monitored by Vice-Premier Liu He, the President's top economic adviser. Moreover, Yi is a part of Central Financial and Economic Affairs Commission (formerly Central Leading Group for Financial and Economic Affairs) which is led by the President. Given the role of LSGs in centralization of policymaking, the central bank governor will be under greater pressure to accommodate the policy stance of the central government. Hence the relative increase in the "de facto" independence of the PBOC garnered by the former PBOC Governor Zhou Xiaochuan, may be lost in the new era.

International economic affairs

Since the 18th Congress, China has adopted a more assertive stance in international relations emphasizing protection of its "core interests" (Zhou, 2019). This is a departure from the policy positions of the previous leaderships who emphasized China's "peaceful rise" and adhered to Deng Xiaoping's famous quote on keeping a low profile (*taoguangyanghui*) (Yan, 2014). At the 19th Party Congress, the Chinese leadership presented the "major–country diplomacy with Chinese characteristics" vision which emphasized China's status as a "great power" and urged a more confident predisposition in country's foreign relations (Shin, 2018). China's diplomatic position in the new era would adopt a more confrontational approach and challenge the existing hegemon, the United States, if necessary, to pave way for its "great rejuvenation". Another important aspect of the new era diplomacy is the use of inclusion or exclusion in the China–generated economic and potential security benefits as a foreign policy tool (Yan, 2014). China already offers alternative institutions and initiatives for economic cooperation to other countries to build deeper relationships and form lasting alliances with the Belt and Road Initiative and establishment of the Asian Investment and Infrastructure Bank. On the other hand, countries that defy China in international relations face exclusion or sanctions as the cases of South Korean retailers (The Straits Times, 2017) or Philippine banana exporters experienced in the last couple of years (Peel and Ramos, 2017).

China's vision to be recognized as a "major power" requires China to establish itself as the regional economic hegemon in Asia. China attempts to achieve this objective by increasing cooperation and generating interdependencies with other Asian countries in trade, investment and finance with greater speed in the new era. This diplomatic tack has ramifications for China's financial architecture and its relatively closed financial system. One of the main pillars of this strategy is the internationalization of RMB and the PBOC is tasked with leading the change in this area. Before the 18th Party Congress, PBOC has already taken steps to encourage the use of RMB by private sector and official institutions outside China. After the Congress, the pace of these steps has accelerated and become bolder. The number of currency swap agreements and RMB clearing banks increased, more foreigners were allowed to issue RMB denominated bonds, and to allow faster, cheaper RMB transfers Cross-Border Inter-bank Payment System (CIPS)was established (Bouman, 2016). The opening of investment connection corridors from Hong Kong to Mainland stock and bond markets and inclusion of Chinese stocks to MSCI index allowed more foreigners to invest in RMB assets. More strikingly, RMB was included in the International Monetary Fund's reserve asset SDR (Special Drawing Rights) basket at the end

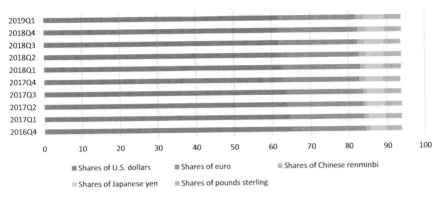

Figure 12.1 The share of Chinese Renminbi in foreign exchange reserves

Source: Currency Composition of Official Foreign Exchange Reserves (COFER), International Financial Statistics (IFS)

of 2015 (see Figure 12.1 for RMB reserve positions since). These policy initiatives have strengthened regionalization of RMB in Asia as more than half of the currency swap agreements were with Asian nations and central banks in Asia could now hold more RMB reserves as a part of their holdings (Song, 2019).

PBOC also pushed for further internationalization of RMB through the Belt and Road Initiative (BRI) which is a signature project of the new era diplomacy aiming to develop regional and global economic corridors connecting China to the globe. The BRI involves huge infrastructure and construction projects worth of 900 billion USD (Xu and Chen, 2018). In an attempt to promote the use of RMB, as declared by the former governor Zhou, the PBOC encouraged use of local currencies in transactions with the BRI countries, promoted the use of CIPS and China based payment systems and proposed to work with regulatory authorities in those countries to allow Chinese financial institutions' operations (Dai, 2017). PBOC supported "going out" policy in finance promoting overseas expansion of Chinese banks and development of major state investment fund for BRI projects such as the 40 billion USD Silk Road Fund. These efforts paid off and China was able to increase RMB transactions with BRI countries by 51% in 2018 compared with the previous year (PBOC, 2019).

A critical pitfall in China's RMB internationalization efforts is the illiberal nature of the capital account and the managed exchange rate. China has recently introduced more measures to open its capital account to allow foreigner investors' access to its capital markets. On 11 August 2015, PBOC also briefly adopted a more market-based exchange rate mechanism which allowed current trading day's exchange rate to be set by the previous day's closing price at the interbank foreign exchange market. However, as the RMB depreciated 3% in two days following the introduction of the new rule, the PBOC quickly reversed its decision and adopted a more ambiguous exchange rate mechanism that granted the PBOC greater control over the exchange rate first with the introduction of "theoretical RMB exchange rate" in 2016 and "countercyclical factor" in 2017 (Yu, 2018). The rapid capital outflows from the country in 2015 and 2016 may have prompted the PBOC to take a more hands-on approach in the exchange rate market after the IMF technical standards were accommodated for RMB's inclusion into the SDR basket. Interestingly, the "countercyclical factor" was removed from the equation determining the exchange rate once China needed a weaker currency to quell the negative impact of the "trade war" with the United States.

China's "new era" vision intends to challenge dollar's hegemony in Asia and beyond. Chinese leadership understands that such attempt will require further reforms in financial opening and diminish country's control over its finances. When the diminished control exacerbates the risk for financial instability or threatens the domestic economic objectives of the Party, a reversal takes place. Overall, as the PBOC is not an independent organization in conventional terms and the exchange rate management is a domestic political economy issue that involves multiple stakeholders, complicating PBOC's efforts to adopt a more market-based approach.

Conclusion

The Chinese economic development model is seeking a new path that will allow the country to continue its economic growth sustainably and deliver prosperity to millions who have enjoyed relative improvements in their living conditions in the last forty years of economic reform. China's "new era" and goal of "national rejuvenation" extend the country's leaders' horizons beyond the domestic political economy and encourage regional and global leadership aspirations. The challenges within the current domestic environment and surfacing resistance to China-centric international political economy demand deeper changes to both domestic economic organization and international economic engagement.

Hence, the next set of reforms will need to target institutional inefficiencies and path-dependencies breeding inertia for China's further development and acceptance as a fair partner outside the country. Among these, the need for reforms in the field of finance are more pressing than ever and the current leadership seems to have a good grasp of the options ahead and the possible leading paths. The efforts of the current leadership in centralizing economic governance can improve chances of success for reforms. However, it would be naïve to think a big-bang approach will open the country's capital account, float the exchange rate or ensure implementation of a "de facto" interest rate liberalization. The Chinese political economy cannot afford mistakes or mishaps that will lead to questioning of the current leadership's role in guiding the country.

Furthermore, to carry out these reforms, multiple stakeholders with different policy preferences need to be convinced. These constraints make reform process gradual, deliberative and open to reversals.

The PBOC plays a crucial role in the midst of financial reforms in China. Despite its weakened organizational capacity in the "new era", the PBOC is a major stakeholder in devising financial policies and an advocate for greater efficiency in allocation of financial resources and policies that will address country's external imbalances. On the other hand, their capacity in driving change is limited as the PBOC is ideologically and politically embedded within the Chinese domestic political economy and their actions have to reflect policy preferences of the Party or its leadership.

Regional and global aspirations of China's leadership may offer an opportunity for the PBOC to push for further reforms. The relationship that the current PBOC Governor, Yi, develops with the top leadership and top economic lieutenants in the coming years will be crucial for determining the weight of the PBOC input in policy development process. Lastly, the challenges that the PBOC faces in managing slower economic growth, achieving an orderly deleveraging, regulating old and new branches of finance and managing a relatively more open financial system amid de-globalization will test its capacity and impact its institutional evolution.

References

Berentsen, A. and Schar, F. (2018). The Case for Central Bank Electronic Money and the Non-Case for Central Bank Cryptocurrencies. *Review*, 100(2), pp. 97–106.

Bloomberg News (2019). China's PBOC Says Its Own Cryptocurrency Is 'Close' to Release – BNN Bloomberg. [online] *BNN*. Available at: www.bnnbloomberg.ca/china-s-pboc-says-its-own-cryptocurrency-is-close-to-release-1.1300194 [Accessed 14 September 2019].

Borst, N. (2015). *China Sets the Rules for Internet Finance*. [online] Federal Reserve Bank of San Francisco. Available at: www.frbsf.org/banking/asia-program/pacific-exchange-blog/china-sets-the-rules-for-internet-finance/ [Accessed 12 September 2019].

Bouman, J. (2016). Internationalisation of the RMB. In: G. Davies, J. Goldkorn and L. Tomba, eds., *The China Story Yearbook 2015: Pollution*. Canberra, Australia: ANU Press, pp. 60–64.

Bradsher, K. (2017). China Moves to Stabilize Currency, Despite Promise to Loosen Control. [online] *The New York Times*. 26 May. Available at: www.nytimes.com/2017/05/26/business/dealbook/china-currency.html [Accessed 14 September 2019].

Brunnermeier, M.K., Sockin, M. and Xiong, W. (2017). China's Gradualistic Economic Approach and Financial Markets. *American Economic Review*, 107(5), pp. 608–613.

Caijing.com.cn. (2019). 央行货币政策委员会调整财政部副部长邹加怡加入_经济_宏观频道首页_财经网 – *CAIJING.COM.CN*. [online] Available at: http://economy.caijing.com.cn/20190625/4597708.shtml [Accessed 12 September 2019].

Cassou, P.-H. (1974). The Chinese Monetary System. *The China Quarterly*, 59, pp. 559–566.

Chen, J. (2018). New Regulator is also the PBOC Party Chief – Chinadaily.com.cn. [online] *Chinadaily.com.cn*. 27 March. Available at: www.chinadaily.com.cn/a/201803/27/WS5a-b99a2ca3105cdcf651477c.html [Accessed 14 September 2019].

Chen, K., Ren, J. and Zha, T. (2018). The Nexus of Monetary Policy and Shadow Banking in China. *American Economic Review*, 108(12), pp. 3891–3936.

Chin, G.T. (2013). Understanding Currency Policy and Central Banking in China. *The Journal of Asian Studies*, 72(3), pp. 519–538.

China Banking News. (2018). Shadow Banking is a Necessary Adjunct to China's Financial Markets: PBOC Head. [online] Available at: http://www.chinabankingnews.com/2018/12/17/shadow-banking-necessary-adjunct-chinas-financial-markets-pboc-head/ [Accessed 12 September 2019].

Chorzempa, M. (2018). Massive P2P Failures in China: Underground Banks Going Under. [online] *PIIE*. Available at: www.piie.com/blogs/china-economic-watch/massive-p2p-failures-china-underground-banks-going-under [Accessed 12 September 2019].

Dai, T. (2017). Belt and Road Financing Welcomes Local Currencies, Says PBOC Chief – Business – Chinadaily.com.cn. [online] *Chinadaily.com.cn*. Available at: www.chinadaily.com.cn/business/2017-05/05/content_29219235.htm [Accessed 14 September 2019].

FSB (2014). Global Shadow Banking Monitoring Report 2014. [online] Available at: https://www.fsb.org/wp-content/uploads/r_141030.pdf?page_moved=1 [Accessed 12 September 2019].

Gabrieli, T., Pilbeam, K. and Shi, B. (2017). The Impact of Shadow Banking on the Implementation of Chinese Monetary Policy. *International Economics and Economic Policy*, 15(2), pp. 429–447.

Han, M. (2016). *Central Bank Regulation and the Financial Crisis A Comparative Analysis*. London Palgrave Macmillan UK: Imprint: Palgrave Macmillan.

Hau, H., Huang, Y., Shan, H. and Sheng, Z. (2019). How FinTech Enters China's Credit Market. *AEA Papers and Proceedings*, 109, pp. 60–64.

He, W. (2018). The One Bank – Three Commissions Regulatory Structure. *The Regulation of Securities Markets in China*, pp. 171–207.

Hsiao, K.H.Y.H. (1982). Money and Banking in the People's Republic of China: Recent Developments. *The China Quarterly*, 91, pp. 462–477.

IMF (2019). *The Currency Composition of Official Foreign Exchange Reserves (COFER)*. [online] Available at: http://data.imf.org/?sk=E6A5F467-C14B-4AA8-9F6D-5A09EC4E62A4.

Iwamura, M., Kitamura, Y., Matsumoto, T. and Saito, K. (2019). Can We Stabilize the Price of a Cryptocurrency?: Understanding the Design of Bitcoin and Its Potential to Compete with Central Bank Money. *Hitotsubashi Journal of Economics*, 60, pp. 41–60.

Johnson, C.K., Kennedy, S. and Qiu, M. (2017). Xi's Signature Governance Innovation: The Rise of Leading Small Groups. [online] *Csis.org*. Available at: www.csis.org/analysis/xis-signature-governance-innovation-rise-leading-small-groups [Accessed 14 September 2019].

Ju, L., Lu, T.J. and Tu, Z. (2015). Capital Flight and Bitcoin Regulation. *International Review of Finance*, 16(3), pp. 445–455.

Jun, M. (1996). Monetary Management and Intergovernmental Relations in China. *World Development*, 24(1), pp. 145–153.

Law of the People's Republic of China on the People's Bank of China (2003 Amendment). [online] Available at: http://en.pkulaw.cn/Display.aspx?lib=law&Cgid=50973 [Accessed 14 September 2019].

Li, T. (2019). PBOC to Cut RRR for Rural Commercial Banks as a Support for the Economy. [online] *SHINE*. Available at: www.shine.cn/biz/finance/1905064181/ [Accessed 12 September 2019].

Liao, S. (2018). Chinese Internet Users Employ the Blockchain to Share a Censored Story About Vaccines. [online] *The Verge*. Available at: www.theverge.com/2018/7/24/17607690/chinese-internet-users-blockchain-share-censored-news-article-vaccines [Accessed 14 September 2019].

Lu, Y., Guo, H., Kao, E.H. and Fung, H.-G. (2015). Shadow Banking and Firm Financing in China. *International Review of Economics & Finance*, 36, pp. 40–53.

Moody's Quarterly China Shadow Banking Monitor (2017). Moody's Investor Service. [online] *Moodys.com*. Available at: www.moodys.com/research/Quarterly-China-Shadow-Banking-Monitor – PBC_1124347 [Accessed 12 September 2019].

Naughton, B. (2017). *The Regulatory Storm: A Surprising Turn in Financial Policy*. [online] Hoover Institution. Available at: www.hoover.org/research/regulatory-storm-surprising-turn-financial-policy [Accessed 12 September 2019].

PBOC Annual Report 2017 (2018). *People's Bank of China*. [online] Available at: www.pbc.gov.cn/eportal/fileDir/english/resource/cms/2018/10/2018102918484953963.pdf [Accessed 12 September 2019].

Peel, M. and Ramos, G. (2017). Philippine Banana Bonanza Sparks Debate on Shift to China. [online] *Financial Times*. Available at: www.ft.com/content/3f6df338-056b-11e7-ace0-1ce02ef0def9 [Accessed 14 October 2019].

Pei, M. (2019). Rewriting the Rules of the Chinese Party-State: Xi's Progress in Reinvigorating the CCP. [online] *China Leadership Monitor*. Available at: www.prcleader.org/peiclm60 [Accessed 12 September 2019].

People's Bank of China (2018). The People's Bank of China Annual Report 2017. [online] *Pbc.gov.cn*. Available at: www.pbc.gov.cn/eportal/fileDir/english/resource/cms/2018/10/2018102918484953963.pdf [Accessed 14 September 2019].

People's Bank of China (2019). 中国人民银行年报 2018. [online] *People's Bank of China*. Available at: www.pbc.gov.cn/chubanwu/114566/115296/3869784/3870296/2019080610410891150.pdf [Accessed 14 September 2019].

Ray Chaudhuri, R. (2018). *Central Bank Independence, Regulations, and Monetary Policy*. New York: Palgrave Macmillan US.

Shadow Banking is a Necessary Adjunct to China's Financial Markets: PBOC Head (2019). [online] *China Banking News*. 9 September. Available at: http://www.chinabankingnews.com/2018/12/17/shadow-banking-necessary-adjunct-chinas-financial-markets-pboc-head/ [Accessed 12 September 2019].

Shih, V. (2011). "Goldilocks" Liberalization: The Uneven Path Toward Interest Rate Reform in China. *Journal of East Asian Studies*, 11(3), pp. 437–465.

Shin, J. (2018). China's Great Power Identity and Its Policy on the Korean Peninsula in the Xi Jinping Era. *Pacific Focus*, 33(2), pp. 284–307. [online] Available at: https://onlinelibrary.wiley.com/doi/abs/10.1111/pafo.12119 [Accessed 14 September 2019].

Smith, C. (2019). US Treasury Officially Labels China a Currency Manipulator. [online] *Financial Times*. Available at: www.ft.com/content/9d24c1ca-b7cd-11e9-96bd-8e884d3ea203 [Accessed 14 September 2019].

Song, G. (2019). China's Economic Strategy in Asia. *Asian Education and Development Studies*, 8(1), pp. 2–13. [online] Available at: www.emeraldinsight.com/doi/full/10.1108/AEDS-08-2017-0083 [Accessed 14 September 2019].

State Council (1993). *Decision of the State Council on Reform of the Financial System*. [online] Available at: http://en.pkulaw.cn/display.aspx?cgid=2ba7392c53b3a024bdfb&lib=law [Accessed 14 September 2019].

State Council (2015). Premier Li Keqiang and Internet Plus. [online] *www.gov.cn*. Available at: http://english.www.gov.cn/policies/infographics/2015/12/31/content_281475263938767.htm [Accessed 14 September 2019].

The State Council Information Office of the People's Republic of China (2016). Full text: China's Progress in Poverty Reduction and Human Rights. [online] *English.gov.cn*. Available at: http://english.gov.cn/policies/latest_releases/2016/10/17/content_2814754 68533275.htm [Accessed 12 September 2019].

The Straits Times (2017). *South Korea's Lotte to Sell China Shops in Face of Boycott.* [online] Available at: www.straitstimes.com/asia/south-koreas-lotte-group-says-4-retail-stores-in-china-closed-amid-political-tension. [Accessed 14 October 2019].

Strengthening Oversight and Regulation of Shadow Banking Regulatory Framework for Haircuts on Non-Centrally Cleared Securities Financing Transactions (2014). [online] Available at: www.fsb.org/wp-content/uploads/r_141013a.pdf [Accessed 14 September 2019].

Wu, H., Zhang, Y. and Lin, J. (2018). Central Bank to Turn Clock Back to 1998, Give Each Province Own Branch – Caixin Global. [online] *Caixinglobal.com.* Available at: www.caixinglobal.com/2018-08-20/central-bank-to-turn-clock-back-to-1998-give-each-province-own-branch-101316939.html [Accessed 12 September 2019].

Wu, Y. (2017). Central Bank to Regulate Rapidly Growing Fintech – Business – Chinadaily.com.cn. [online] *Chinadaily.com.cn.* Available at: www.chinadaily.com.cn/business/2017-08/08/content_30365345.htm [Accessed 14 September 2019].

Xu, J. (2017). China's Internet Finance: A Critical Review. *China & World Economy,* 25(4), pp. 78–92.

Xu, S. and Chen, L. (2018). Embracing the BRI ecosystem in 2018 | Deloitte China. [online] *Deloitte China.* Available at: https://www2.deloitte.com/cn/en/pages/soe/articles/embracing-the-bri-ecosystem-in-2018.html [Accessed 14 September 2019].

Yan, X. (2014). China's New Foreign Policy: Not Conflict But Convergence Of Interests. *New Perspectives Quarterly,* 31(2), pp. 46–48. [online] Available at: https://onlinelibrary.wiley.com/doi/pdf/10.1111/npqu.11449 [Accessed 14 September 2019].

Yi, G. (1992). The Money Supply Mechanism and Monetary Policy in China. *Journal of Asian Economics,* 3(2), pp. 217–238. [online] Available at: www.sciencedirect.com/science/article/pii/104900789290014P [Accessed 12 September 2019].

Yi, G. (2008). Renminbi Exchange Rates and Relevant Institutional Factors. *Cato Journal,* 28(2). [online] Available at: https://object.cato.org/sites/cato.org/files/serials/files/cato-journal/2008/5/cj28n2-2.pdf [Accessed 14 September 2019].

Yi, X. (2019). 当前央行发行数字加密货币意义不大_法币. [online] *Sohu.com.* Available at: www.sohu.com/a/333069889_651494?scm=1002.0.0.0-0 [Accessed 14 September 2019].

Yu, Y. (2018). The reform of China's exchange rate regime. In: *China's 40 Years of Reform and Development:1978–2018.* Canberra, Australia: ANU Press, pp. 313–328.

Zhou, J. (2019). China's Core Interests and Dilemma in Foreign Policy Practice. *Pacific Focus,* 34(1), pp. 31–54. [online] Available at: https://onlinelibrary.wiley.com/doi/10.1111/pafo.12131 [Accessed 14 September 2019].

Conclusion

New avenues of research on central banking in emerging economies

Mustafa Yağcı

This volume has examined an extensive number of emerging economy central banks with diverse theoretical and methodological orientations. The interdisciplinary orientation of the chapters has illustrated that we have so much to learn about the central banks. The chapters highlighted several dimensions of the political economy of central banking in emerging economies. These findings can be summarized as follows:

- The interactions between international and domestic forces shape the political economy context within which central banks are embedded. We need to unravel how local and global forces are translated into monetary policy practices in divergent contexts.
- The political economy context that shapes the central banking activity includes several variables such as the political regime type, the historical legacy behind the foundation of the central bank, the organization of bureaucracy, the structure of the financial system, state-business relations, political struggles within the country, external relations with other states and international organizations, dominant international norms and the macroeconomic institutional framework, such as the economic growth model, the exchange rate and capital account regime, the legal independence status of the central bank and regional currency arrangements.
- While the political economy context shapes the central banking activity, central banks do also influence the political economy context and the overall institutional setting within the country.
- In addition to the structural and institutional variables, the individual agency has a crucial role in central banking, and this dimension should not be overlooked in contextualization efforts.
- The de jure and de facto distinction should be contemplated in the analysis of central bank independence.
- In addition to independence, transparency and accountability are critical dimensions of central bank governance regimes.
- Central bank policies have significant distributional consequences within society.

- Emerging economy central banks are subject to spillover effects from the monetary policies conducted by advanced economy central banks, and central bank coordination mechanisms should be developed at the international level.
- Central banking can and should be studied from diverse theoretical and methodological orientations to enrich our understanding.
- A comparative historical analysis perspective can be utilized in contextualizing central banking activity within specific historical periods and divergent political economy contexts.

Based on these findings, it can be deduced that there is a long way to go for developing a global perspective on the political economy of central banking. We suggest future research in the political economy of central banking to take advantage of interdisciplinarity, methodological pluralism, and going beyond single case studies to regional and global comparative studies.

Interdisciplinarity

Central banking activity should be scrutinized from different angles, and an interdisciplinary perspective is needed to enrich our understanding. This volume has illustrated that sociological, organizational, historical, legal, and gender-related approaches can be integrated into a political economy framework to study central banking. In doing so, the influence of both international and domestic forces can be identified to grasp the multidimensionality of central banking. This would enable bridging macro- and micro-level analysis, answering questions of why and how central banks operate the way they do, and what is the relevance of international and domestic forces in this respect.

In terms of theoretical interdisciplinarity, different strands of institutional theory, organization theory, theoretical perspectives in public policy, and public administration can be used for central banking research. In institutional theory, different forms of institutional change (Campbell 2004; Mahoney & Thelen 2009; Hall & Taylor 1996), varieties of capitalism research stream (Hall & Soskice 2001; Hall & Thelen 2009), and the scholarship on how ideas are translated into policy practices (Blyth 2002; Ban 2016) offer novel means to explain central banking. Organization theory can be employed to study organizational dynamics of how a central bank makes decisions (Abolafia 2010) and learns (Yağcı 2017). Theoretical perspectives on public policy and public administration would guide researchers to examine policy processes at the micro-level by identifying the political struggles and relevant actors in the policy process stages of agenda-setting, policy formulation, decision-making, policy implementation and policy evaluation (Howlett & Giest 2012); how policy change happens in central banking (Capano 2009; Real-Dato 2009); and how reactions to the monetary policy implementation create adverse feedback effects for monetary policy regimes (Yağcı 2018).

The bridge between macro-level structural and institutional analysis with a micro-level agency-based analysis on tensions and struggles in the policy processes would unravel new avenues of research on central banking. This would help to distinguish between de jure and de facto independence of the central banks, identify relevant actors in different stages of the policymaking, and juxtapose the interlinkages of political and economic factors in different countries.

Methodological pluralism

Methodological pluralism would take advantage of multiple orientations to explore central banking activity. Quantitative approaches, which dominate central banking research in orthodox economics scholarship, would be better suited to understand causal effects, whereas qualitative approaches would enlighten causal mechanisms in central banking activity (Brady & Collier 2010; Mahoney & Goertz 2013). Moreover, qualitative approaches may be more suitable to answer 'big questions' on central banking and its normative dimensions.

A comparative historical perspective can be employed to examine central banking activity and to contextualize historical specificities and political economy dynamics in various contexts (Mahoney & Rueschemeyer 2003). In addition to the comparative historical analysis, process tracing would offer a useful analytical lens to identify relevant variables for the research question under investigation (Bennett & Checkel 2015). The interview method is widely used in qualitative research, and the newly emerging qualitative data analysis brings transparency and rigor to interview research (Yağcı 2018).

Going beyond single case studies to regional and global comparative studies

Bringing regional and global comparative perspective to central banking research would strengthen empirical validity in qualitative methodology by identification of relevant variables in diverse contexts. Case selections based on justification criteria would enhance theoretical development in central banking research and would facilitate verification and testability of theoretical propositions (Bennett & George 2005). Justifications based on 'most similar', 'most different', 'least likely', 'most likely' cases would help determine the relevant variables in different countries. Furthermore, the artificial division among scholars about studying either advanced or emerging economy central banks should be repealed. Scholarship on the political economy of central banking should strive to explain the global phenomenon of central banking with a global orientation. Relatedly, the rising research themes on climate change, inequality, emerging financial technologies, crypto currencies, digital currencies and their relation to the central banking and monetary policy practices would require a global orientation to understand the key dynamics in these areas.

References

Abolafia, MY 2010, 'Narrative construction as sensemaking: how a central bank thinks', *Organization Studies*, vol. 31, no. 3, pp. 349–367.

Ban, C 2016, *Ruling ideas: how global neoliberalism goes local*, Oxford University Press, Oxford, UK.

Bennett, A & Checkel, JT (eds.) 2015, *Process tracing*, Cambridge University Press, Cambridge, UK.

Bennett, A & George, A 2005, *Case studies and theory development in the social sciences*, MIT Press, Cambridge, MA.

Blyth, M 2002, *Great transformations: economic ideas and institutional change in the twentieth century*, Cambridge University Press, Cambridge, UK.

Brady, HE & Collier, D (eds.) 2010, *Rethinking social inquiry: diverse tools, shared standards* (2nd ed.), Roman & Littlefield Publishers, Inc, Plymouth, UK.

Campbell, JL 2004, *Institutional change and globalization*, Princeton University Press, Princeton, NJ.

Capano, G 2009, 'Understanding policy change as an epistemological and theoretical problem', *Journal of Comparative Policy Analysis*, vol. 11, no. 1, pp. 7–31.

Hall, PA & Soskice, D 2001, 'An introduction to varieties of capitalism', in PA Hall & D Soskice (eds.) *Varieties of capitalism: the institutional foundations of comparative advantage*, pp. 1–70, Oxford University Press, Oxford, UK.

Hall, PA & Taylor, RC 1996, 'Political science and the three new institutionalisms', *Political Studies*, vol. 44, no. 5, pp. 936–957.

Hall, PA & Thelen, K 2009, 'Institutional change in varieties of capitalism', *Socio-Economic Review*, vol. 7, no. 1, pp. 7–34.

Howlett, M & Giest, S 2012, 'The policy-making process', in E Araral Jr, S Fritzen, M Howlett, M Ramesh & X Wu (eds.) *Routledge handbook of public policy*, pp. 17–28, Routledge, London, UK.

Mahoney, J & Goertz, G 2013, *A tale of two cultures: qualitative and quantitative research in the social sciences*, Princeton University Press, Princeton, NJ.

Mahoney, J & Rueschemeyer, D (eds.) 2003, *Comparative historical analysis in the social sciences*, Cambridge University Press, Cambridge, UK.

Mahoney, J & Thelen, K (eds.) 2009, *Explaining institutional change: ambiguity, agency, and power*, Cambridge University Press, Cambridge, UK.

Real-Dato, J 2009, 'Mechanisms of policy change: a proposal for a synthetic explanatory framework', *Journal of Comparative Policy Analysis*, vol. 11, no. 1, pp. 117–143.

Yağcı, M 2017, 'Institutional entrepreneurship and organisational learning: financial stability policy design in Turkey', *Policy and Society*, vol. 36, no. 4, pp. 539–555.

Yağcı, M 2018, 'The political economy of central banking in Turkey: the macroprudential policy regime and self-undermining feedback', *South European Society and Politics*, vol. 23, no. 4, pp. 525–545.

Index

Note: Page numbers in *italic* indicate a figure and page numbers in **bold** indicate a table on the corresponding page.

Index

Note: Page numbers in *italic* indicate a figure and page numbers in **bold** indicate a table on the corresponding page.

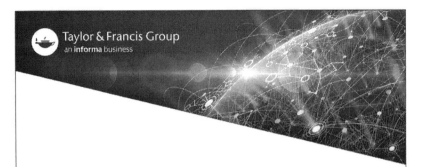